An Encyclopedia of
Cultivated Palms

Washingtonia filifera. Etching/aquatint by James Ebersole

AN ENCYCLOPEDIA OF
Cultivated Palms

by
Robert Lee Riffle

and
Paul Craft

TIMBER PRESS

Published in 2003 by
Timber Press, Inc.
The Haseltine Building
133 S.W. Second Avenue, Suite 450
Portland, Oregon 97204, U.S.A.
www.timberpress.com
For contact information regarding editorial, marketing, sales, and
distribution in the United Kingdom, see www.timberpress.co.uk.

Printed in China

Fourth printing 2007

Library of Congress Cataloging-in-Publication Data

Riffle, Robert Lee.
    An encyclopedia of cultivated palms / by Robert Lee Riffle and Paul Craft.
        p.   cm.
    Includes bibliographical references (p.   ).
    ISBN-13: 978-0-88192-558-6
    1. Palms—Encyclopedias. I. Craft, Paul, 1950– II. Title.

SB317.P3 R54 2003
634.9'74'03—dc21

                                                                    2002067604

To the two Ds in my life,
Diana Gabaldon and Diane Laird
RLR

———

To my wife, Patty, who has
stood by me throughout my palm lunacy
PC

Contents

Preface

The intended audience: This book is intended primarily for gardeners and horticulturists. Although it includes the latest taxonomic thinking about the family and the delineation of species, it is not a systematic treatment of the palms. Rather, it is scientific only to the extent that it needs to be for an adequate understanding of the plant descriptions. Some technical jargon is unavoidable and the glossary is, we believe, mercifully short.

The authors' biases: No nonfiction work is free of its author's biases, even if the biases only be evident in the way the material is organized, and we think we should declare ours up front.

First, we are not fond of common names and, although we have included them for reference, they are probably the least dependable part of a palm's description. Doubtless many vernacular names are missing as we endeavored only to include English names.

Second, given the limited amount of space in this work and the inevitability of having to sometimes choose what to include and what to eschew, we have opted for the species of larger landscape proportions to the exclusion of smaller species, where such a choice existed.

Third, we are not fond of sports, cultivars, and mutations and believe that most variegated examples of palm species are less than aesthetically thrilling. Furthermore, the last-mentioned prejudice also extends to man-made hybrids. It is our conviction that palm lovers should first be concerned with knowing, saving, and maintaining what nature has given us before we journey down the path of "creation" and alter the original species, which in some cases may never be recovered.

Hardiness zones: Although they are inadequate, we have resorted to using the United States Department of Agriculture growing zones for general indications of a

given palm's cold hardiness. These zone ratings are based on average minimum winter temperatures. The inadequacies of these artificial zones have mostly to do with factors that cannot be included in simplified terms—factors such as microclimates, the amount of summer heat, the frequency and duration of cold outbreaks for a given zone, and the accompanying conditions of such outbreaks, such as the amount of precipitation. We have tried to overcome these limitations of the zones by amplifying the relevant and specific text. The zone numbers and their corresponding temperatures are as follows:

Temp °F	Zone	Temp °C
−20 to 10	5	−28.8 to −23.4
−10 to −5	6a	−23.3 to −20.6
−5 to 0	6b	−20.5 to −17.8
0 to 5	7a	−17.7 to −15.0
5 to 10	7b	−14.9 to −12.3
10 to 15	8a	−12.2 to −9.5
15 to 20	8b	−9.4 to −6.7
20 to 25	9a	−6.6 to −3.9
25 to 30	9b	−3.8 to −1.2
30 to 35	10a	−1.1 to 1.6
35 to 40	10b	1.7 to 4.4
40 and Above	11	4.5 and Above

Pronunciation guides: A guide to the pronunciation of scientific names follows the descriptions.

Synonyms: Synonyms of the genera and species are listed in the index to not clutter up the plant descriptions in the body of the book.

That which is lacking: We have not included separate chapters on the structural biology, economic importance, natural history (pollination, seed dispersal, animal interactions), cultivation, diseases and pests, indoor cultivation, and the art of propagation. What we have done instead is to include in the descriptions of the individual species the relevant information. For further reading, we recommend *Genera Palmarum* (Uhl and Dransfield 1987), *Ornamental Palm Horticulture* (Broschat and Meerow 2000), and *Palms Throughout the World* (Jones 1995).

The International Palm Society: No introduction to the palms would be complete without mention of the International Palm Society (IPS). Founded in 1956 the society is dedicated to the study and conservation of the entire family of palms. It now has chapters worldwide whose members meet on a regular basis to discuss their experiences with palms grown in their own region as well as in areas they have visited.

The society's quarterly journal *Palms* (formerly *Principes*) features articles for enthusiasts of every level from novice to researcher. These articles cover newly discovered palms, the latest scientific research and taxonomy, palm horticul-ture, travelogues, book reviews, and news from the many chapters.

The IPS web site (www.palms.org) offers information on many aspects of growing and learning about palms. The site includes a discussion board where anyone can get questions answered from fellow enthusiasts located throughout the world, and a list of links to other palm-related web sites as well as commercial web sites. Besides the web site discussion group, an email discussion list is available for people to exchange information worldwide. A mail-order bookstore sells hard-to-find books and papers.

In addition, the IPS maintains an endowment fund that finances various palm projects throughout the world. The money is not just for researchers but for any worthwhile palm project. We encourage all to join the society; it's an ongoing encyclopedia of palms.

For those without access to the internet, the society may be contacted by mail at International Palm Society, P.O. Box 1897, Lawrence, Kansas 66044, or by fax at 785.843.1276.

Errata

Plate 28. *Roystonea regia*
Plate 41. *Areca catechu*
Plate 93. *Bactris* sp.
Plate 111. *Pinanga* sp.
Plate 114. *Basselinia favieri*
Plate 133. *Bismarckia nobilis*
Plate 173. *Veitchia filifera*
Plates 200–202. *Caryota gigas*
Plate 208. *Caryota rumphiana*
Plate 240. *Chamaedorea elegans*
Plate 281. *Coccothrinax scoparia*

Plates 373, 375. *Pseudophoenix sargentii*
Plate 431. *Archontophoenix purpurea*
Plate 498. *Kentiopsis pyriformis*
Plate 504. *Livistona mariae*
Plate 533. *Licuala* sp.
Plate 601. *Bactris* sp. or *Calamus* sp.
Plate 660. *Astrocaryum mexicanum*
Plate 734. *Ptychosperma wotoboho*
Plate 780. *Veitchia joannis*
Plate 786. *Wodyetia bifurcata*
Plate 866. *Chamaedorea pinnatifrons*

Acknowledgments

A volume of this scope is not the work of a single person. It is rather analogous to film making in which the directors are but a part of the larger whole:

Neal Maillet, executive editor at Timber Press, long suffered the many delays and missed deadlines in the production of this inclusive work.

John L. Dowe of Queensland, Australia, reviewed the manuscript for many genera on which he is expert and provided invaluable comments.

Martin Gibbons of Richmond, Surrey, United Kingdom, and Tobias Spanner of Munich, Germany, have traveled to most regions where palms grow.

Rolf Kyburz of K-Palm Nursery, Queensland, Australia, submitted several important photographs.

Larry Noblick of Montgomery Botanical Center, Miami, Florida, accompanied Bob on several tours of the grounds of that marvelous institution.

Chuck Hubbuch, formerly of Fairchild Tropical Garden and presently creating a garden for the zoo in Jacksonville, Florida.

Tim Hatch of Sarawak, Indonesia, contributed several photographs.

Dave Witt of Orlando, Florida, made many suggestions from his years of growing palm species in that city.

Geoff Stein of Thousand Oaks, California, kindly contributed some excellent drawings of palm parts.

Scott Zona of Fairchild Tropical Garden, Miami, Florida, made suggestions on some American palm species and contributed several great photographs from his travels.

Mike Dahme of Grant, Florida, and Puerto Rico reviewed parts of the manuscript and initiated the contact with John L. Dowe.

Bryan Laughland of Auckland, New Zealand, contributed a number of excellent photographs of palm species in New Caledonia and New Zealand.

Daryl O'Connor of Queensland, Australia, read much of the manuscript and offered insights on growing palms in his country.

Laura Tooley, horticulturist at Flamingo Gardens, Broward County, Florida, accompanied Bob on several tours through that wonderful old garden.

Katherine Maidman, curator of palms at Fairchild Tropical Garden, Miami, Florida, came running out into the garden a number of times from her office to show Bob a particular plant.

Gaston Torres-Vera of Argentina, in spite of present economic and political turmoil in his country, managed to send several excellent photographs of *Trithrinax* species.

Linda Willms, editor at Timber Press, who in spite of the authors' missed deadlines, delays, and irascible opinions, kept valiantly on with the project.

This book would never have been completed without the three women in our lives, and, although the book is dedicated to them, they deserve much more than a dedication.

Introduction

A palm is first of all a flowering plant, or angiosperm. Plants that produce flowers include species as tiny as *Wolffia*, an almost microscopic, aquatic floating plant related to the duckweeds (*Lemna*), and as large as the 350-foot-tall *Eucalyptus regnans* of Tasmania.

Secondly, a palm is a monocot, which is one of two divisions of the flowering plants. Monocots have one embryo or seed leaf, mostly nonwoody tissues, and flower parts in threes or multiples of three. Dicots, the other division of flowering plants, have two seed leaves, mostly woody tissues, and flowering parts in fours or multiples of four. Palms are among the few monocot families with woody tissues. Other monocot families are bananas, aroids (for example, philodendrons, dieffenbachias, calla lilies), orchids, bromeliads, heliconias, cannas, and all grasses including corn. Dicot families include oaks and beeches, eucalypts, daisies (one of the many exceptions to the woody characteristic), scheffleras, magnolias, and roses, among others.

What is not a palm? The answer is cycads, aloes, yuccas, and similar looking large and usually woody plants, all of which outwardly resemble palms. Cycads especially look like palms but are not even flowering plants; rather they are more closely related to conifers, another ancient plant group. Aloes and yuccas are flowering plants belonging to the monocot division.

Palm Structure

Palm species may be shrublike, treelike, or vinelike. Most gardeners are surprised to learn of climbing palms, but such plants exist in the tropics and some of them have developed unique structures to aid in their growth upwards on other vegetation. Only one genus of palm naturally produces branching trunks, but many abnormally produce subsidiary stems from points above the ground, the ab-normality usually caused by an injury to the stem. Leaves of all types are produced only from the ends of the stems or trunks. The only growth form not represented in the family is that of the true epiphyte.

Palm species include those with a solitary trunk and those with clustering or clumping stems. Dimensions range from an ultimate height of 6 inches to at least 150 feet and a stem diameter of less than 0.5 inch to 6 feet. Palm trunks are graced with the scars of former leaves in the crown; these scars may or may not be prominent and are semicircular in general form. Otherwise the stems may be more or less smooth or variously adorned with the bottom parts of old and dead leaves, as well as spines or other protrusions. They may be straight as an arrow, leaning (usually necessarily the case in densely clumping species), recumbent, or even subterranean.

As monocots, palms do not increase their trunk size by growing new wood. Rather, if the trunk enlarges, it does so by expanding the tissues first formed. This characteristic has one important implication for gardeners: injuries to palm trunks are permanent and not repaired by the plants. Also, since few trunked palms naturally branch, killing or removing the growing point means the death of that stem and, in the case of solitary-trunked species, the death of the plant.

Similar to other tropical rain forest plants, some palms develop aboveground stilt roots to support the main trunk. These structures are usually associated with species which begin their lives as undergrowth subjects and grow quickly upwards to attain the sunlight they need to mature. Most palms have relatively shallow root systems compared to those of dicot trees. This fact is important to remember when growing palms: they are mainly surface feeders and need regular applications of moisture.

A palm leaf consists of a sheath (the bottommost part), which is a broadened tubular part, at least until the leaf has emerged entirely from the growing point. After emergence, the sheath may remain large and more or less tubular or may split as the blade or lamina of the leaf expands. Beyond the sheath is the petiole or leafstalk, which may be long or so short as to not be apparent. Beyond the petiole is the blade, the most obvious part of the palm leaf. It may be entire (unsegmented), feather (pinnate) shaped, or fan (palmate) shaped.

Segments making up the feather of pinnate leaves may be completely free of each other or may be fused or partly fused; they may also be further segmented or entire. The individual segments of this type of leaf are referred to as the leaflets. They may grow in one plane from the rachis to create a flat or nearly flat leaf in cross-section, or they may grow from the rachis at an angle that creates a V-shaped leaf in cross-section. In the palmate leaf the lamina may be entire or divided into segments of various widths and lengths; these segments may, as in the pinnate leaf, be further segmented or not.

The length of leaf in palm species, including sheath, petiole, and lamina ranges from less than a foot to more than 70 feet, the largest leaf among the flowering plants; only giant kelps in the Pacific Ocean have longer leaves and they are not flowering plants. Like the stem, the leaf of a palm may bear spines or other protrusions; notably in the palmate-leaved species is often a protrusion termed a *hastula*. The sheaths of palm leaves may form a crownshaft at the top of the trunk. This is a cylindrical, pillar-like organ that may be tiny or grand and may be green or beautifully colored and may also bear hairs, threads or spines, exactly like the rest of the leaf.

Palm flowers are, in relation to those of most other flowering plant families, small, most being significantly under an inch in diameter; however, they are invariably formed in large clusters or inflorescences, and one palm genus (*Corypha*) boasts the largest inflorescences in the world. The inflorescences may grow from the leaf crown in the same manner as the leaves, may be borne below the leaves at nodes on the trunks, or may grow directly from the top of the stem. The latter phenomenon results in the slow death of the stem from which the inflorescence grows; an example of this last phenomenon is seen in the genus *Corypha*.

Palm fruits range from small to gigantic and, like the inflorescences, are borne in clusters. They may be smooth or covered in scales or spines, and their surfaces may be soft or wooden. They normally contain only one seed in the center of the flesh, but the flesh may be almost nonexistent and there may be as many as 10 seeds in one fruit. The seed of one palm species, *Lodoicea*, is the largest in the world.

Palm Habitats

Palms are indigenous to every continent except Antarctica. The northernmost naturally occurring species (*Chamaerops*) is in southern Europe and the southernmost naturally occurring species (*Rhopalostylis*) is found in northern New Zealand.

Their habitats include all types except cold montane regions and polar regions. There are species in mangrove coastal environments, estuaries, and fresh water swamps, the oases of deserts, tropical and subtropical coastal plains and grasslands, deciduous tropical forests, rain forest (both lowland and montane and both tropical and warm temperate), and even in the drier regions of mountains; at least one species is a true submerged aquatic. The greatest diversity of palms occurs in tropical forest regions, especially humid and moist forests where many smaller palm species are undergrowth subjects, the larger species at home in clearings and along riverbanks.

Relations in the Palm Family

Present taxonomy puts the number of genera (singular "genus") in the palm family (Palmae or Arecaceae) at 192, and the number of palm species (singular and plural) at about 2500 (see table, pp. 14–15). In trying to better understand the relations between the species, modern taxonomists have divided the family into subfamilies, tribes, subtribes, and genera, all of which are natural groups with progressively closer affinities. Since most of the relations involve the structure not only of the leaves and trunks but also more importantly the flowering parts of the palms, the affinities are not always that obvious to nonbotanists. For example, the subfamily Coryphoideae includes only palmate-shaped leaves, with one salient exception, *Phoenix*, the date palms; all other subfamilies consist of pinnate-leaved palms.

While an understanding of the tribes into which palms are divided may seem superfluous for the gardener, it does have a practical application for anyone who wants to grow palms from seed. The genera of a given tribe all germinate similarly. Thus, for example, species in the tribe Corypheae send down a radicle from the seed, which, when it reaches a certain depth, becomes the starting point for both the roots (which continue downward from that point), and the first leaf (which sprouts up from this depth). This fact informs the gardener to start such seed in a deep pot.

Until the advent of airplane travel and nearly instant communication, the palm family was probably the most poorly known among the large families of flowering plants. Taxonomy is based on specimen collection and palm parts include the biggest leaves and inflorescences among the flowering plants. Add to this the fact that plant classification was, until the 20th century, mostly a product of the Western world and the fact that most of the species in the family originate in remote to greatly remote (to Europe and North America) areas of the globe, and it is not hard to understand why most of the advancement in palm taxonomy has occurred recently. The present trend has largely been to lump formerly discrete genera and species and, in the future, there will doubtless be more combining, especially within the subtribes. For example, *Ceroxylon* and *Oraniopsis* are similar in so many ways that, if they were not separated by the Pacific Ocean, they would doubtless have already been combined into a single genus.

Palms in the Landscape

Palms are the most underused design elements in nearly every garden, even most of those in the tropics or subtropics. Fortunate indeed are gardeners who live in regions where at least a few palms grow, as their unique variety of forms cannot begin to be simulated by anything other than massive ferns, yuccas, and cordylines, which themselves are tropical or subtropical.

The biggest reason these princes of the plant world are eschewed even where they can be grown is probably lack of space: most palm species are relatively large. This problem is compounded by the gardener's desire for color. The desire is, of course, an important one, but color is greatly overused at the expense of variety of form. The smaller the garden, the more the use of color alone tends to become overwhelming and even tiring, somewhat analogous to eating a diet of cake and ice cream only, or listening to only one type of music. *Variety* is the operative word and is what palms excel at with their ineluctably different forms. In addition, palms are often colorful, especially the tropical species. Their crownshafts, inflorescences, and leaf colors are sometimes extraordinary. Palms lend to the landscape a more controlled and subtle color palette than that of most "flowering plants."

A few points should be considered when incorporating palms into the landscape. First, palms don't look good planted in straight lines, but what type of plant does? This arrangement is unnatural in the sense that it doesn't occur in nature. The larger palms are magnificence itself when lining streets or avenues, but the dictum still applies: a curving street, path, or driveway is infinitely more aesthetically pleasing than a straight one where variety is the missing element.

Second, palms generally look their best when planted in small groups or groves rather than as a single tree surrounded by space. Again, the reason is that palms do not occur singly in nature. Furthermore the discrete groups look best when the number of individuals therein is three or more and the individuals are of varying heights; if each palm is the same height, the crowns visually "fight." Variety is the missing element in groups of same-height palms.

Third, a landscape whose horizon is basically at one level is incredibly less interesting and beautiful than one of varying levels. Nothing fixes the imbalance better than using palms as *canopy-scapes*, where the crowns of trees float above the general level of the surrounding vegetation. Such palms substitute remarkably well for a lack of mountains. Again, variety of form!

Fourth, the wall of vegetation that constitutes the horizon of the garden is so much less appealing if it is of one form or of one color. There are no plants better suited to fix this than palms, whether large or small, fan leaved or feather leaved. Palms are the *sine-qua-non* elements to create the needed form and texture. Again, variety of form!

A few palm species are so large and impressive that they can be advantageously planted alone as specimen plants surrounded by space and still look good. They would look even better if planted in groups, but the size or other limitations of a given landscape or garden can often make this difficult or impossible.

Finally, no palm species has an uninteresting or ugly silhouette, so palms can be planted in front of walls or other structures, especially if the structure has a contrasting color. In this situation even small palms can look wonderful planted singly.

Pruning

While it is true that palms are underutilized in nearly every landscaping situation, it is also the case that, once planted, they tend to be lamentably overpruned. This is partly because they are unlike other garden trees and shrubs with which most gardeners are more familiar. Most people agonize all too much about whether or not to prune a palm tree, thinking, naturally enough, that a palm is like a hydrangea bush, an oak tree, or a morning-glory vine that needs diligent guidance from youth to old age to make a presentable landscape specimen. This is not the case. A palm occasionally requires some pruning, but the type and frequency of pruning requirements are unlike those of other landscape subjects. A palm is, except for some special aesthetic concerns, human safety, or the health of the plant itself, a low-maintenance landscape subject.

The Palm Family

Subfamily	Tribe	Subtribe	Genera
Coryphoideae	Corypheae	Thrinacinae	*Chamaerops, Chelyocarpus, Coccothrinax, Cryosophila, Guihaia, Itaya, Maxburretia, Rhapidophyllum, Rhapis, Schippia, Thrinax, Trachycarpus, Trithrinax, Zombia*
		Livistoninae	*Acoelorraphe, Brahea, Colpothrinax, Copernicia, Johannesteijsmannia, Licuala, Livistona, Pholidocarpus, Pritchardia, Pritchardiopsis, Serenoa, Washingtonia*
		Coryphinae	*Chuniophoenix, Corypha, Kerriodoxa, Nannorrhops*
		Sabalinae	*Sabal*
	Phoeniceae		*Phoenix*
	Borasseae	Lataniinae	*Borassodendron, Borassus, Latania, Lodoicea*
		Hyphaeninae	*Bismarckia, Hyphaene, Medemia, Satranala*
Calamoideae	Calameae	Ancistrophyllinae	*Eremospatha, Laccosperma*
		Eugeissoninae	*Eugeissona*
		Metroxylinae	*Korthalsia, Metroxylon*
		Calaminae	*Calamus, Calospatha, Ceratolobus, Daemonorops, Eleiodoxa, Pogonotium, Retispatha, Salacca*
		Plectocomiinae	*Myrialepis, Plectocomia, Plectocomiopsis*
		Pigafettinae	*Pigafetta*
		Raphiinae	*Raphia*
		Oncocalaminae	*Oncocalamus*
	Lepidocaryeae		*Lepidocaryum, Mauritia, Mauritiella*
Nyphoideae			*Nypa*
Ceroxyloideae	Cyclospaeae		*Pseudophoenix*
	Ceroxyleae		*Ceroxylon, Juania, Oraniopsis, Ravenea*
	Hyophorbeae		*Chamaedorea, Gaussia, Hyophorbe, Synechanthus, Wendlandiella*
Arecoideae	Caryoteae		*Arenga, Caryota, Wallichia*
	Iriarteae	Iriarteinae	*Dictyocaryum, Iriartea, Iriartella, Socratea*
		Wettiniinae	*Wettinia*
	Podococceae		*Podococcus*
	Areceae	Oraniinae	*Orania*
		Manicariinae	*Manicaria*
		Leopoldiniinae	*Leopoldinia*

AESTHETIC CONCERNS. Several palm species, like *Washingtonia filifera* and *W. robusta*, have a characteristic and mostly picturesque shag, sometimes called a *petticoat*. These petticoats consist of the adherent dead leaves whose leaf bases often refuse to fall from the trunk. In the palms' native desert and arid grassland regions, natural fires commonly burn off the old leaves. In cultivation, the palms seldom retain enough dead leaves in moist and humid climes to form the petticoat but, in more arid regions, they usually do. Some palm owners love the shag, while others detest the "ugly haystack." The easiest way to remove the shag is, of course, one leaf at a time, as the individual leaves die and become pendent.

Then there is the manicurist mentality of those who want palms like *Washingtonia robusta* to have clean and smooth trunks from the bottom all the way to the leaf crown. This look is popular, especially in fantasy parks and Las Vegas. Removing all adherent leaf bases (or boots) from these palms creates an undeniably handsome look because of the elegantly thin and smooth, tall trunks, but

Subfamily	Tribe	Subtribe	Genera
[Arecoideae]	[Areceae]	Malortieinae	*Reinhardtia*
		Dypsidinae	*Dypsis*
		Lemurophoenicinae	*Lemurophoenix*
		Euterpeinae	*Euterpe, Hyospathe, Neonicholsonia, Oenocarpus, Prestoea*
		Roystoneinae	*Roystonea*
		Archontophoenicinae	*Actinokentia, Archontophoenix, Chambeyronia, Hedyscepe, Kentiopsis, Rhopalostylis*
		Cyrtostachydinae	*Cyrtostachys*
		Linospadicinae	*Calyptrocalyx, Howea, Laccospadix, Linospadix*
		Ptychospermatinae	*Adonidia, Balaka, Brassiophoenix, Carpentaria, Drymophloeus, Normanbya, Ptychococcus, Ptychosperma, Veitchia, Wodyetia*
		Areninae	*Areca, Gronophyllum, Gulubia, Hydriastele, Loxococcus, Nenga, Pinanga, Siphokentia*
		Iguanurinae	*Actinorhytis, Alloschmidia, Alsmithia, Basselinia, Bentinckia, Brongniartikentia, Burretiokentia, Campecarpus, Clinosperma, Clinostigma, Cyphokentia, Cyphophoenix, Cyphosperma, Dictyosperma, Heterospathe, Iguanura, Lavoixia, Lepidorrhachis, Moratia, Neoveitchia, Pelagodoxa, Physokentia, Rhopaloblaste, Satakentia, Sommieria, Veillonia*
		Oncospermatinae	*Acanthophoenix, Deckenia, Nephrosperma, Oncosperma, Phoenicophorium, Roscheria, Tectiphiala, Verschaffeltia*
		Sclerospermatinae	*Carpoxylon, Marojejya, Masoala, Sclerosperma*
	Cocoeae	Beccariophoenicinae	*Beccariophoenix*
		Butiinae	*Allagoptera, Butia, Cocos, Jubaea, Jubaeopsis, Lytocaryum, Parajubaea, Polyandrococos, Syagrus, Voanioala*
		Attaleinae	*Attalea*
		Elaeidinae	*Barcella, Elaeis*
		Bactridinae	*Acrocomia, Aiphanes, Astrocaryum, Bactris, Desmoncus, Gastrococos*
	Geonomeae		*Asterogyne, Calyptrogyne, Calyptronoma, Geonoma, Pholidostachys, Welfia*
Phytelephantoideae			*Ammandra, Aphandra, Phytelephas*

Adapted from Jody Haynes' Virtual Palm Encyclopedia Website.

the procedure is both time consuming and labor intensive, especially for tall specimens. *Washingtonia robusta*, for example, can grow rather quickly to a height of 40 feet, and old palms may attain a height of 100 feet.

The leaf bases of some palms fall off at various times, but many other palms have leaves whose laminae (blades) fall off while the boots themselves, and sometimes most of the petiole, adhere to the trunk for some time. A prime example of the latter is *Sabal palmetto* in the southeastern United States. The dead leaf bases may adhere for most of the life of this slow-growing palm, turning woody and much lighter colored than the actual "bark" of the palm, and giving a picturesque wicker look to the trunks. Often these woody boots are trimmed with a chain saw to conform one to the other in appearance and to create an even more elegant and manicured look.

Some popular palms like *Phoenix canariensis* produce immense, rounded canopies of long pinnate leaves. We personally consider this aspect of the species its most desirable trait, but others feel the palm looks better when the pendent leaves are removed, so that only the leaves that do not fall below the horizontal plane remain on the trunk. Removing the pendent leaves is no more difficult than removing the petticoats of *Washingtonia* palms and, since *P. canariensis* grows more slowly than either *Washingtonia* species, the task need not be done as often. Most pruners leave the boots of the just-cut crop of leaves, which practice results in a picturesque, large rounded knobby cluster (called the "bulb" or "pineapple") of leaf bases directly beneath the leaf crown; by the time of the next leaf pruning, the bulb of boots will have mostly fallen away from the trunk naturally. Other pruners remove the bulb also, which results in an even more picturesque tree with a more tropical and more airy aspect. But many palm owners or the landscapers they hire go far beyond these pruning practices: they remove enough leaves to create leaf crowns that look like feather dusters, leaving only the most erect living leaves therein. This is a truly abominable practice which completely ruins the wonderful appearance of these species. It is also inimical to the overall health of the tree which must struggle to photosynthesize enough food to maintain itself. Alas, this misguided practice is not limited to *Phoenix* species. It is all too common to see *Washingtonia, Syagrus romanzoffiana,* and many other species cropped in this manner, especially by plant maintenance contractors who, of course, make more money by recommending the monthly butchering of these beauties.

Several palms are clustering species that have unique aesthetic and maintenance characteristics. A prime example is *Phoenix reclinata,* which forms many suckers or subsidiary trunks throughout its life, and a single specimen may have as many as two dozen trunks. The trunks are not straight but lean gracefully outward from their points of origin. Few natural phenomena are as beautiful as a large "tuft" of this palm, but the clumps are made even more graceful and dramatic if a few trunks are thinned out as the mass develops, leaving trunks of differing heights. This allows the individual beauty of each trunk and the exquisitely graceful tableau of trunks and crowns to be seen and appreciated to its fullest. The trunks should be thinned when they are young and short, using a large pair of lopping shears to cut off the growing point; when the trunk decays sufficiently, it can be easily pulled apart. Alternately, a chain saw can be used to carefully cut at the base of the developing stem.

HUMAN SAFETY. For most palms the rapidity with which the dead leaf parts fall from the trunks is a matter of environmental conditions, as already implied in the discussion of the two *Washingtonia* species. The factors which influence the fall are wind, abrasion, fire, rain, and humidity, the latter two of which precipitate the breakdown of the dead leaf; and then there is vandalism. In many parts of the southwestern United States, juvenile (and sometimes not so juvenile) miscreants are wont to create "fireworks" by setting ablaze the shags of *Washingtonia* and other petticoat-forming species. The conflagration may be induced not by vandalism alone, but also by the careless tossing of live cigarettes and cigars by passersby as well as lightning strikes and even (in rare instances) damaged live electrical wires. In addition these masses of dead and dry leaves can be a habitat for all manner of vermin, including roaches, obnoxious bird species like starlings, scorpions, rats, mice, and even small snakes.

Of course, it is better to not plant any tree where it is or can become undesirable, looking crowded and cramped, or obstructing a desirable view. In practice, however, it is often done because the person who planted the palm did not know the ultimate dimensions of the particular species or just wanted its juvenile look for a certain period of time. In many instances the desirable, ultimate, and overall landscape use of the palm warrants temporary pruning of its leaves, so that, in time, it becomes a positive component of the landscape. In such instances it should be remembered that, as with any other type of tree, the palm needs a certain amount of functioning leaves for proper photosynthesis and health, the amount of which varies slightly from one species to another but, in general, is about 50 percent of the total. If too many leaves are constantly removed over a given period of time, the palm's trunk is subject to exhibiting varying trunk calipers because of the varying amounts of sugar it could produce at a given point in time; and the sight of a palm trunk with constrictions and bulges in what should be a columnar or naturally tapering stem can ruin an otherwise beautiful landscape subject.

Few palms produce large enough leaves or grow tall enough for their falling leaves to be much of a danger, but some, like the coconut (*Cocos nucifera*) and large date palms (for example, *Phoenix canariensis*), attain great heights and have large, heavy leaves with massive petioles and rachises. In addition, the coconut produces clusters of large, heavy fruit whose natural abscission (upon completely ripening) from the fruit stalk and consequent rapid descent can (in rare instances) be deadly. Removing the leaves and fruits from tall specimens is labor intensive, especially if there are many trees to deal with.

A few tropical palm species have natural rings of large spines at regular intervals around their trunks. Among these are the macaw and gru-gru palms, *Acrocomia* species. Such spines are easily removed with shears or small branch cutters. Much more common in the United States are those palm species whose leaves have vicious spines for a part of their length. Prime examples are all *Phoenix* species (date palms) whose lower (basal) leaflets are always metamorphosed into spines of varying lengths and viciousness. When young, the older, lower, and more spreading leaves of these palms are often removed if they are near human pathways.

HEALTH OF THE PALM. There are only two instances in which pruning is involved in the good health of a palm: transplantation and disease cure or prevention. Leaf pruning, especially of bare-root or balled-and-burlapped plants, is usually a necessity when transplanting. Removing at least half the leaf crown is almost always recommended in these cases to reduce moisture loss through transpiration because of the inevitable root loss. Indeed, with all *Sabal* species the recommendation is to remove all leaves except the "spear" or newest unfurled leaf, as the roots of this palm die under such circumstances and the palm will have to grow an entirely new set from the trunk.

Several types of fungus infestations are cured or prevented by leaf removal. The two most common fungus problems are graphiola or false smut and diamond scale. The latter, in spite of the name, is not a scale insect but rather a fungus which produces scalelike lesions. The fungus problem must first be identified and then the leaves with the worst infestations should be completely removed and burned before finally applying the proper fungicide to the tree. In California, a deadly and incurable fungal disease (*Fusarium* wilt) is transferred by pruning tools, as the fungus organism resides in the sap of the tree. In all cases, but especially in California, pruning tools should be sterilized between pruning one palm tree and another.

Gallery of
Palms

PLATE 1. *Acanthophoenix rubra*, crownshaft and leaf crown of mature individual. In habitat, Réunion. Rolf Kyburz

PLATE 2. *Acoelorraphe wrightii*. Florida. Robert Lee Riffle

PLATE 3. *Acoelorraphe wrightii*, stems. Florida. Robert Lee Riffle

PLATE 4. *Acrocomia aculeata* (*A. totai*). Florida. Robert Lee Riffle

PLATE 5. *Acrocomia aculeata* (*A. totai*), trunk and spines. Florida. Robert Lee Riffle

PLATE 6. *Acrocomia aculeata* (*A. mexicana*). Texas. Robert Lee Riffle

PLATE 7. *Actinokentia divaricata*, crownshaft and inflorescences. In habitat, New Caledonia. Paul Craft

PLATE 8. *Actinokentia divaricata*, new leaf color. In habitat, New Caledonia. Paul Craft

PLATE 9. *Actinorhytis calapparia*. Singapore. Chuck Hubbuch

PLATE 10. *Actinorhytis calapparia*, crownshafts and leaf crowns. Papua New Guinea. Rolf Kyburz

PLATE 11. *Adonidia merrillii*. Big Pine Key, Florida. Paul Craft

PLATE 12. *Adonidia merrillii*, in bloom. Florida. Robert Lee Riffle

PLATE 13. *Adonidia merrillii*, infructescence. Florida.
Robert Lee Riffle

PLATE 14. *Aiphanes aculeata*, inflorescences and infructescence.
Florida. Robert Lee Riffle

PLATE 15. *Aiphanes minima*. Cuba. Paul Craft

PLATE 16. *Aiphanes minima*, leaf crown. Florida. Robert Lee Riffle

PLATE 17. *Aiphanes minima*, leaf outline. Cuba. Paul Craft

PLATE 18. *Aiphanes minima*, infructescence. Cuba. Paul Craft

PLATE 19. *Allagoptera arenaria*. Florida. Robert Lee Riffle

PLATE 20. *Allagoptera arenaria*, leaf. Florida. Robert Lee Riffle

26

PLATE 21. *Allagoptera arenaria*, inflorescence. Florida.
Robert Lee Riffle

PLATE 22. *Allagoptera arenaria*, infructescence. Florida.
Robert Lee Riffle

PLATE 25. *Alsmithia longipes*, long petioles. Florida. Robert Lee Riffle

PLATE 23. *Alloschmidia glabrata*, inflorescences. Australia.
Daryl O'Connor

PLATE 24. *Alloschmidia glabrata*, leaf. In habitat, New Caledonia.
Rolf Kyburz

PLATE 26. *Aphandra natalia*. In habitat, Ecuador.
Martin Gibbons and Tobias Spanner

PLATE 27. *Archontophoenix cunninghamiana*. Florida.
Robert Lee Riffle

PLATE 28. *Archontophoenix cunninghamiana*, crownshaft.
Florida. Robert Lee Riffle

PLATE 29. *Archontophoenix cunninghamiana*, inflorescences. California. Paul Craft

PLATE 30. *Archontophoenix myolensis*. In habitat, Queensland, Australia. Chuck Hubbuch

PLATE 31. *Archontophoenix myolensis*. Florida. Robert Lee Riffle

PLATE 32. *Archontophoenix purpurea*. Australia. Paul Craft

PLATE 33. *Archontophoenix purpurea*, crownshaft. Australia. Paul Craft

PLATE 34. *Archontophoenix tuckeri*. Florida. Robert Lee Riffle

PLATE 35. *Areca catechu*. Australia. Paul Craft

PLATE 36. *Areca catechu*, mature tree. In habitat, Vietnam.
Gary Dahme

PLATE 37. *Areca catechu*, inflorescence. Florida. Robert Lee Riffle

30

PLATE 38. *Areca catechu*, infructescence of yellow crownshaft form. Australia. Paul Craft

PLATE 39. *Areca guppyana*. New Caledonia. Paul Craft

PLATE 40. *Areca ipot*, trunk, infructescences, crownshaft, and leaf crown. Rolf Kyburz

PLATE 41. *Areca latiloba*. New Caledonia. Paul Craft

PLATE 42. *Areca latiloba*. Florida. Robert Lee Riffle

PLATE 43. *Areca macrocalyx*. Florida. Robert Lee Riffle

PLATE 44. *Areca mammillata*. Florida. Robert Lee Riffle

PLATE 45. *Areca mammillata*, crownshaft. Florida.
Robert Lee Riffle

PLATE 46. *Areca minuta*. Australia. Paul Craft

PLATE 47. *Areca vestiaria*. Australia. Paul Craft

PLATE 48. *Areca vestiaria*, single-trunked form. Florida.
Robert Lee Riffle

PLATE 49. *Areca vestiaria*, single-trunked form, crownshaft and infructescences. Hawaii. Chuck Hubbuch

PLATE 50. *Areca vestiaria*, crown-shafts. Australia. Paul Craft

PLATE 51. *Areca vestiaria*, new colored leaf. Mexico. Paul Craft

PLATE 53. *Arenga australasica*, leaf. Florida. Robert Lee Riffle

PLATE 52. *Arenga australasica*. Florida. Robert Lee Riffle

PLATE 54. *Arenga australasica*, leaf underside. Florida. Robert Lee Riffle

PLATE 56. *Arenga brevipes*, leaf underside. California. Paul Craft

PLATE 55. *Arenga brevipes*. California. Paul Craft

PLATE 57. *Arenga caudata*. Australia. Paul Craft

PLATE 58. *Arenga engleri*. Florida. Robert Lee Riffle

PLATE 59. *Arenga engleri*, fibrous stems. Mexico. Paul Craft

PLATE 60. *Arenga engleri*, inflorescence. Robert Lee Riffle

PLATE 63. *Arenga hookeriana*, leaf. New Caledonia. Paul Craft

PLATE 61. *Arenga hastata*. In habitat, Sarawak. Tim Hatch

PLATE 62. *Arenga hookeriana*. Florida. Robert Lee Riffle

PLATE 64. *Arenga microcarpa*. Florida. Robert Lee Riffle

PLATE 65. *Arenga microcarpa*, leaf. Florida. Robert Lee Riffle

PLATE 66. *Arenga obtusifolia*. Florida. Robert Lee Riffle

PLATE 67. *Arenga pinnata*. Australia. Paul Craft

PLATE 68. *Arenga pinnata*. Florida. Robert Lee Riffle

PLATE 69. *Arenga pinnata*, inflorescences. Florida. Robert Lee Riffle

PLATE 70. *Arenga pinnata*, infructescence. Florida. Robert Lee Riffle

PLATE 71. *Arenga porphyrocarpa*. Rolf Kyburz

PLATE 72. *Arenga tremula*. Florida. Robert Lee Riffle

PLATE 73. *Arenga tremula*. Florida.
Robert Lee Riffle

PLATE 74. *Arenga undulatifolia*, leaf outline. Florida. Robert Lee Riffle

PLATE 75. *Arenga westerhoutii*, seedling.
Florida. Robert Lee Riffle

PLATE 76. *Asterogyne martiana*, showing new leaf color. Australia.
Paul Craft

PLATE 77. *Asterogyne martiana*, infructescence. In habitat, Belize. Paul Craft

PLATE 78. *Asterogyne spicata*. In habitat, Venezuela. Paul Craft

PLATE 79. *Asterogyne spicata*, young plant. Florida. Paul Craft

PLATE 80. *Astrocaryum alatum*. In habitat, Costa Rica. Paul Craft

PLATE 81. *Astrocaryum alatum*, juvenile tree. Florida. Robert Lee Riffle

PLATE 82. *Astrocaryum mexicanum*. Florida. Robert Lee Riffle

PLATE 83. *Astrocaryum mexicanum*, petioles and inflorescence. Florida. Robert Lee Riffle

PLATE 84. *Astrocaryum standleyanum*. In habitat, Costa Rica.
Paul Craft

PLATE 85. *Attalea amygdalina*, young tree. Australia. Paul Craft

PLATE 86. *Attalea butyracea*. Costa Rica. Chuck Hubbuch

PLATE 87. *Attalea butyracea*, leaf crown with main flowering
bracts and fruits. Florida. Robert Lee Riffle

PLATE 88. *Attalea cohune*. Belize. Paul Craft

PLATE 89. *Attalea cohune*, leaf crown with fruit. Florida.
Robert Lee Riffle

PLATE 90. *Attalea cohune*, infructescence. Florida. Robert Lee Riffle

PLATE 91. *Attalea crassispatha*. Florida. Robert Lee Riffle

PLATE 92. *Attalea humilis.* Florida. Robert Lee Riffle

PLATE 93. *Attalea phalerata.* Florida. Robert Lee Riffle

PLATE 94. *Attalea speciosa.* Florida. Robert Lee Riffle

PLATE 95. *Attalea* species, male inflorescence. Paul Craft

44

PLATE 96. *Bactris brongniartii*, Brazilian form. Florida. Robert Lee Riffle

PLATE 97. *Bactris brongniartii*, Venezuelan form. Florida. Robert Lee Riffle

PLATE 100. *Bactris gasipaes*, leaves. Florida. Robert Lee Riffle

PLATE 98. *Bactris concinna*. Florida. Robert Lee Riffle

PLATE 99. *Bactris gasipaes*. Florida. Robert Lee Riffle

PLATE 101. *Bactris gasipaes*, trunks. Florida. Robert Lee Riffle

PLATE 102. *Bactris major*. Florida. Robert Lee Riffle

PLATE 103. *Bactris major*, seedling. Florida. Robert Lee Riffle

PLATE 104. *Bactris militaris*. Rolf Kyburz

PLATE 105. *Bactris plumeriana*. In habitat, Cuba. Paul Craft

PLATE 107. *Basselinia deplanchei*. New Caledonia. Paul Craft

PLATE 106. *Bactris plumeriana*, stem. In habitat, Cuba. Paul Craft

PLATE 108. *Basselinia deplanchei*, crown-shaft and inflorescence. New Caledonia. Paul Craft

PLATE 109. *Basselinia deplanchei*, crown-shaft and infructescence. New Caledonia. Paul Craft

PLATE 110. *Basselinia favieri*. In habitat, New Caledonia.
Bryan Laughland

PLATE 111. *Basselinia gracilis*. Hawaii. Chuck Hubbuch

PLATE 112. *Basselinia pancheri*. In habitat, New Caledonia.
Paul Craft

PLATE 113. *Basselinia pancheri*, crownshaft. In habitat,
New Caledonia. Paul Craft

PLATE 114. *Basselinia velutina*. In habitat, New Caledonia. Paul Craft

PLATE 115. *Beccariophoenix madagascariensis*. Florida. Robert Lee Riffle

PLATE 117. *Beccariophoenix madagascariensis*, leaf base fibers. Florida. Robert Lee Riffle

PLATE 118. *Beccariophoenix madagascariensis*, inflorescences and spathes. Rolf Kyburz

PLATE 116. *Beccariophoenix madagascariensis*. Florida. Robert Lee Riffle

PLATE 119. *Bentinckia nicobarica*. Florida. Robert Lee Riffle

PLATE 120. *Bentinckia nicobarica*. Florida. Robert Lee Riffle

PLATE 121. *Bentinckia nicobarica*, crown-shaft of young tree. Florida. Robert Lee Riffle

PLATE 122. *Bismarckia nobilis*. Florida. Robert Lee Riffle

PLATE 123. *Bismarckia nobilis*, leaf sheaths and infructescences. Florida. Robert Lee Riffle

PLATE 125. *Borassodendron borneense*. In habitat, Sarawak. Tim Hatch

PLATE 124. *Bismarckia nobilis*, leaf crown. Florida. Robert Lee Riffle

PLATE 126. *Borassodendron borneense*, infructescences and leaf petioles. Rolf Kyburz

PLATE 127. *Borassodendron machadonis*. Australia. Paul Craft

PLATE 130. *Borassodendron machadonis*, infructescence. Florida. Paul Craft

PLATE 128. *Borassodendron machadonis*, trunk and leaf crown. Florida. Robert Lee Riffle

PLATE 129. *Borassodendron machadonis*, leaf. Florida. Robert Lee Riffle

52

PLATE 131. *Borassus aethiopium*. Florida. Robert Lee Riffle

PLATE 132. *Borassus aethiopium*. Florida. Robert Lee Riffle

PLATE 133. *Borassus flabellifer*, young tree. Texas. Robert Lee Riffle

PLATE 134. *Borassus flabellifer*, young adult tree. Australia.
Paul Craft

PLATE 135. *Brahea aculeata*. California. Paul Craft

PLATE 136. *Brahea armata*, green form, mature tree. Florida. Robert Lee Riffle

PLATE 138. *Brahea armata*, silver form, inflorescences. California. Paul Craft

PLATE 137. *Brahea armata*, green form, inflorescences. California. Paul Craft

PLATE 139. *Brahea brandegeei*, infructescences. California. Paul Craft

PLATE 140. *Brahea decumbens*. California. Robert Lee Riffle

PLATE 141. *Brahea dulcis*, young adult tree. California.
Robert Lee Riffle

PLATE 142. *Brahea edulis*. California. Paul Craft

PLATE 143. *Brahea edulis*, infructescence. Paul Craft

PLATE 145. *Brassiophoenix drymophoeoides*, leaf. Australia. Paul Craft

PLATE 144. *Brassiophoenix drymophoeoides.* Australia. Paul Craft

PLATE 146. *Burretiokentia hapala*. In habitat, New Caledonia.
Bryan Laughland

PLATE 147. *Burretiokentia hapala*, inflorescence. Florida. Robert Lee Riffle

PLATE 149. *Burretiokentia vieillardii*. In habitat, New Caledonia. Bryan Laughland

PLATE 148. *Burretiokentia koghiensis*. In habitat, New Caledonia. Rolf Kyburz

PLATE 150. *Burretiokentia vieillardii*, crownshaft and leaf crown. In habitat, New Caledonia. Rolf Kyburz

PLATE 151. *Burretiokentia vieillardii*, crownshaft. Rolf Kyburz

PLATE 152. *Butia archeri*. In habitat, Brazil. Paul Craft

PLATE 153. *Butia capitata*. California. Paul Craft

PLATE 154. *Butia capitata*, with Rolf Kyburz. Australia. Chuck Hubbuch

PLATE 155. *Butia capitata*, boots. California. Paul Craft

PLATE 156. ×*Butiagrus nabonnandii*. Texas. Robert Lee Riffle

PLATE 158. *Butia yatay*. Queensland, Australia. Paul Craft

PLATE 157. *Butia eriospatha*. Texas. Robert Lee Riffle

PLATE 159. *Butia* × *Jubaea*. Florida. Robert Lee Riffle

PLATE 160. *Butia* × *Jubaea*. Florida. Robert Lee Riffle

PLATE 161. *Calamus moti*. Cape Tribulation, Queensland, Australia.
Paul Craft

PLATE 162. *Calamus* species. Australia. Paul Craft

PLATE 164. *Calamus* species, stem. Australia. Daryl O'Connor

PLATE 165. *Calyptrocalyx*, colored new growth of clumping species. Robert Lee Riffle

PLATE 166. *Calyptrocalyx*, colored new growth of clumping species. Robert Lee Riffle

PLATE 163. *Calamus* species. Singapore. Chuck Hubbuch

PLATE 167. *Calyptrocalyx albertisianus*. Australia. Paul Craft

PLATE 168. *Calyptrocalyx arfakiensis*. Australia. Paul Craft

PLATE 171. *Calyptrocalyx hollrungii*, inflorescence. Florida. Paul Craft

PLATE 172. *Calyptrocalyx hollrungii*, leaf underside. Australia. Paul Craft

PLATE 169. *Calyptrocalyx forbesii*. Australia. Paul Craft

PLATE 170. *Calyptrocalyx hollrungii*, seedling with new leaf color. Australia. Paul Craft

Plate 174. *Calyptrocalyx pachystachys*. Australia. Paul Craft

Plate 173. *Calyptrocalyx hollrungii*, crownshaft and leaf crown of mature plant. Rolf Kyburz

Plate 175. *Calyptrocalyx pachystachys*, leaf. Australia. Paul Craft

Plate 176. *Calyptrocalyx pauciflorus*. Rolf Kyburz

PLATE 177. *Calyptrocalyx polyphyllus*. Australia. Paul Craft

PLATE 178. *Calyptrocalyx polyphyllus*, new leaf color. Australia. Paul Craft

PLATE 179. *Calyptrocalyx spicatus*. In habitat, Ambon, Moluccas. Clayton York

PLATE 180. *Calyptrocalyx* 'Briauu'. Australia. Paul Craft

PLATE 181. *Calyptrocalyx* 'Kainlas'. Australia. Paul Craft

PLATE 182. *Calyptrocalyx* 'Kainlas', leaves. Australia. Paul Craft

PLATE 184. *Calyptrocalyx* 'Sobriawe'. Australia. Paul Craft

PLATE 185. *Calyptrogyne ghiesbreghtiana*. In habitat, Honduras. Chuck Hubbuch

PLATE 183. *Calyptrocalyx* 'Siterum'. Australia. Paul Craft

PLATE 186. *Calyptrogyne ghiesbreghtiana*. In habitat, Belize. Paul Craft

PLATE 187. *Calyptronoma occidentalis*. Florida. Robert Lee Riffle

PLATE 188. *Calyptronoma occidentalis*, leaf crown and inflorescence. Florida. Robert Lee Riffle

PLATE 189. *Calyptronoma plumeriana*. In habitat, Cuba. Paul Craft

PLATE 190. *Calyptronoma rivalis*. Florida. Robert Lee Riffle

PLATE 191. *Calyptronoma rivalis*. Florida. Robert Lee Riffle

PLATE 192. *Campecarpus fulcitus*. In habitat, New Caledonia.
Chuck Hubbuch

PLATE 193. *Campecarpus fulcitus*, crownshaft. In habitat, New Caledonia. Chuck Hubbuch

PLATE 194. *Campecarpus fulcitus*, stilt roots. In habitat, New Caledonia. Paul Craft

PLATE 195. *Carpentaria acuminata*. Florida. Robert Lee Riffle

PLATE 196. *Carpentaria acuminata*, juvenile leaves. Florida. Robert Lee Riffle

PLATE 197. *Carpoxylon macrospermum*. Florida. Robert Lee Riffle

PLATE 198. *Caryota gigas*. California. Paul Craft

PLATE 199. *Caryota gigas*. Florida. Robert Lee Riffle

PLATE 200. *Caryota maxima*. In habitat, Thailand. Chuck Hubbuch

PLATE 202. *Caryota maxima*, infructescence and dead stem. In habitat, Thailand. Chuck Hubbuch

PLATE 201. *Caryota maxima*, leaf. Chuck Hubbuch

PLATE 203. *Caryota mitis*. Florida. Robert Lee Riffle

PLATE 204. *Caryota mitis*, leaflets. Florida.
Robert Lee Riffle

PLATE 205. *Caryota no*. In habitat, Sarawak. Tim Hatch

PLATE 206. *Caryota ochlandra*, in bloom. California. Paul Craft

PLATE 207. *Caryota rumphiana*, inflorescence. Paul Craft

PLATE 208. *Caryota urens*. Florida. Robert Lee Riffle

PLATE 209. *Caryota urens*, in flower and fruit. Australia. Paul Craft

PLATE 210. *Caryota zebrina*. Australia. Paul Craft

PLATE 211. *Caryota zebrina*, stem and petioles. Australia. Paul Craft

PLATE 212. *Caryota* species, dying tree in flower and fruit. Florida. Robert Lee Riffle

PLATE 213. *Ceroxylon alpinum*. In habitat, Venezuela.
Martin Gibbons and Tobias Spanner

PLATE 214. *Ceroxylon amazonicum*. In habitat, Ecuador.
Martin Gibbons and Tobias Spanner

PLATE 215. *Ceroxylon ceriferum*. In habitat, Venezuela. Martin Gibbons and Tobias Spanner

PLATE 216. *Ceroxylon echinulatum*. In habitat, Ecuador. Martin Gibbons and Tobias Spanner

PLATE 217. *Ceroxylon parvifrons*. In habitat, Ecuador. Martin Gibbons and Tobias Spanner

PLATE 219. *Ceroxylon quindiuense*, trunks in excess of 100 feet in height. In habitat, Ecuador. Martin Gibbons and Tobias Spanner

PLATE 218. *Ceroxylon parvum*. In habitat, Ecuador. Martin Gibbons and Tobias Spanner

PLATE 220. *Ceroxylon ventricosum*. In habitat, Ecuador. Martin Gibbons and Tobias Spanner

PLATE 221. *Ceroxylon vogelianum* (foreground) and *C. quindiuense* (background). Jose Celestino Mutis Botanic Garden, Bogota, Colombia. Martin Gibbons and Tobias Spanner

PLATE 223. *Chamaedorea amabilis*. In habitat, Costa Rica. Paul Craft

PLATE 222. *Chamaedorea adscendens*. Belize. Paul Craft

PLATE 224. *Chamaedorea cataractarum*. Belize. Paul Craft

PLATE 225. *Chamaedorea deckeriana*. Paul Craft

PLATE 226. *Chamaedorea ernesti-augustii*. Venezuela. Paul Craf

PLATE 227. *Chamaedorea fragrans*. Paul Craft

PLATE 228. *Chamaedorea geonomiformis*. In habitat, Belize. Paul Craft

PLATE 231. *Chamaedorea metallica*, segmented leaf form. Belize.
Paul Craft

PLATE 229. *Chamaedorea graminifolia*. In habitat, Belize.
Paul Craft

PLATE 232. *Chamaedorea metallica*, used as large groundcover. Belize.
Paul Craft

PLATE 230. *Chamaedorea metallica*. Belize. Paul Craft

PLATE 233. *Chamaedorea microspadix*. Paul Craft

PLATE 236. *Chamaedorea plumosa*. Paul Craft

PLATE 237. *Chamaedorea pumila*. Costa Rica. Paul Craft

PLATE 234. *Chamaedorea microspadix*. Texas.
Robert Lee Riffle

PLATE 235. *Chamaedorea oblongata*. In habitat, Belize.
Paul Craft

PLATE 238. *Chamaedorea radicalis*. Venezuela. Paul Craft

PLATE 239. *Chamaedorea radicalis*, aerial-trunked form. Florida. Robert Lee Riffle

PLATE 240. *Chamaedorea radicalis*, with inflorescences. Florida. Robert Lee Riffle

PLATE 241. *Chamaedorea seifrizii*. Florida. Robert Lee Riffle

78

PLATE 242. *Chamaedorea seifrizii*, broad leaflet form. Florida.
Robert Lee Riffle

PLATE 246. *Chamaedorea tepejilote*. California. Paul Craft

PLATE 243. *Chamaedorea stolonifera*. In habitat, Chiapas, Mexico. Paul Craft

PLATE 244. *Chamaedorea tenella*. Paul Craft

PLATE 245. *Chamaedorea tepejilote*. In habitat, Chiapas, Mexico.
Paul Craft

PLATE 249. *Chamaedorea tuerckheimii*. Australia. Paul Craft

PLATE 247. *Chamaedorea tepejilote*, inflorescences. Florida. Robert Lee Riffle

PLATE 248. *Chamaedorea tepejilote*, leaf. Belize.
Paul Craft

PLATE 250. *Chamaerops humilis*, single-trunked form. Texas. Robert Lee Riffle

PLATE 251. *Chamaerops humilis*, pendent segment form. Florida. Robert Lee Riffle

PLATE 252. *Chamaerops humilis*, very large clump. California. Paul Craft

PLATE 253. *Chamaerops humilis*, with fruit. Texas. Robert Lee Riffle

PLATE 254. *Chambeyronia macrocarpa*. Australia. Paul Craft

PLATE 256. *Chambeyronia macrocarpa*, watermelon-colored crownshaft. Paul Craft

PLATE 258. *Chuniophoenix hainanensis*. Florida. Robert Lee Riffle

PLATE 255. *Chambeyronia macrocarpa*. New Caledonia. Paul Craft

PLATE 257. *Chelyocarpus chuco*, leaf. Robert Lee Riffle

PLATE 259. *Chuniophoenix nana.* Rolf Kyburz

PLATE 260. *Clinosperma bracteale*, trunk, inflorescence, and crownshaft. In habitat, New Caledonia. Bryan Laughland

PLATE 261. *Clinostigma harlandii*, trunk and crownshaft. Australia. Daryl O'Connor

PLATE 262. *Clinostigma samoense.* Florida. Robert Lee Riffle

PLATE 263. *Clinostigma savoryanum*. Florida. Robert Lee Riffle

PLATE 264. *Coccothrinax argentea*. Robert Lee Riffle

PLATE 265. *Coccothrinax argentata*. In habitat, Big Pine Key, Florida. Robert Lee Riffle

PLATE 266. *Coccothrinax "azul."* In habitat, Cuba. Paul Craft

PLATE 267. *Coccothrinax "azul,"* leaf. In habitat, Cuba. Paul Craft

PLATE 268. *Coccothrinax barbadensis*. Florida. Robert Lee Riffle

PLATE 269. *Coccothrinax borhidiana*. In habitat, Cuba. Paul Craft

PLATE 270. *Coccothrinax borhidiana*. In habitat, Cuba. Paul Craft

PLATE 271. *Coccothrinax borhidiana*. In habitat, Cuba. Paul Craft

PLATE 272. *Coccothrinax borhidiana*, with Horace Hobbs. Cuba. Paul Craft

PLATE 273. *Coccothrinax crinita*. Cuba. Paul Craft

PLATE 274. *Coccothrinax crinita*, leaf. Florida. Robert Lee Riffle

PLATE 275. *Coccothrinax crinita*, stem. Florida.
Robert Lee Riffle

PLATE 277. *Coccothrinax gundlachii*. Santiago, Cuba.
Paul Craft

PLATE 276. *Coccothrinax gracilis*. In habitat, Dominican Republic. Paul Craft

PLATE 278. *Coccothrinax clarensis* (*gundlachii* of Henderson et al. 1995). In habitat, Cuba. Paul Craft

PLATE 280. *Coccothrinax miraguama*, leaf. Cuba. Paul Craft

PLATE 279. *Coccothrinax miraguama*, trunk. Cuba.
Paul Craft

PLATE 281. *Coccothrinax miraguama*, leaf underside.
Cuba. Paul Craft

PLATE 282. *Coccothrinax pseudorigida* (*pauciramosa* of Henderson
et al. 1995). In habitat, Cuba. Paul Craft

PLATE 283. *Coccothrinax salvatoris*. In habitat, Cuba. Paul Craft

PLATE 284. *Coccothrinax salvatoris*. In habitat, Cuba. Paul Craft

PLATE 285. *Coccothrinax spissa*. In habitat, Dominican Republic. Paul Craft

PLATE 286. *Cocos nucifera*. Costa Rica. Nancy Landau

PLATE 287. *Cocos nucifera*, leaf sheath and lower petiole. Robert Lee Riffle

PLATE 288. *Cocos nucifera* 'Golden Malayan Dwarf'. Florida. Robert Lee Riffle

PLATE 289. *Cocos nucifera* 'Maypan'. Florida. Robert Lee Riffle

PLATE 290. *Cocos nucifera* 'Samoan Dwarf'. Florida. Robert Lee Riffle

PLATE 291. *Cocos nucifera* 'Tall Jamaican'. Florida. Robert Lee Riffle

PLATE 292. *Colpothrinax wrightii*. In habitat, Cuba.
Paul Craft

PLATE 294. *Colpothrinax wrightii*, before forming a "belly."
Florida. Robert Lee Riffle

PLATE 293. *Colpothrinax wrightii*. In habitat, Cuba.
Paul Craft

PLATE 295. *Colpothrinax wrightii*, infructescences. Cuba.
Paul Craft

PLATE 296. *Copernicia alba*. Florida. Robert Lee Riffle

PLATE 297. *Copernicia baileyana*, young adult. Florida.
Robert Lee Riffle

PLATE 298. *Copernicia baileyana*, mature grove. Florida.
Robert Lee Riffle

PLATE 299. *Copernicia baileyana*, trunk and underside of leaf crown. Florida. Robert Lee Riffle

PLATE 300. *Copernicia berteroana*. Dominican Republic. Paul Craft

PLATE 301. *Copernicia brittonorum*. In habitat, Cuba. Paul Craft

PLATE 305. *Copernicia cowellii*, leaf. Paul Craft

PLATE 302. *Copernicia cowellii*. In habitat, Cuba. Paul Craft

PLATE 303. *Copernicia cowellii*. In habitat, Cuba. Paul Craft

PLATE 304. *Copernicia cowellii*. In habitat, Cuba. Paul Craft

PLATE 306. *Copernicia ekmanii*. Florida. Paul Craft

PLATE 307. *Copernicia fallaensis*. Cuba. Paul Craft

PLATE 308. *Copernicia fallaensis*, leaf bases and petioles. Cuba. Paul Craft

PLATE 310. *Copernicia gigas*. In habitat, Cuba. Paul Craft

PLATE 309. *Copernicia fallaensis*, leaf outline. Cuba. Paul Craft

PLATE 311. *Copernicia glabrescens*. Robert Lee Riffle

PLATE 312. *Copernicia hospita*. Florida. Robert Lee Riffle

PLATE 313. *Copernicia hospita*. Florida. Robert Lee Riffle

PLATE 314. *Copernicia macroglossa*, with full "skirt." Florida. Robert Lee Riffle

PLATE 315. *Copernicia macroglossa*, with partial "skirt." Florida. Robert Lee Riffle

PLATE 316. *Copernicia prunifera*. Florida. Robert Lee Riffle

PLATE 317. *Copernicia prunifera*, with spiraling leaf sheath stubs. Florida. Robert Lee Riffle

PLATE 318. *Copernicia rigida*. Cuba. Paul Craft

PLATE 319. *Copernicia rigida*, young adult tree with partial skirt. Cuba. Paul Craft

PLATE 320. *Copernicia* ×*textilis* (*tectorum* of Henderson et al. 1995). In habitat, Cuba. Paul Craft

PLATE 321. *Copernicia tectorum*. Florida. Robert Lee Riffle

PLATE 322. *Corypha umbraculifera*. Cuba. Paul Craft

PLATE 323. *Corypha umbraculifera*, in bloom. Panama. Paul Craft

PLATE 324. *Corypha utan*. Costa Rica. Paul Craft

PLATE 325. *Corypha utan*, boots. Australia. Paul Craft

PLATE 326. *Cryosophila guagara*. Florida. Robert Lee Riffle

PLATE 327. *Cryosophila stauracantha*. In habitat, Belize. Paul Craft

PLATE 328. *Cryosophila stauracantha*, trunk. Belize.
Paul Craft

PLATE 329. *Cryosophila stauracantha*, infructescences. Belize. Paul Craft

PLATE 330. *Cryosophila warscewiczii*. Costa Rica. Chuck Hubbuch

PLATE 331. *Cyphophoenix elegans*. New Caledonia. Paul Craft

PLATE 332. *Cyphophoenix nucele*. Florida. Robert Lee Riffle

PLATE 334. *Cyphosperma balansae*, leaf crown. In habitat, New Caledonia. Chuck Hubbuch

PLATE 333. *Cyphosperma balansae*. New Caledonia. Paul Craft

PLATE 335. *Cyrtostachys ledermanniana*. Florida. Robert Lee Riffle

PLATE 336. *Cyrtostachys renda*. Australia. Paul Craft

PLATE 337. *Cyrtostachys renda*, stems. Florida. Robert Lee Riffle

PLATE 338. *Cyrtostachys renda*, growing in pond.
Florida. Robert Lee Riffle

PLATE 339. *Daemonorops curranii*. Florida. Robert Lee Riffle

PLATE 340. *Daemonorops jenkinsiana*. In habitat, Bengal, India.
Martin Gibbons and Tobias Spanner

PLATE 341. *Daemonorops melanochaetes*. Australia. Daryl O'Connor

PLATE 342. *Deckenia nobilis*, mature tree. Grenada. John Criswick

PLATE 343. *Deckenia nobilis*, crownshaft and inflorescences. Hawaii. Chuck Hubbuch

PLATE 344. *Deckenia nobilis*, juvenile tree. Florida.
Robert Lee Riffle

PLATE 345. *Deckenia nobilis*, stem and petiole spines.
Florida. Robert Lee Riffle

PLATE 346. *Desmoncus orthacanthos*. Florida. Robert Lee Riffle

PLATE 347. *Desmoncus* species. In habitat, Belize. Paul Craft

PLATE 348. *Desmoncus* species. In habitat, Mexico. Paul Craft

PLATE 349. *Desmoncus* species. In habitat, Mexico.
Paul Craft

PLATE 350. *Desmoncus* species. Cuba. Paul Craft

PLATE 352. *Dictyosperma album*. Florida. Robert Lee Riffle

PLATE 351. *Dictyocaryum lamarckianum*. In habitat,
Ecuador. Martin Gibbons and Tobias Spanner

PLATE 353. *Dictyosperma album*, crownshaft. Florida.
Robert Lee Riffle

PLATE 354. *Dictyosperma album*, leaves. Florida. Robert Lee Riffle

PLATE 355. *Drymophloeus litigiosus*. Australia. Paul Craft

PLATE 356. *Drymophloeus litigiosus*, leaf outline. Australia. Paul Craft

PLATE 357. *Drymophloeus pachycladus*. Florida. Robert Lee Riffle

PLATE 358. *Drymophloeus subdistichus*. Hawaii. Chuck Hubbuch

PLATE 359. *Dypsis ambositrae*. In habitat, Madagascar. Rolf Kyburz

PLATE 360. *Dypsis ambositrae*, seedling trees with colored petioles. In habitat, Madagascar. Rolf Kyburz

PLATE 361. *Dypsis baronii*. California. Paul Craft

PLATE 362. *Dypsis baronii*, stems. California. Paul Craft

PLATE 363. *Dypsis cabadae*. Cuba. Paul Craft

PLATE 364. *Dypsis cabadae*, leaves. Florida. Robert Lee Riffle

PLATE 365. *Dypsis cabadae*, crownshafts. Florida. Robert Lee Riffle

PLATE 366. *Dypsis cabadae*, trunk. Florida. Robert Lee Riffle

PLATE 367. *Dypsis ceracea*. Australia. Paul Craft

PLATE 368. *Dypsis crinita*, nearly mature trees. Florida. Paul Craft

PLATE 369. *Dypsis crinita*, trunk. Paul Craft

PLATE 370. *Dypsis decaryi*. Australia. Paul Craft

PLATE 371. *Dypsis decaryi*, leaf bases and inflorescences.
Robert Lee Riffle

PLATE 372. *Dypsis decaryi*. In habitat, Madagascar. Rolf Kyburz

PLATE 373. *Dypsis decipiens*. Cuba. Chuck Hubbuch

PLATE 376. *Dypsis lanceolata*. Florida. Robert Lee Riffle

PLATE 374. *Dypsis decipiens*. California. Paul Craft

PLATE 375. *Dypsis decipiens*, trunks and crownshafts. Cuba. Chuck Hubbuch

PLATE 377. *Dypsis lanceolata*, stems and crownshaft. Florida.
Robert Lee Riffle

PLATE 378. *Dypsis leptocheilos*. Florida. Robert Lee Riffle

PLATE 379. *Dypsis leptocheilos*, trunk and crownshaft. Paul Craft

PLATE 380. *Dypsis leptocheilos*, crownshaft. Florida.
Robert Lee Riffle

112

PLATE 381. *Dypsis louvelii*. Australia. Paul Craft

PLATE 382. *Dypsis lutescens*, crownshafts and infructescences. Florida. Robert Lee Riffle

PLATE 383. *Dypsis madagascariensis*, single trunked. Florida. Robert Lee Riffle

PLATE 384. *Dypsis madagascariensis*, single trunked, stem and crownshaft. Paul Craft

PLATE 385. *Dypsis madagascariensis*, multiple trunked. Florida.
Robert Lee Riffle

PLATE 386. *Dypsis onilahensis*. In habitat, Madagascar. Rolf Kyburz

PLATE 387. *Dypsis pinnatifrons*. Costa Rica. Paul Craft

PLATE 388. *Dypsis pinnatifrons*, pink crownshaft form. Australia.
Paul Craft

PLATE 389. *Dypsis pinnatifrons*, pink crownshaft form, detail. Australia. Paul Craft

PLATE 390. *Dypsis pinnatifrons*, pink crownshaft form, new leaf color. Australia. Paul Craft

PLATE 392. *Dypsis rivularis*, trunk and crownshaft. Australia. Paul Craft

PLATE 391. *Dypsis rivularis*. In habitat, Madagascar. Rolf Kyburz

PLATE 393. *Dypsis rivularis*, leaf. Australia. Paul Craft

PLATE 394. *Dypsis utilis.* In habitat, Madagascar. Rolf Kyburz

PLATE 395. *Elaeis guineensis*. Florida. Robert Lee Riffle

PLATE 396. *Elaeis guineensis*. Costa Rica. Paul Craft

PLATE 397. *Elaeis guineensis*, trunk and infructescence. Florida. Robert Lee Riffle

PLATE 399. *Elaeis oleifera*. Florida. Robert Lee Riffle

PLATE 398. *Elaeis oleifera*. Florida. Robert Lee Riffle

PLATE 400. *Eugeissona insignis*. Australia. Paul Craft

PLATE 401. *Eugeissona insignis*, leaf bases and petioles. Australia. Paul Craft

PLATE 403. *Eugeissona utilis*. In habitat, Sarawak. Tim Hatch

PLATE 405. *Euterpe oleracea*, crownshafts and stems. Florida. Robert Lee Riffle

PLATE 402. *Eugeissona tristis*. Australia. Paul Craft

PLATE 404. *Euterpe oleracea*. Florida. Robert Lee Riffle

118

PLATE 406. *Euterpe oleracea*, inflorescence.
Robert Lee Riffle

PLATE 407. *Euterpe precatoria*. Australia. Paul Craft

PLATE 408. *Gastrococos crispa*. Florida. Robert Lee Riffle

PLATE 409. *Gastrococos crispa*. In habitat, Cuba. Paul Craft

PLATE 410. *Gastrococos crispa*, young adult. Cuba. Paul Craft

PLATE 411. *Gastrococos crispa*, in fruit. Florida. Robert Lee Riffle

PLATE 412. *Gastrococos crispa*, spines on leaves of juvenile plant. Florida. Robert Lee Riffle

PLATE 413. *Gaussia attenuata*. Florida. Robert Lee Riffle

PLATE 414. *Gaussia maya*. In habitat, Belize. Paul Craft

PLATE 415. *Gaussia maya*, inflorescences. Florida. Paul Craft

PLATE 416. *Gaussia princeps* In mogote habitat, Cuba. Paul Craft

PLATE 417. *Gaussia princeps*. In habitat, Cuba. Paul Craft

PLATE 418. *Gaussia spirituana*. In habitat, Cuba. Paul Craft

PLATE 419. *Geonoma congesta*. Australia. Paul Craft

PLATE 420. *Geonoma densa*. Australia. Paul Craft

PLATE 421. *Geonoma deversa*. In habitat, Costa Rica. Paul Craft

PLATE 422. *Geonoma interrupta*. Australia. Paul Craft

PLATE 423. *Geonoma interrupta*, leaf. In habitat, Belize. Paul Craft

PLATE 425. *Geonoma longivaginata*, leaf. Australia. Paul Craft

PLATE 426. *Geonoma longivaginata*, leaf. Australia. Paul Craft

PLATE 424. *Geonoma longivaginata*. Australia. Paul Craft

PLATE 427. *Geonoma undata*. In habitat, Venezuela. Paul Craft

PLATE 428. *Gronophyllum microcarpum*. Australia. Paul Craft

PLATE 429. *Gronophyllum pinangoides*. Australia. Paul Craft

PLATE 430. *Gronophyllum pinangoides*, inflorescence and infructescence. Australia. Paul Craft

PLATE 431. *Gronophyllum ramsayi*. Cuba. Paul Craft

124

PLATE 433. *Guihaia argyrata*, needlelike
fibers of leaf crown. Florida. Robert Lee Riffle

PLATE 432. *Guihaia argyrata*. Florida. Robert Lee Riffle

PLATE 434. *Gulubia costata*. Florida. Robert Lee Riffle

PLATE 435. *Gulubia costata*. Florida. Robert Lee Riffle

PLATE 436. *Gulubia microcarpa*. Florida. Robert Lee Riffle

PLATE 437. *Hedyscepe canterburyana*. New Zealand. Bryan Laughland

PLATE 438. *Heterospathe cagayanensis*. Australia, Daryl O'Connor

PLATE 439. *Heterospathe delicatula*. Australia. Daryl O'Connor

PLATE 440. *Heterospathe delicatula*. Australia. Daryl O'Connor

PLATE 441. *Heterospathe elata*. Florida. Robert Lee Riffle

PLATE 442. *Heterospathe elata*, crownshaft and inflorescence. Florida. Robert Lee Riffle

PLATE 443. *Heterospathe elmeri*. Florida. Robert Lee Riffle

PLATE 444. *Heterospathe minor*, inflorescence. Australia. Paul Craft

PLATE 445. *Heterospathe negrosensis*. Florida. Robert Lee Riffle

PLATE 446. *Heterospathe philippinensis*. Australia. Daryl O'Connor

PLATE 447. *Heterospathe woodfordiana*. Australia. Paul Craft

PLATE 448. *Heterospathe woodfordiana*, new leaf color. Paul Craft

PLATE 449. *Howea belmoreana*. Australia. Scott Zona

PLATE 450. *Howea belmoreana*. Patty Craft

PLATE 451. *Howea forsteriana*. Robert Lee Riffle

PLATE 452. *Howea forsteriana*, leaf crown. California. Paul Craft

PLATE 453. *Howea forsteriana*, infructes-cences. California. Paul Craft

PLATE 454. *Hydriastele microspadix*. Rolf Kyburz

PLATE 455. *Hydriastele rostrata*. Florida. Robert Lee Riffle

PLATE 456. *Hydriastele rostrata*. Florida. Robert Lee Riffle

PLATE 457. *Hydriastele wendlandiana*. Australia. Chuck Hubbuch

PLATE 458. *Hyophorbe indica*. Costa Rica. Chuck Hubbuch

PLATE 459. *Hyophorbe indica*. Florida. Robert Lee Riffle

PLATE 460. *Hyophorbe indica*, mature trunk and infructescences. Rolf Kyburz

PLATE 461. *Hyophorbe lagenicaulis*. Florida. Robert Lee Riffle

PLATE 462. *Hyophorbe lagenicaulis*, bottle base of trunk. Paul Craft

PLATE 463. *Hyophorbe lagenicaulis*, crownshaft. Florida. Robert Lee Riffle

PLATE 464. *Hyophorbe verschaffeltii*. Florida. Robert Lee Riffle

PLATE 465. *Hyophorbe verschaffeltii*, upper trunk, crownshaft, and inflorescence buds. Florida. Robert Lee Riffle

PLATE 466. *Hyospathe elegans*. Cuba. Paul Craft

PLATE 467. *Hyphaene compressa*. Australia. Paul Craft

PLATE 468. *Hyphaene coriacea*. Florida. Robert Lee Riffle

PLATE 469. *Hyphaene coriacea*, bases of stems and suckers. Florida. Robert Lee Riffle

PLATE 470. *Hyphaene dichotoma*. Florida. Robert Lee Riffle

PLATE 471. *Hyphaene dichotoma*, boots and fruits. Florida. Robert Lee Riffle

134

PLATE 472. *Hyphaene petersiana*. Florida. Robert Lee Riffle

PLATE 473. *Hyphaene thebaica*, very old specimen. Costa Rica. Paul Craft

PLATE 474. *Hyphaene thebaica*. Florida. Robert Lee Riffle

PLATE 475. *Hyphaene thebaica*, infructescences. Australia. Paul Craft

PLATE 476. *Hyphaene* species. Florida. Robert Lee Riffle

PLATE 477. *Iguanura bicornis*. Australia. Paul Craft

PLATE 478. *Iguanura bicornis*, new leaf color. Australia. Paul Craft

PLATE 479. *Iguanura elegans*. Australia. Paul Craft

PLATE 480. *Iguanura palmuncula*. In habitat, Sarawak. Tim Hatch

PLATE 481. *Iguanura wallichiana* var. *major*. Australia. Paul Craft

PLATE 482. *Iguanura wallichiana* var. *major*, new leaf color. Australia. Paul Craft

PLATE 483. *Iriartea deltoidea*. Costa Rica. Paul Craft

PLATE 484. *Iriartea deltoidea*, stilt roots. Costa Rica. Paul Craft

PLATE 485. *Itaya amicorum*, with John L. Dowe. Australia. Chuck Hubbuch

PLATE 486. *Johannesteijsmannia altifrons*. Costa Rica. Paul Craft

PLATE 487. *Johannesteijsmannia altifrons*, inflorescence. Costa Rica. Paul Craft

PLATE 489. *Johannesteijsmannia magnifica*, leaf underside. Paul Craft

PLATE 488. *Johannesteijsmannia magnifica*. Australia. Chuck Hubbuch

PLATE 490. *Johannesteijsmannia perakensis*. Singapore Botanic Garden. Martin Gibbons and Tobias Spanner

PLATE 491. *Jubaea chilensis*. Australia. Chuck Hubbuch

PLATE 492. *Jubaea chilensis*. California. Paul Craft

PLATE 493. *Jubaeopsis caffra*. California. Paul Craft

PLATE 494. *Jubaeopsis caffra*, trunks. California. Paul Craft

PLATE 495. *Kentiopsis magnifica*. In habitat, New Caledonia. Bryan Laughland

PLATE 496. *Kentiopsis oliviformis*. Florida. Robert Lee Riffle

PLATE 497. *Kentiopsis oliviformis*, crownshaft. Florida. Robert Lee Riffle

PLATE 498. *Kentiopsis piersoniorum*, young tree. New Caledonia.
Paul Craft

PLATE 499. *Kerriodoxa elegans*. Florida. Robert Lee Riffle

PLATE 500. *Korthalsia* species. Australia. Paul Craft

PLATE 501. *Laccospadix australasica*. In habitat, Mt. Lewis, Queensland, Australia. Paul Craft

PLATE 502. *Laccospadix australasica*, leaf. Paul Craft

PLATE 503. *Latania loddigesii*. Florida. Robert Lee Riffle

PLATE 504. *Latania lontaroides*. Florida. Robert Lee Riffle

PLATE 505. *Latania verschaffeltii*. Florida. Robert Lee Riffle

PLATE 506. *Lemurophoenix halleuxii*. Australia. Paul Craft

PLATE 507. *Lemurophoenix halleuxii*, petioles. Australia. Paul Craft

PLATE 508. *Lepidorrhachis mooreana*. California. Martin Gibbons and Tobias Spanner

PLATE 509. *Licuala beccariana*. Rolf Kyburz

PLATE 510. *Licuala bintulensis*, leaf. In habitat, Sarawak. Tim Hatch

PLATE 511. *Licuala cordata*. Australia. Paul Craft

PLATE 512. *Licuala cordata*, unsegmented leaf form. Australia. Paul Craft

PLATE 513. *Licuala cordata*, segmented leaf form. Australia. Paul Craft

PLATE 514. *Licuala grandis*. Australia. Paul Craft

PLATE 516. *Licuala mattanensis* 'Mapu'. Australia. Paul Craft

PLATE 518. *Licuala naumanii*, leaf. Australia. Paul Craft

PLATE 515. *Licuala lauterbachii*. Florida. Robert Lee Riffle

144

PLATE 517. *Licuala naumanii*. Australia. Paul Craft

PLATE 519. *Licuala orbicularis*. Australia. Paul Craft

PLATE 520. *Licuala paludosa*. Florida. Robert Lee Riffle

PLATE 523. *Licuala peltata* var. *sumawongii*, infructescences. Australia. Paul Craft

PLATE 521. *Licuala peltata* var. *peltata*. Australia. Paul Craft

PLATE 522. *Licuala peltata* var. *sumawongii*. Florida. Robert Lee Riffle

PLATE 526. *Licuala radula*. Australia. Paul Craft

PLATE 524. *Licuala petiolulata*. In habitat, Sarawak. Tim Hatch

PLATE 525. *Licuala platydactyla*. Australia. Paul Craft

PLATE 527. *Licuala ramsayi*. Australia. Paul Craft

PLATE 528. *Licuala ramsayi*, stilt roots of mature tree. Australia. Paul Craft

PLATE 532. *Licuala spinosa*, leaf. Paul Craft

PLATE 533. *Licuala triphylla*. Australia. Paul Craft

PLATE 530. *Licuala sarawakensis*. In habitat, Sarawak. Tim Hatch

PLATE 529. *Licuala ramsayi*, leaf outline. Australia. Chuck Hubbuch

PLATE 531. *Licuala spinosa.* Panama. Paul Craft

PLATE 536. *Livistona australis.* In habitat, Australia. Chuck Hubbuch

PLATE 534. *Linospadix microcarya.* In habitat, Australia. Paul Craft

PLATE 535. *Linospadix minor,* leaf. Paul Craft

PLATE 537. *Livistona benthamii.* Florida. Robert Lee Riffle

PLATE 538. *Livistona carinensis*. Florida. Robert Lee Riffle

PLATE 539. *Livistona chinensis*. Florida. Robert Lee Riffle

PLATE 540. *Livistona chinensis*, leaf crown. Florida.
Robert Lee Riffle

PLATE 541. *Livistona chinensis*, leaf. Texas. Robert Lee Riffle

PLATE 542. *Livistona decipiens*. Florida. Robert Lee Riffle

PLATE 543. *Livistona drudei*. Florida. Robert Lee Riffle

PLATE 544. *Livistona drudei*, mature trees. In habitat, Australia.
Chuck Hubbuch

PLATE 545. *Livistona fulva*. Florida. Robert Lee Riffle

PLATE 546. *Livistona halongensis*. In habitat, Vietnam. Gary Dahme

PLATE 547. *Livistona jenkinsiana*, a mature tree. India. Martin Gibbons and Tobias Spanner

PLATE 548. *Livistona jenkinsiana*, leaf. Martin Gibbons and Tobias Spanner

PLATE 549. *Livistona lanuginosa*. Australia. Paul Craft

PLATE 550. *Livistona mariae*. Florida. Robert Lee Riffle

PLATE 551. *Livistona merrillii*. Florida. Robert Lee Riffle

PLATE 552. *Livistona muelleri*. Cuba. Paul Craft

PLATE 553. *Livistona muelleri*, young adult. Florida. Robert Lee Riffle

PLATE 554. *Livistona nitida*, trunk, leaf crown, and inflorescences. Florida. Robert Lee Riffle

PLATE 555. *Livistona rotundifolia*. Florida. Robert Lee Riffle

PLATE 556. *Livistona rotundifolia*, young trees. Florida. Robert Lee Riffle

PLATE 557. *Livistona rotundifolia*, trunk. Florida. Robert Lee Riffle

PLATE 558. *Livistona rotundifolia*, leaf crown. Florida.
Robert Lee Riffle

PLATE 559. *Livistona rotundifolia*, infructescences. Paul Craft

PLATE 560. *Livistona saribus*. Florida. Robert Lee Riffle

PLATE 561. *Livistona saribus*, juvenile plants in shade. Paul Craft

PLATE 562. *Livistona saribus*, trunk and fibers, leaf crown. Florida. Robert Lee Riffle

PLATE 563. *Livistona saribus*, toothless petiole and fruit. Florida. Robert Lee Riffle

PLATE 564. *Livistona victoriae*, seedling. Florida. Robert Lee Riffle

PLATE 565. *Lodoicea maldivica*, seed with remote germination of seed leaf. Robert Lee Riffle

PLATE 566. *Lodoicea maldivica*, seed. Paul Craft

PLATE 567. *Lodoicea maldivica*, young but mature tree with fruit. Sri Lanka. Rolf Kyburz

PLATE 569. *Lodoicea maldivica*, fruits of female tree. Sri Lanka. Rolf Kyburz

PLATE 570. *Loxococcus rupicola*. Florida. Robert Lee Riffle

PLATE 568. *Lodoicea maldivica*, seedling. Sri Lanka. Rolf Kyburz

PLATE 571. *Lytocaryum weddellianum*. Australia. Paul Craft

PLATE 572. *Manicaria saccifera,* leaf outline. In habitat, Belize. Paul Craft.

PLATE 573. *Manicaria saccifera,* fruits. Paul Craft

PLATE 574. *Marojejya darianii*, young plant. Australia. Paul Craft

PLATE 575. *Marojejya darianii*, leaf. Australia. Paul Craft

PLATE 576. *Marojejya insignis.*
Rolf Kyburz

PLATE 577. *Marojejya insignis*, leaf petioles. Rolf Kyburz

PLATE 578. *Mauritia flexuosa*. Australia. Paul Craft

PLATE 579. *Mauritia flexuosa*, petioles and inflorescences. Australia. Paul Craft

PLATE 580. *Mauritiella armata*. Australia. Paul Craft

PLATE 581. *Mauritiella armata*, base of large clump. Australia. Paul Craft

PLATE 582. *Mauritiella armata*, stem. Australia. Paul Craft

PLATE 583. *Mauritiella armata*, leaves. Australia. Paul Craft

PLATE 584. *Maxburretia furtadoana*. In habitat, Thailand. Rolf Kyburz

PLATE 585. *Medemia argun*, mature trees. In habitat, Wadi Shigrib, Nubian Desert, Sudan. Martin Gibbons and Tobias Spanner

PLATE 586. *Medemia argun*, seedling. Florida. Robert Lee Riffle

PLATE 587. *Metroxylon amicarum*. Australia. Paul Craft

PLATE 588. *Metroxylon amicarum*, leaf sheaths. Australia. Paul Craft

PLATE 590. *Metroxylon sagu*, new leaf color. Australia. Paul Craft

PLATE 592. *Metroxylon salomonense*, leaf sheath. New Caledonia. Paul Craft

PLATE 589. *Metroxylon sagu*. Australia. Paul Craft

PLATE 591. *Metroxylon salomonense*. Australia. Paul Craft

PLATE 593. *Metroxylon salomonense*, in bloom. Australia. Paul Craft

PLATE 594. *Metroxylon vitiense*. Australia. Paul Craft

PLATE 595. *Metroxylon vitiense*, leaf sheaths. Florida. Robert Lee Riffle

PLATE 596. *Moratia cerifera*. In habitat, New Caledonia. Scott Zona

PLATE 597. *Nannorrhops ritchiana*. Paul Craft

PLATE 598. *Nannorrhops ritchiana*, unusual weeping form. Florida. Robert Lee Riffle

PLATE 599. *Nannorrhops ritchiana*, leaf. Florida. Robert Lee Riffle

PLATE 600. *Nannorrhops ritchiana*, with terminal inflorescences. Florida. Robert Lee Riffle

PLATE 601. *Neonicholsonia watsonii*. Robert Lee Riffle

PLATE 602. *Neoveitchia storckii*. Venezuela. Paul Craft

PLATE 603. *Nephrosperma vanhoutteanum*. Sri Lanka.
Rolf Kyburz

PLATE 604. *Nephrosperma vanhoutteanum*, young trunk and petioles with spines. Australia. Paul Craft

PLATE 605. *Normanbya normanbyi*. In habitat, Australia. Paul Craft

PLATE 606. *Normanbya normanbyi*. In habitat, Australia. Paul Craft

PLATE 607. *Nypa fruticans*. Florida. Robert Lee Riffle

PLATE 608. *Nypa fruticans*, infructescence. Florida. Robert Lee Riffle

PLATE 609. *Oenocarpus bataua*. In habitat, Ecuador. Martin Gibbons and Tobias Spanner

PLATE 610. *Oenocarpus mapora*. Costa Rica. Chuck Hubbuch

PLATE 611. *Oenocarpus mapora*. Panama. Paul Craft

PLATE 612. *Oenocarpus mapora*, stem and leaves. Australia. Paul Craft

PLATE 613. *Oncosperma tigillarium*. Florida.
Robert Lee Riffle

PLATE 614. *Oncosperma tigillarium*, leaves. Florida. Robert Lee Riffle

PLATE 615. *Oncosperma tigillarium*, stem. Florida.
Robert Lee Riffle

PLATE 616. *Orania disticha*. Clayton York

PLATE 618. *Orania palindan*, leaf crown. Florida. Robert Lee Riffle

PLATE 617. *Orania palindan*. Costa Rica. Paul Craft

PLATE 619. *Orania sylvicola*. Tim Hatch

PLATE 620. *Orania trispatha*. In habitat, Masoala Peninsula, Madagascar. Rolf Kyburz

PLATE 621. *Oraniopsis appendiculata*. In habitat, Australia.
Paul Craft

PLATE 622. *Oraniopsis appendiculata*, leaf. In habitat, Australia. Paul Craft

PLATE 623. *Parajubaea coccoides*. Paul Craft

PLATE 624. *Parajubaea cocoides*. Ecuador.
Martin Gibbons and Tobias Spanner

PLATE 625. *Parajubaea sunkha*. In habitat, Bolivia.
Martin Gibbons and Tobias Spanner

PLATE 626. *Parajubaea torallyi*. Bolivia.
Martin Gibbons and Tobias Spanner

PLATE 627. *Parajubaea torallyi*. Bolivia.
Martin Gibbons and Tobias Spanner

PLATE 628. *Pelagodoxa henryana*, leaf underside.
Florida. Robert Lee Riffle

PLATE 629. *Pelagodoxa henryana*, infructescence. Hawaii. Chuck Hubbuch

PLATE 631. *Phoenicophorium borsigianum*. Bahamas. Paul Craft

PLATE 630. *Phoenicophorium borsigianum*. Australia. Paul Craft

PLATE 632. *Phoenicophorium borsigianum*, inflorescence. Australia. Paul Craft

PLATE 633. *Phoenix acaulis*, in bloom. Florida. Robert Lee Riffle

PLATE 634. *Phoenix canariensis*. Florida. Robert Lee Riffle

PLATE 636. *Phoenix loureiri*. Florida. Robert Lee Riffle

PLATE 635. *Phoenix dactylifera*, in fruit. Texas. Robert Lee Riffle

PLATE 637. *Phoenix loureiri*, infructescences. Florida.
Robert Lee Riffle

PLATE 638. *Phoenix paludosa*. California. Paul Craft

PLATE 639. *Phoenix paludosa*, infructescence. Singapore. Chuck Hubbuch

PLATE 641. *Phoenix reclinata*. Florida. Robert Lee Riffle

PLATE 640. *Phoenix pusilla*. Florida. Robert Lee Riffle

PLATE 643. *Phoenix reclinata*, leaf crown. Florida. Robert Lee Riffle

PLATE 644. *Phoenix reclinata*, acanthophylls at bases of leaves. Florida. Robert Lee Riffle

PLATE 642. *Phoenix reclinata*, mature clump. Florida. Robert Lee Riffle

PLATE 645. *Phoenix rupicola*. Paul Craft

PLATE 646. *Phoenix sylvestris*. California. Robert Lee Riffle

PLATE 647. *Phoenix sylvestris*. Florida. Robert Lee Riffle

PLATE 648. *Pholidocarpus macrocarpus*, petioles. Australia. Daryl O'Connor

PLATE 649. *Pholidocarpus maiadum*. In habitat, Sarawak. Tim Hatch

PLATE 650. *Pholidostachys dactyloides*. In habitat, Ecuador. Martin Gibbons and Tobias Spanner

PLATE 651. *Pholidostachys synanthera*. In habitat, Ecuador. Martin Gibbons and Tobias Spanner

PLATE 655. *Phytelephas macrocarpa*, male inflorescence. Ecuador. Chuck Hubbuch

PLATE 652. *Pholidostachys* species. Australia. Paul Craft

PLATE 653. *Phytelephas aequatorialis*. Venezuela. Paul Craft

PLATE 654. *Phytelephas macrocarpa*. Australia. Paul Craft

PLATE 656. *Phytelephas seemannii*. Australia. Paul Craft

PLATE 657. *Phytelephas seemannii*, female inflorescence. Australia. Paul Craft

PLATE 658. *Phytelephas tenuicaulis*. Australia. Chuck Hubbuch

PLATE 659. *Phytelephas* species, male inflorescence. Costa Rica. Paul Craft

PLATE 660. *Phytelephas* species, fruits. Costa Rica. Paul Craft

PLATE 661. *Pigafetta* species, silhouette. Costa Rica. Chuck Hubbuch

PLATE 662. *Pigafetta* species, seedling tree. Costa Rica Paul Craft

PLATE 663. *Pigafetta* species, trunk. Cuba. Paul Craft

PLATE 664. *Pigafetta* species, leaf sheaths and petioles. New Caledonia. Paul Craft

PLATE 665. *Pigafetta* species, in bloom. Australia. Paul Craft

PLATE 666. *Pinanga adangensis*. Florida. Robert Lee Riffle

PLATE 667. *Pinanga bataanensis*. Australia. Paul Craft

PLATE 668. *Pinanga caesia*. Cuba. Paul Craft

PLATE 669. *Pinanga caesia*, inflorescence. Costa Rica.
Paul Craft

PLATE 671. *Pinanga chaiana*. Australia. Paul Craft

PLATE 670. *Pinanga caesia*, new leaf color. Florida.
Robert Lee Riffle

PLATE 672. *Pinanga copelandii*. Indonesia. Scott Zona

PLATE 673. *Pinanga coronata*. Florida. Robert Lee Riffle

PLATE 676. *Pinanga curranii*. Florida. Robert Lee Riffle

PLATE 674. *Pinanga coronata*, inflorescence. Cuba. Paul Craft

PLATE 675. *Pinanga coronata*, infructescence. Cuba. Paul Craft

PLATE 680. *Pinanga javana*, inflorescences, infructescences, and crownshaft. Rolf Kyburz

PLATE 677. *Pinanga dicksonii*. Australia. Paul Craft

PLATE 678. *Pinanga disticha*. Australia. Paul Craft

PLATE 679. *Pinanga insignis*. Venezuela. Paul Craft

PLATE 681. *Pinanga maculata*. Australia. Paul Craft

PLATE 682. *Pinanga maculata*, trunk, crownshaft, and inflorescence. Australia. Paul Craft

PLATE 683. *Pinanga maculata*, leaf. Australia. Paul Craft

PLATE 684. *Pinanga negrosensis*. Florida. Robert Lee Riffle

PLATE 685. *Pinanga negrosensis*, stem. Florida. Robert Lee Riffle

PLATE 686. *Pinanga patula*. Venezuela. Paul Craft

PLATE 687. *Pinanga sclerophylla*. Australia. Paul Craft

PLATE 688. *Pinanga sclerophylla*, infructescence. Australia. Paul Craft

PLATE 689. *Pinanga scortechinii*. Rolf Kyburz

184

PLATE 690. *Pinanga speciosa*. Mexico. Paul Craft

PLATE 691. *Pinanga veitchii*. Australia. Paul Craft

PLATE 692. *Plectocomia himalayana*. In habitat, northeastern India. Martin Gibbons and Tobias Spanner

PLATE 693. *Polyandrococos caudescens*, whitish undersides of mature leaves. Florida. Robert Lee Riffle

PLATE 694. *Polyandrococos caudescens*, new "spear." Florida. Robert Lee Riffle

PLATE 695. *Prestoea acuminata*. In habitat, Puerto Rico. Scott Zona

PLATE 696. *Prestoea acuminata*. In habitat, Puerto Rico.

Jerry Hooper

PLATE 697. *Pritchardia affinis*. Hawaii. Chuck Hubbuch

PLATE 698. *Pritchardia hardyi*. Hawaii. Chuck Hubbuch

PLATE 699. *Pritchardia hillebrandii*. California. Paul Craft

PLATE 700. *Pritchardia hillebrandii*, leaf. Florida.
Robert Lee Riffle

PLATE 701. *Pritchardia lanaiensis*. Hawaii. Chuck Hubbuch

PLATE 702. *Pritchardia martii*. Venezuela. Paul Craft

PLATE 703. *Pritchardia pacifica*. New Caledonia. Paul Craft

PLATE 704. *Pritchardia pacifica*, leaf crown. Australia. Paul Craft

PLATE 705. *Pritchardia remota* var. *aylmer-robinsonii*. Hawaii. Chuck Hubbuch

PLATE 706. *Pritchardia thurstonii*. Paul Craft

PLATE 707. *Pritchardia thurstonii*, inflorescence.
Paul Craft

PLATE 708. *Pritchardia woodfordiana*, young tree.
Florida. Robert Lee Riffle

PLATE 709. *Pritchardiopsis jeanneneyi*.
New Caledonia. Bryan Laughland

PLATE 710. *Pseudophoenix ekmanii*. In habitat, Dominican Republic. Paul Craft

189

PLATE 711. *Pseudophoenix lediniana*. Florida. Robert Lee Riffle

PLATE 712. *Pseudophoenix lediniana*. Florida.
Robert Lee Riffle

PLATE 713. *Pseudophoenix sargentii*, old tree. Florida.
Robert Lee Riffle

PLATE 714. *Pseudophoenix sargentii*, young tree. Florida. Robert Lee Riffle

PLATE 715. *Pseudophoenix sargentii*, inflorescence. Paul Craft.

PLATE 716. *Pseudophoenix vinifera*. Florida. Robert Lee Riffle

PLATE 717. *Ptychococcus lepidotus*. Australia. Daryl O'Connor

PLATE 718. *Ptychococcus paradoxus*. In habitat, Papua New Guinea. Rolf Kyburz

PLATE 719. *Ptychosperma burretianum*. Florida. Robert Lee Riffle

PLATE 720. *Ptychosperma burretianum*, new leaf color. Florida. Robert Lee Riffle

PLATE 721. *Ptychosperma caryotoides*. Florida. Robert Lee Riffle

PLATE 722. *Ptychosperma cuneatum*. Florida. Robert Lee Riffle

192

PLATE 723. *Ptychosperma elegans*. Robert Lee Riffle

PLATE 724. *Ptychosperma elegans*, leaf crown. Florida.
Robert Lee Riffle

PLATE 725. *Ptychosperma elegans*, inflorescence, in-fructescence, and peduncular bract. Robert Lee Riffle

PLATE 726. *Ptychosperma lauterbachii*. Florida. Robert Lee Riffle

PLATE 727. *Ptychosperma ledermannianum*. Florida.
Robert Lee Riffle

PLATE 728. *Ptychosperma macarthurii*. Florida. Robert Lee Riffle

PLATE 729. *Ptychosperma macarthurii*, infructescence.
Belize. Paul Craft

PLATE 730. *Ptychosperma salomonense*. Florida. Robert Lee Riffle

PLATE 731. *Ptychosperma salomonense*. Florida. Robert Lee Riffle

PLATE 732. *Ptychosperma salomonense*, seedling. Florida. Robert Lee Riffle

PLATE 733. *Ptychosperma schefferi*. Rolf Kyburz

PLATE 734. *Ptychosperma waitianum*, newly expanded leaf color. Australia. Paul Craft

PLATE 735. *Raphia australis*. Australia. Paul Craft

PLATE 736. *Raphia farinifera*. Australia. Paul Craft

PLATE 737. *Raphia farinifera*, leaf rachis and leaflets of young tree. Florida.
Robert Lee Riffle

PLATE 738. *Raphia farinifera*, infructescence. Florida. Robert Lee Riffle

PLATE 740. *Raphia hookeri*, trunk and petioles with fibers. Australia. Paul Craft

PLATE 739. *Raphia hookeri*. Venezuela. Paul Craft

PLATE 743. *Raphia humilis*. Florida. Robert Lee Riffle

PLATE 741. *Raphia hookeri*, fibers. Australia. Paul Craft

PLATE 742. *Raphia hookeri*, infructescence. Australia. Paul Craft

PLATE 744. *Raphia humilis*, inflorescences. Florida. Robert Lee Riffle

PLATE 745. *Raphia vinifera*. Florida. Robert Lee Riffle

PLATE 746. *Ravenea glauca*. Rolf Kyburz

PLATE 747. *Ravenea hildebrandtii*. Florida. Robert Lee Riffle

PLATE 748. *Ravenea hildebrandtii*, male inflorescence. Florida. Paul Craft

PLATE 749. *Ravenea julietiae*. In habitat, Madagascar. Rolf Kyburz

PLATE 750. *Ravenea lakatra*. California. Paul Craft

PLATE 751. *Ravenea madagascariensis*. Australia. Paul Craft

PLATE 752. *Ravenea musicalis*. In habitat, Madagascar. Rolf Kyburz

PLATE 753. *Ravenea rivularis*. Florida. Robert Lee Riffle

PLATE 754. *Ravenea rivularis*, mature trees. In habitat, Madagascar. Rolf Kyburz

PLATE 755. *Ravenea rivularis*, young tree. Florida.
Robert Lee Riffle

PLATE 756. *Ravenea robustior.* In habitat, Madagascar. Rolf Kyburz

PLATE 757. *Ravenea sambiranensis*, leaf crown. In habitat, Madagascar. Rolf Kyburz

PLATE 758. *Ravenea xerophila*. In habitat, Madagascar. Rolf Kyburz

PLATE 760. *Reinhardtia gracilis*, leaf. Robert Lee Riffle

PLATE 761. *Reinhardtia latisecta*. Rolf Kyburz

PLATE 763. *Reinhardtia latisecta*, leaf showing "windows." Rolf Kyburz

PLATE 759. *Ravenea xerophila*, seedling. Florida.
Robert Lee Riffle

PLATE 764. *Reinhardtia paiewonskiana*, with Larry Dietrich of Earthworks Nursery. In habitat, Dominican Republic. Paul Craft

PLATE 762. *Reinhardtia latisectus*, young nursery plant.
Paul Craft

PLATE 765. *Reinhardtia paiewonskiana*. In habitat, Dominican Republic. Paul Craft

PLATE 766. *Rhapidophyllum hystrix*. In habitat, Torreya State Park, Florida. Robert Lee Riffle

PLATE 767. *Rhapis excelsa*, cultivar. Australia. Paul Craft

PLATE 768. *Rhapis humilis*. California. Robert Lee Riffle

PLATE 769. *Rhapis laosensis*. Florida. Robert Lee Riffle

PLATE 770. *Rhapis multifida*. Florida.
Robert Lee Riffle

PLATE 771. *Rhapis subtilis*. Australia. Daryl O'Connor

PLATE 772. *Rhopaloblaste augusta*. Australia. Paul Craft

PLATE 773. *Rhopaloblaste augusta*, trunk and crownshaft. Cuba. Paul Craft

PLATE 774. *Rhopalostylis baueri*. Australia. Bryan Laughland

PLATE 775. *Rhopalostylis sapida*. In habitat, New Zealand. Chuck Hubbuch

PLATE 776. *Rhopalostylis sapida*, trunk and crownshaft. Paul Craft

PLATE 777. *Rhopalostylis sapida*, inflorescence. New Zealand. Chuck Hubbuch

PLATE 779. *Roscheria melanochaetes*, crownshaft. Florida. Paul Craft

PLATE 778. *Roscheria melanochaetes*. Florida. Paul Craft

PLATE 780. *Roystonea altissima*, young tree. Florida.
Robert Lee Riffle

PLATE 781. *Roystonea oleracea*. New Caledonia. Paul Craft

PLATE 782. *Roystonea oleracea*, lining a path. Venezuela.
Paul Craft

PLATE 783. *Roystonea princeps*. Florida. Paul Craft

PLATE 784. *Roystonea regia*. In habitat, Cuba. Paul Craft

PLATE 785. *Roystonea regia*. In habitat, Florida.
Robert Lee Riffle

PLATE 786. *Roystonea regia*, infructescence. Florida.
Robert Lee Riffle

PLATE 787. *Roystonea violacea*. Cuba. Paul Craft

PLATE 788. *Roystonea violacea*, stem and crownshaft. Cuba. Paul Craft

PLATE 789. *Sabal causiarum*. Florida. Robert Lee Riffle

PLATE 790. *Sabal domingensis*. In habitat, Cuba. Paul Craft

PLATE 791. *Sabal domingensis*. Florida. Robert Lee Riffle

PLATE 792. *Sabal domingensis*, boots and leaf crown. Robert Lee Riffle

PLATE 793. *Sabal etonia*. Florida. Paul Craft

PLATE 794. *Sabal maritima*. In habitat, Isla de la Juventud, Cuba.
Robert Lee Riffle

PLATE 795. *Sabal mauritiiformis*. Florida. Robert Lee Riffle

PLATE 796. *Sabal mexicana*. Florida. Paul Craft

PLATE 797. *Sabal minor*. In habitat, Texas. Robert Lee Riffle

PLATE 798. *Sabal palmetto*. Florida. Robert Lee Riffle

PLATE 799. *Sabal uresana*. Florida. Robert Lee Riffle

PLATE 800. *Sabal yapa*. In habitat, Isla de la Juventud, Cuba. Paul Craft

PLATE 801. *Sabal yapa*. Florida. Robert Lee Riffle

PLATE 802. *Sabal yapa*, trunk and leaf bases. Florida. Robert Lee Riffle

PLATE 804. *Salacca magnifica*. Florida.
Robert Lee Riffle

PLATE 805. *Salacca magnifica*, leaf underside. Florida. Robert Lee Riffle

PLATE 806. *Salacca multiflora*. Rolf Kyburz

PLATE 803. *Salacca magnifica*. New Caledonia. Paul Craft

PLATE 807. *Salacca wallichiana*. Australia. Paul Craft

PLATE 808. *Salacca zalacca*. Florida. Robert Lee Riffle

PLATE 812. *Satakentia liukiuensis*. Florida. Chuck Hubbuch

PLATE 809. *Salacca zalacca*, thorny petioles. Australia. Paul Craft

PLATE 810. *Salacca zalacca*, underside of new leaf. Florida. Robert Lee Riffle

PLATE 811. *Salacca zalacca*, infructescence. Costa Rica. Paul Craft

PLATE 814. *Satakentia liukiuensis*, detail of stem and crownshaft. Florida. Robert Lee Riffle

PLATE 813. *Satakentia liukiuensis*, stem and crownshaft. Florida.
Robert Lee Riffle

PLATE 815. *Schippia concolor*. In habitat, Belize. Paul Craft

PLATE 816. *Schippia concolor*. Florida. Robert Lee Riffle

213

PLATE 817. *Schippia concolor*, infructescences. Florida.
Robert Lee Riffle

PLATE 818. *Serenoa repens*, ancient 18-foot clumps. Lake June, Florida. Robert Lee Riffle

PLATE 819. *Serenoa repens*, silhouette. Lake June, Florida.
Robert Lee Riffle

PLATE 820. *Serenoa repens*, leaves. Robert Lee Riffle

PLATE 821. *Serenoa repens*, leaf outline. Robert Lee Riffle

PLATE 822. *Siphokentia beguinii*. Australia. Paul Craft

PLATE 823. *Siphokentia beguinii*, trunk, crownshaft, and inflorescence. Florida. Robert Lee Riffle

PLATE 824. *Siphokentia dransfieldii*. Florida. Robert Lee Riffle

PLATE 825. *Socratea exorrhiza*, with Katherine Maidman of Fairchild Tropical Garden. Costa Rica. Chuck Hubbuch

PLATE 826. *Socratea exorrhiza*, stilt roots. Costa Rica. Chuck Hubbuch

PLATE 830. *Sommieria leucophylla*. Indonesia. Scott Zona

PLATE 827. *Socratea exorrhiza*, crownshaft. Australia. Paul Craft

PLATE 828. *Socratea exorrhiza*, leaf. Australia. Paul Craft

PLATE 829. *Sommieria affinis*, inflorescence. In habitat, Papua New Guinea. Clayton York

PLATE 832. *Syagrus amara*, leaf crown and infructescence. Florida. Robert Lee Riffle

PLATE 831. *Syagrus amara*. Florida. Robert Lee Riffle

PLATE 833. *Syagrus botryophora*. Florida. Robert Lee Riffle

PLATE 834. *Syagrus botryophora*, inflorescences and grooved bracts. Florida. Robert Lee Riffle

PLATE 835. *Syagrus "cearensis."* Florida. Robert Lee Riffle

PLATE 836. *Syagrus "cearensis,"* trunks and inflorescences. Florida. Robert Lee Riffle

PLATE 837. *Syagrus "cearensis,"* infructescence. Robert Lee Riffle

PLATE 838. *Syagrus cocoides*, leaf. Florida.
Robert Lee Riffle

PLATE 839. *Syagrus comosa*, young tree.
Florida. Robert Lee Riffle

PLATE 842. *Syagrus coronata*, inflorescence and its primary bract.
Australia. Paul Craft

PLATE 840. *Syagrus coronata*. Florida. Robert Lee Riffle

PLATE 841. *Syagrus coronata*, leaf bases and scars. Florida.
Robert Lee Riffle

PLATE 843. *Syagrus* ×*costae*. Florida. Robert Lee Riffle

PLATE 844. *Syagrus flexuosa*. Florida. Robert Lee Riffle

PLATE 845. *Syagrus flexuosa*, trunk. In habitat, Brazil.
Paul Craft

PLATE 846. *Syagrus glaucescens*. In habitat, Brazil. Paul Craft

PLATE 847. *Syagrus glaucescens*, infructescence. In habitat, Brazil. Paul Craft

PLATE 848. *Syagrus macrocarpa*. Florida. Robert Lee Riffle

PLATE 849. *Syagrus orinocensis*. Florida. Robert Lee Riffle

PLATE 850. *Syagrus orinocensis*. Florida. Robert Lee Riffle

PLATE 851. *Syagrus pseudococos*. Florida. Robert Lee Riffle

PLATE 852. *Syagrus pseudococos*, trunk, leaf crown, and inflorescences. Florida. Robert Lee Riffle

PLATE 853. *Syagrus romanzoffiana*. Robert Lee Riffle

PLATE 854. *Syagrus ruschiana*. In habitat, Brazil. Paul Craft

PLATE 855. *Syagrus ruschiana*, young tree. Florida. Robert Lee Riffle

PLATE 856. *Syagrus sancona*. Florida. Robert Lee Riffle

PLATE 857. *Syagrus schizophylla*. Florida. Robert Lee Riffle

PLATE 858. *Syagrus schizophylla*, trunk. Florida. Robert Lee Riffle

PLATE 859. *Syagrus schizophylla*, infructescences. Florida.
Robert Lee Riffle

PLATE 860. *Syagrus stenopetala*. Florida. Robert Lee Riffle

PLATE 861. *Syagrus stenopetala*, trunks. Robert Lee Riffle

PLATE 862. *Syagrus stenopetala*, inflorescence formation. Florida. Robert Lee Riffle

PLATE 863. *Syagrus vagans*. Florida. Robert Lee Riffle

PLATE 864. *Syagrus* hybrid. Florida. Robert Lee Riffle

PLATE 865. *Synechanthus fibrosus*. Australia. Paul Craft

PLATE 866. *Synechanthus fibrosus*, infructescence. Costa Rica. Paul Craft

PLATE 867. *Synechanthus warscewiczianus*. In habitat, Costa Rica. Paul Craft

PLATE 868. *Thrinax ekmaniana*. In habitat, Cuba. Paul Craft

PLATE 869. *Thrinax ekmaniana*. In habitat, Cuba. Paul Craft

PLATE 870. *Thrinax ekmaniana*, leaf crown. In habitat, Cuba. Paul Craft

PLATE 871. *Thrinax ekmaniana*, leaf crown with fibers. In habitat, Cuba. Paul Craft

PLATE 873. *Thrinax excelsa*, infructes-cence. Robert Lee Riffle

PLATE 875. *Thrinax morrisii,* in bloom. Florida. Robert Lee Riffle

PLATE 872. *Thrinax excelsa*. Florida. Robert Lee Riffle

PLATE 874. *Thrinax morrisii*. Florida. Robert Lee Riffle

PLATE 876. *Thrinax radiata*. In habitat, Isla de la Juventud, Cuba. Paul Craft

PLATE 877. *Thrinax radiata*. Florida. Robert Lee Riffle

PLATE 878. *Thrinax rivularis*. In habitat, Cuba. Paul Craft

PLATE 879. *Trachycarpus fortunei*. In habitat, Yangtze, China. Martin Gibbons and Tobias Spanner

PLATE 880. *Trachycarpus fortunei*. Naturalized in Switzerland.
Rolf Kyburz

PLATE 881. *Trachycarpus latisectus*. In habitat, Kalimpong, India.
Martin Gibbons and Tobias Spanner

PLATE 882. *Trachycarpus martianus*. India.
Martin Gibbons and Tobias Spanner

PLATE 883. *Trachycarpus martianus*. In habitat, India.
Martin Gibbons and Tobias Spanner

PLATE 884. *Trachycarpus nanus.* In habitat, Yunnan, China.
Martin Gibbons and Tobias Spanner

PLATE 885. *Trachycarpus oreophilus.* In habitat, Thailand.
Martin Gibbons and Tobias Spanner

PLATE 886. *Trachycarpus princeps.* In habitat, Yunnan, China.
Martin Gibbons and Tobias Spanner

PLATE 887. *Trachycarpus princeps*, leaf. In habitat, Yunnan,
China. Martin Gibbons and Tobias Spanner

PLATE 888. *Trachycarpus takil*. India. Martin Gibbons and Tobias Spanner

PLATE 889. *Trachycarpus takil*. In habitat, India.
Martin Gibbons and Tobias Spanner

PLATE 890. *Trachycarpus wagnerianus*. Martin Gibbons and Tobias Spanner

PLATE 891. *Trithrinax brasiliensis*. California. Robert Lee Riffle

PLATE 892. *Trithrinax brasiliensis*, leaves. Florida. Robert Lee Riffle

PLATE 893. *Trithrinax brasiliensis*, trunk. California. Robert Lee Riffle

PLATE 895. *Trithrinax campestris*. In habitat, Argentina. Gaston Torres-Vera

PLATE 894. *Trithrinax campestris.* In habitat, Argentina.
Gaston Torres-Vera

PLATE 896. *Trithrinax campestris*, juvenile plant. California.
Paul Craft

PLATE 897. *Trithrinax schizophylla.* In habitat, Bolivia.
Martin Gibbons and Tobias Spanner

PLATE 898. *Trithrinax schizophylla*, young palm. In habitat,
Paraguay. Martin Gibbons and Tobias Spanner

234

PLATE 900. *Veillonia alba*, inflorescences, crownshaft, and petioles. Bryan Laughland

PLATE 901. *Veillonia alba*, older crownshaft and inflorescences. California. Paul Craft

PLATE 902. *Veillonia alba*, new reddish brown leaf sheaths. In habitat, New Caledonia. Paul Craft

PLATE 899. *Veillonia alba*, partially new crownshaft. In habitat, New Caledonia. Paul Craft

PLATE 903. *Veitchia arecina*. Florida. Robert Lee Riffle

PLATE 904. *Veitchia joannis*. Florida. Robert Lee Riffle

PLATE 905. *Veitchia joannis*. Florida. Robert Lee Riffle

PLATE 906. *Veitchia spiralis*. Florida. Robert Lee Riffle

PLATE 907. *Veitchia spiralis*, leaf crown. Florida. Robert Lee Riffle

PLATE 908. *Veitchia spiralis*, in bloom. Florida. Robert Lee Riffle

PLATE 909. *Veitchia spiralis*, inflorescence. Florida. Robert Lee Riffle

PLATE 910. *Veitchia vitiensis*, crownshaft. Rolf Kyburz

PLATE 911. *Veitchia winin*. Florida. Robert Lee Riffle

PLATE 913. *Verschaffeltia splendida*, young tree. Florida. Robert Lee Riffle

PLATE 914. *Verschaffeltia splendida*, spiny trunk. Florida. Robert Lee Riffle

PLATE 916. *Wallichia disticha*, stem fibers and petiole arrangement. Florida. Robert Lee Riffle

PLATE 912. *Verschaffeltia splendida*. Australia. Paul Craft

PLATE 915. *Wallichia disticha*. Florida. Robert Lee Riffle

PLATE 917. *Washingtonia filifera*. In habitat, California. Robert Lee Riffle

PLATE 918. *Washingtonia filifera*. In habitat, California. Robert Lee Riffle

PLATE 919. *Washingtonia robusta*. Robert Lee Riffle

PLATE 920. *Washingtonia robusta*. Robert Lee Riffle

PLATE 921. *Washingtonia robusta*, stem.
Robert Lee Riffle

PLATE 922. *Welfia regia*, leaf. Robert Lee Riffle

PLATE 923. *Wendlandiella gracilis*
var. *polyclada*. Florida. Paul Craft

PLATE 924. *Wettinia maynensis*. In habitat, Ecuador. Chuck Hubbuch

PLATE 925. *Wettinia quinaria*. In habitat, Ecuador. Chuck Hubbuch

PLATE 926. *Wodyetia bifurcata*. Australia. Paul Craft

PLATE 927. *Zombia antillarum*. Paul Craft

PLATE 928. *Zombia antillarum*, whitish leaf undersides. Florida.
Robert Lee Riffle

PLATE 929. *Zombia antillarum*, spiny stem. Florida.
Robert Lee Riffle

Palm Descriptions A to Z

ACANTHOPHOENIX is a monotypic genus of solitary-trunked, pinnate-leaved, monoecious palm. The only common name is barbel palm. The genus name translates from the Greek as "spine" or "thorn" and "date palm." The epithet is Latin for "reddish" and refers to the color of the crownshaft. PLATE 1.

Acanthophoenix rubra is endemic to the islands of Mauritius and Réunion in the Indian Ocean, where it is nearly extinct due to the harvesting of its edible growing point in the past. Dominic Strasberg, a conservation scientist in Réunion, told Chuck Hubbuch (pers. comm.) that the remaining plants on the island are restricted to steep, rocky cliffs and their growth is stunted. At one time, the two island populations were considered distinct enough to warrant the status of separate species, but modern taxonomists now combine them; and, in truth, there is little outward difference in the two populations.

This palm grows naturally from sea level to an elevation of 2640 feet in the wetter (eastern) parts of the islands and, because of the volcanic origin of these islands, is found on sloping ground. It forms a straight, columnar, light-colored trunk and a large, rounded crown of coconut-like leaves and can attain a height of 60 or more feet. The stem is often spiny, especially when young, on the newer growth, the older parts being light gray to almost white and conspicuously ringed except for the oldest part. The crownshaft is 2 to 3 feet tall, bulging at the base, and covered with greenish gray to reddish brown tomentum. The nearly spherical leaf crown is 20 feet wide and tall and has leaves 6 to 10 feet long but usually 8 feet. The many dark green leaflets are 2 feet or more in length, with pointed tips, and are borne in a flat plane off the rachis, which itself is often twisted at its midsection to make the leaflets vertical in orientation from that point on. The leaflets of young plants often have a red midvein with small prickles, while those of older plants have a yellow midvein and often no spines; leaves of any age have lighter colored, waxy undersides. The petioles are short, less than 1 foot long, and clothed in black spines, especially in younger palms. The inflorescences grow from beneath the crownshaft and often carry black spines, especially near the base of the main flower stem. Numerous light pink, red, or purplish male and female flowers are borne on the same tree in the same inflorescence. The globose fruits are less than 0.5 inch in diameter and are always black when mature.

The barbel palm needs at least half a day's sun to thrive, but seedlings require protection from the midday sun, especially in hot climates. The palm also needs adequate and regular moisture. A neutral or slightly acidic, nonsaline, and well-drained soil is ideal. This palm is a reasonably fast grower, especially when younger, if given proper soil and moisture but is not hardy to cold and is impossible outside of zone 11, and even marginal in 10b. It does well but grows slowly in the warmest parts of southern coastal California (Geoff Stein, pers. comm.).

While not closely related to *Archontophoenix*, *Dictyosperma*, and *Veitchia* species, this beauty has many visual similarities to them, with a leaf that is as beautiful as that of the coconut. It is large and imposing enough to be planted singly, especially as a canopy-scape, but is even more glorious in groups of three or more individuals of varying heights.

ACOELORRAPHE is a monotypic genus of clustering, palmate-leaved, monoecious palm. Common names include Everglades palm and paurotis palm. The genus name is derived from Greek words meaning "without," "hollow," and "fold" or "seam," a reference to the physical characteristics of the seed covering. The epithet honors a 19th-century American botanist, Charles H. Wright. PLATES 2 & 3.

Acoelorraphe wrightii grows naturally in southern Florida, the Bahamas, Cuba, the Atlantic coastal plain of Central America, and the Gulf coastal plain of tropical and subtropical Mexico, in moist or even swampy and monsoonal areas that are often flooded with fresh or brackish water. It is not threatened globally, but it is rare or unknown in the extreme southern parts of its natural range in Costa Rica and on the Caribbean coast of Colombia.

It readily forms clumps 10 to 15 feet tall and wide. The stems grow 4 inches per year under optimum conditions to 20 feet tall, or sometimes 40 feet, with a diameter of 4 inches. The oldest parts of mature stems are ringed with closely set leaf base scars, and the other parts of the trunk are covered in a beautiful pattern of light-colored old leaf bases and dense dark brown matted fibers. The leaf crowns are spherical or nearly so and contain 10 to 16 leaves. The leaves are 3 feet or more in diameter on 3-foot-long petioles that are armed with short, vicious teeth, and are semicircular or more in outline. The blade is deeply segmented more than halfway to the petiole into many stiff, narrow, and tapering segments, each of which is again split at its tip. Leaf color is bright green above and silvery beneath. Erect 3-foot-long inflorescences grow from and reach above the leaf crown in summer. The flower clusters are densely packed with small whitish bisexual blossoms. The fruits ripen in midsummer to early fall and are in drooping clusters; each is 0.5 inch wide and rounded, maturing from bright orange to shiny black.

A dry woodland form grows with oaks and cacti in western Cuba but is not cultivated off the island (Chuck Hubbuch, pers. comm.). It appears to have a higher tolerance to drought and may be solitary trunked or few stemmed, with grayish green leaves.

The paurotis palm thrives in full sun but tolerates partial shade. It is a true water lover, although its survives in dry soil. It thrives in neutral to slightly acidic, heavy or sandy soils with lots of organic matter. Alkaline soils must be amended with organic matter or the palms need to be heavily mulched; they tolerate saline soil and air. The species is hardy in zones 9b through 11 and has been known to resprout from its roots after freezing to the ground at 15°F. Damage to the leaves starts with any temperature below 25°F, and the trunks are usually killed to the ground by 20°F or lower. Plants grown in poor or dry soil are subject to rot, especially older specimens, and manganese and potassium deficiencies can develop in plants that do not receive adequate moisture. Because it is native to Florida, the paurotis palm often is thought to handle dry conditions and is sometimes planted in unwatered street medians. Under these conditions the palms suffer, grow slowly, and sometimes die. Propagation by division of the suckers from clumps is possible if the individual sucker is taken with roots and planted quickly.

Nothing is more beautiful than a mature clump of this palm with its slender trunks of varying heights—the essence of the tropical look with a wild yet elegant aspect. The Everglades palm looks better with some judicious thinning of its stems in older clumps. Because the clumps are clothed from foot to head with leaves, this palm can be used as an isolated specimen in an expanse of lawn; its best use, however, is as part of a border or swath of lower vegetation above which its beautifully elegant trunks and relatively small heads of stiff palmate leaves can punctuate the skyline. The palm is not a good candidate for the average house, but it can be grown successfully in conservatories and atriums. It needs as much sunlight as it can get and good air circulation.

ACROCOMIA is a genus of two solitary-trunked pinnate-leaved, monoecious palms in tropical America, both of which are armed with vicious spines on the trunks, leaf petioles, and leaves. The species differ from one another: one is large and variable in form, with columnar straight trunks that resemble royal palms (*Roystonea*); the other species is small and unassuming in the landscape with underground trunks. The genus name translates from the Greek as "highest" and "tuft of hair," an allusion to the larger palm's crown of prickly leaves atop the trunk.

We are here using the taxonomy and nomenclature of Henderson et al. (1995), which reduces the two dozen previously described species to two. Many hobbyists, growers, and even a few scientists do not agree with this controversial lumping, although they readily agree that the genus, like *Brahea*, has, in the past, been over described. (All the controversy surrounds what we list as *A. aculeata* below.) In this regard it may be interesting to note that (1) the 1914 edition of Liberty Hyde Bailey's *The Cyclopedia of Horticulture* lists four species: *A. media*, *A. mexicana*, *A. sclerocarpa*, and *A. totai*, with mention of *A. havanensis*; (2) *Hortus Second* (1946) lists eight species: *A. aculeata*, *A. armentalis* (now *Gastrococos*), *A. fusiformis*, *A. media*, *A. mexicana*, *A. sclerocarpa*, *A. totai*, and *A. vinifera*; and (3) *Hortus Third* (1976) lists five species, *A. aculeata*, *A. hospes*, *A. mexicana*, *A. spinosa*, and *A. totai*.

The primary reasons against the latest lumping have to do with leaf color and hairiness, amount of spininess, growth rate, and cold tolerance, all of which can be merely the expression of the variable morphology of a single, widespread species. The epithets most often mentioned are *A. mexicana* and *A. totai*, the former being shorter with marcescent leaves, the latter being taller with a clean, spiny trunk. David Witt (pers. comm.) points out that seedlings of *A. aculeata* have bifid leaves while those of *A. totai* are simple and unsegmented; *A. aculeata* has noticeably larger fruits and seeds, is significantly less hardy to cold, and is much faster growing when younger than is *A. totai*, often surpassing the queen palm (*Syagrus romanzoffiana*) in growth speed. Plates 4–6.

Acrocomia aculeata is a widespread and variable species extending from Cuba and the Caribbean Islands to southwestern Mexico and the Yucatán Peninsula, Central America, northern Colombia, most of Venezuela, and the eastern half of Brazil. It occurs in savannas and open places in monsoonal areas, and its range has probably been greatly influenced by the prehistoric peregrinations of the native peoples of these regions. Common names are macaw palm, which is also used for *Aiphanes aculeata*, and gru-gru palm. The epithet translates from the Latin as "prickly."

Mature trunks grow 15 to 35 feet high and are 9 to 16 inches in diameter. The stem is mostly columnar and straight but occasionally shows a slight to definite bulge near its middle. Some plants have trunks that are free, or nearly so, of dead leaves and are covered in all but their oldest parts with closely set rings of 1- to 3-inch-long black or lighter-colored needlelike spines. An approximately equal number of plants have trunks that retain many of the old dead leaves, with the bulk of the light gray to almost white trunk free of spines and smooth. The leaf crown is mostly full and rounded. The 20 to 30 leaves are 10 to 12 feet long with 3-foot-long mostly limp and drooping leaflets growing from the rachis at different angles, giving to the leaf a plumose, full aspect. They are borne on short, 3-inch-long, spiny and hairy petioles, and the leaf rachis is very spiny. Leaf color is deep grayish green to deep pure green and even bluish green, sometimes with a grayish to silvery pubescence beneath. The 5-foot-long inflorescences grow from the leaf crown and are usually partly hidden therein. This is a monoecious palm with separate yellowish male and female flowers in the same flower cluster and accompanied by a large woody bract (spathe) that is usually covered in reddish brown tomentum. The small yellowish green to brown, rounded fruits hang in pendent clusters half hidden in the crown and are usually produced without benefit of adjacent individuals.

The palm is moderately slow to fast growing. It is always found in open, sunny areas in habitat and demands at least half a day's sun to thrive. It is drought tolerant but grows faster and looks better with adequate and regular irrigation. It seems to thrive in many soils, from calcareous to rich and acidic, as long as they are well drained. It has a slight tolerance to salinity in the soil and air. Cold hardiness varies greatly, depending on the provenance of a given plant, but in general, this palm is adaptable to zones 9b through 11, although some individuals are more tender.

Overall, this princely palm resembles royal (*Roystonea*) or robust queen palms (*Syagrus romanzoffiana*). It is wonderful in specimen groups of three or more individuals of varying heights and is especially well suited to lining avenues; however, young plants pose a threat to unwary humans, especially children, because of their complete spininess. The species is not a good candidate for indoor cultivation as it demands intense light and good air circulation. In addition, its nearly complete spininess makes it difficult to site in all but the largest spaces. It is occasionally grown in atriums and conservatories.

The species has many uses in its natural range. Its very hard wood is sometimes used for house construction, carving, and furniture making. The pith of the trunk has been used as a source of sago. The spiny leaves are used as temporary fencing and as a source of fibers for weaving hammocks. The spiny leaf stalks have been used as protective fencing. The growing point, fibrous fruit pulp, and seed kernels are sometimes eaten. Oil from the seed has been used locally as a soap; and the oil and seed residue is used as livestock feed. Chuck Hubbuch (pers. comm.) heard stories in Panama of a potent alcoholic beverage that was made from the sap of the tree. Since the sap-collecting process requires the felling of the palm, he recommends the less-potent local beers. In Colombia, fallen flowers of the species have been used medicinally to treat respiratory tract disorders. According to one author, the fruits are particularly attractive to cattle that swallow the seeds whole. Hubbuch (pers. comm.) offers the controversial theory that the palm's fruits are adapted for distribution by now-extinct large mammals: "I have observed fallen seeds under wild plants that are cleaned of the sweet pulp, apparently by modern rodents." Plates 4–6.

Acrocomia hassleri occurs naturally in southwestern Brazil and barely into adjacent Paraguay, an upland and mostly xeric area with a short wet season and long dry periods. It is listed as rare.

It has a short, subterranean trunk with a few spiny leaves, each of which is 2 or 3 feet long and grasslike due to the few leaflets which are, themselves, thin and grasslike. Although the leaflets grow from the rachis at different angles, like those of *A. aculeata*, they do not produce the same plumose effect. The leaflets, rachis, and petiole are sparingly armed with 0.5-inch-long, black spines. The flowers and fruits are similar to those of *A. aculeata* but borne on or near the ground.

The cultural requirements of the two species are similar, but *A. hassleri* is likely to be hardier to cold than *A. aculeata* and, because of its subterranean stem, would most likely grow on even if the leaf crown were killed to the ground. Its growth rate is probably very slow. It is an interesting species but not necessarily in a horticultural sense as it is, to be honest, not overly attractive. It is probably no more suited to indoor cultivation than is *A. aculeata*.

ACTINOKENTIA is a genus of two small, solitary-trunked pinnate-leaved, monoecious, slow growing palms in New Caledonia. The two species are similar in appearance. One species has been introduced to cultivation; the other (*A. huerlimannii*) is nonexistent in cultivation and is rare and threatened in the wild. The genus name consists of the Greek word for "rayed" or "radiating" and *Kentia*, an out-of-date name for species of *Gronophyllum*, *Gulubia*, and *Hydriastele*. PLATES 7 & 8.

Actinokentia divaricata is endemic to low mountainous rain forest of central and southern New Caledonia. The species is listed as threatened by the World Conservation Union (IUCN), although it is widespread in New Caledonia. The epithet translates from the Latin as "spreading," a reference to the branching inflorescences and probably to the spreading leaves, which characteristic is exaggerated by the exceptionally long petioles.

The palm grows to a maximum height of 25 feet with a slender, prominently ringed gray to light brown trunk that is never more than 3 inches in diameter, and atop which the 2-foot-tall yellowish green to brownish green or even reddish brown crownshaft is scarcely thicker. The leaf crown is relatively sparse, never sporting more than six 3-foot-long, strongly arching leaves. The widely spaced leaflets grow from the pinkish red to reddish brown, 3-foot-long, cylindrical rachis at a single angle, making the leaf nearly flat. Each 18- to 36-inch-long leaflet is linear-oblong, with a pointed apex, and matures to a glossy light to dark green with a fuzzy, often slightly waxy underside. New leaves are usually pink or red until they mature. The inflorescences grow from beneath the crownshaft, usually encircling the shaft. The blossoms are light pink to light reddish brown and either male or female, all in the same inflorescence. The 1-inch-long egg-shaped fruits are light to medium violet when mature.

The palm grows slowly, cannot withstand drought, and needs protection from the midday sun, especially in hot and dry climates. It requires a free-draining, humus-rich acidic soil. While the palm's habitat is frostless, the little trees are reported to have withstood 30°F without much harm and seem adaptable even to frostless Mediterranean climes if irrigated on a regular basis.

This elegant and refined small landscape subject must be planted in an intimate setting to be effective. It has good color and is almost architectural in its appeal, with a beautiful silhouette that cries out for up-close inspection, making it perfect for patio gardens where its need for semi-shade and moisture can be attended to and its small-scale charm most enjoyed. It was supposedly widely grown in European greenhouses in the 19th century and is undoubtedly well suited to such treatment.

ACTINORHYTIS is a genus of two tall, slender, and solitary-trunked pinnate-leaved, monoecious palms with prominent crownshafts. They are native to New Guinea and the Solomon Islands, where they are found in lowland rain forest, beginning in the undergrowth but towering above the forest canopy at maturity. The genus name is derived from two Greek words meaning "ray" and "fold" and alludes to the folds in the seed's endosperm. PLATES 9 & 10.

Actinorhytis calapparia grows naturally in Papua New Guinea and the Solomon Islands in rain forest from sea level to 3000 feet elevation. The epithet is a Latinized form of the aboriginal name for the coconut palm (Dransfield 1994). The common name is calappa palm.

The palm grows to 40 or 50 feet in habitat with a slender, light-colored trunk that is never more than 8 inches in diameter. The trunk is closely ringed with leaf base scars and topped by a 3-foot-tall, light green crownshaft that is slightly bulging at its base and is scarcely thicker than the nearly white trunk. The base of the trunk is slightly swollen and usually bears a mass of roots anchoring the thin stem. The leaf crown is spherical but also open. The leaves are remarkably beautiful: 7 to 10 feet long, greatly arching, and recurved feathers of dark green with many 18-inch-long linear leaflets arching up from the rachis at an angle that creates a V-shaped leaf. The petioles are relatively long in juvenile plants but become shorter as the tree adds height, resulting in a beautifully rounded mature crown. The inflorescences form a ring around the base of the crownshaft and are many branched with masses of cream-colored flowers of both sexes. The palm, when in flower or fruit, has a thrilling visual aspect because of the extraordinarily tall crownshaft, the effect being one of a small crown beneath a large crown. The large egg-shaped fruits are 3 inches long and are borne in heavy, pendent masses; each one is red or reddish brown to purplish olive when ripe.

This tropical beauty has a modicum of hardiness to cold, and some specimens in central Florida have survived unscathed a temperature of 30°F. It does not tolerate the extended periods of cool winter nights in southern California (Geoff Stein, pers. comm.). The palm is adapted to sun or partial shade, although young plants prefer semi-shade or even shade. It is a true water lover and cannot withstand drought. It performs poorly in soil lacking nutrients and needs organic matter amended into calcareous soils to thrive. It grows moderately fast under optimal cultural conditions.

This is among the world's most beautiful palms. It has an almost formal elegance because of the gracefully recurving, almost circular fronds, and yet the aspect is stately because of the height of the palm at maturity. The tree makes a beautiful silhouette. It is effective as a canopy-scape, and the nearly complete circles of the crowns of a group of individuals of varying heights against the sky are breathtaking. It should perform well in bright conservatories and atriums with enough space, good air circulation, and high levels of moisture, light, and humidity.

The seeds are reportedly used locally in much the same manner as are those of *Areca catechu,* and the pulverized seed kernel has been used as a baby powder. PLATES 9 & 10.

Actinorhytis poamau is endemic to the Solomon Islands. The epithet is one of the aboriginal names for the species. Not much is known about this species. Compared with *A. calapparia,* it has a taller, more slender trunk and its fruits are smaller and green instead of red. It is most likely not in cultivation.

ADONIDIA is a monotypic genus of solitary-trunked, monoecious, pinnate-leaved palm. It was placed in the genus *Veitchia* as *V. merrillii* until taxonomic studies by Scott Zona indicated it should be returned to its own genus, *Adonidia,* the name by which it had been known in the early 20th century. Common names include adonidia palm, Christmas palm, Manila palm, and dwarf royal palm. The genus name translates from the Latin as "little Adonis" and was selected because the name *Adonis* was already in use for a genus in the ranunculus family; *Adonis* has red blossoms and *Adonidia* has red fruits. The epithet honors Elmer D. Merrill, 20th-century botanist, plant explorer of the Asian tropics, and former director of the Arnold Arboretum. PLATES 11–13.

Adonidia merrillii is widespread in lowland regions of the Philippine Islands and occurs in several soils from coastal forests to limestone slopes.

It can grow to a height of 50 feet with age and in habitat but is usually no more than 30 feet tall in cultivation. The light to dark gray trunks are less than 1 foot in diameter and are stout looking in younger plants but elegantly slender appearing in taller specimens. They are ringed in their newer and younger parts but not strongly so. The light green crownshaft is 1 to 3 feet high and columnar with only a slight basal bulge. The leaves arc 6 to 8 feet long with a decidedly arching rachis and a relatively short petiole that is less than 1 foot long. The light to dark green leaflets grow from the rachis at an angle which creates a V-shaped leaf. The ends of the leaflets are pendent, which fact tends to relieve the slightly stark formal appearance of the leaf crown, and the ones nearest the trunk usually bear long threads from their apices because strips of tissue (termed *reins*) connect the edges of leaflets in new leaves and hang loosely from fully unfolded leaves. There are usually 12 strongly arching leaves per plant. The many-branched inflorescences grow from beneath the crownshaft and bear small, whitish unisexual flowers of both sexes in the same cluster. The fruits are in large grapelike clusters and when mature are brilliant red or scarlet. Their maturation coincides with the end of the year in the Northern Hemisphere, which has led to one of the common names, Christmas palm.

The species is very susceptible to lethal yellowing disease, limiting its landscape value in Florida and the Caribbean Basin. At Fairchild Tropical Garden in Miami, Florida, the oldest survivors are growing in a site shaded by an immense *Enterolobium* tree and it may be that the insect that transmits lethal yellowing (the leaf-hopper, *Myndus crudus*) prefers sunny areas (Chuck Hubbuch, pers. comm.). The tree grows moderately fast, especially when young. It also flowers and fruits with as little as 3 feet of trunk. It is adapted to full sun or partial shade but is not drought tolerant and needs regular and adequate moisture. It tolerates salt spray but is not a candidate for saline soils. It is adaptable to a range of soils with good drainage. It does not tolerate freezing temperatures and is adaptable only to zones 10b and 11, although it sometimes recovers from temperatures slightly below freezing, making it marginal in 10a.

Because of its neatly abscissing old leaves and stiffly arching leaf crown, the palm has a formal, architectural appearance. It is striking in silhouette and, if this characteristic can be emphasized, works well in groups of individuals of varying heights even planted in the middle of a lawn. It is especially wonderful in a patio or other intimate site and is endearing in front of a contrasting background that allows its form and silhouette to be seen. The Christmas palm is easily grown indoors and is among the most frequently used palms in shopping malls and atriums. It needs good light and a constantly moist medium.

AIPHANES is a genus of 22 spiny, pinnate-leaved, monoecious palms in tropical America. Most are indigenous to lower elevation forests on the eastern slopes of the Andes, but others are in the adjacent lowlands and a few in Central America and the Caribbean. Some species in Colombia and Ecuador are in great danger of extinction.

Most have aboveground, solitary trunks, although a few are clustering. All the trunks are covered with spines arranged in closely set rings and usually the leaf stalks as well as the leaflets are spiny. The leaflets are often wedge shaped and have jagged apices. The inflorescences grow from among the leaf sheaths and are spikelike or once branched, the flowering branches bearing both male and female flowers.

Among the most ornamental aspects of these species is the red or orange fruit of most. Every species in this genus is worthy of cultivation, but few are grown. All of them need a rich soil and at least average and regular moisture. None are hardy to cold and most appreciate protection from the midday sun, especially in hot climates and especially when young.

The genus was at one time known as *Martinezia*. The present genus name translates from the Greek as "always obvious" and probably alludes to the brightly colored fruits of most species. PLATES 14–18.

Aiphanes aculeata has the widest distribution in the genus and grows naturally in the drier forests of the Andes Mountains in Venezuela, Colombia, Peru, Bolivia, western Brazil, southeastern Peru, and central Bolivia, from sea level to an elevation of 5280 feet. Common names are coyure palm and ruffle palm. The epithet is Latin for "prickly."

This solitary-trunked palm grows to 35 feet tall and 6 inches in diameter; the stems are ringed in black spines. The leaf crown consists of 10 to 15 leaves and has a wonderful globular aspect due to the beautifully pendent older leaves. Each 5- to 8-foot-long, linear-oblong leaf has 50 to 80 leaflets that are irregularly obdeltoid and abruptly widened at the apex; the leaflets are arranged in groups of four to six, have jagged apices, and grow from different angles out of the rachis, giving the leaf a ruffled, plumose effect. There are squat black spines on the short petioles, leafstalks, and leaflets. Leaf color is deep glossy green above and paler green beneath. The large, arched and pendent inflorescences are accompanied by a spiny spathe and grow from among the leaf crown, bearing both male and female flowers. Each small blossom is yellowish white, and the edible fruits are globose, usually less than 1 inch wide, and bright orange or bright red when mature.

The palm is fast growing if its basic requirements are met. Juvenile trees require shade, while older plants do fine in sun to partial shade. This palm needs regular, adequate moisture and a rich, humus-laden, and well-drained soil but flourishes in calcareous soil if mulched and fertilized. It is adaptable to zones 10b and 11, although it is infrequently successful in the warmer parts of 10a.

The tree is exceptionally beautiful as a canopy-scape. Its crown is among the most satisfying shapes in nature,

being full and round but with much contrast within the orb because of the jagged, plumose leaflets. It is unsatisfactory as an isolated specimen in lawns or other open spaces, even in groups of individuals of varying heights; it needs something at the bases of its trunks. It is successfully grown indoors and especially in greenhouses and conservatories if given good light, good air circulation, a fertile medium, water, and humidity. It is also often grown in containers. PLATE 14.

Aiphanes eggersii is indigenous to the dry, semideciduous coastal tropical thorn forests of Ecuador. The epithet honors the palm's original collector, Henrik F. A. von Eggers, a 19th-century Danish professional soldier and amateur botanist.

This large species grows to 25 feet and is similar to *A. aculeata* but has a clustering habit and many more leaflets to each leaf. The leaves are 3 to 5 feet long and bear narrow, wedge-shaped leaflets in clusters of 4 to 10. Each leaflet is widened and jagged at its apex, is usually lighter colored beneath, and grows at a slightly different angle from the rachis to give a wonderful ruffled look to the leaf.

The palm is not yet widely cultivated and is probably as tender to cold as is *A. aculeata*. It is doubtless tolerant of drought and even salinity.

Aiphanes erinacea is indigenous to the western foothills of the Andes Mountains in southern Colombia and central Ecuador, where it grows in the rain forest at elevations of 2200 to 6700 feet. The epithet is from a Latin word meaning "hedgehog" and alludes to the plant's spininess: every part except the leaves has spines, even the inflorescences.

This densely clustering species has an overall height of 25 feet. The leaves have widely spaced clusters of wedge-shaped, jagged leaflets growing at different angles from the spiny rachis.

This palm is adapted to partial shade and requires it in hot climates. It also needs copious moisture and a soil that is not too calcareous.

Aiphanes gelatinosa is native to the foothills of the western slopes of the Andes Mountains of southern Colombia and northern Ecuador, where it grows in rain forest from an elevation of 2500 to 5280 feet. The epithet is Latin for "gelatinous" and refers to the jellylike substance that usually envelops the densely clustered fruits.

This palm grows to an overall height of 25 feet. Individuals from the northerly parts of the palm's range have linear, wedge-shaped leaflets growing in one plane and are all solitary trunked, while those from southerly parts of the range have clustering stems and widely spaced clusters of narrow, wedge-shaped leaflets growing in several planes to give a ruffled look to the leaf. The fruits are round and 0.5 inch in diameter.

Aiphanes grandis is a rare and endangered, solitary-trunked species growing in the mountainous rain forest of southwestern Ecuador at elevations of 3000 to 5500 feet. The epithet is Latin for "grand" or "large."

This palm is the tallest species in the genus, reaching 70 feet high. The trunk is 6 or 7 inches in diameter, light colored, and ringed with black spines in all but its oldest parts. The leaves are to 10 feet long, and the many large leaflets are grouped into clusters of five to eight. Each leaflet is narrowly lanceolate and jagged at its apex, the ones in the middle of the rachis being to 30 inches long; they all grow from the rachis at slightly different angles to give the leaf a beautiful, almost plumose effect. The many white flowers are of both sexes and are borne in pendent inflorescences, each of which is accompanied by a large, spiny, and woody spathe. The 0.5-inch-wide round fruits are dark green when mature and are covered in an easily removed black, prickly fuzz.

The palm is not known in cultivation but would also seem to be eminently worthy of it because of its stature, especially in cool but frostless Mediterranean regions. Because of the mostly plumose leaves, the magnificent silhouette or canopy-scape of this species looks a lot like that of larger species of *Wettinia*.

Aiphanes hirsuta is extremely variable, and some taxonomists divide it into at least four different species, while others make of it four subspecies. The natural range of this palm is from southwestern Costa Rica down through Panama, into central Colombia, and southwards into extreme northern Ecuador, mainly at elevations of 2000 to 6500 feet, although infrequently in the lowlands. The epithet is Latin for "hairy," an allusion to the tiny, bristly hairs of the inflorescences.

All forms are clustering. The trunks are 6 to 30 feet tall, and there may be 2 to 20 trunks per clump. Stem diameter ranges from 0.5 to 4 inches, and the trunks are always ringed with black spines except in their oldest parts. The leaves are relatively long. The broad to linear leaflets are always wedge shaped and may be arranged on the rachis in a single plane or be plumose and arranged in groups, the terminal pair are larger than the others. The inflorescences are covered in tiny spinelike hairs, and the fruits are red, purple, or white.

Aiphanes lindeniana is endemic to mountainous rain forest of Colombia, where it grows to an elevation of 8600 feet. The epithet honors Jean J. Linden, a 19th-century German botanist and collector in South America.

This palm is usually clustering and attains an overall height of 25 feet. The gray trunks are an ethereally slender 2 to 3 inches in diameter and covered in their younger parts with large, vicious 4-inch-long black spines. The 8-foot-long leaves bear closely spaced, jagged-ended, linear wedge-shaped stiff leaflets that have prickly margins; the leaflets grow at a slight angle from the rachis to create a V-shaped leaf.

This is among the most beautiful species in the genus, and its diaphanous silhouette makes the most wonderful canopy-scape. The palm is slightly susceptible to lethal yellowing disease. It flourishes in hot, tropical or nearly tropical climates and is adaptable to zones 10 and 11. It also is amazingly adapted to various soils, even calcareous ones, and tolerates near drought conditions, although its grows slower and less robustly.

Aiphanes linearis is endemic to the mountainous rain forest of central Colombia, where it grows to an elevation of 8000 feet. The epithet is Latin for "linear," a reference to the shape of the leaflets.

This large, densely clustering species has an overall height of 40 feet and a trunk diameter of 4 or 5 inches. The 8-foot-long leaves have clusters of 2-foot-long, narrow and linear, jagged-ended, pendent leaflets, which grow in different planes from the rachis to create a slightly plumose leaf. Except for the leaflets, every part of this palm is spiny. The fruits are packed into dense clusters and are 1.5 inches wide, round, and covered in reddish golden spines.

It is a beautiful species, almost noble in its stature and form. In cultivation, it looks better if some of the stems of equal or nearly equal height are removed to emphasize each trunk and leaf crown. Although rarely grown, it should be more widely planted; unfortunately, it is now exceedingly difficult to find seed.

Aiphanes macroloba is indigenous to mountainous rain forest of western Colombia and northwestern Ecuador at elevations of 500 to 4500 feet. It occurs in the undergrowth and is in danger of extinction. The epithet is Greek and Latin for "large" and "lobe," an allusion to the leaf form.

This unusual undergrowth clustering species has an overall mature height of 12 feet and leaves that are 6 feet long, undivided (unless mechanically segmented by wind), and pinnate, each with a deeply bifid apex.

It is as beautiful as any of the *Geonoma* or *Calyptrogyne* species but rare in cultivation. Its sparse spininess makes it more desirable, but it's not for the neat or tidy garden.

Aiphanes minima is a variable, solitary-trunked, undergrowth rain forest species found in most islands of the West Indies other than Cuba. The common name, macaw palm, is also used for *Acrocomia aculeata*. The epithet translates from the Latin as "smallest."

According Borschsenius and Bernal (1996), familiar names such as *A. acanthophylla*, *A. corallina*, *A. erosa*, *A. lu-*

ciana, and *A. vincentiana* are listed under one name, *A. minima.* Chuck Hubbuch (pers. comm.) could identify most of these old Caribbean species by their leaves but was confused by their free hybridization in the collection at Fairchild Tropical Gardens. Borschsenius's decision to lump all of these into *A. minima* makes sense: populations of *A. minima* on some Caribbean islands are rare due to habitat destruction. The threat of their loss is significant when one considers that some of these populations are distinct enough in appearance that they were once considered separate species.

The trunk is 20 to 50 feet tall and covered in closely set rings of sharp black spines in all but its oldest parts. The leaf crown is exceptionally rounded and full because of the pendulous older leaves. The leaves are 6 to 8 feet long. They are basically similar to those of *A. aculeata,* but the leaflets are narrower, there are more of them to a leaf, they are more regularly spaced along the rachis, and they are less ruffled at their apices than are those of *A. aculeata.* The petiole and the rachis are covered in black spines, and leaf color is medium dark green above and much paler green beneath. Leaves *A. minima* seedlings are spiny on both sides, while the leaves of *A. aculeata* seedlings are spiny on the underside only (Kurt Decker, pers. comm.). Older plants of both species tend to have spineless leaf upsides (Chuck Hubbuch, pers. comm.). The plant is monoecious with 3- to 6-foot-long inflorescences growing from among the leaves. Blossoms are fragrant and yellowish white. The fruits are rounded, 0.5 inch wide, red, and reportedly edible.

Adult plants do well in sun or partial shade, but juvenile plants need partial shade or mostly shade. The palm is not finicky about soil type as long as drainage is unimpeded, but a decent medium with humus is best. It can withstand some drought if it is not prolonged, but it does not tolerate saline conditions.

The macaw palm is exceptionally graceful and elegant with its full, rounded crown of pendent pinnate leaves. It is more aesthetically adaptable to specimen planting than *A. aculeata,* especially in groups of three or more individuals of varying heights. The palm takes well to indoor cultivation if given bright light and high relative humidity. PLATES 15–18.

Aiphanes ulei is indigenous to southern Colombia, eastern Ecuador, northern Peru, and western Brazil, where it occurs in mountainous rain forest to an elevation of 6000 feet. The epithet honors Ernst H. G. Ule (1854–1915), a botanist and collector in South America.

This small, solitary-trunked species grows to 10 or 12 feet in overall height. The slender trunks are 1 inch in diameter and graced with rings of black spines. The sparse leaf crown has six leaves, each bearing black spines on its base, petiole, and rachis. The 6-foot-long leaves are large for such a short trunk and give a most appealing, ruffled aspect to the palm. The leaflets are arranged in pairs along the rachis and to 1 foot long but, in a pair, one is always longer than its companion; they are wedge shaped with oblique, jagged apices, medium to deep green above and silvery green beneath, and they grow in a single flat plane from the spiny rachis.

This gem is undeservedly rare in cultivation. It is among the prettiest in the genus and makes a perfect close-up subject, especially sited against a contrasting background.

ALLAGOPTERA is a genus of four similar-looking, pinnate-leaved, monoecious palms in eastern South America, all with solitary, short or subterranean trunks. These palms appear to be clustering, because the leaf petioles are short, the leaves are numerous and full, and the growing point of the trunk turns downward at some point in the individual's history and thus is usually lower than the base of the trunk. In addition, the short trunks often bifurcate and produce more than one leaf crown. The leaves of all species consist of clusters of linear leaflets, each leaflet growing in a different plane. The spikelike, erect inflorescences grow from among the leaf bases, with the blossoms tightly packed along the apical half of the spike. The small fruits are yellowish green to brown and are crowded into club-shaped clusters.

The genus was formerly known as *Diplothemium.* The present genus name translates from the Greek as "change" and "feather," an allusion to the plumose leaves. PLATES 19–22.

Allagoptera arenaria occurs naturally along the seacoasts of southeastern Brazil, where it grows in large stands on sand dunes and the adjacent scrublands on sandy to very sandy soils. Because of development and land clearing, the species is now highly endangered. The only common name is seashore palm. The epithet is Latin and translates as "sandy," referring to the palm's habitat.

This palm reaches a height of 8 feet and a width of 15 feet. The 4- to 6-foot-long leaves are dense in the crown. The narrow, ribbonlike leaflets are clustered into irregularly spaced small groups and grow from the rachis at different angles to give a plumose appearance to the leaf. Each leaflet is apically bifid and a deep glossy to dusky green above with a definite silvery cast beneath due to a waxy deposit. The inflorescence is a short, dense, and narrow spike of closely set small greenish yellow flowers, the whole emerging from a paddle-shaped and persistent woody spathe. The orange, round, egg-shaped, 1-inch-wide fruits are densely packed into semipendent narrow club-shaped clusters that are mostly hidden among the leaves. They are not only edible but also delicious in the early stages of ripening (David Witt, pers. comm.).

The species is slightly susceptible to lethal yellowing disease. The palm grows slowly, but to make up for this growth rate it, is one of the most attractive trunkless or nearly trunkless palms and it thrives in poor, sandy soil. It is drought tolerant when established and is relatively hardy to cold, being safe in zones 9 through 11 and probably marginal in 8a. It is not a good shade plant, although it grows reasonably well in semishade.

The shrub is beautiful and useful because of its high salt and drought tolerance. It may be the world's most salt-tolerant palm species. It grows in pure sand along the beach if planted above the high tide line and is useful (if slow) for dune and erosion control. The leaves have a beautiful shimmering quality because of the silvery backed leaflets that move in the slightest breeze. This palm flourishes not only along the immediate shoreline but also farther inland as long as it has sun and the soil is freely draining. It needs almost full sun to thrive, a fact which limits its use indoors, but it is commonly grown in containers outdoors and, if given enough light, should also thrive inside. PLATES 19–22.

Allagoptera brevicalyx is indigenous to a relatively small area of east central Brazil, mainly along the coast but also inland in dry, deciduous forest. The epithet is Latin and Greek for "short" and "calyx."

The principal differences between this species and *A. arenaria* are that it is smaller, has fewer leaves, and has wider leaflets. The leaves are covered in a gray, waxy substance that renders them gray green, and the leaflets are apically bifid. The species is probably not as hardy to cold as is *A. arenaria*, but data are lacking. Otherwise, it should have the same cultural requirements.

Allagoptera campestris grows naturally in southeastern and southern Brazil, the northeastern tip of Argentina, and extreme eastern Paraguay. The epithet is Latin for "of the fields."

This small palm has a subterranean trunk and dull green plumosely pinnate leaves. The thin leaflets are arranged in whorled groups like those of the other species and are grayish green beneath. The immature fruits are reportedly edible.

The palm is weedy looking when combined with larger vegetation but is effective in the landscape if planted against a background of contrasting colors and forms. It is probably hardier to cold than the above two species and is definitely as drought tolerant.

Allagoptera leucocalyx is indigenous to southern-central Brazil and eastern Bolivia, where it forms large colonies in open, grassy, and sunny areas. The epithet is Greek for "yellow" and "calyx."

The plant is slightly smaller than *A. arenaria* and, unlike the other *Allagoptera* species, which have plumose leaves, has stiff, almost rigid leaflets. The leaflets grow from the rachis at an angle which creates a V-shaped leaf.

ALLOSCHMIDIA is a monotypic genus of pinnate-leaved, monoecious, solitary-trunked palm endemic to northeastern New Caledonia, where it occurs in the undergrowth of rain forest. It is threatened because of its small natural range and its growing point, which is harvested for food. The genus name is derived from the Greek word for "other" (in the sense of "different") and the surname of Maurice Schmid, a French botanist in New Caledonia. The epithet is from Latin and translates as "smooth" or "hairless," a reference to the glabrous crownshaft. PLATES 23 & 24.

Alloschmidia glabrata grows to a height of 40 feet in habitat;. The trunk is no more than 6 inches in diameter and is light gray—except for the newest growth that is tan—and indistinctly ringed. The beautiful olive-green crownshaft is 2 feet tall and not much wider than the trunk. The leaves are borne on short petioles, are 6 feet long, and have 24 pairs of slightly S-shaped, light green leaflets, each of which is 2 feet long, and all of which grow from the whitish rachis at a slight angle, resulting in an almost flat leaf. The species exhibits an unusual flowering habit with several inflorescences in various stages of maturity on the upper part of the trunk, commencing beneath the crownshaft. Each inflorescence bears both male and female flowers and consists of thin, ropelike, grayish green and pendent branches with tiny greenish blossoms. The 4-inch-long fruits are black when mature and elliptical.

The palm needs protection from the midday sun, especially in hot climates. It requires a moist, fast-draining soil. It is probably intolerant of frost, but no data are available to confirm this suspicion.

This slender, graceful but slow growing palm is elegance personified. It would seem best planted where its comeliness can be seen against a contrasting background, such as in a patio or as a tableau of specimens towering above lower growing vegetation under high trees.

ALSMITHIA is a monotypic genus of solitary-trunked, pinnate-leaved, monoecious palm in Fiji. It is rare and known only from two sites, each with 100 or so individuals. The genus name honors Albert C. Smith, botanist, plant explorer, and author of a flora of Fiji. The epithet is Latin for "long foot" and refers to the length of the petioles and peduncle. PLATE 25.

Alsmithia longipes occurs on the islands of Taveuni and Vanna Levu, where it grows in low mountainous rain forest. Mature trunks attain a height of 12 feet and a diameter of 3 inches; they are light brown with closely set rings of leaf base scars. The leaves are 8 feet long on 2- to 2.5-foot-long petioles; they are erect, never descending below the horizontal, and are extended down the trunk to create an elongated crown. New leaves are beautiful rose or red, which hue lasts for two weeks. The regularly spaced, linear-lanceolate leaflets are 2 feet long, each with a prominent and lighter-colored midrib. The leaflets grow from the rachis in almost a flat plane and are deep green above and lighter green beneath. The inflorescences grow from among the leaves and are 4 feet long, with several thin, spidery, tan branches, which bear tiny male and female flowers. The 1-inch-long egg-shaped fruits are red when mature.

This palm is barely in cultivation and not many data are available, but it is adaptable only to zone 11 and is marginal in 10b. It needs constant moisture, high humidity, partial shade, and a soil that is not too poor.

AMMANDRA is a monotypic genus of rare and endangered pinnate-leaved palm in northwestern South America. The palm is closely related to and similar in appearance to *Phytelephas* species but smaller.

Until September 2001, the genus was considered to have two distinct species, *A. dasyneura* and *A. decasperma*, separated on flower details and disjunct geographic ranges; Bernal et al. (2001) found a population in an intermediate geographical valley with characters showing a continuum of inflorescence details between the two species. Thus we are here including only *A. decasperma*, the first described species.

The genus name translates from the Greek as "sand man," an allusion to the flowers being formed at or near ground level where they are often hidden by soil or leaf litter. The epithet is derived from Latin words meaning "10" and "seed," the maximum number of seeds in a given fruit.

Ammandra decasperma is native to western Colombia, where it grows in the wet coastal foothills of the Andes Mountains to an elevation of 1500 feet as well as in the intermountain valleys.

This is a clumping species with trunks usually beneath the ground but occasionally emerging into aerial stems that are, nonetheless, recumbent and creep along the ground. The gently arching leaves are large, to 20 feet long, with a 6-foot-long, smooth, and rounded dark green petiole. The leaflets are emerald green, linear, 2 to 3 feet long, and regularly spaced in a flat plane along the rachis. The plants are dioecious; the male inflorescences are long with congested, short flowering branches, and the female inflorescences are compact. The fruits are formed in large globose heads, each with pointed projections.

The palm requires tropical growing conditions (moist and warm) and is not adapted to full sun. It needs a moist but free-draining soil that is well endowed with organic matter. A mature individual looks like a small grove of some gigantic tropical cycad species and is a magnificent sight.

Indigenous peoples reportedly eat the seeds and use the fibers of the large, tough leaf petioles to make baskets. As is the case with *Phytelephas* and *Aphandra*, the hard seeds are used as vegetable ivory to carve objets d'art and in the manufacture of buttons and other utilitarian products.

APHANDRA is a monotypic genus of pinnate-leaved, dioecious palm in eastern Ecuador, northern Peru, and western Brazil, where it grows in the rain forest of the foothills of the Andes to an elevation of 2640 feet. The genus name is a combination of those of *Ammandra* and *Phytelephas* because of the similarities between the inflorescences and infructescences of *Aphandra* and those of the other two closely related genera. It has no common name, but a good one might be mastodon palm. The epithet honors Natalie Uhl, a 20th-century palm taxonomist. PLATE 26.

Aphandra natalia grows to a height of 40 feet in habitat. It is solitary trunked with all but the oldest parts of the 25- to 30-foot stem covered in gigantic, fat, old grayish leaf bases and spinelike black leaf base fibers; it is 1 foot in diameter when shorn of the leaf bases but, with them, it is 3 feet in diameter. Near the top of the trunk, the leaf base fibers are extremely long and pendent, almost ropelike, much like those of *Leopoldinia piassaba*. The 15-foot-long leaves are borne on extremely long, 8-foot robust gray petioles, making the entire leaf (with petiole) 25 feet long. The leaves are erect, slightly arching, and never descend beneath the horizontal; indeed, they are mostly held at a 45-degree angle. The medium to dark green, 3-foot-long linear leaflets are regularly spaced along the rachis and grow in a single plane. The inflorescences are unusual. Male inflorescences are colossal pendent affairs 9 feet long with the 2-foot-long peduncle at the top and short, clustered secondary branches bearing spreading tufts of pure yellow blossoms. Female inflorescences are large, 1-foot-long tufts of wiry, yellowish filaments, surrounded by tough, heavy greenish brown boat-shaped bracts. The fruits are in dense rounded clusters that would look like a medieval club with spikes if the large amount of hairy black fiber were removed from the clusters.

This palm is rare in cultivation outside of Ecuador, where it is grown for the long fibers near the top of the trunks, which are used to make brooms. It is certainly worthy of wider cultivation in tropical climates because of its almost prehistoric appearance.

ARCHONTOPHOENIX is a genus of six solitary-trunked, monoecious, pinnate-leaved palms in warm, moist parts of eastern Australia from sea level to 4000 feet in elevation.

All are noted for their exceptionally beautiful, straight, ringed, and medium to tall trunks, their prominent crownshafts, and their large and graceful leaves. The leaflets grow from the rachis in a single plane, but the rachis twists near its middle, giving a wonderful angle to the leaf and a sense of movement even in still air. The leaflets of all but one species (*A. cunninghamiana*) have silvery undersides. The inflorescences grow in a ring, like a skirt, from the base of the crownshafts and consist of several pendent branches of small purple, yellow, or white flowers, which produce red fruits.

Cold, drought, and hot drying winds are the worst enemies of these palms. Because the growing points are easily damaged when plants of any size are transplanted, these palms should be purchased in containers.

The genus name translates from the Greek as "king" and "date palm." All the species share the common name king palm. PLATES 27–34.

Archontophoenix alexandrae is endemic to rain forest of coastal northern and central Queensland, Australia. It is rare in parts of its range but is overall unthreatened. Common names are Alexandra king palm, Alexandra palm, and, in Australia, the Alex palm and Alexander palm. The epithet honors Princess Alexandra of Denmark (1844–1925).

The palm grows to 80 feet tall but is usually half this stature in cultivation in the continental United States. The trunk bulges slightly at its base and, above that point, is 1 foot in diameter. The leaf crown is 20 feet wide and 10 to 12 feet tall. The crownshaft is to 4 feet tall, slightly bulging at the base, and olive green to purplish brown. The leaves are 6 to 10 feet long with many 3-foot-long, closely spaced, narrow and drooping, strongly ribbed leaflets growing in one plane. Leaf color is bright grassy to deep green above and silvery or gray green beneath; new growth is often bronzy. There are seldom more than 12 leaves in any crown. The many-branched, pendent inflorescences encircle the trunk below the crownshaft. The small blossoms are white or nearly white, and the egg-shaped to round fruits are 0.5 inch in diameter and red when mature.

Two varieties (subspecies of some authors) were described as *A. alexandrae* var. *beatricae* and *A. alexandrae* var. *schizanthera*. Most taxonomists now consider them one variable species. Plants labeled "*A. alexandrae* var. *beatricae*" may exhibit a pronounced "stepped" base to their trunk bases, which feature is attractive enough to be sought after, the form most likely being a cultivar.

In Mediterranean climates this species reportedly withstands unscathed a temperature of 26°F, but in areas subject to wet freezes in winter even large palms die at 28°F; thus it is basically safe only in zones 10b and 11, and marginal in 10a in wet winter climes. Like most other *Archontophoenix* species, it is a true water lover and needs a rich, humus-laden soil that is well drained; it is subject to leaf burn in the hottest part of the day in hot or dry climates, especially when young. It is a fast growing palm, often adding 1 foot or more of trunk annually under good cultural conditions.

No palm is more majestic and yet graceful than a mature specimen of this species with its straight-as-an-arrow, beautifully ringed, light gray trunk and massive crown of leaves. The trunk color is usually light brown when the palm is young. While the tree is spectacular enough to stand alone, it looks better in groups of three or more individuals of varying heights. It is relatively fast growing and difficult to transplant successfully at any size. It has three requirements that mitigate against its use indoors: it needs good air circulation, high relative humidity, and bright light except when young. It is successfully grown in atriums and large conservatories.

Archontophoenix cunninghamiana grows naturally in rain forest of coastal Queensland southwards into southeastern New South Wales. It is rare in parts of its range but is overall unthreatened. Common names are piccabeen palm and bangalow palm. The epithet honors Allan Cunningham, an early 19th-century British botanist in Australia.

Mature trunks attain 60 feet of height and 9 to 10 inches in diameter. The crownshaft is 3 feet or slightly more in height, slightly swollen at its base, and a deep olive to dark green. The leaf crown is 15 feet wide and 10 to 12 feet tall. The leaves are 8 to 10 feet long, with many narrow grassy to deep green 3-foot-long leaflets, each of which is a slightly paler green beneath. The leaflets are more drooping than are those of the Alexander palm and consequently even more graceful. The newly unfurling leaves are often coppery or bronzy hued. The inflorescences are significantly larger than those of the Alexander palm, and the blossoms are lavender. The 0.5-inch-long ellipsoid to rounded pink to red fruits are formed in pendent clusters.

Seed dealers, growers, and nurseries apply the name *Archontophoenix cunninghamiana* 'Illawara' to individuals descending from palms collected in the Illawara area of the mountainous coastal region of New South Wales in Australia. This form is supposedly hardier to cold because of its southerly and elevated provenance. Alas, this has not proved to be the case in central Florida; however, the plant is certainly well adapted to the Mediterranean but nearly frostless regions of coastal California where summer heat is not great; and, according to David Witt (pers. comm.) in Orlando, Florida, this form seems to be the only one which looks good at any age when grown in the shade.

This palm grows as quickly as does the Alexander palm and has the same cultural requirements. It is less heat tolerant, especially when young, but slightly more cold tolerant. Although it has survived several years in zone 9b of the continental United States, it is tender enough that it cannot be relied upon as a landscape subject in that zone, except in the drier Mediterranean climes.

The species serves the same landscape purposes as does Alexander palm but is in even greater need of being planted in groups of three or more individuals of varying heights for the best visual effect. Like Alexander palm, it has three requirements that mitigate against its use indoors, but it is successfully grown in atriums and large conservatories. PLATES 27–29.

Archontophoenix maxima grows naturally in mountainous river valleys of the upper Atherton Tableland (to 3500 feet), west and southwest of the port of Cairns in Queensland, Australia. Before John L. Dowe formally described it in 1994, it was known only as *A.* 'Walsh River'. The common name in Australia is Walsh River king palm. The epithet is Latin for "largest," an allusion to the inflorescence that is the largest in the genus.

This palm grows as tall as piccabeen palm but has a thicker trunk. Other distinguishing features are the short to almost nonexistent petioles and the upright, rigid, scarcely arching leaves. The inflorescence bears creamy white flowers.

The species is probably no hardier to cold than any other species in the genus.

Archontophoenix myolensis is a rare and endangered species endemic to the mountains of northeastern Queensland west of Cairns, along streams and rivers. It, like *A. maxima*, was described by John L. Dowe in 1994 and is possibly the rarest species of the genus in nature. The only common name in English is the one used in Queensland, Myola king palm. The epithet is Latin for "of Myola," a district in Queensland.

The tree is similar to a smaller version of *A. cunninghamiana* but has a bluer crownshaft with more pendent leaflets. It is probably one of the hardier species to cold since it occurs naturally at high elevations and, because of

its riverine provenance, possibly the one requiring the moistest conditions. PLATES 30 & 31.

Archontophoenix purpurea grows naturally in rain forest of northeastern Queensland at elevations to 4000 feet. Before John L. Dowe and Donald Hodel described this species in 1994, it was known as *A.* 'Purple Crownshaft' or *A.* 'Mt. Lewis'. Its common name is purple king palm. The epithet is Latin for "purplish."

Mature trunks attain 50 to 60 feet of height in habitat and 40 feet under cultivation. They usually show diameters of 18 inches, making this species the most massively trunked. The crownshaft is 4 feet tall, slightly bulged at the base, and light violet to reddish purple. The leaf crown is no more than 20 feet wide and 15 feet tall. The leaves are 6 to 10 feet long with many 3-foot-long, closely spaced narrow, drooping leaflets growing in one plane. Leaf color is bright grassy to deep green above, silvery or grayish green beneath. The palm is monoecious and the inflorescences are pendent clusters that encircle the trunk below the crownshaft. The small blossoms are purplish. The 1-inch-wide rounded, scarlet to wine-red fruits are in pendent clusters.

This species has cultural requirements similar to those of Alexandra palm; however, it seems to tolerate cooler conditions better, although it is no more tolerant of frost. It is the slowest growing species in the genus (Daryl O'Connor, pers. comm.). PLATES 32 & 33.

Archontophoenix tuckeri occurs naturally in rain forest and coastal swamps of extreme northern Cape York Peninsula of Queensland, Australia, making it the most northerly occurring and most tropical species. John L. Dowe described it in 1994; before that it was known as *A.* 'Peach River'. The epithet is a Latinized form of the surname "Tucker" and honors the palm's original collector and founder of the Townsville Palmetum.

The palm is similar in appearance to the other species in the genus, especially to Alexandra palm, but is smaller. It is rare in cultivation but in habitat grows to 70 feet. The crownshaft is a typical green, but the new leaves usually are reddish bronze. The inflorescences beneath the crownshaft are held erect and bear white or creamy white flowers from which are formed large, bright red fruits. PLATE 34.

ARECA is a genus of 60 pinnate-leaved, monoecious palms in India, Southeast Asia, Malaysia, Indonesia, the Philippines, New Guinea, the Solomon Islands, and tropical Australia. The seeds of most species are used like that of the most famous member, the betel-nut, *A. catechu*.

The species are generally medium in height, although a few are tall. Most are solitary trunked. All have prominent crownshafts, some of which are outstandingly colored, and all have trunks ringed with prominent leaf base scars. Leaf crowns contain few leaves, and these are arching and usually have relatively wide leaflets, the terminal two usually grown together. The inflorescences grow from beneath the crownshafts, or from the ground in acaulescent species, and consist of short radiating, usually stiff flowering branches bearing both male and female blossoms. The fruits are egg shaped and often colorful.

Most species are undergrowth inhabitants of rain forest, but some (including the most famous) are adapted to growing in full sun in the open. All species are tropical and adaptable to zones 10b and 11, only occasionally being found in warm microclimates of 10a.

The genus name is a Latin form of the aboriginal (southern India) name of one species. PLATES 35–51.

Areca caliso is endemic to the Philippines, where it occurs in mountainous rain forest, mainly along streams at elevations of 1000 to 3000 feet. The epithet is the aboriginal name of the species.

This solitary-trunked species grows to 25 feet tall in habitat. Except in their oldest parts, the trunks are green with widely spaced, light-colored rings of leaf base scars. The dark green crownshaft is 2 feet tall and no wider than the trunk except at its base where it bulges slightly. The 8-foot-long leaves are mostly ascending and usually do not lie beneath the horizontal. The large leaflets are 3 feet long and grow from the rachis at a slight angle but not steep enough to say the leaf is V shaped. They are evenly spaced, deep green above and lighter beneath, linear-lanceolate with mostly oblique apices, and are limp enough that their tips are pendent. The fruits are yellow to red when mature.

The palm is as tender to cold as are any of the other species and needs a humus-laden soil and constant moisture. It thrives in partial shade. The species looks like *A. catechu* but is more choice for intimate sites and, because of the beautiful large leaflets, gives one of the most tropical and lush appearances of any smaller palm. It is rare in cultivation and is probably found only in botanic gardens but deserves much wider acceptance and planting.

Areca catechu is naturalized in India, Southeast Asia, Malaysia, Indonesia, the Philippines, and the South Pacific Islands. The original habitat is unknown but is most likely the wet regions of peninsular Malaysia. Common names include betel palm, betel-nut palm, and areca nut palm. The epithet is a Latin form of the Malayan name for the species.

The solitary trunk may attain a height of 100 feet in habitat but is usually half that under cultivation. Each trunk is less than 1 foot in diameter and usually no more than 8 inches, with prominent whitish rings; trunk color is deep green except for the oldest wood, which is gray to

grayish green. The full, rounded leaf crown is 12 feet wide and tall. The bright green, smooth crownshaft is 3 feet tall, with a slight bulge near its base. Mature leaves are stiffly arching, 8 feet long, with 40 or more shiny medium green leaflets which grow from the rachis at a 45-degree angle, giving the leaf a V shape. The leaflets are linear-oblong to linear-ovate, 2 feet long, and 4 to 6 inches wide with prominent grooves along the upper surface. They are jagged at their apices, and the two terminal leaflets are fused. The palms are monoecious with male and female flowers in each inflorescence, the latter emerging beneath the crownshaft in spreading 2-foot-long panicles. The blossoms are small, fragrant, and whitish yellow. The deep yellow to red fruits are 1 to 2 inches long, egg shaped, and borne in pendent clusters. The seed resembles a miniature coconut.

There is a beautiful selection or cultivar with golden trunks, fruits, and crownshaft; one with a nearly white crownshaft; one with a reddish orange crownshaft; and a dwarf, squat and compact cultivar from Thailand.

The palm flourishes in partial shade or full sun. It is a water lover and a fast grower, luxuriating in rich, humus-laden, moist but well-draining acidic soil; poor and calcareous soils should be amended with organic material or heavy mulches. The tree is slightly tolerant to salt spray. Year-round warmth is essential for this palm, limiting its cultivation to zone 11, but it sometimes can be found in the warmest parts of 10b.

Although it is among the tallest species in the genus, the betel palm is too ethereal to be planted singly and isolated in the middle of space. Groups of at least three individuals of varying heights create a veritable symphony of form and color because of the splash of leaves and the gorgeous, straight dark green trunks with their widely spaced, beautiful light-colored rings. The palm is perfect as a canopy-scape. Mature trees must have a lot of head room and, since betel palm grows quickly, it is soon too large for all indoor spaces except atriums and large conservatories. Commercial nurseries grow it in small flat pots with the seed partially exposed and market it as a miniature coconut. The seed's outward similarity to a small coconut, along with its immature first couple of leaves, makes for a beautiful tabletop plant, but it does not usually thrive for long potted this way.

Betel-nuts contain a mild narcotic, and native peoples have for millennia chewed them mixed with the leaves of one of the pepper vines (*Piper methysticum*) and with lime juice to obtain a high and stain their teeth. The palm and this practice were made famous to the Western world by Bloody Mary in the Rodgers and Hammerstein musical and movie, *South Pacific*. PLATES 35–38.

Areca concinna is endemic to Sri Lanka, where it grows in rain forest at low elevations and is endangered because of agricultural expansion. The epithet is Latin for "elegant" or "orderly."

It is a small sparsely clustering species whose slender, elegant stems grow to 15 feet tall with a diameter of 2 inches at mid height. They are emerald green in their younger parts and light tan to light gray in their older parts. The small crownshaft is hardly wider than the stems, is light green, and bulges slightly at its base. The spreading, slightly arching leaves are 5 feet long. The 18-inch-long medium green leaflets grow in a single plane from the rachis, are slightly limp, 3 inches wide, heavily veined, irregularly spaced along the rachis, and variable, but mostly oblong-lanceolate with slightly jagged apices. The deep red fruits are borne in small pendent clusters.

The palm is tender to cold and adaptable only to zones 10b and 11 and marginal in 10b. It needs constant moisture in a well-drained, slightly acidic, humus-laden soil. It thrives in partial shade, especially when young, and cannot endure full sun in hot climates.

This elegant palm should be planted where its diaphanous stems and heavy-looking leaves can be seen up close. It should also be grown with its few stems at varying heights to show off the beautiful foliage and small trunks.

Areca guppyana grows naturally in low mountainous rain forest of Papua New Guinea and the Solomon Islands. The epithet is a Latin form of the surname "Guppy" and honors a plant explorer.

This solitary-trunked species attains 10 feet high and 3 inches in diameter. Like the trunks of most species in the genus, this one is green with whitish rings of leaf base scars. In spite of the palm's small stature, the base of the trunk usually exhibits prominent stilt roots. The crownshaft is 1 foot tall, light green, and the same girth as the trunk. The few leaves (usually six) consist of four or five widely spaced, broad, deep green, deeply plicate leaflets; the fused leaflets of the terminal pair are largest. The inflorescence is mostly erect and consists of many small greenish white flowers of both sexes. The fruits are bright red when mature and 1.5 inches long.

The palm does not tolerate frost. It needs protection from hot sun and a humus-laden soil that is nearly constantly moist. It must be used in an intimate setting to show up. It makes a good container plant.

Indigenous people use the seed of this palm in the same manner as that of the betel-nut palm, *A. catechu*. PLATE 39.

Areca hutchinsoniana is endemic to the Philippines, where it grows in low mountainous rain forest. The epithet honors W. I. Hutchinson, a 20th-century plant collector in the Philippines.

The stems of this small, solitary-trunked species never grow more than 10 feet tall and are 1 inch in diameter. They are green with widely spaced whitish rings of leaf base scars. The 1-foot-tall green crownshaft bulges slightly at the base. The leaves are 3 feet long but have numerous irregularly spaced leaflets from 1 to 2 inches wide but always S shaped, with a long tapering apex; the two apical leaflets are united at their bases.

This exquisite little palm is suited for a patio, entrance way, or other intimate setting and as a large accent for lower vegetation, such as along a path.

Areca ipot grows naturally in the Philippines in lowland rain forest, where it is threatened because of overcollecting. The epithet is part of the aboriginal name.

This small, solitary-trunked palm does not grow more than 12 feet high and looks like a diminutive betel-nut palm, including the way the leaves are held. The inflorescences are composed of thin, splayed branches of whitish flowers. The tight clusters of ovoid fruits are deep orange or red when mature.

This species cannot tolerate frost and must be protected from the midday sun, especially in hot climates. It is a true water lover and must never dry out. In addition, it needs a rich soil that is neither heavy nor compacted. PLATE 40.

Areca latiloba is indigenous to Thailand, peninsular Malaysia, Sumatra, and Java, where it grows in low mountainous rain forest. The epithet is Latin for "wide lobed," an allusion to the shape of the leaflets.

This small, solitary-trunked, variable species resembles *A. triandra*; indeed, some taxonomists believe it is just that. It reaches a height of 12 feet. The leaf crown is sparse with usually six ascending, slightly spreading leaves borne above a light bluish green 18-inch-tall crownshaft that is no wider than the 2-inch-thick green trunk. The 4-foot-long leaves on 1-foot-long dark green petioles bear either widely spaced, broad, 18-inch-long, glossy deep green, long-tipped leaflets or regularly spaced, more numerous, and narrower leaflets. The starburstlike inflorescences grow from beneath the crownshaft and consist of thin, 6-inch-long whitish branches bearing white flowers of both sexes. The egg-shaped fruits are pink or red.

This small undergrowth palm requires protection from full midday sun, especially in hot climates. It is a true water lover and needs a rich, humus-laden, well-drained soil and a tropical climate. PLATES 41 & 42.

Areca macrocalyx is indigenous to New Guinea and the Solomon Islands, where it grows in dense rain forest from sea level to an elevation of more than 5280 feet. It is sometimes called dwarf betel-nut palm. The epithet is from Greek words meaning "large" and "calyx."

This is a variable species, especially as to leaf form. It grows to 30 feet tall but is often smaller. The trunk is usually straight as an arrow and green in its younger parts, with widely spaced whitish rings of leaf base scars. The elongated crownshaft is usually no thicker than the trunk, even at its base, and is 4 feet tall; most forms are light glaucous green but some are reddish near the base of the shaft. The 6-foot-long leaves are mostly ascending, stiff, and unarching, with many to few deeply pleated leaflets of variable widths and spacings; some individuals have entire or almost entire, unsegmented leaves. They are medium to dark green above and usually lighter green beneath. The fruits may be round or elongated but are invariably deep orange when mature and are said to be used as a betel-nut substitute.

A form of this species with brilliant red on its crownshaft seems well adapted to the climate and soil of southern Florida.

The species does not tolerate frost nor does it need as much heat as many others. It is not tolerant of drought and needs a humus-rich soil. It luxuriates in partial shade at any age and cannot withstand full sun in hot climates. PLATE 43.

Areca macrocarpa is a rare species endemic to lowland rain forest on the island of Mindanao in the Philippines. The epithet is Greek for "large" and "fruit," an allusion to the fruits which are used for the same purposes as is the betel-nut.

The stems of this clustering species grow to 20 feet high and 6 inches in diameter. The crownshafts are slender and 2 feet tall, scarcely of greater diameter than the trunk, and deep green. The leaves are 8 feet long on short petioles, strongly arching, and have closely set, 3-foot-long stiff, erect leaflets growing from the rachis at an angle which gives a distinct V shape to the leaf. The ellipsoid fruits are 3 inches long and red.

The species is wonderfully beautiful and, if the trunks can be kept at different heights, has one of the most thrilling silhouettes in the family. It is tropical in its requirements, needing constant warmth and moisture; it also needs partial shade, especially in hot climates, and a rich, humus-laden soil.

Areca mammillata is endemic to wet forests on the island of Palawan in the Philippines, where it occurs naturally from sea level to an elevation of 1000 feet. The epithet is Latin for "with mammae," an allusion to the teat-shaped fruits.

This small solitary-trunked species grows to 12 feet overall, with a trunk diameter of slightly more than 1 inch. The 1-foot-tall slender crownshaft is medium green and almost unnoticeable. The 3- to 4-foot-long leaves are as-cending and unarched, although the lower ones are spreading; they are borne on 18-inch-long petioles. The 1-foot-long, regularly spaced leaflets are glossy medium green, slightly S shaped, lanceolate overall, with the middle and lower ones long tipped and the ones near the leaf apex thicker, corrugated, and with small apical teeth corresponding to the veins. The fruits are 0.5 inch in diameter.

This choice, intimate-appearing palm needs partial shade, copious moisture, and a tropical climate. PLATES 44 & 45.

Areca minuta is endemic to low mountainous rain forest in Sarawak on the island of Borneo, where it occurs in the undergrowth. The epithet is Latin for "minute" or "tiny."

The stems of this clustering species attain heights of 3 feet. The crownshaft is also tiny and almost white. The 1-foot-long leaves have four to six widely spaced, wide, glossy bright green pinnae that are ovate-elliptical with a drawn-out apex; the leaflets of the terminal pair are apically obtuse and jagged.

The species must have partial shade, regular and adequate moisture, and a humus-laden soil. It makes a beautiful large groundcover and is a perfect container subject. PLATE 46.

Areca multifida is endemic to low mountainous rain forest in Papua New Guinea, where it is an undergrowth subject. The epithet is Latin for "many divisions" and alludes to the numerous narrow leaflets in adult plants.

The solitary-trunked species grows to 10 or 12 feet high. The trunk is hardly more than 1 inch in diameter and is green in its youngest parts and tan in the older parts, with widely spaced light gray or white rings of leaf base scars. The 18-inch-tall crownshaft bulges slightly at the base and is smooth and light mint green. The leaf crown is sparse but has 6-foot-long leaves. The mature leaflets make this palm unusual for an *Areca* species: they number as many as 60 per leaf, are widely spaced, narrowly linear, and 2 feet long with tapering apices; juvenile plants have wider and apically jagged leaflets.

This unusual species is outstandingly beautiful and makes a stunning silhouette against contrasting vegetation. It must be planted in partial shade. Its other cultural requirements are a tropical climate, regular and copious moisture, and a humus-laden soil. Even under ideal conditions, the palm is slow growing.

Areca triandra grows naturally in wet regions at low elevations in eastern India, Southeast Asia, eastern Indonesia, and the Philippines. The epithet translates from the Greek as "three" and "anther."

This clustering species can have up to a dozen trunks per plant, each of which can attain a height of 30 feet. The trunks are green in their newer parts and grayish in their older parts, diaphanously thin and elegant, and are never more than 3 inches in diameter, encircled with widely spaced whitish circles of leaf base scars. The crownshaft is 3 to 4 feet high, smooth, and green, and barely bulging at its base. The leaves are similar to those of betel-nut palm but usually darker green and with larger fused terminal leaflets; there are generally no more than six leaves per trunk. The palms are monoecious with both male and female flowers in each inflorescence, the latter emerging from beneath the crownshaft. The tiny, greenish white, fragrant blossoms produce clusters of 1-inch-wide, ovoid, brownish orange to reddish orange fruits.

The species varies mainly in the ultimate height of the trunks and the amount of suckering; there are even some individuals with solitary trunks. One of these forms has been labeled "*A. aliceae*" in the past.

This palm does not tolerate frost. It requires partial shade when young but, as an adult, can withstand full sun, even in hot climates. It is also a true water lover and needs a rich, humus-laden, friable soil with unimpeded drainage. Because of its suckering habit, the palm resprouts from its roots if frozen back in central Florida (David Witt, pers. comm.). The rooted suckers may be removed with care from the parent plant and grown on.

This relatively small but graceful, almost noble-looking palm is among the few species that can look good planted alone and surrounded by space. It is even more appealing when planted where it can be viewed up close, especially in silhouette. Some individuals form dense clumps of stems and these look better if a few of the trunks are judiciously thinned out so that the beautiful form of the others may be more apparent. The plant grows fast with proper irrigation and nutrients. It makes a fine and easy large houseplant or container subject and needs a soil that never dries out and high relative humidity.

Areca tunku is indigenous to peninsular Thailand, peninsular Malaysia, and Sumatra, where it occurs naturally in low mountainous rain forest. The epithet is the aboriginal name for the palm.

This small solitary-trunked species grows to a maximum height of 15 feet. The closely ringed trunk is 2 inches in diameter and light brown. It is topped by a dark green, 18-inch-tall crownshaft that is slightly wider than the stem. The leaf crown is hemispherical with 6-foot-long spreading leaves that bear closely spaced 2-foot-long glossy dark green, lanceolate-acuminate, and slightly S-shaped leaflets. The fan-shaped inflorescences are borne beneath the crownshaft and consist of erect, coral-colored fleshy branches. The white fragrant flowers produce 2-inch-long greenish brown fruits.

The species is slow growing and needs protection from the hot sun. It also requires copious and regular moisture in a humus-laden, quickly draining soil.

Areca vestiaria occurs naturally in low mountainous rain forest of eastern Indonesia, including Sulawesi and the Moluccas. It is sometimes called orange collar palm. The epithet translates from the Latin as "wrapped" or "clothed," probably a reference to the conspicuous crownshaft.

This species is usually clustering but sometimes solitary trunked. Mature trunks attain a height of 20 feet and a diameter of 3 to 4 inches, often with distinct prop or aerial roots at the base. Clumps may attain a width of 15 feet and a total height of 25 feet. The most striking aspect of the palm is its startlingly beautiful slender crownshaft, which is bright, shiny orange to reddish orange or even red. The leaves are similar in size and form to those of betel-nut palm with the notable exception that the petioles are extremely short and both petiole and rachis are usually an attractive orange or deep yellow. The palms are monoecious with male and female flowers in each inflorescence, the latter emerging from beneath the crownshaft. The flowers are tiny and yellow to orange. The small golden-yellow to orange ovoid fruits are borne in pendent clusters.

A form of this species has a maroon new leaf. By the time the new leaf fades to green, another new leaf is unfurling, giving this cultivar additional color. The crownshaft is more intensely reddish orange than that of the type.

While the species is at home in tropical conditions, it can survive and even thrive in zone 10a and seems able to tolerate extended periods of cool weather. Like most species in the genus, it requires a rich, friable, free-draining, and slightly acidic soil, and it does not tolerate drought. It usually looks its best in partial shade but thrives in full sun except in hot climates. Propagation by division of the suckers is usually unsuccessful.

There is hardly a more beautiful combination of form and color in the plant world, making this palm excellent for almost any landscape circumstance. It excels in close-up situations. With enough moisture, humidity, and light, it works admirably well as a houseplant or in a greenhouse. PLATES 47–51.

Areca whitfordii is endemic to the islands of Luzon and Mindanao in the Philippines, where it grows in low, swampy areas near the coasts. The epithet is a Latinized form of the surname "Whitford" and honors the palm's original collector.

This solitary-trunked species has an overall mature height of 30 feet with an 8-inch-diameter trunk that is green in its younger parts and beautifully ringed with whitish leaf base scars. The 3-foot-tall crownshaft is silvery green and bulges at the base. The ascending leaves on 6-inch-long petioles carry many closely spaced, 3-foot-long, 2-inch-wide leaflets that are deep green above and paler green beneath; they are pleated and leathery, and the larger ones at the midpoint of the blade have long pendent drip tips.

It is undeservedly rare in cultivation.

ARENGA is a genus of 17 mostly monoecious, pinnate-leaved palms in tropical Asia and Australia, some solitary trunked, others clustering. The inflorescences are small and either once branched or spikelike. The trunks of almost all species are monocarpic but do not flower until they are mature (often many years), and the flowering may last for several years because the inflorescences emerge from the leaf base scars around the trunk and progress usually from top to bottom in series of two or three per year. With the clustering species, there are always new trunks forming to take their places. Almost all species produce remarkable amounts of "woven" black and persistent, stringlike fibers around their leaf bases. The flesh of the fruits of all species is poisonous and corrosive to the skin.

The common name of most species is sugar palm because the sap in the trunks of several is used to make sugar as well as alcoholic beverages. The genus name is a Latinized form of an aboriginal name for one species. PLATES 52–75.

Arenga australasica is native to northern Queensland and Northern Territory of Australia, where it grows in lowland forests. The epithet is Latin for "of Australasia."

This clumping species produces one or two stems to 30 feet from the base(s) of which grow several smaller trunks. The tallest stems are light colored in their older parts and are strongly ringed with leaf base scars. The leaf crowns are 15 feet high and wide and consist of a dozen leaves. Each leaf is 10 feet long, including the 1-foot-long petiole. The leaflets are narrow, stiff, pleated, dark green above and a duller and lighter shade of green beneath; they grow from the rachis at a 30-degree angle to create a V-shaped leaf. The inflorescences are large, pendent panicles of yellowish male and female flowers. The black or dark purple, round fruits are less than 1 inch in diameter.

This beauty is tender to cold and adaptable only to zones 10 and 11, being marginal in 10a. It is a water lover, and drought and dry air are its enemies. It needs a soil that drains freely and contains humus. The palm flourishes in sun or shade but looks better in partial shade, especially when younger. About the only fault the palm has is that it is slow growing.

Because of its height and multitrunked habit, this palm is magnificent in the middle of a lawn. It cannot be beat as a giant hedge or barrier, marking the boundary of some garden space, its lower growing trunks creating the barrier, the taller ones a ready-made canopy-scape. This palm would only be adaptable to a large atrium or conservatory with high levels of relative humidity and light. PLATES 52–54.

Arenga brevipes is indigenous to northern Borneo and the adjacent Philippine Islands, where it grows in lowland rain forest. The epithet is Latin for "short foot" and alludes to the trunks.

The short stems of this sparsely clustering species are mostly subterranean, but the large leaves thrust upward to a height of 8 to 10 feet on 2- to 3-foot-long stout dark brown to nearly black petioles. The leaflets are short and congested near the base of the leaf, with the lowermost pointing backwards towards the petiole, but are progressively larger towards the apex where the terminal one is broad and has three to four lobes. The lower leaflets are irregularly wedge shaped with shallow lobes and undulations, and all are deep emerald green above but a startling and shimmering silvery white beneath, with a strong, darker midrib for each lobe of the leaflet.

The palm is not hardy to cold and needs partial shade and a humus-laden, constantly moist but fast-draining soil. PLATES 55 & 56.

Arenga caudata occurs naturally in southern Myanmar, Thailand, northern peninsular Malaysia, Cambodia, Vietnam, and southeastern China, where it is an undergrowth subject in monsoonal tropical forests at elevations mostly under 2500 feet. It is unfortunately also called dwarf sugar palm. The epithet translates from the Latin as "tailed," an allusion to the ends of all the leaflets except the terminal one.

This small, densely clumping species shows remarkable variation of leaf morphology. The stems grow to a maximum height and width of 6 or 7 feet; they are thin, wiry, reclining, and graceful. The leaves are mostly 3 feet long, with slender, wiry 18-inch-long petioles. The 4 to 10 leaflets range from linear to rhomboid; the nonlinear leaflets have an irregularly toothed margin and all but the terminal one have a "tail" of varying length. All forms have silvery undersides. The inflorescences, although mostly hidden by the leaves, bear creamy white, fragrant flowers of both sexes, the female ones producing pendent spikes of small, beautiful egg-shaped, brilliant red fruit, each with an apical pit. The variability of leaflet form has led to the naming of most of these configurations, often with numbers, and some with varietal or cultivar names such as *A. caudata* var. *stenophylla*.

This palm can withstand little cold and is adaptable only to zones 10 and 11, although protected specimens survive in 9b. The plants do not like drought and need a humus-laden, free-draining soil. Filtered sunlight is best, but the palm does reasonably well in full sun, especially in cooler but frostless Mediterranean climates. Alas, this fine landscape subject is slow growing even under ideal conditions.

It must be planted in an intimate setting to be seen, a requirement that can be difficult to achieve due to the palm's small stature. It excels as a giant groundcover in partially shaded sites and is exquisite as a border, as a specimen in a border, or alongside a path in the woods. It makes a good house plant if given bright light, regular irrigation, and good air circulation. PLATE 57.

Arenga engleri is native to the Ryukyu Islands of Japan and to Taiwan, where it grows in moist forests of the low mountains. Common names include dwarf sugar palm and Formosa palm. The epithet honors German taxonomist and plant explorer Heinrich G. A. Engler (1844–1930).

This medium-sized clustering species has trunks to 10 feet tall and clumps to 15 feet tall and wide. The trunks are covered, except in their oldest parts, with a tightly adhering, woven net of black fibers, the older parts being light gray to light tan with distinct rings of leaf base scars. The leaves are 9 feet long on short, stout petioles and exhibit a twist in their orientation from the top of the trunk. The leaflets are to 2 feet long, thick and stiff, linear (except for the apical ones), and irregularly jagged ended at the tips; an inward fold in the center of the leaflet gives it a slight V shape. Leaf color is medium green above but silvery beneath. The orange and yellow fragrant flowers are borne in branched, pendent inflorescences, which grow from the leaf base scars, starting at the uppermost ones until the small, purplish, 0.5-inch round fruits mature on the lowest ones, at which point the entire stem dies.

Two slightly differing forms of this species are known: the one from the Ryukyu Islands is more robust growing with longer and wider leaflets than the one from the more southerly island of Taiwan (David Witt, pers. comm.).

The species is slightly susceptible to lethal yellowing disease. It thrives in zones 9b through 11 and is even possible in 9a with occasional protection; sheltered and well-protected specimens are growing in 8b. It grows moderately fast with adequate water and light but is slow in dry soils. It thrives in clay soils and sandy ones and, even though it grows on mostly limestone soils in habitat, it luxuriates in the acidic clay soils of southeastern Texas where it is often cultivated under pine trees with a thick mulch of needles. It prefers partial or dappled shade but performs amazingly in full sun, even in hot climates if provided with enough irrigation. Suckers may be carefully removed and planted if they are rooted.

A large, well-grown specimen looks good in the center of an expanse of lawn if the mass of trunks is judiciously thinned out to better reveal the appealing form of the stems. The Formosa palm is wonderful as a giant hedge as well as a centerpiece among lower-growing palms or other vegetation. Few palms look as good as large potted specimens, but *A. engleri* must have good light under such circumstances. It is equally at home in well-lit, airy greenhouses, atriums, or conservatories. PLATES 58–60.

Arenga hastata is a small clumping species indigenous to low mountainous rain forest of peninsular Malaysia and western Borneo. The epithet is Latin for "hastate," although the reference is lost as no part of the leaf is shaped like an arrowhead.

The palm forms clumps to 4 feet high (usually less) and 5 feet wide. The light-colored stems are thin and wiry, and the leaves are 2 feet long and pinnate, with 10 diamond-shaped, toothed leaflets; the leaflets of the terminal pair are distinctly wedge shaped with squared-off apices. The spiked inflorescences are erect and carry light orange flowers that form tiny pink or red globose fruits.

The plant is tropical in its requirements and adaptable to zones 10 and 11. It needs partial shade and a moist, humus-rich, free-draining soil. PLATE 61.

Arenga hookeriana occurs naturally in southern Thailand and northern peninsular Malaysia, where it is an undergrowth subject in monsoonal tropical forests. It (or at least the form sought after) is vulnerable in habitat and, although widespread in its distribution, is not common. The epithet honors 19th-century British botanist Sir Joseph D. Hooker.

This small clumping species seldom exceeds 3 feet high in habitat and the local Thai people suspect that all the larger forms have been collected (Hodel 1998). Under cultivation and with ideal growing conditions, a clump may reach 6 feet high and wide. The leaves are 1 to 2 feet long and 9 or 10 inches wide. They are variable but, in the type, are undivided and have an unusual diamond shape with deeply lobed margins, each point between the lobes ending in a short "tail." They are shallowly pleated and deep emerald green above with a beautiful silvery hue beneath. The leaf may also be truly pinnate, with five leaflets, only the terminal one having the above characteristics, the other four looking like the linear leaflets of one form of *A. caudata*. The inflorescences are 2-foot-long spikes (seldom branched) that carry orange or yellow male and female flowers. The small red, round fruits are 0.25 inch in diameter but are sometimes heavy enough to cause the whole infructescence to nod or even droop.

The palm is closely allied to *A. caudata* and hardly distinguishable from some forms of it; indeed, "about 90 percent of wild-collected seeds of *A. hookeriana* grow and develop into typical *A. caudata,* only the remaining 10 percent retaining their simple leaves" (Hodel 1998), which implies that the two are but one variable species. Every collector wants the typical form, as its undivided pinnate leaf is unique in the palm world.

This beauty is adapted to zones 10 and 11. It requires at least partial shade, especially in hot climates, but grows in a range of well-drained soils.

Because of its size and nearly unique leaf form, no other palm needs more judicious placement in the landscape: it cries out for an intimate site where it can be viewed up close. It is an excellent choice for a protected, partially shaded patio, as a specimen along a path, and as a large groundcover. It's hard to imagine a finer container plant. Indoors it needs good light, regular and adequate irrigation, and good air circulation. PLATES 62 & 63.

Arenga listeri is a rare solitary-trunked species endemic to Christmas Island, where it occurs in the undergrowth of low mountainous rain forest. The epithet is a Latinized form of the surname "Lister" and honors a 19th-century British explorer and plant collector.

This is one of three solitary-trunked species in the genus. The straight, columnar, and heavily ringed trunk can attain 60 feet tall but is usually between 30 and 50 feet tall when it flowers. The leaves are ascending, mostly erect, usually few, 10 to 12 feet long, with the evenly spaced leaflets growing along the stout rachis in a nearly single plane; the 2-foot-long linear-elliptic leaflets are deep green above and silvery or grayish green beneath.

This unusual species is difficult to place in the landscape because it grows fast and large but at the same time needs protection from wind as the stout petioles break easily. Another problem is its monocarpic habit and, although it takes up to 50 years from seed to flowering, the inevitable outcome of a flowering specimen creates a mechanical problem.

Arenga micrantha is indigenous to northeastern India, southern Bhutan, and Tibet, where it grows on steep slopes in broad-leaved subtropical mountainous forests at elevations of 4500 to 7000 feet. The epithet is from two Greek words meaning "tiny" and "flower."

The trunks of this medium-sized, sparsely clustering species grow to 10 feet high with a diameter of 6 inches. The leaf crown is hemispherical, with a few 6- to 8-foot-long leaves on 2-foot-long petioles. The leaves are ascending when new but spreading when older. The leaflets are regularly arranged along the rachis, 12 to 18 inches long, narrowly wedge shaped, with a slightly jagged apex. They are medium dull green above with the usual silvery gray hue beneath. New leaves are V shaped with their leaflets growing from the rachis at an angle, but older leaves are flat, their leaflets growing from the rachis in a single plane. The

species is unusual in that it seems to be dioecious with male and female inflorescences on separate trees.

It is a relatively newly described species and is new to cultivation. It is reportedly the most cold-tolerant species in the genus. It may even be adaptable to regions with hot, wet summers and dry winters. It needs a humus-laden soil.

Arenga microcarpa occurs naturally in the Moluccas and on New Guinea, where it grows in mostly swampy regions. The epithet translates from the Greek as "small fruit."

The trunks of this large clumping species are relatively thin, reach 25 feet tall, and are covered in their upper parts in dense black fibers, the lower parts dark green to tan and prominently ringed. The massive leaves are 12 feet long and 5 feet wide, with 6-foot-long petioles. The leaflets are 2 to 3 feet long and linear, with broadened but abruptly pointed tips; they are thick, tough, and evenly spaced along the 8-foot-long rachis. Near the base of the leaves the leaflets are usually in groups and grow from the rachis at different angles, while the outer leaflets lie flat in one plane and are not arranged into groups. Leaflet color is deep green above but silvery beneath. The inflorescences are pendent panicles that are mostly hidden by the leaves and carry fragrant, purplish flowers. The fruits are small, rounded, and red.

The palm requires tropical conditions and is adaptable only to zones 10b and 11. It is a true water lover and requires a rich soil in which it grows moderately fast. While luxuriating in full sun, it grows well in partial shade. It can be propagated most easily by separating the suckers.

This spectacular species works as an isolated specimen as well as a dominant feature of massed vegetation, to which it adds an ineluctable accent. It is unsurpassed as a gigantic hedge or barrier marking property lines or as part of a wall of great foliage, which conditions give a wonderful sense of lushness. Its visual impact is that of a large *A. engleri* specimen. It would be a candidate only for large well-lit atriums or conservatories. PLATES 64 & 65.

Arenga obtusifolia occurs naturally in southern Thailand, peninsular Malaysia, Java, and Sumatra, where it grows in rain forest along the coast and the foothills of the mountains. The epithet is Latin for "obtuse" and "foliage," a reference to the bluntly shaped leaflets.

This is a large, mostly clustering species. The trunks are 1 foot in diameter and can reach a height of 50 feet; they are covered in the typical network of strong, black fibers (some of which are long and pendent) except for the oldest parts which are smooth, light colored, and prominently ringed. The leaves are among the largest in the genus, to 18 feet long, on 3-foot-long petioles. The linear leaflets to 4 feet long are dark green above and silvery beneath, thick and leathery, with wavy margins and rounded but toothed apices; they sometimes grow at different angles from the rachis, especially near the base of the leaf, but are always pendent. The branched inflorescences grow from the leaf base scars on the trunk and bear many white flowers. The mature fruits are egg shaped, greenish, and 2 inches long.

The palm grows mostly in swampy regions and needs constant and abundant moisture, a rich soil, and sun. It does not tolerate frost and is possible only in zones 10b and 11. It grows reasonably fast under ideal conditions. The species is magnificent in almost any site but especially as a canopy-scape because of its usually widely separated stems. As part of a wall of foliage, it is unsurpassed. There are no data relevant to growing this palm indoors, but it requires lots of space and light. PLATE 66.

Arenga pinnata has been in cultivation for so long that its exact origin is uncertain but is probably the rain forest of western Indonesia. The most popular common name is sugar palm, as the trees are felled for the sap in the trunk from which sugar, jelly, and alcoholic beverages are made. The epithet is Latin for "pinnate," which describes the leaves of all *Arenga* species.

The sugar palm is one of three solitary-trunked species in the genus. The trunk is 2 feet in diameter and 50 feet high. It is covered in its younger parts with adherent black fibers but is light colored in its older parts, which usually bear the persistent leaf bases. Several fibers at each leaf base are long, stiff, and spiny. The leaves are 30 feet long on 6-foot-long petioles. They are stiffly erect and never lie below the horizontal plane. The great leaflets are 3 feet long and grow at different angles from the rachis, giving the leaf a plumose effect. They are linear, slightly jagged at their apices but smooth on their margins, and are dark green above but silvery beneath. In addition, they are limp and mostly drooping, which lightens the stiff visual aspect of the erect blades. The branched inflorescences are 7 feet long and bear purplish flowers with a strange aroma. The fruits are oblong, greenish yellow, and 2 or 3 inches long.

The species tolerates various soils, full sun to partial shade and, while a water lover, is also capable of withstanding some drought. It does not tolerate temperatures below 28°F but usually re-leafs and survives from temperatures in the low 20s (F). It is a fast grower if given plenty of water and a rich soil.

The palm looks good in almost any site. It should not be planted singly in areas that must be neat as the entire tree dies over a period of a year or two once it starts flowering. Otherwise it is large and spectacular enough to be sited alone surrounded by space, and it is magnificent as a large canopy-scape. It is rarely grown indoors. PLATES 67–70.

Arenga porphyrocarpa is a small, clumping species native to Java and Sumatra. The epithet is from Greek words meaning "red" or "purple" and "fruit."

The palm attains a maximum height and width of 6 feet. It is similar to *A. caudata*, with variously lobed leaflets carried on thin, limp petioles and rachises. Leaf color is the usual green above and grayish beneath.

It thrives in partial shade or full sun, likes regular and adequate moisture, and cannot endure frost. PLATE 71.

Arenga retroflorescens is a rare and endangered species endemic to Sabah on the island of Borneo, where it grows in lowland rain forest. The epithet is from two Latin words meaning "backwards" and "flowering" and alludes to the unique sequence of inflorescence formation.

The trunks of this clustering species slowly grow to heights of 2 to 2.5 feet. The leaf crown is mostly hemispherical and consists of a few stiff, 4-foot-long leaves on 5-foot-long petioles with densely fibrous bases. The leaflets are regularly and widely spaced along the rachis except the lowermost ones, which are separated from the apical ones and are clustered, more closely spaced, and shorter than the those along the midpoint and apices of the leaf. The middle leaflets are 18 inches long, linear wedge shaped, and stiff, and grow from the rachis in a single flat plane. Leaf color is dusky dark green above and silvery-brownish green beneath. The inflorescences, unlike those of any other species, are formed from the base of the stem first and then successively above at higher nodes along the stem. They are also unusual in being simple unbranched spikes at whose apices are borne elongated masses of single-sexed blossoms, the whole looking like a corncob. The three-lobed orange fruits are less than 1 inch in diameter.

The species has visual affinities to *A. engleri* but is shorter and has narrower leaflets.

Arenga tremula is endemic to the Philippine Islands, where it grows in clearings in the rain forest. The epithet translates from the Latin as "trembling," an allusion to the thin leaflets.

This clumping species is similar to *A. engleri*. The trunks may attain 12 feet of height and a diameter of 3 or 4 inches. They are covered in their youngest parts with the typical netting of black fibers but are smooth, green, and prominently ringed in their older parts. The leaves are similar in size and general shape to those of *A. engleri*, but the leaflets are usually more widely spaced. They are also more limp and drooping (the longer ones even pendent) and usually a lighter green above and below. The inflorescence is a tall spike that usually rises above the mass of foliage but is sometimes pendent, and the small blossoms are greenish white to green. The fruits are 0.5 inch wide, rounded, and red, and are carried on the pendent spike.

The species is adaptable to partial shade or full sun but needs a humus-laden, moist, well-draining soil. It is not as cold tolerant as is *A. engleri* and is adaptable only to zones 10 and 11, although healthy specimens are found in protected sites in 9b. Suckers may be removed and transplanted.

This palm serves the same landscape uses as *A. engleri* but has an overall more delicate, fernlike appearance. The only mitigating factor for indoor use is the palm's need of abundant light. PLATES 72 & 73.

Arenga undulatifolia is found in rain forest clearings of the Philippine Islands, Borneo, and western Indonesia, where it usually grows on sloping ground in the foothills of mostly limestone mountains. The epithet translates from the Latin as "undulating" and "foliage," a reference to the wavy margins of the leaflets.

The species is found in nature as a solitary-trunked or densely clustering specimen. The trunks reach a height of 20 feet with total clump height of 30 feet and a width of 20 feet or sometimes slightly more. The stems are covered in a mat of dark fiber until nearly mature at which time the fiber falls off and leaves a smooth dark green beautifully ringed stem. The leaves are to 10 feet long with relatively widely spaced leaflets that are 18 to 24 inches long, linear-oblong, generally flat or not drooping, and lobed and wavy on the margins. Leaflet color is deep dark green above and silvery green to white beneath. The leaf petiole is short and thick. The branched inflorescences, growing from the leaf bases, are short and mostly hidden by the foliage. The flowers are greenish white, and the fruits are brown, rounded, and 1 inch in diameter.

The palm is of easy culture in tropical or nearly tropical regions with sun, water, and a reasonably fertile, well-draining soil. This species serves the same general landscape use as does *A. microcarpa* but is more vibrant and less somber (but no more beautiful) because of the shape of the leaflets and their silvery bottoms that lend an air of movement to a clump even in still air. It is not known to be grown indoors, but it should do well in atriums or large conservatories with sun, high humidity, and abundant moisture. PLATE 74.

Arenga westerhoutii occurs naturally over a wide area of the Asian tropics, from northeastern India, Thailand, Myanmar, peninsular Malaysia, Cambodia, Laos, and adjacent southern China, where it grows in clearings, often forming colonies, in the rain forest on usually limestone hills. The epithet is a Latinized form of a Dutch surname and commemorates a 19th-century plant explorer in Asia.

This tall, massive palm is one of three solitary-trunked species in the genus. The trunks are to 2 feet in diameter and covered in old leaf bases but usually lack adherent fibers; they attain heights of 60 feet, sometimes more. The leaf crown may be 20 feet tall and 40 feet wide. The 15- to 20-foot-long leaves are flat but exhibit a twist as they grow from the trunk; they are mostly ascending and held above the horizontal. The many 3-foot-long narrowly lanceolate leaflets are regularly spaced along the rachis. Leaf color is deep, bright green, sometimes almost bluish green, above and silvery olive-green to silvery brown beneath. As with *A. pinnata*, the fibers adherent to the younger leaf bases produce several long, stiff, and sharp spines. The palm is monoecious, and the leaves mostly hide the 2-foot-long inflorescences, which are branched and proceed from near the top of the trunk downwards, growing from the leaf base scars. The small flowers are deep red and produce 0.5-inch-wide, round, and black fruits.

This wonderful species can stand no frost and is mostly limited to zone 11 but is marginal in 10b. It is a water lover but can withstand mild drought. The palm is not particular about soil type as long as it is well draining, but it grows faster and more lush in a rich soil.

This is arguably the most beautiful *Arenga* species: it has the size and nobility of *A. pinnata* but is more graceful with its great flat and twisted, bicolored leaves. It is spectacular enough to stand isolated in space but looks better in groups of three or more individuals of varying heights. It also looks better when protected from strong winds. PLATE 75.

Arenga wightii is a moderate-sized, sparsely clumping species from the foothills of the Western Ghat Mountains of India, where it grows in monsoonal forests from elevations of 500 to 3000 feet. It is under threat of extinction because of agricultural expansion. The epithet honors Robert Wight, a 19th-century botanist.

The trunks grow to heights of 12 feet and are densely covered in hairy fibers. The leaves are to 15 feet long on 3-foot-long petioles. The silver-backed leaflets grow from the rachis in a flat plane and have obliquely truncated apices and shallowly lobed margins.

This palm is not particular about soil type as long as it is well drained. It needs a sunny site and is not hardy to cold, being adaptable to zones 10 and 11. Sap from the inflorescences is reportedly used to make an alcoholic beverage.

ASTEROGYNE is a genus of five small, monoecious, pinnate-leaved palms in Central America and northern South America. All but one species are solitary trunked, and all have undivided leaves that are deeply bifid apically. The inflorescences are unusual in that they are a spike, only branched apically. The three to six flowering branches carry small white or nearly white male and female blossoms, which produce red fruits. Only one species is common.

The genus name is derived from the Greek words for "star" and "female," an allusion to the shape of the female flowers. PLATES 76–79.

Asterogyne guianensis is a rare and endangered species endemic to southeastern French Guiana in lowland rain forest. The epithet is Latin for "of Guyana."

This beautiful species is usually taller than *A. martiana* and has a more apparent trunk, a more graceful leaf crown, and slightly more and slightly longer leaves.

Asterogyne martiana has the widest natural distribution of the five species and the only one that is not threatened. It ranges from southern Belize and eastern Guatemala, eastern and northern Honduras, eastern Nicaragua, Costa Rica, Panama, and western Colombia to northwestern Ecuador, where it is an undergrowth subject in low mountainous rain forest. The epithet honors the 19th-century German plant explorer, Carl F. P. von Martius.

The palm forms, with age, a stout, solitary trunk to 6 feet high and 2 inches in diameter. Mature palms have up to 18 leaves, each of which is 3 feet long, generally wedge shaped or spatulate, but with the apex deeply divided into two large, pointed segments. Leaf color is emerald green above and a lighter shade beneath with a darker colored heavy midrib. New leaves are often rosy or coppery colored. The blade is also grooved with prominent transverse veins corresponding to the hidden pinnate segments. The leaves are mostly ascending from the trunk and mostly not held beneath the horizontal. Large specimens in nature have a skirt of brown, dead leaves. The inflorescence is a spike with terminal branches of orange-brown flowers. The fruits are 0.5 inch long, dark purplish, and egg shaped.

This species is unusually sensitive to waterlogged soils, in which the roots often rot. It needs a humus-rich medium and partial shade and does not tolerate frost, being adaptable only to zones 10b and 11. It also needs protection from wind if its elegant undivided leaves are to remain unsplit.

The palm demands an intimate site where its unusual elegance can be appreciated up close. Until it is old, it is wonderful along a curving shady path or as a large groundcover in partial shade. It is one of the best candidates for homes, greenhouses, atriums, or conservatories if given high relative humidity and bright light. PLATES 76 & 77.

Asterogyne ramosa is a rare species endemic to low mountainous rain forest in northern Venezuela. The epithet is Latin for "branch" and alludes to the short flowering branches at the end of the spikelike peduncle of the inflorescence. This large species attains an overall height of 12 feet, with a full leaf crown.

Asterogyne spicata is restricted to Guatopo National Park in northern Venezuela, where it grows in low moun-

tainous rain forest. The epithet is Latin for "spiked," an allusion to the form of the inflorescence of this species as well as the others in the genus.

This palm is much taller than *A. martiana* but has similar vegetative characters. Its new leaves are usually reddish coppery, while its mature leaves are emerald green above and silvery beneath. PLATES 78 & 79.

Asterogyne yaracuyense is a rare and endangered species endemic to a small region of mountainous rain forest in northern Venezuela. The epithet is Latin for "of Yaracuy," a state and a river in the palm's habitat.

It is the only clustering species in the genus. This palm also is the largest, with stems to 20 feet high.

ASTROCARYUM is a genus of 18 very spiny, monoecious, pinnate-leaved palms in the West Indies, Mexico, Central America, and South America. A few are clumping species but most are solitary trunked and a few have subterranean stems. Some have plumelike leaves because the leaflets grow from the rachis at different angles; many others have flat leaves with leaflets in one plane. All the leaflets are silvery or white beneath. The juvenile plants of many species have entire leaves with unseparated leaflets, but the adults invariably have segmented leaves. The inflorescences grow from the leaf sheaths and are accompanied by a large, persistent, spiny paddle-shaped bract. The flowering branches bear male and female blossoms, are usually short, and are formed at the end of long peduncles which elongate and become pendent as the fruits mature. The latter are formed in clusters and are yellow to brown, mostly globular and mostly spiny.

These species are of exceptional beauty at every stage of growth, have stout and vicious spines on most of their anatomy, and are difficult to handle; they are not recommended for planting in high traffic areas. This spininess is one reason these beauties are still rare and difficult to find, but they are worth the effort. Many, mostly the smaller species, are undergrowth rain forest plants and do well in shade or partial shade, while others are more adapted to the sun.

The genus name translates from the Greek as "star" and "nut," a reference to patterns on the seed coat. PLATES 80–84.

Astrocaryum acaule is indigenous to northeastern Colombia, southern Venezuela, and northern and central Brazil, where it grows in lowland rain forest and cleared areas therein, as well as the wet margins of adjacent savannas. The epithet is Latin for "stemless."

The stem of this solitary-trunked species usually remains underground with the giant leaves growing directly from the soil surface; only occasionally does the trunk emerge above ground to a height of perhaps 3 feet. The leaf crown is dense, mainly because of the size of the leaves, which are 10 feet long, erect, and ascending, and arch only near their tips. The 1-foot-long, dark green, narrow leaflets are limp and grow from the light-colored, spiny rachis at several different angles to give an almost fully plumose effect; the overall aspect of the leaf crown is that of a gigantic green shuttlecock. The bright orange fruits are borne in 1-foot-wide rounded clusters.

The species is visually impressive because of the size of its leaves, and it resembles some *Attalea* species. It is rare in cultivation but deserves much wider planting. It needs a tropical climate, copious moisture at all times, and full sun, although it can grow in partial shade.

Astrocaryum aculeatissimum is indigenous to the southeastern coast of Brazil, where it grows in the rain forest and is threatened because of the felling of trees. The epithet is Latin for "spiniest."

This is a mostly clustering species, although a few plants form only one stem. The trunks grow to 30 feet high and 6 inches in diameter, and are covered in rings of black spines. The leaves are 10 feet long with the many linear, 1-foot-long leaflets regularly spaced in a single plane along the spiny rachis. The inflorescences are 2 feet long and pendent, and bear creamy white blossoms. The fruits are 1 inch wide, round, and brown but covered in black spines.

This species is slightly hardier to cold than most others in the genus but is still adaptable only to zones 10 and 11. It is a water lover that nevertheless needs a fast-draining, humus-laden soil. It grows in partial shade or full sun.

The palm is neither elegant nor magnificent enough to be planted in the middle of a lawn but looks good as the taller component of a wall of vegetation and as a small canopy-scape. It would be nice as a small focal point along a walk or street were it not for its complete spininess. No data are available, but this is probably not a good candidate for a house plant and must be judiciously placed even in atriums and conservatories.

Astrocaryum aculeatum is found in open spots in low mountainous rain forest of Trinidad and from Venezuela and Colombia, southwards into Brazil and northern Bolivia. The common name is a direct translation from the Greek genus name, star-nut palm, which refers to markings on the seed coat. The epithet is Latin for "spiny."

This solitary-trunked species grows to 50 feet tall and 1 foot in diameter. The stem is mostly free of old leaf bases and is beautifully ringed with spines. The leaves are 12 to 18 feet long on 6-foot-long spiny petioles. Numerous leaflets grow from the spiny rachis in several planes and in small clusters, creating a plumose leaf. Each leaflet is 3 to 4 feet long, deep green, limp, and pendent. The infrores-

cences are 6 feet long and roughly erect, growing from among the leaves; blossoms are white. The yellow to orange fruits are oval, 2 inches long, and reportedly edible.

The tree grows moderately fast in a humus-laden, moist but free-draining soil. It cannot tolerate frost but does nicely in partial shade to full sun. Moisture and humidity are as important as a nearly tropical climate, and it needs sun to thrive.

This large feather-leaved palm can be sited as a specimen isolated with surrounding space, but it looks its best in groups of three or more individuals of varying heights, or as a canopy-scape. From a distance, mature specimens look like a taller and more elegant *Acrocomia aculeata*. Indoors this palm is only suitable for large conservatories or atriums.

Astrocaryum alatum is indigenous to the rain forest of southern Nicaragua, the Caribbean coast of Costa Rica, and Panama. The epithet is Latin for "winged."

This solitary-trunked palm grows to 20 feet tall and is easily confused with *A. mexicanum*; *A. alatum* usually has slightly larger leaves and is, if possible, even more beautiful. It has the same cultural requirements as *A. mexicanum*. PLATES 80 & 81.

Astrocaryum chambira is indigenous to southeastern Colombia, northeastern Ecuador, northern Peru, and northwestern Brazil, where it grows in lowland rain forest and clearings therein. The epithet is the aboriginal name in Brazil.

The stems of this solitary-trunked species grow to 100 feet high in habitat but are usually 40 feet tall in cultivation. The species is similar in general appearance to *A. aculeatum* but is taller and generally more robust.

It is rare in cultivation outside its habitat, where it is grown for the leaves from which a durable fiber is extracted. Its magnificence should certainly be more widely experienced and planted.

Astrocaryum jauari is indigenous to a large area of the Amazon region in French Guiana, Surinam, southern Guyana, southern Venezuela, northeastern Peru, and northern Brazil, where it grows in lowland rain forest, especially along rivers and streams. The epithet is the aboriginal name in Brazil. In Colombia, it is called *chambirilla*, meaning "little chambira," for its visual affinities to the giant *A. chambiri*.

The trunks of this clustering species reach heights of 40 feet with diameters of 1 foot. They are smooth and white in the older parts but greenish brown with spiny dark brown rings of leaf base scars in the younger parts. The 15-foot-long leaves are stiffly erect and ascending and form a leaf crown resembling a dark green shuttlecock. The 3-foot-long leaflets are arranged in clusters and grow at different angles from the spiny rachis to give an almost completely plumose aspect to the leaf. The round, 1-inch-wide fruits are yellowish orange.

This is one of many Amazonian tree species whose fruits and seeds are dispersed by fish when the rivers along which the trees grow flood and the fish "invade" the land areas. It is a beautiful palm that deserves to be more widely cultivated. It needs a tropical climate, full sun, and uninterrupted and copious moisture.

Astrocaryum mexicanum is a solitary-trunked species that occurs naturally along the tropical Gulf coast of Mexico, southern Belize, northern Guatemala, northern El Salvador, the northern coast of Honduras, and northernmost Nicaragua, where it grows mostly in clearings in low mountains rain forest. The epithet is Latin for "of Mexico," a reference to the palm's primary habitat.

The spiny trunk grows to 20 feet tall with a diameter of 3 inches. It is generally free of leaf bases and indistinctly ringed. The leaf crown is 15 feet tall and wide. Juvenile leaves appear simple but are pinnate, the leaflets essentially fused together unless separated by wind. They are 8 feet long on 2-foot-long, very spiny petioles. The leaflets of older leaves are separated and unequal in width. Their color is yellow-green to a deep grassy green, and they grow from the spiny rachis in one plane, giving a flat appearance to the leaf. The inflorescence is erect but mostly hidden among the leaves. It emerges from a rounded, dark brown, spiny large spathe. The blossoms are whitish and reportedly edible. The 2-inch-long, oblong brown fruits are covered with black spines.

The palm demands a fertile, fast-draining but constantly moist soil. It does not tolerate frost but thrives in gloom when young and in partial shade or full sun when older. It grows moderately fast under ideal conditions.

This exceptional small palm is among the most beautiful in the family, especially when young. It needs a protected, partially shaded spot to keep its gorgeous young leaves from splitting and it is unsurpassed as a patio or close-up subject. Planted in groups of three or more individuals of varying heights there is hardly a more beautiful landscape subject. The species is easy as a large houseplant or greenhouse subject but needs constant moisture and humidity.

Every part of this palm except the roots are used by indigenous peoples in the palm's habitat: the flowers and seeds for food, the leaves for thatch, and the trunks for construction. PLATES 82 & 83.

Astrocaryum murumuru is indigenous to a vast area of Amazonia in South America, where it grows along rivers and in swamps. The epithet is an aboriginal name.

This is mostly a solitary-trunked species, but clumping individuals are occasionally found, and Henderson et al.

(1995) report that some individuals have only subterranean trunks; when arborescent, the trunks can grow to 40 feet. The most distinctive characteristic of this palm is its magnificently long leaves, to 20 feet, with their evenly spaced, long, and limp leaflets that are bright to deep green above but silvery or even pinkish (because of the red hairs in one variety) beneath. They are ascending and erect and form a crown shaped like a shaving brush.

The palm is tropical in its temperature requirements, is a true water lover, and needs a fertile soil. It requires partial shade when young but can endure the full tropical sun when older.

It is truly magnificent because of the immense leaves, looks especially good in colonies, and lends its magnificence to any pond or stream planting.

Astrocaryum standleyanum is a tall, solitary-trunked species indigenous to southeastern Costa Rica, the Caribbean coast of Panama, western Colombia, and northwestern Ecuador, where it grows in lowland rain forest. The epithet honors Paul C. Standley, an early 20th-century taxonomist, collector, author, and curator of the U.S. Herbarium.

The trunks can reach 40 feet high with a canopy of 10-foot-long arching, plumose leaves. This magnificent palm does not tolerate cold and needs a wet, if not soggy, rich soil with partial shade to full sun. PLATE 84.

Astrocaryum vulgare occurs naturally in northeastern Brazil, French Guiana, and Surinam, where it grows in rain forest and wet savannas. The epithet is Latin for "common" and refers to the palm's distribution, not its appearance.

This is a large, sparsely clustering species whose stems attain heights of 25 feet and bear long black spines arranged in beautiful dark rings. The leaves are 10 to 12 feet long and among the most handsome in the genus, with their widely spaced, beautifully arching linear, dark green leaflets growing in several planes from the rachis; the visual effect is plumose but not densely so.

The varying heights of the trunks in any clump give a picturesque aspect. The palm is not tolerant of cold and is adaptable only to zones 10b and 11. It is also a water lover and needs sun.

ATTALEA is a genus of 30 small to large, pinnate-leaved, monoecious palms in tropical America, mostly South America. They inhabit both wet and semiarid climates and vary from acaulescent or subterranean-trunked species to colossally tall and mammoth trunked forms.

The trunks of most species are covered in their younger parts with old leaf bases and, when old, are remarkably straight and columnar but not so relatively thick compared to their heights. All trunked species are solitary stemmed and have remarkably similar, long leaves with long, narrow leaflets, the ones near the bottom of the blade limp and drooping. The petioles and the rachises are robust, stout, and usually light brown, gray, or yellowish, and the unfurled spearlike new leaves are large and imposing. The leaflets have a line of brown tomentum on one of their lower margins. The leaves of all the large, trunk-forming species are erect but usually arching from the midpoint of the rachis, and they rarely descend beneath the horizontal, which characteristic gives a mammoth shuttlecock appearance to the mature palms. The inflorescences are large and accompanied by even larger grooved, woody bracts. The flowers in a given inflorescence are usually either all male or mostly female with a few male blossoms.

The differentiation of the species is based solely on the male flowers and their component parts, especially the number and shape of the stamens. In the past these flower differences were thought significant enough to warrant placing some of these palms into five genera in addition to this one: *Markleya*, *Maximiliana*, *Orbignya*, *Parascheelea*, and *Scheelea*.

All the species are slow growing, especially when younger, and are adaptable to many soils as long as they are fast draining. They need as much sun as they can get for faster growth and better appearance. None of them are hardy to cold or adaptable outside of zones 10 and 11. The growing point of the large, trunk-forming species remains below ground for several years and, in this state, the giant leaves may be damaged or even killed by cold in zone 9 but the palm usually grows back with the return of sustained warmth. It is not unusual to see gigantic specimens in zone 9b (or even 9a) with 20- to 30-foot-tall leaves springing straight from the soil. The same leaf damage and survival phenomenon mostly applies to the subterranean-trunked species as well, with the proviso that, because of their less robust forms, the survival rate from freezes may not be as high.

None of these species are common in cultivation in the United States, although they are among the largest, most magnificent palms in the family. The incredible size of the larger species makes their use in small gardens questionable. These magnificent palms create awe when planted along an avenue, and they dominate the landscape when planted as isolated specimens, but they are nearly unparalleled as a canopy-scape.

The trunk-forming species have several human uses in their habitats: the leaves for thatch, the trunks for construction, and the fruits and seeds for fodder and oil.

The genus name honors an ancient Greek ruler named Attalus. PLATES 85–95.

Attalea allenii occurs naturally in the lowland rain forest of the Caribbean coast of Panama and the Pacific coast of Colombia. The epithet honors Paul H. Allen, 20th-century botanist and former president of the International Palm Society.

This interesting species has subterranean trunks and 15-foot-long plumose leaves with thin, narrow leaflets, except for a few near the end of the leaf that are fused at their apices. The endosperm of the seeds is almost liquid and is eaten or drunk in the same manner as the coconut palm.

Attalea amygdalina is endemic to valleys in the Andes Mountains of Colombia, where it grows in the hilly rain forest. It is endangered because of expanding agriculture. The epithet is Latin for "little almond" and refers to the shape of the edible seeds.

The species never forms an aboveground trunk, but the massive ascending and erect leaves reach lengths of 20 feet or more, only their tips arching. The large rachis holds regularly spaced 2- to 3-foot-long, deep green, linear-elliptic, limp leaflets growing in a single flat plane. PLATE 85.

Attalea butyracea is widespread and occurs naturally from southeastern Mexico, through Central America, into Venezuela, Colombia, eastern Ecuador, eastern Peru, western central Brazil, and northwestern Bolivia. The epithet is Greek for "like butter" and refers to the seed's endosperm.

This species forms trunks to 60 feet high, the overall height of the palm nearing 100 feet. In many parts of its range, it is the most visually dominant plant in the landscape, a towering canopy-scape above the jungle or savanna. The rachis of the giant leaves is twisted to the vertical from its middle to its apex, giving an irresistible appeal of frozen movement. PLATES 86 & 87.

Attalea cohune is indigenous to the west coast of Mexico from the tropic of Cancer southwards and eastwards along the western coast of Guatemala and the southern (Pacific) coast of El Salvador; it is also found in the states of Chiapas and Quintana Roo in Mexico, Belize, northern Guatemala, northern Honduras, and northern Nicaragua. The common name is cohune palm. The epithet is the aboriginal name for the palm.

This species differs little in its vegetative appearance from *A. butyracea* and has the marvelous midpoint twist to the vertical of its great leaves. It is now the most available and widely planted *Attalea* species in the United States. PLATES 88–90.

Attalea colenda occurs naturally in southwestern Colombia and western Ecuador, where it is in danger of extinction because of expanding agriculture; the irony is that most of the clearing has been done to plant the African oil palm, *Elaeis guineensis*, whose quality and quantity of natural oil is slightly superior to that of this indigenous species. The epithet is Latin for "cultivated," an allusion to the importance of the oil extracted from the fruit.

This is one of the largest species in the genus with trunks reaching heights of 100 feet, the total height of the palm to 120 feet. It is also among the most beautiful in the genus, the stout and nearly white columnar trunks supporting an immense and full crown of large, deep emerald green leaves.

Attalea crassispatha is endemic to southwestern Haiti, where it grows on the low limestone hills of dry savannas. It is critically endangered with only a couple dozen trees existing in 1990. This palm is also interesting in a geographical sense as it is the only *Attalea* species in the Antilles. The epithet is from two Greek words meaning "thick" and "spathe."

The trunk of this tall species attains 60 feet high but 1 foot wide. The crown is, unlike almost all other species in the genus, nearly round, and the 10- to 12-foot-long leaves have regularly spaced leaflets growing in a single flat plane. The rachis exhibits the characteristic twist in its apical half, giving this palm a look similar to that of a straight-trunked, massive coconut. PLATE 91.

Attalea cuatrecasana is indigenous to western coastal Colombia, where it grows in lowland rain forest. The epithet honors José Cuatrecasa, botanist and plant explorer of the region.

This species has a subterranean trunk and flat leaves that attain maximum heights of 15 to 20 feet. The brown, rounded fruits are unusually large.

Attalea funifera is endemic to eastern coastal Brazil. The epithet is Latin for "rope-bearing" and refers to the use of the fibers on the leaf bases for making ropes.

The distinctive aspect of this species is its extremely erect giant leaves with long, limp leaflets. The leaves appear to be almost plumose, are borne on long petioles, and are few in number.

Attalea humilis is another species endemic to the eastern coast of Brazil. The epithet is Latin for "humble" or "low."

This palm has a subterranean trunk that seldom grows above ground and, when it does, never attains more than 3 feet of height. The flat leaves are usually 10 and 15 feet long and numerous. PLATE 92.

Attalea insignis is indigenous to southern Colombia, northeastern Ecuador, northern Peru, and northwestern Brazil, where it is an undergrowth subject in the Amazon rain forest. The epithet is Latin for "remarkable."

The trunk is subterranean, but the great leaves reach lengths of nearly 30 feet. Many linear leaflets grow in clusters on each leaf and at different angles from the massive rachis to create a slightly plumose leaf; this characteristic is much more obvious in juvenile plants than it is in adults.

Attalea maripa is native to a large area of northern South America, including southern Venezuela; eastern Colombia, Ecuador, and Peru; northern Bolivia; northeastern Brazil, including Amazonas; and the Guianas. The epithet is one of the aboriginal names in Ecuador.

This palm grows to 80 feet in overall height and has wonderfully large leaves. The long pendent leaflets grow from the rachis at different angles.

Attalea phalerata occurs naturally in eastern Peru, northern Bolivia, and central to northeastern Brazil. The epithet is Latinized Greek for "adorned."

The trunk is among the thickest in the genus, but its overall height is 30 feet. The leaves are typical, but the leaflets may grow from the rachis in either one plane or in different planes, and the leaf itself has the typical midpoint twist to the vertical. PLATE 93.

Attalea speciosa has a disjunct natural distribution in southern Guyana and Suriname, in central and eastern Brazil, and in northeastern Bolivia, where it grows in savannas, clearings in the rain forest, and along rivers and streams at low elevations. The epithet is Latin for "beautiful."

This palm grows to 60 feet overall, with a straight, columnar trunk which is mostly free of leaf bases. The leaves are 15 feet long and show the characteristic midpoint twist to the vertical in their apical half.

This is among the most graceful species in the genus. PLATE 94.

BACTRIS is a large genus of more than 60 mostly spiny, pinnate-leaved, monoecious palms in tropical America. They inhabit every terrestrial biome of this region except the true desert, and they range from subterranean or short-trunked palms to gigantic and clustering forms, mostly with great spininess but sometimes without. The leaflets of most species grow from different angles of the rachis to give a plumose look to the leaf. The inflorescences are either thick spikes or clusters of spikelike and ropelike branches that bear yellow or white flowers of both sexes.

None of the species are tolerant of freezing temperature and, while most are not fussy about soil type, all do much better with a decent soil and adequate moisture.

The genus name is from the Greek and translates as "cane" or "staff," an allusion to a use of the trunks of some of the smaller species (after removal of the spines). PLATES 96–106.

Bactris brongniartii is indigenous to a vast area of the Amazon region in northern and northwestern Brazil, the

Guianas, the southern half of Venezuela, eastern Colombia, eastern Ecuador, eastern Peru, and northern Bolivia, always in low, wet areas and along streams and rivers. The epithet honors Adolphe T. Brongniart, a 19th-century palm botanist from France.

In habitat this densely clustering species forms walls of foliage in open spaces. The stems grow to 25 feet high but are usually shorter and are 2 inches in diameter. They are tan with darker rings of spines. The leaves are 5 feet long with many linear lanceolate, light green leaflets growing from the spine-covered rachis to create a plumose leaf.

The palm is nearly aquatic and makes an impression along the edge of a pond or lake and as part of a wall of other vegetation. It can grow in partial shade but only reaches its full potential in full sun. PLATES 96 & 97.

Bactris coloradonis is indigenous to the Caribbean coastal areas of Costa Rica and Panama and to the Pacific coastal areas of Colombia and extreme northern Ecuador, always in lowland tropical rain forest. The epithet is Latin for "of Colorado," a region of Panama.

This clustering or solitary-trunked species has stems to 30 feet but usually much less; only the solitary-trunked individuals have the tall trunks. The leaves are 5 feet long with linear-lanceolate, deep green leaflets growing at several angles from a rachis covered with tightly woven short, white hairs and bearing 3-inch-long black spines; the visual effect is of basically nonplumose but beautiful leaves.

This palm needs good soil and constant moisture but luxuriates in partial shade or full sun. It is gorgeous as a specimen, and the clustering individuals make some of the most magnificent hedge material and walls of vegetation.

Bactris concinna is indigenous to a large area of the western Amazon region in southeastern Colombia, eastern Ecuador, northern and eastern Peru, northern Bolivia, and western Brazil, where it grows in lowland rain forest. The epithet is Latin for "elegant" or "orderly."

The palm is a clustering species, with stems to a maximum height of 25 feet but usually shorter. The trunks are covered in all but their oldest parts with a dense mat of grayish leaf base fibers and rings of 0.5-inch-long black spines. The leaves are 4 to 5 feet long with regularly spaced, dark green linear leaflets growing in a flat plane from the spiny rachis. The overall appearance of the leaves is akin to those of many of the larger *Chamaedorea* species. The 1-inch-long black fruits are edible.

The palm grows in sun or shade and in almost any moist soil. PLATE 98.

Bactris gasipaes is unknown in the wild, but its origin is probably Central America in open areas of the rain forest. It is now cultivated throughout low wet regions of tropical America. The common name is peach palm because of the edible fruit. The epithet is derived from an aboriginal name for the palm.

This large species is found as clustering and solitary-trunked specimens. The trunks can reach heights of 50 feet or sometimes more. They are beautifully ringed, unusually straight, and relatively slender, never more than 1 foot in diameter, and are invariably spiny. The rounded leaf crowns are 20 feet tall and wide. Leaves are 10 feet or more in length and are held on 1-foot-long, very spiny petioles. The numerous 2- to 3-foot-long leaflets are deep green and mostly limp and drooping. They grow in small clusters from the spiny rachis at different angles to give a rounded, plumose aspect to the leaf; the leaflets of the terminal pair are often larger than the ones beneath them. The many branched inflorescences emerge from among the leaves and from two spathes, one of which is large, spiny, and persistent. The blossoms are cream colored. The 2-inch-long egg-shaped fruits are yellow, orange, or bright red when mature and are edible.

The palm needs warmth, water, and a rich, free-draining soil. It grows fastest in full sun and cannot withstand any but the lightest frost, making it adaptable only to zones 10 and 11, with protected specimens found in 9b. The palm resprouts from the roots in central Florida if frozen to the ground and grows quickly thereafter (David Witt, pers. comm.). It can be propagated by carefully removing the suckers.

This lovely palm looks good as a single specimen, but solitary-trunked forms are always better planted in groups of three or more individuals of varying heights. The clumping specimens are sumptuous with their varying tiers of plumose leaves. The species needs much space, warmth, and sun to do well, and its spininess mitigates against its use as a houseplant.

Few palms are as important to the local peoples: the fruits are still a staple in the diet of many Central and South American indigenous people and the growing point is widely harvested as a vegetable. Because of its importance as a crop, this species has many local cultivars throughout tropical America, including spineless forms and forms with seedless fruits. Some authorities believe the species is a cultivar of the South American *B. macana*. PLATES 99–101.

Bactris glandulosa is indigenous to eastern Costa Rica, Panama, and adjacent northwestern Colombia, where it grows in low mountainous rain forest. The epithet is Latin for "glandular."

This solitary-trunked and clustering species attains an overall height of 20 feet. The 5-foot-long spiny leaves have plumose, linear, dark green leaflets covered in a yellowish or golden feltlike pubescence that gives a shimmering quality to the leaf and has led one grower to give the palm the moniker of gold palm.

A naturally occuring variety, **B. glandulosa var. baileyana**, is less pubescent than the type. The species is undeniably elegant and the more pubescent variety is usually preferred ornamentally.

Bactris grayumi is indigenous to the Caribbean coastal areas of southern Honduras and eastern Costa Rica, where it grows in lowland tropical rain forest. The epithet honors botanist Michael H. Grayum, author of a flora of Costa Rica.

The leaves are similar to those of *B. militaris,* but this species is solitary trunked and the spines on the leaves are shorter. This palm wants the same culture as *B. militaris* and is as beautiful.

Bactris guineensis is a small clustering species from southwestern Nicaragua, the Pacific coastal areas of Costa Rica and Panama into northern Colombia and Venezuela, where it grows in deciduous thorn forests and clearings of the rain forest. The only common name, which is now rarely used, is Tobago cane. The epithet translates from the Latin as "of Guinea," a misspelling of *Guiana* and a heretofore general term for the northern Amazonian region of South America.

The clumps are usually dense with spiny stems, and the trunks are 1 inch in diameter but 10 feet tall. The 3-foot-long leaves have regularly spaced, dark green, linear leaflets that are split at their apices; they grow from the spiny rachis at different angles, creating a slightly plumose leaf.

The palm is adaptable to various soils and exposures but does not tolerate frost. This species reportedly gave the genus its scientific name because its stems, after being stripped of spines, were imported in the 18th century from Trinidad and Tobago to Europe for use as walking staffs.

Bactris hondurensis is a clumping and solitary-trunked species in northeastern Honduras, eastern Nicaragua, the Caribbean coasts of Costa Rica and Panama, and into western Colombia. It is found in the undergrowth of rain forest in low mountainous areas. The epithet is Latin for "of Honduras."

The trunks grow to 6 or 8 feet high and, when clustering, are never dense. The leaves are undivided, 2 feet long, deeply bifid apically, and light green, with grooves corresponding to the cryptic pinnate segments; occasionally the segments are free from each other, especially near the base of the leaf.

The palm must be protected from strong sun and given plenty of moisture in a friable, free-draining, and humus-laden soil. It does not tolerate frost but does well in Mediterranean climates if given enough irrigation.

Bactris longiseta is endemic to the Caribbean coast of Costa Rica, where it grows in lowland tropical rain forest. The epithet is Latin for "long bristle."

This solitary-trunked and clustering species has an overall height of 12 to 15 feet. The 5-foot-long leaves are not plumose, and the deep green leaflets are regularly spaced and linear-lanceolate, with tiny bristles along their margins.

It is beautiful and looks as much like a spiny *Chamaedorea* species as it does most other *Bactris* species. It luxuriates in shade.

Bactris major has a wide distribution, from southern Mexico, through Central America, into northern and eastern Venezuela, the Guianas, central Brazil, and northeastern Bolivia, where it grows in clearings in rain forest and in open savanna regions. The epithet is Latin for "larger." The four varieties are difficult to distinguish from one another; the differences are mostly in the inflorescence morphology and do not seem important to the gardener (Henderson et al. 1995).

The trunks of this large clumping species are covered in black spines until older, when they are shed to reveal dark green smooth stems with prominent white rings. The trunks grow to 30 feet high with a diameter of 2 inches. Total height of the clumps is 40 feet with a width to 30 feet. The leaves are usually 8 feet long on short, spiny petioles, with 36 light green narrowly oblong leaflets growing in a single plane from the intensely spiny rachis. Each leaflet sports a prominent, lighter-colored midrib and may be tapering or blunt at its end; the two terminal leaflets are usually broader but shorter than the others. The much-branched inflorescences emerge from spiny spathes and contain small greenish yellow blossoms. The 2-inch-long purple to black fruits are reportedly edible.

This extremely spiny palm is adaptable to many well-drained soils. It loves sun but grows in partial shade and needs average but regular moisture. It does not tolerate frost and is adaptable to zones 10 and 11, although marginal in 10a.

It is among the finest palms for a large hedge or screen and is exquisite as free-standing clumps or as a strong, large accent in masses of other tropical vegetation. The species is not known to be grown indoors, although given enough light and room it should succeed. PLATES 102 & 103.

Bactris mexicana is a small clumping species from southern Mexico, southern Belize, and northern Guatemala to northern Honduras and northeastern Nicaragua, where it occurs in the undergrowth of rain forest. The epithet is Latin for "of Mexico."

This elegant but spiny palm grows to a maximum height of 10 feet, and the clumps are not dense. The leaves are 3 to 4 feet long with 1-foot-long dark green leaflets growing at slightly different angles from the spiny rachis to form a plumose leaf.

The species is not adapted to cold, full sun, or drought conditions. It is beautiful in a shady and woodsy site and would be exquisite along a path were it not for its spininess.

Bactris militaris is a clustering palm indigenous to northeastern Costa Rica and the Osá Peninsula on the west coast of that Central American country, where it grows in low and swampy regions, mainly in the undergrowth. The epithet is Latin for "armed," a reference to the spiny leaves.

The trunks grow to 10 feet high and 2 inches in diameter in sparse clumps to 15 feet wide. The unsegmented leaves are remarkable: to 10 feet long, dark green, narrow, thick, and grooved (to correspond with the cryptic pinnae); they grow stiffly erect from the trunk and have a distinct, cinnamon-hued midrib, along which are found long, stiff, black widely spaced spines.

This beauty is undeservedly rare in cultivation. It needs warmth, constant moisture, and protection from the hot midday sun and from desiccating, shredding winds. PLATE 104.

Bactris plumeriana is indigenous to Cuba, Jamaica, and Hispaniola, where it grows along the margins of hilly, evergreen forests and in cleared areas. There is reason to believe this taxon should compromise three separate species, namely, *B. cubensis* from Cuba, *B. jamaicana* from Jamaica, and *B. plumeriana* from Hispaniola. The epithet is a Latinized form of the surname "Plumier" and honors a 17th-century French botanist.

It is a clustering species whose mature, slender 6-inch-thick trunks reach 25 feet high. The dark stems are made darker by the whorls of long, black spines covering all but the oldest parts. The leaves are 8 feet long and covered with black spines, with leaflets growing from the spiny rachis at different angles to create a fully plumose leaf.

The palm can form large, dense clumps and is deadly looking but also extremely beautiful. It is hard to imagine a more effective hedge subject, and the crowns are wonderful canopy-scapes. PLATES 105 & 106.

Bactris riparia is indigenous to low elevations of the western Amazon region of southern Colombia, eastern Ecuador, eastern and northern Peru, and western Brazil, where it grows in swamps and on the edges of rivers, streams, and lakes, usually in several feet of water for part of the year. The epithet is Latin for "riverine," an allusion to the palm's habitat preference.

The spiny stems of this clustering species can reach a height of 25 feet with a diameter of 2 to 3 inches. The leaf crown is sparse, but the leaves are beautiful, 5 to 6 feet long, arching, and recurved. Widely spaced groups of 2-foot-long leaflets grow from the rachis at several angles to create a plumose leaf.

Bactris setosa is indigenous to the southern Atlantic coast of Brazil, where it grows in lowland tropical rain forest or clearings therein. The epithet is Latin for "bristly."

The stems of this large, clumping species are almost 20 feet high, 1 inch or so in diameter, and tan with darker rings of black spines. The 6- to 8-foot-long light green leaves have thin, linear leaflets that are plumosely arranged along the sparsely spined rachis, giving the leaf an appearance similar to that of *B. gasipaes*.

The species will, like *B. gasipaes*, resprout from the root if frozen to the ground in central Florida (David Witt, pers. comm.).

BALAKA is a genus of seven small, pinnate-leaved, solitary-trunked, monoecious palms in the Fiji and Samoa island groups. All species have thin trunks and slender, delicate crownshafts, and all are found in the undergrowth of the rain forest.

The leaflets invariably grow from the rachis at an angle to give a V shape to the leaves. The inflorescences grow from beneath the crownshafts and are open, twice-branched panicle-like affairs bearing both male and female blossoms. The fruits are small, ovoid, and brown or red.

All species are tender to cold and adaptable only to zones 10b and 11. They need partial shade when young, protection from strong winds, and a rich, moist but very fast-draining soil. These palms are good candidates for growing in containers or indoors with ample moisture.

The genus is visually similar to and related to *Ptychosperma* and *Drymophloeus*; it is also closely allied to *Veitchia* but not in its general appearance. Few palm groups are more fragile looking; their delicacy is almost ethereal. The genus name is a Latinized form of the aboriginal name.

Balaka longirostris grows to an overall height of 25 feet with an exceedingly thin trunk usually less than 2 inches in diameter. The crownshaft is almost the same diameter as the trunk and is olive to dusky green. The leaf crown is sparse with three to six ascending, erect, and partially arching 5-foot-long leaves. The widely spaced light green leaflets are linear-ovate with oblique, jagged apices. The epithet is Latin for "long beaked," an allusion to the shape of the fruits.

Balaka macrocarpa is similar to but smaller than *B. microcarpa*. The epithet is Greek for "large" and "fruit," alluding to the size of the fruit, which is the largest in the genus.

Balaka microcarpa can grow to 30 feet or more, and the exceptionally thin (3 inches in diameter) and straight trunk gives the tree an ethereal aspect. The crownshaft is deep green and slightly bulging at its base. The leaf crown is sparse and has erect, ascending, slightly arching leaves. The leaflets are widely spaced, grow from the rachis at an angle that creates a V-shaped leaf, and are linear and slightly S shaped with an obliquely cut apex. The epithet is from two Greek words meaning "small" and "fruit."

Balaka seemannii grows to an overall height of 20 feet with a thin and delicate, prominently ringed trunk of 1 or 2 inches diameter. The crownshaft is slender and dark green. The leaf crown usually consists of no more than a half dozen 6-foot-long, glossy dark green leaves, whose leaflets are wedge shaped with deeply and irregularly incised apices; the terminal leaflets are united into two broad but similarly shaped parts. The epithet honors Berthold C. Seemann, a 19th-century German botanist and plant explorer.

BARCELLA is a monotypic genus of pinnate-leaved, monoecious palm in the Amazonas region of Brazil, growing along the banks of the Rio Negro in very sandy scrublands. The origin of the genus name is unknown but may be a Latinized form of a village (Barcelos) near where the palm was discovered (Henderson et al. 1995). The epithet is Latin for "odorous," an allusion to the fragrant male flowers.

Barcella odora is a trunkless palm with 6-foot-long, beautifully arching pinnate leaves growing directly from the ground. The 2-foot-long leaflets are limp and pendent, medium to dark green, linear-lanceolate, with a long tapering apex and are evenly but widely spaced along the arching rachis. The inflorescences grow from the leaf crown, are once branched and erect, and bear all male blossoms or both male and female, the two forms not segregated onto separate plants. The 1-inch-long, ovoid fruits are orange when mature.

This spectacularly beautiful small palm is probably not in cultivation but should be; it has some similarities to a giant tropical cycad or even the kentia palm, *Howea forsteriana*, one with extra wide leaflets. The species would doubtless require tropical conditions and copious moisture but would probably thrive in partial shade as well as full sun. It probably does not require a particularly rich medium.

BASSELINIA is a genus of 11 monoecious, dissimilar species endemic to the islands of New Caledonia. Some are rare with ranges restricted to one mountain or valley. All sport crownshafts and have pinnate leaves, but the segments of some species are undivided and terminally bifid; a few species exhibit both conditions.

In nature the species range from a height of 12 to 70 feet and may be solitary trunked or clustering. Harold E. Moore, Jr., and Natalie Uhl divided the genus into two sections, one for the larger, solitary-trunked species with green crownshafts, the other for the smaller palms with colored crownshafts. The inflorescences grow from beneath the crownshafts and are branched once or twice, bearing both male and female flowers.

Almost all the species are exceptionally beautiful, and some bear colorful, intricately marked crownshafts. None are common in cultivation, and some are virtually unknown.

The genus name honors Olivier Basselin, a 15th-century French poet. PLATES 107–114.

Basselinia deplanchei occurs in the undergrowth and in full sun in low, wet mountainous regions of central and southern New Caledonia. The epithet is a Latinized form of the French surname "Deplanche" and honors a botanist.

This is among the most variable species in the genus and similar in general appearance to *B. gracilis*. It is mostly a clustering species, but some individuals have solitary trunks. It can grow to 20 feet or more in habitat with a slender, dark-colored, and strongly ringed trunk, atop which a small crown of mostly stiffly ascending pinnate leaves grows. Some individuals have undivided and apically bifid leaves. Leaf color is light green with prominent midveins in the undivided leaf. The segmented leaves have lanceolate leaflets, with prominent and lighter-colored multiple midribs. Each leaf is 3 feet long on a 6-inch-long petiole. The crownshaft is usually swollen near its middle and red, orange, or purple with darker striations. The inflorescences grow from beneath the crownshaft and are stiffly spreading and usually the same color as the shaft. They bear tiny flowers. The fruits are small, round, and black when mature.

This species needs uninterrupted and copious water in a free-draining soil. It flourishes in partial shade or full sun except in hot climates where it should be protected from the hottest midday sun. It has a modicum of cold tolerance and should do fine in frostless or nearly frostless Mediterranean climes if given enough moisture. PLATES 107–109.

Basselinia favieri is endemic to rain forest on Mt. Panié in northeastern New Caledonia, at elevations from 1000 to 1700 feet. The epithet honors Joseph Favier, who assisted in collecting the type.

This is a solitary-trunked species whose mature stem attains a height of 30 feet or more. It is dark tan, with darker rings of leaf base scars, and is topped by a 3-foot-long, light green to light greenish gray crownshaft that is slightly swollen at its base. The leaves are to 9 feet long, ascending but gracefully arching, and bear many linear-acuminate emerald green, 4- to 5-foot-long leaflets. In newer leaves, the leaflets grow from the rachis at an angle that gives a slight V shape to the leaf. Older leaflets are more limp and allow the leaf to assume an almost flat cross-section. The large, spidery, and many-branched rose-colored inflorescences grow from beneath the crownshaft. The small fruits are round and black when mature.

The species needs constant moisture in a fast-draining, humus-laden soil. It is not hardy to cold but reportedly withstands light frosts undamaged and is adaptable to zones 10 and 11. It needs partial shade when young and always in hot climates.

It is beautiful enough to serve well as anything but an isolated specimen. In groups of three or more individuals of varying heights, it is magnificent, and its choice form makes it a perfect patio subject. PLATE 110.

Basselinia gracilis occurs naturally on the island of New Caledonia, where it grows in rain forest at elevations from sea level to 5280 feet. The epithet is Latin for "graceful."

Most individuals are clustering. The trunk varies from 5 to 20 feet tall but is always smooth, free of leaf bases and fibers, and distinctly ringed. The color ranges from gray or green to brown and black, and the diameter ranges from 1 to 4 inches. The crownshafts are 4 to 18 inches tall, and they range from green to pink, orange, red, purple, brown, or black. The leaves may be entire and deeply bifid at the apex, with strong and lighter-colored veins, or completely pinnately segmented; the latter condition is associated with leaflets that may be few, fat, oblong, and S shaped with long tips or may be many, linear, and slightly S shaped. The segmented leaves are always spreading but never arching, and the leaf crown may be elongated. Inflorescences grow from beneath the crownshaft and are red to brown or purple, with stringy branches. The fruits are round, 0.5 inch in diameter, and deep red to black when mature.

Some of the palm's vegetative characters are so inconstant that it is nearly impossible for the nonbotanist to realize that one species is being discussed. Interestingly, the leaf forms and trunk heights are related to elevation in the palm's habitat: those forms with segmented leaves and the tallest trunks are found at the lowest elevations, with a continuum of gradual diminution of leaf segmentation and trunk height at higher elevations.

The most important cultural requirement is regular and copious water. The species does not tolerate full sun in hot climates and usually thrives in partial shade in all but cool and nearly frostless Mediterranean climes, where it reportedly withstands unscathed light frosts. The little trees are slow growing but are adaptable to several soils as long as they are well drained and not too acidic.

All forms of this species are eminently suited to intimate sites and are perfect as small to medium-sized patio subjects or, because of their rich colorings, contrasting components of other vegetation. PLATE 111.

Basselinia humboldtiana occurs naturally in wet cloud forest at elevations of 2500 to 3000 feet on the island New Caledonia. The epithet refers to Mt. Humboldt in the palm's habitat.

This solitary-trunked palm grows to an overall height of 30 feet with a uniform trunk diameter of 4 inches. The slender trunks are usually light tan and show closely set darker rings of leaf base scars. The crownshaft is 18 inches tall, mostly cylindrical, slightly wider than the trunk, but sometimes bulging near the base of the shaft. It is covered in a dense light brown or whitish felt. The leaf crown is tight and compact because of the short petioles, which hold mostly ascending but slightly spreading, 5-foot-long, light green leaves that are strongly arching but never descending beneath the horizontal plane. The leaflets are uniformly closely spaced, lanceolate, and slightly S shaped, growing from the rachis at an angle that gives a V-shaped leaf.

The species is not known in cultivation outside of a few botanical gardens and is reportedly slow growing.

Basselinia iterata occurs naturally in cloud forest in northeastern New Caledonia at an elevation of 3000 feet. The epithet is Latin for "repeated" and alludes to the many attempts required to find the rumored species.

It is solitary trunked and grows to a maximum overall height of 30 feet. The slender, gray or tan trunk has a uniform diameter of 3 inches. The crownshaft is light yellowish green, bulging at its base, and 2 to 3 feet tall. The leaf crown is sparse, with 4-foot-long, stiffly ascending and strongly arching leaves on 2-foot-long petioles, which phenomenon gives it the look of a shuttlecock. The leaflets are 4 feet long, linear, dark green above but light yellow-green beneath, with usually pendent, twisted tips.

The species is not in cultivation outside of botanical gardens and is the least attractive in the genus.

Basselinia pancheri occurs naturally in rain forest from sea level to an elevation of 3000 feet on the island of New Caledonia. The epithet honors Isidore Pancher, a 19th-century French botanist in New Caledonia.

This variable species is usually found as a solitary-trunked specimen. The stem can attain a height of 25 feet with a diameter of 4 inches and is mostly green with widely spaced brown rings of leaf base scars, especially in the younger parts; it ages to light gray. The brown to purplish brown crownshafts are 18 inches tall and bulging at their bases. The leaf crown varies in size and shape and may be almost tiny or relatively large, with leaves from 1 to 4 feet long. They may be pinnately segmented or entire and apically bifid, the segmented ones with leaflets that are generally wide and S shaped. In all cases they are dark green above, paler green beneath, and thick and leathery with deeply corrugated veins.

This attractive species warrants wider use in gardens than it at present has. It is easily grown in tropical or nearly tropical climates if given copious and regular moisture and a well-drained, humus-rich soil that is not too acidic. It flourishes in partial shade and full sun except in hot, dry climates. PLATES 112 & 113.

Basselinia porphyrea grows in mountainous, moist but scrubby forest at elevations of 2000 to 3000 feet on the island of New Caledonia. The epithet is Latin for "reddish" or "purplish," an allusion to the color of the inflorescences.

The species occasionally attains a maximum height of 50 feet but usually grows to half that stature. The slender trunks are 4 inches in diameter and light tan to light gray except for the youngest growth which is green. They exhibit closely set darker rings of leaf base scars. The 18-inch-tall crownshaft is slightly bulged at its base and is dark green to brownish green. The leaf crown looks like a tight shuttlecock, with stiffly erect and ascending, deep emerald green, 4-foot-long leaves. The rigid leaflets are 2 to 3 feet long and lanceolate-acuminate, growing from the rachis at an angle that creates a V-shaped leaf. The 3-foot-wide spidery inflorescences grow from beneath the crownshafts and are spectacular because of their color: a deep coral to blood red.

This palm, because of the stiffly ascending leaves, has the overall look of a thin-trunked *Hedyscepe canterburyana* but is possibly more attractive because of the red inflorescences.

Basselinia sordida grows in cloud forests at elevations from 3000 to 5000 feet in northwestern New Caledonia. The epithet is Latin for "dirty" and is an allusion to the dirty white inflorescences.

This solitary-trunked species grows to a maximum height of 40 feet. The slender, light gray trunk is 6 inches in diameter and exhibits darker, closely set rings of leaf base scars. The crownshaft is 2 feet tall, slightly wider than the trunk, almost cylindrical, of nearly uniform diameter from top to bottom, and deep brownish green, tan, or grayish green. The leaf crown is full and spreading but only describes a semicircle as the leaves never lie beneath the horizontal plane. They are each 6 feet long, stiff, and slightly arching on 6-inch-long petioles. The deep green leaflets are 3 feet long, linear-lanceolate with tapering and acuminate, sometimes pendent tips. They grow from the rachis at an angle to create a V-shaped leaf. The spidery inflorescences grow from beneath the crownshaft and bear grayish white, pinkish white, or yellowish white small unisexual blossoms of both sexes that produce small, round, black fruits.

The species is beautiful because of its form and leaf crown. The palm is common in habitat and one of the hardier (to cold) species, reportedly able to withstand undamaged temperatures slightly below freezing.

Basselinia tomentosa occurs in wet forests on ridge tops at elevations of 3000 feet in southern central New Caledonia. The epithet is Latin for "tomentose" and refers to the feltlike hairy covering on the crownshaft.

This solitary-trunked species grows to 50 feet tall and 10 inches in diameter. The gray trunk is marked with closely set, ridged rings of leaf base scars. The crownshaft is 3 feet tall, wider than the trunk, nearly uniformly cylindrical, and covered with a gray or purplish gray tomentum. The leaf crown is dense but describes less than a semicircle because of the stiffly ascending leaves that exhibit little arch. They are 6 or 7 feet long on short, almost nonexistent petioles. The leaflets are 3 feet long, evenly spaced, deep emerald green, stiff, rigid, and lanceolate. They grow from the rachis at a steep angle that creates a distinctly V-shaped leaf. The spidery inflorescences are deep yellow or golden brown.

Basselinia velutina occurs in wet forests at elevations from 1200 to 5280 feet in northeastern New Caledonia. The epithet is Latin for "velvety" and refers to the tomentum on the crownshaft.

The stems of this solitary-trunked species are tan and grow to 30 feet. The crownshaft is 3 feet tall and is gray, reddish, or brown because of its feltlike covering. The leaf crown is full, dense, and rounded because of the greatly arching, almost recurved leaves. Each leaf is 8 or 9 feet long with many 3- to 4-foot-long narrow, rigid, long-tipped, medium green leaflets growing from the rachis at an angle that creates a V-shaped leaf.

The form and silhouette are beautiful and, were it not so slow growing, the palm would probably be more widely cultivated. It is reportedly frost resistant. PLATE 114.

Basselinia vestita occurs in the undergrowth of wet forest at elevations of 3000 feet in central New Caledonia. The epithet is Latin for "clothed," an allusion to the feltlike hairs on the crownshaft and leaf undersides.

This small clustering species attains 10 feet maximum height. The little trunks are 1 inch in diameter and dark colored with indistinct lighter colored rings of leaf base scars. The crownshafts are 6 inches tall, bronzy orange to almost red, with dark, curved striations of purplish black feltlike tomentum; they are narrow at their bases but bulging near their summits. The leaf crown is a semicircle of six tightly packed leaves less than 1 foot long on short, almost nonexistent petioles. The four to six leaflets per leaf are so congested along the short rachis that the leaf looks almost palmate; indeed, some leaves are unsegmented except for their deeply bifid apices. The leaves are a deep, almost bluish green above and are pleated with deep veins, but are a gorgeous silvery purple beneath because of their feltlike covering.

This is a near perfect little thing for an intimate site where it can be seen up close. It is, alas, almost completely unknown in cultivation.

BECCARIOPHOENIX is a monotypic genus of pinnate-leaved, monoecious, solitary-trunked palm in Madagascar. The genus name is derived from the surname of Italian palm taxonomist Odoardo Beccari (1843–1920) and the Greek word for "date palm." Some growers have coined the moniker of window palm for this genus, which would be apt were the name not already applied to most *Reinhardtia* species. It is sometimes called giant windowpane palm because on young plants the leaflets nearest the petiole are partially separated at their bases, creating narrow "windows" on that part of the blade. The epithet is Latin for "of Madagascar." PLATES 115–118.

Beccariophoenix madagascariensis occurs naturally in low, mountainous rain forest, where it grows in sandy soil. Its leaflets are used for hat making and its trunks and rachises for construction (Dransfield and Beentje 1995). It is critically threatened because of development, expansion of slash-and-burn agriculture, and the felling of trees for their edible growing points. Were it not for the wide dissemination of seed in the 1990s, the species would be almost extinct globally.

The trunk attains a maximum height of 40 feet and a diameter of 1 foot or more in habitat. It is covered, except in its oldest parts, with large, persistent leaf bases and tightly woven brown fibers. The grass green leaves are 15 feet long and grow almost directly from the top of the trunk with little or no petiole, although there is a "false petiole" of old fibers adherent to the robust rachis. The leaflets are regularly arranged along the rachis, linear-lanceolate, undulating on their margins, 3 feet long (in mature palms), and usually shortly bifid at their apices. They are bright yellow-green to deep green above and grayish or silvery beneath. In young plants most of the leaflets remain unsegmented, but the leaflets nearest the petiole are partially separated. The leaflets of mature palms are pendent, whereas those of young plants are stiff. John Dransfield describes the inflorescences thus: "When this tree is in bud (and it often is) there seem to be torpedoes poking out of the crown; these are the extraordinary peduncular bracts at the tips of long peduncles" (Dransfield and Beentje 1995). When the bracts open, the much more prosaic 2-foot-long flowering branches emerge with bright yellow blos-

soms. The fruits are 1 inch long, ovoid with pointed ends, and purplish brown.

This palm is not as tender to cold as was first believed; it thrives in zones 10b and 11 and is marginal in 10a. It grows in sandy soils with abundant moisture. It does well in partial shade, especially when young, but can endure sun even at that age.

"[It is a] truly wonderful palm, beautiful, mysterious, and totally special" (Dransfield and Beentje 1995). It is exceptional even as an isolated specimen, especially when younger and exhibiting its "leaf windows." When mature, it is magnificent: the great leaves resemble those of the largest *Attalea* species, and the leaf crown is among the most impressive canopy-scapes. The young plant does fine in greenhouses with enough light and moisture, and older plants would seem to be a good candidates for large conservatories and atriums.

BENTINCKIA is a genus of two tall, graceful, monoecious, pinnate-leaved palms in India and the Nicobar Islands. They are similar to and related to the genus *Archontophoenix* and have prominent crownshafts beneath their leaf crowns. The inflorescences grow from nodes beneath the crownshaft and consist of spreading branches bearing both male and female blossoms. The fruits are red to purplish black when mature. The genus name honors a Dutch governor of the old East Indies. PLATES 119–121.

Bentinckia condapanna is endemic to southern peninsular India in the evergreen forests of the Western Ghat and Palni Hills, where its growing point is so relished by elephants and humans alike that the plant now exists only in the most inaccessible places. The epithet is the Malayan name for the species.

This species grows to an overall height of 40 feet with a slender, smooth trunk that is no more than 6 inches in diameter. The deep green cylindrical crownshaft is hardly wider than the trunk but is 3 feet tall. The sparse leaf crown holds six to eight leaves at a time, none of which usually lie beneath the horizontal plane. They are 5 or 6 feet long, spreading, and slightly arching, with many 2-foot-long stiff, dark green, apically bifid leaflets growing from the rachis at an angle that gives a V-shaped leaf. The inflorescences have a pinkish cast when new and bear beautiful deep red fruits that are ovoid and 3 inches long.

This palm is rare in cultivation, which is a great shame as its silhouette is among the world's most beautiful. It should be much more widely propagated, not only for ornamental purposes but also because of its threatened existence in habitat.

Bentinckia nicobarica is endemic to the Nicobar Islands in the Bay of Bengal, where it grows on low hills in rain forest near the coast. It is threatened because of the lamentably rapid clearing of the forests and the harvesting of the palm's growing point, which is considered a delicacy. The epithet means "of the Nicobar Islands."

The smooth, light brown to deep gray trunks grow to 50 feet and are ringed with circles of whitish leaf base scars. The sparse but beautifully rounded leaf crown is 12 feet wide and tall. The slender, columnar crownshaft bulges slightly at its base, is 6 feet tall, smooth, and light grayish green. The leaves are 6 to 8 feet long on short petioles, with many linear leaflets growing from the rachis in one plane; the rachis itself usually has a slight twist which gives a special appeal to the leaf, similar to the leaves of *Archontophoenix* species. The leaflets are 18 to 24 inches long and are slightly limp and drooping. Although the rachis arches and curves gracefully, the leaf crown is relatively sparse and most of the living leaves do not descend below the horizontal plane. The leaves are deep green on both surfaces. The inflorescences are many branched and pendent and grow in a ring from beneath the large crownshaft. The fruits are round, 0.5 inch wide, in pendent clusters, and red to black.

This lovely species needs a nearly tropical climate, being adaptable only to zones 10b and 11. It is a water lover but not a swamp dweller and needs a humus-rich, free-draining soil. It is fast growing in partial shade and even faster in full sun.

The palm is related to and similar to *Archontophoenix cunninghamiana* and serves approximately the same landscape use, but has a more rounded leaf crown (the leaves descend below the horizontal) and is even prettier than the king palm as a silhouette. The tree is dramatic in groups of three or more individuals of varying heights. PLATES 119–121.

BISMARCKIA is a monotypic genus of large, dioecious, palmate-leaved palm endemic to northern and western Madagascar. The genus name honors the 19th-century German chancellor, Prince Otto E. L. von Bismark-Schönhausen. The common name is Bismarck palm. The epithet is Latin for "noble." PLATES 122–124.

Bismarckia nobilis grows mostly in open grasslands and plateaux. The gray to tan or brown trunk is slightly swollen at its base, 12 to 18 inches in diameter, and at most 80 feet tall for old specimens in habitat but half that for cultivated individuals. It is free of leaf bases for most of its height and is ringed with closely set grooves, the indentations of former leaf bases. The full, rounded to oblong leaf crown is 25 feet tall and 20 feet wide. The leaves are to 10 feet in diameter, nearly round, and divided to one-third the width of the blade into 20 or more stiff, tapering seg-

ments, each of which is a deep to yellowish green, to a grayish green or even bluish gray, often with a thin red margin. Each leaf is carried on a 6- to 8-foot-long petiole that has a few short spines along its margins and is covered with a white waxy substance and patches of cinnamon-colored scales. The leaves are costapalmate and exhibit a wedge-shaped hastula on the upper side at the juncture of blade and petiole. The long, pendent inflorescences bear tentacle-like branches with tiny brownish flowers. The fruits are 1.5-inch brown spheres.

The palm grows fastest in full sun and has better leaf color there. It needs a perfectly draining medium but is not particular about the actual components. Its hardiness to cold is partially dependent on the color of its leaves: bluer color indicates a more hardy leaf—but note that this is only the leaf; the growing points (trunks and roots) are unaffected by leaf color. In general, the blue leaves are safe in zones 9b through 11, while the greener (especially the pale green forms) are more tender to cold, zone 10a being usually the limit. Seedlings of the bluish- or silvery-leaved forms are easily identified by their purplish or maroon young leaves, whereas the plants destined to remain green are green in their seedling stage as well (David Witt, pers. comm.). The palm is drought tolerant but grows faster and bigger with regular and adequate moisture. It is difficult to transplant plants when young and, as such, cannot be done other than with container-grown specimens. Older plants should be root pruned a few months before the scheduled move, and even then great care must be taken to not break the delicate growing point by jostling the plant during the move.

Because of its dimensions and beauty, the Bismarck palm is wonderful as an isolated specimen surrounded by space. It is even more glorious in groups of three or more individuals of varying heights, and is superb as a canopy-scape. This is a tree for large landscapes and it looks crowded in small yards. Nothing but banyans and other giant trees are more imposing in the landscape. Although rarely grown indoors, it could be tried in large, sunny spaces with good air circulation.

BORASSODENDRON is a genus of two palmate-leaved, solitary-trunked, dioecious palms in southern Thailand, peninsular Malaysia, and Borneo. They are closely related to *Borassus* species in details of inflorescences, flowers, and fruits but grow in rain forest rather than in savanna. Ornamentally the two species here are more delicate in appearance and the leaves are distinctively more deeply divided and differently segmented; whereas *Borassus* leaves are similar to other palmate-leaved genera like *Sabal* and *Washingtonia*, *Borassodendron* leaves are more similar to those of *Itaya* and *Chelyocarpus*. The inflorescences grow from among the leaf bases, the males a long thick, pendent branch with secondary branches of wormlike catkins of flowers, the females unbranched and spikelike with large blossoms bunched at the apex, each flower subtended by a bract. The hard, glossy fruits are large and rounded with one side flattened.

Both species are slow growing even under optimum conditions. The genus name combines Greek words for "the flower spike of the date palm" with "tree," a reference to the affinity of this genus to *Borassus*. PLATES 125–130.

Borassodendron borneense is endemic to the rain forest of Borneo. The epithet is Latin for "of Borneo." The palm is similar to the much more widely grown *B. machadonis* but is more ethereal looking and not as robust. It is undeservedly rare in cultivation. PLATES 125 & 126.

Borassodendron machadonis occurs naturally in southwestern Thailand and in northern peninsular Malaysia, where it grows in the wet forests of low, limestone mountains. It is nowhere abundant and is under threat in much of its range because of the harvesting of its edible growing point.

The trunk attains a height of 50 feet in habitat but a diameter of less than 1 foot; it bears conspicuous raised rings in its older parts and is dark gray to brown. The leaves are carried on stout, unarmed petioles, which are 6 feet long and have hard, sharp, knifelike edges. The leaf is usually circular, and the segments are generally deeply cleft to the juncture of the petiole. The barely costapalmate blade is 8 feet wide, and the leaflets, which can number 60 or more, are typically deep green, linear, and apically blunt. The inflorescences are shaped like rough corncobs and bear unisexual flowers on separate trees. The fruits are formed in tight clusters of large, purplish black globes.

This palm has a modicum of cold tolerance and thrives in zones 10b and 11, occasionally in sheltered locations in 10a. It is not particular about soil type as long as it is well drained. It needs regular and adequate moisture, protection from wind, and partial shade to full sun. Cold, dry winds are inimical to its appearance; indeed, strong winds of any temperature or moisture content tatter the leaves.

When mature, the tree has a relatively thin trunk that makes it a remarkably beautiful specimen. When young, the tree is adapted to close-up situations where its form can be appreciated. This species is a good candidate for large, well-lit atriums and conservatories with high relative humidity. PLATES 127–130.

BORASSUS is a genus of six large, dioecious, fan-leaved palms in monsoonal parts of tropical and southern subtropical Africa, Madagascar, southern Pakistan, coastal India, Southeast Asia, Malaysia, Indonesia, New Guinea, and northern Australia, although it is likely not originally indigenous to Australia, probably having been introduced to Cape York in the 19th century. These massive palms have large costapalmate leaves on thick, spiny petioles, and each leaf has a large hastula on both surfaces at the juncture of petiole and blade. Some taxonomists think there is but one variable species in this genus; most, however, put the number at from four to seven species. Only two are in general cultivation.

All the species have many human uses: the trunks in construction, the growing point as a vegetable, the sap for alcoholic beverages, and the leaves for making woven materials.

The genus name is derived from the Greek word for the flower spike of the date palm. PLATES 131–134.

Borassus aethiopium occurs naturally in open, monsoonal woods and savannas of tropical Africa. The only common name is palmyra palm, but this moniker also applies to *B. flabellifer* and the whole genus. The epithet is Latin for "Ethiopian."

Mature palms can attain a trunk height of 80 feet and a trunk diameter of 3 feet. The stems bulge slightly at their bases and sometimes near the middle of the trunk, and they usually have complete or incomplete sets of adherent leaf bases, sometimes at several separate areas. The leaf crown is 20 feet wide and tall. The leaves are 10 to 12 feet in diameter on 6-foot-long stout petioles, which bear large spines along the margin. The blade is nearly circular and is stiff with nondrooping, tapering segments, which extend to more than halfway through the depth of the blade. Leaf color is deep green on both sides. The inflorescence is a pendent panicle growing from among the leaves. Plants are dioecious with male and female flowers on separate trees, the male flowers small, the female blossoms quite large (1 inch wide) for a palm. The large 6- to 8-inch diameter fruits are rounded, brown to yellowish brown, and similar in size and shape to a coconut, each one containing one to three large seeds.

The palm is not hardy outside of zones 10 and 11 but is marginal in warm microclimates of 9b. It is drought tolerant but looks better and grows faster with regular and adequate moisture. It is not particular about soil type as long as it is well drained, but it must have sun.

This massive palm is not for small yards. Mature trees are a dominant part of any landscape and are spectacular from a distance. As a canopy-scape, this palm is superb and tropical looking. It is not a good choice for indoors, even in atriums and conservatories. PLATES 131 & 132.

Borassus flabellifer seems indigenous to open savannas in Africa, Pakistan, India, Southeast Asia, Malaysia, Indonesia, New Guinea, and northern Australia, but its original habitat is unknown. Common names are palmyra palm, toddy palm, and lontar palm. The epithet is Latin for "fan-bearing," an allusion to the palmate leaf.

Mature palms can attain a trunk height of 60 feet in cultivation and a trunk diameter of 3 feet. The stems bulge slightly at their bases and sometimes near the middle of the trunk, and they usually have complete or incomplete sets of adherent leaf bases, which sometimes are found on several different areas of the trunk. The leaf crown is 25 feet wide and tall. The leaves are 8 to 10 feet in diameter on 6-foot-long, stout petioles, which bear large spines along their margins. The blade is nearly circular and is dramatically costapalmate, the intrusion of petiole rendering an almost pinnate look to the leaf blade. The drooping, tapering segments extend to more than halfway through the depth of the blade. Leaf color is deep green on both sides, although the leaves of young plants often exhibit a decidedly bluish cast. The inflorescences grow in pendent panicles from among the leaves. Plants are dioecious with small male flowers and large female flowers on separate trees; at 1 inch wide the female blossoms are large for a palm. The large 6- to 8-inch-diameter fruits are rounded, brown to yellowish brown, and supposedly edible.

The species is slightly susceptible to lethal yellowing disease. The toddy palm is not hardy to cold outside of zones 10 and 11. It is drought tolerant when established but grows faster and looks better with regular irrigation. It is slow growing when young but moderately fast as it matures. It is adaptable to most well-drained soils.

This massive palm is not for small yards. Mature trees are a dominant part of any landscape and are spectacular from a distance. They are sometimes planted when young as if they would never grow to their natural dimensions. As a canopy-scape, this palm is superb and tropical looking. It is not recommended for indoor cultivation.

Not only the fruit but every other part of this palm has been used for millennia by the indigenous peoples of tropical Asia to whom the plant is secondary in importance only to the coconut; and it is of primary importance for some inland peoples where the coconut does not usually grow. It has been used for building materials, writing material (the leaves), baskets and mats, cordage, food, beverage, and pollen for beekeepers. PLATES 133 & 134.

Borassus sambiranensis is a critically endangered species endemic to northeastern Madagascar, where it grows in savannas of low to moderate elevations. The epithet is Latin for "of Sambirano," a region in the palm's habitat.

The massive trunk attains a height of 60 feet in habitat and always has a distinct bulge at or slightly above its midpoint. It is a wonderful light gray to almost white and is graced with fairly widely spaced black rings of leaf scars in its older parts. The leaf crown is large and completely rounded. The individual leaves are 4 to 6 feet wide, deep green on both surfaces, and a half circle or slightly more in outline; they are borne on massive brownish orange petioles that are 4–6 feet long and armed on their margins with 0.5-inch-long teeth.

Mature trees are among the glories of the Malagasy flora and are as dominant in the landscape as the two previously described species. While new to cultivation, the palm appears to thrive under the same conditions as *B. aethiopium* and *B. flabellifer.*

BRAHEA is a genus of 10 fan-leaved, monoecious palms in Mexico and Central America, mostly in the drier regions. Most species are solitary trunked, but a few are clustering and one has a subterranean trunk. The palmate leaves are stiff and usually not pure green, often bluish gray to bluish green. The leaves have a hastula at the juncture of blade and petiole, and one of the most salient characteristics of the genus is the size of the inflorescence, which often greatly exceeds that of the leaf crown.

The larger, arborescent species are similar to each other in appearance and similar to *Washingtonia robusta* in the landscape; the smaller, trunkless species are unusual, especially in the color of their leaves. There is a real need for detailed study of this genus, which, like *Acrocomia*, has been "overly described." Some species names now in use will doubtless become subspecies, varieties, or even synonyms.

Brahea palms are probably one of the worst choices for indoor cultivation. They invariably need sun and good air circulation and are adapted to semiarid open situations.

The genus name honors the 17th-century Danish astronomer Tycho Brahe. PLATES 135–143.

Brahea aculeata is endemic to the desert of northwestern Mexico in the state of Sonora at low elevations. It is sometimes called hesper palm or Sinaloa hesper palm. The epithet is Latin for "prickly," but the species is no pricklier than any other.

The stem of this solitary-trunked palm grows to 30 feet high and 8 inches in diameter. It is usually covered in old, dark gray leaf bases but, when clean, is cinnamon colored. The leaf crown is sparse, and the light green leaves are held on 2-foot-long, spiny petioles and are semicircular. The length of the inflorescences does not exceed the leaf crown. The flowers are white, and the fruits are round and shiny black.

This species is one of the most drought resistant in the genus and must have full sun from youth to old age. It prefers a calcareous soil but grows well in many very well drained soils. It is adaptable to zones 9 through 11 and is marginal in 8b but not in areas subject to wet freezes in winter.

This airy, up-close subject looks good mixed with cactus or succulent plantings. Its size precludes its use as a specimen standing alone, but it looks good in groups of three or more trees of varying heights. PLATE 135.

Brahea armata occurs naturally in Baja California and the Sonoran Desert of northwestern Mexico, where it grows in canyons (where water is available) from sea level to 5200 feet in elevation. Common names are blue hesper palm and Mexican blue palm. The epithet is Latin for "armed."

The trunk is massive, reaching heights of 50 feet or more and diameters of 18 inches; it usually has a slightly bulging base and closely set, indistinct rings, and is usually free of leaf bases. The leaf crown is full, rounded, and 15 to 18 feet wide and 20 feet tall. Leaves are distinctly bluish green, sometimes an icy blue, almost never pure green, and are circular. The blade is 6 feet wide and divided into as many as 50 tapering segments, which each extend half way to the center of the blade and may be stiff to drooping at their ends. The leaves are costapalmate on 4- to 5-foot-long petioles and have margins armed with vicious teeth. The inflorescences grow from among the leaves and are long, arching panicles of cream-colored small bisexual flowers. They extend well beyond the leaf crown and, in younger palms, sometimes reach the ground. The fruits are round, 1 inch wide, and black when mature.

Blue hesper palm demands full sun and a soil with perfect drainage. It does best in slightly calcareous soils but grows in any medium that is not very acidic. It is drought tolerant but grows and looks better when not stressed for long periods with drought. Growth rate is slow to moderately slow under any conditions. The palm is adaptable to zones 8b through 11 but is marginal in areas subject to wet freezes in winter.

It is beautiful enough to be often planted as a single specimen, but it is as a loud accent in a mass of vegetation that it excels, its bluish starburst of leaves lending an almost unmatched fillip to other forms and colors. It is stunningly spectacular in bloom. PLATES 136–138.

Brahea brandegeei occurs naturally in low mountains of southern Baja California and the Sonoran desert area of northwestern Mexico, where it grows in canyons. Common names are San José palm, San José fan palm, and San José hesper palm. The epithet honors Townshend S. Brandegee, an early 20th-century California botanist and the original collector of the species.

Trunks attain a height of 30 to 35 feet and a diameter of 1 foot. The stems usually retain most of the leaf bases and these can be decorative. The leaf crown is 10 feet wide and 8 feet tall. The leaves are 3 feet wide and circular, and are held on 3-foot-long petioles. Leaf segments extend to the center of the blade, and the leaf color is yellow-green to deep green above but waxy grayish green beneath. The inflorescence is 4 to 5 feet long and usually shorter than the leaf crown. The fruits are rounded, 1 inch wide, usually yellow, and reportedly edible when ripe.

This species is adaptable only to zones 9 through 11 unless protected. It is drought tolerant once established but grows more slowly and less robustly when stressed by drought. It is adaptable to various free-draining soils and does not need as much alkalinity as does *B. armata*. San José palm is distinguished by its trunks that are usually covered (except for the oldest parts) in a crisscrossing pattern of leaf bases. PLATE 139.

Brahea decumbens is endemic to the foothills of the Sierra Madre Oriental in northeastern Mexico, where it grows on limestone formations in scrublands. The epithet is Latin for "decumbent" or "reclining."

Trunks are no more than 6 feet high and are usually prostrate to some extent. In addition, the palm is suckering and with time forms extensive thickets in habitat, but in cultivation a mature clump is no more than 15 feet wide and 8 feet tall. The leaves are hemispherical to nearly circular and 2 to 3 feet wide. The leaflets are stiff and extend from halfway to two-thirds into the depth of the blade. Juvenile leaves are green, but older plants have nearly blue leaves. They are held on 2-foot-long petioles that show tiny teeth near their bases. The inflorescence panicles are shorter than the leaf crown and contain bisexual flowers. The fruit was still unknown in cultivation in 2002.

The species is drought tolerant and must have excellent drainage in a calcareous soil, although it seems to do well in any medium that is not very acidic. In dry climates it is hardy in zones 8 through 11 but is probably not as hardy to cold in areas subject to wet freezes in winter.

Although rare, this small palm is desirable as a tall groundcover or as an accent in the cactus and succulent garden. The nearly unique color of its mature leaves is unexcelled. PLATE 140.

Brahea dulcis occurs naturally in the foothills of the mountains of eastern and western Mexico, extreme southern Mexico, Guatemala, southern Belize, the mountains of El Salvador, and Honduras, and is the most widespread species in the genus. It grows in dry, open woods from 1000 to 5280 feet in elevation. Its common name is rock palm. The epithet is Latin for "sweet," a reference to the edible fruit.

The species is mostly a solitary-trunked palm, but rare individuals are found clustering. Trunks attain 20 feet of height and 9 to 10 inches in diameter; they are generally free of leaf bases and deep gray to brown with closely set indistinct rings. The leaf crown is 10 feet wide and 10 or 12 feet tall. The leaves are usually 3 feet in diameter, hemispherical, a dull, yellowish green or sometimes bluish green, and are held on 2-foot-long, spiny petioles. The leaflets are stiff and extend halfway into the blade. The inflorescences are 7-foot-long hairy panicles that extend beyond the leaves and bear bisexual flowers. The fruits are 0.5 inch wide, globular, light brown to greenish brown when mature, and are reportedly edible and sweet.

This species is indifferent to soil type as long as it is well drained and not too acidic. It is drought tolerant when established but grows faster and looks better with regular irrigation. It thrives in full sun in any climate and, when young, enjoys partial shade. Depending on the provenance, the palm is hardy in zones 9 through 11; individuals from the northeastern part of its range have more cold tolerance.

Except for the lack of blue coloration, the palm has the same landscape uses as does *B. armata*. When young and grown in partial shade, the leaves are exceptionally large and tropical looking.

Henderson et al. (1995) have combined several former separate species here, and there is disagreement over such taxa as *B. bella* and *B. salvadorensis*, which are treated here as synonyms of *B. dulcis*. The problem is not helped by collectors and growers who, on the one hand, want as many taxa as possible, and, on the other hand, want them to all be different. In addition, the juvenile forms of this species are often significantly different—as they indeed are in many palm species—and, in the past, separation of species was determined on this sort of phenomenon. Then there is the problem of regional variation.

All parts of the palm are used in habitat: the trunks for construction, the leaves for thatch, and the fruits for food. PLATE 141.

Brahea edulis is endemic to the volcanic desert island of Guadalupe off the northwestern coast of Baja California, where it grows mostly in canyon bottoms but also on slopes. The species is in danger of extinction because of its small natural range and the grazing of sheep and cattle that destroy the few seedlings in this habitat. The common name is Guadalupe palm. The epithet is Latin for "edible."

Trunks grow to 35 feet high with a diameter of 14 inches. They are deep brown to dark gray with closely set almost indistinct rings and are generally free of leaf bases. The leaf crown is 12 feet wide and 10 feet tall. The leaves are hemispherical, from 4 to 6 feet wide with tapering and slightly pendulous leaflets, each of which extends halfway into the depth of the blade. Their color is light to deep green on both sides. Leaf petioles are 5 feet long and often

free of spines. The inflorescences are 4-foot-long panicles that do not exceed the radius of the leaf crown. The fruits are 1-inch-wide, round, and black when mature and are supposedly edible.

This palm needs full sun from youth to old age. It thrives on poor, dry and rocky soils whose main prerequisite should be unimpeded drainage. The palm is not hardy outside of zones 9 through 11 in areas subject to wet freezes in winter but is found in warm parts of zone 8 in drier climes.

Except for the lack of blue coloration, the palm has the same landscape uses as does *B. armata*. This is one of the least adaptable palms for indoor use. PLATES 142 & 143.

Brahea moorei grows in the Sierra Madre Oriental of northeastern Mexico in dry, open woods at an elevation of 5280 feet. Powder palm, a moniker coined by Yucca Do Nursery in Texas, is not yet in wide use but aptly describes the color of the leaf underside. The epithet honors 20th-century palm taxonomist Harold E. Moore, Jr.

The species has underground, nonapparent trunks; some individuals are suckering but most are single stemmed. The leaves are nearly circular and are held on 2-foot-long smooth and spineless petioles. The leaf blade is deeply divided and is light, shiny green above and, in mature plants, chalky white beneath. The inflorescence exceeds the leaf crown.

This species is among the hardiest in the genus, being adaptable in zones 8 through 11. It does not like cold and wet but, if planted high and dry in such climates, usually comes through fine. It is not particular about soil as long as it is well drained; it even tolerates a relatively high pH medium. It seems to thrive in full sun and partial shade.

Brahea nitida is indigenous to the western coastal mountain areas of Mexico, from Mazatlán to Guatemala, where it grows in dry, open woods. The epithet is Latin for "shiny."

The trunks attain a height of 30 feet and a diameter of 1 foot in habitat. The leaf crown is dense with the 3-foot-wide leaves, each of which is borne on a 2-foot-long, unarmed petiole, is circular or nearly so, a deep, shiny green above and a lovely chalky white beneath. The great inflorescences far exceed the leaf crown and are similar to those of *B. armata*. The ripe fruits are yellow or orange.

The palm is adaptable to zones 9b through 11 in areas subject to wet freezes in winter but is probably a good candidate for 8b in the drier climes. It needs more water than many other species and grows on various well-drained soils including calcareous ones. It thrives in full sun or partial shade.

This species is similar to and has the same landscaping uses as *B. armata*.

Brahea pimo is endemic to the southwestern coastal mountains of Mexico, where it grows in dry woodlands. The epithet is an aboriginal name for the supposedly edible fruits.

The trunk attains a maximum height of 15 feet in habitat and is stout and reddish brown. The leaves are 3 feet wide, more than semicircular, and bright green above and dull green beneath. The inflorescences barely exceed the leaf crown, and the fruits are orange.

The palm is not hardy to cold and is marginal in zone 9b, at least in areas subject to wet freezes in winter. It thrives on various well-drained soils and luxuriates in full sun or partial shade.

This one is good up close or as part of a wall of vegetation. Because of its relatively small size, it is not particularly suited as a canopy-scape.

Brahea sarukhanii was described by Hermilio J. Quero from the states of Nayarit and Jalisco in Mexico, where it grows in dry tropical forest in the mountains from 3500 to 5280 feet in elevation. The epithet honors José Sarukhán, a prominent Mexican botanist and ecologist.

This is a solitary-trunked species to 15 feet total height. The trunk is 6 inches in diameter and covered in persistent leaf bases and their attendant black fibers. The petioles are long (to 3 feet) with small spines on the margins, and the 5-foot-wide leaf blade is slightly more than a semicircle of deeply divided, deep green, narrow and shiny segments with bifid apices. The inflorescence barely exceeds the diameter of the leaf crown and bears white flowers that produce 0.5-inch-long, shiny black fruits.

The species is most likely not in cultivation and, if it is, it is known under a different binomial. It most closely resembles *B. aculeata, B. dulcis,* and *B. pimo,* variable taxa themselves, and time alone will determine whether the binomial will stand.

BRASSIOPHOENIX is a genus of two pinnate-leaved, monoecious palms endemic to Papua New Guinea. The outwardly similar species are distinguished only by their disjunct geographical ranges and by the shape and internal structure of the fruits.

These small palms grow to a maximum overall height of 30 feet. The slender trunks are 3 inches in diameter at most; they are green and ringed with darker-colored leaf base scars in their younger parts and are light gray in their older parts. The 2-foot-tall crownshafts are scarcely wider than the trunks, are uniformly cylindrical, and are light green to silvery green. The leaf crowns are sparse, open, and usually rounded because of the ascending and spreading leaves, which are stiff and unarching on short, almost nonexistent petioles. The leaves are 6 feet long, with 1-foot-long, regularly and widely spaced leaflets. The unusual leaflets are diamond shaped with the point of attachment to the rachis a narrow point. They are deeply three lobed, the center lobe extended and with undulate margins, the other two lobes shorter and jagged on their apices; they are a uniform deep green. The inflorescences grow from beneath the crownshaft and are branched twice with ropelike, furry branches bearing flowers of both sexes. The fruits are ellipsoid to round, 1 inch long, and yellow or orange when mature.

The palms need a frost-free climate and copious and regular water in a well-drained, humus-laden soil. They luxuriate in partial shade at any age but, as adults, withstand full sun except in hot and dry climates. They are neither fast growing nor terribly slow growing. The genus has been in cultivation for several years but not widely so and this is a mystery as the species are unusual and tropical looking. Scott Zona has discovered that the species most common in cultivation has been misidentified for years; it has been known as *B. schumannii* whereas it is actually *B. drymophoeoides* (Zona and Essig 1999).

The genus name is derived from the surname of Leonard J. Brass, a 20th-century botanist and the original collector of the genus in New Guinea, and the Greek word for "date palm." PLATES 144 & 145.

Brassiophoenix drymophoeoides occurs naturally in the southeastern peninsular region of Papua New Guinea. The epithet is Greek for "similar to *Drymophloeus.*"

Brassiophoenix schumannii is found in northwestern Papua New Guinea. The epithet honors Karl M. Schumann, the 19th-century original collector of the species.

BRONGNIARTIKENTIA is a genus of two small pinnate-leaved, solitary-trunked, monoecious palms endemic to New Caledonia. One species usually forms only loose, ill-defined crownshafts, but the other produces tight, true shafts. The inflorescences consist of once-branched, panicle-like flowering branches at the ends of long, usually pendent peduncles; they bear both male and female flowers.

Both species are rare in cultivation. They are intolerant of frost and drought and need copious and regular moisture in a humus-laden, fast-draining soil. Both species are adapted to growing in partial shade, especially when young and, in hot climates, must have protection from the midday sun at all ages. They are slow growing.

The genus name is a combination of two words, one of which honors Adolphe T. Brongniart, a 19th-century palm botanist from France, and the other word is an outdated name for species of *Gronophyllum, Gulubia,* and *Hydriastele.*

Brongniartikentia lanuginosa occurs naturally in mountainous rain forest of northeastern New Caledonia from elevations of 2200 to 4000 feet. The epithet is Latin for "woolly" and refers to the tomentose crownshaft.

This palm attains a maximum overall height of 20 feet with a 4-inch-wide dark green or dark brown trunk bearing distinctly indented rings of leaf base scars. The crownshaft is usually tight, distinct, and 18 inches tall; it is covered in ruddy brown tomentum and is slightly swollen at its base. The leaf crown is sparse, and the leaves are short and ascending, never falling beneath the horizontal. They are usually 5 feet long on 2-foot-long petioles. The leaflets are closely and regularly spaced, lanceolate-acuminate, medium to dark green, and thin but stiff; they grow from the rachis at almost a 45-degree angle to give a V-shaped leaf. The fruits are 0.5 inch long, almond shaped, and an attractive red.

Brongniartikentia vaginata occurs naturally in rain forest in southern New Caledonia from sea level to an elevation of 3000 feet. The epithet is Latin for "sheathed," an allusion to the leaf sheaths, which are obvious, because they usually do not form a true crownshaft.

This palm attains a maximum overall height of 30 feet with a slender, delicate trunk that is 3 inches in diameter. It is mostly olive green and bears widely spaced, dark brown rings of leaf base scars. The palm usually forms a loose pseudoshaft of 18-inch-long, deep brownish olive green leaf bases. The leaf crown is more dense than that of *B. lanuginosa* and is a semicircle or dome of 5- to 6-foot-long spreading leaves which arch near their apices and are borne on short, 10-inch-long petioles. The 2-foot-long leaflets are regularly spaced and are wide-lanceolate with drawn-out tips. They are medium to deep green, soft, spreading, and pendent at their apices and grow from the rachis at only a slight angle. The fruits are half the size of those of *B. lanuginosa* but are also an attractive red and are more easily seen as the inflorescences and infructescences are twice the length of those of *B. lanuginosa*.

This species is the prettier of the two, but it is also rare in cultivation.

BURRETIOKENTIA

BURRETIOKENTIA is a genus of six solitary-trunked, pinnate-leaved, monoecious palms endemic to New Caledonia. Three of them were described in 1998. The species are known for their strikingly beautiful trunks and large flat leaves. The former are distinctly ringed and dark green in their younger parts. The inflorescences grow from beneath the crownshafts and are dense with single, ropelike branches bearing both male and female flowers.

The species are relatively fast growing for New Caledonian palms and are usually trouble-free and pest-free. They are among the most beautiful tropical-looking palms in the world.

The genus name is a combination of two words, one of which honors Karl E. Maximilian Burret, a 20th-century palm biologist, and the other a now out-of-date name for species of *Gronophyllum, Gulubia,* and *Hydriastele.* PLATES 146–151.

Burretiokentia dumasii occurs in mountainous rain forest of central and western New Caledonia at an elevation of 2000 feet. It was described by Donald Hodel and Jean-Christophe Pintaud and is rare in habitat and in cultivation. The epithet honors Marc Dumas, founder of Association Chambeyronia, an organization to promote and protect the endemic palms of New Caledonia.

The species attains an overall maximum height of 40 feet in habitat, with a beautiful deep green trunk that is 5 inches in diameter and ringed with widely spaced whitish leaf base scars. The leaf sheaths do not form a true shaft but are broad and a dirty silvery green. The leaf crown is open and dome shaped with 6- to 7-foot-long spreading leaves on 1-foot-long petioles. They are mostly unarching and flat, the 2- to 3-foot-long, lanceolate deep green leaflets growing from the rachis in a single plane. The newly opening leaves are usually deep cherry or wine red.

Burretiokentia grandiflora occurs in mountainous rain forest in southeastern New Caledonia at elevations of 600 to 2900 feet. The epithet is Latin for "large" and "flowered," an allusion to the inflorescences.

The palm is similar in general appearance and size to *B. dumasii,* but the inflorescences are much larger (3 to 4 feet wide), the wider leaflets are slightly more widely spaced, and the newly expanding leaves are green and not reddish; it is nevertheless as beautiful as *B. dumasii.*
This rare and relatively newly described species is not yet in cultivation.

Burretiokentia hapala grows at elevations from sea level to 1600 feet in rain forest in northern New Caledonia. The epithet is Greek for "soft" and alludes to the inflorescences.

The trunk attains a height of 30 feet and a diameter of 6 inches; it is emerald green in all but its oldest parts and is strongly ringed with widely spaced tan leaf base scars. The tan crownshaft is 3 feet tall and is often loose, the upper and mostly separated leaf bases rising above the tightly closed part. The leaf crown is almost spherical with spreading, 7- to 8-foot-long leaves on short petioles that are usually less than 2 inches long; there is often a slight twist to the rachis of older leaves. The leaflets are 3 feet long and are linear-elliptic with a long apical tip. They are medium green and are regularly and closely spaced along the rachis, from which they grow in a single flat plane. The inflorescences grow from beneath the crownshaft and consist of ropelike, pendent, light brown, and furry single branches that are each 1 foot long. There may be as many as six or more at a time growing from several nodes (leaf scar rings) near the top of the trunk. The 0.5-inch-long, reddish brown fruits are ovoid.

The palm does not tolerate drought, but it does tolerate the lightest frosts. It needs a rich, humus-laden, free-draining soil, and it luxuriates in partial shade when young but adapts to full sun in all but the hottest and driest climes when older. It is fast growing.

The distinctly ringed, almost pure green trunks and the large leaves are more than exciting in the landscape and are as tropical looking as the palm world has to offer. This species is a marvelous candidate for up-close and intimate plantings as well as specimen groupings of three or more individuals of varying heights. When young, the leaf crown is beautiful up close. PLATES 146 & 147.

Burretiokentia koghiensis occurs naturally in low mountainous rain forest in southeastern New Caledonia, where it is endangered. The epithet is Latin for "of Koghi," a mountain in the palm's habitat.

This species and *B. vieillardii* are the tallest in the genus, growing to an overall maximum height of 60 feet. It differs from *B. vieillardii* in having erect and ascending leaves that form a shuttlecock-like leaf crown, in having a loosely formed crownshaft that is covered in white tomentum, and in having reddish new leaves which sometimes retain a purplish cast when older.

This is the third relatively new species described by Hodel and Pintaud. It is still rare in cultivation. PLATE 148.

Burretiokentia vieillardii grows in mountainous rain forest of New Caledonia at elevations of 1000 to 4000 feet. The epithet honors Eugène Vieillard, a 19th-century French botanist in New Caledonia.

The trunk grows to 60 feet tall in habitat and is green in the younger parts and light to dark brown in the older parts. It is 6 or 7 inches in diameter and prominently ringed with lighter-colored leaf base scars. The crownshaft is the most distinct in the genus and is 3 feet tall, much bulged at the base, and coppery green to reddish brown with darker striations. The leaf crown is the most rounded in the genus, as the older leaves are spreading and slightly arching. Each one is 8 feet long on an 8-inch-long petiole. The 3-foot-long deep green leaflets are regularly spaced and linear-elliptic with drawn-out apical tips; the leaflets grow from the rachis in a single flat plane. The inflorescences consist of orange-yellow, smooth ropelike, 2-foot-long spreading or pendent branches that produce 0.5-inch-long ellipsoid dark red fruits.

The palm needs copious and regular moisture and partial shade when young. It is not tolerant of freezing temperatures but can succeed in cool but frostless Mediterranean climates if enough irrigation can be supplied. It also needs a humus-laden, moist soil that is freely draining, but it tolerates slightly acidic to slightly alkaline conditions. It is fast growing.

This is the most beautiful species in the genus with its leaf crown of ascending but arching leaves, plump crownshaft, and slender and distinctly ringed trunk. Its silhouette is stunning and, planted in groups of three or more individuals of varying heights, is incomparably attractive. PLATES 149–151.

BUTIA is a genus of eight monoecious, mostly solitary-trunked pinnate-leaved palms in relatively dry grasslands and savannas of South America. A few species have subterranean trunks. The others have aboveground trunks, which are mostly covered with persistent leaf bases. The inflorescences grow from the leaf crown and are branched once or are spikelike, bearing both male and female flowers, and are accompanied by a large, mostly persistent, woody bract that is often tomentose.

Some species are the world's hardiest (to cold) pinnate-leaved palms. Because the plants freely hybridize, many of them are nearly impossible to attach to a specific name; moreover, even the unadulterated species with solitary aboveground trunks are similar enough to make identification difficult. This genus also has the fortunate ability of hybridizing under cultivation with at least two other genera, *Jubaea* and *Syagrus* (to which *Butia* is closely related), producing interesting intergeneric hybrids that are much sought after by collectors (see plates 156, 159, and 160).

The genus name is a Portuguese corruption of an aboriginal term meaning "spiny." PLATES 152–160.

Butia archeri has a small natural range in southeastern interior Brazil, where it grows in sandy savannas. The epithet honors W. A. Archer, an early 20th-century American botanist and plant collector.

The solitary trunks infrequently emerge above ground and then grow no more than 3 feet high and are often recumbent. The leaves are 3 feet long, have short and spineless petioles, and are silvery-grayish green, with leaflets arching from the rachis at a 45-degree angle to give a V-shaped leaf. Overall, the appearance is that of a small and trunkless *B. capitata*.

The species demands a sunny position, is drought tolerant, and would seem appropriate for planting at the base of taller palms or other vegetation or lining a sunny pathway. Its hardiness to cold is uncertain, but it is probably a candidate for zones 9 through 11; because of its underground trunk it will doubtless come back even if the leaves are killed by cold. PLATE 152.

Butia campicola has a natural range in southeastern Paraguay, where it grows in open, sandy savannas and grasslands and is in grave danger of extinction because of agricultural expansion. The epithet is Latin for "inhabitant of the field."

This species is similar horticulturally to *B. archeri* and has the same cultural requirements and landscape uses. The main difference between it and *B. archeri* is that the trunks are sometimes clustering but are hidden underground.

Butia capitata occurs naturally in two disjunct populations in southern Brazil, the northerly population in the southeastern interior, the southern population along the southernmost coast and barely into northern Uruguay. Both regions are monsoonal and consist of mostly savannas and deciduous forests. Common names are pindo palm, jelly palm, and wine palm, the latter unfortunate as it is also the English vernacular for *Jubaea*. The epithet is Latin for "with a head," an allusion to the shape of the leaf crown.

The stems of this solitary-trunked species can measure 18 inches in diameter and 20 feet tall, although cultivated individuals in Argentina reportedly reach 60 feet. The stems are usually covered with old leaf bases unless they are of great age and height, in which case the leaf base scars are incomplete circles of ridges. The leaves are 8 to 10 feet long on short petioles armed with teeth. Many narrow, thin leaflets grow from the rachis at a 45-degree angle, giving the leaf a distinct V shape. The leaf rachis has a pronounced and beautiful arch, sometimes recurving as much as 180 degrees. Leaf color varies from yellowish green to silvery green to almost gray or bluish gray. The stout petioles are 3 to 6 feet long, always with sharp curved spines along their margins. The inflorescence is many branched but relatively short and accompanied by a large spoon-shaped woody bract. The plants are monoecious and bear yellow to orange flowers. The fruits are 1 inch wide, round, yellow to deep orange, and are formed in pendent clusters; they are edible and sweet.

The species is not fussy about soil type as long as it is freely draining. It needs full sun for robust growth and good color and, although drought tolerant, likes moisture. This is probably the world's hardiest pinnate-leaved palm with a trunk, being adaptable to zones 8 through 11 in drier climates. It seems to do well in all parts of Florida but is not much planted in the southern half of that state.

This outstanding landscape subject creates a tropical effect with its pleasing, stiff yet gracefully arching, much recurved, bluish or silvery green feathery fronds and the light to dark gray trunk with adhering leaf bases. Nothing stands out quite like it against the darker greens of other vegetation. The palm is beautiful enough to stand alone and surrounded by space but is more pleasing in groups of three or more individuals of varying heights. It is seldom used indoors because it requires intense light and good air circulation.

There is almost as much difference between individuals of this species as there is between it and other species in the genus. The most common variations from the descriptions above are fatter or more slender trunks, less arching leaves, and the amount of time the old, withered leaves remain attached. The southern population of this species usually has a more compact habit, and Larry R. Noblick has suggested it might be better treated as a separate species named *B. odorata* (Henderson et al. 1995). PLATES 153–155.

In cultivation, the species has hybridized with *Syagrus romanzoffiana* to form one of the most beautiful palm hybrids, ×**Butiagrus nabonnandii**. The epithet honors a French grower who first noticed the cross. In the United States, this hybrid is usually called the mule palm because its seeds are sterile. This palm varies in appearance depending on which species is the male or female parent and whether the individual palm has been further back-crossed. Individuals favoring the *Syagrus* parent are especially desirable as they are faster growing and absolutely the most tropical looking palm for nontropical areas. In southern France, the palm is reported to withstand temperatures in the upper teens (F) without damage. PLATE 156.

Butia eriospatha is indigenous to extreme southeastern Brazil and grows in open, mostly deciduous forests and grasslands. The epithet is Greek for "wool" and "spathe."

The species is similar to *B. capitata* and differs mainly in details of its inflorescence, the most salient of which is the beautiful light brown tomentum that covers the emerging spathe. In addition, the leaves are never as silvery or bluish as are those of *B. capitata*.

The two species have the same cultural requirements and landscaping uses. PLATE 157.

Butia microspadix is native to southeastern Brazil, where it grows in open savannas. The epithet is Greek for "tiny" and "spathe." The trunk remains underground. Except for the woolly spathe of the inflorescence, the species is similar to *B. archeri* and *B. campicola*.

Butia paraguayensis occurs naturally in eastern and southern Paraguay, southern Brazil, northeastern Argentina, and northern Uruguay, where it grows in open, sunny and very sandy areas. The epithet is Latin for "of Paraguay."

While it is often a trunkless palm in habitat, almost all the individuals cultivated in the United States have robust trunks about the height of *B. capitata*. The leaf bases of arboreal specimens seem to be more persistent on the trunks than on trunks of *B. capitata*, and the leaves are even more arched and recurved, almost always bending back to the trunk itself. Leaf color is never as silvery as it is in *B. capitata* but is, at most, only glaucous.

This is a fine substitute for contrast for the ubiquitous *B. capitata* and is pleasing to contemplate up close. The two species have identical cultural requirements and cold hardiness.

Butia purpurascens is native to northeastern Brazil. The epithet is Latin for "purplish." The species is similar to *B. capitata* but lacks teeth on its petioles and has purplish inflorescences and flowers. The fruit is dark purple or almost black. The species is probably the least hardy to cold in the genus.

Butia yatay occurs in southernmost Brazil, northeastern Argentina, and northern Uruguay. The epithet is the aboriginal name in Uruguay.

It is the tallest growing species in the genus and has the longest leaves. These are held on long petioles armed with teeth on their margins. Leaf color is similar to that of *B. capitata*.

Cultural requirements of the two species are nearly identical, but *B. yatay* is probably even more tolerant of cold. It has the most tropical look in the genus because of its large crown and superior height. It should be planted much more widely than it at present is. Plate 158.

CALAMUS is a genus of 370 pinnate-leaved, mostly climbing, dioecious palms from tropical Africa eastwards through the South Pacific. There are both clustering and solitary-trunked species, and a few have no trunks or have subterranean stems. The climbing species do not have a leaf crown; rather the leaves grow along the top parts of the trunks, the lower portions becoming leafless and spineless because, in reality, it is the leaf bases and not the trunk that carry the spines. While the leaf bases clasp the trunks, there is never a crownshaft because of the distance between the leaves on the stem.

Many species climb trees and other vegetation to reach an opening in the forest canopy. All species are spiny or thorny, and the climbers ascend by the spines that attach themselves to supports. In addition, the climbers have specialized organs called "cirri" (singular "cirrus") that are modified and extended leaf rachises. They may also have flagella (singular "flagellum"), a long, whiplike or tail-like modified and sterile inflorescence, an organ that is unique to the genus *Calamus*. Both types of organ have backward-pointing spines or thorns (usually in pairs) on their apical parts that also aid in the climbing process. In almost all cases, these specialized climbing organs are formed only when the palm has attained some age and, more importantly, an aboveground stem.

The inflorescences are also whiplike; long and sparsely branched, the male and female inflorescences are similar in appearance except for the small flowers. The fruits are small, ellipsoid, usually white but also orange, red, or brown, and are covered in distinct, overlapping scales.

Most species are tropical or nearly tropical in their cultural requirements and, because juvenile plants are undergrowth subjects, they need partial shade when young; ironically, most do not climb if kept in dense shade. Indeed many of these climbers simply remain as small clustering palms on the ground for years until enough light reaches them; and many do not flower until they can climb high enough to reach the forest canopy and full sun. They almost all need copious moisture.

This is the largest genus in the palm family, and most of the species are little known. The few species in cultivation are mainly found in the collections of enthusiasts and botanical gardens because of their great spininess and ultimate size. Yet many species are of outstanding beauty; they are best sited to clamber up specimen trees so that their beautiful leaves may be seen without trampling through other vegetation or endangering one's person. Most of the species are easily grown in containers and their stems may be repeatedly cut back to limit their height and to initiate compact clustering. Alternatively, most can be kept in shade, which prevents them from initiating climbing.

The genus name is a Latinized form of a Greek word meaning "reed" or "cane." All species are called "rattans," a Malayan term referring to the use of the pliable stems for making furniture and other articles. Plates 161–164.

Calamus arborescens occurs naturally in Myanmar, Thailand, and peninsular Malaysia. The epithet is Latin for "becoming a tree."

This clustering, nonclimbing species grows to 15 feet high in clumps to 10 feet wide. The short green trunks are 2 inches in diameter. The leaves are erect but arching and 15 feet long (including the spiny petiole), with evenly spaced, 2-foot-long, linear-acuminate leaflets that are deep green above and grayish green beneath. There is no cirrus or flagellum.

Because of the size and form of the leaves, this is a beautiful subject for a wall of contrasting vegetation. It has some similarities to a large clump of areca palm, *Dypsis lutescens*.

Calamus aruensis is a clustering species that can climb to 100 feet in its habitats of northernmost Queensland, the Aru Islands, and New Guinea. The epithet is Latin for "of Aru."

This palm mounts its host by spiny tipped cirri, each of which may be 12 feet long beyond the leaflets. Large, adult plants have a few other spines on the bottom of the leaf rachis, but juvenile plants are completely spiny. The plant clusters from the base, and its stems may root if in contact with the soil. The leaves are to 8 feet long. Immature palms have nearly ovate, long-tipped leaflets that grow from the rachis in a flat plane, whereas adult plants have pendent 18-inch-long leaflets.

Calamus australis is a clustering and climbing species endemic to the rain forest of eastern Queensland, Australia, where it can climb to heights of 80 feet or more. The palm is called wait-a-while and lawyer cane in Australia. The epithet is Latin for "southern," in this case the southern continent.

The very spiny stems are usually 1 inch in diameter and the alternating leaves 6 feet long. The leaflets grow from the rachis in a single plane and are light green, 1 foot long, and linear-acuminate. The palm forms 12-foot-long flagella from the spiny leaf axils.

This climber produces one of the most tropical looking vistas if it can be planted so that its layers of beautifully feathery leaves can be seen.

Calamus caesius is indigenous to Thailand, peninsular Malaysia, Sumatra, and Borneo, where it grows in rain forest. The epithet is Latin for "blue," an allusion to the color of the leaf underside and the spiny leaf sheath.

This large, robust, clustering climber has stems to 150 feet. It ascends a host by 2-foot-long cirri at the ends of the 3-foot-long leaves. The leaflets are irregularly spaced along the rachis, often in small groups, each one linear-elliptic and acuminate, 1 foot long, dark green above and distinctly grayish green or grayish blue-green beneath.

The palm is attractive up close but, because of its long stems, is difficult to place so that it can be seen in the landscape. It can be pruned back to initiate more stems and a better appearance.

Calamus caryotoides is a clustering and climbing species endemic to northeastern Australia, where it grows in the rain forest and in drier forests and clearings. The palm is called wait-a-bit (or wait-a-while) and fishtail lawyer cane in Australia. The epithet is from the Greek meaning "similar to *Caryota*," although the leaflets are not that similar to those of most *Caryota* species.

This palm is capable of making large clumps with as many as 100 stems. It is a smaller plant that usually climbs no higher than 40 or 50 feet mainly by 3-foot-long flagella. The stems are relatively thin, 0.5 inch in diameter, pliable, and not particularly spiny, most of the spines relegated to the leaf sheaths. The leaves are 1 foot long and have 5 to 10 pinnae, each one a glossy dark green, linear to wedge shaped, and jagged at the apex. The deep orange fruits are formed in long, pendent clusters.

Calamus castaneus is indigenous to Thailand, peninsular Malaysia, and Sumatra, where it grows in rain forest.

The epithet is Latin for "chestnut," an allusion to the color of the leaf sheaths and attendant fibers.

This is another nonclimbing, clustering species with little apparent stem or trunk, the great 15-foot-long leaves growing straight from the ground to an overall height of 20 feet. The spines are mainly confined to the 6-foot-long leaf petiole and to the large and felty leaf sheaths. The many leaflets are narrow and pointed, grow in a flat plane, and are each 18 inches long; they are glossy deep green above and a grayish, often bluish lighter hue beneath.

The leaf looks, from any distance, like that of a *Phoenix* species. The palm is spectacular in a wall of vegetation, where its substantial leaves create quite a visual impact.

Calamus diepenhorstii is found in Thailand, peninsular Malaysia, Sumatra, and Borneo. It is a large, robust, clustering, and high-climbing palm with stems to 60 feet long. It clings by 15- to 20-foot-long, slender flagella. The leaves are 6 feet long, with many linear-acuminate, bright green, limp, 1-foot-long leaflets growing in a flat plane from the spiny rachis. The beautiful leaves are reminiscent of those of a giant *Chamaedorea* species.

Calamus hollrungii occurs naturally in Papua New Guinea, in northeastern Queensland, Australia, and in the Solomon Islands, where it grows in lowland rain forest. The epithet is a Latinized form of the surname "Hollrung" and honors a German plant collector in New Guinea.

It is an unusual solitary-trunked climber whose 1-inch-thick, very spiny stem can reach lengths of 80 feet; if it does so, it usually forms stilt roots at its base to anchor its great height. The stem also has the ability to form roots if it contacts the soil. The leaves are 8 feet long, with fairly regularly spaced groups of 1-foot-long, linear-oblong, dark green leaflets along the rachis. The palm clambers up and over by its spiny stems and by its 10-foot-long cirri.

Calamus javensis is indigenous to southern Thailand, peninsular Malaysia, Java, Borneo, and Sumatra, where it grows in rain forest. The epithet is Latin for "of Java." This is among the smallest, most delicate-looking species in the genus.

Although it is a clustering climber, its stems are never longer than 30 feet and are less than 0.5 inch in diameter. It climbs by 3-foot-long flagella at the ends of the 2-foot-long leaves. The dark green, 6-inch-long, elliptic-acuminate leaflets are unusual in that the lowest pair is usually backwards pointing, and the leaflets of the terminal pair are fused.

Calamus manan is indigenous to Thailand, peninsular Malaysia, Sumatra, and Borneo, where it grows in low mountainous rain forest. The species is threatened because it produces the best rattan and has been harvested for generations for that purpose. The epithet is the aboriginal name for the palm.

This solitary-trunked palm is perhaps the largest species in the genus; the 4-inch-diameter stem reaches lengths of well over 300 feet with a cirrus 10 feet long. The immense leaves are 25 feet long and have evenly spaced, 2-foot-long, linear, gray-green, pendent leaflets.

Because of the long stem, it is difficult to see mature plants in nature. Once seen, they are unforgettable.

Calamus moti is endemic to northeastern Australia, where it grows in the rain forest. One of the common names in Australia is yellow lawyer cane. The epithet is a form of the aboriginal name for the palm.

This is another large, clustering and climbing spiny palm whose stems reach lengths of 70 feet. The clumps have many stems, and a single plant can appear like a colony. The leaves are 10 feet long and have deep green, evenly spaced, long, linear leaflets; they much resemble the leaves of the kentia palm, *Howea forsteriana*. The plant hangs onto its supports by 1-inch-long yellow spines on its stems and by 12-foot-long whiplike flagella.

This beautiful species takes readily to container culture with heavy pruning. PLATE 161.

Calamus muelleri is indigenous to the rain forest of southeastern Queensland and northeastern New South Wales, where it is called southern lawyer cane. The epithet honors Sir Ferdinand J. H. von Mueller, a 19th-century German botanist in Australia.

It is a clustering and climbing species with slender stems, 0.5 inch in diameter, that grow to 80 feet or more. The leaves are 3 feet long with 10 widely spaced, lanceolate, deep green leaflets; the leaflets have small spines on their margins and veins, and the rachis has longer and more widely spaced spines. The palm climbs by its 6-foot-long, thin flagella.

Because of its provenance, this species can tolerate cooler conditions than do most others and even occasional freezing temperatures (Daryl O'Connor, pers. comm.).

Calamus ornatus is an immense, clustering and climbing spiny palm indigenous to tropical Southeast Asia, from the Philippines, through Sulawesi, Borneo, Java, Sumatra, and peninsular Thailand. The epithet is Latin for "ornate."

The 3-inch-thick stems grow to 200 feet long. The leaves are 12 to 15 feet long and carry beautiful 3-foot-long, deep green, widely spaced, linear–acuminate leaflets. The palm climbs mainly by its 20-foot-long, slender green flagella.

Calamus scipionum occurs naturally in rain forest of the Philippines, Borneo, Sumatra, and Thailand. The meaning of the epithet is unknown.

It is a clustering and high-climbing palm whose stems can grow to lengths of 150 feet or more by 20-foot-long flagella. The attractive leaves are triangular, dark green, 6 feet long, and widely spaced along the stems. The regularly spaced, 2-foot-long, lanceolate leaflets grow from the rachis in a flat plane and bear small spines.

The palm makes a beautiful isolated specimen if grown in sun and regularly pruned back.

Calamus vanuatuensis is endemic to rain forest on the Vanuatu islands from sea level to 5000 feet elevation. The epithet is Latin for "of Vanuatu."

This is another large species whose solitary stem grows to 100 feet long but is 2 inches or less in diameter. The leaves are 12 feet long and slightly arching, and bear beautiful limp, pendent, broadly lanceolate, glossy dark green, 18-inch-long leaflets. The palm climbs by 6-foot-long cirri at the ends of the leaves.

Calamus vitiensis is indigenous to the Fiji Islands, where it grows in rain forest on sloping ground. The epithet is Latin for "of Viti," one of the Fijian islands.

This solitary-trunked species climbs by 4-foot-long cirri at the ends of the 6-foot-long leaves. The latter are beautifully ascending and arching, with widely and regularly spaced, deep green, pendent, elliptic-acuminate and curved, 1-foot-long leaflets.

Calamus warburgii is indigenous to northern Queensland, Australia, and is found in the Solomon Islands and in Papua New Guinea. The epithet honors German plant collector and botanist Otto Warburg (1859–1938).

This is a large clumper and climber whose many, thin (less than 1 inch in diameter) stems can attain lengths more than 100 feet. The leaves are among the most beautiful in the palm family; they are 8 feet long, are ascending but also gently arching, and have limp, regularly spaced, 1-foot-long grass green, linear and acuminate leaflets. The palm clings to other vegetation by 12-foot-long cirri at the ends of many of its leaves.

This species is beautiful, both as a juvenile plant and when its tiers of great, light green, giant, fernlike leaves can be seen.

CALOSPATHA is a genus of two pinnate-leaved, solitary-trunked, dioecious rattan palms endemic to peninsular Malaysia. They have no specialized climbing organs; rather, they climb to short heights by hooking the recurved spines on their petioles and leaf rachises onto other vegetation. The large leaves are borne on petioles and have numerous linear leaflets with teeth on their margins and bristles along the veins. The inflorescences consist of closely set, two-ranked overlapping boat-shaped and beaked bracts which gradually elongate, each one opening enough for the spikes of male or female flowers to be accessible; the entire inflorescence is visually reminiscent of that of many *Heliconia* species. The fruits are small, rounded, and scaly.

Calospatha confusa and **Calospatha scortechinii** are exceedingly rare in habitat and neither one is well represented in collections, nor has either been seen for many years; they may be extinct. The genus name is from Greek words meaning "beautiful" and "spathe."

CALYPTROCALYX is a genus of 26 mostly small, pinnate-leaved, mostly clustering, monoecious palms, which occur naturally in the rain forest of New Guinea, with one exception from the Moluccas (see *C. spicatus* below). The inflorescences are unbranched spikes of tiny male and female flowers, and the fruits are orange, red, or black. Most of the plants grown today are relatively new to cultivation, and many of them are not taxonomically determined. Thus one finds such names as *Calyptrocalyx* 'Yamu Tumune', which are an attempt at naming something science has not yet gotten around to; in this case a place name is used for separating this new species from the others. Some species have undivided leaves with bifid apices; most newly opened leaves are orange, red, or purple. Almost all these palms are undergrowth subjects, a few rising to or above the forest canopy.

All are tender to cold and adaptable only to zones 10b and 11. All of them need a rich, humus-laden soil that is moist but fast draining, and none are particularly fond of calcareous soil. All are adaptable to partial shade and a few to full sun. Most need protection from strong winds lest their beautiful leaves become marred; dry winds, especially when cold, are inimical and often fatal. All the smaller species make excellent container subjects if given enough water and a fast-draining medium, and all of them are beautiful along a path or as a border to contrasting vegetation.

The genus name is from Greek words meaning "covered" and "calyx." The genus *Paralinospadix* is now incorporated into *Calyptrocalyx*. PLATES 165–184.

Calyptrocalyx albertisianus is a large, beautiful, solitary-trunked or infrequently clustering species, growing ultimately to heights of 25 feet. The epithet honors Luigi d'Albertis, the 19th-century explorer of New Guinea.

The trunk is usually dark tan, less than 1 foot in diameter in mature specimens, and ringed with cream-colored leaf base scars. The leaves are 10 feet long with spreading, glossy deep green, 18-inch-long, elliptic-acuminate leaflets growing in a flat plane from the rachis. The new leaves unfold a beautiful cherry to maroon color that lasts for two weeks before it turns to brownish orange and finally deep green.

The species grows reasonably fast once past the seedling stage and with good soil and abundant moisture. It is tolerant of partial shade to full sun, except in the hottest climates where it needs protection from the midday sun. PLATE 167.

Calyptrocalyx arfakiensis is a small, solitary-trunked species with undivided leaves that are apically bifid. The epithet is Latin for "of Arfak," a mountain range in Western Papua (Irian Jaya).

The species is choice because of the slender, elegant stem that measures 6 feet high and 0.5 inch in diameter when mature. The leaves are a delicious, glossy deep green with corrugations corresponding to the fused pinnae. PLATE 168.

Calyptrocalyx doxanthus is a small clustering species to 6 feet high with thin, delicate stems. The leaves are 3 feet long with 8 to 10 pairs of 6-inch-long, elliptic-acuminate leaflets growing in a flat plane from the rachis. New leaf color is pink to deep rose. The epithet is from two Greek words meaning "glory" or "praise" and "flower," an allusion to the unique arrangement of the flower parts (John L. Dowe, pers. comm.).

Calyptrocalyx elegans is a small clustering species to 15 feet high. The clumps are not dense, and the leaves are either mostly unsegmented and apically bifid or completely pinnate, the latter type of leaf looking much like that of a *Chamaedorea* species, with limp, linear light green regularly spaced leaflets. This species is sought after because of the beautiful dark red newly unfurled leaves. The epithet is Latin for "elegant."

Calyptrocalyx flabellatus is an impressive little solitary-trunked palm. It grows to 9 feet tall with a stem only 1 inch in diameter but with 4-foot-long, deep green leaves that are undivided, very deeply bifid apically, and with corrugations corresponding to the fused pinnae. The new leaves are pinkish orange. The epithet is Latin for "fanned," a reference to the apically divided leaves.

Calyptrocalyx forbesii is among the most beautiful and graceful species in the genus. Two synonyms are *C. petrickianus* and *C. stenoschistus* (John L. Dowe, pers. comm.).

It is a large clustering palm with several elegantly slender, light-colored, ringed trunks that can attain heights of 20 feet or more. The elegance continues with the ascending and beautifully arching pinnate leaves, which are 8 feet long, with many dark green, linear-acuminate, 18-inch-long leaflets that grow from the rachis in a single plane. The new leaf color is dark reddish brown.

A clump of this species is as graceful as an areca palm and, like the latter, benefits visually if some of the densely packed stems are judiciously cut away so that the form of the others is more readily apparent. PLATE 169.

Calyptrocalyx hollrungii is a small species to 8 feet high that forms dense and sometimes large clumps. The leaves are 18 inches long, undivided and apically bifid, medium green, with deep corrugations corresponding to the fused pinnae; some individuals have segmented pinnae of varying widths. The new leaves are a deep maroon or wine color. This species has been cultivated longer than most others have, but it was known as *Paralinospadix hollrungii.* The epithet is a Latinized form of the surname "Hollrung" and honors a German plant collector in New Guinea. PLATES 170–173.

Calyptrocalyx micholitzii is a small, solitary-trunked species with undivided deep green leaves that are apically bifid. The palm grows to 2 feet high and is a true miniature. The new leaves are purplish orange and often show an attractive mottling of dark and lighter green when mature. The epithet honors the plant's original collector, Wilhelm Micholitz.

Calyptrocalyx pachystachys is a small, solitary-trunked species with 6 feet of slender trunk. The gorgeous 3-foot-long leaves are graced with elliptic-acuminate to obovate-acuminate, glossy dark green "fat" leaflets that often have a slight S shape. The newly unfurled leaflets are a beautiful cherry red. A variegated cultivar looks more chlorotic than beautiful. The epithet is from two Greek words meaning "thick" and "spike," a reference to the inflorescence. PLATES 174 & 175.

Calyptrocalyx pauciflorus is a small, solitary-trunked species whose stem usually remains underground. The beautiful 2-foot-long leaves are undivided except for the bifid apex and are deep green, wide at the apex, with a lighter colored midrib and corrugations corresponding to the fused pinnae. The epithet is Latin for "few flowered." PLATE 176.

Calyptrocalyx polyphyllus is a beautiful clustering species whose slender trunks grow to 10 feet. The clumps are neither large nor dense, which makes them more elegantly handsome. The leaves are 3 to 5 feet long with many elliptical, long-acuminate, glossy deep green, 8-inch-long leaflets in mature plants. New growth is typically colored maroon to cherry red. The epithet is two Greek words meaning "many" and "leaf." PLATES 177 & 178.

Calyptrocalyx spicatus is atypical in its origin, being the only species indigenous to the island of Ambon in the Moluccas. The epithet is Latin for "spiked" and refers to the unbranched inflorescence, which is 9 or 10 feet long.

It has a solitary trunk that is atypically large for the genus, growing to a height of 40 feet or more. The trunk is light tan and beautifully ringed with darker leaf base scars; it is typically straight as an arrow and slender, no more than 10 inches in diameter. The leaves are sumptuous, each 12 feet long, pinnately divided into many narrow, lanceolate, pointed 2-foot-long, deep green pendent leaflets. Some people compare the leaves to those of the kentia palm, *Howea forsteriana*, but others see them as much more like *Gulubia costata*. The leaves are glorious and sparse, with never more than 12 per leaf crown. PLATE 179.

CALYPTROGYNE is a genus of eight small, solitary-trunked, pinnate-leaved, monoecious palms in tropical America, all undergrowth subjects in rain forest. Most species are outwardly similar to *Geonoma* and *Asterogyne* species but are not as well represented in cultivation. One wonders why, as they are at least as ornamental as those species. The genus is most closely related to *Calyptronoma* in the technical details of its inflorescences and flowers but not in its vegetative characters. The inflorescences are mostly simple erect spikes held well above the leaf crown, the flowers of most species being pollinated by bats. This last characteristic has led to the far-fetched moniker of vampire palm for the most widely cultivated species. The genus name is derived from two Greek words meaning "covered" and "female," a reference to the pistillate flowers. PLATES 185 & 186.

Calyptrogyne ghiesbreghtiana is the most widespread species, occurring from the state of Chiapas in Mexico, southwards and eastwards through all of Central America except El Salvador and into northern Colombia, where it grows in rain forest from sea level to an elevation of 4800 feet. The species is sometimes called rat's tail palm because of the thin, pendent inflorescences. The epithet honors August B. Ghiesbreght, a 19th-century Belgian botanist.

The stem is subterranean, and the leaves are 3 to 4 feet long. They are pinnately divided into dark green, deeply ribbed segments of varying widths, growing from a stout and lighter-colored rachis; more rarely are the leaves undivided and deeply bifid apically. New growth is usually colored a deep wine or maroon.

This is the only species in cultivation. It is elegant and, because of the color of its new leaves, is widely sought after. Although some populations are found at high elevations, the palm is sensitive to frost and, even under canopy, can be damaged in zone 10a. It wants regular and adequate moisture, partial shade, and a humus-rich soil.

CALYPTRONOMA is a genus of three pinnate-leaved, monoecious, solitary-trunked palms in the Greater Antilles. The species are similar in appearance, and all are denizens of low lying, wet areas. The inflorescences grow from beneath the leaf crown and are a spray of short, congested flowering branches on a stout peduncle. The fruits are small and brown or black when mature.

All three species are wonderfully beautiful feather palms that resemble short coconuts. The genus name comes from Greek words meaning "covering" or "hood" and "tumor," a reference to the petals of the female flowers which are joined to form a cap resembling a small bubble or tumor. PLATES 187–191.

Calyptronoma occidentalis is found only on Jamaica, where it grows in the swampy margins of lakes and streams. The epithet is Latin for "western." The palm grows to a maximum height in habitat of 40 feet. It differs from *C. rivalis* mainly in flower details. PLATES 187 & 188.

Calyptronoma plumeriana is indigenous to Cuba and Hispaniola, where it grows in wet forests and along streams. The epithet is a Latinized form of the surname "Plumier" and honors a 17th-century French botanist.

This species grows to 30 feet tall and, like *C. occidentalis*, differs from *C. rivalis* mainly in details of the inflorescences and flower structure. In the palm's native haunts, the male flowers are eaten for their sweet nectar. PLATE 189.

Calyptronoma rivalis occurs naturally on Hispaniola and Puerto Rico in wet areas along streams. It is exceedingly rare and threatened with extinction. The epithet translates from the Latin as "of the river."

The palm attains a maximum height in habitat of 50 to 60 feet with a light to dark brown or grayish trunk that is 1 foot in diameter and covered in its younger parts with much brown fiber and in its older parts by closely set rings. The leaves are 10 feet long on 2- to 3-foot-long unarmed petioles; they seldom lie below the horizontal and fall quickly after dying. The bright green leaflets are 2 feet long, regularly spaced along the rachis, linear, limp, and pendent. The branched inflorescences have a thick peduncle and bear tiny male and female flowers. The small, pea-shaped fruits are black when mature.

It needs sun except as a seedling, when it prefers partial shade. All three species are water lovers and drought intolerant. They do best on a rich slightly acidic soil. The species is tender to cold and adaptable only to zones 10b and 11, although some protected specimens can be found in 10a. The palm is fast growing once past the seedling stage and if given enough sun and moisture.

It is beautiful up close and as a canopy-scape or part of a massive wall of vegetation. Its elegant silhouette is used to advantage against a contrasting background of differently colored and textured foliage or even man-made structures. PLATES 190 & 191.

CAMPECARPUS is a monotypic genus of rare, pinnate-leaved, monoecious, solitary-trunked palm. The genus name is from two Greek words meaning "curved" and "fruit." The epithet is Latin for "propped up" and refers to the stilt roots. PLATES 192–194.

Campecarpus fulcitus is endemic to southern New Caledonia, where it grows in very wet, low mountainous rain forest.

In habitat, the palm grows to a height of 50 feet, with a smooth and distinctly ringed, green trunk that is 5 inches in diameter and is supported on a massive, 6-foot-tall cone of densely packed stilt roots. The greatly bulging crownshaft is 3 feet tall and is a dull green except the top half, which is covered in a pinkish white feltlike tomentum. The leaf crown is hemispherical, with 8- to 10-foot-long leaves bearing regularly spaced dark green, 4-foot-long stiff, linear leaflets, which grow from the rachis at an angle to give a slight V shape to the leaf. The inflorescences grow from nodes encircling the trunk beneath the crownshaft and consist of ropelike, pendent dingy green branches that bear tiny male and female blossoms. The 0.5-inch-long, egg-shaped cinnamon-colored fruits have curved tips.

The species is almost nonexistent in cultivation. It is surely intolerant of cold and needs a humus-laden soil and partial or full shade when young. Mature palms are beautiful, almost the essence of palmdom, with their elegantly straight, green and smooth, distinctly ringed trunks and handsome leaves; but individuals are so slow growing, especially when young, that planting the species should be looked on as a gift for future generations.

CARPENTARIA is a monotypic genus of tall, pinnate-leaved, monoecious palm. The genus name honors a place in the palm's habitat, the Gulf of Carpentaria. The epithet is Latin for "acuminate," an allusion to the shape of the mature leaflets. PLATES 195 & 196.

Carpentaria acuminata is endemic to the Northern Territory of Australia, where it grows along rivers and streams in the rain forest at low elevations. Common names are Carpentaria palm and, in Australia, simply carpy.

The trunks grow to 50 or 55 feet high and 8 inches in diameter. They are light gray to almost white with widely spaced, prominent rings of the same color. The deep green crownshaft is smooth and 3 to 5 feet tall with a slightly bulging base. The spherical leaf crown is 12 feet wide and tall, and the gracefully arching leaves are 10 to 12 feet long on short petioles and have numerous linear leaflets, growing from the rachis at a slight angle to create a V-shaped blade. Each leaflet is 2 feet long, limp, pendent at its apex, and tapering towards its apex; the lowermost and the uppermost leaflets are larger than the ones near the center of the rachis. Leaf color is deep emerald green above with a decidedly bluish cast beneath. The inflorescences originate beneath the crownshaft, are 3 to 4 feet long, much branched, and pendent. They form a skirt around the base of the crownshaft and bear white flowers of both sexes. The fruits are globose, 0.5 inch wide, and scarlet when ripe.

Carpentaria needs lots of water; its enemies are drought and cold. It thrives in a rich soil and is among the few palms not demanding perfect drainage. It tolerates partial shade when young but needs full sun as it gets older. The species grows quite fast with warmth, sun, and adequate moisture. Its cultivation is limited to tropical or nearly tropical regions, and it is adaptable only to zones 10b and 11, although some mature specimens can be found in protected spots in 10a.

With its relatively diaphanous and straight trunk, the carpentaria palm is elegance personified, and yet it is noble in size and appearance. It is beautiful as an isolated specimen surrounded by space but is even more attractive in groups of three or more individuals of varying heights, and it is stunning as a canopy-scape. It is not known to be grown indoors, but it should be adaptable to large conservatories or atriums with lots of light.

CARPOXYLON is a monotypic genus of rare, pinnate-leaved, solitary-trunked, monoecious palm. The genus name is derived from two Greek words meaning "fruit" and "wood." The epithet is derived from two Greek words meaning "large" and "seed." PLATE 197.

Carpoxylon macrospermum is endemic to the Vanuatu islands, where it grows in the rain forest at low elevations. It is exceedingly rare and was thought to be extinct, known only from descriptions of its fruits and seeds, until the discovery of the trees themselves in 1987 by Australian botanist John L. Dowe, who almost accidentally found it in cultivation on the island of Espíritu Santo. This is a critically endangered species and a governmental organization (PEPP or Profitable Environmental Protection Project) has been established in Vanuatu to try to protect and increase the remaining populations. The organization's retail entity, IPP (Island Palm Products), sells seed to the outside world and uses the profits to further the cause in the archipelago; it also sells other palm seeds native to the island group.

The mature trunks reach heights of 90 feet in habitat with swollen bases and are 1 foot in diameter otherwise; they are deep green in their younger parts, gray in their older parts, and closely ringed with slightly raised, whitish leaf base scars all over. The 4- to 5-foot-tall crownshaft is straight, columnar, and slightly bulging at its base; it is light green or light tan. The beautifully arching leaves are 12 feet long on short (usually less than 1 foot long) petioles.

The leaflets are from 1 foot long at the base of the leaf to 4 feet long in the middle and as short as 8 inches long at the apex. They are olive green above, silvery green beneath, thick, and leathery, and grow at a 45-degree angle from the grooved rachis to create a V-shaped leaf. The infructescences are large and form a circle around the base of the crownshaft, bearing large, bright green, egg-shaped fruits that are each 2 inches long.

This palm seems to thrive in partial shade to full sun in nearly tropical regions. It needs copious and regular moisture. Many young palms grow well in simulated rain forest of Vanuatu (Dowe 1989a). Dowe also reports that the growing point of the palm is sometimes harvested.

This species has one of the most beautiful forms in the palm family and its silhouette is alluring with the much arched, almost recurving leaves and relatively thin trunk. There could be no more beautiful canopy-scape. *Carpoxylon macrospermum* is undoubtedly suited to large greenhouses, atriums, and conservatories with bright light, warmth, moisture, and humidity.

CARYOTA is a genus of 12 bipinnate-leaved, monoecious, monocarpic palms in tropical Asia, India, Malaysia, Indonesia, the Philippines, New Guinea, the Solomon Islands, Vanuatu, and northeastern Australia. This is the only genus of palm with bipinnate or doubly pinnate leaves. Because of their unique leaves, all species are immediately recognizable, whether they be solitary trunked or clustering, and they are called fishtail palms because of their wedge-shaped, jagged-ended leaflets. Most species have elongated leaf crowns in which the triangular-shaped leaves grow not only from the top of the trunk but also and sometimes considerably down its length. The trunks die off after they finish flowering and the fruits mature. This phenomenon is not a great problem for the clumping types as there are always new trunks to fill the void; but, for the single-trunked species, a mechanical problem is created as these species are almost invariably of large size. The beginning of flowering does not, however, signal the immediate death of a trunk because the complete efflorescence may take several years to come to fruition, the inflorescences forming at each leaf node, from the top down. While each palm produces both male and female blossoms, almost always in separate inflorescences, the male flowers tend to produce viable pollen when the pistils of the female flowers are not receptive; thus seed is not always forthcoming from a single, isolated individual.

All species are relatively fast growing when past the juvenile stage and with commencement of trunk production. All are indigenous to forests and need rich, humus-laden soils. The fruits of all species have oxalic acid crystals, which are irritating to the skin and mucous membranes. In spite of this poisonous aspect of the fruit, most species have edible terminal buds and the sweet sap exuding from incised inflorescences is used to make sugar or liquor while the pith of the larger trunks is processed to produce sago.

Because herbarium specimens are difficult to create, many of the species names are tentative and the listings that follow are bound to change in the future. The genus name is from a Greek word that means "a nut," the allusion being obscure. PLATES 198–212.

Caryota cumingii is a solitary-trunked species from the rain forest of the Philippines. The epithet is a Latinized form of the surname "Cuming" and honors a 19th-century plant collector.

It grows to 30 feet with a stout, whitish and prominently ringed, straight trunk. The leaves are 10 feet long and 6 feet wide, in two or three closely set tiers atop the trunks; the apices of the leaves are slightly pendulous as are the secondary rachises, giving a fine, ruffled appearance to the blade.

The species is tropical in its cultural requirements and adaptable only to zones 10b and 11. It needs copious water, a rich but well-draining soil, and full sun or partial shade. Because of its gorgeous trunk, this one makes a fine specimen or canopy-scape.

Caryota gigas is indigenous to wet, mountainous forests in southern China, northern Laos, and northeastern Thailand, where it grows usually in colonies from elevations of 4000 to 5280 feet. There is no widely accepted common English name, but mountain fishtail and giant fishtail are sometimes used, although the latter sobriquet is also applied to at least one other *Caryota* species. One has to wonder about the need for a common name, so short and sweet is the epithet, which is Latin for "gigantic."

In nature, the trunks of this enormous species attain heights of more than 100 feet. The tan stems are straight and columnar, wider near their midpoints than at either end, and usually supported by a cone of stilt roots at their bases. The canopy is sparse with leaves which grow only from the top of the trunk; each triangle-shaped leaf is enormous, 20 feet long and half as wide. The leaf apex is pendent as are the secondary rachises. The inflorescence is among the largest for a flowering plant; it is much branched, pendent, and to 20 feet long. The red seeds are globose.

The species has a modicum of cold tolerance, although none so great as some of the growers' claims; it has endured temperatures as low as 30°F with little or no damage and is a good species for the cooler tropical or nearly tropical regions, such as coastal southern California, if it receives enough moisture. It needs a rich, humus-laden soil

and copious moisture but is adapted to full sun in all but the hottest regions.

One can only think of a tall and massive tree fern when considering the landscape potential of this palm. It is large and beautiful enough to be a specimen plant, especially in groups of three or more individuals of varying heights; its only fault is the slightly grotesque spindle shape of the trunks, a characteristic which is ameliorated by group planting. As a canopy-scape nothing could be more impressive, its incredibly beautiful leaf silhouette absolutely magical against the sky. It can be grown indoors in a truly monstrous atrium or conservatory with lots of light and moisture. PLATES 198 & 199.

Caryota maxima has a large natural distribution, from southern China, Myanmar, Thailand, peninsular Malaysia, Laos, Vietnam, Sumatra, and Java, where it grows in low mountainous rain forest. Common names are giant fishtail palm and black palm. The Latin epithet means "largest."

In habitat, the solitary trunks can reach heights of almost 100 feet. They are 1 foot in diameter and gray to tan. The leaves grow in an extended crown. Each triangular leaf is 10 to 20 feet long on a 4-foot-long petiole. They are mostly stiff and flat but usually pendent at their apices. The leaflets are linearly obdeltoid to almost linear and jagged on the ends with a long point on one side. They are 1 foot or sometimes more long and are generally pendulous. The inflorescences are 6 feet long, many branched, and pendent, and bear 1-inch-long, elliptical, pink to red fruits in 8-foot-long, pendent clusters.

This water lover is adaptable only to zones 10b and 11, although a few good specimens are found in favorable microclimates of 10a. It needs a rich, humus-laden soil but can endure the full sun of any but the hottest climates, even when young.

Caryota maxima is closely allied visually and genetically to *C. rumphiana*. Because of the elongated leaf crown, it has as much in common visually with narrow-crowned dicot trees as it does with other palms. It is almost unbelievably spectacular and tropical looking in groups of three or more individuals of varying heights to give a great tiered effect to the massive fernlike leaves. It is also large and sensational enough to stand isolated, although it looks better either in groups of individuals of varying heights or as a canopy-scape. It can be grown indoors in a truly monstrous atrium or conservatory with lots of light and moisture.

The sap is used to make sugar and alcoholic drinks, and the pith of the trunks for sago. PLATES 200–202.

Caryota mitis is widespread and indigenous to open and cleared areas in the rain forest of the Philippines, southern China, the Andaman and Nicobar Islands, Thailand, peninsular Malaysia, Southeast Asia, Sumatra, Borneo, Java, and Sulawesi. The only common English name is the somewhat trivial clustering fishtail palm. The epithet is Latin for "unarmed," the application unclear as all *Caryota* species are unarmed.

This is one of the few clustering species in the genus. Clumps can be 20 feet tall and 15 feet wide with densely packed stems to 12 feet tall. The leaves are 8 feet long and triangular on 3-foot-long petioles. The leaflets are 6 inches long, obdeltoid with usually three large indentations, and always with a jagged end. There are but few leaves atop any trunk but, because the clumps are dense, the visual effect is a wall of leaves. The inflorescences are 2 feet long and pendent, with many tiny whitish flowers. The fruits are 0.5 inch wide, rounded, and deep red to black when mature.

The species is slightly susceptible to lethal yellowing disease. The palm is tropical in its climate requirements and is adaptable only to zones 10b and 11, although nice specimens are found in favorable microclimates of 10a. It needs abundant water and a rich, humus-laden, free-draining soil, and it thrives in full sun or partial shade. The plants are fast growing under ideal conditions. Propagation is via seed and rooted division of the suckers.

This species is most beautiful as a large element in masses of other vegetation, but is effective standing alone if sited as a focal point. The palm is adaptable to indoor cultivation if given enough light and space.

The starchy pith of the trunks is (or was) used to make sago. PLATES 203 & 204.

Caryota no is endemic to the rain forest of Borneo, where it is endangered because the trees are felled for their edible growing points. The only common English name seems to be giant fishtail palm. The epithet is the aboriginal name.

The gray to almost white solitary trunks attain 75 feet of height. They are 12 to 18 inches in diameter except for a bulge in the middle that is 2 feet in diameter. The stems are beautifully ringed on their older parts, the rings widely spaced, and the upper portions of the trunks are covered in giant leaf bases. The leaf crown is 25 feet wide and 20 feet tall. The triangular leaves are 15 feet long and 12 feet wide, erect, and mostly ascending; while the rachis is unbending, the subsidiary stalks are pendulous, giving the palm a lush, tropical look. The leaflets are narrowly obdeltoid, 1 foot long, and irregularly toothed on their apices. They are slightly pendent. The inflorescences are 6 feet long and pendent. The blossoms are yellowish white, and the fruits are black when mature.

The palm is not hardy to cold and is adaptable only to zones 10b and 11. It needs a lot of water and a rich,

humus-laden, well-drained soil. It grows well in full sun or partial shade when young.

This startlingly beautiful species looks as much like a colossal tree fern as a palm. It is unsurpassed when planted in groups of three or more individuals of varying heights to create a stunning tiered, fern effect, and is even effective as an isolated specimen. Because it needs immense space, only the largest atriums or conservatories would be able to accommodate this species. PLATE 205.

Caryota ochlandra is indigenous to the low mountainous forests of southeastern China. It is sometimes called Chinese fishtail palm. The epithet is Latin for "ochre" and "anther."

The solitary trunks reach 20 feet high and 6 inches in diameter, and are straight and nearly white. Total height of the mature palm is usually 30 feet, and the leaf crown is from 10 to 20 feet tall and 8 feet wide. Older trunks are beautifully ringed. The leaves are 4 to 5 feet long, broadly triangular, with short, stout petioles. The 4- to 5-inch-long leaflets are relatively narrow, a deep, almost bluish green, obdeltoid, and slightly jagged at their apices, with the terminal leaflet larger and broader than the others. The inflorescences are 3 feet long, with many branched pendent clusters of greenish white to yellowish white flowers. The 0.5-inch-wide fruits are rounded and black.

The species is certainly one of the cold hardiest in the genus and is adaptable to zones 10 and 11 and marginal in 9b; mature palms have withstood 28°F without damage for short periods. The palm thrives in partial or full sun, needs average but regular moisture, and is not particular about soil type as long as it is well draining. It grows moderately fast.

When young, the palm looks like a large bamboo species because of the short petioles and narrow leaflets. It is at its best in groups of three or more individuals of varying heights. PLATE 206.

Caryota ophiopellis is a rare, solitary-trunked palm from the Vanuatu islands, where it grows in lowland rain forest near the coast. It was described by John L. Dowe in 1996. The common name is snakeskin palm, which is a literal translation of the Greek epithet and refers to the palm's distinctive characteristic, the color of its leaf sheath and petioles.

The palm grows to 20 feet high, but the trunk is 18 inches in diameter, white with wide, dark rings of leaf base scars spaced 1 foot apart. The leaf crown is sparse and the leaves 10 feet long, with deep green leaflets regularly spaced along the secondary rachises; the leaflets have a smooth margin on one side and are shaped like an irregular triangle, with the shorter sides jagged. The leaf sheath and petioles are deep green to almost black and irregularly circled with white or pinkish bands of tomentum, which extend to the rachis and secondary rachises. The round fruits are 0.5 inch in diameter and, when ripe, are deep crimson.

This undergrowth palm is not good in full sun or in calcareous soils but can thrive with regular water. It is adaptable only to zones 10b and 11.

Caryota rumphiana is a variable species occurring naturally in open, cleared areas of the rain forest of the Philippines, eastern Indonesia, New Guinea, the Solomon Islands, and northern Queensland, Australia. The epithet honors 17th-century herbalist and botanist Georg E. Rumpf (Rumphius).

Mature trunks attain 60 feet of height and are 12 to 18 inches in diameter. They are deep tan to light gray, with beautiful widely set rings on the older parts. The leaf crown is large and extended, from 20 to 40 feet high and 20 feet wide. The triangular leaves are 20 feet long and 15 feet wide on 3-foot-long petioles. The leaflets are linearly obdeltoid to almost linear and are jagged on the ends. They are 18 inches long and generally pendulous. The inflorescences are pendulous, 6 feet long, and many branched, with yellowish flowers. The fruits are 0.5 inch wide, rounded, and black when mature.

The palm is slightly susceptible to lethal yellow disease. This species does not tolerate cold and is possible only in zones 10b and 11. It is a true water lover and needs a humus-rich soil as well as full sun when older. The species is fast growing, which is good and bad: bad because the palm can start flowering and therefore dying when it is 15 years old.

The landscaping attributes of this majestic palm are the same as those of *Caryota no*. Indoors it would need an extraordinarily large space and good light. PLATE 207.

Caryota urens occurs naturally in open, cleared areas of the rain forest of Sri Lanka, India, and Myanmar. This species seems to have more common English names than any other, although none are that apt: solitary fishtail palm, toddy palm, jaggery palm, and wine palm. The epithet is Latin for "stinging," a reference to the irritating juice in the fruits.

Mature trunks grow to 40 feet high and about 1 foot in diameter. They are light to dark gray with widely spaced rings on the older parts. The leaf crown is extended and from 15 to 20 feet tall and 20 feet wide. The leaves are generally 12 feet long and widely triangular on 2-foot-long, stout petioles. The leaflets are narrowly obdeltoid and jagged on one of the wide ends, drawn out into a point on the other; they are usually 1 foot long and are a grassy to glossy deep green. The inflorescences are large, much branched and pendulous, to 10 feet long, with whit-

ish flowers. The fruits are 0.5 inch wide, round, and red.

The species is adapted only to zones 10b and 11 and is marginal in 10a. It needs abundant and regular water and a well-draining soil rich in humus. It is a moderately fast grower in partial shade to full sun.

As the common names imply, the sap in the trunks is tapped to make sugar, alcoholic beverages, and sago. The trunks are also used for construction. PLATES 208 & 209.

Caryota zebrina was described in 2000 by Dransfield et al. as a "snakelike" species with parti-colored sheaths, petioles, and rachises. It has been a collector's item and quite the rage. The common name is zebra fishtail palm. The epithet is Latin for "zebralike."

This solitary-trunked species is endemic to New Guinea, where it grows in the Cyclops Mountains from 2500 to 4600 feet in elevation. The species has a remarkable similarity to *C. ophiopellis*: the petioles of both are striped. Otherwise the trunk of *C. zebrina* can attain 50 feet of height, and the leaflets are more diamond shaped, thicker, and glossier than are those of *C. ophiopellis*. The secondary rachises have few leaflets, while the apical one is much larger than the others and also heavily red veined. PLATES 211 & 212.

CERATOLOBUS is a genus of six pinnate-leaved, densely clustering, spiny, climbing dioecious palms in Thailand, peninsular Malaysia, Sumatra, Borneo, and Java, where they grow in low mountainous rain forest, often forming nearly impenetrable thickets.

The palms climb mainly by their spiny vinelike stems sprawling and leaning against supports; they do not have flagella but they do exhibit short cirri. None of the species reach the giant dimensions of some *Calamus* and *Laccosperma* species and other rattans. The leaflets may be diamond shaped or linear, and new growth is usually tinged pinkish. The unusual inflorescences grow from a single large, usually pendent and persistent woody bract that opens partially to allow access to them; they are slender and branched.

None of the species are in cultivation, and the genus is doubtless exceedingly rare in enthusiasts' collections and in habitat. The genus name is from Greek words meaning "horn" and "capsule" and refers to the unusual inflorescences.

CEROXYLON is a genus of 11 tall, solitary-trunked, pinnate-leaved, dioecious palms in rain forest of the Andes Mountains. The genus contains not only the tallest palms in the world but also those growing at the highest elevations. Some of these species are beyond spectacular in appearance.

The straight, columnar trunks are heavily ringed and are covered thinly or thickly with wax in all but their oldest parts. There is no true crownshaft, but the leaf bases are large and sheathing and, from a distance, often appear to form one. The large inflorescences are obvious even from a distance because they project well beyond the leaf crown, as do the large clusters of red or orange fruit.

All species are difficult to grow outside their native habitats and are impossible in hot, humid climes in which the nighttime temperatures do not drop much; they are most at home in cool, moist climates and, while the ones from high elevations are frost tolerant, they do not tolerate heat. All species are extremely slow growing, often taking many years to develop a trunk.

The vernacular name wax palm or Andes wax palm is applied to most species. The genus name is derived from Greek words meaning "wax" and "wood." PLATES 213–221.

Ceroxylon alpinum occurs naturally in six disjunct regions of the central Andes Mountains in Venezuela, Colombia, and Ecuador, where it grows in wet forests at elevations of 4500 to 6500 feet. Because of land clearing, the species is almost extinct. The epithet is Latin for "alpine."

The trunks grow to 100 feet high but are usually half that stature, tan to almost white with widely spaced darker rings, and covered in a thin layer of wax. The leaves are 8 to 10 feet long with many 18-inch-long, pendent leaflets that grow in a single plane and are evenly spaced along the rachis; they are bluish green above but gray and felty beneath. PLATE 213.

Ceroxylon amazonicum is endemic to southeastern Ecuador, where it grows in the rain forest at elevations of 2640 to 3800 feet. The epithet is Latin for "of Amazon."

This is one of the smaller species with whitish trunks attaining 30 feet. The beautiful leaves resemble those of the coconut palm and exhibit a twist to the apical half of the rachis which causes the leaflets in that part of the leaf to be held vertically; they are deep green above and have a gray, yellowish, or whitish tomentum beneath. PLATE 214.

Ceroxylon ceriferum is indigenous to northern Colombia and Venezuela, where it grows in the rain forest at elevations of 6000 to 9000 feet. The epithet is Latin for "wax-bearing."

The tan trunks reach heights of 75 feet. The leaves are similar to those of the preceding two species except that the rachises are much more ascending or erect and the leaf crown is never fully rounded. PLATE 215.

Ceroxylon echinulatum is endemic to Ecuador, where it grows in rain forest on the eastern and western slopes of the Andes at elevations from 5800 to 6200 feet. The epi-

thet is Latinized Greek and translates as "hedgehog-like," an allusion to the spiny fruits.

The trunk grows to 60 feet in habitat and 1 foot in diameter. The leaf crown is spherical or nearly so, and the individual 10-foot-long leaves bear many regularly spaced linear leaflets that are completely pendent from the rachis and have distinct and whitish tomentum beneath. The reddish orange fruits hang in conspicuous clusters and are covered with soft, tiny spines. PLATE 216.

Ceroxylon parvifrons occurs naturally in the wet Andes of Colombia and Peru at elevations of 6000 to 10,000 feet, the greatest naturally occurring elevation of any palm. The epithet is from two Latin words meaning "small" and "frond."

It is one of the smaller species with a tan trunk to 40 feet tall. The smallish, sharply ascending, arching leaves are unusual for the genus in having stiff, bluish green leaflets. These grow from the rachis at an angle which gives the leaf a V shape. The leaf crown is sparse and never forms more than a semicircle; the leaf bases are large and prominent and almost form a crownshaft. PLATE 217.

Ceroxylon parvum occurs naturally in two disjunct regions of the Andes: the eastern slopes in Ecuador and also in southern Peru and western Bolivia, where it grows in rain forest and the clearings therein from 4500 to 5700 feet elevation. The epithet is Latin for "small."

This is the smallest *Ceroxylon* species, the trunk attaining only a maximum of 30 feet in habitat, with a diameter of 4 to 7 inches. The leaf crown is globular and the individual 6-foot-long leaves bear narrow leaflets which grow at several angles off the rachis to create a plumose leaf. PLATE 218.

Ceroxylon quindiuense is endemic to the Andes of Colombia, where it grows at elevations of 6000 to 10,000 feet under wet conditions. The epithet is Latin for "of Quindío," a region in the western Andes.

This is the tallest palm in the world, the trunks growing to 200 feet high. They are straight, columnar, and white, and bear beautiful dark and widely spaced rings in their younger parts; their whiteness is due to a thick coating of wax. The leaf crown is nearly round, and the leaves are 15 to 18 feet long, with 2-foot-long, pendent, dark green leaflets bearing a thick white or yellowish tomentum underneath.

There is no more spectacular palm tree but, even if one has a favorable climate, one would not live long enough to see such grandeur on one's property. The good news is that even young individuals are massive and splendid with their great ascending leaves. PLATES 219 & 221.

Ceroxylon ventricosum is indigenous to the Andes of Ecuador and southern Colombia at altitudes of 6000 to

10,000 feet in wet forests. The epithet is Latin for "bulged" or "swollen."

This species is similar in general appearance to *C. quindiuense*, differing mainly in its height, leaf form, and trunk size. The trunks grow to half the height of the above species and seem more massive because they are as thick or even thicker; they are also usually slightly swollen or bulging near their middles, are white or nearly so, and bear beautiful undulating dark rings of leaf base scars. The leaf crown is possibly the most rounded in the genus, and the leaves are sumptuous because they are plumose, almost like a royal palm (*Roystonea*).

One is tempted to call this the alpine royal, and it is as beautiful as the royal. Alas, it grows nowhere near where a royal does. PLATE 220.

Ceroxylon vogelianum has the largest natural range in the genus and is indigenous to the Andes in Venezuela, Colombia, Ecuador, Peru, and western Bolivia, where it grows in the rain forest at elevations from 6000 to 10,000 feet. The epithet honors Julius R. T. Vogel, a 19th-century botanist and collector in South America.

It is one of the smaller species, to 50 feet overall, with relatively thin, indistinctly ringed trunks that are brown in their older parts and light green in their younger parts. The leaves are the most plumose in the genus because the bluish green leaflets grow in clusters and from all directions around the rachis. PLATE 221.

CHAMAEDOREA is a genus of about 100 mostly small to quite small, pinnate-leaved, dioecious palms in tropical America, with most species in Mexico and Central America. Many species are solitary trunked but a few are clustering and some are truly trunkless; one is a climber. Some of them exhibit true crownshafts; others have rudimentary crownshafts, but most have no crownshaft. All the trunked species, whether solitary or clustering, have prominent rings on their stems and, because of this characteristic, are usually referred to as bamboo palms.

Many species exhibit a greater variation of leaf detail among their individual forms than between separate species, and most of this variation occurs between young and adult individuals of the given species. The leaves are either pinnate or undividedly pinnate, and all have an even number of leaflets. Some species have the unusual characteristic (for palms) of producing adventitious roots on their stems, which allow them to be air-layered or even grown from cuttings—the original part of the stem, however, almost always dies.

The inflorescences are either male or female and grow from stem nodes beneath the leaf crown. Their form ranges from simple spikes to severally branched, and the tiny flowers are often fragrant. Almost all species, like those of *Caryota*, have fruits, which contain calcium oxalate crystals that are irritating to the skin.

Many *Chamaedorea* species are critically threatened because of expanding agriculture and other forms of development, but some are also in great danger because of overzealous collecting.

Almost all the species hail from mountainous rain forest or cloud forest regions and are undergrowth subjects, which allows them to thrive in shade or partial shade. (In the following descriptions, only the cold hardiness of the individual species is mentioned unless the particular palm's other cultural requirements are different from the majority.) Few large palm genera have as many cultivated representatives as does this one. Virtually all species make excellent subjects for indoors or greenhouses, atriums, and conservatories.

At one time 12 of these species were described in *Morenia*, which is now subsumed into *Chamaedorea*. The present genus name is derived from two Greek words that mean "dwarf" and "gift." PLATES 222–249.

Chamaedorea adscendens is a small, rare, solitary-trunked species indigenous to northern Guatemala and southern Belize, where it grows in rain forest up to 2000 feet elevation. The epithet is Latin for "ascending," the allusion unclear.

The trunks grow to 6 feet high. The leaves are mostly divided pinnately in mature individuals, but some individuals have entire and apically bifid leaves. They are 6 inches long and have obovate leaflets with rounded ends that are thick and leathery, a distinct bluish green, with a velvety texture, which characteristic adds even more to the unusual color and sheen of the leaves.

This little beauty is not hardy to cold but, because of its small size, is easily protected from occasional frosts and is adaptable to zones 10b and 11 and marginal in 10a. PLATE 222.

Chamaedorea amabilis occurs naturally in the cloud forests of Costa Rica and Panama, where it is nearly extinct because of land clearing and overly zealous collecting. The epithet is Latin for "lovely."

This is a solitary-trunked species whose stems are never more than 6 feet tall or 0.5 inch in diameter; they are green and indistinctly ringed. The obovate leaves consist of fused pinnae and are deeply bifid apically. They are bright green and toothed on their margins, and exhibit S-shaped ridges corresponding to the margins of the unseparated pinnae.

It is a deliciously beautiful little thing for undergrowth planting, needing copious moisture and a rich, well-drained soil. The palm is not hardy to cold and is adaptable only to zones 10b and 11, although its diminutive size makes it possible with protection in 10a, and it struggles to survive in hot, tropical climates. PLATE 223.

Chamaedorea angustisecta is indigenous to central western Brazil, central Peru, and western Bolivia, where it grows in lowland rain forest. The epithet is Latin for "narrow" and "segment," although the leaf segments are not extraordinarily narrow.

This is a solitary-trunked species whose green stems grow from 4 to 10 feet tall and usually less than 1 inch in diameter, with lighter-colored rings of leaf base scars. The pseudo-crownshaft is 1 foot tall and is deep green but marbled with white blotches. The spreading and slightly arching leaves are 5 feet long on 3-foot-long petioles that are a dark green mottled with white or yellowish white as is the rachis. The linear-lanceolate, slightly curving dark green leaflets are regularly spaced, 18 inches long at the midpoint of the leaf, and 1 inch long at their widest, and have long tapering tips.

This species is certainly one of the most beautiful and has the look of a small kentia palm, *Howea forsteriana*. It does not tolerate frost.

Chamaedorea arenbergiana is a solitary-trunked species indigenous to southern Mexico, central Guatemala, and northeastern Honduras, where it grows in low mountainous rain forest. The epithet is a Latinized form of the surname "Arenberg" and honors a German duke from whose garden the palm was first scientifically described.

The little trunks sometimes attain a height of 10 feet but only 1 inch in diameter. They are light to dark green, with long internodes, and are gorgeously ringed with golden-brown leaf base scars. The leaves are 5 to 6 feet long with handsome, widely spaced glossy dark green ovate-lanceolate leaflets, each with a long "drip tip" and 2 feet long and 6 inches wide; they are more closely spaced and more definitely S shaped in juvenile plants.

This is one of the choicest "bigger" species in the genus and is irresistibly magnificent when planted in an intimate site. It cannot tolerate frost and needs a humus-laden soil, lots of water, and partial shade; it does well in frostless Mediterranean climates.

Chamaedorea brachypoda is a clustering species indigenous to low mountainous rain forest in northeastern Honduras, where it is now threatened with extinction because of agricultural expansion and collection of plants for the nursery trade. The epithet is derived from Greek words meaning "short" and "foot," an allusion to the rhizomes.

The separate clumps can be large, wide, and dense with stems which grow to 5 or 6 feet, and atop which reside the 18-inch-long mostly undivided and apically bifid leaves. The latter are obdeltoid, dark green, and heavily ribbed. The lower leaves are sometimes partially segmented.

The palm does not tolerate cold and is adaptable only to zones 10b and 11, although with protection it does nicely in microclimates of 10a. It needs constant moisture, partial to nearly full shade, and a rich and slightly acidic soil.

This species makes a wonderful groundcover as each plant spreads far by creeping rootstocks.

Chamaedorea cataractarum occurs naturally in the Mexican states of Oaxaca, Chiapas, and Tabasco, where it grows along rivers and streams in the rain forest. Common names are cat palm, cataract palm, and cascade palm, all of which are good to rough translations of the only somewhat more clumsy Latin epithet which translates as "of the cataracts."

The trunks of this clustering species are usually not visible because they are prostrate. They are unique in that they are forked near their bases. Clumps reach heights of 6 feet and widths of 10 feet. The leaves are 4 feet long with many narrowly lanceolate, dark green shiny, 1-foot-long leaflets growing in a flat plane along both sides of the rachis. The 18-inch-long inflorescences are much-branched and grow near the ground from the leaf nodes, bearing small yellow blossoms. The fruits are 0.5 inch wide, round, red to black, and are borne in pendulous clusters.

It is adaptable to zones 10 and 11 and in favorable microclimates of 9b. It thrives in full tropical sun if given regular water. The cat palm is used as a clump of contrasting foliage within a larger mass of vegetation or as a tall groundcover. It is delicate and ferny in appearance and lends a beautiful gracefulness to any site in which it is planted. Unlike most species, this one needs so much water and humidity that it is a less-than-ideal houseplant. PLATE 224.

Chamaedorea costaricana occurs in southern Mexico and throughout Central America except for Belize, where it grows in lowland to mid-elevation rain forest. Plant size in habitat is related to rainfall amounts: individuals which grow in areas of abundant rainfall (usually at the higher elevations of the palm's range) are larger in all aspects than are those in areas of more seasonal and less total rainfall (Hodel 1992). One common name is the Costa Rican bamboo palm. The epithet is Latin for "of Costa Rica."

This is a clumping species whose mature trunks grow to 20 feet high and 1 inch in diameter. Mature clumps are 6 to 10 feet wide and 12 to 25 feet tall. The trunks are dark green with light green rings; the crownshaft is indistinct. The leaves are 4 feet long and beautifully arching on 2-foot-long thin petioles. The slightly pendent leaflets are many, linear-lanceolate, 8 inches long, olive green to deep green, and thin. They arise from the rachis in one plane, giving a flat appearance to the blade. From below the leaves emerge the 3-foot-long, many thin and pendent branches carrying the yellow to light orange small unisexual flowers. The fruits are usually less than 0.5 inch in diameter, round, and black.

The palm is adaptable to zones 10 and 11 and is occasionally found in favorable microclimates of 9b. It often regrows new canes if the old ones are frozen to the ground and the ground itself does not freeze. It does well in frostless or nearly frostless Mediterranean climates.

Few plants are as robustly graceful as a well-grown clump of *C. costaricana*. This is one of the finest landscape subjects for shade or partial shade, and it is simply superb as a patio specimen or as a large accent in masses of vegetation. There are many stems to a clump, causing the trunks to be usually obscured by the wall of foliage created by the trunks of varying heights; the clumps are much more beautiful if judiciously thinned to allow the lovely trunks to show.

Chamaedorea deckeriana is a solitary-trunked species from Costa Rica and Panama, where it grows in rain forest. The epithet is a Latinized form of the surname "Decker" and honors a 20th-century German botanist.

The 1-inch-thick trunk sometimes attains a height of 8 feet but is usually shorter; it is medium green and bears widely spaced dark rings of leaf base scars. The 2-foot-long leaves are undivided except for the bifid apex; they are borne on 2-foot-long petioles, are dark, and show corrugations that correspond to the fused pinnae.

The palm languishes and even dies in calcareous soils and needs a humus-laden, acidic medium. PLATE 225.

Chamaedorea elegans grows naturally in the rain forest and cloud forests of Mexico, Guatemala, and Belize from sea level to 4500 feet in elevation. It is exceedingly rare in much of its original habitat (primarily Mexico) because of overcollecting. Common names are parlor palm and neanthe bella, the latter an invalid binomial that was never scientifically described or recognized. The epithet is Latin for "elegant."

The stems of this solitary-trunked palm seldom exceed 6 feet but can reach 10 feet. They are 0.5 to 1 inch in diameter and light green with closely set dark green rings. The leaf crown is never more than 5 feet wide and 3 feet high. The leaves are 18 inches to 3 feet long on 6- to 12-inch-long thin petioles. They are erect but gracefully arching and seldom lie below the horizontal. The leaflets are narrowly ovate to linearly ovate, 8 inches long, and light to deep green; they grow from the rachis in a flat plane. The inflorescences are erect and branched, growing from among the leaves, and usually are longer than the crown. The tiny flowers are bright yellow, and the stems of the cluster turn orange to red after the flowers fade. The 0.25-inch-wide, round, black fruits are in erect clusters.

The palm is adaptable only to zones 10b and 11 and is marginal in 10a. Because the stems of older plants form adventitious roots, the palm may be air-layered, but the old stems do not normally put forth leaves after being cut.

No species more deserves its descriptive epithet than this lovely little palm: it is delicate and elegant from youth unto old age. It is unexcelled as an accent in shady borders and, if expense is not a problem, makes one of the most beautiful tall groundcovers; few things are more striking than an area devoted to this palm with small plants on the perimeter and larger plants towards the center of the mass. It is worth plunging pots of this palm into shady borders during the frostless seasons in almost any zone for the great beauty they lend to such areas. This is probably the world's most widely grown indoor palm, most being sold as houseplants.

Chamaedorea ernesti-augustii occurs naturally in lowland rain forest of southern Mexico, northern Guatemala, western Belize, and northern Honduras. The epithet is a Latinized form of the name of a 19th-century German ruler.

Mature stems of this solitary-trunked species sometimes attain a height of 10 feet but are usually 6 feet, and their diameters are rarely more than 0.5 inch. They are light to dark green with closely set rings of a much lighter color. The leaf crown is small and compact, 2 feet wide and 12 to 18 inches tall. The leaves are pinnate but undivided. They are held on 4-inch-long, thin petioles and are broadly obovate with bifid apices very deeply cleft into two fishtail-like wedges. Leaf color is light to deep green, and the surface is glossy and has longitudinal grooves corresponding to the fused leaflets. The inflorescence is an erect spike arising from the leaf bases, with tiny white to yellow unisexual flowers. The spikes are significantly taller than the leaves, and they turn orange or red after the flowers fade. The fruits are egg shaped, 0.5 inch long, and black.

The palm is not hardy to cold and is adapted only to zones 10b and 11 and marginal in 10a. Because stems of older plants form adventitious roots, the palm may be air-layered, but the old stems do not normally put forth leaves after being cut. This little palm is attractive as a single-specimen accent in masses of vegetation of a border; however, it is almost unsightly planted alone and surrounded by space, although it makes a nice silhouette. In groups of three or more individuals of varying heights, it makes a lovely tableau of leaves and stems. PLATE 226.

Chamaedorea fragrans is indigenous to the eastern foothills of the Andes in Peru, where it grows in rain forest to an elevation of 2500 feet. The epithet is Latin for "fragrant" and refers to the flowers.

This clustering species makes large, dense clumps to 15

feet wide and looks as much like a small bamboo as it does a palm. The green stems grow to 10 feet tall with widely spaced internodes. The dark green leaves are unsegmented except for the deep apical cleft, which is so pronounced that one must look closely to tell that the two resulting segments are not separate leaves. PLATE 227.

Chamaedorea geonomiformis occurs naturally in two regions of tropical America, the first being southern Mexico, central Guatemala, southern Belize, and northeastern Honduras, and the second in southwestern Costa Rica. It grows in rain forest from sea level to 3000 feet elevation. This disjunct natural distribution and the fact that individuals from the northern and southern extremes of the distribution are different have led some taxonomists to separate these forms into distinct species. The epithet is a combination of Latin words meaning "formed like *Geonoma*," another genus of tropical American palms.

The palm grows to 6 feet high and has leaves that are 1 foot long, glossy green, and entire, with corrugations corresponding to the fused pinnae. The leaves are narrowly obovate and deeply bifid apically.

This beauty is not adapted to sun and needs regular moisture. It is adaptable to zones 10 and 11. PLATE 228.

Chamaedorea glaucifolia is endemic to the state of Chiapas in Mexico, where it grows on limestone hills in the rain forest at elevations of 1600 to 3200 feet and is in danger of extinction because of land clearing for coffee plantations. The epithet is Latin for "glaucous foliage."

The thin stems of this solitary-trunked species grow to 12 feet high. The leaves are 6 feet long and mostly ascending. The petiole is 1 foot long and it and the rachis are usually covered in a waxy white bloom that is easily rubbed away to reveal a dark green surface. The leaflets are thin, grasslike, dark green, and irregularly arranged in clusters along the rachis from which they also grow at different angles to give a diffuse plumose effect.

In spite of its relatively tall stature, this palm needs to be sited where its sheer leaves can be appreciated: a strongly contrasting background is recommended.

Chamaedorea graminifolia has a disjunct distribution in southeastern Mexico, central Guatemala, and southernmost Belize, but also in northwestern Costa Rica, where it grows in mountainous rain forest from elevations of 2200 to 5000 feet. The epithet is from two Latin words meaning "grass" and "foliage" and alludes to the leaflets.

This clustering species has stems to 10 feet tall. The tan papery pseudo-crownshafts are 1 foot tall. The 4- or 5-foot-long leaves are beautifully arching on 10-inch-long petioles. The evenly and widely spaced, slightly pendent leaflets are 1 foot long or longer, deep green on both surfaces, and linear-lanceolate.

This species has a beautiful silhouette and needs to be planted against a wall or contrasting foliage where its form can be seen. PLATE 229.

Chamaedorea hooperiana is endemic the state of Veracruz in Mexico, where it grows at elevations of 3000 to 5000 feet in the last remaining fragments of tropical rain forest in North America. The epithet honors Louis Hooper, who grew this species for years in his California garden before Donald Hodel identified it and scientifically described and named it.

It is a branching palm with 12-foot-long trunks. The clumps are to 12 feet or more wide, and the stems bend gracefully outwards from the center of the mass. They are very dark green and ringed with light brown leaf base scars. Their upper parts are covered with the brown, tightly held, and persistent woody leaf sheaths to give an impression of a crownshaft, although there is no true shaft of living leaf base tissue. The leaf crown is sparse with 3-foot-long leaves on 1-foot-long petioles. The many leaflets are evenly spaced in a single flat plane, each one linear-elliptic. The inflorescences grow from among the leaves with coral-colored branches and bear small, round green fruits which mature to jet black, giving a festive combination of hues.

There is no more beautiful species in the genus, and it is glorious sited almost anywhere in partial shade. Alas, it is not cold tolerant and needs good soil that is continuously moist and yet well drained; however, the palm is well adapted to frostless Mediterranean climates.

Chamaedorea klotzschiana is endemic to the rain forest of the Mexican state of Veracruz, where it is in danger of extinction because of land clearing and overcollecting for the nursery trade. The epithet honors the 19th-century German botanist Johann F. Klotzsch.

It grows to 12 feet, with a slender, dark green trunk that is distinctly ringed with raised, nearly white leaf base scars. The crownshaft is small, plump, and endearing. The 3-foot-long leaves are unusual because of the arrangement of the leaflets, which grow in irregularly spaced groups along the rachis and, within each group, grow at slightly different angles from the rachis. Each leaflet is linear-elliptic, glossy medium to deep green, strongly nerved, and long tapering apically. The shiny, black little round fruits are borne on coral-colored infructescences.

This palm is not hardy to cold and is at home only in zones 10b and 11. It is delicious in a site where it can be viewed up close, especially against a contrasting background.

Chamaedorea linearis is indigenous to eastern Venezuela, northern and western Colombia, western Ecuador, the western slope of the Andes in Peru, and west central

Bolivia, where it grows in rain forest from sea level to 9000 feet in elevation. The epithet is Latin for "linear," a reference to the leaflets.

This is a solitary-trunked species to 30 feet tall and never more than 3 inches in diameter. The stem is yellow-green to pure yellow in its older parts and has widely spaced brown rings of leaf base scars and a small cone of aerial roots at its base. A crownshaft is obvious in most individuals. The leaves are 10 feet long, with many 2-foot-long, slightly limp, linear but wide and pointed, bright green leaflets growing in a nearly flat plane from the rachis. The branches of the spidery inflorescences grow from the leaf base scars or rings around the upper part of the trunk and bear white flowers. The fruits are round and bright red when mature.

The palm's wide natural distribution results in a natural variability among individual plants, mainly in leaf size, number of leaflets, and trunk height. Some individuals even show fused pinnae and a bifid leaf.

The palm is adaptable to zones 10 and 11 and is an excellent choice for cool but frostless Mediterranean climates. It grows faster than most other species, especially with adequate moisture and a good soil.

It is among the most beautiful and largest *Chamaedorea* species, making it good even as a specimen planted alone. It is wonderful in groves of individuals of varying heights under a canopy.

Chamaedorea metallica has a small natural range in the rain forest of southern Mexico and is near extinction because of overcollecting for the nursery trade. The palm is sometimes called miniature fishtail palm and metallic palm. The epithet is Latin for "metallic," a reference to the color and sheen of the leaves.

This is a solitary-trunked species. Mature trunks sometimes grow to 8 feet high but 3 to 4 feet is more common, with a diameter of 0.5 inch. The stems are dark green and ringed. The leaf crown is 3 feet wide and 2 feet tall. The leaves are usually 1 foot long, undivided, and pinnate, but some plants have three to eight S-shaped leaflets of unequal widths. Unsegmented leaves usually exhibit a slight to pronounced cup shape, the margins of the blade higher than the center or rachis. The leaf is obovate but, like that of *C. ernesti-augustii*, has a bifid apex that is deeply cleft into two fishtail-shaped wedges. The leaves are carried on petioles from 2 to 6 inches long and are held half-erect, never descending below the horizontal plane. Leaf color is a remarkable deep blue-green with a distinct metallic sheen, especially on the upper leaf surface. Although the leaves are not usually variegated, the grooves corresponding to the fused leaflets in the undivided parts of the blade may create a two-toned hue because of the different lev-

els of light reflection; some plants show a definite difference in the color of the leaflets' veins. Male flowers are borne on thin pendulous branched inflorescences, females on erect spikes. The flowers are deep yellow to bright orange. The fruits are 0.5 inch wide, round, and black, and are carried on erect, orange spikes.

This palm is not hardy to cold, being adaptable only to zones 10b and 11 and marginal in 10a. It thrives in shade and is not adapted to full sun. It may be air-layered due to the production of adventitious roots along the older stems; the original stem does not re-foliate.

Because of its form and unique coloration, this little palm is unexcelled in the landscape. It is beautiful in silhouette and, planted in groups of individuals of varying heights, makes a shimmering mass of beauty. Planted en masse, it is one of the most exquisite large groundcovers. PLATES 230–232.

Chamaedorea microspadix is endemic to the foothills of the Sierra Madre Oriental in central eastern Mexico, where it grows in thin forest. A common name is hardy bamboo palm. The epithet is from Greek words meaning "small" and "spathe," which description seems inaccurate as the inflorescences are not that small.

This clustering species makes clumps to 12 feet tall and 8 feet wide. The individual trunks are to 8 feet tall but 0.5 inch in diameter and so relatively slender that they often recline because of the weight of the leaves. The stems are dark green with widely spaced whitish rings. The narrowly cordate leaves are 2 feet long, with widely spaced, narrowly elliptical leaflets, each 8 to 10 inches long and S shaped; the terminal two are slightly wider than the others, and all grow from the rachis in a flat plane, although the leaf is beautifully arching and its leaflets are slightly pendulous at their ends. Leaf color is usually dark green above with a soft, almost satiny feel and silvery beneath. The inflorescences are erect spikes of tiny yellowish white flowers; they grow from beneath the leaf crown. The fruits are 0.5 inch wide, rounded, deep orange to scarlet, and are borne in drooping clusters. Female plants bear fruit several times per year, usually in the warmer months.

This is one of the most cold hardy species in the genus. It takes a temperature in the mid 20s (F) without damage, and its trunks usually survive temperatures in the low 20s; colder temperatures are likely to cut it to the ground, but it almost always grows new trunks and it has reportedly resprouted from temperatures in the low teens.

It is a wonderful landscape subject. The clumps are dense, and the leaves on each thin trunk are widely spaced and cover a good part of the stem's length. The palm is used as a screen or an accent in borders and other massed vegetation. It has a remarkable architectural look when its trunks are thinned (so that each one is visible) and pruned (so that they are of varying heights); its silhouette under such conditions is extraordinarily pleasant. PLATES 233 & 234.

Chamaedorea nubium is indigenous to the west coastal mountains of southern Mexico, southern Guatemala, and western Honduras, where it grows in rain forest. The epithet is Latin for "cloud" and probably alludes to the palm's elevated habitat.

The trunks of this clustering species grow to 9 feet high and are so thin (less than 0.5 inch) that they are often prostrate on the ground. The leaf crown is sparse but usually elongate and consists of deeply bifid leaves with fused leaflets. The blade is 6 inches long on an equally long yellow-green petiole. The yellow-green midrib contrasts with the dull green reverse of the leaf as well as the glossy deep green, grooved upper surface.

The palm is suited only to intimate sites or as a giant groundcover under the shade of larger plants.

Chamaedorea oblongata occurs naturally in southern Mexico, northern Guatemala, western Belize, central Honduras, and north central Nicaragua, where it grows in lowland rain forest. The epithet is Latin for "oblong" and refers to the leaflets, although the leaflets of most of the specimens we've seen are not this shape.

It is a solitary-trunked species to 10 feet tall with a diameter of scarcely 1 inch. The ascending leaves are 2 feet long on 1-foot-long petioles. The leaflets are always thick, leathery, and glossy; they are 1 foot long, ovate to lanceolate, with a long, tapering point, and may be closely set or widely spaced. PLATE 235.

Chamaedorea pinnatifrons has one of the widest areas of distribution in the genus, from southern Mexico, Belize, and Central America into Venezuela, Colombia, Ecuador, Peru, Brazil, and Bolivia, where it grows in wet forests from sea level to 8000 feet elevation. The epithet is Latin for "pinnate" and "leaf," a characteristic common to the whole genus.

This solitary-trunked species grows to 12 feet high. There is usually a loose, indistinct crownshaft, above which the 4- to 6-foot-long leaves form a sparse and often elongated crown. Each leaf has eight pairs of wide S-shaped to lanceolate, tapering bright green leaflets that are thin but crinkly; rare individuals have leaves with fused leaflets and bifid apices. The inflorescences are much branched, and the round fruits are red or black when mature. Morphological variety is to be expected in such a widespread species and, in this one, it is the form and size of the leaves.

The species is adaptable to zones 10 and 11 and does well in nearly frostless Mediterranean climates. It is a picturesque palm that should be planted where it can be

viewed up close. It is truly delicious as a miniature canopy-scape, especially if it can be sited against a contrasting background.

Chamaedorea plumosa is endemic to the Mexican state of Chiapas, where it grows in deciduous forests from 2000 to 4000 feet in elevation. The epithet translates from Latin as "plumose."

This solitary-trunked species grows to 10 feet tall and 1.5 inches in diameter, with a loose, indistinct crownshaft. The leaves are almost unique for the genus because of the thin, grasslike leaflets that grow in clusters irregularly spaced around the rachis.

The palm is not hardy to cold and is adaptable only to zones 10 and 11 but is adaptable to full sun (David Witt, pers. comm.). PLATE 236.

Chamaedorea pochutlensis is a clustering species indigenous to the rain forest and evergreen forests of the Sierra Madre Occidental in western Mexico from the southern half of the state of Nayarit down to the Isthmus of Tehuantepec. The epithet is Latin for "of Pochutla," a town in the state of Oaxaca near where the species was first collected.

The species is so similar in appearance and floral details to *C. costaricana* that Andrew Henderson (1995) is led to write that it "is the northern counterpart of and similar to *C. costaricana*." The stems of *C. pochutlensis*, however, are not as tall as those of *C. costaricana*.

Both species are among the most beautiful in the genus and have the same cultural requirements.

Chamaedorea pumila is endemic to the mountainous rain forest of Costa Rica, where it is highly endangered because of collecting for the nursery trade and agricultural expansion. The epithet is Latin for "dwarf."

This solitary-trunked small palm often looks trunkless because the stem grows to a maximum of 18 inches and the short-petioled leaves are large enough to hide it. The latter are 2 feet long, very deeply cleft apically, and light green, with distinct corrugations corresponding to the fused pinnae as well as indentations along the margins corresponding to the fused segments; the blades usually show a variegation of darker green radiating from the attachment of the petiole, which hue creates an almost luminous effect. PLATE 237.

Chamaedorea radicalis is endemic to the foothills of the Sierra Madre Oriental in northeastern, Mexico, where it grows in oak forests. The epithet translates from the Latin as "from the root," an allusion to the inflorescences which, in the most common form of the palm (trunkless), grow from the base of the plant.

The palm occasionally produces a light green, ringed stem as tall as 12 feet and 1 inch or slightly more in diameter. These trunked individuals usually exhibit a distinct crownshaft. The leaf crown is 5 feet tall and 6 feet wide. The leaves are unusually broad for a *Chamaedorea* species, 3 or more feet long and 2 or more feet wide, and are held on 6-inch-long, thin petioles. The 1-foot-long, linear-lanceolate leaflets grow from the rachis in not quite a single plane, giving a slight V shape to the leaf. Their color is medium to dark green but they are slightly glossy. The leaf crown is sparse, open, and more fernlike than that of most other *Chamaedorea* species; there are seldom more than six leaves in a crown. The inflorescences grow from beneath the leaves. They are 4 feet long and erect to arching. The small unisexual flowers are pale yellow to orange. The fruits are 0.5 inch wide, round, densely clustered, and orange to red when mature.

This is among the cold hardiest species in the genus. It endures temperatures in the mid 20s (F) without leaf damage and regrows from temperatures in the mid teens. It has one of the most beautiful leaf shapes in the genus. Plants with little or no apparent trunk often look like clustering palms, especially when there are several leaves in a crown, and they make choice large groundcovers. Those with apparent trunks are uncommonly graceful and tropical looking and are simply superb in groups of three or more individuals of varying heights. Single-trunked specimens are not good isolated in space, but they are beautiful as canopy-scapes. PLATES 238–240.

Chamaedorea seifrizii is indigenous to the Yucatán and adjacent areas in Mexico, all of Belize, northern Guatemala, and northeastern Honduras, where it grows in lowland monsoonal forest. This is the species most often referred to as bamboo palm; another moniker is reed palm. The epithet honors German botanist William Seifriz, who first collected the species.

This is a clumping species with trunks to 10 feet high and usually less than 1 inch in diameter. They are light to dark green and indistinctly ringed, with an elongated but indistinct crownshaft. A mature clump can reach 12 feet high and 6 feet wide. The leaves are 3 feet long and composed of several mostly linear-lanceolate leaflets, the terminal two of which are often wider and shorter than the others. Leaflets are broadly lanceolate to narrow and linear but usually 8 inches long. They are sometimes straight and stiff looking but also often (for the wider ones) soft and half-pendulous. The leaves are carried on 2-inch-long petioles. The inflorescences are short and erect with fragrant, tiny greenish yellow flowers densely packed along the few branches. The fruits are 0.25 inch wide, rounded, and black.

The species is variable in leaf form; some plants formerly classified as *C. erumpens* have a pair of unusually wide and fat leaflets. Some forms have narrow, almost grasslike leaflets, while others are wider, looser, and even pendent.

The species is tender to cold and adaptable only to zones 10b and 11 and is marginal in 10a. The clumps usually have a stiff but elegant aspect that is best as an accent or silhouette. Unpruned, the stems are densely clustered and usually provide a wall of leaves from top to bottom of the clump; if judiciously thinned the beauty of the silhouette is greatly enhanced. PLATES 241 & 242.

Chamaedorea stolonifera is endemic to the state of Chiapas in Mexico, where it grows in rain forest from elevations of 2000 to 2640 feet. It is highly endangered as its habitat is being cleared primarily for coffee growing. It was thought to be extinct until David Besst rediscovered it in the 1980s. The epithet is Latin for "stolon-bearing."

This is a clustering species whose stems sprout from creeping stolons near the surface of the soil, creating single clumps to 30 feet across. The stems can grow to 6 feet high but are 0.25 inch in diameter; they are a solid deep green with widely spaced nodes that each produce a single leaf. The few leaves extend downwards from the top of the trunk for several nodes like those of a bamboo or other type of grass. They are each 1 foot long on 2-inch-long thin petioles. The blade is simple, unsegmented, very deeply bifid apically; and medium to deep green, and the two segments are grooved and bear widely spaced shallow indentations.

The little palm makes one of the best groundcovers for a shady or partially shady site, needing only lots of moisture and a nearly tropical climate. It thrives on slightly alkaline soils but adapts to slightly acidic ones also and, while it doesn't grow terribly fast, can nevertheless cover a lot of space in a year's time. PLATE 243.

Chamaedorea stricta occurs naturally in three disjunct regions: in Mexico in the state of Chiapas and adjacent Guatemala, in northeastern Costa Rica, and in central Panama, where it grows in low mountainous rain forest. The epithet is Latin for "erect" and refers to the inflorescences.

The solitary trunk grows to 4 feet high but is stumpy and usually nonapparent in habitat because of other vegetation as well as leaf litter. The leaves are outstandingly beautiful and are undivided except at the bifid apex. They are stiff, ascending, 2 or more feet long on 1- to 2-foot-long petioles, and are linear-oblong, a glossy dark green above and beneath, and deeply corrugated—they look like those of bird-of-paradise, *Strelitzia reginae*. Growing from the leaf crown, the inflorescences usually appear to spring from the ground itself. They are taller than the leaves and consist of a long erect peduncle at the end of which is a spray of a few short, spidery branches. Female plants exhibit coral-colored branches and small, white berrylike fruits.

Chamaedorea sullivaniorum is a small solitary-trunked species from the rain forest of Costa Rica and western Panama, where it is in danger of extinction because of collecting for the nursery trade. The epithet honors Pauline and Joe Sullivan of California.

The short trunk is usually less than 1 foot tall, decumbent, and not readily apparent. The 1-foot-long leaves on 6-inch-long petioles are undivided and generally oblong, broken only by the 4-inch-long apical cleft. The thick, leathery blade is deep green with a velvety sheen and bears distinct ribs corresponding to the fused pinnate segments; its margin is toothed. There is often a suffusion of darker hues from the midrib, and the refraction of light along the ribs sometimes results in a reddish or purplish tint.

This little gem does not tolerate cold and is adaptable only to zones 10b and 11 and in 10a with protection. It is also intolerant of full sun in any climate and needs constant moisture in a free-draining, humus-laden soil.

Chamaedorea tenella is a rare and endangered species with a disjunct distribution in the Mexican states of Veracruz and Chiapas and in southeastern Costa Rica, where it grows in mountainous rain forest from sea level to an elevation of 3200 feet. The epithet is Latin for "little slender."

This palm is one of the smallest species in the genus, growing slowly to a maximum height of 6 feet. The leaves are 8 inches long on 1- to 3-inch-long petioles. The leaf is entire and apically bifid, glossy deep green, with heavy striations of nerves. PLATE 244.

Chamaedorea tepejilote is widespread from the rain forest of southern Mexico, through Central America, and into extreme northwestern Colombia. The epithet is the aboriginal name for the palm in El Salvador.

This species is usually found in nature as a solitary-trunked tree, but there are many clustering individuals. Mature trunks may be 10 to 22 feet tall and 0.5 to more than 3 inches in diameter; most individuals have a loose, indistinct crownshaft. Even when very tall, the stems are straight and noble looking. They are light to medium green and prominently ringed. The leaf crown is sparse and 10 feet wide but 3 feet tall. The leaves are beautifully arching, 5 to 6 feet long, on short thin petioles that are no more than 18 inches long and usually less than 12 inches. The leaflets are 2 feet long, lanceolate with long tapering ends, and S shaped. They are light to dark green and mostly pendent from the rachis, although they grow in only one plane. The edible inflorescences are 2 feet long with pendent branches arising from beneath the crownshaft and carrying yellow flowers; the male inflorescences are thinner than the females. Cultivars in Central America

are grown for their larger, tastier inflorescences. The fruits are 0.5 inch wide, rounded, and black. A species with such a widespread natural range must be expected to be variable in form; in this case the variation is in the size of the leaves and the shape and number of leaflets.

This palm does not tolerate cold and is adaptable only to zones 10b and 11 with some specimens found in favorable microclimates of 10a. Because of its large, beautifully arching leaves, it is among the most tropical looking species in the genus. It is unparalleled as a canopy-scape, and it is stunning in groups of three or more individuals of varying heights. PLATES 245–248.

Chamaedorea tuerckheimii occurs naturally in the premontane rain forest of the Mexican states of Oaxaca and Veracruz and in northeastern Guatemala. The species is nearly extinct in the wild due to collection for the nursery trade. Common names are potato chip palm and ruffled palm, the latter of which is often applied to *Aiphanes* species. The epithet is a Latinized form of the surname "von Tuerkheim" and commemorates the original collector of the plant.

This species is solitary trunked but usually under 3 feet tall overall, with stems that are 0.25 inch in diameter and often recumbent. The leaf crown is compact because of the short petioles and in many specimens is almost a rosette. The leaves are 7 inches long, 3 inches wide, undivided, shortly bifid apically, and obovate, with shallowly toothed margins; they are strongly grooved above and beneath and exhibit a prominent, lighter colored midrib. Leaf color is light to dark green above and grayish green beneath; the grooves are so deep that they often create highlights and shadows in a way that the blade seems to be variously hued. The inflorescences are sparsely branched and bear white blossoms that yield small, egg-shaped black fruits.

This palm is not hardy to cold and is adaptable only to zones 10b and 11, being marginal in 10a. It is small enough to be easily protected in even colder climates. Because it is so small, it should only be planted in intimate sites and, if possible, with other foliage of a contrasting color. PLATE 249.

Chamaedorea warscewiczii is indigenous to mountainous rain forest in Costa Rica and Panama. The epithet honors Josef Warscewicz, a 19th-century palm botanist in South America who introduced this species to cultivation.

It is a solitary-trunked species to 12 feet high but 1 inch in diameter. There is no true crownshaft, but the leaf sheaths are prominent and persistent. The leaf crown is extended along the upper part of the trunk with 2-foot-long leaves on 1-foot-long petioles. The widely spaced leaflets are broadly ovate with long drip tips and are glossy, deep emerald green on both surfaces; the apical pair of leaflets is usually significantly wider than the others. The inflorescences grow from the extended leaf crown and consist of long, erect peduncles at the tips of which are the long, pendent, spidery ropelike yellow-green branches. The fruits are round, black, and 0.5 inch wide.

Chamaedorea woodsoniana has a large natural range from southern Mexico, through Central America, and into Colombia, where it grows in montane rain forest. The epithet honors a 20th-century plant collector, Robert E. Woodson.

This species grows to 40 feet high with a green and distinctly ringed trunk to 4 inches in diameter, atop which sits an attractive green crownshaft that is usually swollen at its base. The leaves are 3 to 4 feet long on 1-foot-long petioles. The linear leaflets grow from the rachis at an angle to form a V-shaped leaf; they are deep green above and slightly paler beneath. The inflorescences are much branched and coral red, as are the pendulous clusters of fruit.

This beautiful tree is adaptable only to zones 10 and 11.

CHAMAEROPS is a monotypic genus of variable fan-leaved, mostly dioecious palm in dry parts of the Mediterranean region. It is usually a clumping species, but some individuals remain naturally solitary trunked. It has the distinction of being the world's most northerly occurring palm species. The genus name is derived from two Greek words meaning "dwarf" and "shrub," an allusion to the size of the plant. PLATES 250–253.

Chamaerops humilis occurs naturally on the Atlantic coasts of Spain, Portugal, and extreme northwestern Africa; the Mediterranean coasts of Spain, France, Italy, Albania, and northwestern and north central Africa; and the islands of Corsica, Sardinia, Sicily, and Malta. It grows mostly in coastal areas, including rocky foothills near the sea, but also extends up into the Atlas Mountains of Morocco to elevations slightly above 5280 feet. Two common names are European fan palm and Mediterranean fan palm. The epithet is Latin for "humble" or "small."

The trunks vary from almost dwarf sized to 20 feet high. The mature larger trunks usually have a diameter of 1 foot and are covered in all except the oldest parts with a dense mat of dark gray to dark brown or almost black fibers from the old leaf bases, which create the effect of large, dark, tightly packed scales. The leaf crown is 10 feet wide and tall. Mature clumps are 25 feet tall and 30 feet wide, with full rounded crowns, the dead leaves adherent only near the base of the crown. Leaves are 3 feet wide, a little more than half circular, with several dozen narrow, stiff, and tapering segments which extend two-thirds or

more into the blade. They are carried on stiff petioles from 2 to 5 feet long and are margined with vicious forward-pointing spines. Leaf color ranges from deep grassy green through shades of grayish green and bluish green. The small, erect panicles of yellow flowers grow from the leaf crown and are 6 inches long; they are mostly hidden by the leaves. The plants are usually dioecious, but some individuals bear both male and female blossoms. The fruits are 0.5 inch wide, round, yellow-orange or brown, and are formed in slightly pendulous clusters.

The species is slow growing and drought tolerant, and succeeds in several well-drained soils. It withstands temperatures to 15°F, especially in dry climates; suckering individuals survive even lower temperatures but lose most of their aboveground growth and take a long while to grow back, while solitary-trunked individuals are usually wiped out. The European fan palm is not at home in moist, tropical climates where its growth is slower and where it fails to develop its full set of characteristics. Transplanting of rooted suckers is occasionally successful.

Single-trunked plants are best used as a canopy-scape; they look unnatural as isolated specimens, although a sort of architectural effect is obtained from them, especially as outdoor tub subjects. Clustering plants are picturesque enough to be planted as isolated specimens or as formal architectural specimens in large raised planters. Old clumps create a tableau that is the essence of luxuriance and the semiarid tropical look. As a silhouette against a large wall or differently colored foliage, nothing is better. This palm is not a good choice for growing indoors as the plants tend to decay without good air circulation and bright light.

This variable species has at least one naturally occurring form with waxy and silvery leaves: *Chamaerops humilis* **var.** *cerifera*. The epithet is Latin for "wax-bearing." In most individuals, the leaves are silver on both surfaces. This variety seems to be slower growing than the type but also may be hardier to cold and drought. *Chamaerops humilis* **var.** *elatior* never suckers. The epithet is Latin for "tall," although the single trunks grow no taller than do those of the largest clumping forms.

CHAMBEYRONIA is a genus of two pinnate-leaved, solitary-trunked, monoecious palms in New Caledonia. One is rare in habitat and reportedly difficult in cultivation. The other species is gaining popularity because of its unique beauty. The genus honors a 19th-century naval officer, Charles M.-L. Chambeyron, who mapped the coast of New Caledonia and assisted Eugène Vieillard with the latter's palm collecting therein. PLATES 254–256.

Chambeyronia lepidota is endemic to wet mountainous forests in northeastern New Caledonia. The epithet is

Latin for "scaly," a reference to the surface of the large crownshaft.

The brown, indistinctly ringed trunk grows to 35 feet high and 6 inches in diameter. The remarkable crownshaft is 3 feet tall, fat, and distinctly bulging at the base, and covered in a chocolate-red feltlike tomentum with lighter striations. The leaf crown is mostly a semicircle, and the 6-foot-long, arching leaves are reminiscent of those of *Hedyscepe*; they are stiffly arching, with many dark green linear-lanceolate leaflets growing from the reddish brown rachis at an angle that gives a V-shaped leaf. The red fruits are produced on inflorescences that are the color and texture of the crownshaft.

Because of the unusual soil on which it grows in habitat, this palm is difficult to establish in cultivation and few individuals exist outside their native haunts. It doubtless needs copious moisture and probably partial shade when young. It is not tolerant of frost but would probably do well in cool but nearly frost-free Mediterranean climates.

The tree has an unusually beautiful architectural aspect and would be stunning as a small canopy-scape or an intimate close-up subject.

Chambeyronia macrocarpa is endemic to rain forest on the island of New Caledonia at elevations from 2000 to 3000 feet. Several growers have coined the moniker redleaf palm because some specimens have a colored new leaf; alas, many pinnate-leaved palms have this characteristic. The names red feather palm and flame palm are also gaining acceptance. The epithet is Greek for "large" and "fruit."

Trunks grow to at least 40 feet tall and have a diameter of 10 inches. They are gray to greenish gray with widely spaced light-colored rings. The crownshaft is 3 to 4 feet high, bulging at its base, and deep emerald green. The circular leaf crown is 8 feet wide and tall. It is among the most beautiful forms in the palm family and has 8 or 10 leaves, which are 12 feet long and wonderfully arching up, down, and back towards the trunks. Each of the widely spaced 3- to 5-foot-long linear-oblong leaflets tapers to a full point and grows from the rachis in a single plane. The petiole is usually less than 1 foot long, and the leaflets are heavily veined with a prominent midrib and two lateral veins, giving an almost pleated look to each pinna. Mature leaves are deep bluish green, but newly emerging leaves are often highly colored in shades of carmine red, orange, scarlet, purplish red, or bronzy purple. The inflorescences are 1-foot-long erect panicles that emerge from beneath the crownshaft and carry green and white large flowers. The fruits are 2 inches wide and round or slightly egg shaped, and deep red when mature, hanging on pendent branches.

The species is a water lover and needs a rich, humus-laden, well-drained soil. It is relatively fast growing but not hardy outside of zones 10 and 11 without protection. It relishes partial shade, especially when young or in hot climates.

Besides having gorgeously colored leaves, this palm has an even more incredibly beautiful form: a tall and straight, light-colored trunk topped by a perfectly round crown of a few large and gloriously arching leaves with their widely spaced and wide leaflets—circles within circles. It should receive a favored spot in any planting and is unparalleled for up-close viewing. It looks best as a canopy-scape but is so slow growing that it will probably be first planted as an isolated specimen, and it is extraordinarily beautiful enough to be aesthetically pleasing as such. The species is well adapted to cultivation under glass with abundant moisture, a well-draining medium, and lots of light.

Chambeyronia macrocarpa is morphologically variable in nature, and this variability mostly corresponds with particular geographical locations in New Caledonia. Pintaud (2000) points out that there are very tall forms to 90 or more feet in the southern part of the island, a form with a green- and yellow-striped crownshaft (known as the watermelon type), a form with a yellow crownshaft, a form which never has red new growth, and a form that is especially stout and robust and has a crownshaft covered with white tomentum. PLATES 254–256.

CHELYOCARPUS is a genus of four palmate-leaved, monoecious palms in lowland rain forest of South America. The species are solitary trunked and clustering, with trunks that are smooth and clean except for their newest parts. All species have circular leaves divided nearly to the petiole into pleated and wedge-shaped segments; the overall appearance of a leaf is like a pinwheel with 40 or more marginal indentations. Anatomically the blade has two main segments, but they are not always obvious to the untrained eye. Because of their long petioles, the two taller species have sumptuously beautiful leaf crowns with the "pinwheels" gloriously displayed. The inflorescences grow from the leaf sheaths and are branched once or twice. The flowers of some species are perfect, and all but one is pleasantly fragrant. The attractive fruits are green, brown, or yellowish and succulent looking.

These palms are beautiful because of their large pinwheel-like leaves. All species are tender to cold and adaptable only to zones 10b and 11. They need copious water and a rich, humus-laden, well-drained soil. The palms luxuriate in partial shade (especially when young) or full sun. They are still rare in cultivation.

The genus name is from Greek words meaning "turtle" and "fruit," a reference to the corky, cracked surface of the fruits of *C. ulei*, the most widespread species. PLATE 257.

Chelyocarpus chuco is found in the Amazon regions of extreme northern Bolivia and west central Brazil, where it grows in swamps and seasonally inundated forests. The epithet is one of the aboriginal names for the palm.

This primarily clustering species has stems to 60 feet high. It sports a sparse crown of 5-foot-wide, circular leaves with 40 or more segments; leaf color is deep green on both sides. The leaf segments are the most uniform in size of the genus.

The species is slightly susceptible to lethal yellowing disease. PLATE 257.

Chelyocarpus dianeurus is endemic to the low mountainous rain forest of western Colombia. The epithet is derived from Latin words meaning "two" and "nerve," an allusion to the leaf segments.

The palm attains heights of 50 feet or more and is similar in general appearance to *C. ulei*. The leaves are 4 or 5 feet wide, deep green above, and grayish green beneath; the blade is divided into 10 wedge-shaped segments of varying widths, one of which is usually significantly wider than the rest. Each segment has a deep but rounded apical cleft.

Chelyocarpus repens is endemic to northern Peru near the city of Iquitos, where it grows in lowland rain forest near the Amazon River, often in the seasonally inundated parts. The epithet is Latin for "creeping" and refers to the trunks.

The trunks are 3 feet long and 4 inches in diameter. The leaves are 4 to 6 feet in diameter and have 10 wedge-shaped segments that are cut to the petiole and incised apically into four to six deep triangular indentations. The segments are pale olive green above but grayish green to almost bluish green beneath; they resemble the leaves of many *Licuala* species.

Chelyocarpus ulei is indigenous to western Ecuador, southeastern Colombia, and Peru, where it occurs in the lowland rain forest of the Amazon region. The epithet honors Ernst H. G. Ule (1854–1915), a botanist and the original collector of the species.

This palm grows to 20 feet high and has beautiful, 4- or 5-foot-wide leaves with 6 to 12 segments that are cleft to the petiole. Leaf color is deep green above and silvery or even bluish green beneath because of the white tomentum. These leaves give the typical and thrilling pinwheel effect. The blossoms are not pleasantly fragrant to most people; Harold E. Moore, Jr. (1972), described the odor as that of fishmeal or burning rubber.

CHUNIOPHOENIX is a genus of two clustering, monoecious palms in China and Vietnam. It is among the few genera of palmate-leaved palms whose leaves do not have hastulas. The leaves are deeply divided almost to the peti-ole into segments of varying widths and numbers. The inflorescences grow from the leaf bases and are spikelike and once branched, but the important character for ornamental plantings is that they produce deep orange to red fruits; alas the latter are mostly hidden by the leaf crown.

These palms are amazingly hardy for their tropical origins; both species have withstood temperatures in the mid and upper 20s (F) in central Florida without damage.

The genus name is derived from the surname of W. Y. Chun, a director of the botanical institute in Canton, and the Greek word for "date palm." PLATES 258 & 259.

Chuniophoenix hainanensis is indigenous to the island of Hainan, off the southern coast of China, and the adjacent mainland, where it grows in low mountainous evergreen forest. It is highly endangered because of expanding agriculture. The epithet is Latin for "of Hainan."

Although this palm is a robust-looking clumper, the clumps are not that wide. The trunks grow to 10 feet high and 6 inches in diameter. The leaves are 4 feet wide on 3-foot-long petioles. The many segments are roughly equally sized and deep grayish green; they extend almost to the petiole and are mostly shallowly bifid at their apices. The inflorescence is not noticeable because it grows from the center of the leaf crown and is short. What is usually noticeable is the unpleasant odor of the maroon blossoms it bears. The fruits are 1 inch wide, deep red when mature, and more readily visible in larger specimens than smaller ones.

The species seems at home on calcareous soils but needs supplemental water in drought. It also relishes partial shade but grows well in full sun except in the hottest climates. It should be sited where the wind does not tear its paperlike leaves. PLATE 258.

Chuniophoenix nana is indigenous to southernmost China and adjacent Vietnam, where it grows in low mountainous rain forest. The epithet is Latin for "diminutive."

This species grows to 3 or 4 feet high. It looks like a small clump of lady palm (*Rhapis excelsa*) with its tightly clustering, slender canes and similar leaves. The circular leaves have six widely separated segments, which are thin, glossy medium green, and distinctly ribbed.

This tiny undergrowth species does not like full sun, especially in hot climates. It also prefers a slightly acidic, humus-laden soil, although a mulch usually works well. The palm is not drought tolerant. PLATE 259.

CLINOSPERMA is a monotypic genus of pinnate-leaved, monoecious palm. The genus name is derived from two Greek words meaning "slanted" and "seed." The epithet is Latin for "with bracts," referring to the inflorescence. PLATE 260.

Clinosperma bracteale is endemic to rain forest of southern and central New Caledonia from sea level to an elevation of 3800 feet.

It is a solitary-trunked species whose stems attain heights near 50 feet and uniform diameters of 4 inches. The stems are light gray to light tan and show distinct darker rings of leaf base scars except in their oldest parts. The unusual and loosely formed 2-foot-tall crownshaft is often white, sometimes greenish and white, because of the waxy covering of small scales, but it may also be mauve or light brown to dark brown due to the amount of chocolate tomentum thereon. Its most unusual feature, however, is its almost triangular shape, as it usually bulges near the base but on one side only. The leaf crown is sparse and open with spreading light green leaves that seldom lie beneath the horizontal. The petioles are 1 foot or slightly more in length and hold 5-foot-long leaves that arch only near their tips. The leaflets are regularly spaced along the rachis, are 3 feet long, stiff, and linear-lanceolate, and grow from the rachis at a slight angle to give a shallow V shape to the leaf. Beautiful once-branched inflorescences grow from beneath the crownshaft. The flowering branches are knobby and deep wine red maturing to medium red; they look like an undersea branching coral. The tiny yellowish white flowers of both sexes, followed by the shiny, round green fruits that mature to black, add to the general colorfulness.

The palm needs copious and regular moisture but is not fussy about soil type as long as it is well drained and not too calcareous. It luxuriates in partial shade or full sun except in hot, especially dry climes.

In spite of its tall stature, this beauty has a miniature look about it that is neat, orderly, and appealing. It's hard to misplace it in the landscape. It's also hard to find it for sale and it is, alas, slow growing, especially when young.

CLINOSTIGMA is a genus of 13 pinnate-leaved, monoecious palms in the South Pacific islands. They are solitary-trunked, mostly tall species that inhabit rain forest, from sea level to an elevation of more than 5280 feet. All have prominent crownshafts and leaves with usually pendent leaflets, and most have stilt roots at the bases of their trunks. The short-peduncled inflorescences grow from beneath the crownshafts, are much branched, and bear unisexual flowers of both sexes.

These species are still rare in cultivation, especially in the Western Hemisphere, but are among the most beautiful things the natural world has to offer, and all are more than worthy of cultivation in tropical climates. None are frost tolerant and, while some can adapt to the temperatures of frostless Mediterranean climates, they need such abundant and regular moisture as well as such high hu-

midity that they are seldom grown there. They do not like alkaline soils, which limits their use in southern Florida, unless the soil is amended with humus or the trees are mulched with organic material. Since they start out as undergrowth plants, they relish shade when young and are not adapted to hot and dry climates at any age. None of these species are fast growing but neither are they terribly slow. The species from higher elevations are at their prime in regions similar to the wetter parts of the Hawaiian Islands.

The genus name is from Latin words meaning "inclined" and "stigma," an allusion to details of the female blossoms. PLATES 261–263.

Clinostigma exorrhizum is endemic to the Fiji Islands, where it grows in mountainous rain forest at elevations of 800 to 4000 feet. The epithet is from Greek words meaning "outside of" and "root," an allusion to the prominent stilt roots.

This species grows to a maximum overall height of 70 feet with a diameter of 1 foot. The palm anchors itself to the wet slopes on which it grows by spiny stilt roots at the base of its trunk that may be 10 feet tall. The crownshaft is 6 feet tall, light green to light bluish green, of slightly greater diameter than the trunk, and usually uniform in diameter. The spreading leaves are slightly but beautifully arching, 15 feet long, and borne on 2-foot-long petioles; the rachises do not usually fall below the horizontal but the great pendulous leaflets create nevertheless an almost globular crown. The regularly spaced 3-foot-long deep green leaflets are linear-lanceolate, long tipped, and pendulous from the rachis. The small ovoid fruits are red or pink when mature.

No palm has a more beautiful leaf crown than this one.

Clinostigma gronophyllum is endemic to the tiny island of Guadalcanal in the Solomon Islands, where it grows on ridges at elevations of 4000 to 6000 feet in wet rain forest. The epithet was bestowed by Harold E. Moore, Jr., because the leaf crown is similar to that of *Gronophyllum chaunostachys* and because the leaves are unusual for the genus *Clinostigma*.

The trunk grows to a height of 70 feet but is less than 1 foot in diameter. It is green and waxy in its youngest parts with lighter-colored rings of leaf base scars, but gray and smooth in its older parts. A 4-foot-tall tight cone of thick, reddish brown stilt roots supports it. The crownshaft is 4 feet tall, slightly bulging near its base, and tapering gently to its summit. It is light green except near its summit where it is usually suffused with light purple. The leaf crown is full and rounded because of the 8- or 9-foot-long leaves that are greatly arching on 1-foot-long petioles. The stiff, 4-foot-long leaflets are pendent at their tips and grow from the rachis at a steep angle, giving a V-shaped leaf. They are generally similar to the leaves of *Actinorhytis calapparia*.

This species is reportedly extremely sensitive to cold.

Clinostigma harlandii is endemic to the Vanuatu islands, where it grows in rain forest at elevations of 1300 to 4500 feet. The epithet honors A. E. Harland, the palm's 19th-century original collector.

The trunk attains a height of 80 feet and a diameter of 1 foot. It is green in its youngest parts with closely set whitish rings of leaf base scars, and is light gray in the older parts. A 6-foot-tall cone of stilt roots supports it. The 4-foot-tall crownshaft bulges at the base but above that is scarcely wider than the trunk and is cylindrical; it is light yellowish or even orange glaucous green to pure emerald green at the base but light green or almost white near its summit. The leaf crown and leaves are similar to those of *C. exorrhizum* but lighter colored. The tiny round fruits are deep red when mature. PLATE 261.

Clinostigma ponapensis is endemic to Ponapei, one of the Caroline Islands east of the Philippines, where it grows in mountainous rain and cloud forest. The epithet is Latin for "of Ponapei."

The trunk is mostly light grayish green except for the oldest parts that are almost white. It attains a height of 60 feet in habitat and is beautifully ringed with brownish leaf base scars in its younger parts. A spreading, 4- or 5-foot-tall mass of stilt roots supports the trunk. The crownshaft is 6 feet tall, slightly bulging at its base, and a uniform mint green. The leaf crown is sparse and hemispherical, with no more than 10 leaves at any time. The leaves are 15 feet long, spreading, and arching at their tips. The many evenly spaced glossy dark green leaflets are 4 or 5 feet long, linear-lanceolate, S shaped, and, as in most of the other species in the genus, pendent in trees past the seedling stage, making them one of the world's most beautiful palm leaves.

The species is extraordinarily beautiful and, in silhouette, looks like a gigantic tree fern. It does not tolerate drought or freezing temperatures and is hardy in zones 10b and 11.

Clinostigma samoense is endemic to Samoa, where it grows in low mountainous rain forest. The epithet is Latin for "of Samoa."

The tan, heavily ringed trunk attains a height of 50 feet and a diameter of 1 foot. The leaf crown is among the most beautiful in the palm world: it is semirounded and slightly more than hemispherical, with 15- to 20-foot-long spreading, ascending leaves that are slightly arched at their tips. The many leaflets are a uniform deep green, regularly spaced along the rachis, and 3 to 4 feet long; they are also linear-lanceolate and pendent.

There is no more beautiful palm species. PLATE 262.

Clinostigma savoryanum is endemic to the Bonin Archipelago (Ogasawara Islands) southeast of the main Japanese islands, where it grows in low mountainous rain forest. The epithet honors Nathaniel Savory, a 19th-century adventurer from Massachusetts and founder of one of the first colonies in the archipelago.

This is among the smaller species in the genus, the trunks attaining a height of 40 feet. They are tan in their older parts, deep green in their younger parts, and relatively slender at 10 inches in diameter. The 4- to 5-foot-tall crownshaft bulges slightly at its base and is a light glaucous mint green to almost white. The 10-foot-long leaves on short petioles form a slightly more than hemispherical crown; they are typically ascending, spreading, and slightly arching, with 3-foot-long narrowly lanceolate pendent leaflets that are regularly spaced along the rachis.

While the habitat of the species is mostly extratropical geographically, it is climatically tropical, and the palm is as tender to cold as are the other species in the genus. PLATE 263.

COCCOTHRINAX is a genus of 14 to 49 palmate-leaved, small to medium, monoecious palms. Many are probably naturally occurring hybrids or minor gradations of a type; indeed, *Coccothrinax* is even reported to hybridize with *Thrinax* in cultivation. All the species are indigenous to the Caribbean Basin, southern Florida, and the Yucatán Peninsula of Mexico. They include solitary-trunked as well as clustering species, whose trunks are covered in the younger parts with long, spinelike fibers. The leaves are mostly circular and usually silvery beneath. A salient characteristic is that the branched inflorescences usually exceed the leaf crown and are twice branched, bearing bisexual flowers.

All species are drought tolerant and of unusual beauty, their only drawback being that they are uniformly slow growing. They are relatively cold hardy, most of them being adaptable to zones 9b through 11. Almost all species tolerate salinity in the soil and air.

The genus name comes from the Greek word for "berry" and the related genus name *Thrinax*, which these palms resemble. The species are all called thatch palms for their use in making thatched roofs. PLATES 264–285.

Coccothrinax argentata occurs naturally in southern Florida and the Bahamas, where it grows in open woods, grasslands, and coastal dunes. Common names are silver thatch palm, silver palm, silvertop palm, and Florida silver palm. The epithet is Latin for "silvery."

This is a solitary-trunked species whose mature trunks grow to 20 feet with a diameter of 6 inches; the upper part of the stem is covered with matted dark brown fiber that often hangs in wide patches from the leaf axils. The leaf crown is no more than 6 feet wide and 8 feet tall. The leaves are circular to half-circular on 2-foot-long petioles, 3 feet wide, with deep lanceolate segments that are pendulous at their tips, a shiny deep green above and a silvery to a metallic brownish green beneath. The 2-foot-long inflorescences are branched and borne among the leaves, and bear yellowish white bisexual flowers. The fruits are 0.5 inch wide, rounded, and black.

Like most other *Coccothrinax* species, this one relishes full sun and is not particular about soil type, thriving under limey conditions. Being drought tolerant, it needs a quickly draining medium. It is adaptable to zones 9b through 11 and, while sometimes briefly surviving in colder regions, grows slowly enough that its long-term survival in the landscape is doubtful, especially in wetter climates, where fungus attacks can be fatal.

There is something alluring about the beautiful rounded, glossy dark green and silvery leaves of almost all *Coccothrinax* palms, and this one is no exception. It looks especially good in groups of three or more individuals of varying heights and is superb in a patio or courtyard where it can be seen up close. This one, like all the others, is superb as a canopy-scape, and few landscape subjects are as beautiful and as immune to saline conditions as the thatch palm, making it a perfect candidate for the seashore. It is not known to be grown indoors and would seem to be a poor candidate for such.

Coccothrinax argentea is endemic to Hispaniola, where it grows in grasslands and low altitude pinelands. Common names are Hispaniolan silver thatch palm and Dominican silver thatch palm. The epithet is Latin for "silver," an allusion to the leaf underside.

The trunks of this mostly solitary-trunked species can attain a height of 30 feet but are more commonly 20 feet tall. They are 8 inches in diameter, and the younger parts are covered with a mat of tightly woven dark gray to dark brown or black fibers from the old leafstalks. Total height of a solitary-trunked specimen is 35 feet with a crown width to 15 feet and a height of 8 to 10 feet. The leaves are to 5 feet wide, perfectly circular, with many narrowly lanceolate, long tapering segments divided nearly to the center of the blade; the segments are slightly pendent at their tips and are a deep, shiny green above with a striking silvery hue beneath. The leaves are carried on petioles that are 4 to 5 feet long, which gives an open, graceful appearance to the crown. The 1-foot-long branched inflorescence hangs slightly below the leaf crown and bears small yellow–white bisexual blossoms. The fruits are 0.5 inch wide, round, and black when mature, and are borne in small pendent clusters.

Individuals on the northern coast of the Dominican Republic are larger than the others and usually have trunks with swollen bases (Henderson et al. 1995).

The species grows well in most well-draining soils, even calcareous ones. It is not hardy to cold and is adapted to zones 10 and 11. Full sun is important even for seedlings.

This is among the most graceful palms, and it is taller than most other *Coccothrinax* species. Its leaf crown is perhaps the most beautiful in the genus, providing breathtaking little starburst effects when the tree is planted en masse, and scintillating in the breeze to show off the silvery undersides. A single plant works well in an intimate space and is superb as a canopy-scape. It is not known to be grown indoors and would probably be difficult to do so; without extremely good air circulation, it would be subject to disease. PLATES 264 & 265.

Coccothrinax "azul" is an unnamed species from central Cuba, where it grows in serpentine soils with *C. clarensis*. The name *azul* comes from the coloration of the leaves, which are bluish silver above and whitish silver below. Many palms that grow in serpentine soils show unusual bluish tendencies, but no other *Coccothrinax* species has leaves that are this blue, which is as at least as intense as that of the blue forms of *Bismarckia*.

The palm grows slowly to a height of perhaps 20 feet with a trunk diameter of no more than 5 inches. The fiber is particularly stiff and needlelike. The leaves are V shaped and not as stiff as those of some other species.

Whether this palm becomes a separate taxon or is lumped with another species, it appears to have several distinct taxonomic characters. It would be a stunning addition to the landscape even though it would take years to grow from seed to a size where it could be really appreciated. PLATES 266 & 267.

Coccothrinax barbadensis occurs naturally in the Lesser Antilles, including the islands of Barbados, Trinidad, and Tobago, and northernmost Venezuela, where it grows on calcareous soils in scrubland not far from the coast. It is sometimes called silver palm. The epithet translates from the Latin as "of Barbados."

This is a solitary-trunked species with trunks to 40 feet high, making it one of the largest species in the genus, although the trunk is never more than 6 inches in diameter and thus very delicate looking. The leaf crown is 6 feet wide and 5 feet tall. The leaves are 3 feet wide, circular, with the narrowly lanceolate, tapering segments reaching only halfway to the center of the blade; they are pendulous at their ends. Leaf color is deep, shiny olive green to emerald green above but with an almost chromium-like silvery and shiny hue beneath. Inflorescences are 2 feet long and pendent, drooping slightly below the leaf crown. They bear small white bisexual flowers. The fruits are 0.5 inch wide, round, and black when mature.

The palm has the same cultural requirements as the two previously described species. It is not hardy to cold outside of zones 10 and 11, although some protected specimens exist in 9b. PLATE 268.

Coccothrinax borhidiana is an endangered species endemic to Cuba, where it grows in scrublands near the ocean. The epithet honors Hungarian botanist Atilla Borhidi, who wrote a flora of Cuba.

This is a solitary-trunked species growing, with great age, to a maximum height of 15 feet in habitat, the trunk usually clothed in a heavy skirt of dead leaves. The leaves are borne on short petioles, and the leaf crown is tight and dense and, from any distance, causes the palm to look much like a yucca. Each leaf is almost circular with stiff linear, pointed segments that are a deep to bluish green above and a lighter hue beneath. From the side, the leaves appear to be in tight tiers. The inflorescences rise well above the leaf crown and become pendulous when the round, purplish fruits mature.

The palm is hardy in zones 10 and 11, needs full sun, and is drought tolerant and somewhat accepting of salinity. It grows in well-drained alkaline soils.

The small tree is distinctive looking with its tight leaf crown and is suitable for the cactus or succulent garden or, when immature, set near a path or other site where it can be seen up close. Although it grows in sparse stands in open areas in its native haunts, it does not lend itself to specimen planting in an open space. PLATES 269–272.

Coccothrinax crinita is endemic to Cuba, where it grows in monsoonal grasslands and hillsides, and where it is threatened because of its few numbers and restricted range. Common names are old man palm, old man thatch palm, and mat palm. The epithet is Latin for "hairy."

This is a solitary-trunked species whose stems attain a height of 25 feet with great age and a diameter of 10 inches; if the trunk retains its fibrous covering, it appears to be of greater width. The most distinctive characteristic is the shag of light to dark brown, long fibers that envelop the trunks; the fibers look like a loosely combed brown wig up close. Only old trunks that are subject to wind lose this covering. The rounded leaf crown is 8 feet wide and tall. The leaves are to 5 feet wide and circular, and are carried on 4-foot-long petioles. The segments extend to three-fourths of the way to the center of the blade and are narrowly lanceolate and rigid. Leaf color is dark, shiny green above and silvery green beneath. Flower clusters are 5 feet long and extend beneath the leaf crown, bearing yellow bisexual flowers. The fruits are rounded, 1 inch

wide, and black when mature. Some taxonomists recognize two subspecies based on the length of the leaf base fibers.

The palm has the same cultural requirements as the preceding three species with the possible exception that it is not as drought tolerant. It also seems to be more cold tolerant than the other species and is grown successfully in zones 9b through 11.

Because of its unusual trunk, old man palm is not as easy to place in the landscape as are the other species. It is nice in small groups of individuals of varying heights, and can be a conversation piece when planted where it can be enjoyed up close. It is not known to be grown indoors. PLATES 273–275.

Coccothrinax ekmanii occurs naturally in southwestern Dominican Republic, where it grows on limestone hills in scrublands near the coast. The epithet is a Latinized form of the surname "Ekman" and honors a 20th-century plant collector.

This is one of the tallest solitary-trunked species, attaining a maximum height of 50 feet in habitat. The leaves are no more than half circular, with narrow, stiff segments that are deep green above, distinctly silvery hued beneath, and accompanied by numerous spiny fibers. The inflorescences are short, heavy, and pendent, hanging beneath the leaf crown. The fruits are round and brown.

The palm is hardy only to zones 10 and 11. It thrives in alkaline soil, needs full sun, and is drought tolerant once established.

The size of this species makes it suitable for specimen plantings in groups of three or more individuals of varying heights. It also is a wonderful canopy-scape.

Coccothrinax gracilis is endemic to Hispaniola, where it grows in open coastal areas on limestone near sea level. The epithet is Latin for "graceful."

The palm grows to 30 feet in its native haunts. It has leaves that are circular and bright green above but silvery beneath.

It has an airy appearance because of its height and relatively thin trunks. The palm is well suited as a canopy-scape or even in specimen groups of individuals of varying heights. It thrives in full sun in any well-drained soil, but it is not hardy to cold and is only good in zones 10 and 11. PLATE 276.

Coccothrinax gundlachii is endemic to Cuba, where it grows in open savannas or scrublands near the coasts on alkaline soil. It is rare.

The solitary trunk in habitat grows to 30 feet high and 8 inches in diameter and is covered in all but its oldest parts with a beautiful woven pattern of light gray to nearly white closely adhering and often needlelike fibers. The sparse leaf crown is hemispherical or nearly spherical and contains 8 or 10 leaves, which are 3 to 4 feet wide, circular or nearly so, with deeply cleft, long, and narrow pendent segments. Leaf color is glossy deep green above and chalky, light bluish green beneath. The inflorescences are long and mostly erect, extending above the leaf crown. PLATES 277–278.

Coccothrinax hiorami is endemic to eastern Cuba, where it grows in arid calcareous soil.

The trunk grows to 30 feet tall, and the leaves tend to be deeply divided with leaflets somewhat lax. The fiber is open and soft and, with the remnants of the old leaf bases, forms a distinct pattern on the trunk.

This palm would do best in full sun on well-drained alkaline soils.

Coccothrinax miraguama is indigenous to Cuba, where it grows in savannas, open woods, and near the coast. The epithet honors a province in Cuba.

This is a solitary-trunked species whose mature trunks reach a height of 40 feet or more in habitat but under cultivation grow no more than 30 feet with a diameter of 6 inches. An exceptionally beautiful woven mesh design of old leaf fibers and narrowly triangular leaf bases covers younger parts of the stems, while older parts are bare and show closely set rings. The leaf crown is more rounded than that of most other species of *Coccothrinax* and is a maximum of 12 feet wide and 8 feet tall. The leaves are circular or nearly so and to 5 feet wide on 3- to 4-foot-long petioles. The segments extend halfway to the center of the blade, are linear-lanceolate, rigid with a nondrooping end, and slightly V shaped. Leaf color is shiny deep green to almost bluish green above and silvery gray or grayish green beneath. The inflorescences are 3 feet long, branched but barely hanging beneath the leaf crown. The small bisexual flowers are whitish yellow. The fruits are 0.5 inch wide, rounded, and red, maturing to a deep purple or black.

The palm is hardy only in zones 10b and 11 and is marginal in 10a. It needs full sun and grows in most well-drained soils, including calcareous ones.

This species is generally considered the most beautiful in the genus. Its attractions are the wonderful crown of separated, round starburst-shaped leaves with their silvery undersides, the beautiful design of the trunk fibers, and the colorful fruit. The slight V shape to the surfaces of the leaflets creates another beautiful shadow design within each leaf. The palm is exceptionally beautiful in groups of three or more individuals of varying heights and is unexcelled as a canopy-scape. It is among the best close-up landscape subjects or silhouettes for patios, courtyards, and other intimate sites. In addition, the plants are faster grow-

ing than most other *Coccothrinax* species. It is not known to be grown indoors and is probably not a good candidate for such. PLATES 279–281.

Coccothrinax pauciramosa is endemic to eastern Cuba, where it grows in open, serpentine savannas and on limestone hills at low elevations. The epithet is Latin for "few branches," a reference to the inflorescences.

The slender stems of this solitary-trunked species can attain a maximum height of 40 feet but are usually much shorter. They are covered in all but their oldest parts with dense woven dark fibers, some of which are long and spiny. The leaf crown is sparse, each leaf nearly circular with stiff segments that extend more than halfway to the petiole; the blade usually has a silvery sheen on its lower surface.

The little tree needs full sun and is hardy only to zones 10 and 11. It needs a well-draining soil. PLATE 282.

Coccothrinax salvatoris is endemic to eastern Cuba, where it grows along the coast on low limestone hills adjacent to salt marshes. The epithet is a Latinized form of a province in the palm's habitat.

It is a solitary-trunked species whose stems reach 20 to 30 feet high with much thick, woven, and spiny fiber on all but the oldest parts. The leaves are nearly circular with silvery undersides and have stiff segments. PLATES 283 & 284.

Coccothrinax spissa is an endangered endemic of Hispaniola, where it grows in savannas and cleared forest areas. The epithet is Latin for "thick," an allusion to the swollen trunk.

The trunk attains a height of 20 to 30 feet. It is light colored, usually free of leaf bases, smooth, robust, and usually but not always showing a slight to pronounced bulge near the middle of the stem. The leaf crown is sparse and the leaves are semicircular, with deep but limp, pointed, light to deep green segments that exhibit a silvery sheen beneath. The inflorescences grow from among the leaves and are prominent because of the sparse canopy. They are short and branched, and carry yellow blossoms. The fruits are round, 0.5 inch in diameter, and deep purple to nearly black.

The palm is hardy only to zones 10 and 11, being marginal in 10a. It is drought tolerant and not particular about soil type as long as it is well drained. It is slow growing even in full or nearly full sun. PLATE 285.

COCOS is a monotypic genus of pinnate-leaved, monoecious palm now found on all tropical seashores. The genus name is a Portuguese corruption of an aboriginal name meaning "monkey," an allusion to the three facelike depressions at one end of the nut. The common name is coconut palm. The epithet is Latin for "nut-bearing." PLATES 286–291.

Cocos nucifera has been cultivated for so long and was carried to tropical regions at such an early date that its exact places of origin are obscured but are probably the seacoasts of the South Pacific Islands.

The species is solitary trunked, although rarely young plants sucker. Mature trunks can reach a height of 90 to 100 feet. The base of the stem is always swollen and its diameter above that point is nearly constant at 1 foot. The trunks of large palms lean or curve and, especially near the shore, are often prostrate and contorted. They are picturesquely ringed with crescent-shaped leaf base scars, and some individuals exhibit a beautiful color pattern of light gray or almost white trunk with darker scars. The leaf crown is usually round, full, and to 30 feet wide and tall. The leaves are 20 feet long on 3- to 4-foot-long stout yellowish petioles. The leaflets are to 3 feet long and narrowly lanceolate, and arise in one plane from the rachis. Young leaves have stiff leaflets, but older ones tend to be pendulous. The younger leaves also tend to have a twist of the rachis, which renders the leaflets vertical for the apical half of the blade. Leaf color varies according to environmental conditions and the variety of the palm, ranging from deep, shining green to yellowish green. The palms start blooming and fruiting at an early age, often with no more than 3 feet of trunk growth. The inflorescences appear in 5-foot-long panicles below the crown of leaves and are accompanied by a large tubular woody spathe, which is usually deciduous before the fruits form. The flowers are tightly packed on the flowering branches, and their color ranges from white to almost yellow. The coconut is 1 foot long, three-sided, and, when fully mature, bright yellow to green or brown depending on the cultivar and the age of the fruit.

Coconuts are exceedingly handsome on the tree, hanging in great clusters below the crown of leaves; and, yes, they can be fatal if they fall from any height onto one's head, although this is a rare phenomenon. The edible nut must be liberated from its brittle, brown, hairy shell before consumption. The coconut is undoubtedly the world's most important palm economically. Every part of the tree is used and some of the uses, like copra (the dried endosperm from which coconut oil is expressed) and the edible nuts, constitute major industries in the Philippines, Indonesia, Trinidad, Tobago, Jamaica, and Mexico. The trunks are used for construction and the leaves for thatch and for weaving many utensils.

The species is susceptible to lethal yellowing disease. It is drought tolerant when established and extremely tolerant of saline conditions. It survives in dry, poor, and limey soil but looks and grows much better with good soil and adequate water. In tropical coconut plantations, the trees are fed and irrigated regularly. They grow moderately fast under optimal conditions, especially when younger. The palm is almost intolerant of cold and is adaptable only to zones 10b and 11.

The coconut palm is the paradigm of the tropics and tropical beauty. While it is commonplace in tropical areas, it is yet the most beautiful tree on earth. One of the most picturesque palm tableaux is created by planting a number of coconuts of varying heights in a group; siting them no more than 10 feet from each other encourages them to naturally bend towards the optimum lighting conditions for each tree, and the result is a natural-appearing island. The coconut palm is unsurpassed as a canopy-scape, and its silhouette is both stunning and a universally recognized emblem of the tropics. This palm is difficult to maintain in any enclosure, as it needs good air circulation and bright light. In spite of this, it is often successfully grown for years in large atriums and conservatories.

Many cultivated forms exist, several of which are readily available. *Cocos nucifera* **'Tall Jamaican'** (synonym 'Jamaican Tall'), one of the tallest growing and reportedly the most tender to cold, is very susceptible to lethal yellowing disease, as is *C. nucifera* **'Panama Tall'**. Three varieties are seemingly much less susceptible to lethal yellowing: *C. nucifera* **'Green Malayan Dwarf'**, to 60 feet high with deep green leaves; *C. nucifera* **'Golden Malayan Dwarf'**, also to 60 feet high but with beautiful yellow-green leaves, dazzling golden fruit, and golden to almost orange petioles and rachises; and the outstandingly spectacular *C. nucifera* **'Maypan'**, tall growing and robust with leaves that are longer and broader than those of the type.

COLPOTHRINAX is a genus of three palmate-leaved, monoecious palms in tropical America. The leaves are costapalmate but, unlike those of many *Sabal* species, not so much that they appear semipinnate. The inflorescences are much branched, extend beyond the leaf crown, and bear orange-red bisexual flowers. The fruits are black when mature.

All the species are slow growing and not hardy to cold, being adaptable only to zones 10 and 11. Despite horticultural myth, these palms do not like calcareous soils and dry conditions, although *C. wrightii* is able to withstand periods of drought.

The genus name combines the Greek word meaning "swollen," referring to the trunks of the Cuban species, and *Thrinax*, a similar genus. In reality, *Colpothrinax* is much more closely related to *Pritchardia*. PLATES 292–295.

Colpothrinax aphanopetala was described in 2001 by Randall J. Evans. It is indigenous to southern Nicaragua, Costa Rica, and Panama, where it grows in rain forest at low to moderate elevations. The epithet is from Latin and Greek words meaning "without," "apparent," and "petal," an allusion to the small corolla lobes of the flowers.

The palm looks like *C. cookii,* but the leaves are usually smaller with more deeply divided segments and smaller petioles, and the flowering branches of the inflorescences are a beautiful pink.

Colpothrinax cookii is indigenous to four disjunct and small areas in central Guatemala, southern Belize, Costa Rica, and Panama, where it grows in mountainous rain forest. The epithet honors Orator F. Cook, a 20th-century American botanist.

This palm grows to an overall height of 40 feet with trunks 1 foot in diameter; the newer parts are usually covered in a tangled mass of long fibers. The 3-foot-wide leaves are borne on 4-foot-long petioles and are circular; the linear segments are yellowish green above and grayish green to almost white beneath, extend almost to the petiole, and are pendulous at their apices.

The palm has exceptionally beautiful circular leaves and is slow growing enough so that it may be used as a closeup subject in partial shade or full sun; older trees make specimen plantings when spaced in groups of three or more individuals of varying heights.

Colpothrinax wrightii is endemic to western Cuba and the adjacent Isle of Youth, where it grows in open savannas. Common names are Cuban bottle palm, Cuban belly palm, Cuban barrel palm, and, in Cuba, barrigona. The epithet honors a 19th-century American botanist, Charles H. Wright.

The trunks can attain a height of 30 feet with age. They almost invariably have a distinct bulge near or beneath the middle of the stem; a few individuals in habitat even have a second bulge often twice the diameter of the trunk above and beneath the "belly." It is assumed that this swelling stores water for the palm in times of drought; Scott Zona has observed that cultivated specimens which receive regular and ample amounts of moisture usually have smaller bulges. The leaves are similar in size and form to those of *C. cookii* but have generally stiffer segments and are a darker, almost bluish green above.

The species does not take kindly to calcareous soils; it prefers red clays and quartz sands. It grows faster and looks better with regular and ample moisture. It also needs full sun from youth unto old age but seems more tolerant of cold than does *C. cookii,* although it is still tender. The "belly" is to some persons grotesque, but, if one can get beyond it or doesn't agree, the palm is as beautiful as and more majestic than most *Pritchardia* species; it also looks from a distance like a stout, robust palmetto (*Sabal* species). It is probably at its best as a specimen, especially in groups of varying heights. This species is not known to be grown indoors and is probably a poor candidate for such as it requires much sunlight. PLATES 292–295.

COPERNICIA is a genus of 13 to 24 mostly solitary-trunked, palmate-leaved, monoecious palms in the drier regions of Cuba, Hispaniola, and South America, with most species endemic to Cuba. Usually a significant skirt of dead leaves hangs on the trunks, and the undersides of living leaves are often covered with wax. The leaves are held on usually short, sometimes almost nonexistent, very spiny petioles, and a hastula is often present at the juncture of petiole and leaf blade. The inflorescences are much branched, grow from the leaf crown, and are often longer than the leaf crown is wide. They bear bisexual blossoms that produce rounded black fruits.

All but two species (*C. alba* and *C. prunifera*) are slow to exceedingly slow growing, especially when young. A popular misconception is that *Copernicia* species like truly dry conditions. In habitat, most grow in lowland conditions that are seasonally flooded. Even during the dry season they generally receive occasional rain but can tolerate a couple of months without rain because the water table where they grow is high. The soils they grow in may also have some bearing on their moisture requirements as well: *C. baileyana, C. fallaensis, C. glabrescens,* and *C. hospita* grow in alkaline red clay soils that can hold water; other species such as *C. brittonorum, C. gigas, C. macroglossa,* and *C. rigida* grow in coastal sand close to, and often in, mangrove swamps that stay wet at all times—these last-named species are also very salt tolerant. While copernicias can tolerate dry conditions, they grow best with regular and adequate moisture. Regular feedings with a good palm fertilizer are sufficient and all but perhaps *C. cowellii* do not require any additional trace elements. In southern Florida and similar climates, copernicias have proved cold hardy, only minor leaf burn occurring on specimens when temperatures reach the high to mid 20s (F) during the infrequent cold snaps.

The Cuban species hybridize frequently in some areas of the island, often making it difficult to determine their parentage. Some of the most incredibly beautiful specimens can be found in these habitats. The genus name honors the 16th-century Polish astronomer Mikolaj Kopernik, better known as Copernicus. PLATES 296–321.

Copernicia alba occurs naturally in eastern Bolivia, Paraguay, northern Argentina, and southeast Brazil, where it grows in monsoonal savannas. The species is commonly called caranday palm. The epithet is Latin for "white," an allusion to the undersides of the leaves as well as the trunks.

The palm can attain a height of 100 feet in habitat. The trunks of large specimens are less than 1 foot in diameter and retain many old leaf bases in their younger parts; the older parts are mostly smooth, sometimes indistinctly ringed, and light gray to almost pure white. The 3-foot-wide leaves are borne on long petioles and are deeply divided into linear, pointed segments that are grayish green to pure green above, silvery green beneath, and glaucous and waxy on both surfaces. The length of the inflorescence exceeds the leaf crown, and the fruits are egg shaped and black when mature.

The species extends farther south than any other species in the genus and is the hardiest to cold. It is adaptable to zones 9b through 11, and protected specimens are occasionally found even in 9a. It adapts to a range of soils, including calcareous and heavy clays and, while drought tolerant once established, can endure flooded soil for a short time. It is among the fastest growing species in the genus and needs full sun. It also is the tallest growing *Copernicia* species.

This palm is noble, yet graceful. Its dense leaf crown is beautiful up close and from afar, and it works wonderfully as a canopy-scape. It is probably most picturesque in groups of three or more individuals of varying heights, simulating its colonial habit in the wild where great stands of the palm occur. It is not known to be grown indoors, but could be given a sunny and airy site in a conservatory or atrium. PLATE 296.

Copernicia baileyana is endemic to Cuba, where it grows in savannas and open woodlands. The common name is Bailey fan palm. The epithet honors horticulturist and palm taxonomist, Liberty H. Bailey (1858–1954).

Mature trunks attain a height of 60 feet in habitat but are usually no more than 40 feet under cultivation, with a diameter of about 2 feet. The trunks are usually of even diameter from within 1 foot of the ground to the leaf crown but sometimes show a slight swelling in the middle. They are remarkably smooth below the few pendent dead leaves and are light gray to pure white. The leaf crown is usually rounded and 15 to 20 feet wide and tall. Leaves are 5 feet wide and nearly circular, with many stiff narrowly lanceolate and tapering but erect segments extending one-third of the way to the center of the blade. The leaves are held on 4-foot-long stout petioles that extend into the blade, making the leaf costapalmate. Leaf color is light to deep green above and lighter, grayish green beneath, where the leaf is covered in a waxy bloom. The leaf crown is dense and fully packed, with stiff segments in the highest leaves. The much-branched inflorescence panicles are 7 feet long,

curving down from the center of the leaf crown, and bear whitish blossoms. The fruits are rounded, brown to black, and less than 1 inch in diameter.

This species is not hardy to cold and is limited to zones 10 and 11. Although drought tolerant when established, it grows faster and looks better with regular and adequate moisture. It is not particular about soil type as long as it is well drained, but it needs full sun, especially when past the juvenile stage.

The first thing one notices about mature specimens of this magnificent palm are the concretelike columnar and massive trunks. The second thing noticed is the dense crown of large deep green rounded leaves with their almost startling halo effect of stiff, comblike segments. The palm is eminently suited to specimen planting in large areas and to planting in groups of individuals of varying heights. It should not be used as part of a foundation planting. The palm is not known to have been grown indoors and is probably a poor candidate for such. PLATES 297–299.

Copernicia berteroana is endemic to the driest parts of Hispaniola. The epithet honors a 19th-century Italian plant collector, Carlo L. G. Bertero.

The palm grows to a height of 30 feet in habitat with a slender, brownish gray trunk 8 or 9 inches in diameter, which is mostly smooth and free of leaf bases. The leaves are 3 feet in diameter, a pure, grassy green on both surfaces, and circular, the segments divided to two-thirds of the way to the petiole and pendulous on their margins, at least in older specimens. The inflorescences are slightly longer than the diameter of the leaf crown, and the mature fruits are black.

The species is drought tolerant but looks better and grows faster with regular and adequate moisture. It is not hardy to cold and is adapted only to zones 10 and 11. It needs full sun from youth to old age but is not fussy about soil type as long as it is well drained. It is one of the faster growing species but could never be considered fast.

It resembles the much taller and faster-growing Mexican fan palm, *Washingtonia robusta*. *Copernicia berteroana* is wonderful as a canopy-scape or even isolated in expanses of lawn if planted in groups of three or more individuals of varying heights. PLATE 300.

Copernicia brittonorum is endemic to western Cuba, where it grows in a restricted area of savanna, open dry woodland, and almost on the beach. It is a critically endangered species.

Its appearance is similar to that of *C. hospita*, differing mainly in the much longer inflorescences and in its leaves that are always circular, green, and with segments whose apical ends are deeply divided and pendent. PLATE 301.

Copernicia cowellii is endemic to eastern Cuba, where it grows in dry pine scrub and open savannas. It is rare and endangered. The epithet is a Latinized form of the surname "Cowell" and commemorates the original collector of the species.

The trunk attains 6 feet of height but is seldom seen because of the adhering dead leaves; the overall height of old individuals is 8 feet, making it the smallest species in the genus. The leaf crown is dense and compact, causing the plant to look like a yucca. The leaves are circular but do not readily appear so because they are held on short petioles and are packed tightly in the crown. Each thick, rigid leaf is 3 feet in diameter and deep olive green above but a waxy bluish gray beneath. The inflorescences are much longer than the leaf crown and bear round, black fruits.

This palm is adaptable only to zones 10 and 11 and is marginal in 10a. It needs full sun, is drought tolerant, and grows in habitat on serpentine soils, which are high in magnesium, iron, and nickel and are generally toxic to plants except those that have over the eons adapted to them. The species has only been in cultivation for a few years, and it will be interesting to see how it adapts to cultivation outside its habitat.

It is not large enough to be planted as a specimen isolated in the middle of a lawn or other open space. It works well as a border for larger vegetation but must not be combined with water-loving plants, and it looks good in a cactus or succulent garden as a focal point. Displayed against a contrasting background, it is incredibly effective, as it is planted along a wide, sunny path where it can be viewed up close. PLATES 302–305.

Copernicia ekmanii is endemic to northern Haiti, where it grows near the coast. It is rare and threatened with extinction because of its small range. The epithet is a Latinized form of the Swedish surname "Ekman" and honors the palm's original collector.

The palm attains a maximum height of 15 feet in habitat, with trunks that are usually smooth and free of old leaves, but under cultivation the trunk can grow to 30 feet. The stiffly segmented leaves are circular, 3 feet across, and dusky green above and a waxy bluish gray beneath, and are borne on 2- or 3-foot-long, spiny petioles. The inflorescences do not usually project beyond the leaf crown. The fruits are small, ovoid, and a shiny black.

The palm is drought tolerant but not hardy to cold and is adaptable only to zones 10 and 11. It requires a well-drained soil and full sun. Because of its leaf color, the palm is wonderful against a background of contrasting colors and textures. PLATE 306.

Copernicia fallaensis is endemic to Cuba and is known from a single location, where it is threatened with extinction. The epithet is Latin and translates as "of Falla," a small town in northern central Cuba near the palm's habitat.

This is the largest species in the genus, and it is similar in appearance to *C. baileyana* but larger. The trunks attain a height of 60 feet and a diameter of 3 feet. The leaves, in contradistinction to those of *C. baileyana*, are always silvery blue-green, are diamond shaped, and are 8 feet wide. Some taxonomists think this is a more robust form of *C. baileyana*. PLATES 307–309.

Copernicia gigas is endemic to southeastern coastal Cuba in open woodlands, savannas, and salt marshes. The epithet is Latin for "gigantic," an apt appellation.

This palm is similar in all respects to *C. baileyana* except for its leaf size and shape: its leaves are slightly larger with much larger leaf bases and much longer petioles, and they are shaped like a wedge or a triangle. PLATE 310.

Copernicia glabrescens is endemic to western Cuba, where it grows in open savannas at low elevations. The epithet is Latin for "smooth" or "hairless."

This species is similar to *C. hospita*, except that it clusters with time and it always has pure green leaves; the few differences of floral details are important only to taxonomists. The thin trunks can grow to 30 feet in habitat and are covered in old leaf bases and petiole parts.

The species has the same cold tolerance and general cultural needs as *C. hospita* but, in clustering individuals, is an even more desirable garden subject. PLATE 311.

Copernicia hospita is endemic to Cuba in savannas and open woodlands. The epithet is Latin for "host" and is probably an allusion to the large shag of dead leaves adhering to the trunk in which rodents and often birds make a nest.

Mature trunks grow 20 to 25 feet high with a diameter of 1 foot and are smooth on the older parts. The leaf crown is 18 feet wide and tall. The leaves are 5 to 7 feet wide, circular to wedge shaped, with many rigid segments extending to one-third of the way to the petiole, becoming slightly pendulous at their ends when they mature. Leaf color is grayish green to bluish green to almost pure white or silver, and both surfaces are covered in a waxy bloom; there are tiny teeth along the margins of each segment. The petiole is short but extends into the leaf blade making it costapalmate, and there is a distinct hastula on the top of the juncture of leaf and petiole. The leaf crown is densely packed, with leaves that almost overlap. The 6-foot-long panicles extend beyond the leaves and bear small brownish yellow bisexual flowers, which produce 0.5-inch-wide round, black fruit.

The form of *C. hospita* formerly known as *C. yarey* is much more tolerant of cold than the type, has leaves that are not as silvery, and is a strong, dependable grower in central Florida (David Witt, pers. comm.). *Copernicia hospita* is known to hybridize in nature with several other *Copernicia* species.

The palm is adaptable to zones 10 and 11, needs sun, and is drought tolerant but looks and grows better with regular moisture.

The color and form of the leaves, especially in young plants, make this small palm choice for patio or courtyard settings. It is also beautiful in groups of three or more individuals of varying heights. It is not known to be grown indoors but is probably adaptable to large and sunny conservatories. PLATES 312 & 313.

Copernicia macroglossa is endemic to northwestern Cuba, where it grows in savannas and in salt marshes near the coast. The common name is Cuban petticoat palm. The epithet is two Greek words meaning "large" and "tongue," an allusion to the flaplike hastula at the junction of leaf blade and petiole.

Mature trunks attain a height of 15 feet. They are 8 inches in diameter but, especially in younger plants, are covered with a shag of dead leaves that render them seemingly as wide as the leaf crown, which is 12 to 15 feet wide and tall but does not look that size if the petticoat is intact. Leaves are 5 to 7 feet wide, wedge shaped or half circular, and are carried on short petioles that extend only a little distance into the blade. A third of the way into the blade they are divided into many stiff narrowly lanceolate segments. Leaf color is light to deep green above and grayish green and waxy beneath. There is a distinct and relatively long hastula protruding from the top of the leaf at the juncture of blade and petiole, and the leaf segments are margined with tiny teeth. The leaf crown is unusually round and full in older palms, and the leaves are so densely packed that the visual effect is more like that of a yucca than that of most palms. In addition, the persistent petticoat of dead leaves on all but old plants looks like a haystack, reminding viewers of a giant yucca. The panicles are at least 6 feet long and extend beyond the leaf crown, bearing brownish yellow bisexual blossoms. The fruits are 0.5 inch wide, rounded, and black.

The species is adaptable to zones 10 and 11 and is marginal in 9b. It needs sun and a well-draining soil.

It is dramatic in the landscape. It may be used as a large accent in a wide border and, even when it grows up (which takes a long while), its height is not too great to remain visually "in place." Its character makes it adaptable to the cactus or succulent garden, and a group of these palms is stunning if the individuals are of differing heights. It is not known to be grown in enclosures and is probably a poor candidate for such. PLATES 314 & 315.

Copernicia prunifera is endemic to northeastern Brazil, where it grows in low lying monsoonal areas, especially along rivers and lakes. The common name is carnauba wax palm. The epithet translates from the Latin as "pruinose," referring to the whitish, powdery covering on the leaves.

Mature trunks grow to a height of 50 feet in their native haunts but are usually no more than 35 feet tall under cultivation. They are 10 inches in diameter and often retain the spirally arranged knobby leaf base scars, mostly on the lower parts of the trunks rather than the upper portions as is the case with most other palm species. The full, rounded leaf crown is 15 feet wide and open. The leaves are 5 feet wide, circular, and are carried on 3-foot-long petioles that are margined with strong teeth. The many linear, tapering rigid segments extend halfway to the center of the blade. Leaf color is deep yellow-green to blue-green, and both surfaces are covered in a tough gloss of wax, especially the lower surface. The 7-foot-long narrow panicles extend well beyond the leaves and bear brownish yellow bisexual flowers. The fruits are 1 inch wide, brown to black, and round.

This species has unusual hardiness to cold considering its tropical origins. David Witt (pers. comm.) reports that it seems hardy in Orlando, Florida (zone 9b/10a). It is slow growing but significantly faster than most other *Copernicia* species except for *C. alba*. It needs sun and, unlike many other species in the genus, appreciates regular and adequate moisture, although it is drought tolerant when established. It seems to thrive on almost any soil type except the quite acidic or quite alkaline.

This moderately sized palm is excellent in a large patio or courtyard, where the form of its trunk and leaf crown may be appreciated. It looks especially wonderful in groups of three or more individuals of different heights and its silhouette is extraordinarily beautiful. It is probably a better candidate than most other *Copernicia* species for atriums or conservatories.

The wax from the leaves was formerly a valuable commodity, and refineries in Brazil still process it. PLATES 316 & 317.

Copernicia rigida is endemic to eastern Cuba, where it grows in savannas, open pinelands, and salt marshes near the coast. The epithet is Latin for "rigid," an allusion to the leaf segments.

The palm grows to 50 feet high in habitat. The trunk is covered near its summit with a skirt of dead leaves and in all but its oldest parts in old leaf bases, and it tends to have the shape of a lollipop when older. The stiff, erect, narrow, and wedge-shaped leaves are medium green above and waxy and grayish underneath, with small thorns along the margins of the rigid, linear segments. The petiole extends into the blade to form a prominent costa. The inflorescences extend beyond the leaf crown and bear small brown flowers, which produce small, round, black fruits.

This palm is not hardy to cold and does not survive unprotected outside of zones 10 and 11. It is drought tolerant and needs full sun and a well-drained soil

The species is most unusual looking, especially when smaller, as it usually has a long leaf crown and the erect and stiff leaves resemble a cross between a *Yucca* species and a *Pandanus* species. Because of its slow growth, it can be sited as a curiosity or specimen for a long time; in old age, it is magnificent as a canopy-scape, the crown then usually globular atop the stout, straight trunk. This is probably not a good candidate for indoors, but no data are available. PLATES 318 & 319.

Copernicia tectorum is indigenous to northern Colombia and northwestern Venezuela, where it grows in monsoonal savannas (*llanos*), often forming great colonies. The epithet is Latin for "of the roofs," an allusion to the use of the leaves as thatch.

The palm grows to 40 feet in habitat. The trunks are 1 foot in diameter and are covered in an attractive pattern of old leaf bases except in their older parts which are smooth and light to dark gray. The leaves are 3 feet wide and circular; they are carried on thorny petioles that are 5 feet long. Leaf color is medium to deep green on both surfaces. The inflorescences are as long as the diameter of the leaf crown and are not as apparent as in other *Copernicia* species, where the panicles extend beyond the crown. The fruits are egg shaped, brown to black, and 1.5 inches long.

This species is tender to cold and adaptable only to zones 10 and 11. It thrives in heavy clay, sandy, and calcareous soils. It can withstand waterlogged soil as well as drought conditions but grows faster and looks better with regular moisture. It needs full sun.

This palm does not have the strange attributes of many other *Copernicia* species; it looks a lot like a *Livistona* species from a distance and is excellent as a canopy-scape or as a specimen group of three or more individuals of varying heights. It is not known to be grown indoors but can probably adapt to a sunny, airy conservatory. PLATES 320 & 321.

CORYPHA is a genus of eight gigantic solitary-trunked, palmate-leaved, monoecious palms in tropical Asia, Malaysia, Indonesia, and Australia. The plants are monocarpic, which means their large trunks, the largest in the world, die after producing enormous terminal inflorescences, posing a major mechanical problem in the landscape. Were it not for the spectacular beauty of the leaves, especially when young, and the fact that it takes many years for the palms to flower, they would be outcasts. Even so, they are best relegated to estate-sized gardens, botanical gardens, and wherever the death of the trunks does not pose a threat to adjacent gardens or structures. The palms grow slowly when young but faster with the advent of trunk formation. Only two species are commonly planted. Both dominate the landscape. The genus name is Greek for "summit," an allusion to the giant terminal inflorescence. PLATES 322–325.

Corypha umbraculifera is of unknown origin because of its long history of cultivation and is no longer found in the wild except in association with human habitation; it probably originated in the monsoonal plains and open forests of southern India and Sri Lanka. While not strictly an English name, talipot palm is a commonly used name. The epithet is Latin for "shade-bearing," an allusion to the giant leaves and immense crown.

Mature trees grow to 90 feet high with a trunk diameter to 3 feet. They are mostly free of leaf bases and ringed when older, but younger parts have many immense leaf bases resembling rhino horns. The leaf crown is 40 feet wide and tall when young but half those dimensions when mature. The plants take many years to form a trunk and grow slowly (but are nevertheless massive) until trunk formation is initiated. The leaves are 20 feet wide, circular but folded into a trough, and are carried on 10-foot-long stout petioles armed with black teeth. They are the largest palmate leaves in the world. The leaves are costapalmate with the petiole projecting several feet into the blade, resulting in a deep V shape. There is a large hastula on the blade at the juncture of leaf and petiole. The segments extend one-third of the way into the blade and are stiff, tough, and 3 inches wide and 7 feet long. Leaf color is light to deep green on both sides. The terminal panicle is 30 feet tall with great branches that make it 40 feet wide. This is the largest inflorescence among flowering plants. The flowers are creamy white to almost yellow and number in the millions, creating a Christmas-treelike affair with enormous white plumose branches. The round 2-inch-wide green to brown fruits create a show almost as spectacular as the flowers since they form on the hardening branches of the inflorescence.

The palm is tender to cold and adaptable only to zones 10b and 11, although specimens are found in microclimates of 10a. It needs average but regular moisture and, although drought tolerant when established, does not attain its spectacular proportions if constantly deprived of moisture. The palm is adaptable to most soils with good drainage but only looks its best with adequately fertile soil.

This spectacular and colossal palm is not for small gardens. Its leaf crown is as large as some small houses. Its massive proportions make it marvelous as a specimen, but it is simply breathtaking if room can be found to plant groups of three or more individuals of varying heights; such practice also ensures the perpetuation of its landscape role. Its slow growth when young and before it forms a trunk allows it to be used as a tropical-appearing giant shrub and accent for many years, and some gardeners have it cut out as it begins to form a trunk since the inevitable outcome necessitates removing the trunks after they bloom and fruit. The life span of a single tree is from 30 to 80 years. Only as an immature plant could the palm be considered for a large atrium or conservatory, and it would need lots of light.

Talipot palm has many nonornamental uses. The trunks are felled for the starchy pith and the sap from which alcoholic beverages are made; the leaves are used for thatch and for making many household items; and the growing point is harvested as a vegetable. At one time the great leaves were used for writing paper. Plates 322 & 323.

Corypha utan is native to a vast area from northeastern India through Southeast Asia and northwards to the Philippine islands and south to northern Australia. The epithet is one of the aboriginal names.

The species is similar to *C. umbraculifera* but smaller in all its parts, has spiraling leaf bases, and has much more deeply segmented leaves. It is also less hardy than *C. umbraculifera*. It is slightly susceptible to lethal yellowing disease. Plates 324 & 325.

CRYOSOPHILA is a genus of nine palmate-leaved, monoecious, spiny trunked palms in Mexico, Central America, and northwestern Colombia, some of them rare in habitat. The spines are often branched and are actually aerial roots that harden into spinelike protrusions from the trunk, especially the lower parts; they usually root if they reach the soil. The circular leaves are borne on long petioles and usually are silvery on their undersides. As in the genus *Chelyocarpus*, the leaves are divided into two halves, which are split into numerous segments. The two main divisions are not overly obvious in most cases to the untrained eye as all the segments are close together; they become more obvious when spread apart. The short, congested, and much branched inflorescences are mostly hidden in the leaf crown; they bear small, white bisexual flowers. They are initially covered in overlapping, tomentose bracts that form a tube. The fruits are unusual in that, when mature, they are either white or green.

The plants generally grow on limestone soils, and most species are similar and difficult to distinguish one from another. All the species are intolerant of freezing temperatures, and all need nearly constant moisture.

The genus was formerly named "*Acanthorrhiza.*" The current genus name is from Greek words meaning "cold loving," an allusion that is obscure. The common English name, rootspine palm, applies to the whole genus. Plates 326–330.

Cryosophila cookii is a rare and endangered palm native to a small area of the Caribbean coastal rain forest of Costa Rica. The epithet honors a 20th-century American botanist, Orator F. Cook. This species is slightly taller than *C. stauracantha*.

Cryosophila grayumii is another rare species, indigenous to the coastal rain forest of southwestern Costa Rica. The epithet honors botanist Michael H. Grayum of the Missouri Botanical Garden. This species is slightly shorter than *C. stauracantha*.

Cryosophila guagara is native to the Pacific coastal rain forest of Costa Rica and adjacent Panama. The epithet is an aboriginal name. This species differs from *C. stauracantha* in being a sometimes clustering species and in having more numerous and generally longer root spines. Plate 326.

Cryosophila kalbreyeri is native to the eastern half of Panama and northeastern Colombia, where it grows in low, mountainous rain forest. It is in danger of extinction. The epithet is a Latinized form of the surname "Kalbreyer" and honors a 20th-century German palm collector in South America. This species differs from *C. stauracantha* in being a sometimes clustering species as well as having a smaller stature.

Cryosophila macrocarpa is native to a small area of northeastern Colombia, where it grows in Pacific coastal rain forest. The epithet is Greek for "large" and "fruit." This species is shorter than *C. stauracantha* and has larger white fruits.

Cryosophila nana is indigenous to the western coast of Mexico from Mazatlán to almost the border of Guatemala, where it grows in mountainous, semiarid deciduous forests and pine and oak woodlands. The epithet is Latin for "small," although one wonders how it was meant to apply to this palm. This species differs from *C. stauracantha* in its shorter stature, its leaves that are green on both surfaces, and in not needing constant moisture.

Cryosophila stauracantha occurs naturally in lowland rain forest of southern Mexico, northern Guatemala, and Belize. The palm is called give-and-take in Belize (Henderson et al. 1995). The epithet is from Greek words meaning "crossed" and "spine."

Mature trunks may attain a height of 30 feet with a diameter of 4 to 5 inches. They are mostly covered, and densely so, with gray to almost white short root spines, although the upper parts often are free of the roots, which either do not form at these levels or have been worn away. The sparse but beautifully rounded leaf crown is 15 feet wide and tall. The leaves are perfectly circular and 6 feet wide, and are carried on delicate and slender 6-foot-long petioles. The segments are clustered in groups of two to four and extend halfway to the center of the blade. Leaf color is dark green above and grayish green to gray beneath. There is a small but distinct hastula at the junction of leaf blade and petiole. The inflorescence is 2 or 3 feet long and grows from among the leaves, bearing small, white bisexual flowers. The fruits are 1 inch long, round, and green to white.

The species is almost tropical in its requirements and is adaptable only to zones 10b and 11, although sometimes found in favorable microclimates in 10a. It is a true water lover. It thrives in a rich soil but is adaptable to those that are sandy if fertilized and mulched with compost; it prefers slightly alkaline or slightly acidic soils. It likes partial shade, especially when young, but can adapt to full sun when older.

Because of the shape and form of the leaves dancing on their slender stalks and because of the delicate and thin trunk, there is no more graceful palm. It has one of the most beautiful silhouettes of any plant and nothing in the landscape sings more alluringly than a canopy-scape of rootspine palm. It is perfect also in a courtyard or patio, and groups of three or more individuals of varying heights create a veritable oratorio of grace and movement. It is not known to be grown indoors, although there would seem to be no reason why it couldn't be if given enough light, space, and moisture. PLATES 327–329.

Cryosophila warscewiczii is native to the Caribbean coastal rain forest of Costa Rica and northern Panama. The epithet honors Josef Warscewicz, a 19th-century palm botanist in South America. This species is taller than *C. stauracantha* and is slightly susceptible to lethal yellow disease. PLATE 330.

Cryosophila williamsii is a rare and endangered species indigenous to northeastern Honduras, where it grows in low mountainous rain forest. The epithet honors Louis O. Williams, a 20th-century botanist and collector. This species is shorter than *C. stauracantha*.

CYPHOKENTIA is a monotypic genus of solitary-trunked, pinnate-leaved, monoecious palm. The genus name is formed from a Greek word meaning "tumor" or "swelling" and an out-of-date name for species in the genera *Gronophyllum*, *Gulubia*, and *Hydriastele*. The epithet is formed from two Greek words meaning "large" and "spike," an allusion to the inflorescences.

Cyphokentia macrostachya is endemic to New Caledonia, where it grows in mountainous rain forest at elevations from sea level to 3000 feet.

In habitat the light gray or tan trunk attains a height of 50 feet but is 6 inches in diameter except at its expanded base. The elegant cylindrical crownshaft is 3 feet tall, slightly wider than the trunk, and is light gray to almost pure white. The leaf crown is sparse, and the leaves are borne on short, 2-foot-long petioles. They are 10 feet long and beautifully recurved, with evenly and widely spaced, 4-foot-long, light green stiff and narrowly lanceolate leaflets that grow from the rachis at an angle to give a V-shaped leaf. The inflorescences grow in a circle from nodes beneath the crownshaft and are 3-foot-long, thin, rope-like, and pendulous branches bearing both male and female flowers. The fruits are 0.5 inch long, egg shaped, and bright red when mature.

This beautiful palm is rare in cultivation and slow growing. It needs partial shade when young, a frost-free climate, and constant moisture in a rich, humus-laden soil. Its silhouette is as beautiful as that of any palm. This palm makes a perfect canopy-scape but is so slow growing as to be planted for future generations.

CYPHOPHOENIX is a genus of two solitary-trunked, pinnate-leaved, monoecious palms in New Caledonia. The inflorescences grow from beneath the crownshaft and are large, spreading, multibranched, and succulent; they bear both male and female blossoms, which produce 0.5-inch-long ellipsoid red or reddish brown fruits.

The genus name is formed from Greek words for "swelling" or "tumor" and "date palm" and probably alludes to the shape of the fruits. PLATES 331 & 332.

Cyphophoenix elegans is endemic to northeastern New Caledonia, where it grows in low mountainous rain forest. The epithet is Latin for "elegant."

The trunk attains a height of 50 feet in habitat and is 6 inches in diameter. It is a light green in its younger parts and a light to deep gray in its older parts, with distinct whitish rings of leaf base scars. The bulbous crownshaft is 2 to 3 feet high, markedly swollen at its base, and olive green to light silvery green. The leaf crown is less than a semicircle because of the short-petioled, ascending but also beautifully arching and recurved 6-foot-long leaves. The 3-foot-long leaflets are a deep yellow-green on both sides, linear-lanceolate, and stiffly ascending, growing from the rachis at an angle which gives the leaf a V shape.

The tree is relatively fast growing for a New Caledonian palm, needing only year-round warmth and copious and regular moisture in a free-draining, humus-laden soil. Its silhouette is almost breathtakingly beautiful and makes one of the finest canopy-scapes. PLATE 331.

Cyphophoenix nucele is endemic to the small island of Lifou in the Loyalty Islands, east of New Caledonia, where it grows at low elevations near the coast on limestone outcrops. It is rare and endangered, with fewer than 100 individuals in habitat. The epithet is the aboriginal name, which translates as "nut" and "sling"; at one time on Lifou the fruits were used as ammunition for hunting birds with slingshots.

The trunk attains a height of 50 feet in habitat and is slightly more than 6 inches in diameter. It is light green in its younger parts and tan in its older parts with distinct white rings of leaf base scars. The crownshaft is 2 feet high, barely thicker than the trunk itself, and is almost pure white because of the dense, feltlike tomentum that covers it. The leaves are deep emerald green on short petioles and are ascending and erect, forming a crown shaped like a shaving brush with usually eight 6-foot-long leaves. The linear-lanceolate, long-tipped, stiff 2.5-foot-long leaflets grow almost in a single plane from the rachis.

The species is still rare in cultivation but has the same cultural requirements as *C. elegans* with the exception that it is tolerant of limey soils. PLATE 332.

CYPHOSPERMA is a genus of four pinnate-leaved, solitary-trunked, monoecious palms in the islands of Fiji, Vanuatu, and New Caledonia. Only one species forms a true crownshaft, and the inflorescences of the other three species, while growing from the leaf crown, usually persist and eventually are found beneath the leaf crown. They consist of elongated peduncles from the ends of which grow the flowering branches bearing both male and female blossoms. All species are wonderfully tropical looking and exotic.

The genus name is derived from Greek words meaning "swelling" or "tumor" and "seed," and is an allusion to the form of the seeds. PLATES 333 & 334.

Cyphosperma balansae is endemic to New Caledonia, where it grows in mountainous rain forest from 1300 to 3200 feet elevation. The epithet honors Benedict Balansa, a 19th-century plant collector and botanist in New Caledonia.

The trunk attains a height of 50 feet in habitat and is 8 inches in diameter. It is deep green in its younger parts but chocolate to nearly black in its older parts, with beautifully distinct light yellow rings of leaf base scars, making this one of the most beautiful stems of any palm. The 2-foot-long leaf sheaths are prominent but do not form a crownshaft; they are the color of the trunk at their bases with light green summits. The leaf crown is shaped like a shaving brush because of the erect and ascending, unarching 8- to 10-foot-long leaves on short petioles that are generally less than 1 foot long. The 3-foot-long light green stiff leaflets are linear-lanceolate with acuminate tips, and

grow from the rachis at an angle that creates a V-shaped leaf. The inflorescences are extraordinarily long—to 7 or 8 feet—and consist of a sturdy 6-foot-long peduncle with many apical reddish brown branches bearing both male and female flowers. The large pendent clusters of 0.5-inch-round fruits are deep red when mature.

This species is one of the most strangely beautiful palms and is more tropical looking than it actually is with its incredibly exotic trunk; it looks as though it belongs in Hawaii rather than New Caledonia. It is still rare in cultivation but is reportedly easily and quickly grown if given ample, regular moisture and a humus-laden soil. It seems to thrive in partial shade when young and is adaptable to full sun in all but hot and dry climates. It needs, alas, a nearly tropical climate and is not frost tolerant. Seedlings with entire, unsegmented leaves are much sought after (Hodel and Pintaud 1998). PLATES 333 & 334.

Cyphosperma tanga is endemic to the island of Viti Levu in the Fiji Islands, where it grows in low mountainous rain forest. The epithet is the aboriginal name for the species.

The trunk attains a height of 20 feet in habitat and a diameter of 6 inches. It is chocolate brown in all but the oldest parts and is graced with wavy yellowish rings of leaf base scars. The leaf crown is in the form of a shaving brush because of the stiffly ascending and erect 6-foot-long leaves, which are deep green above and paler green beneath. They are borne on short light green petioles, are wedge shaped, and are unsegmented except at their apices where there are irregularly sized segments—one is led to wonder if the leaves would remain unsegmented if planted in a protected site. The blade shows deep corrugations above and below corresponding to the fused segments. The inflorescence consists of a 6-foot-long erect, unarching peduncle whose apex terminates in a spray of 2-foot-long thin branches bearing greenish yellow blossoms of both sexes. The fruits are 0.5 inch long, ellipsoid, and yellow.

This species is undeservedly rare outside of botanical gardens. It is exotic and tropical looking and is on a par with *Phoenicophorium* and *Verschaffeltia* in beauty. It needs constant warmth and moisture, a humus-laden and slightly acidic soil, and full sun once past the seedling stage.

Cyphosperma trichospadix is endemic to the Fiji islands of Vanua Levu and Taveuni (the genus was formerly known as *Taveunia*), where it grows in mountainous rain and cloud forests at elevations of 2000 to 4000 feet. The epithet is derived from Greek words meaning "hair" and "spadix," an allusion to the hairy spathe of the inflorescence.

The trunk grows to a maximum height of 18 feet in habitat with a diameter of 3 inches. It is a beautiful smooth light green in all but the oldest parts where it is a light tan with indistinct lighter-colored rings of leaf base scars. This is the only species in the genus to form a true crownshaft, which is 3 feet tall, scarcely wider at any point than the trunk itself, and a beautiful silvery green. The leaf crown is open and almost hemispherical with only a few ascending but gracefully arching 6- to 7-foot-long leaves on bright green 4-foot-long petioles. The leaflets are widely spaced, each one 2 feet long, deep green on both sides, and lanceolate-acuminate, and grow from the rachis in a nearly single flat plane.

This is the most typical looking species in the genus because of its open, full leaf crown and colored trunk. It is nevertheless of great beauty. It is extremely rare in cultivation but not deservedly so and should do well in all but the hottest and driest nearly tropical climes if given substantial and regular moisture, partial shade, especially when young, and a free-draining, humus-laden soil.

Cyphosperma voutmelense is endemic to Vanuatu on the island of Espíritu Santo, where it grows in mountainous rain forest at elevations of 2800 to 3500 feet. It is a rare species; only seven individuals were known in 1989. The epithet is Latin for "of "Voutmélé," a mountain near the site where the species was collected.

This small species has closely ringed trunks attaining in habitat a height of 20 feet. The palm forms no crownshaft. The leaves are 5 feet long on short petioles, erect, and ascending; they form a crown shaped like a shaving brush. The widely spaced leaflets are 18 inches long, S shaped, and not as stiff as those of *C. balansae* to which the species has many visual similarities.

CYRTOSTACHYS is a genus of nine monoecious, pinnate-leaved palms in Thailand, Indonesia, New Guinea, and the South Pacific Islands. There are both clumping and solitary-trunked species. The spreading inflorescences form beneath the crownshaft and are much branched, the flowering branches bearing both male and female blossoms.

Only two species are cultivated outside of tropical botanical gardens but, if the others are at all comparable in beauty, then this is one of the most badly neglected palm genera for horticulture. All species need tropical growing conditions and abundant moisture.
The genus name is derived from Greek words meaning "curved" and "spike," referring to the inflorescence. PLATES 335–338.

Cyrtostachys elegans is indigenous to rain forest of New Guinea. The epithet is Latin for "elegant." This species differs from *C. glauca* in having larger clumps with pure green crownshafts and leaves with more pendent leaflets.

Its cultural requirements are the same as those for *C. renda,* except that it is not as demanding of moisture.

Cyrtostachys glauca is a sparsely clustering species from low mountainous rain forest in Papua New Guinea. The epithet is Latin for "glaucous" and refers to the crownshaft.

The tallest trunks attain a maximum height of 30 feet but usually number only two or three, most of the suckers being much shorter. The younger parts of the stems are a beautiful green with prominent rings, the older parts a light gray. The prominent crownshafts are 3 feet tall, glaucous blue-green, and smooth. The bright green leaves are 10 to 12 feet long and flat or nearly flat because the leaflets grow from the rachis in one plane.

Although not as demanding of moisture as is *C. renda,* this species is a water lover and needs sun and a rich soil. It grows faster than does *C. renda* but is as tender to cold. It is a wonderfully picturesque and beautiful palm because of the form of the clumps with their levels of leaves and heights of trunks. It looks best in a wall of vegetation, where it also serves as a marvelous canopy-scape.

Cyrtostachys kisu is indigenous to rain forest of the Solomon Islands, east of New Guinea. The epithet is one of the aboriginal names.

This solitary-trunked species of noble proportions grows to 50 feet. The crownshaft is 5 feet tall, slightly bulging at its base, and olive green. The leaves are, unlike those of *C. renda,* spreading but have stiff rachises that arch only near their tips; while not stiff and arching like those of *C. renda,* the leaves almost never lie beneath the horizontal. The 2-foot-long leaflets are medium green and pendent.

The palm has the same cultural requirements as does *C. renda* but needs less moisture and grows faster.

Cyrtostachys ledermanniana is endemic to New Guinea, where it grows in low mountainous rain forest in the northern central region of the island, near the border of Papua New Guinea and West Papua. The epithet honors Carl L. Ledermann, an early 20th-century Swiss botanist and collector.

According to Ken Foster of Fairchild Tropical Garden, Miami, who collected it in 1981, this solitary-trunked species grows to an overall height of 60 feet, with a dark green, slightly bulging crownshaft beneath a crown of 10-foot-long mostly stiff, slightly arching leaves. The regularly spaced, deep green lanceolate leaflets are pendent in mature individuals.

The species is probably adaptable only to zones 10b and 11 and doubtless needs copious and regular moisture. It is probably not fussy about soil type; a young specimen at Fairchild Tropical Garden is flourishing in calcareous soil with a mulch of decomposing leaves. This palm needs a site in full sun. PLATE 335.

Cyrtostachys loriae is a solitary-trunked species from the rain forest of New Guinea.

Its beautifully slender, dark green trunk has prominent and widely spaced white rings of leaf base scars; it grows straight as an arrow to 30 feet high. The leaves are 6 to 8 feet long on 2-foot-long petioles; they are medium to deep green, and the pendent leaflets grow in one plane from the rachis to create a flat or nearly flat leaf.

Cyrtostachys peekeliana is native to the rain forest of the island of New Britain off the northeast coast of Papua New Guinea. The epithet is a Latinized form of the German surname "Peekel" and honors a Catholic missionary to New Guinea who, as an amateur botanist, wrote about the island's flora.

This is among the largest, if not the largest, species in the genus, with a solitary trunk to 50 feet high and more than 1 foot in diameter. The tall, green crownshaft is scarcely wider than the trunk, and the long, erect leaves are composed of many pendent leaflets.

Cultural requirements are like those of *C. renda*.

Cyrtostachys renda is native to lowland rain forest and coastal swamps in Thailand, Sumatra, Malaysia, and Borneo. Common names are sealing-wax palm and lipstick palm. The epithet is an aboriginal name for the palm.

The trunks of this clustering species grow to 60 feet high in habitat but under cultivation are usually no more than half that with diameters of only 2 to 3 inches. The younger parts of the stems are green, but the older portions are light brown to gray or sometimes almost white and are beautifully ringed. The leaf crown is 10 feet wide and 6 feet tall; and mature clumps may attain a total height of 35 feet and a width of 20 feet. The crownshaft is 3 feet long, smooth, and slender, and slightly bulging at the base. It is a brilliant reddish orange to vivid scarlet. The leaves are 4 to 5 feet long and are held on short petioles less than 1 foot long. The petiole and rachis are the color of the crownshafts. The leaflets are narrowly elliptical, tapering, and 1 foot long; they are narrowly grooved and stiff and grow from the rachis at an angle that creates a V shape to the blade. Leaf color is light to deep green above and a distinctly lighter grayish green beneath. There are usually only six to eight leaves on any given trunk, and they almost never descend below the horizontal plane. The inflorescences grow from beneath the crownshaft and are short, sparsely branched with whiplike branches, and a beautiful red. They bear small greenish white or greenish yellow male and female flowers. The fruits are 0.5 inch wide, round, and black.

The palm needs abundant and constant moisture and constantly tropical temperatures. It is almost aquatic and is often grown in ponds, potted or free of containers. It is marginal in zone 10b. While it readily adapts to full sun when mature, it likes partial shade when young. Cold or dry winds are inimical to this species. The richer the soil, the better; in fact, it grows in peat swamps in most of its habitat. There are forms of this species with light green as well as orange or deep yellow crownshafts.

This is one of the most beautiful palm species; every part of the plant is choice. The slender diaphanous trunks are heartbreakingly beautiful and so thin and lissome as to often bend as if they were the long stalks of big blossoms in a bouquet. The clumps are usually open enough that the trunks do not need to be thinned, and the younger stems add incredibly beautiful tiers of leaves from top to bottom; however, it is the magnetic attraction of the long, red crownshafts that makes this species irresistible. It is hard to imagine a site in which it would not be the center of attraction, but it looks exceptionally beautiful when made a part of other vegetation. The palm does well in large, humid, and constantly warm enclosures with good light. PLATES 336–338.

DAEMONOROPS is a large and diverse genus of 115 spiny, mostly climbing, dioecious palms from India eastwards to New Guinea and the Philippines, primarily in peninsular Malaysia, Sumatra, and Borneo.

Some species are solitary trunked, but most are clustering. A few are dwarf in stature; many others are gigantic and high climbing. A few of the trunkless species have no specialized climbing organ, but most others develop a cirrus at the ends of the leaf rachises. A few species are monocarpic (or hapaxanthic), and the stems die after flowering and fruiting. The stems of all species are spiny, and several species have sets of interlocking spines that form "ant galleries" in which the insects make their homes, a symbiotic relationship between palm and insect.

The inflorescences grow from the leaf axils and are usually accompanied by large boat-shaped and podlike, erect or pendent, spiny woody bracts that open by splitting lengthwise to reveal much-branched but short stalks of male or female blossoms. The fruits are scaly, 1 inch wide, usually globose, and light brown to dark brown to reddish brown or black. The "pods" often have a sharply pointed beak that may be as long as the part of the bract that holds the inflorescences themselves.

All species require a tropical or nearly tropical climate and copious, regular moisture, but almost all flourish in full sun or partial shade. The high climbing species may be pruned to remain in bounds. Like other rattan species, the juvenile plants are much smaller, are less viciously spiny, and make wonderful rosettes of pinnate leaves, especially for containers.

The genus name is derived from two Greek words meaning "deity" or "demon" and "bush" or "shrub," an allusion to the red (devilish) exudate that emerges from between the scales of the fruits (John L. Dowe, pers. comm.). PLATES 339–341.

Daemonorops angustifolia is indigenous to peninsular Malaysia, peninsular Thailand, Sumatra, and Borneo, where it grows mostly in clearings and along banks of streams and rivers. In Malaysia, it is called *rotan ayer* or "water rattan." The epithet is Latin for "narrow leaf" and refers to the shape of the leaflets.

The species grows from sea level to an elevation of 2640 feet. It is a giant clustering climber, the beautiful stems with their long internodes growing to lengths of 100 feet but only 1 inch or slightly more in diameter. The spreading leaves are 6 to 8 feet long and bear numerous, narrowly lanceolate 1-foot-long subglossy leaflets that grow from the rachis in a flat plane and are semipendent, making for an extremely handsome leaf. The cirrus is another 3 feet long and bears widely spaced grapnel-like backward-pointing pairs of 2-inch-long spines. The 18-inch-long woody inflorescences are erect.

Daemonorops calicarpa is indigenous to peninsular Malaysia and Sumatra, where it grows in lowland rain forest in dense large colonies. The epithet is derived from Greek words meaning "crowded" and "fruit," an allusion to the congested inflorescences and fruits.

This is a clustering species whose short trunks often remain underground; in any case, they are invisible because of the number and size of the spreading leaves, which grow to 15 feet long. The leaves occasionally produce a short, nonfunctional cirrus at the apex of the rachis. The many leaflets are 1 foot long and narrowly lanceolate, grow from the rachis in a flat plane, and are slightly pendent. A single plant may have to 10 clusters of leaves, creating a mass that is 20 feet wide and almost as tall. The unusual inflorescences grow from the top of the diminutive or subterranean trunks, making this species monocarpic (or hapaxanthic). They are never more than 6 feet above the ground level and are thus mostly hidden among the large leaves. They are monstrous-looking club-shaped affairs, the podlike bracts of the inflorescences congested at the apices of the flowering stem, with vestigial and much reduced leaves and even rudimentary cirri growing from their tips.

What a wonderful palm this is! The leaves are beautiful and the plant makes one of the most useful, handsome hedges or barrier plantings, in and out of shade, for tropical or nearly tropical climates.

Daemonorops curranii is endemic to Palawan Island in the Philippines, where it grows in dense rain forest at low elevations. It is a small clustering and short climbing species whose flat leaves are 6 feet long and terminate in a short cirrus. This beautiful clumper is easily kept in bounds and in its rosette stage by pruning. It makes an incredibly nice large groundcover or hedge or barrier planting in shade or sun. PLATE 339.

Daemonorops jenkinsiana is indigenous to northeastern India, Bhutan, Myanmar, and northern Thailand, where it grows in low mountainous rain forest. The epithet commemorates the original 19th-century collector, Major-General F. Jenkins.

It is a large clustering climber whose stems grow to lengths of 60 feet or more. The leaves are 6 to 8 feet long, spreading in posture, with 18-inch-long closely and regularly spaced, linear and pendent leaflets.

This extremely spiny but gorgeous species is best planted in outlying areas of a garden where its marvelous leaves can be appreciated. PLATE 340.

Daemonorops melanochaetes is indigenous to peninsular Thailand, peninsular Malaysia, Sumatra, and Java, where it grows in rain forest from sea level to an elevation of 1000 feet, often forming large colonies. The epithet is from Latin and Greek words meaning "black" and "bristle" and alludes to the long spines that cover the sheaths, petioles, and leaf rachises.

The densely clustering stems grow to 100 feet long, the 10-foot-long leaves are borne on 2- to 3-foot-long petioles, and the terminal cirrus is 3 feet long. The many dark green, 2-foot-long leaflets are regularly spaced along the rachis, grow in a single plane, and are narrow and pendent.

The palm is easily kept at a manageable height and, as such, makes a beautiful large component in other vegetation. PLATE 341.

Daemonorops mollis is endemic to the Philippines, where it grows in rain forest from sea level to an elevation of 2640 feet. The epithet is Latin for "soft" and refers to the pliable stems which are used to make objets d'art.

This is a sprawling, clustering, partially climbing small species. It has 6-foot-long leaves sporting 1-foot-long deep green linear leaflets that grow from the rachis in a single flat plane. Because of its small size and sprawling habit, the palm needs to be pruned to make an acceptable garden subject, which feat is easy to accomplish.

DECKENIA is a monotypic genus of spiny, solitary-trunked, pinnate-leaved, monoecious palm in the Seychelles Islands. The genus name honors a 19th-century German explorer of Africa, Karl K. von der Decken. The epithet is Latin for "noble" and refers to the size and appearance of the species. PLATES 342–345.

Deckenia nobilis grows in rain forest on hills, slopes, and low mountains, usually within sight of the coast but also to an elevation of 2000 feet. In some areas, it forms large, dense colonies, whose individuals litter the ground so that no other vegetation, including their own seedlings, can grow. The species is endangered because of habitat destruction and the harvesting of its growing point as a vegetable.

This is a large and magnificent species whose trunk can attain a height of 100 feet or more but a diameter of no more than 18 inches. It is straight as an arrow, light gray or light tan, and beautifully and distinctly ringed with darker leaf base scars; it sports a 3- or 4-foot-tall smooth, cylindrical crownshaft that is bulging at its base and is usually a light green but may also be bluish green or purplish. Young trees are invariably covered on their trunks, crownshafts, and petioles with 2- to 3-inch-long golden spines, but these gradually disappear as the palm ages and, usually by the time the trunk is 12 feet tall, most are gone. The leaf crown is large and rounded, and the 10- to 12-foot-long leaves bear 3- to 4-foot-long, linear-lanceolate, long-tipped, deep green, limp, and half-pendent leaflets. The leaf rachis usually exhibits a twist near its midpoint so that the apical half of the leaf is oriented in a vertical plane, much like that of *Archontophoenix* and *Cocos* (coconut) species. The bracts of the inflorescences are spiny no matter what the age of the palm, and these buds grow from nodes beneath the crownshaft. The inflorescences are sprays of yellow branches bearing both male and female blossoms. The small ovoid fruits are black.

This magnificence is one of the most beautiful palm species but is very tender to cold and is marginal even in zone 10b. It also needs constant moisture, a fast-draining and humus-laden soil, full sun when past the seedling stage, and constantly high humidity. It is fast growing when past the seedling stage and up until the trunk attains 20 feet of height. There is no finer subject for tropical climates.

DESMONCUS is a genus of seven variable, pinnate-leaved, monoecious, spiny palms in tropical America. All but one species are climbers and use cirri to get a footing on other vegetation, rocks, or whatever.

The stems of these species are mostly lacking spines, but all have extensions of the leaf bases that are like tough sleeves extending from one petiole or node to the next above, and these sheaths are invariably spiny; technically they are called *ochreas*. Unlike the leaves of nonclimbing palms, the leaves of these climbers extend from the top of the stem to its bottom in some instances, but more rarely

are found on the top third or half of the stem. The inflorescences are elongated with few or many short flowering branches bearing both male and female blossoms, or often only male flowers. All these palms produce attractive clusters of red or orange rounded fruits.

The few species in cultivation grow best with a rich soil, copious water, and partial shade or full sun. All species are indigenous to lowland rain forest and none are cold tolerant.

The genus name comes from two Greek words meaning "band" and "hook" and refers to the cirri at the ends of the leaves. PLATES 346–350.

Desmoncus giganteus is indigenous to southern Colombia, eastern Ecuador, northern Peru, and extreme western central Brazil, where it grows in lowland rain forest. The epithet is Latin for "gigantic," an allusion to the immense leaflets.

The stems grow to 80 feet, with leaves confined to the upper parts thereof. The leaves are soft and limp and, therefore, pendent, and look, from any distance, as much like leaves of a *Dracaena* species or a large aroid than those of a palm. Each leaflet is 2 feet long and 3 inches wide, linearly ovate-lanceolate, glossy deep green above, and waxy, whitish green beneath. Straight black spines cover the leaf rachis and the ochreas.

This species is most likely not in cultivation but is so interesting and even attractive that it needs to be. The stems could be cut back regularly, as is done with several *Calamus* species, to keep the handsome leaves at eye level.

Desmoncus orthacanthos is the most far ranging species of the genus, from southeastern Mexico southwards through Central America and most of the northern half of South America east of the Andes, from sea level to elevations near 3000 feet; it is found mostly along rivers, in cleared areas of the rain forest, and in coastal forests. The epithet is from Greek words meaning "straight" and "spine."

This is a clustering species with stems attaining lengths of 40 feet but widths of 1 inch. The leaves are 3 to 6 feet long and grow only on the upper part of the stem. The leaflets vary in size, shape, and arrangement and may grow in clusters or singly, be regularly or irregularly spaced, bear short spines or not, and be linear-elliptic or ovate; they may be straight and stiff or limpish and curling. Two invariable characteristics are the rachis, which is erect, stiff, and straight as an arrow, and its attendant spines, which are straight, stiff, black, and 2 inches long.

The stems are used in the palm's habitats to weave baskets. PLATE 346.

Desmoncus polyacanthos is indigenous to a large area of northern South America east of the Andes, where it grows in almost every type of habitat below 3000 feet elevation. The epithet is derived from two Greek words meaning "many" and "spine," an apt allusion to the prickly stems, petioles, and rachises.

The stems grow to maximum lengths of 50 feet, clambering over and hooking onto other vegetation by the cirri. The leaves are 6 feet long with evenly spaced 1-foot-long dark green elliptic and wavy margined leaflets.

DICTYOCARYUM is a genus of three large, mostly solitary-trunked, pinnate-leaved, monoecious palms in the rainy cloud forests of the mountains of northern South America, although one species is also found at lower elevations.

All three species have large cones of spiny stilt roots at the bases of their trunks, enormous plumose leaves held on short petioles in a sparse crown, tall crownshafts, and unusually large inflorescences growing from beneath the shafts. The inflorescences are once branched, the flowering branches pendent in a curtainlike fashion from the stiff and horizontally held peduncle. The 1-inch-wide fruits are globose and yellow when ripe.

The species are related to and closely resemble those of the genus *Iriartea*. All require great and regular amounts of moisture and a noncalcareous soil. They are not frost tolerant, but the ones from high elevations should do well in frostless but cool, Mediterranean climates if given enough water.

The trunks of these palms are used by the native peoples for construction.

The genus name is from Greek words meaning "net" and "nut," an allusion to the markings on the seed coat. PLATE 351.

Dictyocaryum fuscum is endemic to the mountain ranges of northern Venezuela, where it grows in rain forest at elevations of 3000 to 5500 feet. The epithet is Latin for "reddish brown," an allusion to the color of the horn-like spathes.

This species is similar to *D. lamarckianum* except for its slightly shorter stature, columnar and nonbulging stem, and its giant downward-curving inflorescence spathes.

Dictyocaryum lamarckianum is the most widespread species, occurring in the rain forest of easternmost Panama, the high Andes of Colombia, Ecuador, Peru, and into western Bolivia at elevations of 3000 to 6000 feet, where it often grows in immense colonies on mountain slopes. The epithet honors French naturalist Jean B. P. M. de Lamarck (1744–1829).

The trunks grow to 70 feet high in habitat but slightly more than 1 foot in diameter and sit atop a massive cone of spiny stilt roots; they usually exhibit a slight bulge near the middle of the stems and are light gray to white, with distinct and widely spaced darker rings of leaf base scars in their younger parts. The smooth, light green crownshafts are 6 to 8 feet tall and are bulged at their bases but otherwise hardly exceed the girth of the trunks. The 12- to 16-foot-long leaves are in a sparse crown that never has more than six leaves, and are borne on short petioles that, from any distance (like the ground) are mostly invisible. The leaves are erect and slightly arching near their apices, never lie beneath the horizontal, but are plumose with linear, 2-foot-long leaflets that are deep green above and silvery glaucous beneath. The immense inflorescences burst out from large, upwardly-curving horn-shaped spathes beneath the crownshafts and are yellowish white with unisexual blossoms of both sexes.

The palm is a true water lover. It also needs a rich soil that is slightly acidic and contains humus; these requirements keep it from being grown in hot, nearly tropical climates like southern Florida where the nighttime temperatures remain high in the summer and where the soil is mostly alkaline. It flourishes in partial shade when young but, when older, needs lots of light. It withstands temperature near freezing for short periods but is also killed by short periods of freezing temperatures.

The palm is truly magnificent and unparalleled as a specimen tree. It looks best in groups of three or more individuals of varying heights. Its skyline silhouette is second to none and matches the *Iriartea* and *Wettinia* species. The only drawback to the species is that it is not particularly fast growing. PLATE 351.

Dictyocaryum ptarianum is indigenous to four disjunct areas of rain forest in northern South America: western and north central Peru and adjacent extreme western Brazil, southeastern Colombia, the Guyana Highlands of southern Venezuela, and adjacent Guyana. In Brazil, Peru, and Colombia the species occurs in mountainous rain forest at elevations of 600 feet whereas it grows at elevations of 2500 to 5280 feet in Venezuela and Guyana. The epithet is a Latinized form of the name of the table mountain in Venezuela (Ptari-tepuí) where the species was first collected. This palm is similar to *D. lamarckianum* except for its shorter stature (60 feet overall), nonbulging trunks, downward-curving floral spathes, and often sparsely clustering habit.

DICTYOSPERMA is a monotypic genus of pinnate-leaved, solitary-trunked, monoecious palm. The genus name is from Greek words meaning "net" and "seed," an allusion to the marking on the seed coat. Common English names are hurricane palm (because it reputedly resists strong winds by losing its leaves) and princess palm. The epithet is Latin for "white," an allusion to the most common color of the crownshaft. PLATES 352–354.

Dictyosperma album is endemic to the Mascarene Islands, where it grows in coastal forests. It is in danger of extinction because of the felling of trees for their edible growing points; only one individual is left in habitat of one of its naturally occurring varieties.

Mature trunks grow to a height of 30 feet but can reach 40 feet and are 6 inches in diameter except for a swollen base. The trunks are light to dark gray or light to dark brown and closely set with rings. The crownshaft is distinctive but partially hidden by the rounded crown of leaves. It is 4 feet tall, bulbous at its base, light green to gray or almost white (and sometimes with a reddish hue), and usually smooth but sometimes covered in a short felt. The beautifully full and mostly rounded leaf crown is 15 feet wide and 10 feet tall. The leaves are 8 to 12 feet long on petioles usually less than 1 foot long. The rachis of young leaves has a beautiful rounded arch and is twisted to 90 degrees for the last third or so of its length, resulting in the leaf plane being almost vertical from this point on. The leaflets are 2 to 3 feet long and narrowly lanceolate, tapering to a point; they grow from the rachis in a single flat plane. The new leaves are slow to unfold their leaflets and remain in a great thick, needlelike shoot before the leaflets unfurl. The latter are deep green, with a prominent midrib, and are usually drooping on older leaves. Young plants often have a reddish petiole whose color is lost when the plant is older. The inflorescences are 2 feet long and usually form a ring around the trunk below the crownshaft. They carry creamy white to yellow to reddish brown single-sexed small, fragrant flowers. The fruits are 0.5 inch wide, deep purple to black, and ovoid.

This species was at one time thought to encompass four separate varieties, all in danger of extinction in habitat. The varieties were separated according to color of flowers and veins in the leaflets.

The species is slightly susceptible to lethal yellowing disease. The palm is a water lover and, while it survives in poor, dry soil, its growth is so changed that it is scarcely recognizable to specimens grown under optimum conditions. It is adapted to full sun but grows readily in partial sun. It needs a good, well-draining soil. It is nearly tropical in its temperature requirements and is adapted to zones 10b and 11, although some nice specimens are to be found in favorable microclimates of 10a. The palm grows moderately slow to moderately fast, depending on the conditions.

The species is allied genetically and visually to *Archontophoenix cunninghamiana* and serves generally the same landscape uses, but it seems slightly heavier and more noble in appearance. While good as an isolated specimen surrounded by space, the palm is incredibly tropical and lush looking when planted in groves or in groups of three or more individuals of varying heights. It is seldom grown indoors but is adaptable to large, sunny conservatories with good air circulation.

DRYMOPHLOEUS is a genus of seven pinnate-leaved, solitary-trunked, monoecious, stilt-rooted palms in the Moluccas, New Guinea, the Solomon Islands, and Western Samoa. These are lovely, mostly small palms with straight, beautifully ringed trunks, elegant crownshafts, and variously incised leaflets; the terminal pair of leaflets is often united. The inflorescences are small and sparsely branched, and the fruits are orange or red.

All the species are water lovers, need protection from the midday sun, especially when young, and need a humus-laden, free-draining soil. They are all intolerant of cold and are adaptable to zones 10b and 11.

The genus name is from two Greek words meaning "wood" and "bark," the allusion unexplained. PLATES 355–358.

Drymophloeus hentyi is endemic to rain forest on the island of New Britain. The epithet honors E. E. (Ted) Henty, 20th-century botanist and curator of the herbarium at Lae, Papua New Guinea. The species grows to 15 feet and has a beautiful medium green crownshaft. The recurving leaves have wedge-shaped leaflets with oblique, jagged apices.

Drymophloeus litigiosus is indigenous to northwestern New Guinea, where it occurs in the undergrowth of rain forest.

This choice little palm grows to 12 feet high. The light green crownshaft bulges at its midpoint in a sort of spindle shape. The leaves have regularly spaced leaflets growing in a flat plane and apices that are usually jagged; the leaflets of the terminal pair are larger than the others. PLATES 355 & 356.

Drymophloeus oliviformis occurs naturally in West Papua and is in great danger of extinction. The epithet is Latin for "formed like an olive" and alludes to the shape of the fruit.

The species is similar in most respects to *D. litigiosus* except that the terminal pair of leaflets is united to form a single, large segment that may or may not be itself cleft. David Fairchild (1943) described the texture of the leaflets as rubbery when he found the palm on Amboina in 1940.

Drymophloeus pachycladus is indigenous to the Solomon Islands in the South Pacific, where it grows in low mountainous rain forest. The epithet is derived from two Greek words meaning "thick" and "branched."

It is one of the larger species in the genus with trunks growing as tall as 20 feet. The prominent crownshaft is 3 feet tall, olive green, and slightly bulging at its midpoint. The leaves are 6 to 8 feet long, beautifully arching, with widely spaced, large, and wide, wedge-shaped leaflets that are variously incised and lobed apically.

This one is perfection as a small canopy-scape and, because of its near ravishing form, even works as a specimen palm, albeit on a small scale. PLATE 357.

Drymophloeus subdistichus is endemic to the Solomon Islands in the South Pacific, where it grows in rain forest at elevations below 1000 feet. The epithet is from Latin words meaning "almost two-ranked," an allusion to the arrangement of the flowers in the inflorescences.

It is one of the largest species in the genus, the light brown to grayish trunk attaining a height of 30 or more feet and a diameter of less than 1 foot, with closely set darker rings of leaf base scars; it grows atop a small, 10-inch-tall cone of stilt roots whose diameter is scarcely wider than the base of the actual trunk. The crownshaft is 4 feet tall and a beautiful silvery green except at its top, which is suffused with black or dark purple. The 7- to 8-foot-long leaves are borne on short petioles and are ascending but arched from their midpoints. The 1-foot-long, 2- to 3-inch-wide leaflets are light to deep green, oblanceolate, and obliquely jagged at their apices; they grow from the rachis at an angle which gives a slight V shape to the leaf.

This palm, because of its more than delightful overall form, is striking enough to be used as a specimen, even surrounded by space; in groups of three or more individuals of varying heights, it is a magnificent canopy-scape. Few forms are lovelier. PLATE 358.

DYPSIS is a large genus of 140 pinnate-leaved, massive to tiny, monoecious, solitary-trunked or clustering palms growing in open savannas as well as dry and wet forests throughout Madagascar, the Comoro Islands, and Pemba Island in the far western Indian Ocean. Almost all the species have a crownshaft and many have plumose leaves. The inflorescences mostly are formed from within the leaf crown but sometimes beneath it, and the flowers are invariably unisexual, with both sexes present. The fruits are mostly brightly colored, but some species produce black or brown fruits.

Before the groundbreaking work of John Dransfield and Henk Beentje in Madagascar, 7 to 24 small, mostly undergrowth species had been placed in the genus *Dypsis*. Between 1986 and 1994 the two scientists almost revised the palm flora of that part of the world, and especially the genus *Dypsis*, which presently includes more than 80 per-

cent of the total palm species in the area studied. Why this occurred is because so much of Madagascar was botanically unknown. Another reason is that the palms especially were unknown scientifically, and several genus names created in the past (when only a few species of native palm had been collected) were thought to represent distinct genera, such as *Chrysalidocarpus, Macrophloga, Neodypsis, Neophloga, Phloga,* and *Vonitra.* The research of Dransfield and Beentje clearly showed that descriptions of the just-mentioned genera constituted but points in a spectrum of characters that should unite them all into one genus and that the scientific description of *Dypsis* best fits them all.

Collectors have been at work in the palms' native haunts for a century and many of the species have been in cultivation for almost that long. This phenomenon has led to at least some of the pre-existing binomials being of uncertain validity and, in many cases, likely erroneous. Alas, only time and more scientific study will remedy the situation; and, in the case of Madagascar, time is of the essence, as most of the island's present ecosystems are in a state of irreversible degradation. The etymology of the present genus name is obscure. PLATES 359–394.

Dypsis ambositrae is endemic to the central highland of Madagascar, where it grows in forest at elevations of 4200 to 4800 feet. It is in danger of extinction, there being fewer than 10 individuals left in habitat in 1995. The epithet is Latin for "of Ambositra," a town in the palm's habitat.

It is a sparsely clustering species with trunks attaining a height of 20 feet and a diameter of 4 or 5 inches. They are light brown or gray in their older parts but green and distinctly ringed with whitish leaf base scars in the younger parts. The grayish green and glaucous crownshaft is 3 feet tall and is hardly wider than the trunk. The leaf crown is round and dense with 6-foot-long leaves on 1-foot-long grayish green petioles; the leaves are beautifully arching and recurved. The leaflets grow from the rachis at an angle of almost 90 degrees to create a V-shaped leaf; they are 3 feet long and erect, except near their apices where they are also shortly bifid.

This beauty is reportedly easy of cultivation and has some hardiness to cold. PLATES 359 & 360.

Dypsis baronii is endemic to northern, central, and eastern Madagascar, where it grows on steep slopes in wet forest from 2500 to 4500 feet elevation. The edible growing point is still harvested. The epithet honors Richard Baron, a 19th-century plant collector.

This clustering species is rarely found with solitary trunks. Mature stems attain heights of 25 feet and diameters of 6 inches. They are deep green on all but their oldest parts and are encircled with widely spaced white or gray rings of leaf base scars. The crownshaft is 1 foot tall, light green to yellow-green, slightly bulging at the base or sometimes the middle, and waxy and smooth. The leaf crown is sparse, usually containing six blades, with each leaf 6 feet long on a 1-foot-long petiole which, when newly expanded, is often red. The leaves are erect but arching, and the 1-foot-long, stiff, deep green leaflets grow from the rachis at an angle that gives the leaf a V shape. The much-branched inflorescences may grow from atop or beneath the crownshaft. They are coral colored and bear brown or whitish single-sexed small blossoms. The fruits are 0.5 inch wide, globose, and bright yellow.

The palm is better adapted to nearly frostless Mediterranean climates than to those that are constantly warm or tropical. It needs a lot of moisture and is not hardy to cold, being adaptable only to zones 10 and 11. It loves a rich, humus-laden, well-drained soil and flourishes in full sun or partial shade. There is no more graceful landscape subject. The palm should be planted against a contrasting background so that its diaphanous form can be appreciated. It is superb as a canopy-scape and nothing could be choicer than a clump of this palm in a patio or courtyard. It is not known to be grown indoors but is probably adaptable to such conditions. PLATES 361 & 362.

Dypsis bejofo is, in its habitat of the rain forest of northeastern Madagascar, an endangered species because of its few numbers. The epithet is the aboriginal name for the palm.

The mature trunks in habitat reach heights of 80 feet with diameters of 1 foot or slightly more. The crownshaft is 4 or 5 feet tall, slightly bulging at its base, and glaucous bluish green or almost greenish white. The leaf crown is sparse, but the leaves are massive, each as long as 20 feet, with 3- to 4-foot-long, linear deep green leaflets growing from the rachis at all angles to create a plumose leaf.

The palm may not be in cultivation, and many plants labeled as such do not seem to fit the scientific description by Henk Beentje.

Dypsis cabadae is not known in the wild, but its origin is presumed to be Madagascar. Plants were first identified growing in Cuba. The only common English name seems to be cabada palm. The epithet is a Latinized form of the surname "Cabada," honoring a Cuban medical doctor who probably brought the seed from Madagascar and in whose garden the palm was first identified as a separate and valid species.

This is a large, clustering species. Mature trunks grow to 25 feet high but are less than 6 inches in diameter. They are olive green to deep dull green and are graced with widely spaced light gray to almost white rings. Leaf crowns are 10 to 15 feet wide but 8 feet tall. Total height of a mature clump is 35 feet and the width is 20 to 25 feet. The green

to almost silvery gray crownshaft is 3 to 5 feet tall, smooth, and slightly bulging at its base. The leaves are 8 to 10 feet long on 1-foot-long petioles. The rachis arches stiffly upward and results in a crown of half erect leaves, none of which descend below the horizontal plane. The leaflets grow at a 20- or 30-degree angle, creating a slight V shape to the blade. They are bright medium green, 2 feet long, and pendent at the tip. The inflorescences are 5-foot-long pendent panicles of small yellow flowers. The 0.5-inch-wide, rounded red fruits are borne in pendent clusters.

The species is slightly susceptible to lethal yellowing disease. The palm is tender to cold and adaptable only to zones 10b and 11, although mature specimens are found in the most favorable microclimates of 10a. The tree is a water lover but can endure average amounts of moisture. It looks better in full sun but is adaptable to partial shade. It never makes a dense clump and often takes several years to start suckering, which phenomenon but emphasizes the extraordinary beauty of the trunks.

The palm's moderate size and gorgeous trunks make it one of the most successful tropical or subtropical large patio or courtyard landscape subjects. It is wonderfully attractive in silhouette against a large wall of vegetation of contrasting color or form. As a canopy-scape, it is unsurpassed. The only landscape use to which it is not suited is as an isolated specimen surrounded by a large space. The palm is successfully grown in conservatories and atriums. PLATES 363–366.

Dypsis catatiana is endemic to northern and eastern Madagascar, where it grows in rain forest from sea level to an elevation of more than 6000 feet. The epithet is a Latinized form of the French surname "Catat" and commemorates the original 19th-century collector of the species.

The green stem of this solitary-trunked, small undergrowth palm attains a height of 4 feet and a diameter of 0.5 inch. It forms no true crownshaft, but the sheaths are prominent. The leaves are glossy deep green above but paler and usually with a brownish hue beneath. They are up to 4 feet long and are usually unsegmented and apically bifid, although many specimens exhibit segmented leaves with three to five pairs of variably sized slightly S-shaped pinnae.

This choice little thing must be protected from the midday sun, especially in hot climates. It probably luxuriates in frostless Mediterranean climes if given constant moisture, partial shade, and a humus-laden, quickly draining soil. No data are available for cold hardiness, but the species is probably sensitive to frost.

Dypsis ceracea may not exist in or out of cultivation. The epithet is Latin for "waxy" and alludes to the glaucous crownshaft. John Dransfield writes that it has not been collected since 1949 (Dransfield and Beentje1995). When it was collected, it was found in two disjunct areas of the eastern coast of Madagascar in low mountainous rain forest. The binomial is still listed on several seed and nursery stock lists, and plants labeled as such are growing in several places in the tropics. It is possible that individuals in private and botanical gardens are *D. ceracea* as the palm's habitat is nearly devastated due to population expansion.

In any case, the palm last seen and described as *D. ceracea* was reported to be a solitary-trunked species whose stems attain a maximum height of 50 feet. The plants in cultivation now are robust looking but slow growing, with leaves 10 to 12 feet long, a distinct olive green to bluish green glaucous crownshaft, and regularly spaced deep green, limp leaflets growing in a single flat plane. The newly unfurling leaves are reported to be, in most cases, a beautiful pink to yellowish bronze, and this agrees roughly with the description quoted by Dransfield.

The plants in cultivation are not frost tolerant, as is to be expected of plants from lowland tropical rain forest, but they are magnificently beautiful and robust appearing. PLATE 367.

Dypsis concinna is endemic to eastern Madagascar, where it grows in rain forest at elevations of 2640 to 3600 feet. The epithet is Latin for "elegant" or "orderly."

This small undergrowth species is found as solitary-trunked and clustering specimens. The stems grow to 6 feet, and the leaf crown is usually extended. The leaves vary in form from unsegmented and very deeply bifid at the apex to finely segmented with leaflets narrowly elliptical, shiny medium green, and growing from the rachis in irregular, widely spaced groups at slight angles from the horizontal.

Dypsis crinita is a sparsely clustering species from northwestern and northeastern Madagascar, where it grows in mountainous rain forest along banks of streams and rivers at altitudes from 600 to 800 feet. The epithet is Latin for "hairy," an allusion to the persistent leaf base fibers.

The species is sometimes found as a solitary-trunked specimen in nature; the trunks also are sometimes branched above ground. The dark brown trunks grow to 40 feet in their native haunts, but none in cultivation are this large. The most distinctive feature of the species is the great amount of persistent light brown to cinnamon-colored leaf fibers on the younger parts of the stems. The most beautiful feature of the species is its leaves. These are an elongated ellipse in shape, usually 6 to 8 feet long, borne on 3-foot-long petioles, with regularly arranged, glossy medium to dark green, and limp, narrowly elliptic-

lanceolate leaflets growing from the rachis in a single flat plane. The rachises invariably twist 90 degrees in their apical halves to give the leaf and its leaflets a vertical orientation for half their length. The visual effect is reminiscent of a large cycad or *Phoenix roebelenii* but even lovelier. The new leaves are usually a beautiful orange brown to pinkish brown shortly after they unfold.

This palm is a true water lover, almost an aquatic. It needs a rich, humus-laden soil with pH that is not too high. It does not tolerate full sun in hot climates and is best in partial shade in any clime. While not hardy to cold, the palm has survived temperatures in the upper 20s (F) in central Florida, under canopy. Nothing could be more beautiful as part of a wall of vegetation and as an accent or focal point therein. PLATES 368 & 369.

Dypsis decaryi is endemic to a small area of extreme southeastern Madagascar, where it grows in dry forest on poor soil. The species is gravely threatened because of its small natural range and because so many of its seeds are collected for export to the nursery trade that the palm is not regenerating itself in habitat. The common name is triangle palm. The epithet honors the original collector, Raymond Decary.

This solitary-trunked species grows to 35 feet in habitat and 25 feet under cultivation. The trunks are free of leaf bases beneath the pseudo-crownshaft and are dark gray with closely set rings of leaf base scars. The stems are stocky and to 20 inches in diameter. The leaf crown is 15 feet wide and tall. The leaves grow from the trunk in three distinct vertical rows and the wide, overlapping leaf bases of the living leaves form a large triangle at the top of the trunk that is 3 feet tall and 2 feet wide. The leaves are 10 feet long and stiffly erect with only the tips pendent. The leaf petiole is short, 1 foot long, its base expanded into a large, plump, and broadly triangular sheath. It is covered when young in a fine felty rusty-colored tomentum that is soon shed to reveal a chalky bloom on the older bases. The 2-foot-long leaflets grow at a steep angle from the rachis to give a definite V shape to the leaf, and only the tips of leaflets near the tip of the blade are pendent. The lower leaflets are extended at their tips into long and thin threadlike filaments called "reins." Leaf color is grayish green to bluish green. The dead leaves tend to fall cleanly from the trunk, giving a distinctive inverted triangle to the leaf crown. The inflorescence grows from among the lower leaves, is much branched and 4 to 5 feet long, and bears small yellow unisexual flowers of both sexes. The fruits are 1 inch long, ovoid, and greenish yellow to white.

The species is slightly susceptible to lethal yellowing disease. It is safe only in zones 10 and 11, although it is found in 9b as a protected individual. It wants full sun but endures partial shade. It is drought tolerant but grows better with regular moisture. It needs a well-draining soil but is not particular as to type.

This is a sensational landscape subject whose great fountain sweep of grayish leaves is seen to best advantage against a dark green background. One of the most dramatically beautiful placements was at Leu Botanical Gardens in Orlando, Florida, where the triangle palm was planted in a widened circle in the middle of a broad cement walkway and surrounded on all sides by other palms and cycads; this siting not only allows a close-up view of its form but also singles it out from its surroundings, and the color of its leaves is striking against the darker greens around it. The silhouette of the triangle palm is almost amazingly decorative. The palm can work well in almost any landscape but should not be crowded into a small space where it looks quite uncomfortable. It is not known to be grown indoors, but it should succeed given lots of light and good air circulation. PLATES 370–372.

Dypsis decipiens is endemic to the plateau region of Madagascar, where it grows in exposed, rocky sites at elevations from 4000 to 6000 feet and is endangered because of habitat destruction due to agriculture and wildfires. The epithet is Latin for "deceiving," a term usually applied to plants that look remarkably like other species: "in this case, it is a particularly inappropriate name" (Dransfield and Beentje 1995).

The species is mostly found in nature as a solitary-trunked individual, but individuals with two or more stems are known. The mature trunks can attain heights of 60 feet in habitat and are encircled in their younger parts with wide, dark rings. The dark gray stems are massive and columnar, resembling those of royal palms (*Roystonea*) but even more so those of gigantic specimens of *Hyophorbe*. They are usually bulging in their middle portions but may also have a distinct, often grotesque bulge only near the base of the column; with age the upper stem invariably tapers. The crownshaft is 2 feet tall, a light, waxy green, sometimes almost white, and often scarcely thicker than the adjacent trunk, although many individuals show a slight bulge near the base of the column. The arching leaves are borne on short petioles less than 1 foot long. The stiff leaflets are usually deep green on both surfaces but sometimes are bluish and glaucous. They grow from the rachis at a steep angle to give the leaf a V shape, but this phenomenon is obscured because of the short petioles and the arrangement of the leaflets in plumose groups. The short but much branched inflorescences grow from beneath the crownshaft and bear many small yellow blossoms of differing sexes. The globose 0.5-inch fruits are yellow.

This species seems temperamental in its climatic requirements, flourishing in nearly frostless Mediterranean climates but languishing in hot and moist tropical or subtropical climes. The trees reportedly are immune to light frosts and are drought tolerant but slow growing. They seem to be not particular about soil type as long as it is well drained. From all reports, they need full sun when past the seedling stage. David Witt (pers. comm.) reports that the species is a "tillering" palm that tries to pull itself downwards as a seedling and therefore needs to be planted high to counteract this tendency in wet climates.

This imposing palm works even as an isolated specimen, surrounded by space. It is more pleasing in groups of three or more individuals of varying heights; and it is visually arresting as a canopy-scape. It is not known to be grown indoors and may not be amenable to such conditions. PLATES 373–375.

Dypsis fibrosa is endemic to mountainous rain forest of eastern Madagascar at elevations from sea level to 2640 feet. The epithet is Latin for "fibrous."

This palm is a sparsely clustering species whose individual fiber-laden trunks attain heights of 20 feet in nature and are often branched above ground. The stems are usually covered with a mass of long, deep brown fibers, which in the youngest parts are especially long and are pendent. The leaves are 6 feet long, with widely but regularly spaced dark green, narrow, linear-elliptic, and S-shaped leaflets growing in a flat plane. The leaf rachis, like that of *D. crinita*, is twisted in its apical half to give a vertical orientation to the leaf and the leaflets from that point on; new leaves are usually light red or pink.

The species does not tolerate cold, is adaptable only to zones 10b and 11, and is marginal in 10a. It is a water lover and likes a humus-laden soil. It thrives in partial shade or full sun except in the hottest climates. The palm is robust looking enough to be used as a specimen, a contrasting component of other vegetation, or a close-up subject.

Dypsis hovomantsina is endemic to the lowland rain forest of northeastern Madagascar, where it is rare and threatened because of agricultural expansion. The epithet is the aboriginal name that, according to Dransfield and Beentje (1995), means "stinking," a reference to the smelly but edible growing point.

The stem of this solitary-trunked palm attains a height of 40 feet and a diameter of 1 foot; it is a light cinnamon color in its older parts, the younger parts a grayish green with widely spaced rings of brown leaf base scars. The bulging crownshaft is 3 feet high and is a beautiful waxy white except near its summit where it has a reddish brown feltlike tomentum. The leaf crown is hemispherical with spreading 10-foot-long, barely arching leaves on 18-inch-long, thick petioles and bearing narrow, long dark green leaflets that grow at all angles from the rachis to give a wiry plumose effect.

This odd-looking palm is not always beautiful or tidy looking but is fascinating to contemplate because of the unusually colored crownshaft and the large wiry leaves. It is tender to cold and needs copious and regular moisture in a humus-laden soil.

Dypsis lanceolata is endemic to the elevated rain forest of the Comoro Islands, east of Mozambique and northwest of Madagascar, where it grows from elevations of 1000 to 3000 feet. The epithet is Latin for "lanceolate," in reference to the shape of the leaves.

This palm is a small, mostly clustering species with trunks attaining a maximum height of 20 feet; they are olive green in all but their oldest parts and bear widely spaced, darker rings of leaf base scars. The elongated crownshaft is light silvery green or even white and is covered in tiny whitish scales. The leaves on older palms are 8 feet long, borne on short petioles, and carry wide, glossy light green, tapering and pointed leaflets which grow from the rachis at an angle when young but from nearly the same plane when older.

This exceptionally beautiful species resembles *D. cabadae* but is of smaller stature. It needs abundant and nearly constant moisture, a tropical climate, full sun to partial shade, and a moist, well-drained, rich soil. PLATES 376 & 377.

Dypsis lastelliana is endemic to northwestern and northeastern low, mountainous rain forest and lowland wet forests of Madagascar. Common names are teddy bear palm and redneck palm. The epithet honors the original collector, de Lastellé.

The palm is solitary trunked. Mature trunks can grow to 65 feet in habitat but usually attain half that height under cultivation. They are 10 to 15 inches in diameter and have phenomenal color in their younger parts: the stems are deep brown to reddish brown with wide, closely spaced pure white rings of leaf base scars. The leaf crown is 12 feet wide and 8 feet tall and is the glory of the palm. It is loosely formed and 2 feet tall, but it has an outstanding color of deep orange-brown to reddish brown and is felty to the touch. The leaf crown is nearly rounded with leaves that are 10 feet long, erect, and slightly arching but some of which fall beneath the horizontal and are carried on short pet ioles that are never more than 1 foot long. The many narrowly lanceolate 18-inch-long leaflets grow from the rachis in a flat plane but are pendent and glossy deep green on both sides. The leaf crown is not dense, and the old leaves fall cleanly, leaving only a half crown. The inflorescences are borne from among the lower leaves and are 2 feet long and much branched. They bear small whitish unisexual flowers. The fruits are 1 inch long, ovoid, and orange.

This species has been confused with *D. leptocheilos* (see following). Almost all growers in Florida still think they are growing *D. lastelliana*, although there are exceedingly few representatives of it in that state; most so-named individuals are actually *D. leptocheilos*.

Dypsis leptocheilos is endemic to Madagascar but precisely where seems unclear. It was first described from a garden in Tahiti and, because it was thought to be a cultivar, was named *D. lastelliana* 'Darianii'. The epithet *leptocheilos* is from two Greek words meaning "thin" and "lip."

This species is generally similar to *D. lastelliana* but has a lighter-colored, even looser crownshaft, is shorter, and has 12-foot-long leaves that are elongated ellipses with flatter, much more spreading leaflets. The leaves are as beautiful as those of *D. lastelliana*. Horticulturally the difference is that *D. leptocheilos* endures cooler temperatures at or slightly below freezing and does not require as much moisture or as good a soil as *D. lastelliana*; it thrives in southern Florida and coastal southern California on soils that are alkaline.

The species is tender to cold and adaptable only to zones 10b and 11. It needs regular moisture and a humus-laden, well-drained, slightly acidic soil. It is a "tillering" palm that tries to pull itself downwards as a seedling (David Witt, pers. comm.) and therefore needs to be planted high to counteract this tendency in wet climates.

This beautiful palm does not work well as an isolated specimen surrounded by space; it needs to be in groups of three or more individuals of varying heights or used as a canopy-scape. Old, tall specimens look much like a straight-trunked coconut from any distance. This palm needs space and good light to do well indoors and is only suited to large greenhouses, atriums, or conservatories. PLATES 378–380.

Dypsis louvelii is endemic to the rain forest of central eastern Madagascar at elevations of 1000 to 3500 feet. The epithet is a Latinized form of the French surname "Louvel" and honors a 19th-century forester in Madagascar.

This small undergrowth palm has a thin trunk to 3 feet high in nature. The leaf crown is sparse, but the leaves are beautiful, each one being 3 feet long, linear wedge shaped, deep dark green, entire and undivided except for the deep single apical cleft, and heavily ribbed throughout. The new growth has a beautiful orange or reddish brown hue. The slightly branched inflorescences are long and form beautiful scarlet fruits, which cause the infructescence to become pendent.

The palm does not tolerate frost but succeeds in the cooler but frostless Mediterranean climates. It needs partial shade in all climates and a constantly moist but well-draining soil. PLATE 381.

Dypsis lutescens is endemic to sandy riverbanks and clearings in the wet forests of eastern Madagascar. Because of its small distribution in isolated areas and, mainly because of development and the expansion of agriculture there, the species is critically threatened. In its long history under cultivation, the palm has acquired several common names, including areca palm, yellow bamboo palm, butterfly palm, and golden cane palm. The epithet is Latin for "growing yellow," a reference to the petioles.

This is a clustering species whose trunks can attain a height of 25 feet with a diameter of 2 to 3 inches. The younger parts are deep green to yellow or even orange, depending on how much light they receive; the yellow color results from high light levels. The rings are relatively closely set. The leaf crown is 12 feet wide and 10 feet tall. A mature clump can reach a height of 35 feet and a width of 20 feet. The 3-foot-long crownshaft is grayish green to almost silvery gray and slightly bulging at its base. The leaves are 6 to 8 feet long, narrowly ovoid, and beautifully arched. They are carried on lissome 2-foot-long petioles, and the 2-foot-long, thin and narrowly lanceolate yellow-green to dark green leaflets grow from the rachis at a 40-degree angle, creating a distinct V shape to the blade. The petiole and rachis are light green to almost orange, depending on the amount of light the plant receives, and the lightweight leaf moves in the slightest breeze. There are only six to eight leaves in a single crown, but their great arches give a full visual effect. The flower stalks are pendent and branched and grow from beneath the crownshafts. The flowers are yellow. The ovoid fruits are 1 inch long and yellow-orange to purple or black.

The palm is tender to cold and is restricted to zones 10b and 11, although its fast growth and clumping habit allow it to be widely grown in 10a with occasional damage. It loves water and needs sun to look its best but is not particular about soil type as long as it is well drained. Rooted suckers are easily transplanted but may sulk for a while after being planted.

Few plants are as breathtakingly graceful as a well-grown clump of this palm. It is so common in tropical areas that it is often overlooked, especially by palm collectors, in favor of less common and often harder to grow palms, most of which are not as beautiful. There is no more handsome screen than mature clumps of this species planted 10 feet apart; its wall of leaves from top to bottom creates a world unto itself, one of unexcelled grace and frozen movement. As a patio or courtyard subject, it is impossible to beat. The areca palm even looks good in the midst of a lawn surrounded by space, and as a major accent among other masses of vegetation it is more than eye-catching. Like many other clustering palm species, the clumps are more beautiful, especially as a silhouette, if judiciously and occasionally thinned so that the trunks and their lovely forms may be better seen. This is one of the commonest indoor subjects. It needs high light levels to look good. It is also subject to spider mite infestation in low humidity situations. PLATE 382.

Dypsis madagascariensis is endemic to northern and northeastern Madagascar, where it grows in dry, open areas of semideciduous forest as well as in rain forest. There are both clustering and solitary-trunked individuals. The clumping forms are known as **D. madagascariensis var. lucubensis**. This species is endangered because of habitat destruction and harvesting of its edible growing point. The epithet is Latin for "of Madagascar."

Mature trunks reach a height of 25 feet and a diameter of 6 inches and are slightly swollen at their bases. They are gray to greenish (especially the younger parts) with prominent and widely spaced rings. The leaf crown is 20 feet wide and 15 feet tall. The clustering forms produce few trunks, and they are not dense, attaining a total width of 30 feet. The crownshaft is only 1 foot or so in height, smooth, light green, and thicker at the top than at the bottom. The leaves are 10 feet long and stiffly arching, and are held on 6- to 8-inch-long petioles. The 2-foot-long dark green leaflets grow from the rachis in small groups, emanating from the stem at different angles to give a plumose appearance to the blade. The arrangement of the leaflets, their width, and even their color vary, some plants have plumose leaves with narrow leaflets, others having leaves whose leaflets spring from the rachis at a 40-degree angle, giving a V shape to the blade. The inflorescences are densely branched, grow from beneath the crownshaft, and bear yellow flowers. The fruits are 0.5 inch long, ovoid, and black.

This species is intolerant of cold and is adaptable only to zones 10b and 11. It relishes full sun and is drought tolerant but looks and grows much better with regular and adequate moisture. It seems not particular about soil type as long as it is well drained.

This species has more in common visually with *D. cabadae* than it does with *D. lutescens*, but its trunks are less attractive. It is (or should be) used in the landscape as is *D. cabadae*; it can, however, look better as an isolated specimen. It is difficult to maintain indoors in any but the brightest and airiest of large glasshouses. PLATES 383–385.

Dypsis malcomberi is a rare and endangered species endemic to southeastern Madagascar, where it grows in wet forest at elevations of 1000 to 2640 feet. The epithet honors Simon Malcomber, a member of the Dransfield-Beentje expeditions to Madagascar.

This is a large solitary-trunked palm whose distinctly ringed trunk attains a height of 80 feet in habitat. The mint green, wax-covered crownshaft is 5 to 6 feet tall and slightly bulging at its base, mostly cylindrical otherwise. The leaf crown is sparse and hemispherical with 10- to 12-foot-long spreading and slightly arching, deep green, plumose leaves.

This beautiful species looks from a distance like an elegant version of a queen palm (*Syagrus romanzoffiana*) and should serve the same landscaping purposes as the queen, except that it is tropical in its requirements. It grows fast with regular and adequate moisture in a humus-laden, well-drained soil, and withstands full tropical sun once past the juvenile stage.

Dypsis mananjarensis is endemic to eastern Madagascar, where it grows in dry and wet habitats at low elevations. The epithet is Latin for "of Mananjary," a region of the palm's habitat.

This is a solitary-trunked palm whose straight stem attains a height of 80 feet in habitat and a diameter of 1 foot. It is ringed with whitish widely spaced leaf base scars and is greenish in its youngest parts but gray in its older parts. The glaucous crownshaft is 4 feet tall, bulging at its base, and varies from silvery green to yellow or orange-yellow because of large, waxy scales that cover it; the scales give the palm a palpable gritty appearance, which has led to the common name of mealy bug palm. The sparse leaf crown is hemispherical or less and consists of 10-foot-long leaves that are spreading, unarching, and arranged in three ranks. They are borne on short petioles, which are covered in the same scales as the crownshaft and bear many 3- to 4-foot-long dark green narrowly lanceolate leaflets; the leaflets grow from the scaly rachis in groups and from different angles to give a plumose effect.

This is an impressive palm when mature and a fast, robust grower until mature. It is not frost tolerant but should grow well in frostless Mediterranean climates as it does not need copious moisture or humidity.

Dypsis onilahensis occurs in small pockets of evergreen forest throughout Madagascar. The epithet is Latin for "of Onilahy," a river in southwestern Madagascar. The species is closely related to, similar in appearance to, and has the same cultural requirements as *D. baronii*. PLATE 386.

Dypsis pembana is a rare clustering species endemic to the island of Pemba off the coast of Africa, where the borders of Kenya and Tanzania meet. It grows in a single lowland rain forest. The epithet is a Latinized form of the name of the palm's habitat.

The palm grows to 40 feet, with a light brown or gray trunk that is straight and encircled with widely spaced whitish rings of leaf base scars. The plump crownshaft is 1 foot tall, olive green, and bulging at its base. The 6-foot-long leaves are borne on short petioles, with deep green, linear, and tapering leaflets that grow from the rachis at a steep angle to create a V-shaped leaf.

The species does not tolerate cold and is adaptable only to zones 10b and 11. It needs abundant and nearly constant moisture and a rich but well-draining soil. It thrives in full sun to partial shade.

Dypsis pilulifera is endemic to northern and eastern Madagascar, where it grows in rain forest at a moderate elevation of 2640 feet and is endangered because of being felled for its edible growing point. The epithet is Latin for "bearing little globes," a reference to the fruits.

This is a solitary-trunked species whose stem in habitat can attain 100 feet high but is scarcely more than 1 foot in diameter. It is brown or dark gray in the older parts but greenish in the younger parts and distinctly ringed with brown leaf base scars in all parts. The crownshaft is 3 to 5 feet tall, bulging at its base, and green, brown, or yellowish according to the age of most sheaths. The leaf crown is sparse and slightly more than hemispherical. The leaves are 12 to 15 feet long, spreading and slightly arching, and borne on short petioles. The 3- to 4-foot-long leaflets are deep green on both surfaces, grow in widely spaced groups, and are pendent.

This is one of the most attractive palms in Madagascar and is beautiful in silhouette. It is fast growing if given a decent soil, regular and adequate moisture, and a tropical climate.

Dypsis pinnatifrons is endemic to eastern Madagascar, where it occurs in the undergrowth layer of rain forest at elevations from sea level to 3000 feet. The epithet is a combination of two Latin words meaning "pinnate" and "leaf."

The stems of this solitary-trunked species can attain 40 feet of height in its native haunts, are never more than 6 inches in diameter, and are as straight as an arrow. All but the oldest parts of the trunk are light to dark green with distinct and widely spaced white encircling rings of leaf base scars. The crownshaft is swollen at its base and light green to nearly white. The leaf crown is elongated, and the leaves are widely spaced along the upper part of the stem. Each one is borne on a short petiole and has widely spaced, S-shaped or obovate, medium green, tapering and long-tipped leaflets arranged in widely spaced groups, except near the apex of the leaf where they are usually more closely set. The newly unfurled leaves are usually purplish red or pink. The inflorescences grow from the top of the crownshaft and consist of many thin, light yellow branches carrying tiny flowers. The small fruits are brown when mature.

The species is not tolerant of cold and needs a site in partial shade, with abundant and regular moisture and a rich, fast-draining soil. A natural form with a rosy hued crownshaft and wine-colored new growth is one of the most beautiful plants in the genus. PLATES 387–390.

Dypsis prestoniana is endemic to central eastern and southeastern Madagascar, where it grows in low mountainous rain forest. The epithet "honors Mr. Paul Preston, president of McDonald's Restaurants Limited (UK), who sponsored the four-year Palms of Madagascar fellowship" (Dransfield and Beentje 1995).

It is a solitary-trunked species whose straight stem attains a height of 35 feet in habitat, with a diameter of slightly more than 1 foot. It is light grayish green to dark gray and has distinct dark gray rings of leaf base scars in all but its older parts. There is no true closed crownshaft, but the leaf sheaths form a loose inverted pyramid that is 4 feet high and green, often with brownish maroon tomentum near the summit of the mass and sometimes covering most of it. The leaf crown is usually less than hemispherical because of the erect 7-foot-long leaves. The latter are borne on short petioles and are erect but gracefully arching near their apices. The 4-foot-long dark green leaflets grow from the rachis in groups and at different angles and are mostly erect but have arching and pendent apices; the overall effect is that of a partially plumose V-shaped leaf.

This beautiful and robust-appearing palm is still rare in cultivation. All that is currently known is that it seems slow and need lots of water and a tropical or nearly tropical climate.

Dypsis procera is a sparsely clustering, variable species endemic to the low mountainous rain forest of northeastern Madagascar. The epithet is Latin for "tall."

The trunks can grow to 15 feet high and are usually less than 1 inch in diameter; because of the long internodes, they are elegantly reminiscent of bamboo stems. The 4-foot-long leaves range from entire but apically bifid to several broad leaflets to pinnate in segmentation but are always deep green.

The palm is intolerant of cold and drought. It needs a rich, moist, fast-draining soil.

Dypsis pusilla is a small undergrowth, mostly solitary-trunked but occasionally clustering species endemic to northeastern Madagascar, where it grows in moist coastal forest at low elevations. The epithet is Latin for "very small," an allusion to the palm's overall size.

The trunk grows to only 3 to 6 feet and is covered in fibrous leaf bases and small aerial roots. There is no crownshaft, and the leaf crown is hemispherical with erect and spreading, slightly arching 3-foot-long leaves on 1- to 2-foot-long petioles. The 12- to 18-inch-long dark green, lanceolate leaflets are regularly spaced in a nearly flat plane along the rachis.

This little palm is rare in cultivation but is reported to be slow growing and to need partially shady and moist conditions in a frost-free climate. It is fernlike in general appearance and makes a wonderful display in small groups under canopy.

Dypsis rivularis is a rare, solitary-trunked, stilt-rooted species endemic to northwestern Madagascar, where it grows along streams and rivers. The epithet is Latin for "of rivers" and refers to the palm's habitat.

The trunks are usually 6 or 8 feet high but in habitat may reach 15 feet. The crownshaft is loose and ill defined in younger plants but often distinct and red at its base in older trees, at which age it is usually deep olive green to brownish green. The leaves are 6 to 8 feet long with a gracefully arching rachis. According to John Dransfield (Dransfield and Beentje 1995), they appear "untidy" up close because the medium to dark green, slightly S-shaped, linear-lanceolate, and pendent leaflets tend to grow in irregular groups along the rachis; the leaflets of some leaves are almost regularly arranged. From any distance this "untidy" effect is not noticeable and, especially when planted in groups, the palm has a lovely, graceful appearance.

This species is another true water lover and is intolerant of alkaline soils. It does not tolerate frost and is adaptable only to zones 10b and 11 and probably marginal in 10a. PLATES 391–393.

Dypsis saintelucei is a sparsely clumping species endemic to extreme southeastern Madagascar, where it grows in coastal forest on sandy soil at elevations near sea level. It is rare and critically threatened because of its few numbers and development of its single site of nativity. The epithet is a Latinized form of the name of the region in which the species is native.

The trunks grow to 30 feet in habitat with a diameter of 6 inches and are usually straight as an arrow in cultivation. They are distinctly ringed with undulate, whitish leaf base scars and are brown or gray except for the youngest parts, which are wax covered. The outstanding crownshaft is light green, almost white or bluish white in many specimens, and is waxy, 1 or 2 inches wider than the trunk, nearly cylindrical, and 2 feet tall. The leaf crown has the form of a shaving brush because of the erect 6- to 7-foot-long leaves. The latter are borne on short petioles, arch apically, and grow in three ranks, but this fact is usually obscured visually because of their density in the crown. The medium to dark green leaflets are stiff and grow from the rachis at an angle to create a V-shaped leaf.

This outstandingly attractive palm, with visual affinities to both *D. cabadae* and *D. madagascariensis,* is reportedly easy of cultivation and seems to do well in frostless Mediterranean climates. It needs moderate moisture and full sun except for hot climates. It is not tolerant of freezing temperatures.

Dypsis sanctaemariae is a small clustering species endemic to the island of Sainte-Marie off the northeastern coast of Madagascar in the Indian Ocean. It occurs as an undergrowth subject in windswept coastal forest near sea level, and is rare and critically endangered because of its few numbers and real estate development. The epithet is Latin for "of Sainte-Marie."

The stems grow to 3 or 4 feet high and 0.5 inch in diameter. There is no crownshaft, but the persistent leaf bases clasp the stem and usually have a reddish patch of color near the beginning of the rachis (there is no true petiole). The leaf crown is extended, and the leaves to 4 feet long. They are either entire and very deeply bifid or divided into a few wide, stiff segments and are medium to deep green on both surfaces.

This attractive little species is still rare in cultivation. It seems to be intolerant of cold, needs partial shade and regular and adequate moisture, but is not fussy about soil type as long as it is well drained.

Dypsis schatzii is a small, rare and endangered, clustering or solitary-trunked species endemic to northeastern Madagascar, where it grows in lowland rain forest. The epithet honors George Schatz of the Missouri Botanical Garden.

The stems grow to 10 feet high in habitat and are less than 0.5 inch in diameter. The tiny crownshaft is 4 to 5 inches tall and is a glossy green overlain with tiny reddish scales. The leaf crown is hemispherical with usually 12 obovate, unsegmented, highly glossy 10- to 18-inch-long leaves, each with undulate and slightly jagged margins, shortly bifid at the apex and exhibiting a wine-colored midrib; occasionally the leaves are segmented into two unequally sized pinnae.

This is one of the world's most attractive small palms. It is rare in cultivation, and no data are available regarding its culture. It probably needs a tropical or nearly tropical climate, constant and adequate moisture, partial shade, and a humus-laden soil.

Dypsis tsaravoasira is a large, rare, solitary-trunked species endemic to northeastern Madagascar, where it grows in rain forest at elevations up to 3400 feet. It is under threat of extinction because of its few remaining individuals and agricultural expansion. The epithet is the palm's aboriginal name.

In habitat, the trunk grows to a height of 80 feet and a diameter of 18 inches. It is smooth, straight and, in its younger parts, green and distinctly ringed with lighter-colored leaf base scars. The 4- or 5-foot-tall crownshaft is cylindrical, a few inches wider than the trunk beneath it, and yellowish green. The leaf crown resembles a giant shuttlecock because of the 10-foot-long, erect leaves on short petioles. The leaves are beautifully arching and recurved in the apical third of their length. The 4-foot-long leaflets are stiff and grow from the rachis at a slight angle from the horizontal.

This great palm has one of the most beautiful silhouettes in the world. Alas, it is almost unknown in cultivation and no data are available on its cultural requirements, although it cannot be immune to frost and doubtless requires a humus-laden soil and copious moisture.

Dypsis utilis is a clustering or solitary-trunked, branching species endemic to eastern Madagascar, where it grows in low mountainous rain forest usually along streams and rivers. The epithet is Latin for "useful" and alludes to the long, tough fibers from the leaf bases, which are used for rope production and were profitably exported in the past.

The stems grow to 50 feet tall and 1 foot in diameter. They often branch dichotomously well above the ground but usually only twice per stem, and the branches grow parallel and close together. The trunks are light gray or light brown and exhibit many pendent, thin, brown leaf base fibers near the leaf crowns but form no true crownshafts. The crowns are hemispherical, with many densely packed 10- to 12-foot-long leaves on 2- to 3-foot-long petioles. The leaves usually exhibit a twist of the rachis at the midpoint so that the leaflets are aligned vertically from that point to the apex of the leaf. The 2- to 3-foot-long leaflets are linear-lanceolate, deep green, usually pinkish orange when new, and are slightly limp when old.

The species needs constant and copious water and is not hardy to freezing temperatures. It seems to not be fussy about soil type but needs full sun once past the juvenile stage. PLATE 394.

ELAEIS is a genus of two large, monoecious, pinnate-leaved solitary-trunked palms, one in Central America and South America and the other in Africa. The trunk of the American species creeps along the ground (or sometimes underneath it) for a time when young and then turns upright. The genus is not cultivated much, although it is worthy of being so. The genus name is based on the Greek word for the olive tree, an allusion to the valuable oil extracted from the fruits of both species. PLATES 395–399.

Elaeis guineensis is native to western and central tropical Africa, usually in cleared or open spaces and along streams and rivers and sometimes in swampy areas. It is often referred to as African oil palm. The epithet is Latin for "of Guinea," a country in West Africa.

Mature trunks reach a height of 60 feet or sometimes more in habitat but, under cultivation, are often no more than 40 feet tall. Diameter of the stem is 2 feet, and older parts are covered in rings of knobby leaf base scars, which create a chiseled look, while the younger trunks are usually densely covered in the tough wedge-shaped leaf bases. The full, rounded leaf crown is 25 feet wide and 20 feet tall. The leaves are 15 feet long and erect but gently arching near their ends. The stout green petioles are 3 to 5 feet long and armed with long, fibrous spines. The deep green 3-foot-long leaflets are limp and drooping and grow from the rachis in small clusters at slightly different angles, giving a plumose effect. The inflorescences usually consist of single-sexed flowers, but both types occur on the same tree, and a few inflorescences have both sexes in the same cluster; they are 1 foot long and wide and grow from among the lower leaves, carrying densely packed small whitish blossoms. The 2-inch-long fruits are densely packed into 1-foot-wide clusters, each one ovoid and black when mature.

A rich, humus-laden soil is best, although the palm can adapt to many soils. It luxuriates in full sun but adapts to partial shade. It is not hardy to cold and is adaptable only to zones 10 and 11. It is moderately slow growing but grows faster with ample moisture and a rich soil.

The African oil palm is one of the few palms that looks decent as an isolated specimen, so massive and spectacular is it; it is not for a small space, however. It looks better planted in groups of three or more individuals of varying heights. Young palms with little trunk do not show the characteristics of older plants with some trunk; their leaves are stiff and not as graceful. The palm has been called the poor man's Canary Island date palm as it is significantly cheaper to obtain than is *Phoenix canariensis*, it grows faster, has the same visual impact, and is not subject to lethal yellowing disease; it is, of course, only good for tropical or nearly tropical regions. The palm is not known to be grown indoors but, given enough space and high light levels, it should be possible.

The oil extracted from the seeds is a valuable commodity second in economic importance only to the coconut. Vast plantations in western Africa and southeastern Asia are devoted to its cultivation. This oil is used in the manufacture of many products, such as margarine, detergent, and soap, and is used as a fine lubricating agent in industry. PLATES 395–397.

Elaeis oleifera occurs naturally in two disjunct regions of tropical America: the first is primarily in Central America (Honduras, Nicaragua, Costa Rica, Panama, and northern Colombia), and the second in South America (northern Peru, Ecuador, the northern Amazon region of Brazil, Surinam, and French Guiana). It grows in wet, low lying areas near streams, rivers, and lakes, and was probably introduced eons ago into Brazil by the native peoples. The common name is American oil palm. The epithet is Latin for "oil-bearing."

Mature trunks are prostrate near their bases and to 20 feet long and 1 foot in diameter; they are covered in old leaf bases. The leaves are 12 feet long, erect but beautifully arching, on 4- to 5-foot-long spiny petioles. The deep green, 2-foot-long, linear leaflets grow from the rachis in one plane that would create a flat leaf were they not mostly pendent from the rachis. The inflorescences grow in tight, compact, and rounded clusters from among the leaves and bear either male or female flowers. The 0.5-inch-long, egg-shaped fruits remain in tight clusters and are yellow, orange, or red, often all three colors.

Because the lower portion of the trunk is prostrate, the entire trunk forms aerial roots, and the base of the stem often dies and rots away while the upper portion is erect, the species can actually move its location to a small extent. It seems to have the potential of being immortal unless destroyed by mechanical factors, because the stem avoids the stresses of great vertical height, which supposedly cause other aerial, solitary-trunked palms to eventually die.

This species is more tender to cold than its African relative and is adaptable only to zones 10b and 11. It needs copious water, as it is nearly aquatic, and a soil that incorporates some humus. It grows in full sun or partial shade but is always slow growing. This unusual palm is beautiful as a part of a wall of vegetation, from which its beautiful leaves with their drooping leaflets stand out in a tropical-looking contrast; its half-prostrate manner prevents it from being well used in most other situations. PLATES 398 & 399.

ELEIODOXA is a monotypic genus of clustering, pinnate-leaved, dioecious palm in Thailand, peninsular Malaysia, and eastwards to Borneo and Sumatra. The genus name is from Greek words meaning "water" and "glory," an allusion to the size, beauty, and natural habitat of the species. The epithet is Latin for "congested" and refers to the inflorescences.

Eleiodoxa conferta occurs naturally in lowland tropical swamp forests, often forming extensive colonies.

It is a densely clustering species with subterranean stems. The leaves arise directly from the ground and are each 12 feet long, stiffly ascending, and barely arching, on 10-foot-long deep green petioles. The leaf sheath near the base of each petiole bears partial rings of 2- to 3-inch-long spines that are black when new but age to almost white. The regularly spaced leaflets are 5 feet long, linear-lanceolate, with an obliquely terminated apex, medium to dark green, and margined with short spines; they grow in an almost flat plane from the rachis. The leaves look overall similar to those of a large *Arenga* species. The inflorescences grow from the underground trunks and are compacted short spikes of male or female flowers. The fruits on female plants are in compact clusters and are small, scaly, and reddish brown. The underground stem which produced the inflorescence dies off after the fruits mature but, since the species is so densely clustering, the dying leaves are soon replaced by those from another underground trunk.

The species must have copious water and a rich acidic soil, and it is intolerant of frost or even cold, being adaptable only to zone 11 and marginal in 10b. The palm is tropical looking and its large leaves make a stunning contrast with other vegetation when it is incorporated into same. Its size and clustering habit lend themselves to the palm's being sited as a specimen plant.

The seeds of this species are reportedly eaten (usually pickled) on Borneo.

EREMOSPATHA is a genus of possibly 12 pinnate-leaved, clustering, monoecious, spiny climbing palms in wet tropical Africa. Most species are large and high climbing with relatively slender stems. Juvenile leaves are entire except for the bifid apex and are borne on petioles, while the adult leaves are pinnately segmented, lack a petiole, and form cirri at their apices. Spines are confined to the leaf rachis, the margins of the leaflets, and the cirri. The inflorescences grow from the leaf axils, are relatively short, and sparsely branched, and bear bisexual flowers that produce small oblong scaly fruits.

None of the species seem to be in cultivation, and the genus is not well known even to taxonomists. All species are tropical in their temperature requirements and all need copious and regular moisture.

The genus name is derived from two Greek words meaning "lack of" and "spathe."

Eremospatha hookeri is indigenous to low mountainous rain forest in West Africa, where it grows in clearings and along riverbanks. The epithet honors 19th-century British botanist Sir Joseph D. Hooker.

It is a large species with stems to 150 feet long but usually around 75 feet. The leaves are small, 1 foot long, with an equally long cirrus. The leaflets are obovate and bear tiny spines on their margins.

Eremospatha macrocarpa is indigenous to low mountainous rain forest of West Africa, where it is found in forest clearings. The epithet is Greek for "large" and "fruit."

This is a large, densely clustering species whose slender stems reach lengths of 150 feet or more. The leaves are 5 feet long and bear long, narrow, slightly pendent leaflets with tiny prickles along their margins. The cirrus is almost as long as the leaf.

Eremospatha wendlandiana is indigenous to the low mountainous rain forest of coastal Nigeria and Cameroon, where it grows in swampy areas and forest clearings. The epithet honors Hermann Wendland, a 19th-century German botanist and gardener.

This is one of the smaller species, the stems usually growing to 70 feet long. The leaves are 7 feet long including the terminal cirrus. The large leaflets are 8 inches wide, dark green, widely spaced, plicate, triangular or wedge shaped, with notched or toothed apices.

EUGEISSONA is a genus of six unusual, clustering, spiny, monoecious palms in peninsular Malaysia, Thailand, and Borneo. There are both trunk-forming and trunkless species, and the species forming aerial stems usually have basal stilt roots supporting the trunks. The latter species are unusual in that the junction of aerial roots and trunks forms a basket in which much leaf litter can collect as well as various insect nests and other small animal residents. The trunks, petioles, and rachises bear spines, which, on the petioles, can be large. The leaves are large and borne on long petioles. The inflorescences are erect and spikelike, and bear large male and bisexual flowers; the inflorescence stem and bracts turn woody and persistent as the ovoid scaly fruits form. The stems flower terminally and die after the fruits ripen.

Some consider the trunking species like *E. tristis* untidy looking because of the masses of stilt roots and leaf litter, others find the large, feathery leaves to be gorgeous and, when incorporated into other vegetation, the ungainly trunk bases are hardly noticeable; they are, however, weedy in habitat. All the species are tropical and adaptable only to zones 10b and 11.

The genus name is from two Greek words meaning "good" and "roof," an allusion to the use of the leaves of most species for thatching roofs. PLATES 400–403.

Eugeissona brachystachys is endemic to peninsular Malaysia, where it grows in low mountainous rain forest. The epithet is from two Greek words meaning "short" and "spike," a reference to the inflorescences.

This is a trunkless species. The leaves are to 15 feet long with beautiful pinkish rachises and 6-foot-long petioles. The leaflets are regularly and widely spaced, each one 3 feet long, lanceolate, long tipped, and growing from the rachis in a single, almost flat plane.

Eugeissona insignis is endemic to the rain forest in Sarawak on the island of Borneo. The epithet is Latin for "remarkable."

It is another trunkless or nearly trunkless species whose great leaves are rigidly ascending and slightly arching when new but are later spreading and gently arching. They are 20 feet long. The regularly spaced thin leaflets are 3 feet long and pendulous, creating one of the most beautiful leaves of any palm. PLATES 400 & 401.

Eugeissona minor is endemic to Sarawak, where it grows in wet, low mountainous forests. The epithet is Latin for "smaller," a reference to the comparison of this species to *E. tristis,* which has similar leaves.

This clumping palm forms aerial stems or obvious aboveground short trunks on stilt roots that are taller than the trunks themselves. The leaves can reach 18 feet long on petioles almost as long. They are stiff, unarching, and completely ascending. The widely spaced leaflets are 3 feet long, narrow, and long tipped, and grow from the rachis in a single flat plane.

Eugeissona tristis occurs naturally in peninsular Malaysia and southern Thailand, where it grows in low mountainous rain forest or in low and swampy areas but usually on sloping ground. The Latin epithet translates literally as "sad" and, by extension, as "dull" or "colorless," an allusion to the drab brown and purple inflorescences.

It is a trunkless or almost trunkless species, which in habitat often forms large and impenetrable thickets of petioles and leaves. The latter are 20 feet long and bear regularly spaced 3-foot-long leaflets that grow from the rachis in a nearly flat plane.

This species is considered by many to be "untidy" because, in habitat, giant colonies of the palm usually have several dead leaves. The landscaping solution to this dishevelment is to limit the size of the individual clumps and therefore make it much easier to remove the unsightly deceased leaves. The living leaves are as beautifully magnificent as are those of any species in the genus. PLATE 402.

Eugeissona utilis is widespread on the island of Borneo and is found in peninsular Malaysia, where it grows in hilly rain forest. The epithet is Latin for "useful" and alludes to the usefulness of almost every part of the plant in habitat. The pith of the trunks is important in the palm's habitat for making sago.

The stems of this truly gigantic species grow to heights of 40 or more feet. The leaves are commensurably large and may reach 30 feet long. They are ascending but also beautifully arching and bear 4-foot-long pendulous leaflets, a truly magnificent sight. PLATE 403.

EUTERPE is a genus of seven monoecious, solitary-trunked or clustering pinnate-leaved palms in tropical American rain forest. The inflorescences grow from beneath the crownshaft and are sparsely branched, covered in short hairs, and whitish; they bear both male and female blossoms, which produce small, round black fruits.

These are some of the world's most beautiful palms and all have tall, slender crownshafts that may be green, yellow, or orange, and gorgeous pinnate leaves with pendulous and widely spaced long leaflets. They are without exception intolerant of frost and drought. Few tropical plants are as wonderfully graceful as these palms: their long drooping leaflets are comblike against the sky and create a constant visual effect of movement even in still air.

According to Henderson et al. (1995), the "genus is considered by many people to contain the most beautiful American palms" and yet only three of the species are in cultivation. In Florida one reason for their rarity is that, in the parts of the state with winters warm enough to grow them, the soil is usually not to their liking: they need an acidic or slightly acidic medium.

Many species once known under the name of "*Euterpe*" are now segregated into a closely related genus *Prestoea.* The genus name honors one of the Greek Muses and translates as "good delight." PLATES 404–407.

Euterpe edulis occurs naturally in the Atlantic coastal forests of eastern Brazil, southwards to extreme southeastern Paraguay and extreme northeastern Argentina. It is nearly extinct because of the felling of trees for their edible growing points. The epithet is Latin for "edible," a reference to the growing point.

The species is mostly a solitary-trunked palm but is rarely found clustering. Mature trunks grow to 30 feet high and 6 inches in diameter. They are light gray to light brown and are graced with widely set darker rings of leaf base scars. The crownshafts are 3 feet tall and 6 inches in diameter. They are deep green but often show a suffusion of orange or red. The leaf crown is 15 feet wide and 10 feet tall. The leaves are 10 feet long with unarching stiff rachises and 2- to 3-foot-long drooping narrowly lanceolate, widely spaced and tapering leaflets. They are light to medium green and carried on short, 1-foot-long petioles. Few if any of these elegant leaves descend below the horizontal plane. The inflorescences consist of many thin and furry branches, growing from beneath the crownshaft, bearing tiny whitish flowers. The unopened inflorescence is reportedly edible. The edible fruits are 0.5 inch wide, round, and dark purple to black when mature.

The species does not tolerate cold and is adaptable only to zones 10b and 11, although a few specimens are found in protected sites in 10a. It needs constant moisture and a rich acidic soil. The palm thrives in partial shade to full sun except in tropical desert regions where it needs lots of irrigation and protection from the hottest midday sun. The palm is moderately fast growing under optimal conditions.

All *Euterpe* species have exquisitely lovely leaves. They are extraordinarily beautiful planted in groups of three or more individuals of varying heights. They look good as solitary individuals only when used as a canopy-scape. The palm looks like a delicate and straight-trunked coconut. It is eminently adaptable to growing under glass if provided with ample moisture, humidity, light, and space.

Euterpe oleracea is indigenous to two disjunct regions of northern South America, one being western and northern central Colombia and extreme northern Ecuador, and the other being coastal areas of northeastern Venezuela, the island of Trinidad, the Guianas, and northeastern Brazil. It grows in low, wet areas along rivers and streams. The palm is usually called the assai (a-SAH-ee) palm in English-speaking countries, from the Portuguese name (*açaí*) for a popular drink made from the fruits in the Amazon region. The epithet is Latin for "vegetable-like," an allusion to the plant's edible growing point.

The species is clustering but often grows only a solitary trunk until that stem (almost) reaches its total height; then it produces suckers. It produces pneumatophores under swampy conditions in its habitat. Mature clumps may be 50 feet wide and 90 feet tall, while mature trunks attain a height of 80 feet in habitat but are usually no more than 60 feet under cultivation. They are never more than 6 inches in diameter and are green on their younger parts and light gray to light brown on the older parts. The crownshaft is 3 to 4 feet tall, smooth, and slender, and almost 6 inches in diameter throughout. Its color is usually a light to medium green, but some plants have crownshafts tinged with yellow, brown, or even purple. Leaf crowns are 15 feet wide and 10 feet tall. The leaves are 8 to 12 feet long, with straight, stiff rachises along which grow the 3-foot-long, narrow, widely spaced light to dark green pendulous leaflets. The leaves seldom descend beneath the horizontal and, like all the other species of *Euterpe*, fall cleanly from the trunk after dying and leave a neat appearing crown. The inflorescences are 3 feet long, growing from beneath the crownshafts, and are many branched; the branches are furry and bear tiny white flowers. The fruits are 1 inch wide, rounded, and dark purple when mature.

This species has the same cultural requirements as those of *E. edulis* but needs even more moisture. There is no more beautiful and spectacular palm. It combines grace and nobility like few other things in nature do, and mature clumps are beautiful enough to stand isolated but look better as canopy-scapes. The assai palm is eminently adaptable to cultivation under glass if enough space, humidity, moisture, and light can be provided. PLATES 404–406.

Euterpe precatoria has the widest distribution in the genus—from eastern Belize, eastern Guatemala, all the rest of Central America, into Colombia, eastern Ecuador, eastern Peru, northern Bolivia, north central Brazil, and the eastern Guianas. In the mountain regions of its range it occurs to elevations of more than 5280 feet, in wet forests, while in the lower areas of its range it grows along rivers, in swamps, and along lakes, often in areas that are seasonally inundated. A common name seems to be mountain cabbage palm. The epithet is Latin for "of supplication" or "relating to prayer," the allusion unclear.

In nature, the palm is usually found as a solitary-trunked specimen, only rarely as a clustering individual. The mature trunks are less than 1 foot in diameter but can attain heights of 60 feet. They are gray with widely, regularly spaced dark rings and a cone of stilt roots at their bases. The crownshaft is 6 feet tall, bright green, smooth, and barely wider in diameter than the trunk. The leaf crown is sparse and open with erect leaves whose rachises arch and droop at their apices. The leaves can be as long as 15 or 20 feet and are carried on relatively short petioles. The pendulous, medium green leaflets are numerous, regularly spaced, linear and tapering, and as long as 3 feet. The inflorescences form a large, encircling skirt beneath the crownshaft and consist of many branches carrying bright yellow blossoms. The fruits are 1 inch wide, round, and purplish black when mature.

A naturally occurring variety, ***E. precatoria* var. *longivaginata***, occurs in elevated areas; it has leaves with nearly flat and nonpendulous leaflets and generally shorter trunks. The word *longivaginata* is Latin for "long-sheathed." The type, ***E. precatoria* var. *precatoria***, hails from lower elevations and has taller and always solitary trunks and larger inflorescences.

The species needs constant and abundant moisture, a humus-rich acidic soil, and partial to full sun. It is not cold tolerant and succeeds only in zones 10 and 11 but can adapt to cool but frostless Mediterranean climates if enough moisture is provided. There is no more beautiful species of palm. It has every virtue of the family except for bright coloration. It is fetching enough to be planted in almost any site, including as an isolated specimen, but looks its best when used as a canopy-scape or mixed in a wall of contrasting vegetation. The palm is adaptable to large conservatories or atriums if enough light, space, and moisture can be provided.

The trunks are used for construction, the fruits in beverages, and Henderson et al. (1995) write that the roots are used medicinally. PLATE 407.

GASTROCOCOS is a monotypic genus of spiny, pinnate-leaved, solitary-trunked, monoecious palm. It is closely related to and similar in appearance to *Acrocomia* *aculeata* and will probably be incorporated into *Acrocomia* as soon as more study is done on both genera (Henderson et al. 1995). The palm was known as *A. crispa, A. armentalis,* and before that (1865), *Gastrococos.* The common name is Cuban belly palm, which has unfortunately been applied to another Cuban species, palmate-leaved *Colpothrinax wrightii.* The genus name combines the Greek word for "belly" with *Cocos.* The epithet is Latin for "curled" or "rippled." PLATES 408–412.

Gastrococos crispa is endemic to Cuba and the much smaller Isle of Youth, where it grows in open savannas at low elevations.

The trunk grows to 60 feet in habitat and is light gray to almost pure white. It invariably exhibits a distinct bulge (or belly) near the midpoint of the stem; this bulge is usually long and not very often rounded, giving to the trunk a distinct spindle shape. The trunk is graced with closely spaced darker rings of leaf base scars and, in the younger parts, spines that were associated with the leaf bases. The slightly arching, 8- to 10-foot-long leaves are numerous and produce a beautiful rounded crown that looks much like that of a royal palm (*Roystonea*); the leaves of most individuals are plumose with leaflets that grow from the spiny rachis in all directions and are deep green above but silvery or grayish green beneath. The leaves of juvenile plants have spiny rachises and leaflets, but the spininess is lost as the palm matures. The inflorescences grow from the leaf crown and bear unisexual yellowish orange flowers that produce clusters of round orange fruits.

The palm is slow growing when young but moderately fast after forming a few feet of trunk. It is wonderfully tolerant of calcareous soils but is also adaptable to those with a lower pH. It needs full sun from youth to old age and, while drought tolerant, grows faster and looks better with regular and adequate of moisture. Like *Roystonea regia,* this species is truly magnificent lining an avenue or other promenade, and its canopy-scape effect is one of the best. As a specimen it is best in groups of three or more individuals of varying heights, but it is always splendid and imposing as an adult. Being tolerant of such a range of soils, it is extremely valuable for adding the spice and variety to a given palm planting that everyone craves. The palm is not known to have been grown indoors and is probably a poor candidate for doing so as it requires such great amounts of light and good air circulation, not to mention space.

No one has come up with a good explanation for the bulges in the trunks of this species. Arthur C. Langlois (1976) suggests that they might be an "organ" for storing nutrient tissue in younger individuals to provide energy for the flowering process. If this is the case, why is it that other palm species from the same types of habitat do not exhibit the same phenomenon, and why do mature individuals of this species retain the bellies? Plants grown in shade are skinnier and often with only a small belly, while those grown properly in full sun with enough room always get a nice fat belly. Again, no one has an adequate explanation of why this is so.

GAUSSIA is a genus of five medium-sized, solitary-trunked, pinnate-leaved, monoecious palms in the West Indies and Central America. All the species have trunks with swollen bases, tapering tops, sparse leaf crowns, and cones of roots at their bases; they form indistinct, loose crownshafts. The inflorescences grow from the leaf sheaths and consist of a stiff, elongated peduncle at the end of which radiate the much-branched flowering branches bearing both male and female blossoms. The fruits are red when ripe.

These species are mostly found on mogotes (limestone hills). They are intolerant of real cold and are adaptable only to zones 10 and 11, although some specimens are found in protected areas of 9b.

The genus name honors the 19th-century German mathematician and physicist Karl Gauss. PLATES 413–418.

Gaussia attenuata is a rare species endemic in western Puerto Rico, where it grows on steep hillsides of the monsoonal limestone plains and is in danger of extinction because of its few numbers. The epithet is Latin for "attenuated," a reference to the top of the trunk, including the crownshaft.

The trunk can, with time, attain a height of 50 feet and a diameter of 1 foot. It tapers dramatically near the light green crownshaft that, in comparison with the rest of the trunk, sometimes seems almost grotesquely thin. The few leaves are 6 feet long on 8-inch-long petioles, with deep green, 2-foot-long, wide lanceolate leaflets that grow at an angle from the rachis, giving a V-shaped leaf.

The species is drought tolerant and slow growing. It needs full sun and a free-draining alkaline soil. The species is slightly susceptible to lethal yellowing disease. PLATE 413.

Gaussia maya occurs in scrublands on rocky, limestone outcrops and hills in Belize, the adjacent Mexican state of Quintana Roo, and in the Petén region of Guatemala. The common name is Maya palm. The epithet refers to the ancient Maya people who lived in the palm's habitat.

Mature trunks attain a height of 60 feet and are enlarged at their bases, the rest of the stem columnar and of unvarying diameter, light gray or light brown, with widely spaced, whitish rings of leaf base scars; they are never more than 1 foot in diameter above their bases, and usually less, which characteristic often sees them leaning gracefully because of the weight of the leaf crown. The crownshaft is smooth and deep green. The leaves are erect from the trunk but gracefully arching; they are 8 to 10 feet long on short petioles and have narrow light to deep green, 18-inch-long leaflets growing in groups at different angles from the rachis to give the leaf a plumose effect. The species has an interesting method of flowering: the inflorescences arise from the leaf base scars on the trunk and stop developing until several others form above them, at which point the first (lowest) inflorescence commences with anthesis. This process results in 12 or more branched inflorescences on the trunk at one time, spaced spirally around the upper part of the stem, and in various stages of flowering and fruiting.

The species is possibly more tolerant of cold than the others and has been successfully used in Orlando, Florida (David Witt, pers. comm.). It also likes more moisture than the other species, and the soil need not be as alkaline. This is one of the most beautiful species in the genus and certainly the most "typical" looking. It is excellent as a canopy-scape and equally wonderful as a specimen grouping of three or more individuals of varying heights. This is probably the only species of *Gaussia* adaptable to indoor cultivation; it needs lots of light and good air circulation. PLATES 414 & 415.

Gaussia princeps is endemic to extreme western Cuba, where it grows in monsoonal forest areas on limestone hills. The epithet is Latin for "chief" or "prince."

The mature trunks attain a height of 30 feet; they are light gray or even white, with greatly expanded bases, the remainder of the stem tapering to the crownshaft.

The palm is similar to *G. attenuata* but twice as tall and faster growing. It is extremely nice as a canopy-scape. PLATES 416 & 417.

Gaussia spirituana is endemic to central Cuba where it grows on limestone cliffs in monsoonal savannas. The Latin epithet is based on the name of one area in the palm's habitat, Sancti Spiritus. This is a somewhat grotesque appearing palm because of the greatly swollen trunk that tapers—until it is mature—to the slim crownshaft. Its maximum height is 18 feet, and it grows slowly. PLATE 418.

GEONOMA is a large genus of some 50 mostly small, pinnate-leaved, monoecious palms in tropical America. Most are found in the undergrowth of wet regions from sea level to 10,000 feet elevation.

There are both solitary-trunked and clustering species, and a few are tall and rise above the canopy. Almost all species have trunk "wood" that is extremely hard and durable for small palms. Some of the larger species have loose or rudimentary crownshafts. They are similar in many respects to species of *Chamaedorea* and *Calyptrogyne* and, as in *Chamaedorea*, some species vary in morphology, exhibiting a greater variation of leaf detail among the individual forms of a given species than exists between the species itself and other species in the genus. Within a given species, leaves may be undivided or divided and leaflet form may vary greatly. Many species have colorful newly emergent leaves from light pink to bright red to deep maroon. Most species do not form a true crownshaft. Furthermore, their similarities to species of the other two genera have led to some erroneous labeling in the nursery trade. The inflorescences are as variable as the leaves and may be much branched or simple spikes; they may grow from among the leaves or beneath the leaf crown and crownshaft. They bear flowers of both sexes, and the female blossoms produce fruits that are blue or black when mature.

Almost all these species are at least as beautiful as those in *Chamaedorea* but are not nearly so well represented in cultivation; the larger and often more beautiful species of *Geonoma* are especially rare in gardens. This is most likely due to their more remote habitats and their slow growth habit. Only species from high elevations can withstand frost, but several others perform well in cool, frostless Mediterranean climates. Their most important requirement is constant moisture and, for most, constantly high humidity. Few are adaptable to limey soils, and all need one that is fast draining.

The genus name is from two Greek words meaning "earth" or "ground" and "province" or "colony" and refers to the low or small habit of many species, which often grow in large colonies. PLATES 419–427.

Geonoma congesta is a mostly clustering undergrowth species indigenous to northeastern Honduras, eastern coastal Nicaragua, Costa Rica, Panama, and western central Colombia. It is found in low mountainous rain forest. The epithet is Latin for "congested" and alludes to the inflorescence, which is 2 feet long, including the peduncle.

The stems grow to 20 feet high but are 1 inch in diameter. They are green in their younger parts but light brown in their older parts. In habitat they are sometimes reclining on the ground and rooting at the leaf base scars. The leaf crown is full but not usually rounded as most leaves are erect or horizontally spreading. Each one is 5 feet long in mature individuals and nearly that size in juveniles, and each is borne on a wiry, 1-foot-long petiole that has sharp margins. They are occasionally found entire with deeply bifid apices, but mostly are segmented into 6 to 10 pinnae of varying widths, each deeply grooved and apically tapering.

Because of its size, this is one of the most attractive species in the genus. It is neither fast growing nor hardy to cold, being adaptable to zones 10b and 11, but is lovely at all stages of growth. PLATE 419.

Geonoma cuneata is indigenous to extreme southern Nicaragua, Costa Rica, Panama, and central western Colombia, where it occurs in the undergrowth of low mountainous rain forest to an elevation of 3800 feet. The epithet is Latin for "cuneate," an allusion to the wedge-shaped leaf.

The palm is found mostly solitary trunked but occasionally as a clustering specimen. The stem is often short or even subterranean but sometimes is aerial and as tall as 5 or 6 feet. The leaf crown is full and nearly rounded, with 3- to 4-foot long glossy leaves that are obovate and either entire and deeply bifid apically, or segmented into 6 to 14 broad, slightly falcate, acuminate and deeply grooved pinnae; the leaflets of the terminal pair are usually much wider than the rest.

This is one of the more variable species in the genus, and at least four separate varieties have been named to describe different sizes of the leaf, whether or not the individual is clustering or solitary trunked, and the differing shapes of the leaflets. There is a continuum between these forms, and most taxonomists believe that they indicate a variable single species.

This is a beautiful little palm for underplanting in partial shade. It is adaptable to zones 10 and 11 and seems to grow well in frostless Mediterranean climates if given enough moisture.

Geonoma densa is a solitary-trunked, sometimes suckering species with a disjunct distribution in northern South America: in northwestern Venezuela; in northwestern and in north central Colombia, on both sides of the Andes; in extreme southern Ecuador and adjacent northwestern Peru; and in extreme southeastern Peru and adjacent west central Bolivia. In all cases, it is an undergrowth subject in mountainous rain forest or cloud forests at elevations from 4800 to 8000 feet. The epithet is Latin for "dense" and alludes to the short, almost congested, yellowish green branches of the inflorescences.

The trunks grow to heights of 20 feet in habitat, are 1 to 3 inches in diameter, and exhibit beautiful undulating rings of leaf base scars. While no true crownshaft is formed, the leaf sheaths are persistent and the inflorescences are borne at the nodes beneath them. The leaf crown is mostly hemispherical, the leaves 4 to 5 feet long on 8- to 12-inch-long hard, slender petioles. They bear many, regularly and widely spaced, lanceolate to ovate-acuminate, glossy dark green, and leathery, pleated leaflets; new growth is usually bronzy pink.

This beauty is not completely adaptable to hot tropical regions like southern Florida, although it usually survives there. It readily grows in frostless or nearly frostless Mediterranean climes if provided with regular and copious moisture. PLATE 420.

Geonoma deversa has one of the most widespread distributions in the genus, from southern Belize through northern South America, where it grows mostly in low mountainous rain forest, but occasionally is found up to an elevation of 3800 feet.

It is a clustering species whose stems attain heights of 12 feet in habitat but are usually less than 1 inch in diameter. The leaf crown is extended along the upper part of the stem, and the leaves generally spreading and arching. As is to be expected, the leaf form of such a widespread species is variable but, in general, leaves are 2 feet long. They may be undivided except for the bifid apex but are usually segmented into four to eight fat and wide, S-shaped, widely spaced, and long-tipped pinnae; the new growth is deep rosy bronze.

The species does not tolerate frost but is otherwise easy to grow if given regular and generous moisture, partial shade, and a humus-laden soil. PLATE 421.

Geonoma epetiolata is indigenous to the Caribbean coasts of Costa Rica and Panama, where it is an undergrowth subject in low mountainous rain forest. The epithet is from two Latin words meaning "without a petiole."

This is a small solitary-trunked species whose stem grows to 5 feet in habitat. The leaves are undivided with a bifid apex, are borne on short or nonexistent petioles, and are erect in the crown. Each one is to 2 feet long and obovate, the apical points S shaped. New growth is rosy colored as is the leaf underside.

The species does not tolerate frost.

Geonoma interrupta is the most widespread species in the genus and occurs naturally from southeastern Mexico into northern South America, as well as in the Caribbean Basin in Haiti and the Lesser Antilles. It mostly grows in lowland rain forest and swamps but is also found to an elevation of 4500 feet. Vegetatively it is among the most variable species.

It is found both as a solitary-trunked and as a clustering palm in habitat and is one of the largest in the genus, with stems to 30 feet high and 4 inches in diameter. The leaves are never undivided in specimens past the seedling stage, but the variation in leaf form between young plants and (nearly) mature individuals is large, the younger ones having as few as two wide, S-shaped leaflets. Older plants usually bear leaves with 12 to 40 differently sized leaflets, all glossy deep green and generally S shaped with long tips and distinct grooves corresponding to the leaflet veins.

This is certainly one of the most beautiful species in the genus, and a large clump is a veritable symphony of leaf form from the ground upwards. It does well in frostless Mediterranean climes if given enough irrigation. PLATES 422 & 423.

Geonoma laxiflora is a clustering species indigenous to the western Amazon region of southeastern Colombia, eastern Peru, western Brazil, and northern Bolivia, where it occurs in the undergrowth of lowland rain forest and along the rivers and streams. The epithet is Latin for "loose flowered" and alludes to the inflorescences, which are borne beneath the leaf crown.

Individual plants often form colonies of distinctly ringed stems, each capable of growing to a height of 12 or even 15 feet but with a diameter of less than 0.5 inch. The leaves are entire and unsegmented, 1 to 2 feet long, deeply bifid apically, and wedge shaped or obovate. They are usually coppery colored when new but shiny emerald green on both surfaces when older, and they exhibit deep corrugations corresponding to the fused or unseparated segments.

The species is tropical and needs constant and copious moisture.

Geonoma longevaginata is an undergrowth, sparsely clustering species in low mountainous rain forest of Costa Rica and Panama. The epithet is Latin for "long sheathed."

The stems grow to heights of 12 to 15 feet and are usually less than 1 inch in diameter. The leaf crown is sparse and hemispherical, with 3-foot-long leaves that bear glossy deep green leaflets when mature but a beautiful coppery or wine color when new. They are regularly spaced, 8 inches long, and slightly S shaped; the leaflets of the terminal pair are much wider than the others. PLATES 424–426.

Geonoma undata is a large, solitary-trunked species with the second widest distribution in the genus, from Belize into northern South America and on the islands of Dominique, Guadeloupe, and Martinique in the Lesser Antilles, always growing in mountainous rain forest at elevations from 4500 to 7700 feet. The epithet is Latin for "wavy."

The trunk attains a height of 30 feet and a diameter of 4 inches in habitat. The loose reddish brown crownshaft bulges near its midpoint and is cylindrical and 2 feet high. The leaf crown is full and slightly more than hemispherical, with 6- to 8-foot-long leaves that bear many 2-foot-long, sickle-shaped and deeply corrugated leaflets that are usually of differing widths and may or may not grow from the rachis at different angles but almost always have pendent tips. The inflorescences are large and grow from beneath the crownshaft.

This beautiful species is still rare in cultivation and few data are known about its requirements. It would probably be a good candidate for frostless or nearly frostless Mediterranean climates. PLATE 427.

GRONOPHYLLUM is a genus of 33 pinnate-leaved, monoecious palms in the Moluccas, Sulawesi, Australia, and especially New Guinea. They grow in varied habitats from lowland rain forest to near alpine conditions.

There are both solitary-trunked and clustering species as well as small undergrowth and tall emergent species. All form crownshafts of varying size, texture, and color. The inflorescences are formed beneath the crownshafts and consist of a short, fat peduncle and single, pendent flowering branches bearing both male and female flowers. The fruits are round or ellipsoid and red, purple, or black.

At one time, the genus included only tall, solitary-trunked palms with generally linear leaflets, but it now includes smaller, mostly undergrowth and clustering palms with broader, wedge-shaped leaflets, formerly known as *Nengella*. The two genera are united by their floral and fruit/seed details; the species of the *Nengella* alliance bear remarkable visual similarities to *Hydriastele* species.

The taller species here include some of the most magnificent palms, with straight, columnar trunks and great, usually arching leaves, while the smaller clustering species of the *Nengella* alliance are luscious subjects for intimate sites. The genus is undeservedly rare in cultivation, especially in the Western Hemisphere.

The genus name is from two Greek words meaning "chewed away" and "leaf" and refers to the form of the apices of the leaflets of most species. PLATES 428–431.

Gronophyllum apricum is endemic to northwestern Papua New Guinea, where it grows in low mountainous rain forest on limestone ridges. The epithet is Latin for "in the sun" and alludes to this palm's habitat on exposed hillsides.

This is a small solitary-trunked species in the *Nengella* alliance. The slender (1 inch in diameter) and distinctly ringed trunk grows to 15 feet high. The crownshaft is 9 inches tall, silvery green, and bulging near its summit, the widest part being 2 inches in diameter. The leaf crown is sparse but is almost rounded, with 18- to 24-inch-long arching leaves bearing widely spaced groups of dark green, narrowly wedge-shaped leaflets with oblique, jagged apices.

This little beauty is not known to be in cultivation but is eminently worthy of it. It doubtless is not hardy to cold, needs copious and regular moisture, and probably flourishes in nonacidic soils and in full sun.

Gronophyllum brassii is endemic to southwestern Papua New Guinea, where it grows in lowland rain forest. The epithet honors Leonard J. Brass, a 20th-century botanist and collector in New Guinea.

It is a moderate-sized clustering species whose stems attain heights of 25 feet and diameters of 4 inches. Its crownshaft is 1 foot tall, slightly bulging at its base, and medium green but covered in a white tomentum. The 6-foot-long leaves bear wedge-shaped leaflets that grow in widely spaced groups along the rachis, the apical and basal groups having clustered leaflets that grow from the rachis in a single plane, but the leaflets in the middle of the frond grow at several angles.

Gronophyllum cariosum is endemic to northwestern Papua New Guinea in the Bewani Mountain Range, where it grows in low mountainous, wet rain forest. The epithet is Latin for "decays" and alludes to the appearance of the petals of the female flowers.

This is a clustering species in the *Nengella* alliance whose stems grow to 12 feet high and 0.5 inch in diameter. The tiny crownshafts are 6 inches tall and olive green. The leaf crowns are extended along the upper parts of the stems, and the 2-foot-long leaves are borne on 6-inch-long wiry petioles. The individual leaf blade is usually entire and undivided except for the deeply bifid apex, obovate, deep emerald green on its surface, and slightly paler green beneath. The leaf surfaces are wavy and bear boldly distinct darker veins corresponding to the margins of the fused segments. Occasionally leaves are found that are once segmented into two pinnae; the leaflets of the terminal pair are much wider than the leaflets of the lower pair.

Described by John L. Dowe and Michael Ferrero in 2000, this species was previously named *Gronophyllum* 'Filiawoi Yamu', which is the Bewani name for the species. It is as choice as any other species in the *Nengella* alliance. It should need constant warmth, great and regular moisture, partial shade, and a humus-rich soil.

Gronophyllum chaunostachys is endemic to Papua New Guinea, where it grows in mountainous rain forest at elevations of 5280 to 6500 feet. The epithet is from Greek words meaning "lax" and "spike," an allusion to the large, once-branched, whiskbroom-like inflorescences which grow from beneath the crownshaft and produce large clusters of small red fruits.

The trunk attains a height of 60 feet in habitat. It is tan in its older parts but glossy green in the younger parts and is ringed with widely spaced light gray leaf base scars. The beautiful crownshaft is 3 to 4 feet tall, slightly thicker than the trunk at the base of the shaft, and tapering upwards. Its color is a deep green, and it is covered with feltlike brown tomentum. The leaf crown is large, hemispherical, and extended above the crownshaft. The leaves are 8 to 10 feet long, including the 1- to 2-foot-long petiole. They are wonderfully arching and recurved and bear many, stiff, 2-foot-long linear-lanceolate, deep green leaflets that grow from the rachis at an angle which gives a V-shaped leaf.

There is hardly a more beautiful palm. This wonderful example of the vegetable kingdom is almost completely absent from gardens and little data are available regarding its requirements. It is probably well adapted to elevated tropical regions but is not frost tolerant. It doubtless require copious and regular moisture and a rich soil.

Gronophyllum gibbsianum is a tall, solitary-trunked species endemic to Arfak, a mountain range in Western Papua (Irian Jaya), where it grows in rain forest at elevations from 5000 to 7000 feet.

The trunk attains a height of 40 to 50 feet in habitat and a diameter of 18 inches. It is smooth, olive green in its younger parts and light tan in its older parts, most parts having widely spaced and distinct whitish rings of leaf base scars. The crownshaft is 3 to 4 feet high, slightly bulging at its base and tapering to its summit; it is olive to yellowish green near its summit but deep green, almost black, near its base. The leaf crown is sparse but rounded, and the leaves are 10 feet long on short petioles, beautifully arching and recurved. Each of the 2-foot-long, evenly spaced, medium to deep green narrowly obovate and long-tipped leaflets is pendent at its apex. The leaflets grow from the rachis at an angle that creates a V-shaped leaf.

This species is incredibly beautiful with its columnar, stout, and beautifully ringed trunk supporting the rounded crown of leaves. It is rare in cultivation but is probably not adapted to hot tropical or nearly tropical climates.

Gronophyllum ledermannianum is endemic to north central Papua New Guinea, where it occurs in the undergrowth of low mountainous rain forest. The epithet honors Carl L. Ledermann, an early 20th-century Swiss botanist and collector.

The stem of this moderate-sized solitary-trunked species grows to 30 or 40 feet but is usually less than 3 inches in diameter. The 2-foot-tall crownshaft is slightly bulging at its base and is otherwise cylindrical and a beautiful silvery green to nearly white. The 8-foot-long leaves are spreading and borne on 18-inch-long petioles, and form a crown that is slightly more than hemispherical. They bear widely spaced groups of 1-foot-long wedge-shaped, pendent leaflets with jagged apices and beautiful silvery undersides.

This is another species that is undeservedly rare in cultivation. It is reportedly tropical in its temperature requirements. It seems to need constant and copious moisture and a humus-laden, free-draining soil in partial shade.

Gronophyllum mayrii is endemic to the Cyclops Mountains of New Guinea, in northeastern West Papua, where it grows in mountainous, wet and dense rain forest at an elevation generally under 2000 feet. The epithet honors Heinrich Mayr, a 19th-century palm collector.

This is a solitary-trunked species to 40 or more feet tall and usually 1 foot in diameter. The trunk is straight as an arrow, smooth, and columnar, with distinctly beautiful and widely spaced whitish rings of leaf base scars. The crownshaft is 2 to 3 feet tall, uniformly deep green, and scarcely thicker than the trunk. The leaf crown is full and rounded with several 10-foot-long leaves on 2-foot-long stout petioles. The leaves are spreading and wonderfully arching near their apices. The leaflets grow in closely spaced groups, are 2 to 3 feet long, linear-lanceolate, deep green, and pendent at the apex. The terminal group of leaflets is fanned with closely set segments growing in a nearly flat plane, which creates a squared-off apex to the leaf. All the other leaflets grow from the rachis at an angle that creates a slight V shape to most of the leaf.

The palm has an incomparably beautiful silhouette that is more than thrilling to contemplate. It is rare in cultivation but would need a tropical climate, copious and regular moisture, and a humus-laden soil.

Gronophyllum microcarpum is indigenous to the Moluccas and Ceram between Sulawesi and New Guinea, where it grows in low mountainous rain forest. The epithet is from Greek words meaning "small" and "fruit," an allusion to the clusters of small, round, red berrylike fruits that are reportedly used as a betel-nut substitute in habitat.

It is a solitary-trunked species whose stem attains a height of 30 feet. The crownshaft is 2 feet tall, slightly bulging at its base and slightly tapering to its summit, and an even dark green. The leaf crown is slightly less than hemispherical with ascending, slightly arching 6- to 8-foot-long leaves. The many stiff and erect, dark green leaflets grow from the rachis at a 45-degree angle to give a V-shaped leaf.

The species is tropical in its requirements and needs abundant moisture. It thrives in partial shade or full sun except in hot, dry climes. PLATE 428.

Gronophyllum montanum is endemic to Arfak, a mountain range in Western Papua (Irian Jaya), where it grows in rain forest at moderate elevations. The epithet is Latin for "mountainous" and refers to the palm's habitat.

This is a sparsely clustering species of the *Nengella* alliance, whose stems grow to 30 feet but have diameters of 2 inches. The silvery green to nearly white crownshafts are 2 to 3 feet tall and scarcely wider than the trunk itself. The leaf crown is sparse and less than hemispherical with stiffly ascending, 4- to 5-foot-long leaves on 1-foot-long petioles. The few leaflets occur in widely spaced groups and are linearly to broadly wedge shaped, with jagged

apices; the leaflets of the terminal pair are larger than the others. New growth is rosy to reddish.

The species is almost nonexistent in cultivation, and little is known about its requirements. It probably needs a nearly tropical climate, great and regular moisture, partial shade, and a humus-laden soil.

Gronophyllum pinangoides is endemic to northern West Papua, where it occurs in the undergrowth of low mountainous rain forest. The epithet translates as "similar to *Pinanga*," but the similarity is difficult to see.

This is a densely clustering species in the *Nengella* alliance, whose slender stems grow to 20 feet high and less than 1 inch in diameter. The light green crownshafts are scarcely wider than the stems, and the leaf crowns are extended along the upper parts of the stems. The leaves are 3 or 4 feet long, including the 18-inch-long petioles. The 4 to 10 leaflets grow in oppositely placed pairs along the rachis, each one rhomboidal or obliquely wedge shaped, glossy dark green, with a jagged apex and a generally undulating surface. The leaflets of the terminal pair are united to some extent, and the new growth is usually deep rose or wine red.

The species is as tender as any of the rest, needs partial shade, especially in hot climates, copious and regular moisture, and a humus-laden soil. This is probably the most widely grown species in the genus, although it is still not that common. It should be planted in an intimate site where the individual leaflets may be seen up close. PLATES 429 & 430.

Gronophyllum pleurocarpum is endemic to northeastern Papua New Guinea, where it grows in low mountainous, wet rain forest. The epithet is from two Greek words meaning "rib" and "fruit."

This is a clustering species in the *Nengella* alliance whose individual slender stems grow to 20 feet tall in habitat. The 2-foot-tall crownshaft is scarcely thicker than the stem and is medium to deep green. The 6-foot-long leaves are unusual in that the leaflets grow in widely spaced groups of two or four oppositely paired large, irregularly rhomboid-shaped, glossy deep green leaflets, each one strongly ribbed and apically jagged. They grow from the rachis in a single plane, and each group looks like a giant glossy green butterfly. The new growth is rose colored.

The species does not tolerate frost or cold.

Gronophyllum ramsayi is a tall, solitary-trunked species endemic to the extreme northern region of the Northern Territory of Australia (Arnhem Land), where it grows in low, swampy areas on sandy soils, often in large stands. It is called northern kentia palm in Australia.

The trunk attains a height of 50 feet in habitat and is light gray to nearly white and often bulged at its midpoint.

It is also distinctly ringed with closely set leaf base scars. The 3-foot-tall crownshaft is light green to nearly white and 3 feet high. It is usually bulging at its base and tapering to its summit, although many individuals exhibit a cylindrical shaft that is about as thick as the trunk itself. The leaf crown is wonderfully full and round with 8- to 10-foot-long, greatly arching and recurved leaves on short to nearly nonexistent petioles. The numerous stiff leaflets grow from the rachis at a 45-degree angle to create a distinctly V-shaped leaf. They are linear-lanceolate, long tipped, and slightly pendent at their apices. Their color ranges from deep olive green to more commonly bluish and glaucous green.

This species has great visual affinities to another of the world's most beautiful palm species, *Actinorhytis calapparia*. Its trunk, however, is much more robust, particularly in cultivation. It does not tolerate cold, needs constant and copious moisture, and flourishes in full sun. It is reportedly difficult to grow when young, and the roots are brittle and difficult to transplant. Once established, however, the palm grows fast and robustly. PLATE 431.

GUIHAIA is a genus of two small, clustering palmate-leaved, dioecious palms in southern China and northern Vietnam, where they grow in crevices of steep limestone hills and cliffs. The inflorescences of both sexes grow from the leaf crown and are erect and much branched, the females producing small, ellipsoid bluish black fruits. The genus name is the ancient name of one of the Chinese provinces to which the palms are native. PLATES 432 & 433.

Guihaia argyrata occurs naturally on limestone cliffs in extreme southern China and northern Vietnam. Grant Stephenson, a palm broker in Houston, Texas, has coined the apt vernacular names Vietnamese silver-backed fan palm and Chinese needle palm. The epithet is Latin for "silvery."

Mature trunks grow slowly to 3 feet. They are covered in brown fibers, and those near the top of the stem are spinelike, reminiscent of the crown of *Rhapidophyllum*. Mature clumps are unknown in cultivation and have not yet been studied in habitat, but they would probably not exceed 6 feet high and wide. The leaves are usually circular, 3 feet wide, with deep, obovate-lanceolate segments extending almost to the 3- to 4-foot-long petiole. There is a small dark hump-shaped hastula atop the center of the leaf, at the juncture of petiole and blade. The narrow segments are light to deep green above and are shallowly once pleated, the fold being roof shaped rather than trough shaped. There is a distinct and lighter-colored vein atop the pleat of the upper surface, and the undersides of the leaf are a beautiful and shiny light tan overlain with a bright and tangible white to silvery sheen, the result of small, silvery scales. The inflorescences grow from among the leaves, are usually erect, and are several-branched with tiny whitish flowers. The fruits are 0.25 inch wide, round, and black when mature.

The species is probably hardy in zones 8b through 11, possibly even hardier. It has survived unscathed a temperature of 22°F in containers in Houston, Texas (Grant Stephenson, pers. comm.). It is drought tolerant but grows better with regular and adequate moisture. It thrives on calcareous soils but seems to like various well-drained soils. It luxuriates in partial shade to full sun. Plants at Fairchild Tropical Garden are smaller, have fewer leaf segments, and have more pleats per segment when grown in sun than those grown in partial shade (Dransfield and Zona 1998). The plants are slow growing no matter what the conditions.

This palm is suited to sites where its color and form can be readily appreciated. It works wonderfully as an accent with other contrasting vegetation but is not suited to specimen planting, isolated with surrounding space. It is not known to be grown indoors but probably could be, given enough light and good air circulation. PLATES 432 & 433.

Guihaia grossefibrosa is indigenous to the same general region as *G. argyrata*. The epithet is from Latin words meaning "fat" and "fibrous," an allusion to the thick fibers of the leaf bases. It differs from the above species in being slightly taller, lacking "needles" in the crown but having more leaf base fibers of greater length that are adherent to the petioles, and in having leaves with thinner segments that extend all the way to the petiole and are of only a slightly paler color on the lower surfaces and are not silvery hued.

GULUBIA is a genus of nine tall, pinnate-leaved, solitary-trunked, monoecious palms in the Moluccas eastwards to the South Pacific islands. The leaves of most species are large and usually arching, but two species have straight leaves with unarching rachises; all have many leaflets. The inflorescences form beneath the crownshafts and are once or twice branched; they bear unisexual blossoms of both sexes that produce red or blue fruits.

Every one of these species is incredibly beautiful and tropical and exotic looking to Western eyes; there is no more beautiful genus of palm. In spite of this, the species are mostly absent in tropical gardens, a situation that should receive the utmost attention.

The genus name is a Latinized form of the Moluccan aboriginal name of one species (*G. moluccana*). PLATES 434–436.

Gulubia costata is indigenous to the Aru Islands of Indonesia, the island of New Guinea, the Bismarck Archipelago, and northeastern Queensland, Australia, where it grows in lowland rain forest and swamps, often forming large stands. The epithet is Latin for "ribbed," an allusion to the fruits.

It is a very tall and magnificent species. The trunk attains heights of 100 feet in habitat, with a diameter of 2 feet. The crownshaft is 4 or 5 feet tall, slightly bulging at its base, and medium to deep green often with purplish hues near its base and a suffusion of brown near its summit. The sparse leaf crown is hemispherical or slightly more so. This is one of two species with straight, unarching rachises, and the leaves are 12 to 15 feet long on 1- to 2-foot-long petioles. The many 3- to 4-foot-long, lanceolate, medium to dark green leaflets are pendent and give to each leaf a sort of curtain appearance. Each leaflet is 2 inches wide at its base and is very deeply bifid at its apex, which characteristic adds to the finely serrate appearance of the curtain of segments. The individual inflorescences are not extraordinarily large, but they produce 3-inch-long, ellipsoid bluish gray, white-striped fruits.

The species is nearly tropical in its temperature requirements and adaptable only to zones 10b and 11. It needs constant and copious moisture and sun when past the juvenile stage. In spite of its preference for a humus-laden soil, the species is thriving at Fairchild Tropical Garden in Miami, Florida, where its site in the rain forest area is heavily mulched and watered. It is slow growing while a seedling, a stage in which the mostly undivided leaves look much like those of an *Areca* species; once past this stage, however, it is fast. This exquisite species stands out in the landscape as hardly any other specimen of vegetation can. It is incomparably spectacular because of its great stiff, curtainlike leaves and, as a canopy-scape, is matchless. Groups of three or more individuals of varying heights create an irresistible tableau of tropical beauty. PLATES 434 & 435.

Gulubia cylindrocarpa is indigenous to the Vanuatu archipelago and the Solomon Islands, where it grows in mountainous rain forest at elevations of 300 to 3200 feet. The epithet is Latin for "cylindrical fruited," an allusion to the shape of the small yellow to orange fruits.

It is one of the tallest palms in the genus with mature trunks attaining heights of nearly 100 feet but diameters of usually less than 1 foot. They are light gray to almost white, exhibit closely spaced rings of leaf base scars, and are basally expanded. The 3-foot-tall crownshaft is light or silvery green, slightly bulged at its base, and cylindrical above. The leaf crown is rounded and contains 15 to 18 greatly arching, recurved 7-foot-long leaves on 1-foot-long petioles. The 3-foot-long linear-lanceolate leaflets are olive green above and grayish green beneath. They are stiff and shortly bifid apically and grow from the rachis at an angle that gives a V-shaped leaf.

Young palms before they grow above the forest canopy have a short cone of stilt roots and usually undivided leaves, a characteristic that leads to the palm's being often misidentified at this stage as a *Pelagodoxa* species. Mature palms are enchantingly beautiful, especially in silhouette.

Gulubia hombronii is endemic to the Solomon Islands, where it is widespread in low mountainous rain forest. The epithet honors Jacques B. Hombron, a 19th-century botanist and collector in the islands.

The trunks of mature palms grow to 60 feet tall in habitat with diameters of 10 to 12 inches and swollen bases. The crownshaft is 2 to 3 feet tall, almost cylindrical, and scarcely thicker than the trunk. It is olive green with a suffusion of orange at its summit. The leaf crown is hemispherical to almost spherical and is dense, with as many as 20 strongly arching 6-foot-long leaves on petioles less than 1 foot long. Juvenile leaves are usually entire and unsegmented. The light green leaflets are 18 to 24 inches long, linear-lanceolate, and shortly bifid apically. They grow from the rachis at a 45-degree angle, creating a V-shaped leaf. The small fruits are ellipsoidal and dull red.

The species has a beautiful silhouette and makes an exciting and lovely canopy-scape. It is tender to cold and needs constant moisture but seems not terribly fussy about soil type.

Gulubia longispatha is endemic to north central West Papua, where it grows in mountainous rain forest at elevations of 500 to 4600 feet. The epithet is Latin for "long" and "spathe" and alludes to the primary leathery, 4-foot-long bract that initially covers the inflorescence before the latter expands and the former falls away.

The trunk attains a height of 80 feet or more in habitat, is less than 1 foot in diameter, is light gray to nearly white, and is smooth, almost shiny, straight as an arrow and ringed with closely set darker leaf base scars. The crownshaft is 3 to 4 feet tall, slightly thicker than the trunk, cylindrical, smooth and glaucous, light green at its base and silvery green, almost white at its summit. The leaf crown is rounded with 18 strongly arching, recurved 8-foot-long leaves on 10-inch-long petioles. The 3-foot-long linear-lanceolate leaflets are stiff and erect, growing from the rachis at a 45-degree angle to create a V-shaped leaf. They are light green or olive green and are deeply bifid and slightly pendent at their apices. The 0.5-inch-wide round fruits are shiny bright red.

The species is still undeservedly rare in cultivation. It should do well in almost any frostless climate if given constant and copious moisture and a humus-laden soil. It is arguably the most beautiful species in a genus that is rife with beauty. Its thrilling silhouette is comparable to that of *Actinorhytis calapparia*. A group of three or more individuals of varying heights is among the most exquisite sights the palm family has to offer.

Gulubia macrospadix is endemic to the Solomon Islands, where it grows in mountainous rain forest at elevations from sea level to 3000 feet. The epithet is from Greek words meaning "large" and "inflorescence," although the inflorescence is no larger than those of most other species.

The tan, slender, and tapering trunk grows to 40 or 50 feet high but is 10 inches in diameter at its midpoint. The crownshaft is 3 or more feet tall and light to medium green except near its top where it is suffused with a purplish black hue. The leaf crown is spherical. The 6- to 7-foot-long leaves are borne on 1-foot-long petioles and are beautifully arching and recurved at their apices. The dark green 2-foot-long leaflets are evenly and widely spaced and grow from the rachis at a 45-degree angle, giving to the leaf a V shape; each one is wide-lanceolate with an obliquely cut apex that terminates in a pendent tip. The 0.5-inch-long ellipsoid fruits are crimson.

Gulubia microcarpa is endemic to the Fiji Islands, where it grows in low mountainous rain forest. The epithet is Greek for "tiny" and "fruit."

This tall, slender-trunked species grows to 80 feet high in habitat with a trunk diameter that is usually less than 1 foot. The light green crownshaft is barely thicker than the trunk, 2.5 feet tall, and cylindrical. The leaf crown is hemispherical and consists of 16 or 17 arching, 7-foot-long leaves on 1-foot-long petioles. The 3-foot-long leaflets are stiff and grow from the rachis at an angle that makes a V-shaped leaf. The small fruits are cylindrical and gray or white when ripe.

The species is still rare in cultivation but needs a humus-rich soil, partial shade when young, full sun when older, and a frostless climate. The palm has a beautiful silhouette and is stunningly attractive in groups of three or more individuals of varying heights. PLATE 436.

Gulubia moluccana is indigenous to the Moluccan islands of Halmahera, Ternate, and Bacan, where it grows in mountainous rain forest from elevations of 1000 to 4000 feet. The epithet is Latin for "Moluccan."

This is possibly the tallest species in the genus, its trunk reportedly attaining the incredible height of 170 feet but a diameter of only 1 foot or slightly more. It is also one of two species in the genus with straight, unarching rachises. The crownshaft is 3 feet tall, light green, and scarcely thicker than the trunk at its base but bulges gradually towards its summit. The leaf crown, like that of *G. costata*, is rounded and large. The leaves are 10 feet long on 2- to 3-foot-long petioles. The leaflets are numerous, narrowly lanceolate, and long tipped, slightly more than 3 feet long and, like those of *G. costata*, are pendent and curtainlike.

The species seems not to be in cultivation and this is unfortunate as it is an almost unbelievably beautiful palm, much like *G. costata* but larger and taller. It should do well in any tropical climate if given enough moisture and a humus-laden soil.

Gulubia palauensis is a rare and endangered species endemic to the Palau islands east of the southern Philippines, where it grows in wet forest at low elevations on limestone soils. It is called Rock Island palm in Palau, and the epithet is Latin for "of Palau."

The trunk attains a height of 60 feet in habitat with a diameter of 6 inches. The smooth crownshaft is 2 feet tall, scarcely thicker than the trunk, cylindrical, and light green. The leaf crown is nearly spherical, with small 3-foot-long arching leaves on 10-inch-long petioles. The 2-foot-long leaflets are stiff, linear-lanceolate, and deeply bifid apically, and grow from the rachis at a 45-degree angle to give a V-shaped leaf.

The species, like the rest in the genus, has a beautiful silhouette but seems not to be in cultivation.

Gulubia valida is endemic to northwestern Papua New Guinea, where it grows in low mountainous rain forest. The epithet is Latin for "valid" or "true" and, according to Fred B. Essig (1982), who first technically described the species and bestowed the epithet, "refers to the strength and robustness of the foliage."

The trunk attains a height of 40 to 50 feet in habitat and is usually less than 1 foot in diameter. The crownshaft is usually 3 feet tall, light green, slightly thicker than the trunk, and cylindrical. The leaf crown is dense and nearly spherical with 20 or more 7-foot-long, slightly arching leaves on stout, 1-foot-long petioles. The 2- to 3-foot-long stiff lanceolate leaflets grow from the rachis at an angle that creates a V-shaped leaf. The 0.5-inch-long ellipsoid fruits are dark red to dark purple.

This extremely attractive species has an exceptionally beautiful leaf crown and an arresting silhouette. The palm is rare in cultivation and should be much more widely planted in tropical or nearly tropical regions.

HEDYSCEPE is a monotypic genus of pinnate-leaved, solitary-trunked, monoecious palm on Lord Howe Island, where it is called umbrella palm or big mountain palm. The genus name is derived from two Greek words meaning "pleasant" and "shade," although one is hard put to understand how the canopy would ever provide much shade or how that the amenity might be needed in such a cool habitat. The epithet honors John H. T. Canterbury, a 19th-century governor of the state of Victoria in Australia. PLATE 437.

Hedyscepe canterburyana grows in mountainous moist forest from 1000 to 2400 feet in elevation. It occurs mostly on cliffs and ridges near the coast where the rainfall is high and there is often cloud cover.

The robust and stout, light brown to dark gray trunk attains a height of 35 feet in habitat, a diameter of 1 foot or more, and has closely set, darker brown rings of leaf base scars. The crownshaft is 2 feet tall, slightly thicker than the trunk, cylindrical, and light green to bluish gray-green. The leaf crown is hemispherical or slightly less, with erect, slightly arching 8- to 9-foot-long leaves on short petioles. The 1-foot-long leaflets are lanceolate, stiff, and rigid, and grow from the rachis at an angle that creates a V-shaped leaf. They are deep green above but paler green beneath. The inflorescences grow from nodes beneath the crownshaft and consist of rigid, fleshy spreading branches bearing male and female flowers. The fruits are obovoid or oblong, 2 inches long, and dark red.

This palm requires a moist Mediterranean or cool tropical climate, such as the mountains of Hawaii, northern New Zealand, and southern coastal Australia. It is not adapted to hot climates, where it only languishes and slowly dies, nor does it stand much cold. It also needs a humus-laden, moist but-fast draining soil. Even under optimum conditions it is slow growing. Love of the appearance of the palm is an acquired taste, one which is nevertheless widespread and popular now. This species is related genetically and visually to the genus *Rhopalostylis;* it is simultaneously architectural and formal appearing, and lends itself to sites where the strong form or silhouette can be seen against the sky or contrasting foliage or structures. It looks good as a specimen planting, even surrounded by space in certain formal sites, but is better in groups of three or more individuals of varying heights.

HETEROSPATHE is a genus of 40 pinnate-leaved, small to large, monoecious palms in the Philippines and islands east of these, New Guinea, eastern Indonesia, the Solomon Islands, Vanuatu, and Fiji.

There are solitary-trunked and clustering species as well as small undergrowth and large emergent species. None of them form a crownshaft, but many have colored new growth. The inflorescences are formed in the leaf crown but are often found beneath it by the time the single-sexed blossoms open. They consist of several short, usually white or yellowish branches and are enclosed by two large, leathery bracts when new, one bract usually persisting until the fruits are formed. The latter are round or oblong and orange to red.

All species are tender to cold and are only possible in zones 10b and 11, although a couple of them (*H. delicatula* and *H. humilis*) hail from the mountains of New Guinea and may be adaptable to frostless Mediterranean climes. They invariably need constant moisture and a soil that is slightly acidic, humus laden, and yet fast draining. Only one species is common in cultivation in the United States, but all would seem more than worthy of growing; they are much more widely grown in Australia but are still not common.

The genus name is derived from two Greek words meaning "varied" and "spathe," an allusion to the two dissimilar bracts enclosing the inflorescence buds. PLATES 438–448.

Heterospathe cagayanensis is endemic to the Cagayan Islands of the southern Philippines, where it occurs in the undergrowth of dense rain forest at low elevations. The epithet is Latin for "of Cagayan."

The palm is found both as an acaulescent and a trunked species, the latter form slowly growing to 20 feet. The beautifully arching 6-foot-long leaves are borne on 2-foot-long petioles and have widely spaced, narrow, 2-foot-long, deep green, S-shaped, narrowly lanceolate, and long-tipped leaflets.

This lovely species is not for the full sun of hot climates. It needs constant and abundant moisture and a humus-laden soil. PLATE 438.

Heterospathe delicatula is endemic to extreme eastern Papua New Guinea, where it grows in mountainous rain forest at elevations of 3000 to more than 5280 feet. The epithet translates from the Latin as "diminutively delicate" and refers to the small stature of the palm.

This species has a subterranean trunk with 5- to 6-foot-long ascending, erect leaves on 18- to 24-inch-long petioles. The deep green leaflets are regularly and widely spaced along the rachis, each one 6 to 10 inches long, linear-lanceolate, limp, and pendent, and a beautifully brilliant cherry to wine in color when new. The inflorescences are colorful with their reddish brown bracts and branches and their brownish and purple flowers. The fruits are bright red. PLATES 439 & 440.

Heterospathe elata is widespread in the Philippines, Micronesia, and the Moluccas in rain forest at low elevations, where it can be undergrowth subject for years before usually ending up as an emergent canopy tree. It is called sagisi palm even in English-speaking countries. The epithet is Latin for "tall."

The mature stems of this solitary-trunked species grow to 50 feet high with a diameter of 1 foot. They are smooth and gray with wide and widely spaced rings of leaf base scars on the younger parts and a swollen base. The leaf crown is 15 feet wide and tall, full, and nearly round. The leaves are 6 to 10 feet long on 2-foot-long petioles with 2- to 3-foot long limp, dark green narrowly lanceolate and tapering leaflets that are pendent with age. They grow from the rachis in a flat plane, and the rachis is usually twisted to an angle of 90 degrees at its midpoints, resulting in the upper half of the blade being almost vertical in alignment. New leaves of younger plants are an unusual shade of pinkish bronze. The 4-foot-long panicles of the inflorescences are much branched and grow from among the leaves, bearing many small whitish single-sexed blossoms of both sexes. The fruits are 0.5 inch wide, rounded, white, and are borne in pendent clusters hanging beneath the leaf crown.

The species does not tolerate frost and is adaptable only to zones 10b and 11. It also needs partial shade when young, full sun when older, a humus-laden soil or a permanent organic mulch, and regular and adequate moisture. Its growth rate is slow when young and until it forms an aboveground trunk, but moderate to even fast afterwards; the young stems usually sit or grow slowly sideways for a few years before they start growth upwards.

This palm is grace and elegance personified. Its leaves are reminiscent of those of *Cocos* (coconut), if not as large, and it is possibly even more attractive than the coconut when it is young as the leaf crown is often extended, with leaves arching out from the trunk at some distance from the palm's growing point. It is beautiful enough to stand as an isolated specimen but looks better in groups of three or more individuals of varying heights. It has a silhouette almost as beautiful as that of the coconut and is stunning as a canopy-scape; against a background of contrasting foliage, it is most delightful. In short, it is hard to misplace it in the landscape. It is possible indoors in a large space with good light and high relative humidity. PLATES 441 & 442.

Heterospathe elmeri is endemic to Camiguin Island, north of the main island of Luzon, in the Philippines, where it grows in dense rain forest at low elevations. The epithet honors Adolph D. E. Elmer, an early 20th-century palm collector.

This is a solitary-trunked species growing to an overall height of 25 feet. The 10- to 12-foot-long mostly erect leaves have numerous narrowly linear-lanceolate dark green, regularly spaced 2-foot-long, limp, and pendent leaflets.

This beautiful species is extremely slow growing. The seeds are reportedly used as a betel-nut substitute in habitat, and the growing point is edible. PLATE 443.

Heterospathe glauca is endemic to the island of Batjan in the Moluccas, where it grows in dense rain forest at low elevations. The epithet is Latin for "glaucous" and refers to the leaf bases or leaf sheaths.

This is a solitary-trunked species growing to an overall height of 30 feet. There is no true crownshaft, but the silvery green leaf bases are persistent and result in a cylindrical pseudo-crownshaft. The leaf crown is hemispherical or slightly more rounded and is composed of 10 to 12 spreading 10-foot-long leaves on a short, stout petioles; the leaves are mostly straight but arch near the apex. The regularly spaced leaflets are deep green, broadly lanceolate, with irregularly truncated apices and 2 or slightly more feet in length; they are limp and pendent when mature.

This is one of the most attractive species in the genus and, although rare in cultivation in the United States, should do well in calcareous soils if kept constantly moist and heavily mulched with organic material.

Heterospathe humilis is endemic to a large area of Papua New Guinea, where it occurs in the undergrowth of mountainous rain forest at elevations of 2800 feet to slightly more than 5280 feet. The epithet is Latin for "humble" or "low."

This trunkless, usually clustering, sometimes solitary-trunked species grows to 10 feet, with ascending, spreading leaves on long petioles. The leaflets grow in groups and are widely spaced along the rachis, the terminal pair usually significantly wider than the others. Each one is 2 feet long, lanceolate to narrowly lanceolate, medium to deep green, thin, and limp but usually not pendent.

Heterospathe macgregori is endemic to eastern Papua New Guinea, where it grows along streams and rivers in lowland rain forest. The epithet honors the original collector of the palm, Sir Walter MacGregor.

This clumping species is a true rheophyte, being found only in shallow water and never on higher, dry ground. The individual gray or tan stems grow to lengths of 20 feet or more but are only 2 or 3 inches in diameter. They are often semiprostrate or found growing horizontally; seldom are they straight. The leaf crowns are hemispherical and dense, with as many as 15 leaves, each of which is 6 feet long. The numerous 2-foot-long leaflets are narrowly linear-lanceolate, stiff, evenly spaced along, and grow in almost a flat plane from the rachis; they are medium to deep green.

This beautiful species is not in cultivation, but it should be. Its requirements are nearly or completely aquatic and tropical.

Heterospathe minor is endemic to the Solomon Islands, where it grows in low mountainous rain forest. The epithet is Latin for "smaller," possibly in comparison to *H. elata*.

This is a solitary-trunked species growing to an overall height of 20 feet. The leaves of older palms are borne on exceptional 6-foot-long petioles and are no more than 8 feet long and usually nearer 6 feet. The leaves form a crown that is less than hemispherical because of their ascending nature. The numerous leaflets are regularly spaced along the rachis, medium to deep green, 3 feet long, narrowly lanceolate, long tipped, and slightly S shaped; they grow from the rachis at an angle which creates a V-shaped leaf and are a beautiful wine or rosy bronze when new. PLATE 444.

Heterospathe negrosensis is endemic to the Philippines, where it grows in lowland rain forest. The epithet is Latin for "of Negros," a large island in the central Philippines.

It is a solitary-trunked species whose stem is 8 feet tall but whose leaves are 15 feet long, including the 4- to 5-foot-long petioles. The numerous leaflets are deep green, 3 to 4 feet long, narrowly lanceolate, limp, and partially pendent. PLATE 445.

Heterospathe philippinensis is endemic but widespread in mountainous rain forest in the Philippines, where it grows to an elevation of 5280 feet. The epithet is Latin for "of the Philippines."

This variable species has both solitary-trunked and clustering individuals. The slender stems grow to heights of 6 feet, and the leaf crown is hemispherical or less. The 4- to 5-foot-long leaves have deep green 1-foot-long leaflets that grow from the rachis at an angle to create a slightly V-shaped leaf. PLATE 446.

Heterospathe phillipsii is a rare and endangered species endemic to low mountainous rain forest on Viti Levu, one of the Fiji Islands, and was described in 1997. It is threatened because of logging activities there. The epithet honors the late Richard H. Phillips, amateur botanist and collector of palms in Fiji.

This solitary-trunked species has a trunk to 40 feet high and 6 to 7 inches in diameter. The leaf crown is nearly spherical with 13- to 14-foot-long sumptuously beautiful, spreading, dark green leaves on 12- to 18-inch-long petioles. The dark green leaflets are 2.5 feet long, wide-lanceolate, closely and evenly spaced along the rachis, and limp and semipendent. The small, oblong fruits are bright red when mature.

This is among the most beautiful species in the genus. It is almost as tall as *H. elata* and its leaves are even more attractive. The palm is faster growing than most other species but, alas, is no hardier to cold.

Heterospathe salomonensis is endemic to the Solomon Islands, where it grows in low mountainous rain forest. The epithet is Latin for "of Solomon." This species is similar in stature and appearance to *H. elata* but is slower growing.

Heterospathe sibuyanensis is a rare species endemic to Sibuyan Island in the Philippines, where it grows in lowland rain forest and may be extinct since it has not been found in the wild since 1919. The epithet is Latin for "of Sibuyan."

The species is similar to *H. elata* in overall appearance but shorter, its trunk growing to 30 feet high, with a diameter of 4 or 5 inches. Its leaf crown is nearly spherical and contains 8-foot-long leaves that are flat and borne on 2-foot-long petioles. The numerous 2-foot-long leaflets are dark green above, paler green beneath, stiff, and thin; the newer leaves are usually twisted to the vertical near their midpoints. The tiny ovoid fruits are bright red.

Heterospathe uniformis is a rare species endemic to Vanuatu on western Ambrim Island, where it occurs in the undergrowth of lowland rain forest. It was described in 1995. The epithet is Latin for "uniform" and alludes to the homogeneous endosperm in the seeds, a characteristic that is unique in the genus.

The solitary trunk attains a height of 18 feet and a diameter of 6 inches. The leaf crown is hemispherical or slightly more and contains six 4-foot-long leaves on 1-foot-long petioles. The 2-foot-long leaflets grow in a single flat plane from the rachis and are deep green above and lighter green beneath. The ovoid fruits are less than 1 inch long and a deep red when ripe.

Heterospathe woodfordiana is endemic to Ysabel Island in the Solomons, where it grows in low mountainous rain forest. The epithet honors C. M. Woodford, an early 20th-century British naturalist and collector as well as government official of the Solomons.

The solitary brown trunk grows to 12 feet and a diameter of 3 or 4 inches. The leaf crown is hemispherical and holds 10 leaves that are each 5 feet long. The regularly spaced, linear-elliptic, long-tipped, soft leaflets are pendent at their tips. New growth is a beautiful maroon, and the small fruits are deep red. PLATES 447 & 448.

HOWEA is a genus of two monoecious, pinnate-leaved solitary-trunked palms on Lord Howe Island off the central eastern coast of Australia. The inflorescences are unusual, 6-foot-long unbranched pendent spikes, growing from the lower leaves and carrying tiny creamy white unisexual flowers of both sexes. The species are slightly susceptible to lethal yellowing disease. The genus name is a Latinized form of the name of the palm's habitat. PLATES 449–453.

Howea belmoreana is endemic to Lord Howe Island, where it grows in hilly, moist forests. Common names are sentry palm and kentia palm. The epithet is a Latinized form of the surname "Belmore," an Australian governor.

Mature trunks attain heights of 40 feet in habitat with a diameter of 6 inches. They are light brown to gray with slightly swollen bases and closely set darker leaf scar rings. The leaf crown is 10 feet wide and 8 feet tall, full, and rounded. The leaves are 7 to 10 feet long, the younger ones strongly arching and forming almost a semicircle. They are held on 3-foot-long, strongly arching petioles. The dark green leaflets are 3 to 4 feet long and grow from the rachis at a 45-degree angle, creating a strong V shape to the leaf. The fruits are 2 inches long, ovoid, and brown to reddish brown when ripe.

The palm needs average but regular moisture and is adaptable to zones 10 and 11. It is slow growing at all stages but thrives in partial shade, especially in hot climates; indeed, it is difficult to maintain in hot or tropical climates. It is magnificent in nearly frostless Mediterranean climates.

Because of its strongly arching and trough-shaped leaves, the palm has unusual grace and a striking architectural aspect. It is unsurpassed for a silhouette display against the sky as a canopy-scape, or large expanses of walls or different background landscape colors. It is accommodating in this respect because of its slow growth, retaining whatever proportions for a relatively long time. It is exceptionally beautiful in groups of three or more individuals of varying heights, and yet is distinctive and appealing enough as an isolated specimen. This is one of the most durable indoor plants, especially when young, adapting to low light as well as some neglect. PLATES 449 & 450.

Howea forsteriana is endemic to low, coastal elevations on Lord Howe Island. Common names are kentia palm and sentry palm. The epithet honors William Forster, an Australian politician.

Mature trunks reach heights of 50 to 60 feet but are usually half that under cultivation. The stem is 6 inches in diameter, swollen at the base, and gray to tan, with closely spaced, grooved rings of leaf base scars. The leaf crown of mature palms is usually 20 feet wide and 12 to 15 feet tall; it is extended down the trunk but never quite rounded. The leaves are 8 to 12 feet long on 4- to 5-foot-long petioles. The rachis arches beautifully, and the many 2- to 3-foot-long dark green, narrowly lanceolate and tapering, limp leaflets are pendent. There is much tightly woven brown fiber associated with the bases of the leaf stalks and it is persistent for each leaf until the leaf dies and falls. The fruits are 2 inches long, ellipsoid, and orange or red when mature.

The species needs average but regular moisture. It is adaptable to a range of free-draining soils. The palm grows in zones 10 and 11; older palms sometimes withstand a temperature of 28°F unharmed, but anything colder is trouble and temperatures in the low or mid 20s (F) can be fatal.

Younger plants have an astoundingly graceful and attractive fountainlike aspect, and there is likely nothing more elegant in all nature than these wonderful curves accented by the great drooping leaflets. The palm should be sited where there are no other prima donna plants to compete with its visual perfection except more of its kind. It is one of the few tall palms that is beautiful enough to stand alone as an isolated specimen, but it is even more choice in groups of three or more individuals of varying heights, and its silhouette is very beautiful. It is the second most (if not the most) popular indoor palm and has been used for more than 100 years as an interiorscape subject. It is a divine diva, thriving and proffering her great beauty in spite of abuse and bad lighting, gracing every imaginable chamber from saloons and cheap hotel lobbies to spacious presidential ballrooms. PLATES 451–453.

HYDRIASTELE is a genus of nine pinnate-leaved, mostly clustering, monoecious palms in northern Australia, New Guinea, and the adjacent Bismarck Archipelago. The species form crownshafts above which the leaf crowns are sparse, especially in clustering forms, but often elongated, with distinctive, relatively short leaves. The leaflets are mostly irregularly wedge shaped with jagged apices; the leaflets of the terminal pair are always larger than the rest, and a few species have typically dissected, linear leaflets (for example, *H. rheophytica*). The inflorescences grow from beneath the crownshafts, are once branched, and look like large whisk brooms; they produce pendent clusters of small red, purple, or black fruits.

Most of these beauties have been in cultivation for many years, but none are common, especially in the United States. All are intolerant of cold and adaptable only to zones 10b and 11. Otherwise the species are mostly of easy culture and seem not fussy about soil type, needing mainly copious and regular moisture. They seem to do best when given partial shade in their youth.

The genus name is from two Greek words, one for a water nymph, the other meaning "column," the allusion supposedly to the size of the palms and the swampy habitats of some species. PLATES 454–457.

Hydriastele beccariana is endemic to low mountainous rain forest in eastern Papua New Guinea. The epithet honors Italian palm taxonomist Odoardo Beccari (1843–1920).

The stem of this solitary-trunked species grows to 12 to 15 feet high and 2 or 3 inches in diameter. The crownshaft is large for such a relatively small species: 3 feet tall, scarcely thicker than the trunk itself, cylindrical, nonbulging at any point, and light grayish to silvery green. The leaf crown is in the form of a shaving brush, with 8 to 10 stiffly ascending leaves, each of which is 4 feet long on a 1- to 2-foot-long petiole. The deep green leaflets are evenly spaced along the rachis and are of varying widths and lengths, but mostly 2 feet long and 2 inches wide, linear-oblong to linear-obovate, always with an obliquely truncated, jagged apex.

Hydriastele kasesa is endemic to the Papua New Guinea islands of New Britain and New Ireland archipelagos, where it occurs in low mountainous rain forest. The epithet is the aboriginal name of the palm.

This densely clustering species grows to a maximum height of 15 feet. The slender stems are topped by 2-foot-tall, slender, light green crownshafts above which the sparse crowns of 3-foot-long leaves grow. The leaflets are widely spaced along the rachis, each one 1 foot long, irregularly wedge shaped, with an obliquely truncated, jagged apex; the leaflets of the terminal pair are usually united and much wider than the others.

This palm looks better if some of the stems are judiciously cut out so that the others may be more readily seen.

Hydriastele microspadix is endemic to northern Papua New Guinea, where it grows in lowland rain forest. The epithet is from two Greek words meaning "tiny" and "spadix" or "inflorescence."

It is a densely clustering species growing to an overall height of 15 to 20 feet. The crownshaft is 2 to 3 feet tall, usually slightly bulging near its midpoint and nearly white except near its summit where it is suffused with greenish brown. The leaves are 5 feet long and bear regularly and widely spaced, linear-oblong, 2- to 3-foot-long leaflets with obliquely truncated, jagged apices; the leaflets of the terminal pair are larger than the others, often significantly so, and all the leaflets are medium to deep green above but duller and paler green beneath. PLATE 454.

Hydriastele rostrata is endemic to eastern and central Papua New Guinea, where it grows in lowland rain forest. The epithet is Latin for "beaked" and refers to the shape of the fruit.

This is a densely clustering, large species, and the stems grow to heights of 30 or more feet. The crownshaft is 3 feet tall, barely thicker than the trunk, not conspicuously bulged at any point, cylindrical, and medium to deep green. The 6-foot-long leaves are borne on 2-foot-long, wiry petioles, and the leaflets are spaced along the rachis in groups and are of varying widths but are all narrowly or widely wedge shaped with obliquely truncated, jagged apices.

This impressive palm looks better if a few of the stems in a clump are judiciously cut out so that the interesting forms and silhouettes of the stems and leaflets may be better seen. It is rare in cultivation and this fact is almost unfathomable as the palm is robust and easy of culture in a tropical or nearly tropical climate. PLATES 455 & 456.

Hydriastele wendlandiana is endemic to Australia in northern and northeastern Queensland and the Northern Territory, where it grows in swampy lowland rain forest. Two common names in Australia honor places in the Northern Territory: Florence Falls palm or Latrum palm (after a small river by that name). The epithet honors Hermann Wendland, a 19th-century German botanist and gardener.

This sparsely clumping species is occasionally found as a solitary-trunked individual. The stems attain heights of 60 feet. They are usually only 6 inches in diameter, light gray to almost white, straight and distinctly ringed in their younger parts with darker rings of leaf base scars. The crownshafts are relatively short considering the heights of the trunks; they are 2 feet tall, swollen near their midpoints, and light silvery green to whitish blue-green. The 6-foot-long leaves bear yellowish green to deep green, wedge-shaped leaflets of varying widths. Wide leaflets are interspersed with narrow ones in no particular pattern, the wider leaflets always fewer in number, and all are shortly or even minutely toothed at their apices; however, the leaflets of the terminal pair are considerably shorter and wider than most of the others.

The species is easy of culture in tropical or nearly tropical climates if given regular and adequate moisture. It is not suited to calcareous soils and must be heavily mulched (or the soil greatly amended) in such sites. PLATES 457.

HYOPHORBE is a genus of five solitary-trunked, pinnate-leaved, usually heavy trunked, monoecious palms endemic to the Mascarene Islands of the Indian Ocean, where they are threatened with extinction. Several species have unusual swollen trunks and all have prominent, colorful crownshafts and distinctive upward-pointing horn-shaped inflorescence buds beneath the crownshafts. The much-branched, spreading inflorescences emerge from these buds, bearing male and female blossoms.

Two species are commonly planted in tropical or nearly tropical climates; a third (*H. indica*) is common; the fourth (*H. vaughanii*) is rare in its habitat and in cultivation; and the fifth species (*H. amaricaulis*) is, in habitat, reduced to one individual which does not produce viable seed.

The genus name is Greek for "pig" and "food," the allusion probably to the fruits being at one time used for fodder. PLATES 458–465.

Hyophorbe indica is endemic to Réunion Island, where it grows in moist lowland forest. The epithet is Latin for "Indian," a reference to the subcontinent from which the plant was thought to originate.

The light gray to light tan trunk attains a height of 30 feet and a diameter of 8 inches, and is beautifully ringed with widely spaced dark leaf base scars. The crownshaft is usually distinctly bulging at its base, 2 to 3 feet tall, and variable in color, especially in younger individuals: from light green to deep dark green to chocolate or reddish brown. The leaf crown is sparse but hemispherical or even rounded, with half a dozen 6- to 8-foot-long leaves on 2-foot-long petioles; the petiole rachis color is usually the same as the crownshaft in young specimens and may be light to dark green or brownish red. The leaves are gracefully arching and bear numerous, regularly spaced, light green to dark green, linear-lanceolate leaflets that, in younger palms, grow from the rachis in an almost flat and single plane but, in older specimens, are more rigid and grow at angles that create a V-shaped leaf.

The species is fast growing and generally carefree in tropical or nearly tropical climates. It prefers a humus-laden, slightly acidic soil but is adaptable to other soils as long as they are fast draining. It makes an attractive canopy-scape and is more than beautiful in groups of three or more trees of varying heights. PLATES 459 & 460.

Hyophorbe lagenicaulis is endemic to coastal savannas and hilly forests of the Mascarene Islands, where it is critically endangered. The common name is bottle palm. The epithet is derived from two Greek words meaning "bottle" and "stem."

Mature trunks sometimes attain a height of 20 feet. They are light gray to almost white with closely set rings around all but the oldest parts, which are smooth. The shape of the trunk is unusual among palms: it is thick, 2 feet in diameter, and is a column for two-thirds of its height and then tapers abruptly to a bottle-neck form until it reaches the crownshaft, which is 2 to 3 feet tall, mint green, and smooth and waxy, with an enlarged base. The leaf crown is 8 feet wide and tall with usually six leaves. The leaves are 6 to 12 feet long and much arching, to the point that they form semicircles. The petiole is short, 10 inches long, and stout at its base. The deep green, linear-lanceolate and tapering 2-foot-long leaflets grow from the rachis at an angle of 45 degrees or more, lending a deep V shape to the leaf. The inflorescences grow in a whorl around the base of the crownshaft and are upward-pointing, horn-shaped, 3-foot-long green buds composed of several bracts which fall, one by one, to emit the much branched greenish yellow panicles which bear small white unisexual flowers. The fruits are 1 inch wide, rounded, and black when mature.

The palm is tender to cold and adaptable only to zones 10b and 11. It needs full sun, average but regular moisture, and a humus-rich, sandy soil that is well drained. The crown of leaves is always beautiful and dramatically architectural. The trunks are an acquired taste; some think them dumpy, insolent, and grotesque, while others think them shapely and dramatically architectural. In any case, they could never be called "graceful." Where they are planted would seem to make all the difference as to whether or not they are pleasing in the landscape. Rather than trying to hide their unusual form, the latter should be accented. They are nice in groups of three or more individuals of varying heights, and the silhouettes of their leaf crowns are handsome. Given enough space and light, the palm makes a remarkably attractive indoor plant. PLATES 461–463.

Hyophorbe verschaffeltii is endemic to coastal savannas and hilly forests of the Mascarene Islands, where it is critically endangered. The common name is spindle palm. The epithet is a Latinized form of the Belgian surname "Verschaffelt" and honors a 19th-century nurseryman.

Mature trunks grow to 25 feet high. Their diameters are from slightly less than 1 foot to 18 inches. The vernacular name well describes the overall shape of the stems: they are spindle-shaped with the greatest diameter anywhere from the middle of the trunk to beneath the crownshaft. The crownshaft is 2 to 3 feet tall, mint green to powdery blue, and smooth and waxy with an enlarged base. The leaf crown is 10 feet wide and tall. The leaves are 6 to 10 feet long and arched almost exactly like those of the above species. The leaflets generally grow from the rachis at a 45-degree angle but, in addition, grow at several angles to give a plumose look to the leaf. They are limp and not as stiff as those of *H. lagenicaulis,* which fact further adds to the fuller, more graceful, and less formal aspect of the blade. There are usually six leaves in the leaf crown but, because of their arch, the crown is quite round. The inflorescence is similar to that of *H. lagenicaulis.*

The species is slightly susceptible to lethal yellowing disease. It is slightly more tolerant of cold than is the bottle palm, but it is still marginal in zone 10a. Given enough space and high light levels, the spindle palm makes a remarkably attractive indoor plant. PLATES 464 & 465.

Hyophorbe vaughanii is endemic to Mauritius, where it once grew in low, hilly forests but today is represented by a few cultivated specimens on that island; it is extremely rare in cultivation elsewhere in spite of its being a much sought-after species. The epithet honors Reginald E. Vaughan, a Welsh botanist and former director of the herbarium on Mauritius. In stature and appearance, this species is similar to *H. indica* but has stiffer leaves and narrower, more erect inflorescence buds.

HYOSPATHE is a genus of two small, pinnate-leaved, monoecious palms in tropical American rain forest. The inflorescences grow from beneath the leaf crown, are once branched, small, and whitish, and look like little starbursts. They bear male and female blossoms and turn a beautiful crimson as the small, purplish black fruits mature. Because the leaves of both species vary greatly in size and segmentation, it was formerly believed there were as many as 17 different species.

The palms are rare in cultivation and generally limited to specialty collectors and a few botanical gardens. They are not tolerant of freezing temperatures and need copious and regular moisture with partial shade and a humus-laden soil. The genus name means "hog" and "spathe" and is a literal translation into Greek of the Brazilian aboriginal name. PLATE 466.

Hyospathe elegans has a wide distribution from Costa Rica, through Panama and into most of northern South America, where it grows under canopy from sea level to 6000 feet. The epithet is Latin for "elegant."

This palm is found mostly as a single-trunked species but sometimes as a clustering specimen. The individual trunks are slender and, in solitary-trunked specimens, may attain a height of 20 feet with a diameter of 1 inch. They form an elongated but skinny tan crownshaft of leaf sheaths. Leaf form and size are extremely varied. Larger plants usually have 3- or 4-foot leaves with 4 wide to 24 narrow, and regularly spaced, sickle-shaped pinnae, while smaller plants often have undivided leaves from 8 to 20 inches long. The wiry petioles are 1 foot long and the leaf blades, whether divided or not, are beautifully corrugated with raised veins.

The larger individuals with segmented leaves are beautiful and are reminiscent of large, robust *Chamaedorea* species, while the smaller individuals resemble *Asterogyne* species.

Hyospathe macrorachis is endemic to Ecuador in mountainous rain forest on the eastern slopes of the Andes, where it grows under canopy at elevations of 3000 to 6000 feet. The epithet is from Greek words meaning "large" and "rachis."

This is mostly a solitary-trunked species with recumbent creeping stems to 6 feet long. It forms no true crownshaft but has loose and persistent tan leaf sheaths. The leaves may be undivided, deeply bifid apically, and 18 inches long, or may have six to eight, broad sickle-shaped leaflets and be 4 feet long.

The species is rare in habitat and even more so in cultivation.

HYPHAENE is a genus of 10 palmate-leaved, dioecious palms in arid or semiarid regions of southern and eastern Africa, Madagascar, Arabia, and western India. Most species are clustering but some are solitary trunked. A few are small but most are moderate to large palms. They grow in dry savannas, along rivers and streams, on the margins of forests, and often in coastal regions inland of the dunes, but always in open, sunny, and mostly hot areas where groundwater is available to the thirsty roots. They are mostly lowland occupants but *H. compressa* can be found at an elevation of 4500 feet in Kenya and Tanzania.

The genus is unique in having species whose trunks naturally and dichotomously branch. The larger species with clustering and branching stems almost always end up with only one main trunk because of the great diameter of the leaf crown which pushes over the less dominant trunks. The stems are covered in Y-shaped leaf bases in their younger parts, but these bases eventually fall away to leave a trunk that is closely ringed. The leaf crown is usually hemispherical, but there are also several dead leaves hanging beneath the crowns that create the visual effect of a spherical crown. The leaves are borne on petioles with marginal forward-pointing thorns, exhibit a distinct hastula on the underside of the juncture of petiole and blade, and are extremely costapalmate with a strong and curving costa (rib) that arches downwards, much like in *Sabal* species, to create an almost pinnate-looking leaf. Leaf color ranges from deep green to silvery green to almost blue in some species, and the blades usually have a thin, glaucous covering of wax on both surfaces. The leaf segments are always stiff and tough and usually have several threadlike segments (again, as in many *Sabal* species) between them.

The short inflorescences grow from the leaf crown, are once branched, and bear tiny creamy white male or female flowers. The large, leathery fruits are usually pear shaped, hourglass shaped, or oblong, and constricted in the middle, often looking like large cashew fruits; they are invariably orange to deep red to dark reddish brown. They usually take a year (sometimes two) to ripen on the tree. The flesh of the fruits of most species is edible, although fibrous and not delicious, and is often fed to livestock, while the sap from the trunks is sometimes fermented to make an alcoholic toddy. The seeds of most species are extremely hard and were, in the past, used as "vegetable ivory" and carved into objets d'art. In some regions of the palms' habitats, the trees formed great colonies with hardly any other tree in sight. In these areas, the palm trunks were felled for construction purposes, but these populations are now so decimated in most areas that this practice is rapidly dying out.

All species are drought tolerant but grow and look better if supplied with regular and adequate moisture. They are tolerant of salinity in the soil and air, especially the coastal species. They are sun lovers from youth unto old age, and most of them die if planted under canopy. In their native haunts, the palms usually grow on poor soils, but if given a decent soil, they grow faster and look better. None are hardy to cold but most are adaptable to zones 10 and 11, especially in drier climates, and many survive as small and shrublike in 9b. They are all slow growing.

All species are generally referred to as doum palms or simply doum, the word being a French transliteration of an Arabic word for one of the species. The genus name is derived from the Greek word for "weaving" and alludes to the fibers in the flesh of the fruits. PLATES 467–476.

Hyphaene compressa is indigenous to eastern tropical Africa in Somalia, Kenya, Tanzania, and Mozambique, where it grows near the coasts and extends inland along streams and rivers to an elevation of 4500 feet. The epithet is Latin for "compressed" and refers to the shape of the fruit, which is flattened on two sides.

This species is mostly solitary trunked with stems to 60 feet tall in habitat, but sometimes produces specimens with two to four main trunks. The trunks branch as many as four or even five times with age and, until they are old, are covered in gray leaf bases. Leaf color is usually deep green but may also be silvery green or even bluish green. The fruits are mostly pear shaped or oblong and deep orange or light brown; they smell like gingerbread when broken apart.

This is one of the tallest, most massive species in the genus, and old, mature palms are incredibly beautiful and interesting with their tall, branched trunks atop which sit the relatively small leaf crowns; few palm species are as picturesque. PLATE 467.

Hyphaene coriacea occurs naturally in tropical eastern Africa (Somalia, Kenya, Tanzania, Mozambique, and northeastern South Africa) and eastern Madagascar, where it grows mostly along the coasts, even among the dunes. The epithet is Latin for "coriaceous" and alludes to the leathery fruits.

In habitat, this species is often shrubby and almost non-descript because of the nearly sterile soils it grows in; but in cultivation with proper care, it can become one of the most attractive species in the genus, with 30-foot-tall trunks. It is mostly a clustering species but can also be found in habitat as a solitary-trunked individual; the trunks do not normally branch. The fruits are oblong, constricted in the middle, and deep orange or light chestnut brown.

The species seems unusually cold tolerant. It is now found in many locations of central Florida, zone 9b (David Witt, pers. comm.). PLATES 468 & 469.

Hyphaene dichotoma is endemic to western India, where it grows in open savannas at low elevations and is endangered because of land clearing. The epithet refers to the branching habit of the species.

The older trunks of this mostly clustering species dichotomously branch three or four times. The leaf crowns are large and globular, and the leaves are deep green to slightly silvery green. They are nearly orbicular if flattened and are 3 or slightly more feet across. The shiny, leathery fruits are pear shaped and light to deep orange-brown.

This massive species is as beautiful and as picturesque as *H. compressa* when it is old, but it grows slowly, and small plants are not likely to assume the branching habit for many years. Reports indicate this species is unusually hardy to cold and may be possible as a tree in drier regions of zone 9b. PLATES 470 & 471.

Hyphaene petersiana is indigenous to central southern Africa in the countries of Tanzania, Congo, Angola, Namibia, Botswana, and Zimbabwe, where it grows in open savannas and along streams and rivers in the desert areas. The epithet is a Latinized form of the surname "Peters" and honors a 19th-century German explorer of southern Africa.

This unusual species is usually found as a solitary-trunked palm and is always nonbranching. The trunk attains a height of 60 or more feet in habitat and is often slightly swollen near or slightly above its middle. The leaf crown is spherical and consists of great grayish green, 6-foot-wide, very deeply costapalmate leaves on 4-foot-long petioles.

The silhouette of this palm is exceptional because of its spherical outline and its airiness due to the exceptionally long petioles that allow the leaves to be seen; it is one of the most beautiful canopy-scapes. It is faster growing than most other species in the genus, especially if provided with moisture and a decent soil.

The species is among the most useful to native peoples who use every part of it: the trunks for construction; the leaves for an extensive basket weaving industry; the sweet flesh of the fruits for food; and the hard seeds as a vegetable ivory for making utensils and objets d'art. PLATE 472.

Hyphaene thebaica is indigenous to northern and northeastern Africa, where it grows near the coasts in open savannas and along streams and rivers inland, always at low elevations. A common name, gingerbread palm, refers to the taste of the fruits. The epithet is Latin for "of Thebes," an ancient city on the Nile River.

The species is sparsely clustering and freely branching, even at a relatively young age. It is similar in general appearance to *H. compressa* and *H. dichotoma* but does not grow as tall, although it is almost as massive in its old age because of its repeated and dense branching. Individual trunks never attain more than 50 feet of height and are usually 30 feet or less. The leaves and leaf crown are smaller than the aforementioned two species and are a deep green to grayish or silvery green. The fruits are 3 inches long, pear shaped, and light brown.

The palm is exceptionally picturesque and appealing at all ages. It is a fabled species with a long record of cultivation and use in ancient Egypt. PLATES 473–475.

IGUANURA is a genus of 20 delicately beautiful, small, pinnate-leaved, monoecious palms in peninsular Thailand, peninsular Malaysia, Sumatra, and Borneo. There are both clustering and solitary-trunked species and all are undergrowth plants in rain forest. The leaves are either entire, with the segments united and apically bifid, or with segments divided; the margins of the leaflets are always toothed, and the newly unfurled leaves of many species are pinkish, reddish, purplish, or bronzy for an unusually long time. The leaves last a long time also, so that in habitat, epiphytes, algae, and fungi often find homes on them. The inflorescences grow from the leaf crown in all species except *I. bicornis* (which has a rudimentary crownshaft) and are elongated and mostly spikelike, but some are branched.

All are tender to cold and adaptable only to zones 10b and 11; they need warmth year-round, even at night, and thus are not suitable for frostless Mediterranean climates. They are water lovers, need a slightly acidic, humus-laden soil, and cannot take the full sun of hot climates. All species are eminently well adapted to greenhouse or container culture.

The genus name is coined from the New World Spanish word for "lizard" (*iguana,* which itself is from a South American aboriginal word) and the Greek word for "tail," alluding to the spikelike, scaly inflorescences of some species. PLATES 477–482.

Iguanura bicornis is indigenous to peninsular Thailand and peninsular Malaysia, where it grows in low mountainous rain forest. The epithet is Latin for "two horned" and refers to the shape of the fruits.

It is a clustering species with stems attaining heights of 8 or 9 feet. The palm forms a slender, loose, light green crownshaft to 1 foot in height. The leaf crown is sparse. The leaves never lie beneath the horizontal, are 18 inches long, and are borne on slender 1-foot-long petioles. The few leaflets are irregularly spaced along the rachis, each 8 to 10 inches long, irregularly trapezoidal, and S shaped; the apex is wider than the point of attachment, obliquely squared, and jaggedly toothed. New growth is a beautiful purplish bronze. The inflorescences grow from beneath the crownshaft and are twice branched, thin and spreading; they bear both male and female flowers that produce 0.5-inch-long, egg-shaped red fruits, each of which has two small lobes at one end. PLATES 477 & 478.

Iguanura elegans is endemic to Sarawak on the island of Borneo, where it grows in lowland rain forest. The epithet is Latin for "elegant."

The leaves of this sparsely clustering species are either entire and undivided with the usual bifid apex, or divided into irregularly spaced and wide, slightly S-shaped segments. Both forms have deeply corrugated blades or segments, and the new growth is a beautiful rosy bronze. An exceptionally beautiful form has leaves variegated in cream and shades of green, the new growth also rose colored. PLATE 479.

Iguanura geonomiformis is endemic to peninsular Malaysia, where it occurs in the undergrowth of low mountainous rain forest. The epithet is Latin for "formed like *Geonoma,*" an unrelated tropical American genus of palms with many vegetative similarities to *Iguanura* species.

This is a densely clustering species whose stems are thin and never more than 3 feet high. The 3-foot-long ascending leaves may be undivided with deeply bifid apices, be divided into a few wide segments with even larger and wider apical segments, or exhibit fine and regular pinnate segmentation.

Iguanura palmuncula is endemic to Borneo, where it grows in low mountainous rain forest. The epithet is Latin for "little palm" and is somewhat humorous as the "-uncula" suffix was previously used only by anatomists of the Leeuwenhoek (the Dutch inventor of the microscope) days to refer to human spermatazoa, *homunculus,* or "little man." The stems of this clustering species are no more than 6 feet tall. The leaves are 2 to 3 feet long and a uniform emerald green, and are either segmented into broad S-shaped leaflets or are entire and apically bifid. PLATE 480.

Iguanura polymorpha is indigenous to peninsular Thailand, Malaysia, and Borneo, where it grows in low mountainous rain forest. The epithet is from two Greek words meaning "many" and "form," although vegetatively the species is not as polymorphous as *I. geonomiformis.*

It is a densely clustering species whose stems attain heights of 10 feet. The sparse leaf crowns have 3-foot-long leaves on 1-foot-long petioles. The leaflets are similar in shape and size to those of *I. bicornis,* and the plant overall, is similar in appearance except for the fruits.

Iguanura speciosa is endemic to peninsular Thailand, where it grows in low mountainous rain forest. The epithet is Latin for "beautiful."

The stems of this densely clustering species grow to heights of almost 12 feet. The leaves are unsegmented except for the bifid apices. They are 3 feet long and an unusual large oblong, dark green above with glossy, deep corrugations and a lighter, duller green beneath.

This is a beautiful little palm. Some taxonomists consider it a form of *I. polymorpha* because of the similar inflorescences, but the leaves of this one are distinct.

Iguanura wallichiana is among the most widespread species in the genus. The epithet honors Nathaniel Wallich, 19th-century superintendent of the botanical gardens in Calcutta, India.

This palm is among the most variable in vegetative characters, and two naturally occurring forms have been identified, both clustering. *Iguanura wallichiana* var. *wallichiana* is indigenous to peninsular Thailand, peninsular Malaysia, and Sumatra, where it grows in low mountainous rain forest. The stems grow to heights of 9 feet and the leaves are 4 to 5 feet long. The latter are spreading and slightly arching, segmented into broad, corrugated, S-shaped and regularly spaced leaflets, which are a most beautiful rosy bronze when new. *Iguanura wallichiana* var. *major* is endemic to peninsular Malaysia, where it grows in low mountainous rain forest. This form is usually not as large as the type and has undivided 2.5-foot-long, stiff and ascending obovate, apically bifid and deeply corrugated leaves that, like the type, are a beautiful purplish or rosy bronze when newly opened. This variety is most sought after in horticulture; in fact, it was so avidly collected and grown in greenhouses and conservatories in Victorian England that it is still endangered in habitat. It is no more beautiful or desirable than the type. PLATES 481 & 482.

IRIARTEA is a monotypic genus of large, solitary-trunked, pinnate-leaved, monoecious palm in tropical America. The genus name honors Don Bernardo de Iriarte, an 18th-century Spanish (Canary Islands) politician and benefactor of explorations to the New World. The genus was once considered to consist of at least three species: *I. gigantea* (named for the size of mature individuals), *I. ventricosa* (named for the swollen trunks of individuals growing in lowland rain forest), and *I. deltoidea* (named for the form of juvenile leaflets). PLATES 483 & 484.

Iriartea deltoidea occurs naturally in extreme southeastern Nicaragua, through Costa Rica and Panama, and into western and southern Colombia, southern Venezuela, northern Ecuador, eastern Peru, northern Bolivia, and the western Amazon region of Brazil, where it grows from sea level to an elevation of 4200 feet, always in rain forest and almost always on the slopes of the hills and mountains where, in some localities, the species forms great colonies.

The trunk attains a height of 80 feet in habitat and is 1 foot in diameter. It is light gray to white in older individuals. The presence of a midpoint bulge seems associated with the elevation at which the palm grows: lowland individuals have the swelling, highland individuals lack it. The base of the stem is, in older palms, supported by a short 4- to 6-foot-tall dense cone of dark colored, almost black, stilt roots bearing short, prickly thorns; young and nonemergent individuals seldom exhibit the prop roots. These roots themselves often branch near their bases, in much the same manner as do the prop roots of the American mangrove (*Rhizophora mangle*).

The crownshaft is a light grayish green, 3 to 4 feet tall, usually bulging at its base but may also, at that point, be the same diameter as the trunk and then expanded near its summit. The leaf crown is sparse with six leaves but is usually spherical because of the great spreading plumose leaves, each of which is borne on a petiole 12 to 15 feet long and is stiff and straight except near its apex where it is slightly arched. The leaflets are narrowly wedge shaped, 2 to 3 feet long, of varying widths, and deep emerald green on both surfaces, with obliquely truncated, jagged apices. They grow from the rachis at different angles to create a plumose, rounded leaf. The leaflets of younger trees are exceptional in having a different form: they are immense, 2 to 3 feet long, flat, lustrous, and irregularly fan shaped or wedge shaped with jagged apices, and grow from the rachis in a single, nearly flat plane. It is only when the young trees grow above the canopy into the full sunlight that the much more narrow and plumosely arranged leaflets are formed, possibly as an adaptation to the winds above the forest cover (falling leaves are reportedly silent because their mass is so relatively small compared to their size).

The inflorescences are formed beneath the crownshaft, and the primary bracts are remarkable, forming before opening 10-foot-long, downward-curving, and narrowly horn-shaped buds of as many as 16 overlapping woody, hirsute bracts. The inflorescences consist of many cream-colored 2- to 3-foot-long pendent branches bearing both male and female flowers. The round, yellowish green fruits mature to bluish black and are less than 1 inch in diameter.

The species has many uses in habitat: the trunks are used for construction of houses, blowguns, and spears (young individuals), and, hollowed out, for canoes; the inside of the leaf sheaths (crownshafts) is administered to women in childbirth to ease the rigors of labor; the leaves are used for thatch; the growing point is edible and eagerly eaten by the native people, as are the seeds.

Mature trees are among the most magnificent palms. The great plumose leaves are incomparably beautiful and create an exceptionally alluring silhouette and canopyscape. Alas, the species does not tolerate frost, and needs copious and constant moisture and a soil that is humus rich, constantly moist, and yet fast draining. It appreciates partial shade as a juvenile but adapts to full sun even then and only comes into its own with full exposure once past its early youth.

IRIARTELLA is a genus of two clustering, pinnate-leaved, monoecious palms in tropical America. These are undergrowth species in low mountainous rain forest.

The slender, reedlike stems are supported atop a small mass of short stilt roots. The species are clustering, often forming colonies. They send up either stems from the creeping rootstocks (rhizomes) or adventitious shoots from original stems at a point well above the ground. The loosely formed crownshafts are covered in a short prickly tomentum that can be irritating to the skin. The inflorescences are once branched and green and bear green flowers of both sexes. The small fruits are orange or red and ellipsoid.

Neither of these species seems to be in cultivation outside of a few botanical gardens, but both are attractive and worthy of being grown. They are intolerant of frost and need regular and adequate moisture as well as partial shade.

The genus name translates as "little *Iriartea*" and alludes to the similarity of the juvenile leaves of *Iriartea* and the mature leaves of *Iriartella*.

Iriartella setigera is indigenous to southwestern Guyana, southern Venezuela, extreme eastern Colombia, and northwestern Brazil. The epithet is Latin for "bristle-bearing" and alludes to the short hairs on the leaf sheaths.

The stems grow to heights of 35 feet but are no more than 2 inches in diameter. They were formerly used in habitat for making blowguns. The trunks are deep green and have widely spaced distinct gray rings of leaf base scars. The little crownshafts are barely thicker than the stems, a bright, light green, and cylindrical. They are covered in a short, stiff tomentum that is irritating to the skin. The leaf crown is sparse and hemispherical with six spreading 4- to 5-foot-long leaves on 1- to 2-foot-long wiry petioles. The 8 to 10 leaflets are large considering the length of the leaf, light to medium green on both surfaces, obliquely wedge shaped or diamond shaped, with an undulating surface and jagged apices; the leaflets of the terminal pair are usually wedge shaped and significantly broader than the others.

Because of the light color of the leaves and crownshaft as well as the shape of the leaflets, this palm would make a stunning contrast with other vegetation or palms under a high canopy.

Iriartella stenocarpa occurs naturally in extreme southeastern Colombia, eastern Peru, and adjacent extreme western Brazil, where it grows in low mountainous rain forest. The epithet is from two Greek words meaning "slender" and "fruit."

This species differs from *I. setigera* in its smaller stature, its smaller and lower (in elevation) natural distribution, its smaller clumps, and its leaves that are sometimes entire and unsegmented but usually with three to five pinnae shaped like those of the *I. setigera*.

ITAYA is a rare monotypic genus of palmate-leaved, monoecious palm in northern South America, where it is in great danger of extinction because of land clearing. It is similar taxonomically and visually to the genus *Chelyocarpus* but is readily distinguished by the petiole bases, which are split in mature leaves. The inflorescences are much branched but shorter than the leaf crown and consist of flowering branches bearing small, white bisexual flowers that produce round, greenish fruits.

The genus name is that of a river in Peru near where the palm was discovered. The epithet is Latin for "of friends" and was bestowed by Harold E. Moore, Jr. (1972), because "of the spirit of the program under which I first encountered it [the species] and for my associates in Peru." PLATE 485.

Itaya amicorum is indigenous to northeastern Peru, southeastern Colombia, and extreme northwestern Brazil, where it occurs in the undergrowth and along rivers and streams in lowland tropical rain forest.

The little palm attains a total height of 15 feet with a clean trunk that is 3 inches in diameter. The leaves are the reason one lusts after this beauty; they are circular, 6 feet in diameter, with wedge-shaped segments that are apically toothed and that extend to the petiole. The 10 to 16 leaf divisions are deeply pleated and light shiny green above and silvery green or even white beneath. The leaves are reminiscent of those of the larger *Licuala* species and are borne on 7- to 8-foot-long petioles, giving the leaf crown the most beautiful aspect of a globular constellation of giant pinwheels spinning in the breeze against the sky.

The species is tender to cold and is adaptable only in zones 10b and 11. It needs a rich soil with unimpeded drainage and nearly constant moisture, although it thrives in partial shade or full sun when older. The palm makes one of the world's most beautiful canopy-scapes.

JOHANNESTEIJSMANNIA is a genus of four unsegmented but palmate-leaved, monoecious palms in southern Thailand, peninsular Malaysia, Sumatra, and western Borneo. These are undergrowth palms in tropical rain forest, where they occur on slopes and ridges, never in swampy areas. One species has a short trunk; the others form no aboveground stem, the leaves growing directly from the ground in immense rosettes. *Johannesteijsmannia* is closely related to *Licuala,* and the two genera may be united in the future.

The genus has the third largest undivided leaves in the palm family; only *Manicaria* of the American tropics and *Marojejya* of Madagascar have larger undivided leaves and, in both cases, the leaves are usually split or segmented by the wind. These are diamond-shaped or lanceolate leaves borne on long petioles, and the blades are strongly pleated and exhibit a distinct midrib or extension of the petiole through the blade. Both petioles and the bottom margins of the leaves bear tiny thorns, and the blade apex is toothed or jaggedly incised, corresponding to the corrugations on both surfaces of the blade. The leaves appear to be more pinnate than palmate, mainly because of the relative narrowness and length of the blades. That they are basically palmate is proved by the small hastula on the undersides of young leaves before they are fully expanded, at the juncture of blade and petiole; the hastula is usually worn off by the time the leaf is unfurled.

The inflorescences are relatively short and are partially hidden in the leaf crowns by the size of the leaves and, in habitat, usually by leaf litter and other debris. They are enclosed in bud by several felty bracts that persist after the short, curved cream-colored branches of the inflorescences emerge. The bisexual flowers smell bad but produce light brown, globose, corky fruits with conical projections.

These palm species are certainly among the world's most beautiful and are almost maniacally sought after by gardeners and collectors in suitable climates. Drawings and photographs seldom convey the extraordinary size and elegance of these palms. Amazingly, although they are adaptable only to tropical or nearly tropical climates, they nevertheless withstand temperatures at or near freezing for short periods. They resent cold dry winds and demand partial shade in all climates but especially hot ones and especially when young. They need a humus-laden, friable soil that is constantly moist but quickly draining, and they are difficult to maintain without constantly high relative humidity.

The genus is called joey palms, mainly because of the length of the scientific name, which honors Johannes E. Teijsmann, a 19th-century Dutch botanist and gardener in Java. PLATES 486–490.

Johannesteijsmannia altifrons has the widest natural distribution of the genus and is found in Sumatra, peninsular Malaysia, southern Thailand, and western Borneo, where it grows in mountainous rain forest at elevations from 1000 to 3000 feet. It is threatened in Malaysia because of forest destruction and the gathering of the leaves for thatch. The species is sometimes called diamond joey. The epithet is Latin for "tall frond" and alludes to the centermost leaf in a rosette that may reach as high as 20 feet.

The petioles are 6 to 10 feet long and are armed with tiny sawlike teeth, which are also found on the lower margins of the younger leaf blades. The diamond-shaped blades are 10 feet long in older plants and 6 feet wide at their broadest points. They are light to medium green on both surfaces and are held erect and slightly spreading, but the older ones near the margins of the rosettes are usually spreading horizontally and pendent. There may be as many as 24 giant leaves in a single rosette.

This is the most widely cultivated species in the genus, and for good reason: it is supremely attractive. PLATES 486 & 487.

Johannesteijsmannia lanceolata is a highly endangered species endemic to southeastern peninsular Malaysia, where it grows in low mountainous rain forest. The epithet is Latin for "lanceolate," referring to the shape of the leaves. The species differs from *J. altifrons* in having 7- to 8-foot-long linear leaves that are 1 foot wide on 3-foot-long petioles.

Johannesteijsmannia magnifica is an endangered species endemic to peninsular Malaysia, where it grows in low mountainous rain forest. The epithet is Latin for "magnificent." This species is similar to *J. altifrons,* but the leaf underside has a gorgeous, almost shimmering, white tomentum, which often has a bluish hue and creates an unbelievably beautiful leaf. PLATES 488 & 489.

Johannesteijsmannia perakensis is endemic to central peninsular Malaysia, where it grows in low mountainous rain forest. The epithet is Latin for "of Perak," a province in the palm's habitat.

This palm forms an aboveground stem, which grows to 12 feet high. The leaves are similar in appearance and dimensions to those of *J. altifrons,* slightly narrower.

A mature or nearly mature specimen is truly glorious, especially when incorporated into other vegetation, but the trunk takes many years to grow very high. PLATE 490.

JUANIA is a rare and endangered monotypic genus of pinnate-leaved, dioecious palm endemic to the Juan Fernandez Islands in the eastern Pacific, 350 miles west of Valparaiso, Chile. It is nearly extinct because of habitat destruction, which was mainly caused by goats until 1977. The genus name alludes to the name of the islands. The epithet is Latin for "southern."

Juania australis grows in moist, cool forests on steep hills and ridges at elevations from 600 to 2500 feet.

The trunks attain heights of 50 feet in habitat and are 1 foot in diameter. They are light to dark gray in all but their youngest parts and are ringed with light colored, closely spaced leaf base scars. There is no crownshaft but, in young plants, the leaf sheaths are persistent and a deep olive green. The leaf crown is hemispherical to nearly rounded, with 6- to 8-foot-long, spreading and slightly arching leaves on short petioles. The medium to dark green leaflets are 2 feet long, stiff, linear-lanceolate, and shortly bifid at their tips. They grow from the rachis at an angle, giving a slight V shape to the leaf. The inflorescences grow from the leaf sheaths and are accompanied by long, woody bracts.

The species is closely related to the genus *Ceroxylon,* but its appearance is more akin to *Jubaea.* The palm seems nearly impossible to grow and there is reportedly only one mature individual outside of the palm's island home, in coastal mainland Chile. It has been tried in southern Europe, Ireland, coastal southern California and San Francisco, New Zealand, and other cool Mediterranean climates but seems to last only a while in any of these regions. Small palms in southern Europe were killed by temperatures of 25 to 29°F and do not last a season in climates that have hot summer temperatures with high nighttime temperatures.

JUBAEA is a monotypic genus of massive, pinnate-leaved, monoecious palm. The genus name supposedly honors Juba, an ancient king of Numidia (present-day Algeria). The common name is wine palm or Chilean wine palm. The epithet is Latin for "of Chile." PLATES 491 & 492.

Jubaea chilensis is endemic to a small area in central Chile, where it grows in the monsoonal savannas and low forests of the foothills of the Andes.

Mature trunks grow to 80 feet or more in habitat with a diameter of 6 feet, making them some of the thickest palm trunks. They sometimes show a slight bulge near their middles and are usually dark gray, retaining their rings of diamond-shaped leaf base scars even on the oldest parts of the stems. The leaf crown is 25 feet wide and 15 to 20 feet tall. The leaves are 8 to 12 feet long on short petioles that are generally less than 1 foot long. They do not arch but are spreading, with the 2-foot-long narrow, stiff leaflets growing from the rachis in one plane to give a flat shape to the blade. Leaf color is a dull green above and a lighter, often grayish green beneath. The leaf crown may be hemispherical or almost completely rounded. The inflorescences are once branched and have large paddle-shaped woody, persistent, felt-covered bracts. The flowering branches are usually 4 feet long and erect, bearing small, dirty purple unisexual blossoms of both sexes. The fruits are 1 inch wide, round, and yellow to orange, and hang in pendent clusters mostly hidden by the leaves.

The species is drought tolerant when established but grows quicker and looks better with average but regular moisture. It is hardy to cold and is adaptable to zones 9 through 11 in areas subject to wet freezes in winter, and to zones 8 through 11 in drier, Mediterranean climes. The Chilean wine palm is not recommended for hot, humid climates like those found in Florida and along the Gulf coast; although it is perfectly hardy in most parts of these areas, it grows slow, is never as large or beautiful, and tends to die out because of year-round high heat and humidity and because of the little difference between daytime and nighttime temperatures. In cooler climates like those of southern California, the Mediterranean, South Africa, and areas of Australia, it is often the most magnificent palm grown. It is not particular about soil type as long as it is fast draining, and it needs as much sun as possible.

Few gardens are large enough to accommodate a mature Chilean wine palm, but since the palm grows so slowly, it is usually planted without regard to its ultimate size. A group of old palms is very impressive. This palm is also one of the few that looks good in straight rows lining a drive or large avenue. There is something massively "Egyptian" about their thick, straight-as-an-arrow columns that is reminiscent of those ancient Nubian temples. They are architectural and yet among the most magnificent subjects for a canopy-scape. This palm is not known to be grown indoors and is not recommended for such situations.

The trunks were formerly used for construction and were felled for their sap, which was made into wine. This practice led to near extinction of the species in habitat. The remaining population has been declared a national sanctuary. The seeds are edible and delicious, tasting much like coconut.

JUBAEOPSIS is a rare monotypic genus of pinnate-leaved, clustering, monoecious palm. The genus name means "similar to *Jubaea,*" although genetically the palm is more closely related to the coconut. The species is sometimes called Pondoland palm. It was once known as kaffir palm, a moniker that should be eschewed as it is a derogatory term for a person of color and comes from an Arabic word meaning "infidel" or "heathen." The epithet is a Latinized form of the word "kaffir" and could also be changed: the rules of nomenclature have, in the past, been bent for equally "invalid" reasons. PLATES 493 & 494.

Jubaeopsis caffra grows at low elevations along three rivers near the coast of Pondoland in northeastern South Africa.

The species is sparsely clumping, and the stems are thick and robust looking. They grow to heights of 20 feet in habitat and are covered in all but their oldest parts with persistent, woody leaf bases. The leaf crowns are, at most, hemispherical and often look like a shaving brush due to the large, erect leaves. The latter are 12 to 15 feet long, gracefully arching from their midpoints, and usually have a twist to the rachis from the midpoint on which results in a vertical alignment of the leaflets in the apical half. The 3- to 4-foot-long, stout petioles may be green, yellow, or deep orange. The leaflets of new leaves and those of juvenile plants are stiff and grow from the rachis at an angle that gives a V-shaped leaf, while those of older leaves in older plants are often nearly pendent. They are light to medium green, 3 feet long, lanceolate to narrowly lanceolate, with obliquely truncated and shortly bifid apices, and are regularly spaced along the rachis. The 3- to 4-foot-long cream-colored inflorescences grow out of the leaf bases and emerge from two bracts, the upper of which is large, woody, and persistent. They carry flowers of both sexes and produce round yellow, 1-inch-wide fruits.

This palm seems to need sun even from an early age and, while not fussy about soil type, does best with a fast-draining, fertile one. It languishes if not provided with regular and adequate moisture. It would seem to be a perfect candidate for Mediterranean climates but is not so good in tropical or nearly tropical regions, where the nighttime temperatures in the summer are high. It tolerates frost moderately and is adaptable to zones 10 and 11.

The species is slow growing, and the trunks take many years to grow to any size. It is a beautiful clumper even when young because of the great arching leaves, and it gives a wonderful contrast when incorporated into other vegetation. It is even beautiful as a specimen surrounded by space, especially when older. It is a close relative of *Cocos* (coconut), and much has been written about the similarities between the two genera. While the leaves may be similar, there is no way the ponderous looking and clumping trunks of *Jubaeopsis* could be mistaken for those of the coconut; they are almost unique.

KENTIOPSIS is a genus of four large, pinnate-leaved, monoecious palms in New Caledonia. All but one species is endangered. The inflorescences are formed beneath the crownshafts and consist of reddish or purplish, much-branched sprays of waxy, furry white blossoms. The fruits are egg shaped, 1 inch long, and bright red or dull purple when mature.

All the species are intolerant of cold and adaptable only to zones 10b and 11. They are slow growing. The genus name translates as "similar to *Kentia*," an out-of-date name for species of *Gronophyllum*, *Gulubia*, and *Hydriastele*. PLATES 495–498.

Kentiopsis magnifica is endemic to northern New Caledonia, where it grows in colonies in mountainous rain forest at elevations of 1000 to 2000 feet. The epithet is Latin for "magnificent."

The trunk can attain a height of 80 feet and is straight, columnar, less than 1 foot in diameter, and strongly ringed, except in the oldest parts. The crownshaft is 3 or 4 feet tall, slightly wider than the stem, of uniform width, and a beautiful bluish green to purplish black. The 8-foot-long leaves on short petioles exhibit a vertical twist from their midpoints to their apices; they often are a handsome reddish brown or cherry red when newly unfurled. The leaflets are a deep green, leathery, regularly spaced along the rachis in a single flat plane and are linear-acuminate and 2 to 3 feet long. PLATE 495.

Kentiopsis oliviformis is endemic to central New Caledonia, where it grows in colonies in wet forests and valleys and drier hillsides under 1000 feet elevation. It is in danger of extinction because of agricultural expansion. The epithet is Latin for "formed like an olive," a reference to the fruits.

It is the tallest palm native to New Caledonia, with trunks reaching to almost 100 feet tall and 1 foot in diameter. The crownshaft is 3 feet tall, scarcely wider than the trunk, and dull purplish to brownish green. The leaves are 10 to 12 feet long, sharply ascending and, except when dying, never lie beneath the horizontal. The deep green, linear-acuminate leaflets are 2 to 3 feet long and grow in a single flat plane from the rachis.

The species seems adaptable to most soils, even alkaline and calcareous ones, and it is becoming popular in southern Florida.

The palm is of exceptional beauty, both as a juvenile and as a mature specimen. It is majestic enough to be an isolated specimen but looks best in groups of three or more individuals of varying heights. It is one of the grandest canopy-scapes. PLATES 496 & 497.

Kentiopsis piersoniorum is endemic on the steep, wet slopes of Mt. Panié in New Caledonia, at elevations between 1000 and 3000 feet. The epithet honors the Pierson family of New Caledonia, who helped Donald Hodel and Jean-Christophe Pintaud explore the palm flora of the territory.

The trunk can reach a height of 50 feet, atop which resides the 3-foot-tall, purplish gray, waxy crownshaft whose diameter is slightly greater than the trunk and does not much vary along its length. The beautifully arching, light to deep grayish green leaves are 8 feet long with regularly spaced, stiff, linear-acuminate leaflets, growing from the rachis at a steep angle to give the leaf a V shape.

This is the only species that is not critically endangered in habitat. The epithet "magnifica" could equally well be applied to this more than beautiful canopy-scape with its globular crown of recurved leaves. Specimen groups of three or more individuals of varying heights are equally aesthetically satisfying. PLATE 498.

Kentiopsis pyriformis is endemic to southeastern New Caledonia, where it grows in rain forest and is much endangered. The epithet is from Latin words meaning "pear" and "formed."

The palm grows to 70 feet overall. Its crownshaft is purplish or coppery colored, and the sparse leaf crown consists of arching, deep green 8-foot-long leaves with sharply ascending stiff leaflets. The palm is still rare in cultivation.

KERRIODOXA is a monotypic genus of palmate-leaved dioecious palm. It is sometimes called white elephant palm. The genus name is a combination of two words, one of which honors Arthur Kerr, the original collector and early 20th-century botanist, and the other of which is Greek for "glory." The epithet is Latin for "elegant." PLATE 499.

Kerriodoxa elegans is endemic to the low mountainous and wet forests of the west coast of peninsular Thailand.

Mature trunks grow to 15 feet high with a diameter of 6 to 8 inches. They are generally light brown and smooth and show closely set rings on the older parts; the younger portions are covered with narrowly triangular leaf bases. The leaf crown is 10 to 12 feet wide but usually 8 or 9 feet tall. The leaves are circular and 6 to 8 feet wide, with the tapering narrowly lanceolate, once-pleated segments extending to a third or almost halfway to the center of the blade. They are carried on stout, 3-foot-long, dark purple or black petioles, and the leaf segments are slightly pendent at their ends. A small hastula sits atop the blade near its center. Leaf color is light to medium green above, but the undersurface is covered in a short but dense white tomentum. The male inflorescences are much branched and about 1 foot long; the females are more sparingly branched and almost 3 feet long. Both are covered in a gray or tawny felt and carry small yellowish flowers. The 2-inch-wide fruits are round and yellow to orange when ripe.

This palm has proven amazingly hardy to cold considering its tropical origins; it is adaptable to zones 10 and 11 and is found in favorable microclimates of 9b. It loves moisture, a rich, well-drained soil, and partial shade, although large palms can adapt to full sun. Constantly high relative humidity seems to be important to the palm's health; the only problem with the species in southern and central Florida comes in the dry season (winter) when the leaves can look ragged and, if not watered every day, the plant can die off.

The great, spreading leaves are astonishingly handsome and spectacular, especially in young plants with little trunk. There are no more beautiful palmate leaves; the nearest comparison to them are those of young *Livistona rotundifolia* or some of the larger-leaved species of *Pritchardia*.

This is a perfect palm for a patio or courtyard. It is also a beautiful accent in a bed of lower vegetation. Planted in groups of three or more individuals of varying heights, it creates a tableau of near rapturous beauty and, if one has a hillside, nothing could be more splendid than having these wonderful leaves seen from above or below. The palm has not been in cultivation long, having been scientifically described and named by John Dransfield in 1983, but its beauty will make it popular in tropical and subtropical regions in the future; seed is now widely distributed. It is not known to be grown indoors, but there should be no reason why it wouldn't succeed with high light and humidity. It would also seem to be one of the choicest palms for containers outdoors.

KORTHALSIA is a genus of 25 pinnate-leaved, clustering, spiny, monoecious, climbing palms in lowland wet forests of the Andaman and Nicobar Islands, Myanmar, Thailand, Laos, Vietnam, Cambodia, southeastern China, Sumatra, Indonesia, and eastwards to New Guinea and the Philippines.

These rattans are mostly large and high climbing, and they are the only rattans whose aerial stems branch. The stems are covered in all but the oldest parts with long, needlelike spines, which are also found (in much smaller sizes) on the petioles and rachises of climbing individuals. The leaves of juvenile plants are unlike those of older plants and are entire, usually linear-lanceolate, with distinct petioles and toothed margins, and are undivided except for the bifid apex in some species. Once the plants begin to climb, the pinnate leaf is formed with an extension of the rachis into a barbed cirrus, allowing stems to hook onto other vegetation in the plant's scramble upwards. The leaflets of climbing individuals are linear, wedge shaped or diamond shaped, and deep green above but silvery or silvery brown beneath; they grow in a roughly flat plane from the rachis until the stem reaches sunlight, at which time they usually become pendent.

Another distinction of the genus is that the leaflets of most species are borne on short stalks, which grow directly from the rachis. Several species have persistent, much swollen leaf sheaths in which large biting ants reside who, when disturbed, first click their large and hard mandibles together as a warning and then rush out to attack whatever occasions the disturbance.

The genus name honors a 19th-century Dutch botanist, Pieter W. Korthals, who collected in Indonesia.

The large inflorescences grow from the ends of the stems, not from the stem's nodes, and, after flowering and fruiting, the stem dies. Each inflorescence consists of stout and robust primary branches that branch once again, the long, felt-covered, wormlike, and pendent flower stalks growing from the second set of branches and bearing bisexual blossoms. The fruits are round or egg shaped, brown, orange-brown, or reddish brown, and are covered with large, overlapping scales.

These plants, after they begin to climb, are viciously spiny in their younger parts, and this is most likely why they are so rare in cultivation. If space can be found for them, however, they are beautiful in a wall of vegetation where they create a lovely contrast to their surroundings. The juvenile, nonclimbing plants would make great container subjects. They require a tropical climate and copious moisture, and, if kept shaded and occasionally pruned, will keep the unsegmented, friendly leaf form for a while.

The stems of many species are used in habitat to make rope, baskets, and other utensils; the stems are not valuable commercially, however, for making rattan furniture because they cannot be polished. PLATE 500.

LACCOSPADIX is a monotypic genus of pinnate-leaved, monoecious palm. The genus name is from two Greek words meaning "reservoir" and "spadix," an allusion to the flowers being formed in depressions on the branches of the inflorescences. In Australia, the species is called Atherton palm (from the Atherton Tableland) and Queensland kentia. PLATES 501 & 502.

Laccospadix australasica is endemic to rain forest in northeastern Queensland, Australia, where it occurs in the undergrowth at elevations from 2500 to 4500 feet. The epithet is Latin for "Australian."

The species is found mostly as a clustering palm, in which case the stems grow to 10 or 12 feet tall and no more than 2 inches in diameter. If solitary, the trunk usually grows to 25 feet tall and 4 inches in diameter. The stems, whether clustered or solitary, are deep green, almost black, in their younger parts and deep tan or brown in their older parts. They are distinctly ringed with lighter leaf base scars and are covered with the persistent leaf bases and short fibers in their younger parts. The leaf crown is never more than hemispherical, even in solitary-trunked forms, because the leaves are ascending, mostly erect, and gracefully arching. They are 6 feet long on 3-foot-long, stout, green petioles. The leaflets are linear-elliptical, long tipped, light to medium green on both surfaces, and widely and evenly spaced along the rachis in a single flat plane. They are also limp and slightly pendent at their apices. New growth is sometimes a beautiful wine to deep bronzy red, and there is some evidence that the solitary-

trunked specimens more often produce the colored growth than do the clustering individuals. The 3- to 4-foot-long inflorescences grow from the leaf crown and are remarkable single, cream-colored, and pendent unbranched spikes that bear tiny male and female flowers. The 0.5-inch-long, oblong, juicy berrylike fruits grow directly on the spike and are bright cherry red when ripe.

The palm needs partial shade at all ages. It does not grow well in hot or tropical climates with warm nighttime temperatures. It wants a moist, relatively cool but frost-free climate with no extreme fluctuations in temperature. It is not well adapted to calcareous soils but needs a friable, humus-laden medium that is constantly moist but not soggy. This is a species for coastal southern California and similar climates.

It is an elegant and graceful small palm. The clustering forms are a veritable symphony of lovely leaf forms among other vegetation, and the solitary-trunked form is scintillating when surrounded by space and a short groundcover, all under canopy. One of the most beautiful sitings is in the Rain Forest Pyramid at Moody Gardens in Galveston, Texas, where a large, curving trunked solitary specimen leans out over a pathway, its beautifully ringed stem and lovely, ethereal leaf crown often with colored new growth.

LACCOSPERMA is a genus of seven pinnate-leaved, clustering, spiny, climbing, monoecious palms in (mostly western) tropical Africa, where they grow in low mountainous rain forest or swamps.

These are mostly large and high climbing palms with large leaves. The stems (actually the adherent leaf sheaths) are invariably spiny as are the petioles and rachises. The leaflets also have small barbs and are linear, usually regularly spaced along the spiny rachis, and mostly pendent. The ends of the rachises are formed into long cirri with pairs of backward-pointing spines. The inflorescences form at the ends of the stems and are usually tall and twice branched with the flowering branches hanging down from the secondary branches like a curtain. After the bisexual flowers form fruits, the stems die.

These species are almost completely unknown to horticulture outside of their native haunts. The leaves are large, striking, and even beautiful, but the plants are so spiny that their use in gardens is limited.

The genus name is from Greek words meaning "reservoir" or "pit" and "seed."

LATANIA is a genus of three large palmate-leaved dioecious palms endemic to the Mascarene Islands, where they are now nearly extinct. They are similar in general appearance, especially as adult plants. They freely hybridize when grown near each other so that it may be impossible to assign a specific name to such seedlings. All three, especially when older, resemble the Bismarck palm, *Bismarckia nobilis,* the salient differences being the greatly flaring trunk base of *Latania,* the larger and less costapalmate leaves of *Bismarckia,* and the latter's stouter but taller trunk.

The latan species are slightly susceptible to lethal yellowing disease. They are not tolerant of cold and are adaptable only to zones 10b and 11, although mature specimens are found in favorable microclimates of 10a. They are drought tolerant but grow faster and look better with average but regular moisture. They are not fussy about soil type as long as its drainage is unimpeded; they even flourish in calcareous types.

These palms are spectacular because of their size and color, and are amenable to almost any landscape situation other than small spaces. Their exceptionally straight trunks and their rounded, dense crowns make them unexcelled as canopy-scapes. They look good as isolated specimens but are at their best in groups of three or more palms of varying heights. They are not known to be grown indoors, but there would seem to be no good reason why they cannot be, given enough light and space.

The genus name is a Latinized form of the aboriginal vernacular. PLATES 503–505.

Latania loddigesii is endemic to savannas and forested hills of the Mascarene Islands, where it is critically endangered because of development and agricultural expansion. The common name is blue latan palm. The epithet honors a late 18th-century British nurseryman, Conrad Loddiges.

Mature trunks grow to at least 35 feet high and are 10 inches in diameter, swollen at the base, and closely set with the rings of deeply indented leaf base scars. The stem is usually deep gray but may be almost black (or sometimes dark brown), and the leaf crown is full, rounded, and 12 feet wide and tall. The leaves are 6 to 8 feet wide but are costapalmate, with the petiole protruding so far into the leaf that the blade is folded and usually does not spread to its full width. The petiole is 4 to 6 feet long and is armed with small teeth along its lower margin when young, and covered in a white tomentum which does not rub off with age; it is heavily tinged with red along its margins in young palms. The lanceolate leaf segments are stiff and armed with fine, tiny teeth along the margins; they are never pendent and they extend halfway to the center of the blade. Leaf color is bluish gray green to silvery blue. The inflorescences are shorter than the leaves but sometimes 6 feet long. The male inflorescences are shorter than the females and are composed of several branches that bear small yellowish brown blossoms, while the female inflorescences are longer single stems with flowers of the same color. The fruits are plum shaped, brown, and 3 inches long and 1 inch wide. PLATE 503.

Latania lontaroides is commonly known as red latan palm. The epithet is Greek for "similar to *Lontarus*," an outdated name for *Borassus.*

It differs from *L. loddigesii* in having distinctly red petioles and red-margined and red-veined stiff leaflets when young; adult leaf color is never silvery blue but rather a deep and dull green above with grayish green beneath. Because young plants of both species have similar leaf and petiole, many growers believe they have this species when they most likely have the much more common *L. loddigesii.* PLATE 504.

Latania verschaffeltii is commonly known as yellow latan palm. The epithet is a Latinized form of the Belgian surname "Verschaffelt" and honors a 19th-century nurseryman.

Young plants have bright yellow petioles covered in white tomentum. Mature plants differ from *L. loddigesii* in having much thinner, much less stiff leaves that are never silvery or bluish but rather yellowish to deep green on both surfaces. PLATE 505.

LAVOIXIA is an extremely rare monotypic genus of pinnate-leaved, solitary-trunked, monoecious palm endemic to New Caledonia, where it is in danger of extinction; only 30 or so individuals remain in habitat. The genus name honors Lucien Lavoix of New Caledonia and his children.

Lavoixia macrocarpa grows in rain forest on the slopes of Mt. Panié at elevations of 1600 to 2200 feet. The epithet is Greek for "large" and "fruit."

The trunk grows to 50 feet high in habitat. It is light to dark brown and distinctly ringed with dark leaf base scars in its younger parts. The crownshaft is 2 feet tall, slightly bulging at its base, midpoint, or even its summit. It is gray to bluish gray or even tan and usually exhibits horizontal dark striations. The leaf crown is usually hemispherical, with erect to spreading 7-foot-long leaves on 1-foot-long petioles. The stiff, 4-foot-long leaflets are medium to dark green and linear-lanceolate with long drawn-out tips, and grow from the rachis at an angle that creates a V-shaped leaf. The inflorescences grow from beneath the crownshaft and are a spray of stiffly spreading 2-foot-long branches, which bear both male and female flowers. The fruits are round, 1.5 inches in diameter, and chocolate-purple.

The species is not in cultivation except for a few immature plants in New Caledonia.

LEMUROPHOENIX is a monotypic genus of large, pinnate-leaved, monoecious palm. The genus name is a combination of "lemur," the endemic primate, and the Greek word for "date palm." According to Dransfield (1994), the aboriginal name for the palm in Madagascar translates as "the palm of the red-tufted lemur." The epithet honors Frenchman Dominique Halleux, one of the first Westerners to discover the species. PLATES 506 & 507.

Lemurophoenix halleuxii is endemic to northeastern Madagascar, where it grows on steep slopes in rain forest at elevations from 600 to 1400 feet. It is critically endangered, with reportedly fewer than 20 individuals left because trees are being felled for construction and firewood.

The trunk attains a height of 60 feet in habitat and a diameter of 18 inches. It is light to dark gray and distinctly ringed with darker leaf base scars. The crownshaft is 4 to 5 feet tall, slightly thicker than the trunk, cylindrical, and light to pinkish gray. The leaf crown is hemispherical with 12-foot-long leaves on 1-foot-long stout petioles. They are erect to spreading and almost completely unarching. The 3-foot-long, deep green leaflets are linear-lanceolate and regularly spaced along the rachis; they are wine colored when new, at least in younger plants. The inflorescences grow from beneath the crownshaft and consist of many 6-foot-long branches on large 3-foot-long peduncles. The branches bear both male and female flowers, and the fruits are brown, globose, and 1 inch in diameter.

This is a truly massive palm which, when immature, has the look of a gigantic majesty palm, *Ravenea rivularis*. It is grand and beautiful at all stages but is reportedly not easy to grow, needing tropical conditions with constant warmth and copious and regular moisture. The palm, while quickly forming an impressive leaf crown, takes a long while to begin trunking. Its great beauty would seem to justify whatever it takes to grow this palm in a tropical climate.

LEOPOLDINIA is a genus of three small, pinnate-leaved, monoecious palms in the Amazon region of South America, where they grow along rivers and in lowlands that are seasonally flooded for months at a time. They are characterized by much fiber among their leaf bases, fibers that in one species obscure the trunk. The inflorescences are much branched, brown, and hairy, and bear tiny, mostly unisexual flowers that produce, in one species, unique flattened fruits.

None of these species are probably in cultivation, but there seems no reason why they couldn't be, given a tropical and wet climate.

The genus name honors an 18th-century archduchess of Austria and empress of Brazil, whose father sponsored an expedition to that South American country for Carl F. P. von Martius to collect specimens of the flora and eventually establish this genus name, among others.

Leopoldinia major occurs naturally in far western Brazil, southern Venezuela, and extreme northwestern Colombia, where it grows along the Rio Negro, often in large colonies. The epithet is Latin for "larger."

The stems of this clustering species may attain heights of 20 feet and are covered in their younger parts with a flat network of interwoven, cinnamon-colored fibers and leaf bases. The leaves are 5 or 6 feet long and the deep green, 1-foot-long, widely and evenly spaced, narrowly lanceolate leaflets grow in a single plane from the ascending and stiff rachis.

In its native haunts, this species grows in large tracts, which are impressive and tropical-looking, virtual walls of feather leaves.

Leopoldinia piassaba is indigenous to the same region as is *L. major* but, unlike most individuals of *L. major*, is an undergrowth subject, never growing in full sun. The epithet is one of the aboriginal names for the tough and long leaf base fibers, which have many uses by the native peoples, including retailing of brooms.

The stem of this solitary-trunked species grows to 15 feet and is 6 inches in diameter but looks as though it is much thicker (2 to 3 feet) because of the large mass of long, hanging brown or reddish brown cordlike fibers that cover it. The 12- to 15-foot-long leaves are borne on long petioles and have widely and regularly spaced, narrowly lanceolate, stiff, light green 2- to 3-foot-long leaflets growing in a single plane; they have undulate margins and are often apically bifid. The fruits are reniform and flattened; they are also edible and used to make an alcoholic beverage in the palm's habitats.

This impressive palm looks larger than it is, especially up close, and would seem to be a perfect landscape candidate for a spectacular specimen or small palm grove in a jungle setting.

Leopoldinia pulchra has a natural range similar to that of the above two species but more extensive. It is similar to *L. major*, but its trunks are rarely clustering and its leaves are more graceful and arching. The epithet is Latin for "beautiful," an apt adjective for the most beautiful species of the genus.

LEPIDOCARYUM is a monotypic genus of palmate-leaved, dioecious palm in South America. The genus name is from two Greek words meaning "scale" and "nut." The epithet is Latin for "thin" or "tenuous" and alludes to the leaf petioles.

Lepidocaryum tenue is indigenous to a large area of the Amazon region in western Brazil and adjacent regions of

Venezuela, Colombia, and Peru, where it occurs in the undergrowth of lowland rain forest.

The species is clustering and usually forms a large colony by its rambling rhizome. The stems grow as tall as 10 or 12 feet, are 1 inch in diameter, and are beautifully ringed with grayish leaf base scars. The leaves are borne on 2-foot-long, wiry green petioles and are divided to the petioles into two parts; each half is split into 2 to 11 (making totals of 4 to 22) narrowly wedge-shaped to lanceolate or oblong segments that are 18 to 30 inches long and 0.5 to 3 inches wide. Each segment is deeply ribbed and lustrous medium green, and bears tiny white prickles along its margins and often veins or ribs. There is no distinct hastula, only (usually) a slight swelling on the top of the juncture of petiole and blade. The leaf is usually less than hemispherical. The inflorescences consist of short branches at the ends of 2-foot-long peduncles that are pendent in fruit. The female inflorescences produce attractive oblong to nearly round, 1-inch-long fruits that are covered in orange to reddish brown overlapping scales.

As many as nine species were formerly recognized but, as the palms have become better known to taxonomists, it seems obvious these are forms of one species. Henderson et al. (1995) recognized three naturally occurring varieties according to the number of leaf segments, number of inflorescence branches, and size and shape of the fruits.

These are delicately attractive little things whose leaves are reminiscent of lady palms (*Rhapis* species) and would make truly beautiful large groundcovers; however, they are almost completely absent from cultivation probably due to their need of a tropical climate, shade or partial shade, copious and regular moisture, and a rich, humus-laden soil that is always moist but freely draining and not limey.

The leaves are widely and heavily used for thatch in habitat.

LEPIDORRHACHIS is a monotypic genus of pinnate-leaved, solitary-trunked, monoecious palm endemic to Lord Howe Island. It is called little mountain palm in Australia. The genus name is from two Greek words meaning "scale" and "rachis," in reference to the scales on the sheaths, rachis, and pinnae of the leaves. The epithet is a Latinized form of the surname "Moore" and honors a 19th-century botanist and horticulturist who was the first director of the Sydney Botanic Gardens in Australia. PLATE 508.

Lepidorrhachis mooreana occurs at an elevation of 2640 feet and above on Gower and Lidgbird mountains in windswept, cool but frostless and constantly moist cloud forests.

The trunk grows to 10 or 12 feet in habitat and is often shorter. It is 6 inches in diameter but, because of the small height, looks thicker and more robust. It is succulent light green in its younger parts and usually light gray in its older parts, always with closely spaced rings of leaf base scars. The thick, succulent-looking leaf sheaths form a pseudo-crownshaft that is loose, split, and light green, often with a pinkish hue. The petioles are stout and short, and hold 5-foot-long leaves. They are ascending but arching and create a less-than-hemispherical leaf crown that is more like a shaving brush. The 2-foot-long leaflets are stiff, leathery but not rigid, medium to dark green, and lanceolate, and grow from the rachis at an angle that creates a V-shaped leaf; older leaves have semipendent leaflets. The inflorescences grow from nodes beneath the loose crownshaft and are short, succulent, densely branched, and spreading, and bear male and female flowers. The small round fruits are 0.25 inch in diameter and red when mature.

The species has visual affinities to another Lord Howe endemic, *Hedyscepe,* but is related to the genera *Clinostigma* and *Clinosperma.* This is among the most alluring palm species, and one made possibly even more alluring because there are so few regions in which it thrives. It requires a cool moist, nearly frost-free climate, such as that in San Francisco, California. It is impossible in warm tropical or hot climates, especially those with warm nighttime temperatures. It grows in poor but constantly moist, free-draining soil. This palm is reportedly extremely slow growing but has endured unscathed temperature in the upper 20s (F), but these temperatures were without drying winds which are also inimical to it.

LICUALA is a genus of more than 100 small to medium, palmate-leaved, solitary-trunked or clustering palms in India, Myanmar, southeastern China, Thailand, Southeast Asia, Sumatra, Malaysia, Indonesia, New Guinea, Borneo, the Philippines, northeastern Australia, the Solomon Islands, and the Vanuatu archipelago, where they are mostly undergrowth subjects in rain forest. The center of natural distribution of the genus is Borneo. In some forests, a single species dominates the undergrowth, leaving room for few other species to grow. A few *Licuala* species grow in exposed sites, especially along riverbanks and in swampy areas.

All have palmate leaves that are circular or diamond shaped. Several have undivided leaves, but most have deeply segmented leaves, and all have deeply corrugated leaf blades. All the species except the largest make excellent container subjects. Most species have armed petioles and all have leaf sheaths with much fiber that is usually adherent to the stem for varying periods. A few species with segmented leaves have the unusual characteristic of leaf blades bearing secondary petioles, with one or more segments borne on the subpetiole. The inflorescences grow from the crown and may be branched or spikelike. They are mostly monoecious plants, but a few are dioecious. They bear mostly bisexual flowers, which produce red, rounded fruits.

The leaves and petioles of a few species have been used for wrapping and weaving.

Several species whose leaves have smaller segments are difficult to distinguish one from the other, especially when not in flower and fruit, but many are among the most desirable ornamental palms. The smaller ones cry out for intimate settings in which their individual beauties may be best appreciated. None are hardy to cold, although a few can tolerate occasional sharp drops in temperature, and fewer still withstand some frost. They invariably need regular and adequate moisture, a well-drained soil, and partial shade. In the following text, no mention of cold hardiness is made unless the species tolerates frost, and no mention is made of exposure requirements unless the particular species has different needs from the majority.

The genus name is derived from a Moluccan aboriginal name for one of the species. PLATES 509–533.

Licuala beccariana is a solitary-trunked species endemic to low mountainous rain forest of Papua New Guinea, where it occurs in the undergrowth. The epithet honors Italian palm taxonomist Odoardo Beccari (1843–1920).

The trunk grows to 12 or 15 feet high and is slender and fiber covered. The leaves are deeply segmented on 3- to 4-foot-long, thin petioles. Each leaf is slightly more than hemispherical and has six, often fewer, widely separated, dark green segments, which are narrowly wedge shaped, deeply corrugated, and obliquely truncated and jagged at the apex; one segment is usually much broader than the rest.

This is certainly among the most desirable species for the garden because of its size and delicately segmented large leaves on long petioles that seem to shimmer in the slightest breeze. PLATE 509.

Licuala bidentata is a solitary-trunked species endemic to the rain forest in Sarawak on the island of Borneo. The epithet is from Latin and Greek words meaning "two teeth," in this case two small indentations on the apices of the segments.

Most individuals have little or no trunk, but occasionally one forms 3 feet of stem and reaches 6 feet in overall height. The leaves are 3 feet in diameter, circular, with 12 to 24 medium green, long, narrow segments, each extending to the petiole and ending in two indentations. The petioles are 5 feet long.

This delicately beautiful species, one of the choicest in the genus because of the diaphanous leaf segments, can lighten up the gloom of an under-canopy site.

Licuala bintulensis is a solitary-trunked species indigenous to swampy areas of rain forest in Sarawak. The epithet is Latin for "of Bintulu," a region of Sarawak.

This lovely palm grows to 10 feet, and that height mainly due to its long and thin leaf petioles. The beautiful deep, bluish green, deeply divided, and circular leaves have six to nine distinctly wedge-shaped, deeply corrugated leaflets. The apex of each leaflet is often slanted and always toothed, with the indentations corresponding to the corrugations of the segment itself. PLATE 510.

Licuala cabalionii is a rare, solitary-trunked species endemic to the Vanuatu islands, where it occurs in rain forest from sea level to 800 feet elevation. The epithet honors Pierre Cabalion, a French ethnobotanist in Vanuatu.

The trunk grows to a height of 15 feet in habitat with a diameter of 3 inches and is smooth and light gray or light brown except near its summit where it holds old leaf bases with attendant fibers. The leaf crown is breathtakingly beautiful and open, with the 3-foot-wide leaves on 8-foot-long thin petioles and armed with short teeth at the leaf base. The circular leaves are divided to the petiole into 12 pleated, glossy deep green segments, the center one of which is much wider than the others. Each segment is soft and slightly pendent at its apex. The deep yellow or orange fruits are round and 0.5 inch in diameter.

John L. Dowe of Australia formally described this species in 1993. It is one of the most beautiful species in the genus, with an incomparable silhouette. It is among the most tropical in its requirements and possible only in zones 10b and 11. It needs copious and regular moisture and a humus-laden soil but grows in partial shade or full sun except in the hottest, driest climates.

Licuala cordata is a small, solitary-trunked species indigenous to the low mountainous rain forest in Sarawak. The epithet is Latin for "heartlike," a reference to the leaf's basal lobes.

The palm grows to 3 or 4 feet high on a short, slender trunk that is sometimes not apparent. The 18- to 24-inch-wide leaves are circular or almost so, sometimes with one or more shallow points and often undulate; the leaf base is usually lobed. The entire blade is deeply corrugated and a glossy light to emerald green. Occasionally specimens have leaves divided into six wide, wedge-shaped segments, but plants with undivided leaves are, by far, more desirable and almost unique. PLATES 511–513.

Licuala densiflora is a small, solitary-trunked species occurring naturally in the rain forest in Sarawak. The epithet is Latin for "dense" and "flowered," an allusion to the placement of the flowers on the inflorescence.

This nearly trunkless palm has few leaves carried on long, thin petioles. Each leaf is hemispherical and has five to seven wedge-shaped, widely spaced, deeply corrugated segments that are light green and toothed at the apex. The indentations correspond to the ribs of the segment.

Licuala distans is a solitary-trunked species endemic to peninsular Thailand, where it grows in low mountainous rain forest. The epithet is Latin for "distant" in the sense of "widely separated" and alludes to the leaf crown of the species.

Mature trunks attain a height of 10 or 12 feet. The 4-foot-wide, deep green leaves are borne on 6- or 7-foot-long stout, armed petioles. The leaf blade is circular, 4 feet wide, and deeply divided into many linear wedge-shaped and corrugated segments. The tip of each segment is oblique and deeply indented, with the indentations corresponding to the corrugations of the segment. The inflorescences are branched and 5 to 7 feet long, and extend up and out of the leaf crown. The globose fruits are deep red.

The palm is simply magnificent and should be sited where its large, pinwheel-like leaves can be best displayed. In spite of its relatively large size, it does not relish full sun, especially in hot climates.

Licuala glabra is a small, solitary-trunked species in southern peninsular Thailand and northern peninsular Malaysia, where it occurs in the undergrowth of mountainous rain forest to an elevation of 4000 feet, often in immense colonies; it also grows in lowland rain forest. The epithet is Latin for "glabrous" and alludes to the smooth inflorescences.

Mature trunks can grow to 6 feet high, and the overall height of the palm can be 12 feet. The leaves are borne on long, thin petioles and are circular or nearly so, with wedge-shaped segments. *Licuala glabra* **var.** *selangorensis* has fewer, generally broader segments (especially the middle ones), which are not as uniformly shaped as those of the type.

Licuala grandis is indigenous to rain forest in the Vanuatu archipelago and the Solomon Islands. It is sometimes called the ruffled fan palm. The epithet is Latin for "grand" or "spectacular."

The solitary trunk of mature trees seldom grows to more than 10 feet tall and 3 inches in diameter. It is usually covered in tightly woven brown fibers from the leaf bases, which are narrowly triangular; old trunks are usually gray to almost white and nearly smooth but exhibit closely set semicircular rings of leaf base scars. The leaf crown is 8 feet wide and 6 feet tall. The undivided, pleated leaves are 3 feet wide on 3-foot-long, heavy petioles with small curved teeth on the margins of their lower parts. The leaf is semicircular to broadly wedge shaped or diamond shaped, and the leaf margins are deeply toothed, the indentations as well as the pleats in the blade approximately

matching the fused segments. Leaf color is medium to deep, shiny green on both sides. The leaves are mostly erect, the older ones pendent, and they usually do not create a fully rounded crown. The blade is usually wavy and undulating, especially along its margins. There are more than 12 leaves per palm (often as many as 20) on relatively long petioles; the visual effect is that of being densely packed into the leaf crown. The flower stalks are 6 inches long and grow from among the leaves. They are sparsely branched and bear small yellowish white bisexual flowers. The fruits are 0.5 inch wide, rounded, and bright red when ripe.

The species does not tolerate cold and is possible only in zones 10b and 11. It needs copious and constant humidity and moisture in a fast-draining, humus-laden soil. It is eminently adapted to partial shade, especially when young, but older plants can take full sun, except in the hottest climates. These small palms are among the choicest in the world of horticulture. They have an exquisite elegance matched by few other palms. This is probably the last palm the gardener should consider planting as an isolated specimen; its penchant for partial shade adds to its usefulness and need to be a part of other vegetation. The leaf crowns are stunning when planted in groups of three or more individuals of varying heights and as accents in masses of other vegetation. As a patio or courtyard subject this palm is perfect anywhere its beauty may be enjoyed up close. The palm is unexcelled for indoors and excellent as container specimens outdoors. It needs good light but not full sun, a rich soil, regular feedings (fish emulsion is good), and should never dry out. PLATE 514.

Licuala lauterbachii is indigenous to the undergrowth of rain forest in Papua New Guinea and the Solomon Islands. The epithet honors Carl A. G. Lauterbach, a 19th-century German plant collector.

The mature solitary trunks grow to 20 feet high and less than 6 inches in diameter. They are mostly free of fibers and leaf bases, are light gray to almost white, and are indistinctly grooved with leaf base scars. The leaf crown is 12 feet tall and wide. The leaves are 3 to 5 feet wide, circular to semicircular to oval, and composed of 15 to 30 segments, each of which is wedge shaped, squared at its apex where it is also pleated and toothed corresponding to the fused segments. The segments extend to or almost to the petiole, and the visual effect is that of a large green pinwheel, made more dazzling because of the offset and not circular leaf. The thin, graceful petiole is 4 to 5 feet long with short marginal spines on its lower portions and gives to the leaf crown a full and nearly rounded aspect. Leaf color is grayish to medium to deep green on both surfaces. The inflorescences are 3 feet long, mostly erect, and sparsely branched, with small whitish bisexual blossoms. The fruits are round, orange to red, and 1 inch wide, and are borne in half-pendent clusters.

The species does not tolerate cold and is adaptable only to zones 10b and 11. It needs an abundance of moisture and a rich, well-draining soil. Young plants should not be subjected to the full sun of hot summer climates. The leaf crown provides one of the most beautiful silhouettes in nature. Its large pinwheel-like blades dance on their delicately long stalks and move in the slightest breeze. It is superbly attractive as a patio or courtyard subject and, in groups of three or more individuals of varying heights, creates a veritable symphony of forms. It is wonderful as a large potted palm, indoors or out, asking only for bright light, never to dry out, and a rich, friable medium. PLATE 515.

Licuala longipes is indigenous to low mountainous rain forest of southern Myanmar and peninsular Malaysia. The epithet is Latin for "long" and "foot," referring to the length of the petioles.

The stem of this solitary-trunked species is usually underground and nonapparent. The leaves are to 7 feet wide, a deep and lustrous green, and divided almost to the petiole into 12 giant wedge-shaped segments. The apical segments are 1 foot wide, while the smaller basal segments are 4 to 5 inches wide. Leaf outline is a giant oval to almost a circle, and the petioles may be 8 feet long.

This species is an amazing sight, so large are the leaves and so tall are the stalks. It is perhaps the grandest and most beautiful trunkless species. It seems to be among the more tender (to cold) species in the genus.

Licuala mattanensis is endemic to Sarawak on the island of Borneo, where it grows in lowland rain forest, usually in acidic peaty soil. The epithet is Latin for "of Mattang," a region of Sarawak.

This solitary-trunked species takes a long time to form a stem and reaches a maximum height of 3 feet. The leaves are 2 feet wide and often smaller, hemispherical or slightly more rounded, and consist of 12 linear wedge-shaped segments. The species has three traits that are not typical of the genus: unarmed petioles; large, linear, and not red fruits; and beautifully variegated forms. The most sought after cultivar is ***Licuala mattanensis*** **'Mapu'**, which has light yellow tessellation and is often referred to as *L. mapu*.

This seems to be one of the more tender (to cold) species in the genus. PLATE 516.

Licuala naumanii is endemic to the island of Bougainville, where it grows in lowland rain forest.

This is among the tallest species in the genus, its trunks growing to 30 feet in habitat. The leaves are 3 feet wide and circular or egg shaped. They are borne on 2- to 3-foot-long petioles that create a rounded leaf crown. The segments usually number a dozen, with the apical three longer and wider than the others, and the single, most apical segment usually much larger and wider. Leaf color is deep, lustrous green, and the segments are shallowly toothed at their apices.

This spectacular species is near to *L. ramsayi* in size and magnificence. Alas, it is still all too rare in cultivation and is probably one of the most tender to cold in the genus. PLATES 517 & 518.

Licuala olivifera is indigenous to lowland rain forest and swamps of peninsular Malaysia as well as Sarawak. The epithet is Latin for "olive-bearing," an allusion to the size and shape of the fruits, but could equally well apply to the color of the leaf segments.

This solitary-trunked species has a short, often nonapparent trunk. The leaves are to 4 feet wide on 3-foot-long petioles and are circular, with 24 (or sometimes more) narrow wedge-shaped, deeply ribbed segments. The uppermost segments are wide and have squared apices, with progressively narrower and shorter segments on both sides towards the base of the circle. The matte, almost olive-green leaf is among the most beautiful in the genus.

Licuala orbicularis is an undergrowth inhabitant of rain forest in Sarawak, where it is nearly extinct because of clearing of the rain forest. The epithet is Latin for "orbicular," an allusion to the leaf shape.

The species is solitary trunked or trunkless with the stem confined beneath the ground. The total height of the plant is 6 to 8 feet. The leaves are to 5 feet wide and 3 feet long and shaped like squared-off fan, although some specimens have orbicular leaves. The segments are fused, and the blade is slightly indented along its margins, corresponding to the fused segments that are deeply pleated within the blade. A prominent midvein in the middle of the blade extends through its entire length, and the leaf margins are undulating and wavy. The dark green, shiny leaves are carried on elegantly thin, long petioles to 6 feet or more in length but 1 inch thick at the base. The lower part of the petiole is margined with small teeth. This little palm seldom blooms in cultivation, but the inflorescence is 3 feet long and pendent, and bears small whitish bisexual flowers. The fruits are 0.5 inch wide, round, and red when mature, and are borne in narrow, pendent clusters.

The species does not tolerate cold and is adaptable only to zones 10b and 11. It needs constant warmth, moisture, and humidity but is no good in full sun in tropical climes. It also needs a humus-rich soil with unimpeded drainage.

It is an astonishingly beautiful accent plant for shady beds, the great shiny, rounded, and corrugated blades adding an almost unique elegance and charm to tropical sites that are difficult to landscape. It should be grown with plants whose leaves are of a different shape and texture, like ferns and small pinnate-leaved palms such as *Chamaedorea elegans*, lest the other leaf forms detract from its exceptional grace and elegance. This is a near perfect choice indoors if given enough water and a rich soil. PLATE 519.

Licuala paludosa occurs naturally in peninsular Malaysia, Thailand, Sumatra, and Vietnam, where it grows in swampy areas at low elevations. The epithet is Latin for "swampy," an allusion to the palm's habitat.

This sparsely clustering species has stems to 12 or 15 feet with a diameter of 1 inch; the overall height of the palm exceeds 20 feet. The trunks are mostly smooth and free of leaf bases except for the youngest parts. The 3-foot-wide leaves are circular and borne on 18-inch-long slender, spiny petioles; they are similar to those of *L. spinosa* but generally larger, a darker green, and the segments are more varied in width with one or two quite wide.

The species is more beautiful than *L. spinosa* because of its leaves and its less dense clumps. In fact, it is arguably the most beautiful divided-leaf *Licuala* species. Compared with *L. spinosa,* it is, alas, more tender to cold, needs more water and a better soil that is on the acidic side, but grows as fast. It grows in partial shade or full sun. PLATE 520.

Licuala parviflora is endemic to northern Papua New Guinea, where it grows in low mountainous rain forest. The epithet is Latin for "small flowered."

The stem of this solitary-trunked species slowly attains 6 feet high. The leaves are borne on 2-foot-long petioles, are 2 to 3 feet wide, and are semicircular or slightly more rounded. They bear 15 to 20 segments, which are diaphanously thin and nearly the same length and width. The leaf crown is also sparse.

The whole aspect of this little gem is fairylike and utterly charming. It is tropical in its requirements and needs copious and regular moisture.

Licuala peltata occurs naturally from northeastern India, Bhutan, Bangladesh, the Andaman and Nicobar Islands, through Myanmar, Thailand, and into peninsular Malaysia, where it grows in low mountainous rain forest. It is threatened with extinction in India and Bangladesh. The epithet is Latin for "peltate," which term describes the condition of a circular leaf attached to its petiole at the bottom center of the leaf blade, as is the case with lotus and nasturtium leaves.

This is a mostly solitary-trunked, rarely clustering species. The trunk slowly grows to 20 feet high. The 6-foot-wide leaves are borne on petioles that may be as long as 12 feet but are more often half that length. This great length creates a large, open, and nearly rounded leaf crown. The leaf blade is hemispherical or slightly greater and often is slightly diamond shaped; it normally is divided into 15 to

25 wedge-shaped, lustrous, deep green segments of nearly equal length and widths except for the most apical ones. All have deeply toothed apices. The inflorescences are 10- to 12-foot-long erect spikes from which pendent flowering branches grow, bearing small yellowish bisexual blossoms. The fruits are 0.5-inch-wide, deep red, rounded berries.

Licuala peltata **var.** *sumawongii* has entire, unsegmented leaf blades, which are so relatively thin that they often fold to some extent because of their own weight. This variety grows naturally only in southern Thailand and peninsular Malaysia, where it may now be extinct. It was named for Watana Sumawong, a Thai collector who introduced it to cultivation as *L. elegans*. It looks much like *L. grandis* and is much sought after by gardeners and collectors almost to the exclusion of the segmented, typical form. Some people find it difficult to believe the two forms can be the same species, but if they could see the Sumawong form in a windy and exposed site, they would have no problems with their imagination as the leaves usually become variously segmented under these conditions. Both varieties are equally beautiful.

This magnificently beautiful and tropical-looking species seems surprisingly hardy to cold, having withstood unscathed temperatures slightly below freezing. It is also adaptable to a range of soils including slightly alkaline ones, as long as they are fast draining. In addition, the species can tolerate a modicum of drought but looks and grows much better if provided regular and adequate moisture. It responds well to a deep organic mulch in southern Florida and luxuriates in partial shade or nearly full sun once past the juvenile stage, always being a healthier and darker green with some shade.

This palm is so attractive that it is hard to misplace in the garden if given enough space; it should not be crowded into tight spaces with other vegetation. It should be planted in a wind-protected site as its leaf blades are relatively thin and become easily tattered, but, even then, it is unusually beautiful. It looks its best as a specimen planting under a high canopy with three or more individuals of varying heights in a single group; in this situation, it is a veritable symphony of shimmering leaf form. Once past the juvenile stage, this palm is unusually fast growing for a *Licuala* species. Indoors it needs a large space and high light and humidity. PLATES 521–523.

Licuala petiolulata is endemic to low mountainous rain forest in Sarawak. The epithet is Latin for "tiny petioled" and alludes to the little "stalks" of some leaf segments.

This solitary-trunked species has a short stem that is often nonapparent but may attain 2 or 3 feet high. The small, nearly perfectly circular leaves are 2 to 2.5 feet wide and borne on 3- to 4-foot-long, thin petioles; they are as beautiful as any in the genus, however. The blade consists of 15 to 20 elegantly thin, wedge-shaped segments divided to the petiole, each with an obliquely truncated, jagged apex. The central segments are usually wider than the others, and their basal portions are narrow and stalklike, looking almost like short, secondary petioles. Their color is a medium, almost olive to deep green on both surfaces.

The species does not tolerate cold. PLATE 524.

Licuala platydactyla is endemic to northern Papua New Guinea, where it grows in lowland rain forest. The epithet is from two Greek words meaning "flat" and "fingered," an allusion to the central and much broader (in older plants) leaf segment.

The stems of this solitary-trunked species grow to 10 feet high in habitat. The leaves are borne on stout petioles that are 3 feet long or sometimes longer. The leaf blade mostly consists of three but sometimes four segments. The central segment is much broader than the others in mature or nearly mature plants and is usually deeply bifid. All segments have obliquely truncated, jagged apices and are a medium to deep green on both surfaces. PLATE 525.

Licuala radula is indigenous to extreme southeastern China, Vietnam, and Cambodia, where it occurs in the undergrowth of low mountainous rain forest. It is under threat of extinction in Vietnam. The epithet is Latin for "little root," an allusion to the clustering habit.

The species is sparsely clustering and forms, with time, short, stout trunks 3 feet high. The 18-inch-wide segmented leaves are borne on 1- to 2-foot-long, thin petioles. Leaf outline is circular, and the blade consists of 9 or 10 segments, each with an obliquely truncated and toothed apex. The middle segments are the broadest, the ones adjacent to them progressively more narrow and slightly shorter as they approach the basal portion of the leaf. They are a lustrous medium to dark green and are mottled with lighter green. Unlike other *Licuala* species, this one is dioecious, with male and female blossoms on separate plants.

This is a gem of a palm, its beautiful little round leaves as pretty in a small way as any in the genus. It is also one of the more cold tolerant in the genus, being adaptable to zones 10 and 11, and even in warm microclimates of 9b. PLATE 526.

Licuala ramsayi is endemic to low, swampy rain forest of northeastern Queensland, Australia. The epithet is a Latinized form of the surname "Ramsay" and commemorates the original collector.

This solitary-trunked species starts as an undergrowth subject but, in maturity, reaches and usually overtops the tree canopy. It sometimes attains a height of 60 feet in habitat but is usually no more than 30 to 40 feet tall under cultivation. Stem diameter is never more than 8 inches, and the almost-white trunk is smooth and free of leaf bases except for the youngest parts. The leaf crown is 18 feet wide and tall. The leaves are 5 to 6 feet wide and nearly circular (often shaped like a scallop's shell) but are divided into 10 or more wedge-shaped segments that are squared off on their jagged ends. The segments vary in width, but each one extends to the petiole, giving a visual effect like that of a pinwheel. Leaf color is light to medium green on both sides, and each segment is deeply pleated, the pleats corresponding to fused segments. The elegantly thin petioles are 6 feet long and armed with short teeth along the lower margin. The leaf crown usually has 12 leaves. The inflorescences are unusually long, usually spilling out of the leaf crown; they are much branched and bear small white flowers. The fruits are 1 inch wide, round, and red.

The species does not tolerate cold and is adaptable only to zones 10b and 11 (at least as the magnificence it should be). It needs constant moisture and humidity, as well as a rich soil. It usually survives on drier soils but is always stunted and less colorful. It luxuriates in partial shade, but older plants can take full sun. This is the tallest, most spectacular, and most beautiful species in the genus. Its leaves form incredibly beautiful silhouettes and dance in the slightest breeze. The palm looks its best among or near masses of other darker vegetation against which its light-colored trunks and great pinwheel-like leaves stand out. It is unequalled as a canopy-scape. The species is a good candidate for growing indoors when young, or when planted in large conservatories, if it can receive enough light and moisture. PLATES 527–529.

Licuala reptans is endemic to Sarawak, where it grows in lowland rain forest. The epithet is Latin for "creeping."

This small species has a short, creeping stem. The leaves are circular, borne on 2- to 3-foot-long, thin petioles, and consist of 9 or 10 variably wide segments that extend to the petiole. The central segment is much broader than the others, but all are medium to dark and lustrous green on the top surfaces and lighter green overlain with tiny rusty brown scales on the lower surfaces.

Licuala rumphii is a densely clustering species endemic to the island of Sulawesi, where it grows in low mountainous rain forest. The epithet honors 17th-century herbalist and botanist, Georg E. Rumpf (Rumphius).

The stems grow to 10 feet. The leaves are circular and consist of 8 to 10 segments, which extend to the petiole. The central segment is much broader than the others and is 18 inches long. All segments are obliquely truncated and toothed at their apices, and deep green.

This species looks better if some stems are judiciously pruned out so that the attractive form of the leaves may be seen. It is not hardy to cold but thrives in various soils, including alkaline ones. it seems to luxuriate in partial shade or full sun, needing only a tropical or nearly tropical climate and regular and adequate moisture.

Licuala sallehana is a rare and densely clustering species endemic to peninsular Malaysia, where it grows as an undergrowth subject in lowland rain forest. It was described in 1997. The epithet honors Salleh Mohammad of the Forest Research Institute in Malaysia.

The thin, reedlike stems grow to heights of 4 feet and are covered with a fine, almost woven net of fibers and leaf bases. The leaves are unusual in the genus as they are undivided, lanceolate to an elongated diamond shape, 2.5 feet long and 8 inches wide near their apices. They are deep green and deeply grooved on long petioles armed with triangular teeth on their lower halves. The inflorescences are short and produce small round fruits that are black when mature.

The overall aspect of this extraordinarily beautiful palm is that of a small, clustering *Johannesteijsmannia* species.

Licuala sarawakensis is endemic to lowland rain forest in Sarawak. The epithet is Latin for "of Sarawak."

This small, solitary-trunked species has a short stem that is usually nonapparent. The leaves are 18 inches wide and circular, and consist of six to eight wedge-shaped segments of varying widths. The segments of adult plants are of mixed widths without a pattern to their variation in breadth, wider segments adjacent to narrower ones; juvenile plants usually exhibit a central segment that is significantly broader than the others. Leaf color is medium to light green on both surfaces.

The species is unusually attractive because of the circular leaves and diminutive size of the plants. It is exquisite as a groundcover in tropical climates. PLATE 530.

Licuala spathellifera is endemic to Sarawak, where it occurs in the undergrowth of lowland rain forest. The epithet is Latin for "small spathe-bearing," referring to the size of the bract on the inflorescence.

This solitary-trunked species has a short, usually nonapparent stem. For a diminutive *Licuala* species, it has among the most beautiful leaf forms. The leaves are circular and consist of elegantly thin, linear wedge-shaped segments with obliquely truncated, jagged apices. The 20 to 25 segments are nearly uniform in width, with the center ones longer and the side segments becoming shorter as they progress on both sides to the basal portion of the blade. The leaf is from 18 inches to almost 2 feet wide on a 2-foot-long, thin petiole. There are no more beautiful palm leaves; these are perfect little pinwheels that seem always in motion, so narrow and so numerous are the segments.

Licuala spinosa has one of the largest distributions in the genus and is indigenous to the coastal plains of the Nicobar and Andaman Islands, Myanmar, Vietnam, Thailand, peninsular Malaysia, Sumatra, Java, Borneo, western Indonesia, and the Philippines. The species is sometimes called spiny licuala and in Australia is known as mangrove fan palm. The epithet is Latin for "spiny."

This is a densely clustering species. Mature trunks grow to 15 feet high and are covered with fibers and leaf bases in their upper parts but are almost smooth and light colored on the lower portions. A clump can measure at least 15 feet wide and 20 feet tall. The leaves are almost completely circular and 2 or more feet wide, and consist of 10 to 15 wedge-shaped segments, which are strongly pleated and obliquely squared on its end. The apex of each segment is deeply toothed, the indentations corresponding to the pleats in the blade. Each segment is approximately the same width but not always the same length, which phenomenon creates the visual aspect of a starburst as well as that of a pinwheel. The leaves are carried on 3- to 4-foot-long thin and delicate petioles with stout curved teeth on their margins. The inflorescences are 3 to 8 feet long and sparsely branched, and bear small yellowish white flowers. The fruits are 0.25-inch-wide, round, red berries borne in short pendent clusters.

This species is hardier to cold than most others and is adaptable to zones 10 and 11. It is a true water lover and, while it needs partial shade when young, can readily adapt to full sun when older. It needs a well-drained soil and abundant and constant moisture. This palm is a splendid hedge subject. It also is perfect as a large accent among other vegetation, in which case it looks better if a few of the trunks (especially those of the same height) are judiciously pruned out so that the wonderful silhouette of the leaves is more readily apparent. Like almost all other species in the genus, it is a superb patio or courtyard subject. It is wonderful indoors but needs more light than most other species. PLATES 531 & 532.

Licuala triphylla occurs naturally in Thailand, peninsular Malaysia, and western Borneo, where it grows in low mountainous rain forest. The epithet is Latin for "three leaves."

It is a solitary-trunked species with a subterranean stem. The leaves are borne on 2- to 3-foot-long petioles and are hemispherical or slightly more so. They consist of three to five widely divergent wedge-shaped segments, the middle one of which is much wider than the others with a truncated, jagged apex. The other two to four segments are obliquely truncated and more pronouncedly toothed at their apices. PLATE 533.

Licuala valida is indigenous to eastern Sumatra and is found in Kalimantan and Sarawak on the island of Borneo, where it grows in low mountainous rain forest. The epithet is Latin for "valid" or "true" and refers to the robust appearance of the species.

This beautiful species is solitary trunked and, with time, forms a short 2- to 3-foot-tall stem. The 3-foot-wide leaves are borne on 2-foot-long petioles, are circular, and consist of an average of 20 deep segments, each of which is broadly to narrowly wedge shaped with deeply toothed apices.

This one creates a small mound of perfection because of the abundant segments forming a perfect circle. It is, however, among the most tender to cold in the genus.

LINOSPADIX is a genus of seven small, pinnate-leaved, monoecious, undergrowth palms on the island of New Guinea and in northern and eastern Australia, where they grow from sea level to an elevation of 7000 feet. There are both clustering and solitary-trunked species and a given species may have leaves that vary in size, shape, and number of segments. All the species have one thing in common: a long, spikelike inflorescence bearing both male and female flowers, the latter of which produce pendent strings or clusters of red, berrylike fruits.

All species are intolerant of drought and need shade to partial shade especially in hot climates. They also need a cool but frost-free climate and a soil that is acidic, humus laden, moist, and well drained.

The genus name is from two Greek words meaning "thread" and "spadix." PLATES 534 & 535.

Linospadix microcarya is endemic to northeastern Queensland, where it grows in rain forest from sea level to 5000 feet. The epithet is from two Greek words meaning "tiny" and "nut."

It is a sparsely clustering species whose stems grow to 10 feet high but are usually 0.5 inch in diameter. They are a deep green and have distinct whitish rings of leaf base scars. The loose pseudo-crownshaft is slivery green to almost white or brownish. The leaves and the leaf crowns vary in form and appearance. The former may be undivided and deeply bifid at their apices with a prominent midrib, in which case the leaf crown is usually of a tufted appearance, or the leaves may be divided into as many as 20 irregularly spaced linear pinnae, in which case the leaf crown is open and airy. In either case, the leaves are deep green on both surfaces. PLATE 534.

Linospadix minor is endemic to northeastern Queensland, Australia, where it grows in rain forest from elevations near sea level to 3800 feet. The epithet is Latin for "smaller" and betrays the fact that, when it was first de-

scribed by Karl E. Maximilian Burret, a 20th-century German palm biologist, only one other species (*L. monostachya*) was known and it is taller.

This is the most variable species in the genus: its stem heights range from 2 to 20 feet; clumps may be sparse or dense; and the leaves may be short or long and have few separate pinnae or many separate leaflets. PLATE 535.

Linospadix monostachya is endemic to Australia in the states of Queensland and New South Wales in dense and wet rain forest from elevations of 500 to 3800 feet. The common name is walking-stick palm in Australia. The epithet is Latin and Greek for "single spike," although the species forms more than a single inflorescence at a time.

The stem of this solitary-trunked species grows to a height of 12 feet with a width of 1 inch. It is light to dark green and has closely spaced darker rings of leaf base scars. The leaf crown is dense and hemispherical to three-quarters hemispherical, and the leaves are 2 to 3 feet long and beautifully arching. They are borne on 1-foot-long petioles and carry 10 to 20 deep green leaflets of variable widths and variable spacing; the leaflets of the terminal pair are, however, always broader and have obliquely truncated, jagged apices, whereas the other leaflets are more linear and long tipped.

This is by far the most widely grown and the most beautiful Australian species, making a perfect little palm of exquisite proportions. It is also the most cold tolerant species in the genus, withstanding unscathed temperatures slightly below freezing. It does not, however, endure regions with hot summers.

LIVISTONA is a genus of 34 or possibly more mostly large, palmate-leaved, bisexual or functionally dioecious palms that are widespread in the Old World tropics and subtropics, from Somalia, Djibouti, the extreme southern Arabian Peninsula, India, Bangladesh, Myanmar, southern China, and Indochina to the southern Japanese islands, the Philippines, New Guinea, the Solomon Islands, Australia, Indonesia, and Malaysia. The genus is best represented in Australia, where there are several species in desert as well as mesic and rain forested regions, and most of the species known to horticulture hail from that country.

All these species are solitary trunked but a few are found naturally with branching stems due to injury of the growing point. Most of them are large to massive, and most have leaf segments whose ends are pendulous when the plants are older but often rigid or shallow when young. The leaves are costapalmate, but the phenomenon is indistinct in many species, especially in younger individuals. Another constant in the genus is the ligule, or flap of fiber from the leaf sheath, which often disappears as the leaf ages; the ligule is different in shape, size, color, and even texture in each species, and it may clasp the trunk or be free from it. All species have a fairly distinct hastula on top of the juncture of petiole and blade. The inflorescences grow from among the leaf crown, are branched two or more times, and bear bisexual flowers that often produce colorful fruits.

Most of these species, and especially those from Australia, are unusually hardy to cold considering their mostly tropical origins, even on that continent. The genus name honors Patrick Murray, baron of Livingston, a 17th-century Scottish nobleman and gardener whose plantings later became the Edinburgh Botanic Garden. PLATES 536–564.

Livistona alfredii is endemic to northwestern Western Australia, not far from the Indian Ocean and at low elevations north of the Tropic of Capricorn. The palm is called the Millstream palm in Australia, after a small settlement in that country. The epithet honors Prince Alfred, duke of Edinburgh and son of Queen Victoria.

The solitary, dark gray or brown trunk grows to a height of 30 feet and has a diameter of 1 foot. The leaf crown is dense and circular or even elongated. The leaves are 4 feet long or slightly more and are strongly costapalmate. They are glaucous bluish gray-green on 3- to 4-foot-long light pinkish brown petioles. The narrow leaf segments are thick and rigid and extend to half the depth of the blade. The fruits are rounded, reddish brown to black, and 1 inch or more in diameter.

This species has an attractive robust appearance. It is, however, slow growing. It is also drought tolerant but grows and looks better with adequate and regular moisture, and can grow in the hottest climates. It needs full sun but is not particular about soil type, growing in calcareous as well as slightly acidic types as long as they are freely draining. It is also unusually cold hardy for a palm with tropical origins and is adaptable to zones 9 through 11 in the drier climates. It is tolerant of some salinity in the soil.

Livistona australis is endemic to the east coast of Australia from central Queensland to the state of Victoria, where it grows in hilly as well as swampy forests and the edges of low mountainous rain forest in the northern parts of its range. It is the world's southernmost *Livistona* species and the second most southerly occurring palm species, the honor of first place going to *Rhopalostylis sapida* in New Zealand. Common names for this species are Australian fan palm, Australian cabbage palm, and fan palm. The epithet is Latin for "southern" and refers to the southern continent of Australia.

This is a solitary-trunked species. Mature trunks are straight as an arrow and can grow to heights of 100 feet in habitat but are generally no more than half that under cultivation. They are generally 1 foot in diameter and, while dead leaves adhere to them for a while, the trunk is mostly clear of leaf bases and is light to dark brown or light to dark gray with closely set deep rings of leaf base scars and several vertical fissures. The leaf crown is round and 15 feet tall and wide. The leaves are 5 feet wide and semicircular to almost circular. The many segments extend two-thirds of the way into the blade and are split to half their length; these smaller segments are pendulous and glossy deep to grayish green. The leaves are held on petioles that are 6 feet or more in length and have spines along their margins in younger palms. The inflorescences are 4 feet long and sparsely branched, and bear small white bisexual blossoms. The fruits are 0.5 inch wide and red or black.

Some populations of this species show slight morphological differences and have, in the past, been referred to as *Livistona* 'Eungella Range' or *L.* 'Paluma Range'. The differences are so slight as to warrant no taxonomic status (John L. Dowe, pers. comm.).

This relatively hardy palm is adaptable to zones 9 through 11, although it is marginal in areas of 9a subject to wet freezes in winter. It grows in a range of soils but is indigenous to regions with fertile soil and plenty of year-round moisture, under which conditions it looks its best. The palm needs sun from youth to old age. The Australian fan palm has nobility and, because of the pendent leaf segments, gracefulness. Its straight columnar trunk invites its use as an avenue tree, planted single file along one or both sides. While this practice works if the palms are planted far enough apart so that their large leaf crowns do not conflict with each other, the fan palm looks even better in groups of three or more individuals of varying heights. It is near perfection as a canopy-scape, especially in groups of individuals of different heights. The palm needs a lot of space and nearly full sun but is sometimes grown indoors as a juvenile plant and is often grown in large atriums or conservatories.

The trunks were once used for building houses and the leaves for making hats (John L. Dowe, pers. comm.). PLATE 536.

Livistona benthamii is indigenous to southern Papua New Guinea, and northern Queensland and Northern Territory in Australia, where it grows in lowland rain forest, especially along the edges of lagoons, swamps, and rivers. The epithet honors George Bentham, a 19th-century British plant taxonomist.

The trunk is tan or cinnamon colored in its younger parts but deep gray in its older parts. It attains a height of 50 feet in habitat but is 6 inches in diameter. It is usually covered in its lower parts with persistent petiole stalks which, even with time and weathering, are 2 feet long and give to the trunk a decidedly spiny if not grotesque look unless they are removed mechanically or by hurricane winds. Once the petiole stubs are gone, the stems usually exhibit picturesque knobs, which are similar to those in several *Phoenix* species and are the old, persistent, and lignified leaf bases. The leaf crown is nearly spherical in older trees but is elongated in younger individuals, the leaves growing from an extended area of the upper trunk; in both cases it is open. The leaves are 4 feet wide with deep green pendent segments that extend three-quarters of the way to the petiole, which is 6 feet long and bears perpendicular spines at its base. The leaves of seedling and young individuals are circular with narrow segments extending to the petiole, giving them the appearances of small papyrus plants.

This exceptionally attractive species is fast growing if given a rich, moist soil and is beautiful at all stages. It is tolerant of saline conditions but, alas, not high winds if its appearance is important. It is adaptable to zones 9 through 11 and, while it survives in Mediterranean climes, it grows slowly. PLATE 537.

Livistona boninensis is endemic to the Bonin Archipelago (Ogasawara Islands) southeast of the main Japanese islands, where it grows in low mountainous rain forest. The epithet is Latin for "of Bonin."

The trunk attains a height of at least 60 feet in habitat with a diameter of 1 foot. It is light brown in its younger parts and a light gray in its older parts where it is graced with widely spaced, ridged rings of leaf base scars. The leaf crown is spherical, with many 3-foot-wide leaves on 3- to 4-foot-long petioles. The leaf segments extend two-thirds of the way into the blade and are bifurcated to a distance of 1 foot, with pendent tips. They are glossy light green above and below.

The species has great visual similarity to *L. chinensis* and has been considered a variety of that species. It is at least as hardy to cold as is *L. chinensis* and otherwise has the same cultural requirements.

Livistona carinensis is a highly endangered species from three widely scatted populations in oases of northeastern Africa: Djibouti, northern Somalia, and eastern Yemen in the Arabian Peninsula. The epithet is Latin for "of Carin," one of the oases at which the species was first identified. Until the late 1980s, the species was near extinction, as it was being felled for its durable trunks. In addition, goats were eating the fruits and seedlings and, in one oasis, the groundwater level had lowered to the point that the palms could no longer survive.

In habitat the solitary trunk grows to 80 feet high and 15 inches in diameter, with a heavy, swollen base and aerial roots near the ground and closely spaced rings of leaf base scars near the summit. The leaf crown is spherical or elongated and is open because of the long leaf petioles. The leaves are weakly costapalmate, 3 feet wide, and semicircular; they are borne on 4-foot-long petioles which, on their undersides, are orange to yellow and have backwards-curving teeth along their margins, similar in shape and viciousness to those on the petiole margins of *L. saribus*. The segments extend to three-quarters of the depth of the blade and are stiff, linear-lanceolate, and a deep green on both surfaces. Inflorescences are 7 feet long and usually extend beyond the leaf crown. The tiny fruits are round, brown, and up to 2 inches in diameter.

This is a beautiful species, especially when it is older. Its leaf crown is exceptionally nice and open, and the long petioles allow the leaves to be readily seen, even from a distance. It also seems easy, if slow, to grow and is adaptable to zones 10 and 11 and is marginal in drier climates of 9b. It is salt tolerant and drought tolerant (for short periods). It is adaptable to full sun, even in its youth. PLATE 538.

Livistona chinensis occurs naturally in open woodlands in the southern Japanese islands (as far north as the southeastern part of the island of Shikoku) and in Taiwan, where it is endangered. The common name is Chinese fan palm, and the leaves are still used for making fans (John L. Dowe, pers. comm.). The epithet is Latin for "of China."

The mature stems of this solitary-trunked species grow slowly to 40 feet high with a diameter of 1 foot. They are a deep brown to reddish brown when young (due to the adherence of leaf bases) and gray with indistinct closely set rings of leaf base scars in older palms. The leaf crown is densely packed with 30 to 50 leaves, usually full and almost round, and 18 feet wide and 20 feet tall. The leaves are 6 feet wide on 6-foot-long petioles which, in younger palms, have teeth along their margins. Leaf shape is nearly circular, sometimes diamond shaped, and the segments extend to two-thirds of the way into the blade. The segments are split to at least half their length and these smaller segments are pendulous in older palms but more erect in juvenile plants. Leaf color is bright green to glossy olive green. The inflorescences are 6 feet long and much branched. They bear small whitish bisexual flowers. The fruits are 0.5 to 1 inch long, round to ovoid, and greenish blue to pinkish gray when mature.

The species is slightly susceptible to lethal yellowing disease. The palm is among the hardiest in the genus and is adaptable to zones 9 through 11 and in favorable microclimates of 8b, especially those with drier climates. It withstands drought but only looks its best and grows its fastest with regular and adequate moisture. It is adaptable to and looks wonderful in partial shade as a juvenile but needs full sun to attain its ultimate height. It is not fussy about soil type as long as it is freely draining.

The Chinese fan palm and the Australian fan palm are difficult to distinguish from one another at a distance, especially when past their juvenile stages. The salient differences between the two are that *L. australis* has a taller trunk with much more distinct rings of leaf base scars, leaves that are more of a dusky green, and leaf segments that are usually longer and even more pendulous, at least when *L. australis* is older. The Chinese fan palm has the same landscape uses as the Australian fan palm but is more choice as a young plant because of its wide, nearly circular leaves; when grown in partial shade, the leaves stay rounded and the segments remain shallower and a deeper green for much longer. It is well adapted to indoor cultivation, especially when young, but needs a great amount of space and light when older. PLATES 539–541.

Livistona decipiens is endemic to the eastern Queensland coastal region of Australia, where it grows in open woods or along the edges of forests and in swampy areas near the coast. Common names in Australia are fountain palm and ribbon palm. The epithet is Latin for "deceiving" and alludes to the fact that the species was once incorrectly known in cultivation in France as *Copernicia cerifera* (John L. Dowe, pers. comm.).

This is a solitary-trunked species. Mature trunks grow to 50 feet high with a diameter of 10 inches. They are light brown and, except in young plants, covered in closely set deep rings of leaf base scars. The leaf crown is especially rounded and is densely packed with 40 to 60 leaves, but the visual effect is more diaphanous than most other *Livistona* species because of the thin, long weeping segments which cause the leaves to appear almost pinnate. The leaves are 9 feet wide but are so deeply costapalmate that they are almost V shaped with much of the diameter thus foreshortened and the general leaf a linear diamond shape; the visual length of a given leaf is therefore around 6 feet. The leaf segments extend almost to the intrusive petiole and are divided to half their lengths into finer segments, the latter of which are pendent, resulting in a decidedly weeping visual effect from the curtains of segments that hang vertically for 3 feet or more. The petiole is 6 feet long and has short teeth on its margin. Leaf color is deep green to almost bluish green above and glaucous grayish green beneath. The inflorescences are up to 9 feet long, are much branched, and bear small bright yellow bisexual blossoms. The fruits are 0.5 inch wide, round, and black when mature.

This hardy palm is adaptable to zones 9 through 11 and sometimes 8b in the drier winter climates. Its soil preference is wide as long as the soil is freely draining. It is

drought tolerant when established but looks better and grows faster with regular and adequate moisture. It is adapted to full sun from youth to old age. The ribbon fan palm is more graceful than many *Livistona* species because of the weeping curtain effect of the leaves that look almost pinnate from a distance and are delicate appearing. The leaf crown provides one of the most beautiful silhouettes and its canopy-scape is almost spellbinding. The tree may be planted as a single specimen, even surrounded by space, but is much more attractive in groups of three or more individuals of varying heights. It needs space and high light levels indoors and is not a good subject long term. PLATE 542.

Livistona drudei is endemic to northeastern Queensland, Australia, where it grows in low coastal plains, especially along streams and rivers. The epithet honors Carl G. O. Drude, an early 20th-century German botanist and collector.

The solitary trunk attains a height of 80 feet or more in habitat but is 1 foot in diameter. It is mostly free of leaf bases and fibers except for its uppermost part and is light gray to almost white. It has a beautiful open leaf crown that is circular. The deep green leaves are 4 or 5 feet long on 5- to 7-foot-long petioles, and their segments extend more than halfway to the petiole and are pendent, especially in older leaves. The globular fruits are dull purplish black and 0.5 inch in diameter.

This is an exquisite palm when mature and is certainly one of the most beautiful, if not the most beautiful, in the genus. Its silhouette is thrilling and yet diaphanous because of the open, circular crown with its long leaf petioles. It is adaptable to zones 10 and 11 and marginally so in 9b. It needs full sun, regular and adequate moisture, and a rich soil; it is fast growing if given the proper conditions. PLATES 543 & 544.

Livistona eastonii is endemic to Kimberley Plateau in northern Western Australia, where it grows in flat monsoonal and open, grassy eucalypt forest on laterite soil that is reddish with iron ore. The epithet honors William Easton, the surveyor of the area's first scientific expedition in 1921.

The solitary trunk grows to 40 feet tall with a diameter of 5 inches in habitat. It is dark gray and, in its lower parts, tessellated with the flattish petiole stubs but distinctly and closely ringed in its upper parts. The leaf crown is open and rounded or elongated, the latter condition arising out of the production of the weighty inflorescences; this phenomenon can also create a two-tiered effect. The leaves are strongly costapalmate, broadly wedge shaped, and 2 to 3 feet long, with the stiff and narrowly lanceolate segments usually extending almost to the petiole. The 2- to 3-foot-long petioles are yellowish to light grayish green. The fruits are oblong or ellipsoid, 0.5 inch long, and purplish black.

The palm is the most distinctive plant in its grass-covered habitat, which is often swept by fast-moving fires. It is extremely rare in cultivation. It probably needs a warm to nearly tropical climate, acidic soil, and full sun, and is probably extremely slow growing, as the largest individuals in habitat are almost 1000 years old.

Livistona endauensis is endemic to peninsular Malaysia, where it grows in low mountainous rain forest, usually on top of sandstone ridges, in acidic soil. The epithet is Latin for "of Endau," a region of Malaysia.

The trunk of this relatively small species grows to 20 feet with a maximum diameter of 6 inches. It is deep olive green in all but its oldest parts and is graced with widely spaced light rings of leaf base scars. The leaf crown is open and spherical or nearly so. The 3-foot-wide glossy green leaves are nearly circular and borne on 4-foot-long petioles. The lanceolate, pointed segments extend halfway into the depth of the blade and are stiff and straight in younger plants but become more lax and even pendent on older trees.

Although first formally described in 1987, the species is still rare in cultivation. It is probably not hardy to cold and certainly needs copious and regular moisture and an acidic soil. It is apparently adaptable to full sun even when young as Mike Dahme (pers. comm.) reports that healthy field-grown plants in Malaysia have 1 foot or so of trunk and were grown in full sun.

Livistona exigua is endemic to Brunei in north central Borneo, where it occurs in the undergrowth of low mountainous rain forest on the tops of sandstone ridges in acidic soils. The epithet is Latin for "meager" and alludes to the palm's small stature.

The solitary trunk attains only 12 feet of height and a diameter of 2 or 3 inches; the older parts of the stem are graced with closely spaced rings of leaf base scars. The leaf crown is hemispherical to almost spherical, and the leaves are 18 inches wide, circular, with 10 to 12 narrowly ovate to lanceolate leaflets radiating from the slender 2-foot-long petioles.

The species was described in 1984 by Morgan and Dransfield and is still not in cultivation outside of a few botanical gardens. It is not hardy to cold and needs regular and adequate moisture and an acidic soil. It also needs partial shade when young but is probably adaptable to a more exposed site when older.

Livistona fulva is endemic to Blackdown Tableland in central eastern Queensland, where it grows at springs near the bases of cliffs, in gullies and gorges at elevations of 1200 to 2000 feet. Until A. N. Rodd described it as a species in 1998, it was known as *L.* 'Blackdown Tableland'. The epithet *fulva* is Latin for "tawny colored," an obvious allusion to the undersurface color of the new leaves.

The solitary trunk grows to 40 feet in habitat and is less than 1 foot in diameter. Older stems are usually free of leaf bases and are dark gray and heavily and closely ringed, whereas younger trunks are mostly covered with cinnamon-brown leaf bases and fibers. The leaf crown is usually semicircular and is open because of the long leaf petioles. Individual leaves are almost flat, almost circular, and 3 feet wide, with segments that extend halfway to the petiole and hastula. The leaf stalks are 6 to 8 feet long. Leaf color is light yellowish or grayish green above with a bluish hue beneath. The undersides of new leaves are covered with a beautiful bronzy orange or light golden brown tomentum, which usually disappears as the short hairs are worn off, especially with older trees.

The palm is slow growing but relatively hardy to cold, being adaptable to zones 9 through 11 and possibly marginal in 8b, especially of drier climes. It does well in tropical and Mediterranean climates but not hot desert areas. It seems to thrive in partial shade or full sun and is not fussy about soil type as long as it is freely draining. It is drought tolerant but also languishes and grows more slowly if not provided with adequate and regular moisture. PLATE 545.

Livistona halongensis was described by Nguyen and Kiew in 2000 and is endemic to a few limestone islands in Ha Long Bay in Vietnam, where it grows in rain forest from sea level to 1200 feet elevation. The epithet is Latin for "of Ha Long."

The solitary trunk grows to a height of 30 feet with a diameter of 8 inches and exhibits distinct and closely spaced rings of leaf scars. The leaf crown is large, open, and spherical. The leaves are semicircular and small, 30 inches long, on 4-foot-long petioles that have orange, curved teeth on their lower halves. The segments extend into the blade to within 2 inches of the petiole juncture and are apically bifid. The extraordinary inflorescences are 10 feet long and erect, and extend well above the leaf crown, bearing tiny bisexual blossoms. The fruits are round, less than 0.5 inch in diameter, and glossy, deep green when mature.

This is a striking, tropical-looking species with a beautiful, open leaf crown. It is not in cultivation but should soon be. Although the palm is probably not hardy to cold, it would do well in regions with calcareous soil. PLATE 546.

Livistona humilis is endemic to Northern Territory, Australia, where it grows in open, flat monsoonal *Eucalyptus* woods of low elevations. The epithet is Latin for "humble" or "small."

The solitary trunk grows to 20 feet in habitat, with a diameter of 3 inches, and is dark gray and covered in flattish petiole stubs. The leaf crowns are circular in older trees and open. The small, flat, circular leaves are 12 to 18 inches wide on 2-foot-long petioles. The stiff, nonpendulous segments extend to three-quarters of the way to the petiole and are linear-lanceolate and glossy yellowish to medium green on both surfaces. The trees are dioecious, and the inflorescences bearing female blossoms are long and project out of the leaf crown with thin yellow branches. The fruits are oblong, 0.75 inch long, and dark purple or black.

Although it is the smallest Australian species of *Livistona,* this palm is elegantly picturesque with its neat and tidy round crown and knobby trunks and should be much more widely planted. Its only faults are that it is slow growing and difficult to transplant. It needs sun and, while drought tolerant, grows and looks better with adequate and regular moisture. It is not fussy about soil type and grows well even when occasionally flooded. It is probably not cold hardy.

Livistona inermis occurs naturally in northwestern Queensland and Northern Territory of Australia, where it grows on or at the base of sandstone cliffs at low elevations. It is sometimes called the wispy fan palm in Australia and this moniker is unfortunate as it implies something not overly desirable. The epithet is Latin for "unarmed" and alludes to the petiole margins.

The species is solitary trunked, but some populations show what looks like clustering but is simply branching of the stem due to damage to its growing point (John L. Dowe, pers. comm.). The stems attain maximum heights of 30 feet in habitat with diameters of no more than 4 inches. They are gray and their lower parts usually have flattish petiole stubs. The leaf crown is spherical and open because of the small leaves and relatively long petioles. Individual leaves are nearly circular, 2 feet wide, with narrow light green to grayish green segments that extend almost to the petiole. The leaves are borne on 2- to 3-foot-long petioles that have a pinkish hue and are free of thorns but may have tiny prickles on the margins of their lower halves. The leaf segments are mostly stiff but not rigid and are often pendent near their apices; they are split to three-quarters of their length. The oblong fruits are black when ripe and 0.5 inch long.

The species is reportedly slow growing and resents transplanting. It needs sun and a fast-draining soil. Alas, it is not hardy to cold and is adaptable only to zones 10 and 11. The palm is elegance personified.

Livistona jenkinsiana occurs naturally in northeastern India (Sikkim and Assam), Nepal, Myanmar, northern Thailand, and southern China, including the island of Hainan, where it grows in mountainous rain forest from elevations of 400 to 3800 feet. The epithet honors Major-General F. Jenkins, British commissioner of Assam and collector of the type specimen in the 19th century.

The solitary trunk attains a height of 80 feet in habitat and is 12 to 18 inches in diameter, with flattened petiole stubs on its lower portions. The circular leaf crown consists of many 4-foot-wide nearly circular leaves with stiff but not rigid segments that extend to half the depth of the blade; juvenile plants have larger and much less segmented leaves. Leaf color is deep green above and a glaucous, paler green below. The fruits are globose, 1 inch in diameter, and deep, dull blue.

This noble species is attractive at all stages. Young plants, especially those grown in partial shade, have leaves that much resemble those of *L. rotundifolia* but are smaller. The palm is surprisingly hardy to cold considering its tropical origins and is adaptable to zones 10 and 11 and marginally so in warmer microclimates of 9b. It relishes partial shade when young and needs regular and adequate moisture at all ages. It appreciates a well-drained, humus-laden soil but is known to grow in impoverished soils. PLATES 547 & 548.

Livistona lanuginosa is a rare and endangered species endemic to eastern central Queensland, Australia. Until it was described in 1998 by A. N. Rodd, it was known as *L. 'Cape River'.* The epithet is Latin for "woolly," which alludes to the dense and lengthy white tomentum on the petioles and the inflorescence bracts.

The trunk attains a height of 60 feet in habitat with a diameter of 1 foot, except at the base where it is usually quite swollen. The leaf crown is spherical but beautifully open and airy because of the long leaf petioles. The grayish green leaves are 3 feet wide but 2 feet long, are borne on 5-foot-long petioles, and have segments extending to three-quarters of the way to the petiole. The segments are further divided to three-quarters of their free length and are pendent only at their tips. The young petioles as well as the rachis are covered in a dense white wool on their upper surfaces, and the bottom surfaces of the blades are covered in a thick coating of white wax which gives them a light bluish gray cast. The large fruits are borne on short inflorescences that are half hidden in the leaf crown; they are round, purplish black, and more than 1 inch in diameter.

The species is slow growing no matter what care it receives but does best in full sun from an early age and in a soil that is freely draining; while it is drought tolerant, it cannot be expected to flourish unless given regular and adequate moisture. It is adaptable to zones 10 and 11 and is marginal in warm microclimates of 9b, especially in drier climes. PLATE 549.

Livistona lorophylla occurs naturally in the Kimberley region of northern Western Australia, where it grows in river valleys and gorges, the rims of the plateau, and on top of the cliffs therein, most often in association with sandstone. The epithet is a combination of Latin and Greek words meaning "strap" and "leaf." In the scant literature that has hitherto been available, the epithet is always spelled "loriphylla," but this is incorrect as the combining form of the Latin part of the epithet is "loro-."

The solitary trunk of this small palm grows to 15 feet high and 4 inches in diameter. It is light to dark gray and heavily and closely ringed with ridged leaf base scars. The leaf crown in older plants is spherical, and is open and airy because of the relatively long leaf petioles. The leaves are 3 feet long and strongly costapalmate, on 3-foot-long green to reddish brown petioles. The narrow leaf segments extend almost to the petioles and are light, dusky green on both surfaces, mostly limp, and pendulous at their apices. Mature fruits are obovoid to pyriform, 0.5 inch long, and dull black.

The palm is rare in cultivation but not as rare as *L. eastonii*, its neighbor to the south. It is similar in appearance to *L. inermis*, only larger. It is drought tolerant and slow growing, and needs sun as well as a fast-draining soil. It is reportedly unusually hardy to cold considering its tropical provenance and is probably adaptable to zones 9b through 11, especially in drier climates.

Livistona mariae is endemic to canyon bottoms in mostly desert regions of northern and central Australia: in northeastern Western Australia, northern and southern Northern Territory, and northwestern Queensland. It is sometimes called central Australian cabbage palm. The epithet honors Grand Duchess Marie Alexandrovna, the Russian daughter-in-law of Queen Victoria.

The solitary trunk grows to 90 feet in habitat and 1 foot in diameter, and to 40 feet under cultivation. Older trunks are deep to light gray and are closely set with rings of leaf base scars. Younger trunks are covered in a dense, tight fiber mass and in old leaf bases that impart a dark brown coloration to the stems. The leaf crown is 15 feet wide and tall. The leaves are 6 or more feet wide and are semicircular, with linear-lanceolate segments that extend to two-thirds of the depth of the blade. The segments are essentially split and pendent and, like the rest of the blade, are grayish green on both sides, with a waxy coating on the undersides. The 6- to 8-foot-long, reddish brown petioles have 1-inch-long sharp teeth on their lower margins. The leaves of young palms are usually tinted reddish purple or deep rose, and their leaf segments are stiff and

not pendent. The 6-foot-long inflorescences are mostly erect and are much branched. They bear small yellow bisexual flowers. The fruits are 0.5 inch wide, round, and glossy black when mature.

The species is adaptable to various well-drained soils. It is drought tolerant when established but grows much faster with regular and adequate moisture. It is adaptable to zones 10 and 11 but is probably safe in 9b, especially in drier climates. The palm needs full sun from youth to old age. If given good care in a tropical or nearly tropical climate, this species is fast growing once past the juvenile stage: 25 feet of trunk in 15 years. The palm has the same landscape uses as *L. australis* and *L. chinensis* but is nobler appearing than either of them. It does not look bad even when used as a specimen tree surrounded by space but is much more pleasing in groups of three or more individuals of varying heights. *Livistona mariae* needs room and extremely good light to be grown indoors.

A. N. Rodd considers this species to consist of three subspecies: subsp. *mariae,* subsp. *occidentalis,* and subsp. *rigida,* but we are treating these as three separate species. PLATE 550.

Livistona merrillii is endemic to several islands of the Philippines, where it grows along the edges of and in clearings in the rain forest at low elevations. The epithet honors Elmer D. Merrill, 20th-century botanist, plant explorer of the Asian tropics, and former director of the Arnold Arboretum.

The trunk attains a maximum height of 50 feet and is 1 foot in diameter. The leaf crown is open and spherical. The leaves are 3 to 4 feet wide and semicircular, and are borne on 3-foot-long petioles. The leaf segments extend to halfway into the blade and are medium to deep green on both surfaces.

This beautiful and fast-growing species is rare in cultivation. It is amazingly hardy to cold considering its tropical origins and is adaptable to zones 9b through 11. It needs regular and adequate moisture and flourishes in full sun even from youth. PLATE 551.

Livistona muelleri is indigenous to far northern and northeastern Queensland, Australia, as well as southern New Guinea, where it grows in monsoonal savannas, on the edges of rain forest, and in open and drier woodlands, always at low elevations. It is called dwarf fan palm in Queensland, probably because of its slow growth. The epithet honors a 19th-century German botanist, Sir Ferdinand J. H. von Mueller, in Australia.

Mature trees in habitat are known to form trunks as tall as 60 feet but most are 40 feet or shorter. They are less than 1 foot in diameter, dark gray (often black in habitat due to grass fires), and heavily and closely ringed, the lowest parts covered in rounded stubs of the old petioles. The leaf crown is hemispherical and dense. The leaves are borne on 2- to 3-foot-long petioles and are circular, flat, and 2 feet wide. The segments extend to slightly more than halfway into the depth of the blade and are stiff and nonpendulous; they are a dark grayish green above and a lighter bluish gray-green beneath. The fruits are ellipsoid, 0.5 inch long, and deep brown to black.

The palm is exceptionally slow growing but is adaptable to zones 10 and 11 and may be marginal in 9b, especially in drier climates. It needs sun and copious and regular moisture but is not fussy about soil type, growing in alkaline and acidic soils, and even those that are on occasion waterlogged. This neat and attractive species is especially nice in groups of three or more individuals of varying heights. PLATES 552 & 553.

Livistona nitida is endemic to southeastern Queensland, Australia, where it grows near permanent springs and along banks of rivers and streams at low elevations. Until it was described in 1998 by A. N. Rodd, it was known as *L.* 'Carnarvon Gorge'. The epithet *nitida* is Latin for "shiny" and alludes to the fruits.

The solitary trunk attains a height approaching 100 feet with a diameter of 1 foot, is light gray to light brown, and is distinctly ringed with leaf base scars. The leaf crown is circular and open. The leaves are 5 to 6 feet wide on 5-foot-long petioles. The yellowish green leaf segments extend three-quarters of the way to the petiole and are narrow, limp, and pendent, creating a weeping or curtain effect. The fruits are round, glossy black, and 0.5 inch in diameter.

The species is unusually hardy to cold considering its near tropical origins, is adaptable to zones 9 through 11, and possibly is marginal in 8b, especially in drier climes. It is a beautiful palm, similar in most respects to *L. australis* but more robust. PLATE 554.

Livistona rigida is endemic to northwestern Queensland and Northern Territory, Australia, where it grows near water at low elevations. The epithet is Latin for "rigid," an obvious allusion to the stiff inflorescence branches.

The species is closely related to *L. mariae*, and A. N. Rodd (1998) considers it a subspecies of that taxon. It is, however, distinct in appearance: the leaves are much more rigid, especially in juvenile plants; are much more grayish green or even bluish gray-green; and are covered in a thin coating of wax on their undersurfaces. They are also smaller than those of *L. mariae* and, even when mature, the leaf segments of *L. rigida* are not pendent. The latter extend halfway through the depth of the blade and are shortly but distinctly bifid at their apices.

This palm is amazingly cold tolerant, considering its tropical origins. It survives (with protection when young) in warm microclimates of zone 8b and is dependable for the most part in 9 through 11. It is fast growing and not particular about soil type but does better in a good one. It is drought tolerant but grows slowly and does not look as good under such conditions.

Livistona robinsoniana is endemic to low mountainous rain forest of the Philippines. The species is similar to *L. rotundifolia* and with further scientific study may become synonymous with that taxon or only a variety thereof. The epithet honors Charles Budd Robinson, a 19th-century English botanist and collector.

It is a solitary trunked species whose mature stems reach 80 feet tall and 1 foot or slightly more in diameter. They are mostly free of leaf bases and are deep green in the younger parts where they also exhibit pale green, fairly widely spaced leaf scar rings. The oldest parts of the trunks are light brown to deep gray and are only indistinctly ringed. The youngest parts of the stems are wrapped in a beautiful pattern of spiraling ribbon-like fibers. The leaf crown is about 15 feet wide and 10 feet tall and is not quite rounded. It contains usually about two dozen leaves and is open and spacious looking because of the long leaf petioles. The leaves are 6 feet wide in younger palms and are semicircular to almost circular. The 6- to 8-foot-long deep green petioles re unarmed. Leaf color is medium to deep green on both sides, and the segments extend to about two-thirds of the way into the blade and are slightly pendent at their tips. The branched inflorescences are 6 feet long, are mostly erect, and bear small yellow bisexual blossoms. The fruits are 0.5 inch wide, rounded, and orange when mature.

The palm flourishes in partial shade or full sun, even in hot climates if given enough moisture. It prefers a humus-laden soil that is constantly moist and it should be heavily mulched with organic materials in areas like southern Florida. It is not hardy to cold and is adaptable only to zones 10 and 11.

Because of its relatively thin trunk and open leaf crown, this palm is perhaps the most graceful of the large *Livistona* species. It is well suited to avenue edging as well as standing alone as a specimen tree even surrounded by space. In groups of three or more individuals of varying heights it is exceptional in beauty, and nothing is lovelier as a canopy-scape.

Livistona rotundifolia extends from southern peninsular Malaysia to Sarawak, Brunei, and Sabah in Sulawesi, the Moluccas, and many Philippine islands, where it grows in low mountainous rain forest. It is called footstool palm and round-leaf fan palm. The epithet is Latin for "round leaf" and alludes to the shape of the leaves, mainly on juvenile plants.

The solitary trunk attains a height of 80 feet in habitat but is no more than 1 foot in diameter. Older parts of the trunks are smooth and pale gray to almost white, and show regularly spaced reddish brown rings of leaf base scars except for the oldest parts. In several younger individuals the leaf crown is extended and even reaches to the ground in specimens that are 20 feet tall overall, but it is always rounded, much shorter, and open in older palms. The petioles are 8 feet long and bear curved spines along their lower margins. The leaves are 5 to 6 feet wide and are circular on juvenile palms. In older palms, the leaves are significantly smaller, do not form complete circles, and have stiffer segments that extend to halfway into the blade with a short split at their ends. Leaf color is glossy, deep green on both surfaces. The inflorescences are 8 feet long with many branches bearing small yellow bisexual flowers. The 1-inch-wide, round fruits are deep red, maturing to black.

A naturally occurring variety on the island of Luzon and adjacent islands in the Philippines is known as ***Livistona rotundifolia* var. *luzonensis*** and has several notable differences from the type: the trunks are almost dark green, of shorter ultimate stature, and exhibit beautiful and regularly spaced white rings of leaf base scars, and the fruits are deeper red. The variety is reportedly more tender to cold, slower growing, and definitely much rarer and harder to find.

The species is slightly susceptible to lethal yellowing disease. It is the least cold-tolerant species in the genus, is adaptable only to zones 10b and 11, and is marginal in 10a. It wants copious and regular moisture but is not fussy about soil type. It grows well in partial shade when young but needs full sun when older. Because of the long petioles, the leaf crown is open and exquisitely graceful, and is among the finest canopy-scapes. When planted in groups of three or more individuals of varying heights, it is even more attractive.

Young plants have larger, less deeply segmented leaves than do adults. The leaves are stunningly attractive up close, looking more like disks than fan leaves, and are choice for intimate areas. Alas, they, like other young palms in nature, grow up and reach considerable heights. The juvenile aspect of the leaves is maintained to some extent if the palm is in partial shade. *Livistona rotundifolia* is a good indoor candidate when young. PLATES 555–559.

Livistona saribus is among the most widespread species in the genus, from southeastern China, Vietnam, Laos, Cambodia, Thailand, and peninsular Malaysia to Borneo and the island of Luzon in the Philippines, where it grows in swampy rain forest, clearings, and monsoonal savannas.

It is usually called taraw palm. The epithet is a Latinized form of a Moluccan name for the species.

Mature trunks grow to 90 feet in their native haunts but are usually 50 feet tall under cultivation, with a diameter of 1 foot. Old plants have trunks free of leaf bases and fibers, which are then pale gray, with deep but incomplete circles of leaf base scars and flattened petiole stubs. The leaf crown is dense and hemispherical to spherical, depending on whether the old dead leaves are present, and 15 feet wide and tall. Leaves are generally 4 feet wide on 5- to 6-foot-long petioles that are green or a beautiful deep orange to deep red, and are armed with stout, black, curved teeth that may be as long as 3 inches and have bulbous bases. The segments extend to more than halfway into the blade and exhibit vertically drooping ends. Leaf color is deep green on both surfaces. The leaves of juvenile trees (with less than 6 feet of trunk height) are radically different and consist of fewer, wider segments, which are deeply split once or twice, and are not pendent. The yellow inflorescences are 5 feet long and sparsely branched. They bear small yellow bisexual flowers. The 1-inch-wide, round fruits are an outstandingly beautiful shiny blue or purple.

There seem to be two slightly different forms of this species: one with green petioles and one with red or deep orange petioles in younger plants. The red-petioled forms are more attractive and significantly more tender to cold. No one seems to know where the more highly colored form originated or why it is more tender to cold, but it is safe only in zones 10 and 11.

The species is relatively fast growing when younger and if given regular and adequate moisture and a humus-laden soil. It luxuriates in partial shade when young but needs full sun as it ages if it is to grow as fast as it should and look as good as it can. It is adaptable to zones 9 through 11 and is marginal in 8b. The palm has visual similarities to *L. australis* when older. When juvenile, it is much more interesting because of the larger and less segmented, flat leaves and the beautiful petiole thorns. The leaf segments of older individuals are not as pendulous as those of *L. australis* are and this characteristic gives it another attraction in the landscape. It should not be planted as a single specimen surrounded by space, but groups of three or more individuals of varying heights are beautiful indeed. This is a good candidate for indoor cultivation only when young. PLATES 560–563.

Livistona tahanensis is endemic to a single mountain in peninsular Malaysia, where it grows at elevations of 3000 to 5000 feet on sloping ground and in moist, peaty soil. The epithet is Latin for "of Tahan," the mountain on which the species is found.

The solitary trunk grows to 20 feet high and is less than 1 foot in diameter. It is dark gray to brown and is covered in flattened petiole stubs in its lower portions, the upper portions rough with the remains of leaf bases. The leaf crown is spherical, partly because of the short shag of dead leaves, and is 10 feet wide and high. The leaves are 3 feet wide, with segments extending to half the depth of the blade. The latter are lanceolate, stiff, shortly bifid apically, and a deep, glaucous green above and grayish green beneath. The 4-foot-long petioles have margins rimmed with thorns. The egg-shaped fruits are 0.5 inch long and shiny green dappled with tiny white spots.

The species is exceedingly rare in cultivation and little is known about its requirements, but it probably would do well in frostless Mediterranean climes as well as more tropical ones. It should also need a constantly moist, acidic soil.

Livistona victoriae, described by A. N. Rodd in 1998, was formerly known as *L.* 'Victoria River'. It occurs naturally in far northeastern Western Australia and northwestern Northern Territory, Australia, where it grows in sandstone ravines and intermittent river courses, always where groundwater is available. The epithet is Latin for "of Victoria," a reference to the Victoria River in the palm's habitat.

The solitary trunk grows to 50 feet high with a diameter of 8 inches. It is light gray, straight, and nearly smooth in its older parts. The leaf crown is spherical and open. The 3-foot-long leaves are strongly costapalmate with stiff segments that extend halfway to the 3-foot-long petiole. They are a beautiful bluish gray-green to silvery green and are thick and leathery. The fruits are round, brown, and 0.5 inch in diameter.

This is, because of the leaf color, an especially attractive species. It is amazingly hardy to cold considering its tropical origins and is probably adaptable to zones 9 through 11 in the drier climates. It needs sun and a fast-draining soil. PLATE 564.

Livistona woodfordii occurs in the Solomon Islands and Papua New Guinea, where it grows in low mountainous rain forest. The epithet honors C. M. Woodford, an early 20th-century British naturalist and collector as well as government official of the Solomons.

The solitary trunk attains a height of 40 feet and a diameter of 6 inches. It is gray to tan and heavily ringed with leaf base scars in its younger parts but nearly smooth in its older parts. The leaf crown is spherical and dense with 3-foot-wide leaves that are segmented to two-thirds the depth of the blade. They are deep green on both surfaces and are borne on 4- to 5-foot-long slender petioles armed near their bases. Juvenile trees have rounded leaves with wide segments, similar to those of juvenile plants of *L. saribus*, whereas the leaves of older trees are only hemispherical. The small bluish black fruits are globose and 0.5 inch in diameter.

This is one of the most elegant species in the genus, its lollipop form making an exquisite silhouette and, planted in groups of three or more trees of varying heights, it is almost unparalleled in beauty. Considering its tropical origins, it is surprisingly hardy to cold, being adaptable to zones 10 and 11 and possibly marginal in warm microclimates of 9b. It needs sun when past the juvenile stage and is a true water lover, but it seems satisfied with limey or slightly acidic soils, as long as they are freely draining.

LODOICEA is a monotypic genus of massive, palmate-leaved, solitary-trunked, dioecious palm. The genus name supposedly honors King Louis XV of France, but it may be a corruption of Laodice, a beautiful princess of the legendary city of Troy, as the immense seeds resemble female buttocks. The epithet is Latin for "of Maldive" and was bestowed when only the fruit of the palm was known and that from beaches of the Maldive Islands, southwest of India in the Indian Ocean. PLATES 565–569.

Lodoicea maldivica is endemic to the two small islands of Curieuse and Praslin in the Seychelles Islands northeast of Madagascar, where it grows in large stands in forests and moist valleys at low elevations. It was probably much more widespread in the Seychelles in the past.

The solitary trunk grows to a height of 80 feet or even more with a diameter of 20 inches maximum. The stem is straight, columnar, and light tan in its younger parts but light gray to dark gray in its older parts. It is swollen at the base and, in habitat, the bulbous stem base forms a depression in the ground from which it grows. This basin is probably created to allow the relatively slender trunk to sway in the wind. Male trees reportedly grow taller than female trees, and it is assumed that their loftier statures facilitate wind pollination of the shorter females. The wind is probably assisted by indigenous snails and geckos, which are often seen on the inflorescences of both sexes. The leaf crown consists of 15 to 20 leaves and is mostly hemispherical but sometimes exhibits pendent dead leaves at its base. The leaves are borne on 6- to 12-foot-long robust petioles and are deeply costapalmate, with blades 18 feet long and 12 feet wide. The leaf segments are relatively shallow in younger trees but much deeper in older ones. They are lanceolate, coriaceous, and mostly stiff, but slightly pendent at their tips. Their color is glossy deep green on both surfaces.

The inflorescences grow from among the leaf bases. The male inflorescences are 6-foot-long, 3-inch-thick, fleshy, pendent spikes with sessile starlike whitish blossoms. The female inflorescences are shorter, with several thick, fleshy branches, also bearing sessile but extremely large, fleshy, white cup-shaped blossoms; they are the largest of all palm flowers. The infamous fruits are immense and top shaped, 20 inches long and 12 to 15 inches wide; they are nearly black and are rough on the surface, usually with loose fibers similar to a coconut. They require from five to seven years to reach maturity, at which time they can weigh up to 45 pounds. The seeds inside these fruits are almost as large as the fruit itself and have two hemispherical lobes connected by a deep groove; they are the largest seeds in the world and the subject of much lore.

Europeans encountered the fruits in the early 16th century. Because the fruits were afloat in the ocean or washed up on the shores of the Maldive Islands and because they resembled giant coconuts, they were thought to grow on submarine coconut palms. Since only nonviable fruits float, the palm has never grown anywhere but the Seychelles. It was not until the mid-18th century that the true origin and nature of these trees was known. When the rare fruits were found edible, they were credited with fantastic medicinal and aphrodisiacal properties. James C. McCurrach (1960) wrote:

> They were particularly credited with being a positive antidote for every form of poison. Princes and potentates of the times, much inclined to the poisoning of their enemies, lived in daily dread of themselves being poisoned. It is not surprising that they were willing to offer large sums for these mysterious objects which they firmly believed could purify any fluid, no matter what poison it contained.

In the late 17th century, a British general who visited the Seychelles supposedly associated the palm with the Biblical tree of knowledge and its forbidden fruit when he beheld the trees with their phallic male inflorescences and their suggestive fruits and seeds.

The trees are extremely slow growing, especially when younger: it may take 20 years or even longer for the trunk to start forming. The species does not tolerate frost and is adaptable only to zones 10b and 11. It also needs regular and adequate moisture, partial shade when in seedling stage, and sun thereafter. It is not fussy about soil type as long as it is fast draining.

LOXOCOCCUS is a highly endangered monotypic genus of solitary-trunked, pinnate-leaved, monoecious palm. The genus name is from Greek words meaning "slanting" and "seed." The epithet is Latin for "rock

dwelling" and refers to the habitat in which the species grows. PLATE 570.

Loxococcus rupicola is endemic to Sri Lanka, south of the Indian subcontinent, where it grows in mountainous rain forest at elevations of 1000 to 5000 feet. It is critically endangered because of destruction of the rain forest.

The slender, gray trunk slowly attains a height of 20 feet or slightly more. It is nearly smooth in its older parts and indistinctly ringed in its younger parts. The 2-foot-tall crownshaft is deep green, smooth, cylindrical, and barely thicker than the trunk. The leaf crown is hemispherical or slightly more rounded, open, and airy with 10 or fewer leaves. Each leaf is 10 feet long and is ascending but beautifully arching when new and spreading when older. The stout 10-inch-long petiole holds many widely spaced, narrow, deep green, 2-foot-long leaflets; in young leaves, the leaflets grow from the rachis at an angle which creates a V-shaped leaf but older leaves have spreading leaflets that are almost in a single flat plane. The inflorescences grow from beneath the crownshaft and are short, with stiff but spreading flowering branches that bear both male and female blossoms. The fruits are 1 inch long, egg shaped, and red to reddish brown when mature.

This beautiful palm is almost absent from cultivation outside of a few botanical gardens. It is reportedly slow growing, needs a constantly moist but well-drained acidic soil, and does not tolerate cold.

LYTOCARYUM is a genus of two pinnate-leaved, monoecious palms in southern Brazil. The inflorescences grow from among the leaf bases and are once branched with numerous short flowering branches bearing small unisexual blossoms of both sexes. The fruits are brown, 1-inch-long ellipsoids with shallowly sectioned outer flesh as though they were animal cells in the process of dividing. The genus name is derived from two Greek words meaning "loose" and "nut," a reference to the surface of the fruits. PLATE 571.

Lytocaryum hoehnei is endemic to a small area of wet, mountainous forest in southern Brazil, where it grows at elevations of 2640 to 3200 feet, and where it is nearly extinct. The epithet honors 20th-century Brazilian botanist and collector, Frederico C. Hoehne.

The species differs from *L. weddellianum* mainly in its longer leaflets that are even more silvery on their undersurfaces, and in its slightly larger fruits. It is also perhaps even more beautiful than *L. weddellianum* but is virtually unknown in cultivation. It would have the same cultural requirements, with possibly slightly more cold tolerance.

Lytocaryum weddellianum is endemic to southeastern coastal Brazil, where it occurs in the undergrowth of lowland rain forest to an elevation of 3000 feet. It is endangered because of development along Brazil's coast but is commonly cultivated, especially in containers in Europe, and this may be its only hope of survival. The epithet honors Hugh A. Weddell, a 19th-century British botanist and collector in South America.

The solitary trunk slowly grows to a height of 15 feet with a diameter of 4 inches in habitat but in cultivation is seldom taller than 6 feet. The stem is usually covered in dark fibers from the leaf sheaths and with the pale stubs of the dead petioles. The leaf crown is spherical and open, and has beautifully arching, 2- to 3-foot-long leaves on 1-foot-long petioles with shaggily hairy margins. The leaves resemble those of pygmy date palm, *Phoenix roebelenii,* but are smaller. The newer leaves often show a slight twist of the rachis at its midpoint. The numerous 4- to 6-inch-long, linear-lanceolate leaflets are regularly spaced along the arching rachis. They are deep green above and grayish green to almost completely gray beneath, and grow from the rachis in a single flat plane.

This palm cannot withstand the full sun, especially of hot climates. It has a modicum of cold tolerance and is adaptable to zones 10 and 11 and, if occasionally protected, is possible—because of its diminutive stature—in 9b. It does not tolerate drought and needs regular and adequate moisture as well as a rich, friable, well-drained soil that is slightly acidic; it grows in southern Florida if protected from the sun and if the soil is either amended or heavily mulched. This deliciously elegant miniature palm should be sited in an intimate, under-canopy site in the garden. It makes one of the finest house or container plants. Its only fault is that it is slow growing. PLATE 571.

MANICARIA is a monotypic genus of pinnate-leaved, monoecious palm in tropical America. The genus name is Latin for "gloves" and refers to the large, tough fibrous primary bracts of the inflorescences. The epithet is Latin for "sack-bearing" and alludes to the saclike peduncular bract. PLATES 572 & 573.

Manicaria saccifera occurs naturally in two large and disjunct regions. The northern and western part of its range is centered in Central America (from southern Belize and eastern Guatemala, through the Caribbean coastal regions of northern Honduras, eastern Nicaragua, Costa Rica, and Panama) and the Pacific coastal lowlands of Colombia and extreme northwestern Ecuador, where the species is a denizen of coastal swamps. The other area is east of the Andes in northern South America and includes eastern Colombia, northeastern Peru, eastern and southern Venezuela, Guyana, Surinam, French Guiana, and adjacent Amazonian Brazil; here the species grows in season-ally inundated rain forest, always as a large undergrowth subject in wet areas or along the banks of rivers, often forming dense stands or colonies. It is infrequently found on the wet slopes of the Andean foothills.

The palm forms a solitary or sometimes sparsely clumping trunk to 30 feet tall and 10 inches in diameter but is usually 6 feet high. In nature, several dead leaves persist and mostly hide the fibrous, litter-trapping stem. The erect, elliptical leaves ascend from the trunk and may be 30 feet long but usually are 20 feet long; they are 4 to 6 feet wide and mostly entire and unsegmented until the wind or age separates them into segments of greatly varying widths. The blade is a rich, deep emerald green on both surfaces and is heavily corrugated with the margins of the unsegregated pinnae and serrated on its outer margins with the evidence of their apices. When they are older, the 4- to 6-foot-long soft petioles easily break under the weight of the immense leaf blades. The inflorescences grow from among the leaf bases and are once branched and 3 feet long. In nature they are usually hidden (because of their short length) by the leaf bases and the litter trapped therein. These flower clusters are unique because of the large fibrous, saclike primary bract that covers them like a hood. It is a pyramidal mass of "woven" fibers that is pushed away only as the peduncle of the flowering branches elongates and the fragrant flowers start to open, but it usually remains hanging in the leaf crown. The hard, woody fruits are borne at the ends of the 4-foot-long, lignified peduncle and are round or barbell shaped with one or two lobes and are always covered in pyramidal tubercular, curly tipped projections. They are durable and, in coastal or lowland stands of the species, detach from the trees and float down the rivers to the sea to be often seen on distant shores.

The species is, outside of botanical gardens, rare in cultivation, mainly because of its tropical requirements: it cannot withstand temperatures below 50°F. It needs year-round warmth, copious and constant moisture, a humus-laden acidic soil, and shade or partial shade when young. It grows in the open in full sun, but the rich color and integrity of its blades are compromised: the leaves are always tattered and unsightly when exposed to the elements. If the proper growing conditions can be provided, it makes one of the most startlingly beautiful and impressive plantings possible.

The palm has, in the past, had many human uses. Its great leaves are used in the species' habitat for thatch and, at one time, were used as the sails for canoes. The remarkable peduncular bract is still used to make hats that need no weaving, and nowadays for making hats and other souvenirs for tourists who visit the Amazon. The stems were formerly felled by the Warao people of Venezuela to extract the pith, a source of sago or palm starch; the saclike bract was used for hats as well as loin cloths; and the liquid endosperm of the unripe fruits was imbibed for nourishment and refreshment as well as used as a cough syrup.

MAROJEJYA is a genus of two pinnate-leaved, monoecious palms endemic to eastern Madagascar, one of them extremely rare in habitat, both of unusual beauty and magnificence. The inflorescences are short with thick rope-like flowering branches and are almost hidden by the leaf bases. They are unisexual but both sexes are found on a single tree. The oblong to nearly round fruits are formed in clusters, are less than 1 inch in diameter, and are red or black when mature.

The genus name is derived from "Marojejy," a mountainous region of northeastern Madagascar. PLATES 574–577.

Marojejya darianii is an extremely rare and endangered species endemic to one small site in Madagascar, a swampy valley bottom in dense rain forest at 1300 feet elevation. The epithet honors Mardy Darian, a palm collector in southern California and the first Westerner to track down the location of the species in habitat.

In nature, the species forms a solitary trunk to 50 feet tall with a diameter of 1 foot. Its dimensions under cultivation are not known as it has only been available since 1985. The leaf crown is in the form of a gigantic shaving brush as the leaves grow erect and ascending from the top of the trunk, without benefit of petioles. In individuals past the juvenile stage the leaves are 12 to 15 feet long, 4 feet wide at their midpoints, and are undivided when new, with a linear-obovate outline that is apically bifid. Both surfaces are deep green and deeply grooved with the outlines of the fused or cryptic pinnate segments. The rachis is stout but soft and is much lighter green. Time and the elements usually tatter the blades into pinnae of variable widths.

Although none are in cultivation, mature palms are startling in their beauty and splendor because of the dimensions of their immense and undivided new leaves. The cultural requirements are water and more water, in an acidic, fast-draining soil. This palm is reportedly immune to temperatures at or even slightly below freezing once past the seedling stage. It also seems adaptable to sun from an early age. It is slow growing in its seedling stage but reportedly much faster thereafter. It makes a stunningly beautiful container subject when young and is adaptable to a greenhouse if given enough light and moisture. PLATES 574 & 575.

Marojejya insignis is endemic to the mountainous rain forest on the east coast of Madagascar, where it grows at elevations from sea level to 3700 feet. The epithet is Latin for "remarkable."

This species is smaller than *M. darianii*, its trunk attaining a maximum height of 20 feet in habitat, but its leaves are slightly larger. The leaves are borne on short to 4-foot-long petioles and are segmented in their apical halves into many narrow, regularly spaced dark green leaflets, each of which is 3 feet long, stiff but not rigid, and grows from the rachis at only a slight angle, resulting in a nearly flat leaf.

The species is as beautiful and spectacular as *M. darianii*, but it is not nearly as sought after. It has the same cultural requirements as *M. darianii* but is probably slightly more hardy to cold. PLATES 576 & 577.

MASOALA is a genus of two massive pinnate-leaved, monoecious palms in Madagascar. One has a stout trunk and leaves bearing many linear leaflets; the other species has nearly unsegmented, ascending, and erect leaves. The large inflorescence consists of a long, bract-covered peduncle with long, wormlike yellowish flowering branches at its end. The fruits are round and brownish yellow.

Both species are rare and endangered in habitat and both are still rare in cultivation and reportedly slow growing. They are intolerant of freezing temperatures.

The genus is named for the area in Madagascar where one species (*M. madagascariensis*) has its habitat.

Masoala kona is endemic to central southeastern Madagascar, where it grows in low mountainous rain forest. The epithet is the aboriginal name for the palm.

The solitary trunk grows to a maximum height of 25 feet in habitat but is usually much shorter, with a maximum diameter of 8 inches. It is covered in old leaf bases in its younger parts. The leaf crown looks like a narrow feather duster and contains 15 ascending, 10- to 12-foot-long stiff, unarching leaves. The leaflets are fused into 6 to 15 upswept, pleated segments, the longest and widest being near the bottom of the blade and 6 feet long and 2 feet wide. They grow from the rachis at angles that create a V shape to the blade, and their color is bright emerald green on both surfaces.

This impressive species has strong visual affinities to its relative, *Marojejya darianii*.

Masoala madagascariensis is endemic to northeastern Madagascar, where it grows in lowland rain forest. The epithet is Latin for "of Madagascar."

In habitat the solitary trunk grows to a maximum height of 30 feet but is usually much shorter; its diameter is 8 inches. The leaf crown is dense, less than hemispherical, and shaped like a feather duster, with 24 ascending, straight, and unarching 10- to 12-foot-long leaves on 2-

foot-long, stout petioles. The rachis is often twisted near its base or midpoint so that the plane of the leaf is positioned vertically. The 2-foot-long leaflets are regularly spaced along the rachis and grow from it in a single flat plane but are forwards pointing towards the apex of the blade. They are narrowly elliptic, long pointed, and medium green.

This impressive species is so slow growing that its planting is for future generations.

MAURITIA is a genus of two massive, palmate-leaved, dioecious palms in South America. The leaves are immense with many deeply cut segments which, in individuals past the juvenile stage, grow at slightly different angles from the petiole. The inflorescences are also massive and consist of distichous and horizontally spreading woody branches held at right angles to the stem by an even woodier bract and from which a curtain of smaller flowering branches descends with either male or female blossoms but not both. The oily and edible round or oblong fruits are covered with large scales and are red to reddish brown.

The genus name honors Johan Mauritz van Nassau-Siegen, the 17th-century Dutch governor of the West India Company of Brazil. PLATES 578 & 579.

Mauritia carana is indigenous to western Amazonia in extreme southern Venezuela, southeastern Colombia, northeastern Peru, and west central Brazil, where it grows as a canopy-scape in rain forest, wet savannas, and along rivers on white sands at low elevations. The epithet is one of the aboriginal names for the palm.

The species is similar to *M. flexuosa* but smaller, differing in the following respects: the trunk grows to a maximum height of 50 feet and has a larger shag of dead leaves and fibers below the crown of living blades; the leaves are also smaller (10 feet wide) with fewer segments that are almost completely pendent; the leaf bases are clothed in a mass of fibers which usually hides them from view; the inflorescences are slightly longer; and the fruits are rounded and larger.

The cultural requirements of this extraordinarily beautiful palm are virtually the same as those of *M. flexuosa* save it is not as needy of acidic soil.

Mauritia flexuosa occurs naturally in a great area of northern South America, east of the Andes Mountains, including all of Amazonia except its eastern part, always in open sites. It grows along rivers and streams and in swamps, from elevations of a few hundred to 3000 feet and, in swamps of the flatlands, forms immense colonies to the exclusion of most other trees. The epithet is Latin for "flexible" and alludes to the leaf segments as well as the massive petioles.

The solitary trunks attain heights of 80 feet or more and diameters of 1 or 2 feet in habitat. Their younger portions are grayish green to tan with widely spaced, undulating, dark rings of leaf base scars, while the older parts become light gray or nearly white and are relatively smooth. The giant leaf crown is hemispherical as the living leaves rarely descend beneath the horizontal, but there are usually several (nearly) pendent dying and dead leaves which create, especially from any distance, the visual effect of a spherical mass of leaves. The leaves are 15 feet wide on large light green petioles to 30 feet long with bases 4 feet wide and of an even lighter hue. The great leaves are basically circular and divided into 200 or more narrow and stiff but not rigid segments whose tips are pendent and each of which is 6 to 7 feet long and extends almost to the petiole. They grow at slightly different angles from the leaf stalk to give a three-dimensional, almost pinnate, visual effect, especially in leaves that are strongly costapalmate. The leaves of seedlings and younger individuals are not nearly so massive and are flat, with many fewer segments. The inflorescences are single giant woody branches held horizontal from among the leaf bases by an even tougher woody bract on two opposite sides of the palm; they are 6 feet or more in length. From these distichous branches grow the pendent cream-colored and subsidiary 1- to 2-foot-long branches that descend from the main branch like a curtain and bear the unisexual small blossoms. The woody main bracts gradually break down after the flowers open and, in female trees, the heavy clusters of red fruits are pendent on the single remaining flowering branch that also becomes pendent. The individual fruits are 3 inches long, round or oblong, deep red, and covered in large but not overlapping scales on the outer skin.

This is one of the most grandiose, impressive, and extravagantly beautiful palms. Its majesty must be seen to be appreciated. Alas, the species is cold tender and is adaptable only to zones 10b and 11. It is also nearly aquatic and, while it survives in drier sites of tropical climates, it does not fulfill its potential unless provided with constant and copious moisture as well as nearly constant warmth. It prefers acidic soil.

The species is of great significance to the local peoples: the fruits are eaten raw or made into flour and, when fermented, into alcoholic beverages; the oil expressed from the fruits is an important commercial industry in Brazil; the fibers of the young leaves are used for making ropes, hammocks, and utensils; the pith of the petioles is used to make mats and paper; and wine and sago starch are culled from the trunks of felled trees.

MAURITIELLA is a genus of three palmate-leaved, dioecious palms in South America. It is closely related to and named after *Mauritia*. *Mauritiella* differs from *Mauritia* in its smaller stature, its clustering habit, and its much smaller inflorescences that are not arranged distichously. The juvenile leaves of both genera are radically different from those of mature individuals, with many fewer segments growing a flat plane. Likewise, the male and female blossoms of both genera are found on separate trees. The fruits of the two genera are similar, but those of *Mauritiella* are usually smaller and not so distinctly scaly in appearance.

These lovely species do not tolerate cold and are nearly aquatic, requiring constant and copious moisture. Indeed, in habitat, they often grow either in the streams and rivers or in land that is regularly flooded by the watercourses. They are not so exacting about acidic soil preferences as are the two species of *Mauritia* and do well on several soils, as long as they are constantly moist. They are adapted to full sun even in youth but luxuriate in partial shade. In a much more diminutive way, they are as beautiful as the species of *Mauritia*. PLATES 580–583.

Mauritiella aculeata is indigenous to northern South America, where it grows along the banks of the Orinoco and its tributaries at low elevations, in extreme southern Venezuela, western Colombia, and northwestern Brazil. The epithet is Latin for "prickly," an allusion to the leaflet margins with their tiny little teeth as well as the bases of the stems with their small root spines.

The numerous clustering stems grow to 25 feet, if that, with a maximum diameter of 4 inches. They are light, almost white, and half reclining, sometimes twisting, never straight, and often lean out over the water along the banks of the streams and rivers along which they grow. The lower portions of the trunks bear small root spines and have a small mound of buttressing aerial roots at their bases. The species forms pseudo-crownshafts with its silvery glaucous large leaf sheaths. The leaf crowns are open because of the long petioles and are hemispherical to spherical. The few leaves in the crown are each 30 inches wide and circular with many narrow segments extending almost to the petiole. The segments are dark green above but a beautiful silvery green beneath. They are 0.5 inch wide and pendent in their apical halves, growing from the petiole at slightly different angles. The fruits are oblong, 1.5 inches long, and olive colored, maturing to reddish brown.

This clumper is simply beautiful. Its enchantingly thin, usually sinuous stems and its open, weeping, silvery shimmering crowns are diaphanously exquisite. It is not in cultivation outside of botanical gardens.

Mauritiella armata is the most widespread species in the genus and covers almost all of Amazonia and adjacent uplands in northern South America, where it grows along the rivers and streams, in open savannas, and in rain forest and clearings therein. It is found mostly at low elevations but, in the Guyanas, can be found on mountainous rain forest to an elevation of 4500 feet. The epithet is Latin for "armed" and refers to the stout root spines on the lower trunk.

The trunks attain heights of 60 feet and diameters of 10 to 12 inches. Like the trunks of other species, they have small root spines on their lower portions and a small mound of stilt roots at their bases. The stems are usually straight and almost white but, in their older parts, are indistinctly ringed; their younger parts are distinctly ringed with widely spaced leaf base scars and are reminiscent of the beautiful stems of *Dypsis lutescens* or *D. cabadae*. The leaf crowns are hemispherical because of the mostly ascending leaves and are open because of the long petioles. The leaves are hemispherical to nearly circular and 3 to 4 feet wide. The many narrow segments are glossy deep green above and silvery beneath, extend virtually to the petiole, and are gracefully arching with pendent apices. The fruits are similar to those of *M. aculeata*.

The clumps of *M. armata* are usually more sparse than those of *M. aculeata* and young clumps are endearing while mature palms are noble in appearance. PLATES 580–583.

Mauritiella macroclada is indigenous to the Pacific slopes of the western Andes Mountains in Colombia and northwestern Ecuador, where it grows to an elevation of nearly 3000 feet. The epithet is from Greek and Latin words meaning "large" and "branch" and alludes to the relatively massive petioles and leaf sheaths.

This species is similar in appearance to *M. armata* with the exceptions of its more robust leaf bases and petioles and its stiffer leaf segments. It is not yet in cultivation (2002).

MAXBURRETIA is a genus of three small, clustering, spiny, palmate-leaved, monoecious or dioecious palms in Thailand and peninsular Malaysia. One species has subterranean stems. The leaf bases are fibrous, and the fibers usually persist as spinelike projections on the leaf crown or adherent and persistent on the stem. Inflorescences are sparsely branched, erect, and usually project out of the leaf crown. The flowers are either bisexual or separately sexed on different individuals. The fruits are small, rounded, and black when mature.

The genus is related to *Chamaerops* and *Guihaia*. The genus name honors Karl E. Maximilian Burret, a 20th-century German palm biologist. PLATE 584.

Maxburretia furtadoana is a rare species endemic to open, wet but scrubby forest on limestone cliffs and hills of peninsular Thailand at low elevations. The epithet honors Caetano X. Furtado, an early 20th-century palm botanist and taxonomist.

The sparsely clustering trunks slowly attain maximum heights of 10 feet in habitat. They are 8 inches in diameter with persistent, spiny leaf bases only 2 inches in diameter without the sheaths. The leaf crowns are open and hemispherical to almost spherical. The leaves are borne on 2-foot-long unarmed petioles and are hemispherical to nearly spherical. They are 30 inches wide, with many narrow, half limp, long-tipped segments that extend into the blade nearly to the petiole. Leaf color is glossy deep green above and grayish green beneath.

These little palms, although extremely rare in cultivation outside of their habitat, are picturesque and, if the spiny leaf bases are kept, a real curiosity in the garden. They look especially good in a rock garden, although they are not drought tolerant. They thrive on limestone soils as well as neutral or even slightly acidic ones and grow equally well in full sun or partial shade; however, they are adaptable only to zones 10 and 11.

Maxburretia gracilis is a rare and endangered species endemic to the Langkawi Islands off the northwestern coast of peninsular Malaysia, where it is an undergrowth subject in soil pockets of the limestone hills at low elevations in a manner similar to *Coccothrinax* species on the mogotes (limestone hills) of Cuba. The epithet is Latin for "graceful."

This sparsely clustering species has one to four stems of unequal heights to a clump. The trunks grow to 30 feet in habitat and are covered in their younger parts with a beautiful pattern of leaf base stubs and fibers, while the older parts are light brown and graced with distinct and closely spaced rings of leaf base scars. The leaf crown is hemispherical and open because of the length of the leaf petioles. The leaves are 2 feet wide and circular or almost so. The segments extend two-thirds of the way into the blade, and are elliptic-lanceolate and light green above and grayish green below.

The species is not in cultivation outside of botanical gardens, and this is a shame as it is the most beautiful species of the genus.

Maxburretia rupicola is a rare and endangered species endemic to limestone cliffs and hills of peninsular Malaysia at low elevations, where it grows in wet but scrubby forest. The epithet is Latin for "rock dwelling" and alludes to the palm's habitat.

This species is similar in a horticultural sense to *M. furtadoana*, differing in its smaller stature, longer petioles, stiffer segments, and more sparsely clustering stems; it is often found as a solitary-trunked specimen in habitat. It seems to be absent from cultivation outside of botanical gardens but doubtless has the same requirements as does *M. furtadoana*.

MEDEMIA is a monotypic genus of rare and endangered palmate-leaved, dioecious palm endemic to Sudan. The genus name may come from a Greek word meaning "no one" or "nothing," and, if it does, would doubtless allude to the near wasteland that is now the palm's habitat. PLATES 585 & 586.

Medemia argun grows in wadis of true desert, the lower portions of its trunk often covered in wind-blown sand. It forms a solitary trunk to 30 feet or more in height and a diameter of 1 foot in habitat. The stems of younger individuals are covered in persistent leaf bases, but older trees have brown trunks with closely spaced rings of leaf base scars. The leaf crown is dense and spherical and usually has a short shag of dead leaves at its base. The 4- to 5-foot-long, strongly costapalmate bluish or grayish green leaves lack a hastula and are borne on stout, 3-foot-long yellowish petioles that, in younger individuals, are armed on their margins with black teeth; older palms have unarmed leaf stalks. The yellowish orange petiole (costa) extends well into the blade and causes it to recurve. The leaf segments also extend deep into the blade and are stiff, rigid, and wide-lanceolate, with long tapering and almost threadlike tips. The inflorescences are similar to those of *Bismarckia*. The fruits are egg shaped, under 2 inches long, and glossy black when mature.

The palm is related to *Bismarckia* and *Hyphaene*. It looks like the latter genus but even more like a bonsai *Washingtonia* species. The species was presumed by many botanists to be extinct as scientists had not seen it since 1963, but in 1995 Martin Gibbons of England and Tobias Spanner of Germany found the species in Wadi Delah in Sudan. They returned to the desert in 1996, found more locations for the species, and brought back viable seed, which they have since germinated and distributed through their retail nurseries in England and Germany. Several seedlings now grow around the world, including southern Florida. The palm probably has the same cultural requirements as *Bismarckia* as far as minimum temperatures go (Gibbons 1993). It also should be slow growing and drought tolerant, as well as sun loving and accepting of alkalinity and salinity.

The fruits are reportedly edible. The trees were cultivated in ancient Egypt and the fruits included in graves 3500 years ago as gifts for the dearly departed.

METROXYLON is a genus of five large to massive, pinnate-leaved, monoecious palms in the Moluccas, New Guinea, the Solomon Islands, the Vanuatu archipelago, Fiji Islands, the Carolines, and Western Samoa.

There are clustering and solitary-trunked species in the genus, and all but one species is monocarpic (or hapaxanthic), meaning that the stems flower terminally and then die. The monocarpic species have large inflorescences whose branches are either tiered and have the general shape of a Christmas tree or are upward sweeping and look like gigantic insect antennae but are horizontally spreading or even pendent when the fruits mature. The fruits are relatively large and covered in tough, overlapping scales; they make beautiful knickknacks when polished after hardening off. One universally distinguishing character is the massive leaf sheaths and petioles, all of which exhibit half-ringed markings, consisting of groups of small black spines resembling the record made by a seismograph as it registers a mild tremor. In addition, all the species have spines on petioles and leaf rachises as well as incipient aerial roots growing from the younger rings of leaf base scars.

All species are extremely tender to cold, are adapted only to zone 11 and often are marginal in 10b. They are also all water lovers and, while they grow in poor soil, really appreciate and luxuriate in a rich, organically based medium. All are adapted to full sun when past the seedling stage, and all are invariably fast growing, given enough moisture and a soil that is not too poor.

These great palms are the essence of the tropical look and are exotic and beautiful in the extreme. Some people find them overpowering, primitive, and grotesque looking. One rather refined woman, who saw one of us (Bob) bending over backwards to photograph the awesome crown of *M. vitiense*, remarked with a slight shudder that she thought it was "Jurassic looking." And it is. Bob did not tell her that in a few years the remarkable palm would probably be dead and gone because it would have flowered.

The genus name is derived from two Greek words meaning "heart" and "wood" and alludes to the starchy pith, or sago, in the trunk. PLATES 587–595.

Metroxylon amicarum is endemic to the Caroline Islands in Micronesia, where it grows in mountainous rain forest. The epithet is Latin for "of friends" and was bestowed when the species was thought to hail from the Friendly Islands (now Tonga Islands).

This tall, magnificent species has solitary trunks to heights of 80 feet but seeming to mostly top out at 60 feet. It is usually covered in its younger parts with massive old leaf bases but, in its older parts, is ringed with widely spaced leaf base scars. The leaf crown is hemispherical at most and is usually shaped like a gigantic shuttlecock because of the stiff, ascending, and erect leaves, which are 15 feet long on 3- to 4-foot-long petioles. The leaflets are numerous, 3 feet long, lanceolate, and dark green, and grow from the rachis at several angles to create a plumose leaf. This is the only nonmonocarpic species; the inflorescences are much narrower than those of the monocarpic species, and they grow from amidst the leaf bases and are erect until the large fruits make them pendent. The fruits are ovoid and 3 to 4 inches long, covered in large, glossy brown scales.

The seeds are extremely hard and are still used as "vegetable ivory" as are the seeds of *Phytelephas* species; the palm is called the Caroline ivory-nut palm in certain parts of the world. It is as massive and as striking as the large *Raphia* species and is spectacular in the landscape. It is also probably the hardiest to cold of the species. PLATES 587 & 588.

Metroxylon sagu is probably endemic to New Guinea but is now naturalized all over the Asian tropics. The epithet is the aboriginal name for the starch in the stems.

The stems of this clumping species sometimes attain heights of 60 feet but more often are half that stature before flowering. They are 2 feet in diameter and are clothed in their upper parts with old leaf bases, their lower parts rough but graced with widely spaced rings of leaf base scars. The leaf crowns are shaped like gigantic shuttlecocks and hold erect but arching leaves that are 20 feet or more in length and bear many dark green leaflets, the longest of which are 5 feet. They grow from the rachis at an angle that creates a slight V shape to the leaf. The great terminal inflorescences are 25 feet tall with upward-thrusting primary branches and subbranches. The fruits are the size of baseballs and a light brown or greenish brown, and are covered in large, overlapping scales.

The species varies in form according to how tall the stems grow, the length of the leaves, and the amount of spininess thereon. Some forms have spiny leaf sheaths, petioles, and rachises with partial rings of flexible but vicious golden spines, each of which can be 3 inches long, while others are nearly spineless. This variability is doubtless due to the palm's long history of cultivation. It has been grown for millennia for the sago starch in its trunks; the stems were felled before flowering, as the formation and maturation of the flowers and fruits tend to drain the stem of its reserves.

This is one of the world's most impressive palms. Because of its suckering habit, it can make a great veritable, tiered wall of sumptuously beautiful and tropical-looking foliage. Alas, all forms of the palm are marginal if not impossible even in zone 10b. In addition they need constant and copious moisture and a rich, humus-laden soil; their favored habitat is a mucky swamp. In addition to seed germination, this one can also be propagated by careful removal of the suckers. PLATES 589 & 590.

Metroxylon salomonense occurs naturally in eastern Papua New Guinea, the Vanuatu archipelago, and the

Solomon Islands, where it grows mostly in low, swampy areas but also in lowland rain forest to an elevation of 2640 feet. The epithet is Latin for "of Salomon (Solomons)," a reference to one of its habitats.

Its massive, light brown trunk attains a height of 50 feet before flowering and may be 4 feet in diameter. It is covered in its upper parts with massive leaf bases but with widely spaced rings of leaf base scars otherwise. The great leaf crown is less than hemispherical, generally shaped like a wide shuttlecock. The leaves are 30 feet long on massive 4- to 5-foot-long petioles. The sheaths, petioles, and even the leaf rachises bear large, yellowish spines. The dark green leaflets grow from the rachis at only a slight angle and create a leaf that is nearly flat. The terminal inflorescence is 12 feet tall, with horizontally spreading branches from which descend curtains of whitish tertiary flowering branches. The yellowish green, scaly fruits are apple shaped and 3 inches long.

This is perhaps the most impressive of the solitary-trunked species. PLATES 591–593.

Metroxylon vitiense is endemic to the Fiji Islands, where it grows in rain forest and in low, swampy areas. The epithet is Latin for "of Viti," one of the Fiji Islands.

The solitary trunk attains a height of 50 feet before flowering and a diameter of 3 feet. The stem is mostly free of leaf bases but is strongly ringed with widely spaced leaf scars. The leaf crown is relatively narrow and in the form of a gigantic shaving brush, with erect, 12- to 15-foot-long leaves. The 4-foot-long, dark green leaflets are stiff and grow from the massive rachis in a nearly single flat plane in older leaves. The upper parts of the tree are spiny, as well as the sheaths, petioles, leaf rachises, and leaflets. PLATES 594 & 595.

Metroxylon warburgii occurs in the Vanuatu archipelago and the Solomon Islands, where it grows mostly in low, swampy areas but also on hill slopes, always at low elevations. The epithet honors Otto Warburg (1859–1938), German plant collector and botanist.

It is the smallest of the solitary-trunked species with a stem that only attains 25 feet of height and a diameter of 1 foot. The leaf crown is hemispherical and the leaves are 10 feet long. While the smallest in stature, this species has the most beautiful leaves in the genus as they are more arching and the deep green leaflets are not as stiff with pendent apices. They grow from the rachis at an angle that creates a slightly V-shaped leaf.

MORATIA is a monotypic genus of pinnate-leaved, monoecious palm endemic to central and northeastern New Caledonia. The genus is closely related to *Cyphokentia* and will probably be subsumed under that genus in the future.

The genus name honors French botanist Philippe Morat, the original collector of the species. The epithet is Latin for "wax-bearing" and alludes to the beautiful crownshaft. PLATE 596.

Moratia cerifera occurs naturally in mountainous rain forest from sea level to 2500 feet.

Its solitary trunk grows slowly to 60 feet with a diameter of 6 or 7 inches in habitat. It is light to dark brown with distinct but closely spaced, ridged rings of leaf scars in its upper parts. The crownshaft is 2 feet tall, cylindrical, but slightly bulged at its base and slightly tapering above that point. It is deep orange but covered with a thick layer of pure white wax, which, unless removed, makes the shaft the same color. The leaf crown is open and nearly spherical because of the few leaves that are arched and recurving. They are borne on short (less than 1 foot long) orange to yellow petioles and are 7 feet long. The leaflets grow from the rachis at an angle that creates a V-shaped leaf. They are a deep yellowish to pure emerald green and are linear-lanceolate, long tapering, and stiff. The inflorescences, which grow from beneath the crownshaft, are large, 3-foot-wide, spreading grayish green flowering branches that have a gigantic spidery appearance. The small fruits are reddish, round, and 0.5 inch wide.

This is a stunningly beautiful palm. Its white crownshaft and round crown with recurving leaves create a tableau that seems the essence of what a palm should look like. If only it were easier and faster growing! The trees are so slow growing as to be impractical for the average person, which accounts for this palm's rarity in cultivation.

MYRIALEPIS is a monotypic genus of clustering, pinnate-leaved, dioecious climbing palm in Myanmar, Thailand, Cambodia, Laos, Vietnam, peninsular Malaysia, and Sumatra. The genus name is from two Greek words meaning "ten thousand" (and, by extension, "innumerable") and "scale" and alludes to the myriad tiny scales on the outer skins of the fruits. The epithet is Latin for "paradox."

Myrialepis paradoxa grows at the edges of rain forest and in clearings therein as well as along the banks of rivers and streams from sea level to an elevation of 3500 feet, often forming large thickets and colonies.

Its clustering stems can climb to great heights, are 3 inches in diameter, and are ringed with whorls of vicious, golden spines. The leaves are widely spaced along the reddish brown stems, to 10 feet long, with widely spaced linear and long pointed, dark green, pendent leaflets. The rachises extend beyond their leaves to form 4-foot-long cirri that have a few pairs of backward-pointing barbs. The inflorescences grow from the uppermost leaf axils, including the terminal one, and are 2 feet long and much branched. The fruits are 1-inch-wide greenish brown balls and are covered in minute scales that impart a glistening luster to the skin of each one.

The species is similar in appearance to many *Calamus* species and other rattan genera but is most closely related to *Plectocomiopsis*. It is not in cultivation outside of botanical gardens but, because of its densely clustering habit, would make an effective, tropical-looking wall of foliage from a safe distance. It can, like most other rattans, be pruned severely to try to keep it in bounds, but in a tropical climate, which it requires, is rampant.

NANNORRHOPS is a monotypic genus of palmate-leaved monoecious, monocarpic palm in desert regions of the Middle East. The genus name is a combination of two Greek words meaning "dwarf" and "shrub." The epithet is a Latinized form of the surname "Ritchie" and commemorates the original collector. PLATES 597–600.

Nannorrhops ritchiana occurs naturally in the dry mountainous areas of the Arabian Peninsula, Iran, Afghanistan, and Pakistan, where it grows usually in stream beds or on the sides of hills. The only common name seems to be mazari palm, which is the vernacular in the palm's habitat.

The palm forms clustering trunks that are mostly subterranean but sometimes emerge from the ground and reach heights of 15 feet. Emergent trunks are covered in brown leaf bases and orange-brown fiber and are 8 inches in diameter. A clump can reach 20 feet tall and wide after many years, but most mature clumps are 6 feet tall and 8 feet wide. The leaves are 4 feet wide and are wedge shaped to semicircular. There are 30 stiff, narrowly lanceolate segments extending almost to the petiole, each one split to half its length. The leaves are held mostly erect on 3-foot-long petioles, which usually but not always bear tiny teeth along their margins; they have, when new, patches of light brown fine, woolly fibers. Leaf color is dull grayish green to bluish or grayish green to a chalky blue-gray color. The inflorescence is terminal and the stem bearing it dies off after fruit formation. It is much branched, 6 feet long or tall, and is held erect, bearing small white bisexual flowers. The fruits are 0.5 inch wide, rounded, orange-brown, and reportedly edible.

The species is slightly susceptible to lethal yellowing disease. In dry climates, mazari palm is hardy to cold, being adaptable to zones 8 through 11 and marginal in 7. It is drought tolerant and thrives on many soils, even calcareous ones. It needs full sun at all ages and is slow growing. Because of its form, color, and hardiness, the species is valuable as a strong accent along sunny paths and in sunny borders or the cactus and succulent garden. It makes a nice

potted specimen for outdoors, but the container must have unimpeded drainage. It is not known to be grown indoors and is probably not a good candidate.

NENGA is a genus of five pinnate-leaved, monoecious palms in Myanmar, Thailand, Vietnam, peninsular Malaysia, Sumatra, Java, and Borneo. The genus has both clustering and solitary-trunked species, but all have crownshafts of varying dimensions and tightness. The inflorescences grow from beneath the crownshafts and are small, pendent, and once branched; they bear unisexual flowers of both sexes. The fruits are mostly small and are invariably egg shaped or teat shaped and range from brilliant red to purple or black.

All the species are intolerant of frost and need partial shade, especially in hot climates, abundant and regular moisture, and a decent, fast-draining soil. Only one species (*N. pumila*) is in general cultivation outside of botanical gardens, but all species are deliciously gorgeous palms of unparalleled elegance.

The genus name is a corruption of the Indonesian (Javanese) name for a similar palm in the genus *Pinanga* from which this genus was separated.

Nenga gajah is endemic to Sumatra, where it grows as an undergrowth subject in mountainous rain forest at elevations of 2640 to 3000 feet and is critically endangered because of rain forest destruction. The epithet is a part of the aboriginal name for the palm and translates as "elephant." This is an anomalous species in the genus as it is unlike the others: its inflorescences are borne among the leaf bases and not beneath the loose crownshaft; and the pendent fruit clusters are in a congested form, like a club, and similar to the primitive-looking fruit clusters of the nypa palm, *Nypa fruticans*.

The relatively stout trunk grows to 6 feet high but has a diameter of 6 inches. It is supported by a short mound of stilt roots, is brownish gray with closely spaced rings of leaf base scars, and is mostly covered in leaf base fibers. The loosely formed crownshaft is 18 inches tall and yellowish green to tan. The leaf crown is less than hemispherical with 10 ascending and, later, spreading leaves 8 to 10 feet long. The leaves are borne on stout, 2-foot-long petioles and bear widely spaced, 2-foot-long leaflets that are 3 inches wide, linear-ovate, and slightly S shaped, with tapering apices. They are deep green above and slightly paler green beneath.

This is an exceptionally beautiful species because of the widely spaced, fat leaflets and is as attractive as any small *Areca* species.

Nenga macrocarpa is indigenous to peninsular Thailand and peninsular Malaysia, where it grows in mountainous rain forest from elevations of 700 to 2640 feet. The epithet is Greek for "large" and "fruit."

It is a solitary-trunked species whose light brown to green and beautifully ringed trunk grows to 12 feet high and 2 inches in diameter. Its leaf crown is usually less than hemispherical because of the ascending, slightly arching leaves. The crownshaft is 18 inches tall, cylindrical, slightly thicker than the trunk, and a smooth green overlain with a purplish brown tomentum. The leaves are 6 feet long on 1-foot-long petioles. The leaflets are evenly spaced along the rachis, each one 18 inches long, a deep green above and a paler green beneath, and linear-lanceolate, the apical ones S shaped. The spreading inflorescences grow from beneath the crownshaft, each one 18 inches long and producing 1-inch-long pendent clusters of brownish purple or deep purple fruits.

The species is exquisitely attractive, and it is a mystery why it is not cultivated more widely.

Nenga pumila is endemic to Java, where it grows in low mountainous rain forest. The epithet is Latin for "small," although the species is not diminutive when mature.

It is a clustering species whose stems attain heights of 18 feet with diameters of 2 inches. They are light brown in their older parts but deep green in their newer parts with beautiful, distinct rings of leaf scars. The crownshafts are 2 feet tall and are yellowish to deep green but are overlain with a brown tomentum. The leaf crown is hemispherical and is open with six leaves, each of which is 6 feet long on an 18-inch-long, brown felty petiole. The many 18-inch-long leaflets are emerald green on both surfaces, linear-lanceolate, S shaped, limp, and half-pendent. The tan inflorescences grow from beneath the crownshafts and are 18 inches long and pendent. The 0.5-inch-long fruits are brownish orange.

A naturally occurring variety, **N. pumila var. pachystachya** is, if possible, even more attractive than the type as it grows taller and has brilliant orange-red to scarlet fruits that are slightly larger. The epithet *pachystachya* is from Greek words meaning "thick" and "spike."

There is scarcely a more beautiful palm. The tiers of leaf crowns and the elegant, reedlike stems are beyond enchanting. The only problem with the palm is that it is not fast growing.

NEONICHOLSONIA is a monotypic genus of pinnate-leaved, solitary-trunked, monoecious small palm in Central America. The genus name honors George Nicholson, curator of the Royal Botanic Gardens, Kew, in the late 19th century. The epithet honors William Watson, an American botanist and collector of the same time. PLATE 601.

Neonicholsonia watsonii is indigenous to eastern central Honduras, central Nicaragua, most of Costa Rica, and southwestern Panama, where it occurs in the undergrowth of lowland rain forest to an elevation of 2000 feet.

This small palm has a short trunk usually underground, the leaves appearing to grow directly from the ground. The leaves are 5 feet long, ascending, and slightly arching when new and later spreading. They are borne on short, soft petioles and bear widely spaced narrowly elliptical, long-tipped, 1-foot-long, emerald green leaflets that grow opposite each other on either side of the rachis in a single flat plane. The inflorescences seem to arise directly from the ground in individuals with no aerial stem but grow from among the leaf bases. They are tall, erect spikes that usually rise above the leaves and bear both male and female blossoms. The fruits are ovoid, 0.5 inch long, black when mature, and attached directly to the spike.

The little palm is beautiful as a large groundcover or as an under-canopy specimen, looking something like a giant fern or a tropical cycad. It is tender to cold and is slow growing, most individuals never forming an aerial stem; those that do take many years to do so. It needs partial shade at all stages, especially in hot climates, constant moisture, and a humus-laden, nonacidic soil.

NEOVEITCHIA is a genus of two rare, pinnate-leaved, monoecious palms in the Fiji Islands and the Vanuatu archipelago. The species are visually and genetically related to the genus *Veitchia* but have significantly stouter and straighter trunks. They also do not form true crownshafts, but this is not so visually apparent as the large leaf sheaths clasp the top of the stem and are almost closed. The inflorescences grow from beneath the crownshafts and consist of a thick, succulent-looking peduncle from which a spray of cream-colored, 2-foot-long flowering branches spread. The genus name translates as "new *Veitchia*." PLATE 602.

Neoveitchia brunnea was described by John L. Dowe in 1996 and is a rare and endangered species endemic to Vanuatu, where it grows in mountainous rain forest at an elevation of 1000 feet. The epithet is Latin for "brown" and alludes to the color of the female flowers and the anthers of the male blossoms.

This species differs from *N. storckii* in being slightly shorter in height, in details and color of the flowers, in lacking hairy scales on the undersides of the leaflets, and in pseudo-crownshafts that are green rather than black. Otherwise, it is as impressive and as beautiful as *N. storckii*.

Neoveitchia storckii is endemic to the island of Viti Levu in the Fiji Islands, where it grows in low mountainous rain forest and is critically endangered due to the trunks being felled for use in house construction but is now protected by the government. The epithet is a Latinized form of the surname "Storck" and commemorates the original collector of the species.

The trunk attains 50 feet of height in habitat and 1 foot in diameter except at its base where it is much expanded. It is light brown in its upper parts, where it is also distinctly ringed with undulating deeper brown leaf base scars; its older parts are gray and indistinctly ringed. The pseudo-crownshaft is amazingly distinct to be not a true, closed shaft: it is slightly thicker than the stem and is nearly black except at the summit where it shades into a deep green, the color of the petioles. The leaf crown is hemispherical or slightly more rounded and contains 10 stiff, 15- to 18-foot-long leaves that arch only near their apices. The individual leaf bears many 30-inch-long, deep green leaflets that are linear-lanceolate, long tipped, limp, and mostly pendent. There is a distinct twist to the leaf from its midpoint on which orients the apical half to the vertical plane. The fruits are ellipsoid, not quite 2 inches long, and orange when mature.

Because of its great leaves, which actually look bigger than they really are, with their beautiful vertical twists, the palm is among the most impressive, beautiful, and tropical looking in the family. It has visual affinities with *Veitchia*, the princess palm (*Dictyosperma album*), and the coconut. It is not tolerant of cold, is adaptable only to zones 10b and 11, and, while it survives in frostless Mediterranean climes like coastal southern California, it languishes there and does not grow well. It is also a water lover and must not be subjected to drought conditions at any stage. It appreciates partial shade when young but needs full sun when older to fulfill its landscape potential. It is surprisingly tolerant of various soils and even seems to flourish in the limey ones of southern Florida. PLATE 602.

NEPHROSPERMA is a monotypic genus of pinnate-leaved, monoecious palm in the Seychelles Islands. The genus name is from Greek and Latin words meaning "kidney" and "seed," an allusion to the shape of the seeds. The epithet honors Louis van Houtte, a 19th-century Belgian nurseryman. PLATES 603 & 604.

Nephrosperma vanhoutteanum grows mainly on wet mountain slopes but sometimes in the undergrowth of rain forest at elevations from sea level to 2000 feet. Its solitary trunk attains a height of 30 feet in habitat and is 6 inches in diameter except at its base where it is swollen. It is a light gray and, in its youngest parts, is indistinctly ringed. The leaf crown is hemispherical to nearly spherical and open. It forms no crownshaft, but the grayish leaf sheaths are dramatically large and prominent. The gracefully arching leaves are 6 feet long in mature individuals but to 10 feet long in younger ones; the petioles are 3 to 4 feet long. The individual leaflets are 4 feet long, generally linear-lanceolate but of varying widths, strongly ribbed, and closely spaced along the rachis. They are a light grayish green to bright grassy green and are leathery but soft, limp, and pendent. The extraordinary inflorescences are 10- to 12-foot-long spikes, arching out of the leaf crown, bearing 2-foot-long, spreading flowering branches at their apices, with both male and female blossoms. The cherry red fruits are spherical and 0.5 inch in diameter.

The species is tropical looking and appealing, especially before it is mature, when the leaves are longer and can be viewed up close. Its drawbacks are that it is extremely sensitive to cold and slow growing unless planted in a rich but fast draining soil and constantly watered. Even then, it is not fast. It is adaptable only to zone 11, although it may be possible in the warmest microclimates of 10b when it is small and can be protected.

NORMANBYA is a monotypic genus of pinnate-leaved, monoecious palm indigenous to northeastern Queensland, Australia, and adjacent New Guinea. The genus name and the epithet honor George A. Constantine, marquis of Normanby and a 19th-century governor of Queensland. PLATES 605 & 606.

Normanbya normanbyi grows in wet rain forest, usually along streams or rivers but also in low, swampy areas at low elevations.

In habitat the solitary trunk attains a height of 60 feet, a diameter of 6 inches, and is light tan in its younger parts and graced with widely spaced, nearly white rings of leaf base scars. The crownshaft is 2 to 3 feet tall, bulging at its base, cylindrical, and silvery green to light gray to almost white. The leaf crown is hemispherical to nearly spherical and has about 10 leaves on short petioles. The leaves are 8 feet long and gracefully arching. Leaf color is medium to deep green above but silvery or even bluish silvery green beneath. Older plants have many wedge-shaped leaflets with oblique, jagged apices; the leaflets are split to their bases and radiate at different angles from the rachis to give a plumose aspect to the leaf. Younger palms also have wedge-shaped leaflets with jagged apices, but the leaflets grow in almost a flat plane off the rachis. The inflorescences grow from beneath the crownshaft and are 3-foot-wide sprays of flowering branches bearing both male and female flowers. The fruits grow in pendent clusters and are 2 inches long, ovoid, and pinkish to red or brownish purple.

This distinctive and extremely attractive species is close to *Wodyetia* in appearance but more elegant and refined looking because of its thinner trunk and more diaphanous leaf crown. It is slower growing than *Wodyetia* and more finicky in its cultural requirements, needing constant moisture and a deep, slightly acidic soil that is rich in organic matter. It is possible in the limestone soils of southern Florida with a thick mulch, copious and constant moisture, and an amended soil, but it grows more slowly there than it does in its native Queensland. It must have partial shade when young, especially in hot climates, but is almost as hardy to cold as is the foxtail, surviving short spells of temperatures slightly below freezing. Its great beauty seems worth whatever heroic measures need to be taken if the gardener can provide such; it is the rich man's *Wodyetia*.

NYPA is a monotypic genus of pinnate-leaved, monoecious palm indigenous to a wide area of the Asian tropics and eastwards to Micronesia and Melanesia, as well as the Solomon Islands. It is called nipa or mangrove palm. The genus name is a transliterated form of the Malaysian name for the palm. The epithet is Latin for "fruiting." PLATES 607 & 608.

Nypa fruticans is widespread in the Asian and Pacific tropics, from Sri Lanka, northeastern India and Bangladesh, the coasts of Myanmar, Thailand, peninsular Malaysia, Sumatra, Vietnam, Cambodia, southeastern China, the Philippines, the Ryukyu Islands of Japan, Indonesia, New Guinea, northeastern Australia, the Bismarck Archipelago, the Solomon Islands, Micronesia, and Melanesia. It grows always along the coasts, usually in mangrove estuaries or lagoons, always at low elevations, and often forms vast colonies along the banks of coastal rivers, inland if the rivers are in a flat floodplain.

This is a solitary-trunked species that looks clustering because of its prostrate or subterranean stem that branches dichotomously. It forms adventitious roots when and where it is prostrate on top of the soil and exhibits widely spaced rings of knobby, lighter leaf scars if its thick, succulent trunk is uncovered. The leaf bases are usually covered in mud but, when exposed, are seen to be stout, succulent looking, and a deep chocolate or purplish brown, which characteristics apply to the petioles and leaf rachises as well. The newer leaves are mostly ascending and erect, but older ones are more spreading. They are 20 feet long, including the robust but soft petiole, which may be a third of the length. The many lanceolate leaflets are 3 feet long and regularly spaced, and grow from the rachis at only a slight angle, which gives to the leaf only a hint of a V shape. The leaflets are stiff but not rigid, usually pendent at their tips, and may be light green or even yellowish green to deep emerald green, depending on the soil and amount of moisture the plants get.

The species has remarkable inflorescences and fruits. The former grow from among the leaf bases and are erect and usually 3 to 5 feet high. They consist of a spikelike portion at the top of which is a globular mass of dull purplish female flowers subtended by short catkin-like yellow branches of male blossoms, the whole affair enclosed at first in leathery, ochre bracts. The mahogany-colored infructescence forms atop the spike and is round and club-like with many flattish teat-shaped or conical-shaped fruits packed into the rounded mass. In habitat these individual small fruits separate when ripe, fall into a stream or lagoon, and are carried off to start new nipa colonies. The genus is similar to other monocot plants, including the pandans (*Pandanus*), and was once placed into its own family because of the flowers and fruits.

The most important cultural consideration is constant water, which, contrary to popular belief, need not be saline. In fact, this palm dies in undiluted salt water, although it luxuriates in brackish to mainly fresh water. A lake or pond is not necessary for growing the palm if its soil can be kept constantly moist. It is adaptable to many soils including calcareous ones and needs full sun when past the seedling stage. The second most important cultural factor is temperature: this palm needs a tropical or nearly tropical climate and is adaptable only to zones 10b and 11. The nipa palm is fast growing.

This is a fantastic and fantastic-looking species with a tropical but wild and primitive demeanor. It creates a true "jungle" aspect like no other species can when planted around ponds or small lakes. Fortunate is the gardener who has room to grow it. It would only succeed in a large conservatory or atrium that has full or nearly full sun exposure, an area wide enough, and a soil deep enough to accommodate the thick trunks.

The species has many uses in its native haunts. The primary one is for thatch and weaving baskets and other utensils, but the leaflets are also used for rolling cigarettes. The dried petioles, because they are filled with tiny air sacs, are used for construction of huts, for fuel, and for fishing net floats. The immature fruits and seeds are considered a delicacy in parts of the palm's range, and the peduncles of the inflorescences yield a sugary sap that is used in sugar, alcoholic beverages, and vinegar. The young, unfolding leaves are also sometimes eaten as a salad. The most dramatic use is, however, as a stabilizing plant to thwart erosion of banks along streams, rivers, and ponds or lagoons.

OENOCARPUS is a genus of nine pinnate-leaved, monoecious palms in Central America and northern and northeastern South America. Most species are indigenous to lowland rain forest, but a few on the slopes of the Andes grow to an elevation of 3500 feet.

There are both solitary and clustering species, and some species form loose pseudo-crownshafts with large, prominent leaf sheaths, usually in the form of an inverted triangle. The pinnate leaves are large, often plumose, the leaflets with silvery undersides, and new growth is usually reddish. The inflorescences grow from beneath the leaf sheaths and consist of pendent sprays of single, relatively short flowering branches that resemble a whisk broom; they bear unisexual blossoms of both sexes.

The large species in this genus have strong visual affinities with the large species of *Attalea* and could be similarly used in the landscape. None of the species are tolerant of cold, although reportedly several have survived temperatures slightly below freezing. All are water lovers and appreciate a humus-laden soil that is not too alkaline. They are sun lovers also once past the seedling stage.

The genus name is from two Greek words meaning "wine" and "fruit," the allusion being to the edible fruits from which wine, among other comestibles, is made. PLATES 609–612.

Oenocarpus bacaba is indigenous to northern Amazonia in the Guyanas, the southern half of Venezuela, eastern Colombia, and northeastern Brazil, where it grows in lowland rain forest to an elevation of 3500 feet but is not found in the seasonally inundated forests. The epithet is the aboriginal name for the palm in Brazil.

It is a solitary-trunked species whose stem attains 60 feet of height and a diameter of 1 foot or less. The grayish green pseudo-crownshaft is distinct, like an inverted pyramid, and 4 feet tall. The leaf crown is shaped like a gigantic shuttlecock, with 12 erect and ascending, stiff, slightly arching leaves from 15 to 20 feet long on stout, 1- to 2-foot-long grayish green petioles. The many leaflets are each 3 to 4 feet long, linear, deep olive green to pure emerald green, limp, and pendent; they grow from the rachis at different angles to create a loosely plumose leaf. The gorgeous 4-foot-long inflorescence branches turn brilliant scarlet as the 0.75-inch-long fruits mature to deep purplish black.

The palm is stunningly attractive and grows fast with lots of water and a decent soil. It is adaptable to the full equatorial sun past the seedling stage.

Oenocarpus bataua has the largest range in the genus: from extreme eastern Panama into the western slopes of the Andes in Colombia and Ecuador, into northern Bolivia, the lowland rain forest of northern Colombia, eastern Colombia, northeastern Ecuador, Peru east of the Andes, northeastern Brazil, Venezuela, and the Guyanas. The epithet is a Latinized form of the aboriginal name in

Brazil. This species grows on the eastern Andean slopes to an elevation of 3500 feet, through the seasonally wet *llanos* (savannas) of Venezuela, the seasonally inundated forests of Amazonia, and along the edges of lowland rain forest as well as the banks of streams and rivers.

It is a solitary-trunked species whose stem attains a height of 80 or 90 feet in habitat but has a diameter of 18 inches. It is light tan to light gray, relatively slender and, in its younger parts, is graced with widely spaced darker rings of leaf base scars. The pseudo-crownshaft is 6 feet tall, like an inverted pyramid, and deep olive green to brown, with many long, stiff and almost needlelike black fibers on its margins. The leaf crown is in the form of a gigantic shaving brush and usually contains 12 long, stiff, and erect leaves. The leaves are 30 feet long on short, 1-foot-long petioles. They arch only near their tips, if at all, and bear many, regularly spaced, 4- to 5-foot-long, long-tipped olive green to emerald green, silvery backed leaflets that are pendent but grow in a single plane from the rachis, creating a hanging curtain effect. The new growth is usually dark red or maroon. The 6-foot-long pendent inflorescences bear 1-inch-long black fruits, and the flowering branches turn rusty red as the fruits develop.

There are two recognized varieties of this species, but their differences are in details of the inflorescences and not important in the landscape. This is one of the world's most impressive palms. It grows robustly and fast in a tropical or nearly tropical climate if given ample and regular moisture and a decent soil. It is adapted to full sun once past its seedling stage and has extremely colorful new growth when young. PLATE 609.

Oenocarpus distichus is indigenous to northern central Brazil, from the northeastern tip of Bolivia eastward to the mouth of the Amazon River, where it grows in lowland rain forest. The epithet is Latin for "distichous" and alludes to the two-ranked disposition of the leaves in the crown.

The solitary trunk attains a height of 60 feet in habitat and is 1 foot in diameter. It is light gray to nearly white and is graced with widely spaced dark rings of leaf base scars. The grayish green to grayish brown pseudo-crownshaft is 3 feet tall with the shape of a flat inverted pyramid. The leaf crown is hemispherical to nearly spherical but is also nearly in one plane because the leaves grow only from two opposite sides of the trunk. Individual leaves are mostly erect and slightly arching, 10 to 15 feet long, on short petioles usually less than 1 foot long. The 3-foot-long deep olive green leaflets grow from the rachis in different planes and are pendent, creating a heavy curtain effect. The pendent reddish brown inflorescences have 3-foot-long flowering branches on which form 0.5-inch-long purple-black round fruits.

Because of the flat leaf crown, this is the most distinctive solitary-trunked species. It is also possibly the most attractive.

Oenocarpus mapora has a wide distribution from western Costa Rica, through Panama, the western slopes of the Andes in Colombia and Ecuador, northern Colombia and western Venezuela, central Colombia, eastern Ecuador, Peru east of the Andes, and northern Bolivia, where it grows in lowland rain forest. The epithet is the aboriginal name of the palm in Venezuela.

This is a clustering species whose stems attain heights of 50 feet and diameters of 6 inches. The pseudo-crownshaft is in the shape of a narrow inverted pyramid, 3 feet tall in older plants, and is deep olive green to greenish brown. The leaf crown is hemispherical or nearly spherical and consists of six spreading leaves. Individual leaves are from 4 to 15 feet long on 1- to 3-foot-long petioles and usually show a slight twist near their midpoints that orients the apical half of the leaf into a vertical plane. The leaflets are 2 to 3 feet long, broad, and regularly spaced, and grow from the rachis mostly in a flat plane; they are limp and pendent. Leaf color is medium to deep olive green to almost emerald green. The inflorescences consist of pendent, reddish, 2-foot-long flowering branches that produce 1-inch-long, round to ovoid blackish purple fruits.

The species is extremely attractive because of the tiers of large leaves and slender, graceful whitish trunks. It looks especially good planted near water. PLATES 610–612.

ONCOCALAMUS is a genus of five clustering, pinnate-leaved, spiny, monocarpic, and monoecious climbing palms in western tropical Africa, where they grow in lowland rain forest, clearings therein, swamps, and along banks of rivers and streams.

Seedling palms have unsegmented and apically bifid leaves, those of adults with numerous regularly spaced leaflets mostly growing in a single flat plane. The upper parts of the stems are covered in tightly clasping leaf sheaths that bear spines, and there are spines on the short petioles as well as the rachis and even the leaflet margins. The plants climb mainly by the elongated cirri with their paired backwards-pointing spines at the apices of the adult leaves. The inflorescences grow directly from the tops of the stems and consist of male and female flowers on pendent flowering branches, each blossom enclosed by a papery bract, these bracts overlapping on the branches. The fruits are small, globular, yellowish brown to reddish brown, and covered in overlapping scales. The individual climbing stems gradually die after flowering and fruiting.

The genus is unknown in cultivation outside of a few botanical gardens. The genus name is derived from two Greek words meaning "hook" and "reed."

ONCOSPERMA is a genus of five large, mostly clustering, spiny, pinnate-leaved, monoecious palms in the Philippines, Borneo, Sulawesi, Java, peninsular Malaysia, Sumatra, and Sri Lanka.

The younger parts of the trunks are covered in rings of downward-pointing black spines, and there are spines on the short crownshafts as well as the petioles and leaf rachises. The inflorescences grow from beneath the crownshafts and consist of many pendent flowering branches bearing both male and female blossoms, the whole enclosed in woody and spiny bracts when developing. The round fruits are dark purple or black.

The growing points of all species are edible and considered a delicacy in their habitats. The trunks of most species are durable and are used locally for construction.

Only two species are in cultivation. All require tropical or nearly tropical climates and copious and regular moisture but are not finicky about soil type as long as it is well drained. They are adaptable to full sun from an early age.

The genus name comes from two Greek words meaning "hook" and "seed" and alludes to the shape of the seeds. PLATES 613–615.

Oncosperma fasciculatum is endemic to Sri Lanka, where it grows in low mountainous rain forest. The epithet is Latin for "fascicled" or "bunched together," an allusion to the palm's clumping habit.

This densely clustering species is similar to *O. tigillarium* but has fewer stems per clump, does not grow as tall, and has shorter leaves with less pendent leaflets.

Oncosperma gracilipes is endemic to the Philippines, where it grows in low mountainous rain forest on several islands. The epithet is Latin for "graceful foot" and alludes to the long petioles.

This species is smaller than most others in the genus, its stems only growing to 30 feet high, with a diameter of 4 inches. The crownshafts are deep reddish yellow to orange with striations of small black spines. The leaf crowns are hemispherical with six spreading, 6- to 8-foot-long leaves on 2-foot-long petioles. The leaflets are pendent in older leaves but slightly so in younger ones, which characteristic but lends to the overall beauty of the different tiers of foliage.

The species is wonderfully, elegantly graceful, the most ethereal looking in the genus.

Oncosperma horridum is a sparsely clustering species (often found with a single trunk) with a wide natural distribution in peninsular Malaysia, Sumatra, Borneo, and some islands of the Philippines, where it grows in mountainous rain forest from sea level to an elevation of 1800 feet. The epithet is Latin for "horrid" and alludes to the spiny younger parts of the trunks.

The stems grow to heights of 60 feet in their native haunts with diameters of 1 foot. The crownshafts are 3 feet tall and prominent, being conspicuously swollen near their bases, and tan or greenish brown. The leaf crowns are hemispherical to nearly spherical, and the leaves are 12 to 18 feet long, spreading, stiff, and barely arching. The younger ones usually exhibit a twist near the middle of the rachis, which results in the apical half of the leaf being oriented vertically. The leaflets are numerous, linear-lanceolate, long tipped, and deep emerald green on both surfaces, and grow in a nearly flat plane from the rachis with only their apical tips pendent.

The species is not as beautiful as *O. tigillarium* because of the fewer trunks that usually attain similar statures, the leaf crowns looking congested and in contest with each other. Selecting and pruning out one or two of them could probably remedy this.

Oncosperma platyphyllum is a rare species endemic to the island of Negros in the Philippines, where it grows in low mountainous rain forest. The epithet is from two Greek words meaning "flat" and "leaf."

It is a sparsely clustering species to 20 feet high, making it the most diminutive species in the genus. The small crownshafts are rust colored because of the thick tomentum that covers the sheaths; they are also striated with small black spines. The leaf crown is hemispherical and holds six spreading 6-foot-long leaves, which are slightly arching and linear. The regularly spaced leaflets grow from the rachis in a single flat plane, are deep green on both surfaces, and are linear.

The species is attractive and looks like a giant clumping tropical cycad species. It is not in cultivation outside of a few botanical gardens.

Oncosperma tigillarium is indigenous to peninsular Thailand, peninsular Malaysia, Sumatra, Java, and Borneo, where it grows in low, swampy areas near the coasts, often landward of mangrove forests. The epithet is Latin for "of little stems" and must refer to the relative slenderness of the stems, certainly not their height.

The stems grow to heights of 80 or more feet with diameters of 6 inches. They are light tan and, in their younger parts, exhibit widely spaced darker brown rings of leaf scars accompanied by rings of downward-pointing, long black spines. The crownshafts are 5 feet tall in older individuals and are cylindrical and slightly thicker than the stems beneath them. They are pale green or sometimes grayish green. The leaf crowns are hemispherical and contain as many as 36 leaves, each of which is 10 feet long, gently and gracefully arching, and borne on a 1- or 2-foot-long petiole. The numerous leaflets are 2 feet long and are pendent from the rachis, appearing like a curtain; the lowermost ones are usually accompanied by long, whitish threads called *reins* when newly unfurled. They are medium green and linear-lanceolate. The inflorescences grow from nodes beneath the crownshafts and consist of pendent, bright yellow flowering branches bearing both male and female blossoms. The fruits are small, rounded, and dark purple.

The most important cultural requirements are a tropical or nearly tropical climate and copious and regular moisture. The speciest seems almost indifferent to soil type, even intermittently soggy ones, and it is at home on calcareous soils, especially if the trees are mulched. In regions with distinct dry seasons, such as southern Florida, the clumps suffer and the wonderful leaves become unsightly unless irrigated. The palm resprouts if frozen to the ground and if the soil does not freeze, but this practice is futile as the great beauty of the large clumps is lost and the plant dies out if subjected to such stress in consecutive winters. The clumps are adapted to full sun from an early age and, with enough water, grow quite fast.

There is no more beautiful palm species. The great height and density of the stems clump, as well as the array of different heights of leaf crowns with their beautifully arching leaves and curtains of pendent leaflets, make this palm a veritable symphony, almost a world unto itself, of glorious forms. Some old individuals have one or a few much more dominant stems, which only add to the incredible beauty of the clump. The palm can stand alone as a specimen surrounded by space or be a splendid, large part of other vegetation. A large avenue with this species planted along either side would be one of the most magnificent sights possible, especially if the drive were curving! It is not for small gardens, but plots that are only somewhat larger than average could well accommodate a single clump in an outlying region. This palm is not known to be grown indoors and, because of its great size, would seem to be a poor choice for trying. In addition, it needs lots of light.

The trunks are reportedly immune to marine conditions and the wood is strong and durable and used for pier pilings as well as house construction. The seeds are also reportedly used as a betel-nut substitute in Malaysia. Plates 613–615.

ORANIA is a genus of 19 solitary-trunked, pinnate-leaved, monoecious palms in Madagascar, peninsular Thailand, peninsular Malaysia, Sumatra, Java, Borneo, the Moluccas, Sulawesi, and the Philippines, with most species in New Guinea.

They are mostly tall, robust palms with distinctly stiff leaf rachises and ascending large leaves that exhibit little arching. The leaflets are pendulous in all but the Malagasy species and are usually long, with their apices obliquely truncated and slightly jagged. The palms form no crown-shafts and the inflorescences grow from among the leaf bases and are branched once, twice, or three times and produce large and unusual round fruits with one to three seeds. The number of large seeds creates the form of the fruit: two-seeded fruits with two adjoining globes and three-seeded fruits with three adjoining spheres.

Most parts of these palms are poisonous. Except for the Malagasy species, these palms are similar to each other in general appearance: stiff, barely arching leaves with a curtain of pendent leaflets. They are all extraordinarily impressive and tropical looking. The genus is unaccountably rare in cultivation in the Western Hemisphere. All the species are intolerant of cold and need copious and regular moisture as well as protection from the midday sun when young. They are, however, seemingly adapted to various soils, even calcareous ones.

The genus name honors William, prince of Orange and king of the Netherlands. PLATES 616–620.

Orania archboldiana is endemic to lowland rain forest of southern Papua New Guinea. The epithet honors the late Richard Archbold, an American who funded several natural history expeditions to the area.

This species is one of the smaller ones in the genus, the slender trunk growing to 25 feet high with a diameter of 4 inches. The leaf crown is hemispherical to extended, and the leaves are often separated by 3 feet or more of trunk space. Each leaf is 8 feet long, slightly arching, and borne on a 1- to 2-foot-long petiole. The widely spaced leaflets are 2 feet long, shiny emerald green on both sides, broadly lanceolate, and wonderfully lax and pendent. They grow from several angles off the rachis to create a plumose leaf.

Orania disticha is endemic to southern Papua New Guinea, where it grows in low mountainous rain forest. The epithet is Latin for "distichous," referring to the disposition of the leaves in two ranks at the top of the trunks.

The trunk of this large, magnificent, and elegant-looking species grows to a height of 60 feet and a diameter of 8 inches. The leaf crown is in the form of a gigantic flat green fan with the great leaves growing on opposite sides of the slender stem. They are erect, ascending, scarcely arching, and 8 to 10 feet long on 2- to 3-foot-long petioles; they bear many closely and regularly spaced leaflets, the inner ones much longer (5 feet) than the outer ones (3

feet). The pendent leaflets create the effect of a large green curtain hanging from the unbending leaf rachises.

This is an incredibly exotic and appealing species, and it is a complete mystery why it is not much more obvious in cultivation. PLATE 616.

Orania glauca is endemic to northwestern Papua New Guinea, where it grows in low mountainous rain forest. The epithet is Latin for "glaucous" and alludes to the smooth and waxy inflorescence branches.

The trunk of this tall, massive species attains a height of 50 feet and a diameter of 18 inches. The leaf crown is in the form of a narrow inverted pyramid with a few giant leaves, each one 25 feet long, erect and ascending, with regularly spaced leaflets of varying widths and lengths: those nearest the trunk 7 feet long and often recurved or curling, the outer ones 2 feet long. The leaflets grow in one flat plane from the rachis and are limp and pendent.

Orania lauterbachiana is endemic to northwestern Papua New Guinea, where it grows in low mountainous rain forest. The epithet honors Carl A. G. Lauterbach, a 19th-century German plant collector.

The trunk attains a height of 60 feet in habitat and a diameter of 1 foot. The leaf crown is in the form of a gigantic shaving brush, and the 10-foot-long leaves are erect, ascending, and nicely arching on 2-foot-long petioles. The many regularly spaced leaflets are 2 feet long and are pendent; they are also broad in relation to their length, a characteristic which make this beautiful species (and one other) unusual in the genus.

Orania macropetala is endemic to northwestern Papua New Guinea, where it grows in low mountainous rain forest. The epithet is from two Greek words meaning "large" and "petal." The species is similar in general appearance to *O. lauterbachiana* and may be conspecific with it.

Orania palindan is endemic to a few islands of the Philippines, where it grows in low mountainous rain forest. The epithet is one of the aboriginal names for the species.

This palm is among the smaller species in the genus, the trunk attaining a height of 25 feet but a diameter of almost 1 foot. The leaf crown is hemispherical with typical 10-foot-long, unarching leaves that bear long, narrow, and pendent leaflets.

It seems to be the most cold-tolerant species, surviving brief periods of temperatures slightly below freezing. PLATES 617 & 618.

Orania regalis is a rare species endemic to the Aru Islands, southwest of New Guinea, where it grows in lowland rain forest and swamps. The epithet is Latin for "regal."

The trunk of this massive species grows to at least 30 feet high and a diameter of 2 feet at its base. It is light gray to tan and is heavily ringed with widely spaced darker leaf base scars. The leaf crown is hemispherical with several 16-foot-long, stiff and unarching leaves on 6-foot-long, stout petioles. The many pendent leaflets are 6 feet long and 6 inches wide at their bases.

The species is the most massive looking in the genus because of its robust trunk that is straight as an arrow and slightly tapering from the base upwards. Until the year 2000, it had not been seen in the wild since the 1870s.

Orania rubiginosa is a rare species endemic to the Philippines, where it grows in low mountainous rain forest. The epithet is Latin for "rusty" and alludes to the color of the tomentum on the undersides of the new leaflets. This is one of the smaller species in the genus, growing to 30 feet high overall. The leaves are 8 feet long and bear 2-foot-long, pendent leaflets.

Orania sylvicola is indigenous to peninsular Thailand, peninsular Malaysia, and Sumatra, where it grows in low mountainous rain forest. The epithet is Latin for "inhabitant of the forest."

The trunk attains a height of 60 feet and a diameter of 1 foot. It is gray and distinctly ringed with slightly darker leaf base scars in its upper parts. The leaf crown is spherical or nearly so and usually contains 18 leaves, which are 10 feet long on 2-foot-long petioles. The leaves are stiff and unarching and bear 2- to 3-foot-long pendent leaflets, which are deep green above and silvery brownish gray-green beneath. PLATE 619.

Orania trispatha is one of three species endemic to Madagascar. This rare and endangered palm grows in lowland rain forest and swamps from sea level to an elevation of 1500 feet. The epithet is Latin and Greek for "three spathes."

The trunk grows to a height of 65 feet in habitat with a diameter of 1 foot. There is no crownshaft, but the large leaf bases are distinct, prominent, and almost white. The leaf crown is a giant fan of distichous 6- to 7-foot-long, stiff and unarching leaves on incredibly long, 6-foot petioles. The stiff leaflets grow from the rachis at an angle that creates a V-shaped leaf and are a deep green above but have a glaucous bluish gray-green hue on their undersides.

Because of its distichously arranged leaves in the form of a gigantic flat fan, the species is one of the most exotic-looking palms in the world. PLATE 620.

ORANIOPSIS is a monotypic genus of solitary-trunked, pinnate-leaved, dioecious palm in northeastern Queensland, Australia. The genus name translates as "similar to *Orania*." It may be similar in appearance to *Orania*, but it is closely related to *Ceroxylon* genetically and in appearance. The epithet is Latin for "appendaged." PLATES 621 & 622.

Oraniopsis appendiculata is found naturally in mountainous rain forest at elevations from 1000 to 5000 feet.

The trunk grows to 60 feet in habitat but is usually 20 feet tall. It is typically 1 foot in diameter but may be 18 inches thick and is straight and light to dark gray. The leaf crown is shaped like a shuttlecock to almost hemispherical, usually with several dead and marcescent leaves beneath the crown. The leaves are 12 to 15 feet long on 2-foot-long, stout petioles; they are stiff, nearly unarching, and ascending to spreading. The leaves bear many regularly spaced, narrowly linear leaflets that are stiff and straight but grow in a single flat plane. Their color is deep emerald green above but grayish to silvery green beneath. The pendent inflorescences grow from the leaf bases and are 30 inches long with the flowering branches covered in a long brown tomentum and bearing small white flowers. Female trees produce 1-inch-wide round orange fruits that sometimes have two lobes.

This palm looks like a cross between a coconut and an *Arenga* species, but it grows like neither of those palms. It is likely to not form a trunk for 20 or even 30 years. In addition, it needs constant high humidity with copious and regular moisture and a humus-laden, quickly draining soil. The only good news relative to its cultural requirements is that it has survived unscathed temperatures just below freezing.

PARAJUBAEA is a genus of two or three pinnate-leaved, monoecious palms in the mountains of South America. The leaves are large and their sheaths are fibrous. The leaf rachis is usually twisted near its midpoint so that the apical half of the leaf is oriented vertically. The inflorescences grow from among the leaf bases and are generally similar to those of *Jubaea*, *Syagrus*, and the coconut palm, *Cocos*. They are enclosed at first in large, woody boat-shaped bracts and, at anthesis, are branched but once into stiff, short, erect flowering branches bearing both male and female blossoms. The large, 3-inch-long fruits have edible seeds and are borne in compact, elongated masses. The leaf sheath fibers are used for weaving material, principally in making rope.

The three species are similar in appearance to each other and are massive looking with fibrous stems when young, but, with one exception, quite tall and elegant, with smooth trunks when older. All three species are adapted only to Mediterranean or temperate climates with cool nighttime temperatures and moderate to warm winters. They are impossible to grow in hot, humid tropical regions; indeed, one species is reputed to be the world's highest (altitudinally) growing palm species. The irony is that, considering the great elevations at which they grow in habitat, some species are not as hardy to cold as would be expected. The genus name translates as "similar to *Jubaea*." PLATES 623–627.

Parajubaea coccoides is known only in cultivation and may be a cultivar of *P. torallyi*. The epithet translates as "similar to *Cocos*." It is a relatively common ornamental in Quito, Ecuador, at an elevation of 9400 feet but is also found up to 10,000 feet.

The trunk attains a height of 50 feet and a diameter of 18 inches. It is heavily covered in dark cinnamon-colored leaf bases and fibers when young but is light to dark gray and nearly smooth in older trees. The leaf crown is hemispherical to almost spherical and usually consists of 24 leaves, each 10 to 12 feet long on 3-foot-long petioles. They are beautifully arching and bear many 2-foot-long, linear leaflets growing in a single flat plane from the rachis.

When young, the species has visual affinity with *Jubaea* but when older is more delicate appearing with a much more slender trunk than the Chilean wine palm. Its leaf crown is stunningly attractive and tropical looking—much like that of a coconut palm—and it is almost impossible to believe its nativity is so elevated and nontropical. PLATES 623 & 624.

Parajubaea sunkha is endemic to Bolivia in the foothills of the eastern slope of the Andes at elevations from 5500 to 7000 feet. It grows in deciduous forest of elevated, seasonally dry valleys. The epithet is the aboriginal name, which alludes to the fibers of the leaf sheaths. This little-known species may not deserve specific status but may be only a variety of *P. torallyi*. In any case it is the smallest palm in the genus, its trunk attaining no more than 25 feet of height and 18 inches in diameter. It is reportedly also slower growing than the other species in the genus. Otherwise, it is similar visually to *P. coccoides*. PLATE 625.

Parajubaea torallyi is a rare and endangered species endemic to deciduous forest in the dry valleys of the Andes foothills of western Bolivia. It is similar in stature and appearance to *P. coccoides* but has a slightly more open leaf crown because of the slightly longer petioles; it also has a slightly thinner trunk. Some authorities recognize two varieties based on the size of the fruits: *P. torallyi* var. *microcarpa* and *P. torallyi* var. *torallyi*. PLATES 626 & 627.

PELAGODOXA is a monotypic genus of rare and endangered pinnate-leaved, monoecious palm. The genus name is derived from two Greek words meaning "sea" or "water" and "glory," an allusion to the wet environment and great beauty of this species. The epithet honors Augustine Henry, an early 20th-century French botanist and plant collector. PLATES 628 & 629.

Pelagodoxa henryana is endemic to low mountainous rain forest in the Marquesas Islands, where it occurs in the undergrowth in a single valley, and where it is now almost extinct, with fewer than 12 trees.

The solitary trunk attains a maximum height of 25 feet and a diameter of 6 inches in habitat. It is light brown and usually columnar and straight, with widely spaced, raised rings of leaf base scars. The leaf crown is hemispherical to spherical. The leaves are linear-elliptical to linear-obovate, 6 to 7 feet long, 3 to 4 feet wide, entire and undivided, and shortly bifid apically, with shallow indentations on the margins corresponding to the pinnately disposed veins in the blade. They are borne on stout 2-foot-long petioles, are heavily ribbed on both surfaces, and are deep green above but grayish green beneath. The inflorescences grow out of the leaf bases and are short, erect when new, 1 to 2 feet long, and twice branched; they bear both male and female blossoms. The fruits are round, covered with raised, warty projections, light greenish brown, and to 6 inches in diameter; they are borne in short, pendent clusters in the leaf crown. Fruit size varies considerably and, in the past, has led to the suspicion that there may be two species. The suspicion was abetted when it was recognized that small populations of the tree in the Solomon Islands and the Vanuatu archipelago are the result of 19th-century seed imports and are not a part of the original distribution of the species. The fruits reportedly take three years to mature.

The palm is tropical in its requirements and is marginal in zone 10b. It must have copious and regular moisture, constantly high humidity, and protection from the full sun of hot climates. It does not tolerate hot or cold dry winds and needs protection from any strong breeze if its elegant, undivided leaves are to remain pristine. It prefers a humus-laden soil but does well even in calcareous soil if organic matter or a mulch is added.

Few palms are as beautiful as this species is. Its large undivided, deeply grooved leaves and its nearly rounded crown are more than exciting. It should receive a protected and featured spot under a high canopy.

PHOENICOPHORIUM is a monotypic genus of spiny, pinnate-leaved, monoecious palm in the Seychelles Islands. The genus name comes from Greek words meaning "date palm" and "stolen," a reference to the fact that one of the early (and few) specimens in the Western world was purloined from the Royal Botanic Gardens, Kew. The epithet is a Latinized form of the surname "Borsig" and honors a 19th-century German horticulturist. PLATES 630–632.

Phoenicophorium borsigianum grows from sea level to an elevation of 1000 feet in valleys and on hillsides and ridge tops in rain forest. The species forms extensive stands where forest once stood.

In habitat, the solitary gray trunk attains a height of 50 feet and a diameter of 4 inches. The leaf crown is hemispherical and contains 12 gracefully arching, 6-foot-long leaves on 8- to 10-inch-long stout petioles that extend into the blade as stout, thick, yellowish green midribs. The blade is entire but usually segmented by wind or other mechanical means and is deep emerald green on both surfaces. It is obovate and shortly bifid apical, and bears large indentations along its margins as well as distinct grooves in the blade, each corresponding to a fused pinna. Young leaves are distinctly V shaped, but older leaves are nearly flat. Young trees have many black spines on the leaf sheaths, petiole, and leaf rachis, but older plants usually have few, if any, spines. The 3-foot-long erect inflorescences grow from the leaf bases, are twice branched, and bear both male and female yellow flowers. The individual fruits are ovoid, less than 0.5 inch long, and dull red when ripe.

This beauty does not tolerate cold and is adaptable only to zone 11. It also does not tolerate sustained temperatures below 45°F. It is adaptable to full sun once past the seedling stage and, although a true water lover, tolerates occasional short lapses in its moisture supply. It seems not too fussy about soil type as long as it is well drained. This is one of the world's most beautiful palms. Its gorgeous leaves are nearly incomparable in beauty, especially in young trees that can be protected from wind. It is one of the few palms that can look good even as a single specimen surrounded by space but is much more effective in groups of three or more individuals of varying heights.

PHOENIX is a genus of 13 pinnate-leaved, dioecious palms from the Canary Islands, tropical and subtropical Africa, the Mediterranean region, the Middle East, the Arabian Peninsula, India, Indochina, and eastwards to Hong Kong, Taiwan, and the southern Philippine islands. They grow in habitats as diverse as deserts, mangrove sea coasts, and swampy areas. Most species hail from semiarid regions but grow near springs, watercourses, or high groundwater levels.

Nine species have clustering trunks, but four are solitary stemmed. While most are medium sized to massive or robust in stature, a few are dwarf and one has a prostrate, creeping trunk. Several trunked species do not form an aboveground stem for several years and sometimes refuse to do so under drought or other adverse conditions. All species have leaves whose lowermost leaflets are metamorphosed into often long, vicious spines (technically *acanthophylls*). The petioles are short or nonexistent, which

fact is not too obvious unless one looks closely at the base of the leaf where the spines start—a sometimes dangerous activity. All have leaflets that, unlike almost all other pinnate-leaved palms, are V shaped. The inflorescences of male and female plants are similar in appearance and each inflorescence has several branches that are not branched. They are white or cream colored as are the unisexual flowers and emerge from a leathery, usually boat-shaped bract which falls away shortly thereafter. The fruits are usually in large pendent clusters and mature orange, brown, or sometimes black.

All species freely hybridize one with another, and seed harvested from trees that are grown in proximity with other *Phoenix* species (especially in Florida) are likely to be hybrids. The genus name is a Latinized form of the Greek word for "date palm," which possibly referred to the peregrinating Phoenicians who carried the palm from one location to another. PLATES 633–647.

Phoenix acaulis occurs naturally in northern India and Nepal, where it grows in scrublands and savannas and in the undergrowth of pine forests from 1200 to 5000 feet elevation. The epithet is Latin for "trunkless."

The stem remains mostly underground and, even when emergent, is only a few inches in height. The erect 5-foot-long leaves are grayish green with widely spaced sharply pointed, 1-foot-long leaflets which grow in clusters and from different angles off the rachis; the outermost leaflets are not rigid and in older plants are often semipendulous.

The palm is more of a curiosity than ornamental and doubtless has some hardiness to cold. It would fit into a cactus or succulent garden or other type of xeriscape as it is drought tolerant, its roots growing quite deep in search of moisture. PLATE 633.

Phoenix andamanensis is a rare species, occurring only in the Andaman Islands in the Bay of Bengal, south of Myanmar, where it grows on sloping ground in scrubland at elevations of 1400 to 2200 feet. The epithet is Latin for "of Andaman." The original description in 1999 by Sasha Barrow is close to that of *P. rupicola*. This palm is probably not in cultivation and no cultural data are known, but it seems impossible that it would be hardier to cold than the cliff date.

Phoenix caespitosa is a clustering species from the deserts of Somalia and the Arabian peninsula, where it grows in oases and near underground springs, sometimes in large masses. The epithet is Latin for "clumped" or "tufted." The trunks are short and subterranean, but the leaves attain 10 feet long and have stiff, bluish green, 6- to 18-inch-long pointed leaflets that grow from the rachis in two slightly different planes. The overall appearance is that of a strongly clumping, trunkless edible date palm.

Phoenix canariensis is endemic to the Canary Islands, where it grows in moist and semiarid areas from sea level to an elevation of 2000 feet, always in open areas and where there is abundant groundwater. The only common name is Canary Island date palm. The epithet is Latin for "of the Canaries."

Mature old trunks grow to 70 feet but are usually 40 feet tall in cultivation. They are massive, usually straight as an arrow (unless planted on slopes where, if they do not fall over, become leaning and curved) and columnar, with a diameter of 2 to 3 feet; they often sit atop a mound of densely packed aerial roots in older palms. Young trunks are decidedly bulbous, almost like a pineapple, and are covered with persistent large triangular leaf bases. Old trunks are almost free of the leaf bases except near the beginning of the leaf crown, where they form a "bulb" or "pineapple," and the stems show a beautiful pattern of horizontally elongated diamond-shaped leaf base scars in closely set spiraling rings. The trunks are light or dark brown. The immense leaf crown is densely packed with often well over 100 leaves and is 25 to 40 feet wide and as tall. The leaves are 10 to 20 feet long, narrowly elliptical, and dull olive green to deep green; the pure and unhybridized species never shows a bluish hue. The slightly arching leaves have stiff, sharp-pointed leaflets growing from the rachis at slightly different angles and giving the leaf a slight V shape. The leaves are held on short, almost nonexistent petioles that bear long, vicious spines. The inflorescences are 6 feet or more in length with many deep yellow to light orange single branches that bear small yellow unisexual flowers. The brilliant orange fruits are oblong, 1 inch long, and densely packed into broad, heavy pendent clusters. They are edible but mostly unpalatable.

The species is susceptible to lethal yellowing disease. It is suited to most fast-draining soils. The palm is adaptable to zones 9 through 11 in areas subject to wet freezes in winter but is usually good in 8 through 11 in drier ones, especially when older. It needs full sun from youth to old age and, while drought tolerant when established, grows so slowly under this condition as to be frustrating.

The Canary Island date is among the most massive palms, rivaling even the great talipot (*Corypha*). It has a stately elegance that no other palm can surpass and, at the same time, seems warm and almost motherly and protective. There is no finer plant for lining avenues, and a grove of *P. canariensis* is a wonder to behold. It is beautiful and a welcome sight in all but small and cramped areas. It tolerates salt-laden winds but not soil and is one of the finest trees for planting near the seashore, although it is definitely not a strand plant. The practice of removing older hanging fronds is aesthetically abominable, but some people prefer it, or are taught to think they should by landscapers who need work or homeowner associations suffering from a pathological obsessiveness with "neatness." The usual excuse of both these groups is to expose the "bulb" or "pineapple" beneath the subsequently marred crown of leaves; the bulb is unattractive, especially when compared to the magnificence of the full crown! The only valid excuse for the blemishing crop is in transplanting or moving the tree. This is one of the least likely to succeed in any indoor planting, needing as it does such a vast space and such high levels of light.

In the palm's habitat the leaves are used for weaving baskets and other utensils and for Christian religious services, and the young inflorescences provide sap which is made into honey. Sasha Barrow (1998) points out that the greatest threat to the species in habitat is the importation and cultivation of exotic species of *Phoenix* which hybridize with the endemic. These exotics may also expose the endemics to lethal yellowing disease. PLATE 634.

Phoenix dactylifera would seem indigenous to all dry regions of northern Africa, the Middle East, Turkey, Pakistan, and northwestern India, but was probably originally native only to northern Africa or the Middle East, having been long ago transported by people to regions eastwards and westwards. It grows at oases, along rivers and streams, or anywhere underground water is available in desert areas. The species is universally known as the date palm or edible date palm. The epithet is from both Greek and Latin and translates as "finger-bearing" or "hand-bearing," an allusion to the pendent clusters of fruit.

It is a sparsely clustering species that only suckers with age. Mature trunks grow to 90 feet in their native regions but, under cultivation, do not usually exceed 70 feet, and that would be for old palms. The trunk diameter is never more than 2 feet and is usually 18 inches. Younger trunks are usually clothed with the narrowly triangular leaf bases, but older trunks are often free of them and show a closely set pattern of spiraling wide, flat "knobs." The trunk occasionally branches dichotomously well above the ground level, producing an interesting but not necessarily beautiful tableau. The leaf crown is 20 feet tall and wide. The leaves are 10 to 20 feet long, stiff, and slightly arching. The false petiole is 3 to 4 feet long and is armed with long sharp acanthophylls. The 1- to 2-foot-long leaflets grow from the rachis at several angles and give to the blade a slight V shape. Their color is gray green to almost bluish gray green and they are stiff and nonpendent. The leaf crown is much sparser than that of *P. canariensis* and may have 20 to 40 leaves. The crown is usually less than full and rounded; in warm, humid climes the older leaves are usually fungus ridden and removed because of their unsightliness. The inflorescences are 4 feet long and grow from among the leaves. They are orange and bear many small whitish unisexual blossoms. The fruits are 1 to 3 inches long, oblong, and orange when mature, and are borne in large, spreading handlike pendent masses.

The sweet, edible fruits have been a staple of Middle Eastern peoples for millennia and a source of much commerce for hundreds of years. There are now hundreds, if not thousands, of varieties. The date palm does not fruit well in humid climates, no matter how much heat is apparent during the summer; however, two cultivars now do indeed produce well in such regions as the Gulf coast of the United States: *P. dactylifera* 'Medjool' and *P. dactylifera* 'Zahedii' (Grant Stephenson, pers. comm.).

The species is slightly susceptible to lethal yellowing disease. The date palm is hardy to cold, especially in dry climates where it is adaptable to zones 7 through 11, although marginal in zone 7. In areas subject to wet freezes in winter, it is only good in zones 8b through 11 and is marginal in 8b. Because of its long association with deserts, the date palm is popularly thought to have water requirements similar to that of a cactus. Nothing could be further from the truth. It is always found near groundwater and, while drought tolerant when established, it languishes and even dies under true drought conditions. It seems indifferent to soil type as long as its drainage is unimpeded. It also tolerates salt in the soil and the air and is a good choice for seaside plantings except on the seaward side of dunes. It needs full sun from youth to old age.

The date palm is usually taller but not nearly as massive looking as the Canary Island date palm. It is widely used for lining avenues and is often planted as a specimen tree isolated and surrounded by space. It looks better than many palms do in this situation but is even more beautiful in groups of three or more individuals of varying heights. No more than one palm needs to be planted if it is allowed to keep its suckers. Few other palms are better suited to being used as a canopy-scape.

Phoenix dactylifera and its cultivars became, in the last quarter of the 20th century, one of the most frequently planted landscape palms in the tropical and subtropical areas of the United States, particularly in the southwestern desert areas. This phenomenon is partly due to the rapid development of date plantations in California and Arizona into ever-expanding tracts of suburbia, those great old palm groves now giving way to acres of new houses with many of the former occupants of the groves being transported to adorn further developments around the country and the world. We are assured, however, by Henry Donselman (pers. comm.), that there are now as many com-

mercial date palms as ever, the groves younger and in different locations.

Most of these palms are unfortunately being planted in straight rows of trees of equal height and then trimmed "for neatness" to look like colossal, stiff shaving brushes. This aesthetically abominable habit makes these naturally stiff-looking palms even more stiff and sententious looking, and the visual effect is harsh, hot, and overly energetic, almost frenetic. Considering that these assaults on the sensibilities are often perpetrated in hot, arid climates, the effect is all the more disturbing; instead of lushness and quietude, coolness and gracefulness, these new developments and plantings have an austere and irascible, a regimented and hostile, a tiring and overbearing, demeanor. These noble trees are capable of providing wonderfully graceful landscape accents with their full crowns giving form and texture to the skyline and, in groups of full-crowned trees of varying heights, can add much beauty to warm climate gardening, whether arid or not. It is not a particularly good candidate for growing indoors although, given a bright or sunny situation and good air circulation, it sometimes grows well in large conservatories and atriums.

The date palm's role in the history of the Middle East is analogous to those of the coconut palm and the African oil palm in the tropics. It has been in cultivation for at least 5000 years. Due to the mystery of its place of origin and widespread cultivation, the date palm cannot be considered threatened in the traditional sense; however, as Sasha Barrow (1998) points out, the number of cultivars is decreasing and, once lost, these varieties are irretrievable. PLATE 635.

Phoenix loureiri is indigenous to India, southern Bhutan, and eastwards to Hong Kong, Taiwan, and the southern islands of the Philippines, where it grows from sea level to an elevation of 5280 feet. It is found in low mountainous deciduous or evergreen and open forests but also in cleared areas. The epithet honors Father João de Loureiro, an 18th-century Portuguese naturalist, herbalist, and plant collector in Indochina.

This small species occurs both as a solitary-trunked and as a clustering palm. The stems are 3 to 12 feet tall and to 1 foot in diameter. They are usually covered in all but their oldest parts with a dark brown mat of fiber and the short, stubby remains of the leaf bases. The leaves are variable in morphology but are mostly 6 feet long, arching, and with closely set narrow dark green leaflets that have sharply pointed apices; they grow from the rachis at different angles to create a stiffly plumose leaf. The leaflets may also be much wider at their bases, even more crowded and bluish gray-green. The straw-colored inflorescences are erect and mostly hidden by the leaves, and the bluish black mature fruits are found only at their apices.

The variability of this species is pronounced and seems to be related to types of exposure: in full sun the species tends to be short, slow growing, and more readily clustering, with shorter, bluer leaves and more crowded and fatter leaflets, while as an undergrowth subject in moist, partially shady forests, it grows taller with markedly fewer clustering individuals and with the leaflets less stiff, more widely spaced, and pure green. Sasha Barrow (1998) has subdivided the taxon into two varieties: *P. loureiri* var. *loureiri* and *P. loureiri* var. *humilis*. One would tend to think that the just-mentioned variability would correspond with the separate natural varieties, but not so; according to Barrow's monograph, the distinguishing characteristics are the presence or absence of sclerotic, tannin-filled cells along leaflet margins and midribs. Such is the sometimes esoteric and fascinating world of taxonomists!

Because of its wide range and many differing habitats, the little palm has unusual hardiness to cold for a species confined mainly to the tropics. It has withstood temperatures in the mid 20s (F) unscathed and is probably adaptable to zones 8 through 11. It grows in partial shade or full sun with the exposure variations listed above to be expected. As for soil type, it seems to almost run the gamut, thriving in calcareous as well as acidic media, although always becoming more robust on good ones. It is not fast growing. PLATES 636 & 637.

Phoenix paludosa occurs naturally along the coasts of northeastern India, Bangladesh, the Andaman and Nicobar Islands, Myanmar, Thailand, northern Sumatra, and peninsular Malaysia, where it grows landward of the mangrove forests in swampy areas that are periodically invaded by salt water. The palm's existence in peninsular Malaysia is threatened by habitat destruction. The epithet is Latin for "swampy" and refers to the habitat. The only common name seems to be mangrove date palm.

It is a clustering species with the mostly erect stems growing to 15 feet high. The clumps are dense and usually a wall of foliage, and the trunks are covered in a mass of narrow leaf bases, tightly adhering dark brown fibers, and long needles from the leaf bases; the upper portions of the trunks are not visible unless the thatch of dead leaves is trimmed. Each leaf crown is sparse when it can be seen among the competing ones. The leaves are 6 to 8 feet long and arching, giving the crown a full and rounded aspect. The soft but erect and nonpendent leaflets grow from the rachis in clusters arranged from a different angle, to give a full plumose effect.

The palm is not hardy to cold and needs warmth year-round, making it difficult to maintain in most Mediterranean climates like those of southern California. It does not tolerate drought and must have full sun after its seedling stage. As for soil, as long as it remains moist it works. The species is similar in appearance to *P. reclinata* but differs in the softer leaflets with glaucous undersides, a smaller stature, and much more supple and arching leaves. It can be pruned to look like a miniature Senegal date, although with difficulty and sometimes pain. It is probably best treated in the landscape as a large hedge or barrier. PLATES 638 & 639.

Phoenix pusilla is indigenous to southern India and Sri Lanka (formerly Ceylon), where it grows in monsoonal lowlands that are seasonally inundated and on drier ridges and hills. The epithet is Latin for "tiny" or "weak" and was given in the past when the variability of the species was little known. The common name is Ceylon date palm.

It is a solitary-trunked species for the most part, but clustering individuals are not rare in habitat. The trunk usually grows no taller than 15 feet but may be 1 foot in diameter and is usually covered with numerous, closely set, gray and narrow leaf bases, a distinguishing if not diagnostic characteristic. The 8- to 10-foot-long leaves are erect and ascending, arching only near their apices. The 1-foot-long, shiny light green leaflets are thin, stiff, and acutely pointed; they can be dangerous. The leaflets grow from several angles off the rachis to give the leaf a plumose but stiff appearance.

Attractive mainly because of the wicker-patterned trunks, this species is eminently worthy of cultivation. Alas, it is not cold hardy, being adaptable to zones 10 and 11, with the occasional nice specimen found in the more favorable microclimates of 9b. Like most other species in the genus, it is drought tolerant but grows more slowly and less robustly in dry soil. It grows slowly to begin with. PLATE 640.

Phoenix reclinata grows along rivers and streams in tropical western, eastern, and central Africa, in Zambia, Malawi, and Mozambique in southern Africa, and in Madagascar and the Comoro Islands, from sea level to 10,000 feet elevation, in clearings in the rain forest, seasonally flooded savannas, monsoonal forests, and even rocky mountainsides. Common names are Senegal date palm and African wild date palm. The epithet is Latin for "reclining," an allusion to the angle at which the outer stems of a clump grow.

The species is a large clustering one with trunks reaching 50 feet high but more often, especially in cultivation, 30 feet. Each trunk is 4 to 7 inches in diameter and is covered until old with short leaf bases and matted brown fibers; older trunks show closely set rings of leaf base scars in their lower portions. The palm freely suckers, and a clump may contain 25 separate stems and may be to 55 feet tall and 45 feet wide, but is usually 40 feet tall and 30 feet wide. The trunks are never straight but rather gracefully leaning outwards from the center of the cluster. The leaves are 12 to 15 feet long, narrowly elliptical, and gracefully arching. The 1-foot-long leaflets grow from the rachis at several different short angles, but the leaf appears from any distance flat. Leaf color is bright to deep glossy green on both sides, and the blade is held on short, 1-foot-long pseudo-petioles armed with long, vicious acanthophylls. There are from 20 to 40 leaves in the full, rounded crown. The fruits are 0.5 to 1 inch long, ovoid, and reddish brown. They are reportedly edible but mostly unpalatable.

The species is slightly susceptible to lethal yellowing disease. The palm is not hardy to cold, and the "pure" species is adaptable only to zones 10 and 11. Most plants in cultivation in the United States and especially in Florida are hybrids. This is both good and bad: good because the hybrids are usually more tolerant of cold; bad because some of the hybrids do not have the gracefulness of the nonhybridized individuals. It is impossible to give accurate data for the hardiness of individual hybridized specimens as the degree of cold tolerance depends on how much of the type is there and also what other species might be involved; in general, the hybrids that look enough like the type to be tagged with the binomial are damaged below 25°F and usually die from temperatures much below 20°F, while the pure species is killed at 25°F and below. The palm is indifferent to soil type as long as it is not highly acidic or extremely alkaline. It needs full sun from youth to old age and, with regular and adequate moisture, grows moderately fast; prolonged drought conditions set it back.

Although sometimes disdained in tropical or subtropical regions because of its ubiquity and weediness, this palm makes a beautiful, large clump. The clumps are made even more graceful and dramatic if a few trunks are thinned out as the mass develops so that the remaining trunks are of differing heights and so that their individual beauty can be seen and appreciated to its fullest. One of us (Bob) has seen this palm as a hedge with the many young trunks of evenly spaced plants obscured by a tangled mass of foliage, the visual effect being anything but attractive. If a hedge or barrier is wanted, it is infinitely more aesthetically pleasing to let a few trunks of varying heights form first and then allow the many subsequent suckers to form the desired barrier at the base of the larger ones—this can be a captivating tableau. One of the most beautiful landscape objects is a "wall" of these palms with tall trunks of varying heights above the tiers of lower leaves resulting from the offshoots. There is probably no more perfect candidate for

planting near ponds, lakes, or swimming pools, the gracefully reclining thin trunks lending a tropical and exotic essence that is only matched by something like the coconut. While the clumps are beautiful enough standing isolated in a wide expanse of lawn, they look much better if incorporated into masses of lower vegetation so that their crowns serve as canopy-scapes. The Senegal date palm is only good indoors if great space and high light levels are available.

The trunks are used for construction, and the leaves for thatch and for weaving baskets and other utensils; the fruits are often eaten and the seeds ground into a flour by the native peoples in the palm's habitats. PLATES 641–644.

Phoenix roebelenii occurs naturally in northern Laos, Vietnam, and southern China, where it grows along rivers in areas that are periodically flooded. Common names are pygmy date palm and miniature date palm. The epithet is a Latinized form of the German surname "Roebelin" and honors a 19th-century orchid fancier who first collected the species in Laos.

The form and habit of the pygmy date palm in cultivation are different from those of wild plants. Cultivated specimens have solitary, erect stems, with large, fully rounded crowns of leaves, while those in the wild are clustering palms with curving and twisting, thinner trunks, and sparser crowns. Sasha Barrow (1994) mentions that the form in cultivation is "the product of a series of hybridization events with other cultivated *Phoenix* species, and somewhere along this series the clustering ability was lost." She also theorizes, and rightly so we believe, that the clustering habit and sparser crowns of the wild populations allow the individual palms to withstand the periodic flood stages of the large rivers along which they grow. In cultivation, mature trunks usually grow 6 to 8 feet tall but may reach 10 feet. The stem is 3 inches in diameter near the base to 6 or 8 inches near the leaf crown, and it is usually covered in triangular leaf bases and a mat of brown fiber except near its base where it exhibits closely set spirals of knobby leaf base scars; wind, high humidity, or abrasion usually result in much more ringed trunk space. Older trunks may have a small mass of aerial roots at their bases. The full, rounded leaf crown is usually 6 feet wide and tall and has 50 leaves. The gracefully arching leaves are 3 to 5 feet long and the 10- or 12-inch-long leaflets grow from the rachis almost in one flat plane and are supple, thin textured, and pendent. The false petiole is 5 inches long and spiny. Leaf color is glossy deep green in mature leaves, but new leaves are covered with a fine chalky bloom that gives them a beautiful grayish green cast. The much-branched inflorescences are never more than 2 feet long, and the paddle-shaped spathes from which they emerge are almost as long. The small chaffy looking flowers are light yellow to almost white and produce fruit that is 0.5 inch long, oblong, and black.

The palm is hardy to cold for a tropical species, withstanding temperatures slightly below freezing without damage; it makes a good candidate in zones 10 and 11 and is marginal in 9b in areas subject to wet freezes in winter; Geoff Stein (pers. comm.) reports that, in southern California, the species usually does well even in 8b. The cultural requirement most often neglected with this species is its moisture needs: it is thirsty and needs constant and adequate water, even withstanding occasional flooding. In addition, it relishes a good, friable, and slightly acidic soil. It grows significantly slower in partial shade than it does in full sun.

The cultivated form of this species is unexcelled for using as a silhouette, a small patio tree, or along a walkway where its elegance of form and detail can be appreciated up close. *Phoenix roebelenii* is often sold in containers as a "double palm," meaning that there are two individuals to a pot; this practice is heartily encouraged as few things are lovelier than a planting of two or three palms of varying heights. The pygmy date does not look good in groups of three or more individuals of varying heights if the palm(s) are isolated specimens surrounded by space; its leaves are too delicate and gossamer to be so used unless near a wall or other contrasting form where the silhouette may be appreciated. This is an excellent choice for growing indoors if enough light can be provided.

Phoenix rupicola grows in wet or dry mountainous forests and clearings therein in India and Bhutan from elevations of 1000 to 4000 feet, usually on hillsides, cliffs, or otherwise sloping ground. The only common name seems to be cliff date palm. The epithet is Latin for "inhabitant of rocks" and refers to the palm's general habitat.

This is a solitary-trunked species whose mature overall height is 25 feet with a trunk diameter of 10 inches. The trunks are usually free of leaf bases except near the crown and show closely set spirals of knobby leaf base scars. The leaf crown is 15 feet wide and 20 feet tall. Leaves are 8 to 10 feet long with the 18-inch-long leaflets growing from the rachis in a single flat plane. The false petiole is 2 to 3 feet long and bears spines, which are shorter, fewer, more pliable, and less vicious than those of any other *Phoenix* species. The leaflets are deep olive to glossy emerald green on both surfaces, thin-textured, and limp. The newer leaves usually have a twist to the rachis that has the leaflets oriented vertically for half the length of the blade. The leaf crown is full and round to elongated. The inflorescences are remarkably similar to those of *P. dactylifera* in appearance and in location on the tree, and the 1-inch-long ob-

long fruits are yellow to orange, ripening to a purplish brown.

This is one of the most cold tender species in the genus and is adaptable only to zones 10 and 11 in areas subject to wet freezes in winter and is often marginal in 10a; Geoff Stein (pers. comm.) indicates that it is adaptable to 9b in the drier Mediterranean climate of southern California. It is adapted to partial shade when young but needs full sun when older to look its best and grow its fastest. It is drought tolerant when established but hardly grows under such conditions and is subject to yellowing and disease in poor soil; rather, it requires a humus-laden, fast-draining, and mostly moist soil. The species is slightly susceptible to lethal yellowing disease.

This is arguably the most beautiful solitary-trunked date palm. It combines the grace and elegance of the miniature date palm with the nobility of the Canary Island date, and a group of these palms with trunks of varying heights is one of the most beautiful sights the plant world has to offer. It is attractive enough to stand alone as an isolated specimen tree, and it is small enough to serve as a focal point in a large patio or courtyard, where its lushness and grace remind one of a small coconut. It is excellent as a canopy-scape. It needs space and high light levels if grown indoors. PLATE 645.

Phoenix sylvestris is indigenous to the lower elevations in southern Pakistan and most of India, where it grows in monsoonal plains and scrublands. Common names are toddy palm, wild date palm, silver date palm, and sugar date palm. The epithet is Latin for "of the forest."

It is a solitary-trunked species whose mature trunks may reach 50 feet high and have a diameter of 18 inches. The trunk, while not nearly as massive, looks much like that of *P. canariensis* and is covered until old in broadly triangular leaf bases and thence in the closely set spirals of stretched out diamond-shaped leaf base scars. Old trunks may produce, like those of *P. canariensis*, a dense mass of aerial roots near their bases. The leaf crown is 30 feet wide and 20 to 30 feet tall. The leaves are 8 to 10 feet long, gently arching, and are carried on 3-foot-long spiny petioles. The 18-inch-long, stiff leaflets grow from the rachis at several different angles, but the angles are small and the overall visual effect, especially from any distance, is that of a flat or nearly flat leaf. Leaf color is grayish to bluish green. The crown has, next to that of the Canary Island date, more leaves than any *Phoenix* species (to 100), and is full and rounded. The inflorescence is 3 feet long, with several yellow branches bearing many small whitish unisexual blossoms. The fruits are borne in large, wide, pendent clusters. Each one is 1 inch long, oblong, and orange but maturing to a lovely purplish red. The sap is used in India for making sugar and an alcoholic beverage, and the fruits are used to make jelly.

The species is slightly susceptible to lethal yellowing disease. The palm is not as hardy to cold as is the Canary Island date, being good in zones 9b through 11 and marginal in most areas of 9a. Like *P. canariensis*, it is drought tolerant when established but grows faster and looks better with adequate and regular moisture. It thrives on most fast-draining soils but needs sun, especially when past the juvenile stage.

The wild date palm is similar to the Canary Island date palm but lacks its massiveness, has a different leaf color, and has a stiffer, more compact crown. It serves the same landscape purposes and usually grows significantly faster than *P. canariensis*. It is not known to be grown indoors and is not recommended. PLATES 647 & 648.

Phoenix theophrasti is indigenous to the Mediterranean coasts of Crete and Turkey. The epithet honors the ancient Greek philosopher and botanist Theophrastus. The species has been known for centuries but was only technically described in 1967. It is similar to *P. dactylifera* and may be a form of it. It is, however, more clustering, of smaller stature, and has shorter and more bristly leaves. Its cultural requirements and attributes are identical to those of *P. dactylifera,* and its landscaping uses are, with the exception related to its stature, the same.

PHOLIDOCARPUS is a genus of four or five large, spiny, palmate-leaved, monoecious palms from peninsular Thailand, peninsular Malaysia, and Sumatra eastwards through the Moluccas. All species occur in lowland rain forest or swamps.

These are magnificently tall palms, some of which are reported to form trunks more than 100 feet high. They are usually straight, columnar, and almost white in their older parts, while light tan with closely spaced rings of ridged leaf base scars in their younger parts. The leaf crowns are large, globular, and open because of the long, spiny petioles and consist of numerous large, circular leaves with many wide segments extending nearly to the petiole, each of these again divided or bifurcated, much as in the genus *Livistona* to which this genus is closely related. In overall appearance, these species look like glorified crosses between *Borassodendron* and *Livistona*. The inflorescences grow from the leaf bases and are long and much branched, the primary branches enclosed in octopus armlike fleshy bracts, flowering branches bearing bisexual blossoms. The large fruits are round or ovoid, usually light brown, with a corklike surface shallowly divided into a mosaic of contiguous squares or short, pyramidal projections.

No fan-leaved palms are more beautiful, and it is perplexing why these are not much more widely cultivated in tropical climates. All are similar in general appearance, and all need tropical conditions and are possible only in zones 10b and 11. They are also true water lovers and need copious and regular moisture. They appreciate a humus-laden soil and need full sun when past the juvenile stage, at which time they prove to be robust and relatively fast growers in sufficiently warm climes. The genus name is two Greek words meaning "scaly" and "fruit." PLATES 648 & 649.

Pholidocarpus macrocarpus is indigenous to peninsular Thailand and peninsular Malaysia, where it grows in lowland rain forest swamps and along streams and rivers. The epithet is from two Greek words meaning "large" and "fruit" and alludes to the 3-inch-wide, light brown, globular warty fruits. The trunk attains a height of nearly 100 feet. The 6-foot-wide leaves are borne on 6- to 7-foot-long stout petioles whose lower margins bear a distinct yellow stripe and whose upper margins bear 3-inch-long curved spines with bulbous bases. PLATE 648.

Pholidocarpus maiadum is endemic to Borneo, where it grows in lowland swamps and along the edges of rivers and in clearings in the rain forest. The epithet is a Latinized form of a Sarawak place name. The species is similar in appearance to *P. macrocarpus* except for its stature, which is 70 feet. PLATE 649.

Pholidocarpus mucronatus is endemic to peninsular Malaysia, where it grows in lowland rain forest clearings, along rivers, and in lowland swamps. The epithet is Latin for "pointed" and alludes to the large teeth on the petioles. The species is similar to *P. macrocarpus* except for its stature, which is seldom over 70 feet high.

PHOLIDOSTACHYS is a genus of four pinnate-leaved, monoecious palms in tropical America. They are solitary trunked except for occasional clustering in one species and are not small palms, although they are delicate in appearance and are all undergrowth subjects in rain forest. Their leaf crowns are open and generally hemispherical, the leaves on long petioles and spreading. Newly unfurled leaves are usually light to deep orange in color. The inflorescences grow from the leaf bases and are mostly spikelike and once branched. The flowering branches are distinctive in being ropelike with the tiny flowers in pits. The fruits are borne in congested clusters and are rounded and purplish, brown, or black.

These palms are closely related to and visually similar to those in the genus *Geonoma* and are distinguished technically only by floral details. Of the two species in cultivation, only one is common. All species are cold sensitive and adaptable only to zones 10b and 11. They require constant moisture, high humidity, and a humus-laden soil.

All are adaptable to partial shade, which they absolutely require in hot climates and when young. They are relatively slow growing even under optimum conditions. The genus name is two Greek words meaning "scale" and "spike" and alludes to the pitted flowering branches of the inflorescences. PLATES 650–652.

Pholidostachys dactyloides is indigenous to eastern Caribbean coastal Panama, western coastal Colombia, and western coastal Ecuador, where it grows in rain forest at low to moderate elevations. The epithet is Latin for "fingerlike," the allusion unknown to us.

The solitary trunk attains a height of 30 feet and is 2–3 inches in diameter. The sparse leaf crown is in the form of a feather duster or, at most, is hemispherical. The mostly erect 5- to 6-foot-long leaves bear widely spaced elliptically shaped leaflets that are, after unfurling, green on both surfaces. PLATE 650.

Pholidostachys pulchra is indigenous to extreme southeastern Nicaragua, the Caribbean slopes of Costa Rica and Panama, and the western slope of the Andes in Colombia, where it grows from sea level to 2000 feet in mountainous rain forest. The epithet is Latin for "beautiful," which is an apt description of this delicate-looking species. The slender, solitary trunk attains a height of 25 feet but a diameter of only 1 to 2 inches in habitat, where it is rarely found as a sparsely clustering specimen. The open leaf crown is hemispherical in older plants but usually in the form of a shuttlecock in younger ones. The leaves are 3 to 5 feet long on 2- to 3-foot-long thin, wiry petioles and bear a few widely and irregularly spaced wide leaflets, which grow in a single flat plane from the rachis. The new growth is usually bronzy orange.

Pholidostachys synanthera grows naturally in the intermontane valleys of the Andes of northern and western Colombia and in mountainous rain forest of western Amazonia in eastern Ecuador, northern Peru, and extreme western Brazil. It occurs from sea level to an elevation of 5000 feet, always in wet forest. The epithet is from Greek words meaning "joined" and "flower."

This is a robust and beautiful species whose solitary stem attains a maximum height of 20 feet but is usually much shorter and is 3 inches in diameter. It is covered in many fibrous leaf bases in its younger parts but is smooth with closely spaced, indistinct rings of leaf base scars in its older parts. The leaf crown is dense and hemispherical to nearly spherical, and the leaves are 7 feet long on 4-foot-long thin petioles. The relatively few leaflets are wide and irregularly spaced in a flat plane along the rachis. They are 7 inches wide and 30 inches long and are pendent at their tips. PLATE 651.

PHYSOKENTIA is a genus of eight pinnate-leaved, solitary-trunked, monoecious palms in low mountainous rain forest of the Bismarck Archipelago, the Solomon Islands, the Fiji Islands, and the Vanuatu archipelago in the South Pacific. The beautifully ringed trunks are green in their younger parts and sit atop prominent, prickly, and usually branched stilt roots. All species have distinct crownshafts above which the short-petioled leaves are mostly ascending and beneath which the panicled inflorescences form, bearing both male and female flowers that produce clusters of red or black fruits.

These are some of the loveliest pinnate-leaved palms, their large leaves with large, wide pinnae and their stilt roots the essence of the tropical look. Alas, they are rare in cultivation. All the species are intolerant of cold and adaptable only to zones 10b and 11. All require copious moisture and humidity at all times and a humus-laden soil. As most are undergrowth palms, they relish partial shade and a sheltered site, the larger species tolerating full sun except in the hottest climates. They make some of the most beautiful greenhouse subjects.

The genus name is derived from the Greek word for "bubble" and an out-of-date name for species in the genera *Gronophyllum, Gulubia,* and *Hydriastele.* One of the species (*P. petiolatus*) was formerly the sole representative of the genus *Goniocladus.*

Physokentia dennisii is endemic to mountainous rain forest of the Solomon Islands, where it generally grows at elevations below 1000 feet. The epithet honors Geoffrey F. C. Dennis of the Forestry Department of Honiara in the Solomon Islands, who assisted Harold E. Moore, Jr., in finding the species.

The solitary trunk grows to 30 feet tall and 6 to 8 inches in diameter. It is a beautiful dark green in its younger parts, with widely spaced light brown rings of leaf base scars while, in its older parts, is light gray. It is supported by a dense 4-foot-tall cone of stilt roots and is topped by a yellowish to gray green crownshaft that is 3 feet tall and distinctly bulging at its base. The leaf crown is hemispherical and contains 10 spreading, 6-foot-long leaves on short petioles. The many leaflets are regularly spaced and grow from the rachis in a nearly flat, single plane. The central pinnae are more than 2 feet long, 3 inches wide, linear-elliptic, and dark green above and below, with long tapering and slightly pendent tips. The 3-foot-long, pendent, greenish white, single inflorescence produces 0.5-inch-wide rounded fruits that are deep orange or red when ripe.

Physokentia insolita is endemic to the Solomon Islands, where it grows in mountainous rain forest from elevations of 1700 to 3000 feet. The epithet is Latin for "unusual" and was bestowed by Harold E. Moore, Jr., because the species was, when he first saw specimens, atypical for the genus in details of its inflorescence and fruits.

Its slender solitary trunk attains a height of 50 feet and a diameter of 6 to 8 inches in habitat. It is deep green in its younger parts, with widely spaced gray rings of leaf base scars but, in its older parts, is light brown to deep gray. It is supported on a 5-foot-tall narrow, sparse cone of stilt roots. The crownshaft is 18 to 24 inches tall, slightly bulged at its base, and deep olive green but covered in tan scales which, unless rubbed off, impart their hue to the shaft. The leaf crown is spherical, with eight spreading leaves, each 6 feet long on a 1- to 12-inch-long petiole. The few broad and heavily ribbed leaflets are irregularly spaced, grow from the rachis in a single flat plane, and have obliquely truncated, jagged apices. The 0.5-inch-wide, rounded fruits are deep red when ripe.

Physokentia rosea is endemic to the Vanuatu islands, where it grows in mountainous rain forest from 2500 to 4000 feet elevation. The epithet is Latin for "rosy," an allusion to the newly opened flowers.

Its solitary dark green trunk attains a maximum height of 25 feet with a diameter of 4 inches and shows irregularly spaced and undulating, tan rings of leaf base scars. A narrow, 3-foot-tall cone of stilt roots supports it. The 18-inch-tall crownshaft is deep olive green and is slightly bulged at its base and cylindrical above that point. The leaf crown is hemispherical with eight spreading, 6-foot-long leaves on 8-inch-long petioles. The linear-elliptic, deep green leaflets are regularly spaced and grow in a single flat plane from the rachis, the longest ones 2 feet long. The round, 0.5-inch-wide fruits are glossy black when mature.

PHYTELEPHAS is a genus of six pinnate-leaved, dioecious palms in South America. There are solitary-trunked and clustering species, and the stems are mostly short and stout, covered in leaf bases and fibers, and are often subterranean or recumbent and creeping on the ground. The leaves are large, impressive, and elliptical, but the inflorescences and fruits are distinctive and unusual. The male inflorescences are pendent, ropelike or wormlike, unbranched affairs that bear many small flowers with tiny petals and numerous stamens. The female inflorescences are large, congested heads of large flowers with extremely long, fleshy, curling, ribbonlike sepals and petals. The dark brown fruits are formed in immense and congested heads, and are large, rounded, and covered in small, woody "plates" with horn or spiked projections protruding from the center of each plate. Individual fruits contain several seeds which, when mature, have an endosperm that is pure white or cream colored, hard, and has been and is used as ivory for carving objets d'art, buttons, and other utilitarian

commodities; it is generally called *tagua* in habitat and vegetable ivory in English-speaking regions. The immature endosperm is eaten or drunk as a beverage in its liquid state.

These exotic palms are unusual yet appealing and tropical looking with their large leaves and many leaflets, somewhat resembling gigantic tropical cycads. All are intolerant of enduring frost and need copious and regular moisture; they seem indifferent to soil type although they grow faster and look better in a humus-laden soil. The species are commonly referred to as ivory-nut palms. The genus name is from two Greek words meaning "plant" and "elephant" or, by extension, "ivory." PLATES 653–660.

Phytelephas aequatorialis is endemic to western Ecuador, where it grows in lowland rain forest and on the wet western slopes of the Andes Mountains to an elevation of 5000 feet. The epithet is Latin for "equatorial" and alludes to the palm's habitat, Ecuador, whose boundaries straddle the equator, and whose name is Spanish for "equator."

It is a solitary-trunked species and the tallest in the genus, the stems attaining heights of 50 feet and diameters of 1 foot. The immense leaf crown is spherical, mainly because of the persistent dead leaves that hang beneath the live ones. Individual leaves are linear-elliptical and 25 or even 30 feet long on short, stout petioles. The leaflets are extremely numerous and grow from the rachis in small groups and often at slightly different angles. The center leaflets are 2 or even 3 feet long, but the basal and apical leaflets are much shorter, the ones in between showing a continuum of diminishing lengths. They are all narrowly linear, a deep green on both surfaces, and slightly pendent.

This stupendous and magnificent species deserves to be much more widely planted in tropical regions. PLATE 653.

Phytelephas macrocarpa occurs naturally in the lowland rain forest of western Amazonia in eastern Peru, extreme western Brazil, and northwestern Bolivia. The epithet is Greek for "large" and "fruit."

Its solitary trunk is subterranean or, if aerial, short and usually recumbent. The leaf crown is in the form of a gigantic shuttlecock or nearly hemispherical, with 18 leaves, each 20 feet long, erect, but gently arching. The male inflorescences often reach the ground because of the short or subterranean trunks. PLATES 654 & 655.

Phytelephas seemannii is indigenous to eastern Panama and northwestern Colombia, where it occurs in the undergrowth of lowland rain forest in areas with seasonal flooding. The epithet honors Berthold C. Seemann, a 19th-century German botanist and plant explorer.

This unusual species forms a solitary aerial trunk 1 foot in diameter and to 40 feet long; it is prostrate for most of its length with the apical part and leaf crown erect. The lower portions of the stem usually die off and all parts form aerial roots that grow into the soil on the recumbent parts of the trunk. As the trunk slowly grows in length, the weight of the leaf crown, which can measure more than 50 feet in diameter, pulls the upper part of the trunk to the ground where it roots and eventually grows erect again. After the base of the stem dies off, the process starts again and, in time, results in the peregrination of the palm over short distances, the path usually circular. Because the trunk constantly grows longer but never exceeds 15 feet high before it returns to a recumbent position, the species has the potential of being immortal, eschewing the stresses related to height which cause other erect-growing palm species to eventually die. PLATES 656 & 657.

Phytelephas tenuicaulis is indigenous to extreme south central Colombia, northeastern Ecuador, and northwestern Peru, where it grows along rivers and streams and in swamps at low elevations. The epithet is Latin for "thin stemmed." This clustering species has beautiful, 6- to 8-foot-long, spreading but scarcely arching leaves whose numerous leaflets grow in a single flat plane. It is considered by some botanists to be a form of *P. macrocarpa*. PLATE 658.

PIGAFETTA is a genus of two tall, solitary-trunked, pinnate-leaved, spiny, dioecious palms in Sulawesi, the Moluccas, and Irian Jaya (Indonesian New Guinea), where they grow in clearings, at the edges of the mountainous rain forest, and along wide riverbanks, at elevations from sea level to 3000 feet. The two species are similar to each other in general appearance and only in 1998 did Dransfield recognize the genus to contain two separate taxa, distinguished, among other characters, by their geographical distribution.

There are no more beautiful or magnificent palms. The solitary trunks reportedly attain heights of 120 feet and more but are 18 inches in diameter, which gives old, tall individuals a grand elegance but imparts to younger ones a remarkably beautiful robustness. The stems are unusually smooth and are green in their upper half or even two-thirds, with widely spaced, distinct light gray rings of leaf base scars; they are light gray in their oldest parts. The leaf crowns are open in spite of the large number of leaves therein and are hemispherical or more so. The leaves are 20 feet long, beautifully arching to nearly recurved, and are borne on 6-foot-long, stout petioles with fat sheathing bases. These leaf sheaths vary from deep olive green to pale green or almost white and are covered with closely set rows of dark gray or golden, 3-inch-long flexible spines. The 3- to 4-foot-long leaflets are evenly and closely spaced

along the rachis and grow from it at a slight angle that creates a shallow V-shaped blade. They are deep green on both surfaces, linear-lanceolate, long tipped and pendent at their apices, and armed with bristles on their midribs.

The male and female inflorescences are similar in general appearance and grow from among the leaf sheaths. They are 5 to 6 feet long, and their main axis grows outwards at right angles to the trunk, with the flowering branches descending from it like a curtain; they are similar in appearance to those of the great palmate-leaved palm of South America, *Mauritia*. The female trees produce tiny fruits generally less than 0.5 inch in diameter, yellowish white to orange when mature, and covered in contiguous, diamond-shaped scales.

The species are famous for their rapid growth, which may be the fastest worldwide. After the seedling stage, they add 3 feet of trunk height per year. This growth rate may be due to their colonizing status in habitat: they are never found in primary forest, only in clearings or the edges of the rain forest. Given the fast growth rate of equatorial rain forest, they must grow quickly to outpace the other, competing trees. They therefore require full sun even as seedlings and copious and regular moisture. The palms survive in poor soil if supplied with enough water but only come into their own in a rich medium with humus; an organic mulch and a palm fertilizer with micronutrients help much, the latter especially important in the warmer parts of the year. *Pigafetta elata* (mistakenly named *filaris* at the time) has reportedly withstood temperatures in the upper 20s (F) with little damage in a protected site in Miami, Florida. It cannot be expected, however, to withstand such temperatures regularly as it is doubtless similar to the coconut in that it stops photosynthesizing with temperatures below 60°F. These palms are reportedly shallow rooted, and young plants are definitely top-heavy and need protection from high winds.

Many consider these palms the most beautiful in the world, including David Fairchild, who wrote in 1943 that the sunlight on the leaf sheath spines of the trees "gilded them and made them beautiful indeed, set off as they were against the dark green trunks marked with gray rings where the leaves had fallen off. From that moment I became unreasonable in my admiration for this tree, and I have remained so to this day." These palms are of incredible majesty and are among the few species that look wonderful planted alone as specimens, even surrounded by space. They look even better with other vegetation near or at their bases and, when planted in groups of three or more individuals of varying heights, the tableau is beyond thrilling. These palms are not for small gardens or intimate sites.

The genus name probably honors Antonio Pigafetta, a comrade and biographer of the 16th-century explorer Ferdinand Magellan. Some authors have misspelled the genus name as "Pigafettia." PLATES 661–665.

Pigafetta elata is indigenous to Sulawesi and the Moluccas from elevations of 1500 to 3000 feet. The epithet is Latin for "tall."

The leaves of juvenile plants tend to be spreading. The leaf sheaths and leaf rachises are deep dark olive green and densely covered with closely set rows of nearly black (in older individuals), 3-inch-long spines. The flowering branches of the inflorescences are deep brownish orange to cinnamon in color, and the fruits are orange when ripe.

This species is reportedly hardier to cold than is *P. filaris*.

Pigafetta filaris occurs naturally in the Maluku Archipelago and Irian Jaya from sea level to 1000 feet elevation. The epithet is Latin for "threadlike."

The leaves of young individuals tend to be ascending and erect. The leaf sheaths and leaf rachises are light colored and have few spines compared to those of *P. elata*; the spines are golden in both juvenile and mature trees. The inflorescences are similar to those of *P. elata* but light yellow. The fruits are the size of those of *P. elata* but yellow also.

The species is slightly less hardy to cold than is *P. elata*.

PINANGA is a genus of at least 120 pinnate-leaved, monoecious palms in southwestern and northeastern India, Sri Lanka, Nepal, Bhutan, Myanmar, southern China, Vietnam, Laos, Thailand, Malaysia, Indonesia, the Philippines, and New Guinea. There are both solitary-trunked and clustering species. Although a few are tall, most are small, undergrowth inhabitants of rain forest, and some are acaulescent. Most species grow at relatively low elevations, but a few extend into the cloud forests of tropical mountains, always in wet environments.

Some species show interesting and often beautiful leaf variation, especially when young, and many have nongreen juvenile leaves. Some have entire leaves with the pinnate segments fused together, while others have highly segmented leaves. The trunks are elegantly slender and beautifully ringed and look a lot like bamboo culms. The smaller species usually form aerial roots on their stems and, like some species of *Chamaedorea*, can be propagated with these trunk parts. Several species form stilt roots at the bases of their stems. The aerial-stemmed species have prominent crownshafts that are often colorful and beneath which are formed the short inflorescences, although some of the smaller or acaulescent species have inflorescences that grow from among the leaf sheaths. A few species have spikelike inflorescences but most are once branched. All

have separate male and female flowers on the same plant, and these blossoms are often colorful, in shades of pink, red, and purple. The small fruits are usually red or black.

There are some truly rare species in the genus with natural ranges limited to a certain soil type. All can grow in semishady spots, and indeed, most prefer such sites; a few large species are adaptable to full sun when past the juvenile stage. The species with mottled or variegated leaves are generally more colorful in shade and poor soil. None of the species are drought tolerant, and some are true water lovers that, nevertheless, usually require a fast-draining soil. None are tolerant of cold. These palms are unaccountably neglected in American tropical and subtropical gardens. The genus name is a Latinized form of an aboriginal name for palms in Malaysia that resemble this and other related genera. PLATES 666–691.

Pinanga adangensis is a rare and endangered species indigenous to peninsular Thailand and peninsular Malaysia, where it occurs in the undergrowth of rain forest and along streams and rivers at low elevations. The epithet is Latin for "of Adang," an island in the Straits of Molucca.

It is a clustering species whose stems grow to 18 feet high with a diameter of slightly more than 1 inch. They are dark green with prominent, widely spaced light brown rings of leaf base scars. The loose crownshafts are 2 feet tall, slightly thicker, if at all, than the stems, and light tan with purplish brown hues due to a short tomentum. The gracefully arching 6-foot-long leaves on 2-foot-long petioles bear regularly spaced, dark green linear-lanceolate 18-inch-long leaflets, the apical pair wider than the others. The 0.5-inch-long, teat-shaped fruits are purple when mature.

The species is more beautiful than most *Chamaedorea* species and makes an elegant house or greenhouse plant. As an under-canopy subject in the garden, it is superb lining paths or as an accent in other vegetation. PLATE 666.

Pinanga aristata is endemic to Kalimantan (Indonesian Borneo), where it occurs in the undergrowth of mountainous rain forest at elevations of 500 to 3000 feet. The epithet is Latin for "bearded," an allusion to the white tomentum on the inflorescences.

It is a sparsely clustering species whose stems grow slowly to 6 feet high. A clump seems to always have a single dominant and taller stem, with subsidiary and much shorter ones at its base. The short crownshafts are scarcely thicker than the slender trunks and are grayish green. The leaves are apparently of two types—entire with a bifid apex, or segmented with broad leaflets—but always light, yellowish green with heavy deep green or purplish green mottling and always heavily ribbed. New growth is bluish green or purple greenish with dark purplish or green mottling. The little fruits are scarlet.

It is almost impossible to overwater this little beauty and it even tolerates waterlogged soil for short periods. It is intolerant, however, of full sunlight, especially in hot climates.

Pinanga auriculata is an undergrowth subject endemic to low mountainous rain forest in Sarawak on the island of Borneo. The epithet is Latin for "with an ear" and refers to a small curved protrusion of the leaf sheath.

The stem of this solitary-trunked species grows to 6 or 7 feet high but slightly less than 1 inch in diameter. It is silvery green to light tan and widely but indistinctly ringed with leaf base scars. The crownshaft is silvery green or almost white, 18 inches tall, cylindrical, and half again as thick as the slender trunk. The leaf crown is sparse, open, and hemispherical, with a few arching and spreading leaves, each of which bears 18 pairs of linear-elliptic, widely spaced, long-tipped, and slightly S-shaped, light green leaflets. The leaflets grow from the silvery rachis in a single flat plane, the apical pair wider than the others. The little fruits are borne in pendent, congested masses and are light, silvery green when mature.

Pinanga bataanensis is endemic to the Batan Islands (of the Philippines) north of the island of Luzon, where it occurs in low mountainous rain forest. The epithet is Latin for "of Batan."

The solitary trunk grows to 20 feet with a diameter of 4 to 5 inches and is light brown with widely spaced light gray rings of leaf base scars. The crownshaft is 2 feet tall, light silvery or grayish green, and slightly bulging at its base. The leaf crown is hemispherical to nearly spherical, with spreading, 6- to 8-foot-long, gracefully arching leaves. The numerous and regularly spaced linear-lanceolate, soft, dark green, 2-foot-long leaflets grow from the rachis in a single flat plane. The little 0.5-inch, teat-shaped fruits are deep orange.

This is not a colorful species, but it is beautiful, looking like a cross between a large *Chamaedorea* species and the kentia palm, *Howea forsteriana.* PLATE 667.

Pinanga bicolana is a solitary-trunked species endemic to the island of Luzon in the Philippines, where it occurs in lowland rain forest. The epithet if Latin for "of Bicol" in Luzon.

The green trunk grows to 10 feet, with a diameter of 1.5 inches, and is deep green with widely spaced rings of leaf base scars. The 2-foot-tall crownshaft is cylindrical, slightly thicker than the stem, and light green with a brownish red suffusion. The sparse leaf crown is hemispherical to nearly spherical, with six 3-foot-long spreading leaves on 10-inch-long petioles. The leaflets of adult trees are unequally spaced along the rachis, are unequal in size, and are mostly obliquely ovate with S-shaped ribs and

jagged apices; they are bluish to deep olive green above with mottling of lighter green and are grayish green beneath. The 0.5-inch-long, teat-shaped fruits are red, maturing to purplish black.

Pinanga caesia is a solitary-trunked species endemic to Sulawesi, where it grows in low mountainous rain forest. The epithet is Latin for "slate blue" and alludes to the striking color of the leaf rachis.

The trunk attains a height of 12 feet, a diameter of 3 inches, and is deep olive green with light brown, undulating rings of leaf base scars. The plump crownshaft is 18 inches tall, bulging at its base, and light to dark orange-brown, shading to purple at its summit. The leaf crown is hemispherical or nearly so, and the 5- to 6-foot-long, slightly arching leaves bear numerous regularly spaced, yellowish or bluish green, linear, wedge-shaped leaflets with jagged apice; the leaflets grow from the rachis in a single, nearly flat plane and, as they age, become pendent at their tips. The new growth is a beautiful rusty- or orange-brown. The flowering branches of the inflorescences are light, bright pink at anthesis and turn to coral or scarlet as the little fruits also mature to deep red.

This is a very colorful species. PLATES 668–670.

Pinanga capitata is a sparsely clustering species endemic to Sabah on the island of Borneo, where it occurs in mountainous rain forest from elevations of 2000 to 5000 feet. The epithet is Latin for "with a head" and refers to the swollen base of the leaf sheaths or crownshaft.

The stems grow to 6 feet high with diameters of less than 1 inch. They are dark green with light gray, ridged rings of leaf base scars. The 8-inch-tall crownshafts are yellowish olive green and are swollen at their bases, looking almost tumorous. The open leaf crown is nearly hemispherical, with a few spreading, stiff, and barely arching 4-foot-long leaves. The leaflets are widely spaced linear, light green, long-tipped, slightly S-curved and softly pendent leaflets; the terminal pair of leaflets is joined at the bases and much broader than the others.

A naturally occuring variety, **P. capitata var. divaricata**, has unusual, widely spaced, narrow, and stiff leaflets that are arranged along the rachis opposite each other at right angles in a flat plane; the leaflets of the terminal pair are slightly wider than the others and are not united. The epithet *divaricata* is Latin for "diverging" and alludes to the thin leaflets growing at right angles to each other.

Pinanga chaiana is endemic to low mountainous rain forest in Sabah. The epithet is a Latinized form of the Chinese surname "Chai" and honors a 20th-century botanist in Borneo.

This distinctive little palm is solitary trunked, with a stem to 10 feet high and slightly less than 1 inch in diameter. It is silvery green with widely spaced dark brown or reddish brown rings of leaf base scars. The narrow crownshaft is 2 to 3 feet tall, tapering from its purplish brown summit to its light pinkish tan base. The leaf crown is almost hemispherical, with ascending and spreading, stiff 3- to 4-foot-long leaves that are obovate, entire and unsegmented, apically bifid, and emerald green, with deep pleats in the blade and a light yellowish green, stout midrib. PLATE 671.

Pinanga cochinchinensis is a densely clustering species endemic to northern Vietnam, where it grows in lowland rain forest. The epithet is Latin for "of Cochin, China" and was bestowed by Carl Blume in the 19th century from specimens he thought originated from China.

The stems grow to heights of 20 feet and a diameter of 2 inches. They are deep green with widely spaced light gray rings of leaf base scars. The elongated, 3-foot-tall narrow crownshafts are pale yellow to almost white and scarcely thicker than the trunks. The spreading, slightly arching leaves are 6 feet long and bear numerous linear-lanceolate, 2-foot-long limp and slightly pendent leaflets that are emerald green above and pale silvery green beneath.

The species is stunning in its beauty, and its tiers of foliage are attractive in almost any site. It withstands more sun than most undergrowth species.

Pinanga copelandii is endemic to several islands in the Philippines, where it grows in lowland rain forest. The epithet honors Edwin B. Copeland, a 20th-century botanist. The species is similar in overall appearance to *P. maculata* but is much larger, its solitary trunk attaining a height of 25 feet with a diameter of 4 inches. Its leaves are not as colorful as are those of *P. maculata* and what little mottling they show is green. It is nevertheless a beautiful species. PLATE 672.

Pinanga coronata occurs naturally in the undergrowth of Indonesia's rain forest. The only common name seems to be ivory cane palm. The epithet is Latin for "crowned," an allusion to the shape of the leaf crown.

This is a clustering species whose stems may grow to 20 feet or sometimes more but are usually half this tall, with maximum diameters of 2 inches. They are light green (occasionally gray in the oldest parts) and are beautifully ringed with brown leaf base scars. The leaf crown is sparse and consists of usually no more than six leaves. A mature clump is 12 feet tall and 8 feet wide, although in habitat the palms may be approximately twice those dimensions. The crownshaft is small, less than 1 foot high, light green to nearly yellow, smooth, and of a slightly greater diameter than the trunk. The leaf bases often turn brown before the leaf falls, which makes the crownshaft a papery brown. The leaves are 4 to 5 feet long but 3 feet wide and are held

on 1-foot-long petioles that are covered in small cinnamon-colored scales. The leaflets grow from the rachis at a slight angle and are heavily veined, the veins depressed above, resulting in a grooved look. The leaves grow from the trunk almost erect but later are spreading, and the stout petioles are slightly arching. The shape of the leaflets varies from elliptic-lanceolate and pointed to wide-oblong and truncate with toothed apices, some individuals having only one or the other shape, others having mixed types on the same plant. Leaf color is light green to emerald green on both surfaces. New leaves are usually a beautiful light pink. The inflorescences are 1 foot long, grow from beneath the crownshaft with small pendent branches, and bear small pinkish white flowers of both sexes; they turn a deep red as the fruits mature. The fruits are ovoid, 0.5 inch long, and jet black when ripe.

The species does not tolerate full sun, especially in hot climates. It needs constant and abundant moisture and a rich but fast-draining soil. It is also intolerant of cold and is adaptable only to zones 10b and 11, although there are nice specimens in warm microclimates or protected sites in 10a. The ivory cane palm is comfortable only in partially shaded sites except in areas with mild summers. It is easily overwhelmed by other plant forms and needs to be planted where its graceful aspect can be seen—in sites with rounded or contrasting nonpinnate foliage companions. It makes a beautiful small hedge or wall in semishady sites and is a near perfect accent in borders. It also is unsurpassed in intimate patios and courtyard plantings. This is a fine choice for growing indoors if given enough light (but not full sun) and water. PLATES 673–675.

Pinanga curranii is endemic to the Philippines, where it grows in lowland rain forest. The epithet is a Latinized form of the surname "Curran" and honors a plant collector in the Philippines.

It is mostly found as a clustering species but occasionally as a solitary-trunked specimen. The trunks grow to heights of 20 or 25 feet with diameters of 2 inches. The crownshafts are 3 feet tall, slightly thicker than the stems, cylindrical, and olive green. The open leaf crown is hemispherical with six 2.5-foot-long spreading leaves on 8-inch-long petioles. The numerous leaflets grow from the rachis in a flat, single plane but are of unequal widths and are spaced unequally along the rachis. They are generally linear-elliptic but are curved forwards into a falcate form. They are deep emerald green above but yellowish or grayish green beneath with jagged apices. The 0.5-inch-long, teat-shaped fruits are deep red when ripe.

The species has a beautiful silhouette with its large, open crown of deep green, stiff-leafleted leaves. PLATE 676.

Pinanga densiflora is a densely clustering species endemic to low mountainous rain forest in Sumatra. The epithet is Latin for "densely flowered."

The stems grow to 12 feet high but have diameters of less than 1 inch. The crownshafts are hardly thicker than the stems and are usually tan. The leaf crowns are not obvious unless the clumps are thinned. The leaves are 4 feet long on 2-foot-long petioles in mature plants, with a few broad leaflets of unequal sizes and shapes, the inner ones generally broadly elliptic with pointed tips, the apical ones much broader with truncated, jagged tips; all are hazily ribbed. They are light green with heavy, dark mottling, and the new growth is pinkish hued. Older leaves generally are deep green with little mottling. The young leaves are attractive and unusual, but the mature clumps are dense with leaves. The small fruits are jet black when ripe.

Pinanga dicksonii is endemic to southern India in wet forests of the Western Ghat Mountains, growing at an elevation of 1000 feet. The epithet is a Latinized form of the surname "Dickson" and honors a late 18th- and early 19th-century botanist.

The palm is a clustering species whose stolons may form stems some distance from each other as well as form basal suckers at a "mother plant." They grow to 25 feet high with diameters of 2 inches and are deep green with widely spaced light gray rings of leaf base scars. The crownshafts are 2 feet tall, nearly the same diameter as the trunks, and a rich gold. The leaf crowns are hemispherical and contain six stiffly spreading 4-foot-long leaves on short petioles. The numerous 2-foot-long leaflets are regularly spaced along the rachis and are linear-lanceolate and curved or falcate in overall form. They are pure light green on both surfaces. In younger plants they are stiff and grow from the rachis at an angle which creates a leaf that is slightly V shaped but, in older plants, they are more lax and grow in a single flat plane and are even pendent. The flowering branches of the inflorescences are golden when new but later turn coral colored with pink flowers that produce small red fruits.

This beautiful species is reportedly more tolerant to cold than most other *Pinanga* species. PLATE 677.

Pinanga disticha is a small, clustering species indigenous to Sumatra and peninsular Malaysia, where it occurs in mountainous rain forest from sea level to an elevation of 4000 feet, often forming dense colonies. The epithet is Latin for "distichous" and alludes to the disposition of the fruits on the stalk of the infructescence.

The stems grow to a maximum of 4 feet high with diameters of 0.25 inch. The leaf crowns are sparse, with 1-foot-long, deep green leaves that are mostly obovate with deep apical notches, but some plants have leaves with a few segments. They are mottled to varying degrees with light green to almost white splotches. The little fruits are red when ripe.

The species, especially the more highly colored individuals, makes a stunning high groundcover in the shade of tropical or nearly tropical climates. PLATE 678.

Pinanga elmeri is endemic to the Philippines on several islands, where it grows in mountainous rain forest from elevations of 2000 to 6000 feet. The epithet honors Adolph D. E. Elmer, an early 20th-century American botanist.

This is a beautiful, sparsely clustering species, often found as a solitary-trunked specimen. The stems attain heights of 12 feet and diameters of 2 inches. They are deep grayish green with widely spaced gray rings of leaf base scars. The crownshafts are 3 feet high, cylindrical, slightly thicker than the stems, and a beautiful, light reddish brown. The leaf crowns are hemispherical, with 5- to 6-foot-long, spreading, slightly arching leaves on 1-foot-long petioles. The leaflets are regularly spaced along the rachis and grow in a single flat plane. Each one is 18 inches long, deep but bright green on both surfaces, and linear-lanceolate; the leaflets of the terminal pair are wider than the others. The 0.5-inch-long oblong fruits are light red when ripe.

Pinanga insignis is a solitary-trunked species indigenous to several islands of the Philippines and the Palau islands to the east, where it occurs in low mountainous rain forest. The epithet is Latin for "remarkable."

The trunk grows to 40 feet high with a diameter of 8 inches, making it the tallest species in the genus. The trunk is deep olive green with light brown rings of leaf base scars. The crownshaft is 4 feet tall, bulging at its base, and an even deeper olive green to brownish green. The leaf crown is hemispherical, with as many as a dozen 10-foot-long stiff and spreading, dark green leaves on short, almost nonexistent petioles. The deep green leaflets are 3 feet long and linear-lanceolate, and grow in a single flat plane from the rachis. They have shortly bifid apices and are stiff and straight when new but gradually soften and become pendent. The flowering branches of the inflorescences are 2 feet long and produce pendent clusters of deep red, ovoid fruits.

The species is tender to cold and needs partial shade when young, especially in hot climates. The palm is magnificent and has visual affinities with *Dictyosperma* and even *Archontophoenix*. It is nevertheless not a good candidate for planting as a single specimen surrounded by space but is most attractive in groups of three or more individuals of varying heights. PLATE 679.

Pinanga javana is endemic to mountainous rain forest of western Java, where it is in danger of extinction because of land clearing for agricultural expansion. The epithet is Latin for "Javan."

This is a solitary-trunked species whose mature stems grow to 30 or more feet and 4 or 5 inches in diameter. They are free of leaf bases and fiber, are light gray to almost white except for the youngest parts which may be green, and are wonderfully ringed with dark green leaf base scars. The leaf crown is 12 feet wide and 6 feet tall. The crownshaft is 3 to 4 feet tall, emerald to olive green, bulging at its base, and smooth and shiny. The leaf crown is open and hemispherical with no more than 10 leaves. The leaves are 4 to 6 feet long and 4 feet wide. They are slightly but gracefully arching on short green petioles that are usually no more than 6 inches long. The 2- to 3-foot-long leaflets are uniformly shaped and regularly spaced along the rachis, growing in a single flat plane. They are slightly limp and pendent, narrowly lanceolate and tapering, and a vibrant and glossy green on both sides. The two terminal leaflets are wider than the others. The inflorescences grow from beneath the large crownshaft and are 2 feet long with pendent yellowish green branches bearing small yellowish white flowers of both sexes. They usually form a "skirt" around the trunk. The fruits are 1 inch wide, rounded, and deep orange.

The palm is a true water lover and must never suffer drought. It also needs a rich, humus-laden, well-drained soil but luxuriates in full sun when mature. It does not tolerate freezing temperatures but is well adapted to frostless Mediterranean climes if its moisture requirements can be met. This is one of the choicest and most beautiful palms in the genus but is not a candidate for planting singly as a specimen, isolated with space around itself; instead, it is most enchanting in groups of three or more individuals of varying heights. It looks especially nice with a background of darker green foliage and has an almost overwhelmingly attractive silhouette. It is well suited for a large patio or courtyard, especially if planted in groups, and it is among the finest canopy-scapes. PLATE 680.

Pinanga maculata is endemic to several islands in the Philippines, where it occurs in the undergrowth of dense rain forest and along riverbanks, from sea level to an elevation of 5000 feet. The epithet is Latin for "spotted" and alludes to the new growth.

This is a solitary-trunked species whose stem attains a height of 25 feet in habitat. It is dark green with widely spaced light gray rings of leaf base scars. The crownshaft is 18 inches tall, scarcely thicker than the trunk, and is brownish purple to reddish brown. The leaf crown is hemispherical, and the individual, spreading leaves are 4 feet long on 1-foot-long petioles and bear 8 to 10 pairs of broad, unequally sized and unequally spaced, stiff and

strongly ribbed leaflets, the upper ones deeply incised apically into four to six pointed lobes. Leaf color is deep green above, with a silvery hue beneath. The new growth in young plants is light yellowish green mottled with orange, pink, and red.

This is one of the world's most beautiful small palms; each individual is a little symphony of color and form and needs to be placed where its intimate beauty can be appreciated up close. PLATES 681–683.

Pinanga malaiana is indigenous to mountainous rain forest in peninsular Thailand, Sumatra, peninsular Malaysia, and western Borneo, from sea level to an elevation of 3000 feet. The epithet is Latin for "Malayan."

The stems of this clustering species grow to heights of 20 feet with a diameter of 1.5 inches. They are deep olive green with widely spaced reddish brown rings of leaf base scars. The crownshafts are 18 to 20 inches tall, cylindrical, and slightly thicker than the trunks. They are light green overlain with golden and light to dark purplish hues. The leaf crowns are open and nearly spherical, and contain half a dozen 6-foot-long, spreading and slightly arching leaves on 4-foot-long yellowish petioles. The leaflets are deep emerald green, 3 feet long, regularly spaced along the rachis, and narrowly lanceolate and long tipped. The leaves resemble those of the kentia palm, *Howea forsteriana*. The inflorescences are 1 foot long and turn coral red as the 1-inch-long, teat-shaped fruits ripen to a shiny blackish purple.

Pinanga negrosensis is endemic to the Philippine island of Negros, where it grows in low mountainous rain forest. The epithet is Latin for "of Negros."

It is a large species whose trunks are sparsely clustering and attain heights of 30 feet, with diameters of 3 inches. They are light green in their younger parts, nearly black in their older parts, and beautifully ringed with brown leaf base scars. The leaf crown is in the form of a feather duster or, at most, hemispherical. The 6- to 7-foot-long leaves have 1-foot-long elliptical leaflets that grow from the rachis at an angle to create a slightly V-shaped leaf. The 0.5-inch-long fruits are yellow, ripening to a deep red or shiny black.

This is definitely among the most beautiful species in the genus. PLATES 684 & 685.

Pinanga patula occurs naturally in Sumatra, peninsular Malaysia, and western Kalimantan (Indonesian Borneo), where it grows in mountainous rain forest from sea level to 4000 feet. The epithet is Latin for "spreading," an allusion to the leaf crown.

This variable species has both solitary-trunked and clustering forms. The trunks attain heights of 12 feet but diameters of slightly more than 1 inch. The 2-foot-tall crownshafts are hardly thicker than the stems and are light orange to nearly white. The leaf crowns are nearly spherical, with ten 3-foot-long, spreading, and gently arching leaves with 18-inch-long, S-shaped, light to deep green pinnae that may be broad or narrow but are always deeply ribbed and regularly and widely spaced along the rachis. The little fruits are brown, red, or black when ripe.

This attractive species brightens up shady areas with its form and color. PLATE 686.

Pinanga perakensis is a densely clustering species indigenous to peninsular Thailand and peninsular Malaysia, where it occurs in mountainous rain forest from elevations of 2500 to 3000 feet. The epithet is Latin for "of Perak," a region of Malaysia.

The stems grow to 10 feet with diameters of 1 inch. The elongated crownshafts are 18 inches tall, wider at their summits than at their bases, and a felty orange to brown. The leaf crowns are shaped like shuttlecocks with ascending and erect 6-foot-long leaves on 2-foot-long orange petioles. The dark green leaflets are widely spaced, linear-lanceolate, and slightly S shaped, the longest ones 2 feet. The fruits are black when ripe.

Pinanga philippinensis is endemic to a few islands in the Philippines, where it occurs in dense rain forest at low to moderate elevations. The epithet is Latin for "of Philippines."

The stems of this clustering species grow to 6 or 8 feet, with diameters of 1 inch. They are olive green with widely spaced dark green rings of leaf base scars. The crownshafts are 18 to 24 inches tall, bulging near their summits, and bluish gray to yellow. The leaf crowns are hemispherical with large, 6-foot-long spreading, slightly arching leaves on 8-inch-long golden petioles. The numerous leaflets are deep green, narrowly linear, long tipped, and regularly spaced along the yellowish rachis. They grow in a single flat plane and their long tips are slightly pendent.

The species is one of the more beautiful because of its colors and form, delightful in any partially shaded site.

Pinanga pilosa is endemic to mountainous rain forest in Sabah to an elevation of 6000 feet. The epithet is Latin for "hairy."

It is a small clustering species with slender, wiry 3-foot-tall stems. The leaves are 2 feet long and bear three to four pairs of wide, deeply ribbed, forward-pointing leaflets. The middle pairs are much wider than the others, and all are light to medium green with dark green to brown mottling.

This species is one of the most colorful smaller palms and is stunning as a tall groundcover in partial shade. It is also one of the thirstiest species in the genus, being fussy about constant moisture.

Pinanga polymorpha is a clustering species endemic to peninsular Malaysia, where it grows in mountainous rain forest from elevations of 1500 to 5000 feet, usually forming dense thickets. The epithet is from two Greek words meaning "many" and "form," an obvious reference to the variable leaf morphology.

The stems grow to 10 feet but are usually less than 5 feet high. They are thin and 0.5 inch in diameter. The 6-inch-tall crownshafts are scarcely thicker than the stems, sometimes slightly bulged at the base, and light brown. Leaf shape varies and is not related to age or size of the plants, although the leaves of older individuals are generally 3 to 5 feet long. The leaves may be obovate and unsegmented except for the deeply bifid apex or they may be segmented into three or more pairs of leaflets of varying shapes, from elliptical with pointed apices to wide, forward-pointing oblique parallelograms with truncated, jagged apices, the apical ones always with the last-named form. They are always heavily ribbed. Leaf color is usually dark green above and grayish green beneath and often shows indistinct mottling, especially in the older leaves. The ripe fruits are deep blue to almost black on coral-colored flowering branches.

There is no more beautiful tall groundcover plant. The groves are symphonies of form and color.

Pinanga punicea is endemic to Papua New Guinea, where it occurs in low mountainous rain forest. The epithet is Latin for "red."

It is a solitary-trunked species whose trunk grows to nearly 30 feet high and 4 to 5 inches in diameter. It is light gray to light brown except for the youngest portion, which is green, and it is strongly ringed with darker leaf base scars. The crownshaft is 3 feet tall, slightly thicker than the trunk, cylindrical, and light reddish brown to almost red. The leaf crown is hemispherical with six stiff, spreading 8-foot-long leaves whose leaflets are 2 feet long, linear-lanceolate, and deep olive green. They grow from the rachis in a single flat plane, and the older ones are pendent. The fruits are brilliant scarlet.

This is among the finest and most beautiful species in the genus, almost perfection of form and color. It is, alas, also one of the most tender to cold.

Pinanga rivularis is endemic to Sarawak, where it occurs in lowland rain forest along the banks of rivers and streams. The epithet is Latin for "of the river."

It is a densely clumping species whose stems grow 4 feet high and 0.5 inch in diameter. They are deep green and are distinctly ringed with reddish brown leaf base scars. The little crownshafts are scarcely thicker than the stems, 6 inches tall, cylindrical, and light, silvery green. The leaf crowns are open and hemispherical, with 3- to 4-foot-long, beautifully arching leaves on 6-inch-long petioles. The narrow leaflets are widely spaced along the rachis and are of equal width and form, each one 18 inches long and light to deep silvery green.

The species is a true rheophyte whose stems are often submerged in water. It also needs shade or partial shade. It is among the most beautiful little plants for lining shady ponds or streams, its form and color much brightening the gloom of such sites.

Pinanga sclerophylla is endemic to the Philippine island of Mindoro, where it grows in mountainous rain forest from elevations of 1000 to 5000 feet. The epithet is from two Greek words meaning "dry" or "papery" and "leaf."

The robust, solitary trunk attains a height of 20 feet and a diameter of 2 to 3 inches. It is deep green and graced with prominent light gray rings of leaf base scars. The 3-foot-tall crownshaft is deep olive green to bluish green, smooth and mostly cylindrical, slightly thicker than the trunk. The leaf crown is shaped like a shuttlecock and has steeply ascending, 6-foot-long, dark green leaves with regularly spaced, 2-foot-long linear, stiff leaflets growing in a flat plane from the rachis. The oblong fruits are borne in large pendent masses and are deep orange when ripe. PLATES 687 & 688.

Pinanga scortechinii is a clustering species indigenous to peninsular Thailand and peninsular Malaysia, where it grows in mountainous rain forest from elevations of 1000 to 3000 feet. The epithet is a Latinized form of the Italian surname "Scortechini" and honors a 19th-century Catholic missionary and plant collector.

The stems attain heights of 15 feet with diameters of 1 inch. They are deep olive green with widely spaced reddish brown to gray rings of leaf base scars. The crownshafts are 2 feet tall, plump, elongatedly elliptical, and a beautiful golden yellow to brownish orange. The leaf crowns are sparse and open with mostly ascending, 6- to 7-foot-long leaves on 2-foot-long, yellowish green petioles. The dull green leaflets are widely spaced along the rachis, 18 inches long, narrow, long tipped, and slightly S shaped, and grow from the rachis in a single flat plane. The inflorescences are short, erect, and golden. They produce congested, erect masses of teat-shaped fruits that are white when new, turning pink and later black when ripe. PLATE 689.

Pinanga simplicifrons is indigenous to peninsular Thailand, peninsular Malaysia, and Sumatra, where it grows in lowland rain forest, often forming colonies. The epithet is Latin for "simple frond," an allusion to the mainly unsegmented leaves.

This is a dwarf, clustering species whose stems sometimes attain a height of 4 feet but are usually less than 0.5 inch in diameter. The crownshafts are rudimentary, loose, and ill defined but extended along the upper part of the stems. They are mostly light brown because the sheaths remain on the little trunks until they rot away. The individual 1-foot-long leaves are mostly unsegmented, linear-obovate, apically bifid, the outer margins of the division toothed, glossy deep green, and deeply ribbed; a few plants have leaves with a paucity of variably shaped segments. They are borne on 1-foot-long, thin petioles, making the little leaf crown airy and open. The inflorescences and infructescences are unusual in that they are generally formed inside the persistent, papery and tan sheaths of the ill-defined crownshafts through which they eventually break through. The fruits are scarlet when ripe and are 0.5 inch long, shaped like a bull's horn.

Pinanga speciosa is endemic to the island of Mindanao in the Philippines, where it grows in mountainous rain forest at elevations of 1200 to 4000 feet. The epithet is Latin for "beautiful."

It is a large solitary-trunked species that spends its youth as an undergrowth subject but usually emerges above the canopy as an adult. The trunk attains a height of 30 feet and is 4 to 5 inches in diameter. It is deep bluish green with widely spaced whitish rings of leaf base scars. The crownshaft is 4 or 5 feet tall, slightly thicker than the trunk at the base of the shaft, tapering up to the leaf crown, and an even deeper bluish green, almost black. The leaf crown is open, sparse, and hemispherical to nearly spherical. The leaves are 8 feet long on 2- to 3-foot-long light-colored petioles. The stiff leaflets grow from the rachis in a single flat plane and are 3 or more feet long, linear-lanceolate, long tipped, and deep green on both surfaces. The small fruits are blackish purple and formed in two rows along pendent branches.

This is certainly among the more magnificent species in the genus and is thrilling in groups of three or more individuals of varying heights. It is capable of adapting to full sun once past the juvenile stage except in hot dry climates. PLATE 690.

Pinanga veitchii is endemic to the lowland rain forest in Sarawak. The epithet honors James Veitch, a 19th-century British nurseryman.

Mature plants are similar to *P. simplicifrons,* but young individuals have distinctive, almost startling leaf color, with the background of the blades dark green and mottled with varying amounts and shades of brown, pink, yellow, dark green, and even purple, the blades sometimes almost entirely of one color.

The species is reportedly slow growing and difficult to make happy, even in warm, moist, tropical climates. It requires shade or partial shade at all stages of life and a wet, humus-rich soil. PLATE 691.

PLECTOCOMIA is a genus of 17 pinnate-leaved, spiny, climbing, dioecious, hapaxanthic palms in northern India, Bhutan, Myanmar, southern China including the island of Hainan, Laos, Vietnam, Thailand, Sumatra, peninsular Malaysia, Java, Borneo, and the southern islands of the Philippines. These are, for the most part, large, thick-stemmed, climbing palms, which ascend the heights by cirri that may be half again as long as the long leaves.

There are both clustering and solitary-stemmed species. The leaves have mostly widely spaced, linear-elliptic, and pendent leaflets on thorny rachises. The leaf sheaths that cover the upper portions of the stems are always spiny, sometimes incredibly so. The inflorescences are formed from the topmost nodes or leaf axils of the far-ranging stems and are long, stiff primary branches growing at right angles from the vegetative stems. They bear long curtains of pendent flowering branches with remarkable distichously arranged boat-shaped bracts enclosing either male or female flowers. The fruits are usually oblong, brown or red, always covered in overlapping scales, and have small, spine-like apical projections. The great, pendent infructescences are often spectacular, especially in the red-fruited species.

Unlike many other rattan species, these have no economic importance as the thick stems are pithy and shrink upon drying. These climbing palms are most attractive when they can be seen; as with most other rattans, their leafy portions are often so far up in the trees that viewing them is difficult. They can be constantly pruned to stay within reasonable bounds. Most species are tropical in their temperature requirements, but a few from montane regions, like *P. himalayana,* seem to have some hardiness to cold; this species seems to be the only one in cultivation and it is sought after because of its reputed hardiness.

The genus name is from two Greek words meaning "plaited hair," an allusion to the form of the inflorescences with their overlapping bracts. PLATE 692.

Plectocomia elongata is the most widespread species in the genus, occurring from Thailand, peninsular Malaysia, Sumatra, Java, and Borneo, where it grows in monsoonal, mountainous rain forest at elevations to 6500 feet. The epithet is Latin for "elongate."

The stems are 150 feet long and 8 inches in diameter. The gently arching leaves are 18 feet long, with an 8-foot-long extension of the rachis into a cirrus. The 2-foot-long curtainlike pendent leaflets are dark green above and grayish or even greenish white beneath. The fruits are red and highly ornamental.

Plectocomia griffithii is endemic to peninsular Malaysia, where it grows in low mountainous rain forest.

The stems are 100 feet or more in length and 3 inches in diameter. The arching leaves are 6 to 8 feet long and bear many 18-inch-long, light green, pendulous, widely and regularly spaced elliptical leaflets that hang from the arching rachis like a curtain. The fruits are chestnut brown.

Plectocomia himalayana is endemic to northeastern India (Bengal), where it grows in the foothills of the Himalaya mountains from elevations of 7500 to 8500 feet. The epithet is Latin for "Himalayan."

The stems are 90 feet long, and the 6-foot-long stiff leaves bear widely spaced whorls of light green, elliptic, and pendent leaflets.

Martin Gibbons and Tobias Spanner have promoted this species as being able, in habitat, to endure frost and snow. Growers report, however, that it is hardy only to the upper or, at most, mid 20s (F). It is doubtless a wise choice for a rattan in cool but nearly frostless Mediterranean climates, and may do well in warm, tropical or nearly tropical climes. PLATE 692.

PLECTOCOMIOPSIS is a genus of five pinnate-leaved, spiny, monocarpic, climbing, dioecious palms in peninsular Thailand, peninsular Malaysia, Sumatra, and Borneo. The genus name translates as "similar to *Plectocomia,*" but the genus is more closely related to *Myrialepis* than to *Plectocomia.* Except for the inflorescences, the species are similar in appearance to species of *Plectocomia.* The stems are as long as those of *Plectocomia* but not usually as thick, and the leaflets are generally not pendent as are those of *Plectocomia* species. Like other rattans, these species climb by a cirrus. The inflorescences grow from the topmost nodes of a stem with one thick, upright main axis and two pendent, secondary branches, bearing unisexual flowers. Female plants produce fig-shaped, scaly fruits. Being monocarpic (or hapaxanthic) the flowering stems die off after flowering. None of the species seem to be in cultivation.

PODOCOCCUS is a monotypic genus of clustering, pinnate-leaved, monoecious palm in tropical western Africa. The genus name is derived from two Greek words meaning "foot" and "berry" and refers to the fruits on short stalks.

Podococcus barteri is a small clustering species indigenous to equatorial lowland rain forest in southern Nigeria, western Cameroon, and northwestern Gabon.

The thin stems grow to a maximum height of 15 feet with bases of small, spiny stilt roots and bear leaf crowns that are hemispherical to nearly spherical with arching and spreading leaves. The leaflets are widely spaced, linear diamond shaped, and light green on both surfaces; the terminal leaflet is larger than the others, and all the leaflets are lobed and toothed to varying degrees. The inflorescences are spikelike and, before the fruits form, are erect.

They bear bisexual flowers, which produce small, 1-inch-wide, red, and one- to three-lobed fruits according to the number of spindle-shaped seeds therein.

This diminutive palm is attractive because of its color and leaflet form but is not known in cultivation outside of a few botanical gardens. The species is slow growing and needs copious and regular moisture. It is doubtless tender to cold.

POGONOTIUM is a genus of three spiny, pinnate-leaved, dioecious palms in low mountainous rain forest of peninsular Malaysia and Sarawak on the island of Borneo. These species are closely related to the rattans (for example, *Calamus, Ceratolobus,* and *Daemonorops*) but are not climbing palms, and, except for a sometimes short and rudimentary cirrus, lack both cirri and flagella. The number of leaves varies from as many as 100 narrow, pendent divisions to as few as 9 stiff segments. The short stems are almost completely covered in the spiny leaf sheaths, and there are spines on the petioles and leaf rachises as well as short bristles on the leaflets. The stem spines are long, thin, and hairlike.

The most unusual characteristic of the genus is the unisexual inflorescence, which is spikelike, erect, and, at first, enclosed within two long, narrow, spiny auricles that are narrow extensions of the bases of the petioles. The fruits are small, half hidden in the persistent auricles, red, purplish, or brown, and covered in small scales, looking like succulent raspberries before mature.

The genus is not known to be in cultivation. The genus name is from a Greek word meaning "bearded" and alludes to the hairlike spines on the leaf sheaths and auricles.

Pogonotium ursinum is beautiful, especially as a juvenile plant, with its long leaves and many fine, narrow, and pendent leaflets. The epithet is Latin for "bearlike."

POLYANDROCOCOS is a monotypic genus of solitary-trunked, pinnate-leaved, monoecious palm. The genus name combines two Greek words, "many" and "anther," with the genus name *Cocos* (coconut) and alludes to the numerous stamens of the male flowers. The epithet is Latin for "tail-bearing" and refers to the shape of the inflorescences. PLATES 693 & 694.

Polyandrococos caudescens is endemic to east-central Brazil, where it grows at low elevations in the Atlantic coastal forest. According to Larry R. Noblick, in the northern parts of its habitat, and on poor soils, the palm may form only short, subterranean trunks (Henderson et al. 1995).

The trunk attains a maximum height of 35 feet in habitat but no more than 8 inches in diameter. The older stems are light brown and "stepped" because of the rough leaf base scars, but these are indistinct visually and form incomplete circles. Young trunks are almost entirely covered in fibrous, persistent leaf sheaths. There is no crownshaft, but the leaf sheaths are massive. The leaf crown is hemispherical, and the 8- to 10-foot-long leaves are borne on 2-foot-long petioles often with short "pseudo-spines" and are spreading and slightly arching as they mature. The leaflets of most individuals grow in a single flat plane from the rachis, but the leaflets of others are arranged in indistinct groups, the individual segments growing at slightly different angles from the leaf's rachis, which variance also seems to be geographical. The individual leaflets are 3 feet long, narrowly linear-lanceolate with long tapering points, and a shimmering silvery green beneath, especially the younger leaflets. This color combination of the leaf is unexpectedly demonstrated in the shaft of the unfurled new leaf, which exhibits beautiful horseshoe-shaped dark green markings on an otherwise silvery green spear. That this species is closely allied genetically to *Allagoptera* is proved beyond a doubt by its spikelike inflorescence which, at first glance, looks almost exactly like a larger version of the one that *A. arenaria* sports. While erect before the fruits form, it becomes pendulous as the sausagelike cluster of densely packed, greenish orange to brown fruits mature.

The palm is drought tolerant when established but looks better and grows faster with adequate and regular moisture. It is not fussy about soil type, growing well on sandy and even calcareous ones, but has better color and grows faster if humus is incorporated into the medium; an organic mulch is second best. This species revels in sun, especially when past its juvenile stage. It is not hardy to cold and is adaptable only to zones 10 and 11, although some nice specimens are found in protected and warm microclimates of 9b. Its only fault is that it is not fast growing. This species is extraordinarily beautiful at all stages and is suited, because of its form and color, to being planted even in a wall of vegetation. It is also an attractive specimen planting, even solitary and surrounded by space, but is still more gorgeous in groups of three or more individuals of varying heights.

PRESTOEA is a genus of 11 pinnate-leaved, monoecious palms in tropical America. The genus is closely related to *Euterpe* but is distinguished by not forming crownshafts (except for one species) and in having broader and less pendent leaflets. Most of these species are clustering to some extent and are of only moderate height except for one salient exception. The inflorescences grow from among the leaf base sheaths and are similar to those of the genus *Euterpe* but are not hirsute. They are white when new but change to pink or red as the fruits mature. The fruits are blackish purple.

Only one or two of these palms seems to be in cultivation, and this is a shame considering their great beauty. None of them are tolerant of frost, but those from montane habitats are adaptable to frost-free Mediterranean climates. All of them require copious moisture and a humus-laden soil, and all of them luxuriate in partial shade, some adaptable to full sun except in hot and dry climates. None are tolerant of calcareous soils and usually fail, even with an organic mulch.

The genus name honors Henry Prestoe, a 19th-century British botanist and superintendent of the botanic gardens in Trinidad. PLATES 695 & 696.

Prestoea acuminata is a variable species occurring naturally over a vast area of the American tropics, from eastern Cuba, southwards through the entire Antilles except for Trinidad, into central Guatemala, northern Nicaragua, through all of Costa Rica and Panama, and into northern Venezuela, and the Andean slopes of Colombia, Ecuador, and Peru, growing from elevations of 1200 to 8000 feet. The epithet is Latin for "acuminate" and refers to the tips of the leaflets. The species is most abundant in the mountains of Puerto Rico, where it forms vast colonies on the slopes.

It is found both as a clustering and a solitary-trunked species, the stems growing to maximum heights of 50 feet with maximum diameters of 8 inches. They are light brown, with distinct and widely spaced olive-green rings of leaf base scars in the newer parts of the trunks. The crownshafts are 2 to 3 feet high, cylindrical to a narrow inverted pyramid, and deep green to purplish green or even violet. The leaf crowns are hemispherical or nearly hemispherical and hold 4 to 10 spreading and gently arching 4- to 8-foot-long leaves on 1-foot-long petioles. The leaf often exhibits a twist of the rachis at its midpoint, the apical part of the blade being thus oriented vertically. The numerous leaflets are 2 to 3 feet long, regularly spaced along the rachis in a single flat plane, light to deep green, and broadly lanceolate to linear-lanceolate. They are mostly spreading but are pendent in the older leaves.

Three naturally occurring varieties of this species are distinguished by inflorescence, fruit details, and geographical origin that do not seem important to horticultural or landscaping considerations; ironically **P. acuminata** var. **montana** (the mountain cabbage palm of Puerto Rico) actually occurs naturally at lower elevations than the other two varieties.

This beautiful species is adapted only to frost-free regions that have nights cooler than those of the lowland tropics, such as are found in southern Florida. It languishes in calcareous soils, even when mulched. It needs partial shade and protection from the midday sun when young, wherever it is grown. PLATES 695 & 696.

Prestoea decurrens is indigenous to southern Nicaragua, Costa Rica, Panama, and the western slopes of the Andes Mountains in Colombia and Ecuador, where it grows in rain forest, especially along streams and rivers at elevations from sea level to 5000 feet but mostly below 3000 feet. The epithet is Latin for "running down," in this case referring to the persistent leaf bases that create an elongated but loose and false crownshaft.

It is a clustering species whose stems attain maximum heights of 25 feet but are usually shorter. Their maximum diameters are 4 inches, and they are green in all but their oldest parts and are graced with grayish rings of leaf base scars. The leaf crown is open and hemispherical or slightly less and usually holds half a dozen 6-foot-long leaves on 1- to 2-foot-long petioles. The numerous, light green, 2-foot-long leaflets grow in a flat, single plane from the rachis and are neither stiff nor pendent.

Although rare in cultivation, this especially beautiful species has the overall look of one of the giant tree ferns with which it grows in Costa Rica. It has a handsome clumping habit, which usually includes one, possibly two, dominant stems, the others subsidiary and much shorter.

PRITCHARDIA is a genus of about 30 large, solitary-trunked, monoecious, palmate-leaved palms in the islands of Hawaii and the South Pacific. It is the only genus of palm native to Hawaii, where all but four species are endemic, and where many of these are critically endangered or even extinct. Most species grow in wet rain forest above 1000 feet, but a few are naturally found in drier areas, always at or near natural springs or water seepages.

The leaves are large and stiff, and the blade usually much pleated and, while costapalmate, the condition is not that obvious in most species, the majority having wide and nearly flat leaves. The segments also extend not deep into the blade, giving them a grand appearance akin to leaves of the larger *Licuala* species with unsegmented blades. The petioles are invariably long, stout, and unarmed and are often covered in a dense, almost chalklike, light tomentum, as are the sheaths. The inflorescences, which sometimes extend beyond the leaf crown, consist of a tubular series of bracts from which the stiff and short flowering branches project bearing white, yellow, or orange bisexual flowers. The fruits are large, mostly spherical, and reddish brown or black when ripe; a few are elliptical or ovoid.

Most species hail from wet tropical regions and can stand neither cold nor hot drying winds. All are intolerant of freezing temperatures and adapted to zones 10b and 11. Some of them grow near the seashore and can withstand salt-laden winds and slight salinity in the soil. They are all susceptible to the lethal yellowing disease. These are some of the world's most beautiful palm species and should find a place in any tropical or nearly tropical garden that is large enough to accommodate them and in a region not affected by lethal yellowing.

The genus name honors William T. Pritchard, British consul to the Fiji Islands in the 19th century. PLATES 697–708.

Pritchardia affinis seems to have been endemic to the island of Hawaii but is now probably extinct as a naturally occurring species. It is found on that island from sea level to an elevation of 2000 feet in mesic forests, where it is probably an escape from cultivation. The epithet is Latin for "similar to."

The trunk usually grows to 35 feet high, but some individuals attain 80 feet. The stem has a diameter of 12 to 15 inches and is light to dark tan. The leaf crown in older trees is open and hemispherical unless the dead leaves are retained, in which case it is spherical. Individual leaves are 3 to 4 feet long on 4-foot-long petioles. They are roughly wedge shaped and deeply costapalmate with stiff segments that are deep green above and slightly paler green beneath. The inflorescences are shorter than the leaf crown and produce round, black fruits that are less than 1 inch in diameter. PLATE 697.

Pritchardia arecina is endemic to the Hawaiian island of Maui, where it grows in rain forest at elevations of 2000 to 4000 feet. The epithet is Latin for "little *Areca*."

The trunk attains a height of 40 feet and a diameter of 1 foot or less. The leaf crown is hemispherical, with large, stiff, wedge-shaped, 3-foot-long leaves on 4-foot-long petioles.

Pritchardia beccariana is endemic to mountainous rain forest on the island of Hawaii, where it grows to an elevation of 4000 feet. The epithet honors Italian palm taxonomist Odoardo Beccari (1843–1920).

Mature trunks can grow to 60 feet but are usually no more than 40 feet tall, with diameters of 1 foot. They are free of leaf bases except near the leaf crown and are light to deep brown, with closely set leaf scar rings and narrow vertical fissures. The leaf crown is full and rounded because of the adhering dead leaves and is 15 feet wide and tall. The leaves are 3 to 4 feet wide and semicircular to almost circular. The segments extend to one-third of the distance into the blade and the stout petiole extends into the blade, forming a distinct midrib; the blade is slightly folded and cup shaped when young. Leaf color is bright clear green on both sides of the blade, and the segments are

slightly pendent at their apices. The petiole is stout, light brownish green, covered in a chalky, light brown to almost white felt when young, and 5 feet long. The inflorescences are 5 feet long and many branched, and bear small yellowish bisexual flowers. The fruits are 1 inch wide, round, and glossy black.

The palm thrives in partial shade to full sun except in the hottest climates where it needs protection from the midday sun. It is a water lover and must not suffer drought conditions; it also needs a humus-rich, well-drained soil. This is one of the tallest growing *Pritchardia* species, and old palms are noble in appearance and make wonderful canopy-scapes. As with most other *Pritchardia* species, younger plants are incredibly attractive up close because of the near perfection of the heavy leaves. While this species is attractive enough as an isolated specimen, it is only in groups of three or more individuals of varying heights that the full glory of the leaf crown is achieved.

Pritchardia hardyi is endemic to the Hawaiian island of Kauai, where it grows in wet rain forest at elevations below 2000 feet. The epithet is a Latinized form of the surname "Hardy" and commemorates the original collector.

The trunk attains a height of 80 feet or more and is 1 foot in diameter. The leaf crown is spherical or nearly so, and the stiff, 3-foot-wide leaves are large semicircles of dark green. They are flat and the costa does not extend much into the blade; they tend to fold in down both sides of the blade as they age. The inflorescences are long and extend well out of the crown.
This is among the finest looking palms in the genus with its large, flat deep green leaves. It is fast growing. PLATE 698.

Pritchardia hillebrandii is similar to *P. affinis* in that it is known only from cultivated plants on the Hawaiian island of Molokai, where it is assumed to have originally been endemic. The epithet honors William Hillebrand, a 19th-century physician to the Hawaiian royal family; his property and plantings later became the Foster Botanical Garden in Honolulu. Whatever its true origins, this species is one of the more beautiful in the genus.

The trunk attains a height of 20 or so feet and 10 inches in diameter. The leaf crown is spherical with 4-foot-long emerald green to grayish or bluish green, undulate leaves that are broadly wedge shaped and obviously costapalmate, with long-tipped segments whose ends are often pendent. They are borne on 3-foot-long stout petioles that, when young, are covered in a chalky tomentum. The inflorescences are long and usually extend beyond the leaf crown.

The species is slow growing. PLATES 699 & 700.

Pritchardia kaalae is a rare and endangered species endemic to western Oahu in the Hawaiian chain, where it grows at natural springs in the dry forested mountains at elevations up to 2500 feet. The epithet is Latin for "of Kaala," a mountain in the palm's habitat.

The solitary trunk of this slow-growing smaller species attains a height of 25 feet and a diameter of 1 foot. The leaf crown is hemispherical or slightly more so, and the leaves are semicircular, deep green on both surfaces, with long-tipped segments whose apices are pendulous. The inflorescences extend well beyond the leaf crown.

Pritchardia lanaiensis is endemic to mountains on the Hawaiian island of Lanai, where it grows at elevations of 2000 to 3000 feet. The epithet is Latin for "of Lanai."

The stout trunk slowly grows to a maximum height of 25 to 30 feet and is 18 inches in diameter. The leaf crown is nearly spherical, and the leaves are 3 feet wide on 4- to 5-foot-long stout petioles. Leaf color is medium to dusky green, and the segments are deep into the blade, long, and pendent at their tips. PLATE 701.

Pritchardia lanigera is endemic to the island of Hawaii, where it grows in rain forest on precipitous valley slopes from sea level to an elevation of 3000 feet. The epithet is Latin for "wool-bearing."

This small species grows to 20 feet tall. Its beauty comes from its felty petioles and large, emerald green leaves, which are 4 or more feet wide, are perfect semicircles, and are borne on long, stout petioles. The segments are short and stiff in new leaves but are later pendent at their apices.

Pritchardia maideniana has unknown origins. The epithet honors Joseph H. Maiden, a 19th-century Australian botanist. For many years only two individuals of the species were known, both in the Sydney Botanical Gardens in Australia. They were believed to have come from seed collected in Hawaii, but the species seems to have more genetic affinities with the Fiji and Tonga species.

The light tan trunk is 15 feet high and less than 1 foot in diameter. The small leaf crown is hemispherical with the removal of dead leaves, but nearly hemispherical if these leaves are kept. Individual leaves are wedge shaped, deeply costapalmate, 3 feet long, with deep, rigid segments, and are borne on short, stout, felt-covered petioles. Leaf color is a light and glaucous gray-green, and the segments in the older leaves become more lax, with pendent segments.

Pritchardia martii is endemic to the Hawaiian island of Oahu, where it grows in mountainous rain forest to 3000 feet elevation. The epithet honors the 19th-century German plant explorer Carl F. P. von Martius.

It is a slow growing, short, and stocky species whose trunk attains a maximum height of 12 feet but a diameter of 1 foot. The leaf crown is open and nearly spherical because of the 3- to 4-foot-long, stout, felt-covered petioles. The leaves are 3 to 4 feet wide, semicircular, broad, and flat, with shallow and broad, stiff segments. Leaf color is deep olive to nearly bluish green above but silvery bronze beneath because of a dense covering of felty scales.

This is among the world's most beautiful small palms; it seems the essence of what a palm should look like. PLATE 702.

Pritchardia minor is endemic to wet, mountainous rain forest on the Hawaiian island of Kauai, where it grows from 1000 to 4500 feet elevation. The epithet is Latin for "smaller."

Its slender trunk grows to 20 feet beneath a gorgeous, small, spherical, and dense leaf crown of 2-foot-wide light green, semicircular leaves with stiff, pleated blades and short, wide segments on short, stout petioles.

This is another of the world's most beautiful small palms and seems perfect and jewel-like.

Pritchardia mitiaroana was described by Dransfield and Ehrhardt in 1995 from Mitiaro Island in the remote Cook Islands of the South Pacific, where it grows near sea level in scrubby forest on limestone. The epithet is Latin for "of Mitiaro."

The light brown trunk attains a maximum height of 25 feet and is spindle shaped. The leaf crown is nearly spherical and dense, with 3- to 4-foot-wide, semicircular, light green leaves on 3-foot-long, greenish white, stout petioles. New leaves are stiff with 1-foot-deep segments and are flat, but older leaves become folded with more lax segments that are slightly pendent near their apices.

Although not yet in cultivation, this beautiful, robust species should be nearly perfect for areas with calcareous soils.

Pritchardia munroi is a rare and critically endangered species from the Hawaiian island of Molokai, where only two individuals are left in dry, evergreen scrub forest at elevations of 2000 to 3500 feet. The epithet honors George Munro, an early 20th-century New Zealand naturalist in Molokai.

The trunk of this small, stocky species grows to 20 feet high but is 1 foot in diameter. It is light brown and covered in dense, brown leaf sheath fibers in its younger parts. The leaf crown is nearly spherical and is open because of the 4-foot-long, stout petioles. Individual leaves are deep green, 3 feet long, semicircular to wedge shaped, and deeply costapalmate. The segments are shallow and are stiff in younger leaves, with slightly pendent apices in older leaves.

Pritchardia pacifica occurs naturally in coastal areas of the Tonga islands, 1500 miles east of Australia and 1000 miles northeast of New Zealand. Common names are Fiji fan palm and Pacific fan palm. The epithet is Latin for "of the Pacific."

Mature trunks can grow to 30 feet high with diameters of 1 foot. The upper and younger parts of the stem are usually covered in a dense mat of brown fibers, but the older portions are fiber-free and light to deep bronze with closely set rings of leaf base scars. The leaf crown is 12 feet wide and tall. The leaves are 3 to 6 feet wide on 3-foot-long stout petioles, which are brownish green and covered with a beautiful scurfy white wax coating that imparts a lovely tan coloration. The leaf is semicircular to diamond shaped, and the segments extend a quarter of the way into the blade and are stiff and nondrooping. Younger leaves are cup shaped due to the intrusion of the petiole into the blade, but older leaves are either flat or the two halves are slightly pendent. Leaf color is bright light green to emerald green. The leaf crown is full and rounded with as many as 40 leaves. The inflorescences are 2 to 3 feet long and much branched, and bear small yellow bisexual flowers. The fruits are 0.5 inch wide and glossy black.

The palm is adaptable to most free-draining soils, including calcareous ones. It needs average but regular moisture and thrives in full sun or partial shade. It is especially suited to plantings in groups of three or more individuals of varying heights and loses some of its "warmth" and charm as an isolated specimen tree surrounded by space. It is small enough to be used as a courtyard or patio subject, and young plants are overwhelmingly beautiful. Because it tolerates salt-laden winds and slightly saline soil, the Fiji fan palm is one of the finest landscape subjects for planting near the seashore. It needs space, high light levels, and good air circulation to be grown indoors. PLATES 703 & 704.

Pritchardia remota is a species of four naturally occurring varieties in Hawaii on the islands of Kauai, Maui, Nihoa, and Niihau, all of which are rare and endangered, a few critically so. The epithet is Latin for "remote," an allusion to the small island (of Nihoa) which is home to the type and is some distance from the more famous and larger islands of the Hawaiian chain. *Pritchardia remota* var. *remota* is endemic to Nihoa, or Bird Island, where it grows in dry, evergreen scrub forest at low elevations. It is a small species, its trunk attaining a height of 20 feet. The leaf crown is spherical and dense. The leaves are 2 feet wide, glossy medium green, and semicircular. *Pritchardia remota* var. *aylmer-robinsonii* is endemic to the privately owned island of Niihau, where only two individuals are left in the wild. The epithet honors the island's former owner, Aylmer Robinson. It is a large and noble species whose trunk attains a maximum height of 50 feet and a diameter of 1 foot. The leaf crown is hemispherical to nearly spherical and is open because of the length of the felt-covered petioles. The leaves are semicircular, deep, almost bluish green, with deep and pendent segments. *Pritchardia re-mota* var. *glabrata* is endemic to Maui, where it grows on steep slopes at elevations of 1500 to 2000 feet. It is little known and is not in cultivation. The epithet is Latin for "glabrous." *Pritchardia remota* var. *napaliensis* is endemic Kauai, where it grows in lowland rain forest and is rare and endangered. The epithet is Latin for "of Na Pali," a coastal region of Kauai. The trunk attains a maximum height of 25 feet. The leaves are small, dark green, and wedge shaped. PLATE 705.

Pritchardia schattaueri is a rare and endangered species endemic to the southwestern coast of the island of Hawaii, where it grows at elevations of 2000 to 2600 feet. Donald Hodel bestowed the epithet in 1985 to honor George Schattauer of Kona, Hawaii, the person who discovered the species in 1960. In 1985 only a dozen individuals were left in habitat.

This is one of the tallest species in the genus, the trunk ascending to the astounding height of 130 feet, with a diameter of 1 foot. The leaf crown is spherical and dense. Each of the 30 leaves is 5 to 6 feet wide, semicircular, and glossy deep green on both surfaces. The 6- to 7-foot-long petioles are covered in a light brown, chalky tomentum on their lower surfaces. The leaf segments extend 2 feet into the blade, and their tips are pendent in older leaves.

It is an incredibly elegant and beautiful species that is now in cultivation but still rare.

Pritchardia thurstonii is endemic to coastal regions of the island of Fiji. It is sometimes called Thurston palm. The epithet honors Sir John B. Thurston, a 19th-century planter and governor of Fiji.

Mature trunks grow to 30 feet, although reportedly to 50 feet in habitat. Stem diameters are 8 inches, and the trunks are free of leaf bases and fiber in older stems except near the leaf crown. Trunk color is light brown to deep gray, with closely set rings of leaf base scars and narrow vertical fissures. The leaf crown contains 20 leaves and is frequently more elongated or oblong than round, because the palm does not usually hold onto its dead leaves. The leaves are 4 to 6 feet wide on 3-foot-long petioles that are light green but covered in a gray to white scurfy and waxy bloom. Leaf shape is round to diamond shaped, and the stiff segments extend almost half way into the center of the blade. Younger leaves are cup shaped due to the intrusion of the petiole into the blade, but older leaves are either flat or the two halves are slightly pendent. Leaf color is light to deep green on both sides. The inflorescences are 10 feet long, arching up and out of the leaf crown, and branched near the tip, bearing small yellow bisexual flowers. The fruits are 0.5 inch wide, round, and bright red.

This species is adaptable to various free-draining soils, including calcareous ones. It needs full sun and regular and adequate moisture but is tolerant of salt spray as well as slight salinity of the soil. The palm is visually similar to *P. pacifica* and has the same landscape uses. It has an even more beautiful silhouette and is more tolerant of seaside conditions. It is difficult indoors as it needs high light levels and good air circulation. PLATES 706 & 707.

Pritchardia viscosa is an endangered species endemic to the Hawaiian island of Kauai, where it grows in low mountainous rain forest. There were only three palms left on the island in 1998. The epithet is Latin for "viscous," an allusion to the texture of the inflorescences.

The trunk grows to 20 feet high with a diameter of 8 inches. The leaf crown is open and nearly spherical with 40-inch-wide, semicircular leaves whose segments extend 1 foot into the blade. They are stiff and nonpendent, even in older leaves. Leaf color is glossy and light, grassy green above and a beautiful silvery green beneath.

Pritchardia waialealeana is endemic to wet mountainous rain forest on the Hawaiian island of Kauai at elevations of 1500 to 2600 feet. The epithet is Latin for "of Waialeale," a mountain in the palm's habitat.

This is a tall and robust species whose trunk attains a minimum height of 60 feet and a diameter of 38 inches. The leaf crown is massive, dense, and spherical, with 40-inch-wide, semicircular leaves on large 2-foot-long petioles. The blade is flat and the segments extend into the blade to two-thirds its depth; they are stiff when young but become lax and pendent with age.

Pritchardia woodfordiana is endemic to Florida Island in the Solomons, where it grows in low mountainous rain forest. The epithet honors C. M. Woodford, an early 20th-century British naturalist and collector as well as a government official of the Solomons.

It grows slowly to a height of 25 feet. The trunk diameter is 8 inches, and the leaf crown is open and hemispherical. Individual leaves are 4 feet wide, semicircular, and deep emerald green on 3-foot-long petioles. The segments extend 1 foot into the blade and are stiff and nonpendent. PLATE 708.

PRITCHARDIOPSIS is a monotypic genus of extremely rare and endangered monoecious palm. It is the only palmate-leaved palm native to New Caledonia; all the other palms are pinnate leaved and crownshafted. The genus name translates as "similar to *Pritchardia*," although the palm is more closely related to *Livistona*. PLATE 709.

Pritchardiopsis jeanneneyi is endemic to southern New Caledonia, where it grows in rain forest at 800 feet elevation. In 1998, only one mature individual remained in the wild.

With great age, the solitary trunk reportedly grows to 35 feet high with a diameter of 6 inches. The leaf crown is hemispherical and open because of the relatively long, 4.5-foot-long petioles. The leaves are 5 feet wide, deep green on both surfaces, semicircular to nearly circular, with many stiff segments, each of which extends 18 inches into the blade. The 3-foot-long inflorescences grow from the leaf bases and are similar in general appearance to those of *Pritchardia,* but the flowering branches are longer and not as dense. The 2-inch-wide fruits are round and, when ripe, purplish brown.

The species is beautiful, especially when older, but is slow growing. It needs partial shade when young, copious and regular moisture, and a humus-laden soil. Seedlings are difficult to grow but once plants have established palmate leaves, they seem to do better and can be grown much easier. Young plants established in the ground can take poor soil conditions as well as full sun and wind.

PSEUDOPHOENIX is a genus of four pinnate-leaved, solitary-trunked, monoecious palms in southern Florida, the Florida Keys, the Bahamas, Cuba, Hispaniola, the southern Gulf coast of Mexico and Yucatán, and the Caribbean coast of Belize. It is similar to the genus *Ceroxylon* in that the plants have a lot of wax; even the trunks are often waxy. The leaves are large, and the crowns are open. Unusual is the fact that the inflorescences grow from the leaf crown in contradistinction to most other crownshafted palm species in which they are borne from beneath the shaft. They are much branched and bear bisexual flowers that produce round, red fruits.

All the species are intolerant of cold and adapted only to zones 10 and 11, although specimens are to be found in favorable microclimates of 9b. These palms are denizens of coastal environments where the soil is calcareous and poor, the sun is relentless, and the erratic rainfall is confined mainly to the summer; thus, they are well adapted to seaside planting and hot regions with limey soils. They are all slow growing, some extremely so.

The genus name is from Greek words meaning "false" and "date palm," but the species are not closely related to the date palm species. PLATES 710–716.

Pseudophoenix ekmanii is a rare and highly endangered species endemic to the Dominican Republic, where it grows in open savannas with scrub and cactus species and on low, dry calcareous hills. The epithet is a Latinized form of the surname "Ekman" and honors a 20th-century plant collector.

The white, waxy trunk attains a height of 20 feet and bulges above its midpoint, sometimes extremely and almost grotesquely so. It is also distinctly and beautifully ringed. The crownshaft is of varying thicknesses, dark green, and from 2 to 3 feet high. The leaf crown is spherical but sparse and open, and the 6- to 8-foot-long leaves are ascending and mostly erect—especially when young—and spreading when older. The species is slow growing. PLATE 710.

Pseudophoenix lediniana is endemic to southwestern Haiti, where it is endangered. The epithet honors R. Bruce Ledin, botanist, palm enthusiast, and former president of the International Palm Society.

Mature trunks may attain a height of 65 feet, but this is rare, especially under cultivation, and only half this stature is the norm. The stem diameter is 1 foot, and the trunk slightly bulges near its base and often near the middle. Trunk color is an outstandingly beautiful greenish white to almost pure white, usually with a thin covering of wax and beautiful widely spaced deep green rings of leaf base scars. There are 10 leaves in the crown, which is open and graceful, with a pleasing architectural look. The bluish green, olive green, or grayish green crownshaft is 2 to 3 feet tall, smooth, waxy, and tapering. The leaves are to 12 feet long on stout 6-inch-long petioles. The thin, linear, and deep green leaflets grow from the rachis at slightly different angles, but the angles are short and the overall appearance of the leaf is almost flat. The leaflets are limp and, especially on older leaves, beautifully pendent. The inflorescences grow from among the leaves and are 4 feet long with many short branches bearing small yellowish white bisexual blossoms mixed with a few unisexual flowers. The fruits are 1 inch wide, round, and bright red.

The species is drought tolerant but grows faster and looks better with regular and adequate moisture; under such conditions, it is possibly the faster growing species in the genus. It requires a well-drained soil and full sun at all stages. Because of its relatively fast growth, it is also more capable of recovering from freeze damage than the other species.

The visual aspects of the taller species of *Pseudophoenix*, like *P. ledinii* and *P. vinifera,* are often compared with those of the royal palms, because of the sturdy, mostly light colored trunks and large dark green pinnate leaves that both genera have in common. The practice really does neither genus credit but, if one must indulge in it, this species would seem to invite the correlation as the trunks are tall and straight and the leaves gracefully arching with thin and lissome leaflets. This species grows more rapidly than do the other three and its most salient feature is the wonderfully beautiful trunk and crownshaft, which almost demand that the palm be planted where its stem can be viewed up close. Few things are as beautiful as a grove of this palm planted in groups of three or more individuals of varying heights. It is especially beautiful against a large background of deep green foliage that shows off the light-colored trunks with their wonderful dark rings. The palm is not known to be grown indoors but there would seem no reason it could not be, given high light levels and good air circulation. PLATES 711 & 712.

Pseudophoenix sargentii is the most widespread species in the genus and is indigenous to the Florida Keys, the Bahamas, Cuba, Hispaniola, Belize, and the Caribbean coast (Quintana Roo) of Mexico, where it grows near the sea on sandy, limestone soils. Common names are buccaneer palm and cherry palm. The epithet honors Charles S. Sargent, a 19th-century director of the Arnold Arboretum and original collector of the species.

Mature trunks attain 25 feet of height and a diameter of 1 foot. The stems are grayish green with broad, brown, closely set rings of leaf base scars when young, but eventually turn light to dark gray on the older parts. They have a spindle-shaped bulge at the halfway point. The leaf crown is 10 feet wide and 6 feet tall. There are never more than 12 leaves in a crown and sometimes as few as 8, and the crown is seldom spherical. The tapering crownshaft is 1 to 2 feet tall, smooth, waxy, and bluish to grayish green. The leaves are 8 feet long and gracefully arching on stout, 2-foot-long, green petioles. The stiff and erect bluish green leaflets grow from the rachis at a slight angle to give a shallow V shape to the blade. There is a thin coating of small brown scales on the lower surfaces of the leaflets, but it is not noticeable in the landscape. The inflorescences grow from among the leaves and are 3 to 4 feet long with many short branches bearing small yellow bisexual and single-sexed blossoms. The fruits are 0.5 inch wide, round, and deep red.

The palm is slow growing, even under ideal cultural conditions. It is drought tolerant but looks better with average and regular moisture. Full sun is a necessity but the species is adaptable to most free-draining soils. The buccaneer palm has the same landscape uses as does *P. lediniana* but is smaller, much slower growing, and more generally suitable for intimate sites like courtyards and patios. It is one of the most salt-tolerant palms and does well near the sea, even occasionally tolerating inundation by salt water. The palm is not known to be grown indoors, but there would seem no reason it cannot be if given high light levels and good air circulation. PLATES 713–715.

Pseudophoenix vinifera is endemic to dry hillsides on Hispaniola, where it is in danger of extinction. Common names are cherry palm and wine palm. The epithet translates from the Latin as "wine-bearing," a reference to the sap that is used for making wine.

Mature trunks may attain a height of 70 feet or even more in habitat but usually only half this height under cultivation. Their diameter is 1 foot, except where the stem bulges, which is usually near its midpoint; the trunk above the stem is usually significantly narrower than that below the bulge. Trunk color is brown to deep gray and the stems bear closely set wide, dark (almost black) rings of leaf base scars until they are old, at which time the rings are indistinct. The leaf crown is 15 feet wide and 8 feet tall. There are usually 12 leaves to a crown and the crown is often full and rounded because of the arch of the leaves. The crownshaft is short and 2 feet tall. It is grayish green to almost silver and tapers from its base to its tip. The leaves are 10 to 12 feet long and gracefully arching on 1- to 2-foot-long silvery green to almost white petioles. The leaflets grow from the rachis at several different angles, but the angles are small and the dark green leaflets are limp and pendulous, giving a slightly plumose aspect to the blade. The inflorescence is 6 feet long, pendent, and sparsely branched, and bears small yellowish bisexual and unisexual flowers. The fruits make a spectacular display, hanging in long pendent branches from the leaf crown. Each one is 1 to 2 inches wide, round, and brilliant scarlet.

The palm is adaptable to full sun and most well-drained soils. It is always slow growing. The palm has the same landscape use as does *P. lediniana* with the proviso that its trunks are a bit less traditional appearing and are not as beautiful up close. It is not known to be grown indoors but there would seem no reason it cannot be if given high light levels and good air circulation.

The leaves are used for thatch. The edible but not palatable fruits are fed to livestock in the palm's native haunts. The palms were formerly used for making wine by cutting down the trees and squeezing out the sugary sap from the pith, and then fermenting the juice. The practice has resulted in the near extinction of the tree in habitat. PLATE 716.

PTYCHOCOCCUS is a genus of seven pinnate-leaved, monoecious palms in New Guinea and the Solomon Islands, with all but one species endemic to the island of New Guinea. These are moderate to tall palms with crownshafts atop relatively slender trunks. All the species one of us (Bob) has seen have leaves twisted at their midpoints so that the apical halves of the leaves are oriented to the vertical, a characteristic which is beautiful. The inflorescences grow from beneath the crownshafts, are massive and much branched, and bear flowers of both sexes. The fruits are ovoid and orange to red when ripe.

The genus is closely related to *Ptychosperma*, which fact is evident in its jagged ended leaflets. All except one species is exceedingly rare in cultivation, which is a shame as they are all wonderfully attractive. They are tender to cold and all but one species is impossible outside of zones 10b and 11; the exception is probably safe in 10a. In addition, all species need constant and copious moisture. The good news is that they do not seem fussy about soil type as long as it is fast draining.

The genus name comes from two Greek words meaning "fold" and "berry," alluding to the wrinkled seeds. PLATES 717 & 718.

Ptychococcus archboldianus is endemic to the lowland rain forest of southern Papua New Guinea. The epithet honors the late Richard Archbold, a wealthy American who funded several natural history expeditions to the area.

This is an elegantly tall growing species, the solitary trunk attaining a height of 50 feet with a diameter of 8 inches. It is light gray to nearly white and, except for the youngest parts, is indistinctly ringed with darker leaf base scars. The leaf crown is sparse and open but nearly spherical. The crownshaft is 2 feet tall, scarcely thicker than the stem, cylindrical, and light green, almost white. The leaves are 8 feet long, spreading, and slightly arching, on 1-foot-long petioles. The 2-foot-long leaflets are regularly spaced, grow in a nearly flat plane off the rachis, and are mostly nonpendent. They are linear-oblong with obliquely truncated, jagged apices and are a deep and lustrous green above but have a silvery sheen beneath; the leaflets of the terminal pair are usually broader than the others.

Ptychococcus lepidotus is endemic to mountainous rain forest of New Guinea, from elevations of 3500 to 10,000 feet. The epithet is Latin for "scaled" and alludes to the covering of brown scales on the flower petals as well as the petiole and leaf rachis.

The solitary trunk grows to 30 feet high but is 6 inches in diameter. The crownshaft is 2 feet tall, cylindrical, slightly bulging at its base, and light green. The leaf crown is spherical or nearly so and contains a dozen 10-foot-long leaves on 6-inch-long petioles. The leaves are beautifully arching and exhibit the characteristic midpoint twist to the vertical. The leaflets are regularly spaced along the rachis and grow in a single flat plane from it. They are mostly linear-oblong, with obliquely truncated, jagged apices and are dark green on both surfaces. New leaves emerge in shades of red or rose. The fruits are 2 inches in diameter, round, and brilliant deep orange or crimson when ripe.

This beautiful palm does not like hot, humid tropical conditions, which is to be expected considering its elevated habitat. It survives in tropical conditions but is better in frostless Mediterranean climes, especially those in which there is a significant drop in temperature between night and day. It is probably hardy in zones 10 and 11. PLATE 717.

Ptychococcus paradoxus is endemic to low mountainous rain forest in Papua New Guinea. The epithet is Latin for "tall."

The solitary trunk is straight and columnar and grows to 50 feet with a diameter of 10 inches. It is nearly white and graced, in its younger parts, with widely spaced tan rings of leaf base scars. The crownshaft is 2 feet tall, slightly bulging at its summit, and light silvery green. The leaf crown is mostly spherical, with stiff and unarching, spreading, 8- to 10-foot-long leaves on stout, orange, 1-foot-long petioles. The 2- to 3-foot-long leaflets grow from the rachis in a single flat plane, and vary from linear-oblong with undulate margins and truncated, jagged tips to linear-lanceolate. They are uniformly dark but dull green on both surfaces, and the new growth has a pinkish tinge.

The species is incredibly beautiful because of its large, oversized crown in relation to the slender stem. PLATE 718.

PTYCHOSPERMA is a genus of 28 pinnate-leaved, monoecious, solitary-trunked and clustering palms in the Moluccas, Caroline Islands, Solomon Islands, and northern Australia, with the majority of species in New Guinea. All are indigenous to wet areas, whether rain forest, lowland swamps, or low mountain valleys.

The slender, ringed trunks, prominent crownshafts, and leaflets that are notched or toothed on their apices distinguish these species. Many of them show pinkish, maroon, or bronzy colored new foliage. The inflorescences grow from beneath the crownshafts and are relatively massive, with usually stiff-flowering branches that bear both male and female flowers. The round or ellipsoid fruits are orange, red, or black.

The various species readily hybridize with each other if grown to flowering ages together; this is not a good thing if one is concerned with maintaining what is (or was) originally in nature. Therefore, care should be taken when distributing seeds produced in areas where different species are grown together.

The genus name is a combination of two Greek words meaning "folded" and "seed." PLATES 719–734.

Ptychosperma burretianum is endemic to eastern Papua New Guinea, where it grows in low mountainous rain forest. The epithet honors Karl E. Maximilian Burret, a 20th-century German palm biologist.

It is a clumping species with stems 25 feet tall and 1 inch in diameter. The slender little crownshafts are scarcely thicker than the stems, 1 foot tall, and felty silvery green, almost white. The leaf crowns are open and hemispherical with a few 5- to 6-foot-long, gently arching leaves on 1-foot-long petioles. The widely and regularly spaced leaflets are a lustrous medium green on both surfaces. They are wedge shaped, the longest 10 inches, each one with an uneven and jagged apex. The new leaves are pinkish bronze, and the fruits are a deep orange. PLATES 719 & 720.

Ptychosperma caryotoides is endemic to eastern Papua New Guinea, where it grows in mountainous rain forest from elevations near sea level to 4000 feet. The epithet translates as "like *Caryota*," but the leaves of the species only resemble those of *Caryota* superficially.

It is a solitary-trunked, variable species, but in general the trunk attains a height of 30 feet with a diameter of 1 to 3 inches. The crownshaft is 1 foot tall, usually bulging at its summit rather than at its base, and light green to nearly white. The leaf crown is sparse, open, and less than semicircular, with a few, erect and ascending 2- to 5-foot-long leaves on 2-foot-long petioles. The few leaflets are regularly spaced and grow in a single flat plane from the rachis. They are wedge shaped with an obliquely truncated, jagged apex; the leaflets of the terminal pair are usually much broader than the others. The fruits are bright red. PLATE 721.

Ptychosperma cuneatum is endemic to Irian Jaya on the island of New Guinea, where it grows in lowland rain forest. The epithet is Latin for "wedged," referring to the shape of the leaflets.

The solitary trunk grows to 15 feet high with a maximum diameter of 1 inch. The crownshaft is 18 inches tall, barely thicker than the stem, cylindrical, and white. The leaf crown is hemispherical or nearly so, with a few 4- to 5-foot-long, spreading, and slightly arching leaves. The leaflets are grouped in irregular clusters along the rachis, the largest leaflets 1 foot long, wedge shaped, with deeply incised apices resulting in two "tails" to each apex. The 0.5-inch-long fruits are black when ripe. PLATE 722.

Ptychosperma elegans is endemic to Australia, where it grows in the coastal lowland rain forest of eastern Queensland. Common names are solitaire palm and Alexander palm. The epithet is Latin for "elegant."

This is a solitary-trunked species. Mature trunks may grow to 40 feet in their native haunts but are usually no more than half this height under cultivation. They are 4 inches in diameter, light gray to almost white, and distinctly ringed with widely spaced darker rings of leaf base scars on their younger parts. The crownshaft is 2 feet tall, silvery olive-green to nearly gray, smooth, waxy and slightly bulging at its base. The leaf crown is hemispherical or slightly more so and is 10 feet wide and 6 feet tall. The leaves are 6 to 8 feet long on 1-foot-long petioles, with the leaflets growing from the rachis at a slight angle to create a slightly V-shaped leaf. Each leaflet is 2 feet long, narrowly wedge shaped to oblong with deeply depressed veins above, which give a pleated appearance. It is abruptly squared off at the end and slightly jagged or toothed there. Leaf color is a dark to olive green above and a grayish green beneath. There are usually no more than 8 or 10 leaves in the crown, and they are gently arching but do not stray much below the horizontal plane and fall cleanly after aging. The inflorescence grows from beneath the crownshaft and is 2 to 3 feet long, with many greenish yellow branches bearing small white bisexual blossoms. The fruits are ovoid, 1 inch long, and bright red.

The solitaire palm is adaptable to most well-drained soils but only looks its best with a deep, rich and humus-laden medium. It needs average and regular moisture and does not tolerate freezing temperatures, being adaptable only to zones 10b and 11. It thrives in either partial shade or full sun. The tree is of unsurpassed grace, symmetry, and beauty of form and is even more exquisite when planted two or three to a group of varying heights of trunk. Its silhouette is lovely and notable enough that it should be called the silhouette palm. Among the most splendid sights one of us (Bob) saw was a large Spanish style courtyard with a small group of solitaire palms of varying heights in its center surrounded at their bases with small elephant ears (*Alocasia* species) and ginger relatives; pygmy date palms, self-heading *Philodendron selloum,* and small ferns were planted around the perimeter of the courtyard. The solitaire palm is an excellent choice for growing in large indoor spaces if given enough light and water. PLATES 723–725.

Ptychosperma furcatum is endemic to southeastern Papua New Guinea, where it grows in lowland rain forest. The epithet is Latin for "divided" or "cleft" and alludes to the apices of the leaflets.

This palm is found in nature as a clustering and solitary-trunked species, the stems reaching maximum heights of 18 feet and diameters of 1 to 2 inches. The crownshafts are 1 foot tall, slightly bulging at their bases, and greenish to bluish white. The leaf crowns are hemispherical, with 4- to 5-foot-long arching leaves on 1-foot-long petioles. The regularly spaced leaflets are narrowly wedge shaped or strap shaped and unequally bifid at their apices. Their color is glossy deep green, and the longest ones are 18 inches long. The 1-inch-long ovoid fruits are red when ripe.

The species is attractive, especially the clumping forms, but is tender to cold.

Ptychosperma hosinoi is endemic to the island of Ponapei in the Carolines, where it grows in low mountainous rain forest. The epithet honors an early 20th-century Japanese botanist, Hosino Shutaro.

This is a beautiful solitary-trunked palm whose stem attains a height of 50 feet or more and a diameter of 8 inches.

It is light green in its younger parts, where it is also faintly but beautifully ringed, and is light gray to tan in its older parts. The crownshaft is 2 to 3 feet tall, cylindrical, slightly thicker than the trunk, and a silvery olive green. The leaf crown is hemispherical or slightly more so, with 10 to 12 beautifully arching 10-foot-long leaves. The stiff leaflets are regularly spaced along the rachis and grow from it at an angle that creates a V-shaped blade. They are linearly to widely wedge shaped and 40 inches long and 10 inches wide, with mostly obliquely truncated apices that are always jagged. The 1-inch-long fruits are deep red when mature.

This is one of the world's most beautiful palm species, but it is tender to cold and needs copious and regular moisture as well as high humidity; its enemies are cold, drying winds.

Ptychosperma lauterbachii is endemic to eastern Papua New Guinea, where it grows in lowland rain forest and swamps. The epithet honors Carl A. G. Lauterbach, a 19th-century German plant collector.

It is found as a solitary-trunked and a clustering species, the stems attaining heights as great as 40 feet and diameters of 2 to 4 inches. They are light gray to light tan and are graced with widely spaced, darker rings of leaf base scars in all but their oldest parts. The crownshafts are 18 to 24 inches tall, almost as thick as the stems, and light green to nearly pure white. The leaf crowns are hemispherical or slightly less so, sparse, and open. The leaves are 9 feet long on 1-foot-long petioles. The medium and matte green leaflets are widely and regularly spaced along the rachis from which they grow at slightly different angles to give the leaf a loose, plumose effect. They are linear to linear wedge shaped, the longest ones 70 inches long, all with obliquely truncated and jagged, often bifid apices. The fruits are orange when mature.

The trunks of this species are beautiful, similar to giant bamboo culms, and the clumping forms are exquisite with their levels of foliage, creating beautiful silhouettes. Alas, the palm is tender to cold and is demanding of copious and regular moisture. PLATE 726.

Ptychosperma ledermannianum is endemic to the island of Ponapei in the Carolines, where it grows in low mountainous rain forest. The epithet honors Carl L. Ledermann, an early 20th-century Swiss botanist and collector.

The solitary trunk grows to 60 feet but is usually half that height, with a diameter of 4 inches. The crownshaft is 18 inches tall, bulging at its base, and light olive green to silvery green. The sparse and open leaf crown is hemispherical or slightly less so. The leaves are 10 feet long on 1-foot-long petioles, and are beautifully arching but do not usually descend beneath the horizontal. The stiff leaflets are at least 1 foot long and regularly and closely spaced along the rachis, growing from it at an angle that creates a V-shaped blade. Their shape is generally a narrow wedge, with an obliquely truncated, jagged apex. The spindle-shaped fruits are more than 1 inch long and deep red when ripe.

This is another attractive species, with visual and genetic affinities to *P. hosinoi*. It is stout and robust appearing but also has an elegance and refinement that is nearly formal. A group of three or more individuals of varying heights is one of the handsomest pictures of the tropical world. PLATE 727.

Ptychosperma lineare is endemic to eastern Papua New Guinea, where it grows in lowland rain forest and coastal swamps. The epithet is Latin for "linear" and alludes to the narrow leaflets.

This is a mostly clustering species, but solitary individuals are sometimes found. The stems grow to 50 feet high with diameters of 1 inch or slightly more. They are light olive green in their younger parts and are graced with widely spaced rings of whitish leaf base scars. The slender crownshafts are 2 feet tall and silvery green to nearly white. The leaf crowns are open and nearly spherical, with 8-foot-long arching leaves on 8-inch-long petioles. The leaflets are regularly and closely spaced along the rachis from which they grow in a nearly flat, single plane. Their shape is generally a narrow wedge and their tips are obliquely truncated and unevenly jagged, often with one almost hairlike projection along the margin of the tip. The fruits are jet black and contrast beautifully with the orange or red branches of the infructescence.

This is one of the most elegant species and the tiers of leaf crowns absolutely arresting in appeal.

Ptychosperma macarthurii occurs naturally in rain forest and low swamps of the southern Papua New Guinea and extreme northern Queensland, Australia. It is called Macarthur palm. The epithet honors William Macarthur, a 19th-century Australian politician, explorer, and amateur botanist.

Mature clumps may be 35 feet tall and 25 feet wide and produce trunks to 24 feet tall and 2 inches in diameter. They are light tan to light gray with widely spaced and prominent darker rings of leaf base scars. The crownshaft is 1 to 2 feet tall, bulging at its base, smooth, waxy, and light green to olive green. The leaf crown is hemispherical and can be 10 feet wide but is usually no more than 5 feet tall. The leaves are 3 to 6 feet long on petioles that are usually less than 1 foot long and are held erect and arch slightly. The leaflets are 2 feet long, regularly spaced along the rachis, and narrowly wedge shaped to linear-lanceolate with obliquely squared, toothed ends. Leaf color is me-

dium to deep green on both surfaces. The inflorescences grow from beneath the crownshaft and are much branched but 2 feet long. The branches are yellowish green and bear small yellowish white bisexual blossoms. The fruits are 0.5 inch long, ovoid, and red.

The palm is a water lover and should not be subjected to drought conditions. It does not tolerate frost and is adaptable only to zones 10b and 11. The Macarthur palm survives in poor dry soil but only looks worthwhile in a rich, humus-laden, moist but well-drained medium. It seems to thrive in partial shade or full sun. There are two basic ways of using the Macarthur palm effectively in the landscape: one is to grow the plant only with all tall stems, planting smaller vegetation (such as *Chamaedorea* palms) at and around the base of the trunks; the other way is to have a mass, a wall, of tiered leaves by letting the suckers grow. Both methods are lovely and create wonderful tableaux of tropical luxuriance. The former method exhibits the beautifully ringed trunks more so than the second method, but the tiered layers of tropical-looking pinnate leaves are sumptuous. A clump of the palm is beautiful and elegant enough to stand alone, even isolated in space, but it is as a courtyard or patio feature that it is at its best, a site in which the wonderful trunks (like those of timber bamboo) can be seen close up. The plant's silhouette is as beautiful as that of the Alexander palm. This is a good choice for growing indoors if enough light and space can be provided. PLATES 728 & 729.

Ptychosperma microcarpum is endemic to eastern Papua New Guinea, where it grows in lowland rain forest as well as mountainous rain forest, from sea level to 2000 feet elevation. The epithet is from Greek words meaning "small fruit."

The palm is found as a solitary-trunked as well as a clustering species, with stems that attain heights of 30 feet and diameters from 2 to 5 inches. The crownshafts are 18 to 24 inches tall, silvery olive-green to nearly white, and bulging at their bases. The leaf crowns are hemispherical or slightly less so, with six leaves. Each leaf is 4 to 8 feet long, slightly arching, and borne on a 1-foot-long petiole. The leaflets are 1 to 2 feet long, grow in clusters, and are generally narrowly wedge shaped; the leaflets of the terminal pair are usually much wider than the others. All the leaflets grow from the rachis at slightly different angles, which gives the leaf a plumose effect. Their color is light green on both surfaces and their apices are obliquely truncated and unevenly jagged. The 0.5-inch-long ovoid fruits are brownish red when ripe.

Ptychosperma mooreanum is endemic to extreme eastern Papua New Guinea and adjacent Normanby Island in the D'Entrecasteaux Archipelago, where it grows in mountainous rain forest from sea level to 1200 feet elevation. The epithet honors 20th-century palm taxonomist Harold E. Moore, Jr.

The solitary trunk grows to 25 feet, with a diameter of slightly more than 1 inch. The crownshaft is 1 foot tall, bulging at its base, and brownish olive green. The leaf crown is hemispherical and sparse and open because of the few leaves (five to eight) and their long and slender petioles (2 feet). The leaves are 5 to 6 feet long, gracefully arching and spreading. The leaflets are regularly and widely spaced along the rachis, and the longest ones are 14 inches. They are emerald green on both surfaces and narrowly wedge shaped, with obliquely truncated and bifid or irregularly notched apices. The 0.5-inch-long ovoid fruits are orange when new but deep purplish black when ripe, and are beautiful against the orange branches of the infructescence.

This is an extremely graceful appearing species.

Ptychosperma propinquum occurs naturally on the islands of the Aru Archipelago, south of the western end of the island of New Guinea, where it grows in lowland rain forest. The epithet is Latin for "near to" or "related," the allusion unclear.

The plant is found in nature as a solitary-trunked as well as a clustering species, the stems growing to heights of 25 feet but with diameters of 0.5 inch. The plump crownshafts are 1 foot tall and olive green. The leaf crowns are hemispherical or slightly less so, and the leaves are 2 to 3 feet long on 1-foot-long petioles. The dark green leaflets grow in closely set clusters of two or three but arise off the rachis in a nearly flat plane. They are generally 1 foot long with obliquely truncated, jagged apices. The 0.5-inch-long fruits are bright red when ripe.

Ptychosperma salomonense is endemic to the Solomon Islands from sea level to 1500 feet elevation. The epithet is Latin for "of the Solomons."

The solitary trunk grows to 40 feet high but has a maximum diameter of 2 or 3 inches. The crownshaft is 18 inches tall, cylindrical, slightly thicker than the stem, and deep olive green. The leaf crown is hemispherical with 5 to 10 spreading and slightly arching 5- to 10-foot-long leaves on 5- to 12-inch-long petioles. The leaflets are regularly spaced and grow from the rachis at an angle that gives young leaves a slight V shape. They vary in shape and length, most being strap shaped to wedge shaped and from a few inches long near the base to 20 inches long near the midpoint of the leaf, always with an obliquely truncated, jagged apex. Leaflet color is medium to deep green on both surfaces. The 0.5-inch-long fruits are orange or red when ripe.

The species is visually and genetically similar to *P. elegans* but is, if possible, even more beautiful. Its elegantly thin stems and luscious, large crown of leaves are breathtakingly handsome. PLATES 730–732.

Ptychosperma sanderianum is unknown in the wild but seems to have been endemic to southeastern Papua New Guinea in lowland rain forest. The epithet honors Henry Sander, a 19th-century British nurseryman.

It is a small, clustering species whose stems grow to 10 feet high, with diameters of 1 to 2 inches. The crownshafts are deep olive green, cylindrical, and 19 inches tall. The leaf crown is hemispherical to slightly more with no more than 12 arching 4- to 5-foot-long leaves. The dark green 18-inch-long leaflets are regularly and closely spaced along the rachis from which they grow in a single flat plane. They are narrowly wedge shaped with obliquely truncated, jagged apices. The ovoid, 0.5-inch-long fruits are deep red when ripe.

The species is extremely graceful, with visual affinities to *P. macarthurii* but more delicate appearing.

Ptychosperma schefferi occurs naturally in northeastern Indonesian New Guinea (Irian Jaya) and northwestern Papua New Guinea, where it grows in lowland rain forest. The epithet honors Rudolph H. C. C. Scheffer, a 19th-century Dutch botanist and collector.

In nature, it is found as both a solitary-trunked and clustering species, with stems to 20 feet high and diameters of 2 inches. The plump crownshafts are 18 inches tall, deep olive green, and bulging near their midpoints. The leaf crowns are hemispherical or slightly less, with 10 barely arching, spreading, 5- to 6-foot-long leaves on 18-inch-long petioles. The 18-inch-long leaflets are regularly and closely spaced along the rachis from which they grow at an angle that gives younger leaves a slight V shape. The 0.5-inch-long oblong fruits are reddish brown turning black when ripe.

This is a wonderfully attractive, robust species that has the essence of the tropical look. PLATE 733.

Ptychosperma waitianum is endemic to southern Papua New Guinea, where it grows in lowland rain forest. The epithet honors the late Lucita H. Wait, executive secretary of the International Palm Society and manager of its seed bank.

It is a clumping species with stems to 15 feet tall and less than 1 inch in diameter. The plump, 1-foot-tall crownshafts are silvery green to nearly white and are usually bulged near the midpoint. The leaf crown is hemispherical or slightly more so, with eight 2- to 3-foot-long, arching and spreading leaves on 1-foot-long petioles. The 6- to 8-inch-long leaflets are deep green on both surfaces, broadly wedge shaped, widely spaced in the middle of the leaf, and grow in a single flat plane from the rachis. Their apices are deeply cleft into two irregularly notched main lobes. The new growth is brilliant deep orange to deep salmon. PLATE 734.

RAPHIA is a genus of more than 20 large, pinnate-leaved, monoecious, monocarpic palms in Africa and Madagascar and one in tropical America. Most are denizens of low, swampy areas, but a few grow on hills in rain forest. These palms are mostly massive; indeed, one species (*R. regalis*) has the largest leaves of any flowering plant.

There are both clustering and solitary-trunked species, and a few have subterranean stems. Many species form upward-pointing aerial roots from the leaf bases or nodes on the stem that are assumed to aid in oxygenating the palm when growing in water; these roots are formed even on dry land. The great leaves are erect, ascending, and usually slightly arching near their tips; they are borne on massive orange petioles arising from broad leaf bases that are soon woody and are often accompanied by masses of spiny or long and usually curling black fibers. The leaflet margins as well as the midribs of the leaflets have short bristles and, in several species, grow from the rachis at angles which create a plumose leaf. The inflorescences of these palms are commensurably large and are much branched, the ultimate flowering branches bearing both male and female flowers and all branches subtended by bracts of varying sizes. The fruits are also large, usually brown, and are covered in overlapping scales.

In their respective habitats, all the species have various human uses: the leaflets are used for making baskets and twine, which was formerly important even to the Western world; the pith in the stems is used to make flour; the long, heavy leaf base fibers of *R. hookeri* are used for making brooms and other utilitarian products; the petioles are used for construction; the leaves are used for thatch; and the sap from emerging inflorescences and the stem is used to ferment alcoholic drinks.

All the species are intolerant of cold, and all need copious water to do well. The ones listed below are not fussy about soil type and flourish even in calcareous soils. The genus name is a Latinized form of the aboriginal Malagasy name for *R. vinifera*. PLATES 735–745.

Raphia australis is indigenous to southeastern Mozambique and extreme northeastern South Africa, where it grows in lowland swamps, often in permanent shallow fresh water. The epithet is Latin for "southern."

The stems of this solitary-trunked species sometimes attain a height of 40 feet with a diameter of 18 inches. The leaves are immense, to 60 feet long, on huge orange petioles to 3 feet long. The leaflets are 2 to 3 feet long and deep green to bluish green, and grow from the rachis in pairs, each leaflet in the pair at a different angle from the rachis but always stiff and erect, thus giving the leaf a slightly plumose effect. The single inflorescence grows terminally erect from the top of the trunk, is 10 to 12 feet tall, and looks like a much smaller version of a *Corypha* inflorescence. PLATE 735.

Raphia farinifera is indigenous to Uganda, Kenya, and Tanzania, where it grows in rain forest or swamps from sea level to an elevation of 2640 feet; it is naturalized in Madagascar. The epithet is Latin for "flour-bearing," a reference to the meal obtained from the pith of the stems.

This species is similar to *R. australis* but may be clustering or solitary trunked, has longer and slightly more plumose leaves, and pendent inflorescences. The stems are 5 to 30 feet high with diameters of 2 or more feet. The leaves can attain a length of 70 feet, including a 20-foot-long petiole, with 8-foot-long leaflets, which are deep green above and a glaucous bluish green beneath. The inflorescences are 10 feet long and ropelike, with many congested branches subtended by large triangular bracts.

Mature specimens are nearly overwhelming in their grandeur. They should be kept moist to achieve their incredible potential. PLATES 736–738.

Raphia hookeri is found naturally in tropical western Africa, where it grows in lowland rain forest and swamps. The epithet honors 19th-century British botanist Sir Joseph D. Hooker.

This solitary-trunked and clustering species has stems 30 feet high and 1 foot in diameter. The leaves are 40 feet long, including the 6- to 8-foot-long petioles, and are much more spreading and arching than are those of the two previously described species. The soft, pendent 5-foot-long leaflets grow from different angles off the rachis to create a fully plumose leaf. They are glossy deep green above but glaucous silvery green beneath. The leaf bases are obscured by large, dense masses of both spinelike and long, curling dark gray or black fibers. The inflorescences are 7 feet long and similar to those of *R. farinifera*. PLATES 739–742.

Raphia humilis is indigenous to tropical western Africa in Nigeria and Cameroon, where it grows mainly along rivers and streams at low elevations. The epithet is Latin for "humble" or "small," a reference to the trunk.

This relatively small clustering species has either subterranean or short trunks. The leaf crown is shaped like a shuttlecock, with 15- to 20-foot-long ascending, slightly arching leaves. The dark green leaflets are stiff and mostly erect and grow from the rachis at slightly different angles but do not create a truly plumose effect; the large leaf looks like that of a large *Phoenix* species.

This is a thirsty palm whose needs are almost aquatic. It is stunningly beautiful in or around pools, lakes, or streams. PLATES 743 & 744.

Raphia regalis occurs naturally in rain forest of western tropical Africa. The epithet is Latin for "royal" or "regal."

This species is distinguished by having the largest leaves of any palm, to 80 feet long including the massive petiole. It is also unusual in having, like *R. australis*, erect terminal inflorescences. It is otherwise similar in general appearance to a larger version of *R. vinifera*. Although it is widely quoted in the literature as having the largest leaves in the plant kingdom, this statement is not true unless confined to the flowering plants; kelps of the Pacific Ocean off the coast of southern California reportedly form leaves as long as 200 feet.

Raphia taedigera has two disjunct areas of distribution in tropical America: the Caribbean slopes of Nicaragua and Costa Rica, southwards through Panama and into northwestern Colombia, where it grows in lowland rain forest and swamps; it is also found in the Amazon River estuary of northeastern Brazil, growing in lowland rain forest swamps. The epithet is Latin for "torch-bearing," the allusion unclear.

There is still some controversy whether the species is a variant of *R. vinifera* introduced to the Americas, or whether it is endemic to the Western Hemisphere. In any case it is generally similar to *R. vinifera* and is a clustering species whose stems attain maximum heights of 20 feet and maximum diameters of 1 foot. The leaves are typical of most other *Raphia* species: erect and ascending, with only the tips arching. They are 30 feet long, with plumosely arranged leaflets, each of which is 4 feet long, deep green on both surfaces, and soft and slightly pendent. The 8-foot-long inflorescences are pendent and are similar in general appearance to the other pendulously flowered species.

Raphia vinifera is indigenous to western tropical Africa, where it grows in lowland rain forest and swamps. The epithet is Latin for "wine-bearing" and alludes to the sap that is extracted from the immature inflorescence stalks and fermented into alcoholic beverages. This clustering species is similar in general appearance and dimensions to *R. farinifera,* and has been naturalized in many areas of the tropical world, including the Caribbean. PLATE 745.

RAVENEA is a genus of 17 pinnate-leaved, dioecious, solitary-trunked palms endemic to Madagascar and the Comoro Islands off the southeastern coast of Africa. Most species of this diverse genus are denizens of the rain forest, but a few are found in open drier woods and one in semi-arid conditions. The species form no crownshafts, and the inflorescences grow from the leaf bases and are sparsely branched, the male panicles usually longer, more slender and the branches more congested than those of the fe-males. The genus name honors a 19th-century French official of the Berlin Botanic Gardens, Louis Ravené. PLATES 746–759.

Ravenea glauca is an endangered species endemic to southern central Madagascar, where it grows in dry, evergreen forests and ravines at elevations of 2200 to 4000 feet. The epithet is Latin for "glaucous" and alludes to the texture and color of the new growth.

The slender, light brown, indistinctly ringed trunk attains a maximum height in habitat of 25 feet with a diameter of 3 or 4 inches. The leaf crown is hemispherical, with 18 spreading, 4- to 6-foot-long leaves on 3- to 6-inch-long petioles. The regularly spaced leaflets are 2 feet long, narrowly linear-lanceolate, and glossy deep green on both surfaces when mature; new growth is glaucous and stiff while the older leaflets are more lax and slightly pendent. The 0.5-inch-wide fruits are rounded and yellow when mature.

Some growers have named the species mini-majesty palm because of its supposed visual affinities to *R. rivularis,* but this species is much more delicate, not to mention smaller, in all its parts and its leaves do not exhibit the characteristic midpoint twist that those of *R. rivularis* do. In addition, it is much slower growing than the majesty palm and does not require nearly as much water. It is as hardy to cold as *R. rivularis* and appreciates a decent soil but does not seem as finicky about the quality of the medium. It flourishes in partial shade, especially when young, but is adaptable to full sun when older except in hot climates. PLATE 746.

Ravenea hildebrandtii is a critically endangered species endemic to low mountainous rain forest of the Comoro Islands, where it is an undergrowth subject. The epithet honors Johann M. Hildebrandt, a 19th-century German botanist and the original collector of the species.

The trunk grows to a maximum height of 25 feet in habitat with a diameter of 2 inches; under cultivation; the stature seems to be one-third the habitat height. The leaf crown is hemispherical with 12 to 24 small, 2- to 3-foot-long, mostly spreading leaves on 18-inch-long petioles. Younger leaves sometimes exhibit a twist of the rachis at its midpoint, which gives to the apical half of the blade a vertical orientation. The 12- to 18-inch-long light green leaflets are regularly spaced along the rachis and grow in a single flat plane from it. The 0.5-inch-long fruits are ellipsoidal and a deep yellow when ripe.

This beautiful little miniature palm is slightly susceptible to lethal yellowing disease but flourishes on calcareous soils. It is reportedly slightly hardier to cold than is *R. rivularis,* but not by much, being safe only in zones 10 and 11. It is drought tolerant but looks better and grows faster with regular and adequate moisture, although it is never fast growing. It needs partial shade and protection from the midday sun at all ages. PLATES 747 & 748.

Ravenea julietiae is another rare and endangered species endemic to lowland rain forest in eastern Madagascar. The epithet honors Juliet Beentje, who was the first to point a wild individual out to her husband, Henk.

In habitat, the trunk attains a maximum height of 30 feet with a diameter of 6 inches. The leaf crown is hemispherical or slightly less so and is elongated in younger plants. The 20 leaves per crown are ascending and mostly erect when young, 4 to 8 feet long, and gracefully arch near their apices; the older leaves are more spreading. The dark green, 2- to 3-foot-long, narrowly linear-lanceolate leaflets are regularly but widely spaced along the rachis and grow from it at angles to create a V-shaped leaf.

The silhouette of this palm is extraordinarily beautiful; it resembles a small *Pigafetta*. Reportedly the species is slow growing and difficult. PLATE 749.

Ravenea lakatra is yet another rare and critically endangered species endemic to the lowland rain forest of eastern Madagascar. The epithet is the aboriginal name for the tree and reportedly alludes to the density of the wood.

In habitat, the trunk can attain a maximum height of 45 feet with a diameter of 6 inches. The stems are extremely hard and durable and have steplike leaf base remnants that are 3 inches long. The leaf crown is less than hemispherical because of the ascending leaves. Individual leaves are 12 feet long and slightly arching, exhibit the characteristic twist to the vertical at their midpoints, and are borne on 3- to 5-foot-long petioles. The deep green, 2-foot-long, stiff leaflets are regularly spaced along the rachis, grow from it in a single flat plane, and are narrowly elliptic. The female inflorescences are reportedly 12 feet long and bear 0.5-inch-wide, round fruits that are black when ripe. PLATE 750.

Ravenea madagascariensis is endemic to the central and southern half of eastern Madagascar, where it grows in rain forest and dry evergreen forests from sea level to an elevation of 5280 feet. The epithet is Latin for "of Madagascar."

The trunk attains a height of 60 feet in habitat and a diameter of 6 to 8 inches. The leaf crown is usually less than hemispherical unless the dead leaves are retained. The leaves are ascending and may be straight or spreading and 6 to 10 feet long, and often exhibit the characteristic twist to the vertical at their midpoints. They are borne on stout, 1- to 2-foot-long light-colored petioles. The 2- to 3-foot-long leaflets are medium to dark green and narrowly elliptic; they either grow off the rachis at an angle to create a V-shaped leaf, or grow in a flat, single plane and are often pendent, especially when older. The small fruits are 0.25 inch wide, round, and orange when ripe.

This imposing, noble palm reportedly has a slight tolerance to cold, having withstood unscathed temperatures just below freezing. PLATE 751.

Ravenea moorei is another rare and endangered species endemic to low mountainous rain forest on the Comoro Islands. The epithet honors 20th-century palm taxonomist Harold E. Moore, Jr.

The trunk attains a height of 60 feet in habitat with a diameter of 5 to 12 inches and is much swollen at the base. The leaf crown is hemispherical or slightly less so, with many 4- to 7-foot-long, stiff, straight, and unarching leaves on short, 3- to 4-inch-long petioles. The many leaflets are regularly disposed along the rachis, from which they grow in a single flat plane. They are 2 feet long, deep green on both surfaces, and are narrowly lanceolate and pendent on older leaves. The 0.5-inch-wide fruits are round and orange when ripe.

This majestic species has visual affinities to the Asian *Orania* species. It is still rare in cultivation and little is known of its cultural requirements, but it is definitely neither cold hardy nor drought tolerant but probably is adaptable, except in hot climates, to full sun, even when young.

Ravenea musicalis is a rare species endemic to a single river in southeastern Madagascar at low elevations. The epithet is Latin for "musical," an allusion to the sound of the fruits falling into the stream. This is probably the world's only truly aquatic palm species; the seeds sprout and grow beneath the water.

The trunk attains a height of 25 feet in habitat and is much swollen in its lower half, resembling the stem of *Hyophorbe lagenicaulis*. The leaf crowns of young plants are similar to those of *R. rivularis*, including the twists of the leaf rachises at their midpoints, and the leaf dimensions of the two species are nearly identical. Older plants have leaves with mostly pendent leaflets. The 0.5-inch-wide orange fruits are spongy and split open easily. PLATE 752.

Ravenea rivularis is a vulnerable species endemic to southern and central Madagascar, where it grows along the banks of streams and rivers or in swamps on the edge of the rain forest from elevations of 1200 to 2500 feet. It often forms large colonies along riverbanks. Majesty (or majestic) palm is its common name. The epithet is Latin for "of the rivers."

Mature trunks can grow to 80 feet in their native haunts but are seldom more than half that stature under cultivation. They are free of leaf bases and fibers except for the youngest parts and are light gray to tan. The stems are swollen at their bases and exhibit widely spaced rings of leaf scar rings. The palm forms no true crownshaft, but the purplish brown leaf sheaths are prominent and persistent. There are usually 15 to 25 leaves in a crown, and palms with trunks usually have a full, rounded crown as the older leaves become pendent. The leaves are 6 to 8 feet long and elongated ellipses on stout petioles usually no more than 1 foot long. The leaflets grow from the rachis in a flat plane and are 2 feet long, narrowly elliptic and tapering, and regularly spaced along the rachis. They are thin and supple but not usually pendent. The leaves are erect in young plants but, as the tree develops a trunk, they begin to arch and are usually twisted at the middle of the rachis so that the leaflets along the apical half of the blade are oriented vertically or nearly so. Leaflet color is a smooth deep green on both sides. The inflorescences are 3 feet long and many branched, and bear small white male or female flowers. The fruits are a 0.5 inch wide, round, and bright red when ripe.

The palm is nearly an aquatic and it is difficult, if not impossible, to give it too much moisture. It also wants a rich, even mucky soil and, when older, full sun. It is fast growing when younger if given enough water and a soil that is decent, but it is not hardy to cold and its success is limited to zones 10 and 11.

Majesty palm flourishes in partial shade when young and is a superb subject for planting in such sites where many other large pinnate-leaved palms languish. It is attractive enough to stand alone as a specimen tree but looks better in groups of three or more individuals of varying heights. It had formerly almost displaced the "areca" palm (*Dypsis lutescens*) and the kentia palm (*Howea forsteriana*) as an interiorscape subject as it grows fast indoors and looks good if given lots of light and constant moisture. These conditions are difficult to maintain in the average home. It should not dry out while in a container and should be watered when the top inch or so of the container's soil is dry; it also prefers high relative humidity and becomes ragged looking when grown indoors with artificial dry heat. PLATES 753–755.

Ravenea robustior is endemic to northern and eastern Madagascar, where it grows in rain forest and clearings therein as well as in moist evergreen forests at elevations of near sea level to almost 6000 feet. The epithet is Latin for "more robust," the comparison presumably with other Malagasy palm species.

The trunk attains a height to 100 feet in habitat with a diameter to 2 feet and a swollen base, but these dimensions are rare and the trees are usually half this stature. The leaf crown is dense and shaped like a shuttlecock because of the ascending and erect, 6- to 12-foot-long leaves on 2- to 4-foot-long petioles. They are mostly stiff and unarching, but older leaves may be slightly spreading and some show the characteristic twist to the vertical at their midpoints. The 2- to 4-foot-long, dark green leaflets are regularly and closely spaced along the rachis and grow from it in a single flat plane.

The palm is majestic and beautiful but reportedly slow growing so that one plants it for benefit of future generations; the largest ones in habitat must be very old indeed. Amazingly, it is also reported to take some cold, surviving unscathed temperatures as low as 20°F in Mediterranean climes. PLATE 756.

Ravenea sambiranensis is endemic to and widespread in Madagascar, from the west central part of the island to its northwestern part, with scattered locations up and down the eastern coast. It grows from sea level to an elevation of 6000 feet, in lowland rain forest as well as on drier slopes of the interior. The epithet is Latin for "of Sambirano," a river in northwestern Madagascar.

In habitat the trunk attains a maximum height of almost 100 feet but is usually much shorter and is never more than 1 foot in diameter. The leaf crown is dense and shaped like a shuttlecock because of the erect, ascending leaves. The leaves of young palms are straight and unarching, with leaflets growing from the rachis in a single flat plane; the leaves of older, trunked individuals are beautifully recurved, with dark green, 2- to 3-foot-long, rigid, narrowly lanceolate leaflets growing off the rachis at a steep angle to create a deeply V-shaped leaf. In all cases, however, the crown is never more than hemispherical.

This is another silhouette species whose adult form is extraordinarily beautiful. It is reportedly cold resistant and not overly slow growing but needs fast-draining soil. PLATE 757.

Ravenea xerophila is a rare and endangered species endemic to southern Madagascar, where it grows at elevations from 600 to 2640 feet, mostly on the tops of hills, in dry thorn forests characterized by exotic looking, giant cactuslike *Alluaudia* and *Didierea* species, unique to the island. The epithet is derived from two Greek words meaning "dry" and "loving," an allusion to the habitat. Many palm enthusiasts tend to spell the epithet "xerophylla," which has a different meaning ("dry" and "leaf"). It would help mnemonically to pronounce the word as "ze-RAHF-i-la," reserving the "zer-o-FYL-la" pronunciation for *xerophylla*.

The trunk attains a maximum height of 25 feet but is usually shorter, with a diameter to 1 foot. The younger parts of the stem are covered in dense, persistent, dark gray or black sheets of leaf sheath remnants. The small leaf crown is hemispherical, with 20 ascending, arching, and recurved 5- to 6-foot-long, deep to bluish green leaves on 2-foot-long petioles. The narrow, stiff leaflets are numerous, closely and regularly spaced along the rachis, and grow from it at angles that create a deeply V-shaped blade.

The palm is attractive but agonizingly slow growing. It is, however, unusually hardy to cold, having withstood unscathed temperatures in the upper 20s (F). It is drought tolerant but grows and looks better with adequate and regular moisture; in habitat its aggressive root system goes deep to find underground moisture. PLATES 758 & 759.

REINHARDTIA is a genus of six pinnate-leaved, monoecious palms with both solitary-trunked and clustering species in southern Mexico, Central America, northern Colombia, and the Dominican Republic. They are all undergrowth plants in the rain forest and are mostly small palms. Only one of them ever becomes a canopy tree, and, interestingly enough, it is the only species whose natural range is not in the land mass of Central and South America, where the other five are found.

The leaves of these palms are unusual in that they may be entire and unsegmented or divided into several pinnae, and some have openings or "windows" at the base of the clustered pinnae, which phenomenon has led to their being called window palms or windowpane palms. The species do not form crownshafts, and the leaf sheaths wear down into a network of dark fibers that adhere to the stems, similar to species in the genus *Caryota*, although *Reinhardtia* species are not closely related to the fishtail palms. The inflorescences are spikelike or a cluster of sparsely branched, relatively short flowering branches at the ends of long primary branches. The flowering branches bear both male and female flowers, the latter of which produce mostly small, blackish purple fruits.

All the species are in danger of extinction because the forests in which they dwell are being cut and burned and they cannot exist in nature outside these forests. For such interesting, attractive palms, these species are inexplicably uncommon in cultivation, especially considering their reported ease of cultivation. Their main requirements are a tropical or nearly tropical climate, abundant and regular moisture, a humus-rich soil that is perfectly drained, and partial to near total shade. The genus name is a Latinized form of the surname "Reinhardt" and honors a family of 19th-century Danish biologists. PLATES 760–765.

Reinhardtia elegans has a disjunct distribution in southern Mexico and in northern Honduras, where it occurs in the undergrowth of mountainous rain forest from elevations of 3000 to more than 5280 feet. The epithet is Latin for "elegant."

This is one of only two species in the genus with regularly pinnate leaves, the other four species having leaves that are either simple or with pinnae united into a few leaflets. It is a solitary-trunked species whose stem attains a maximum height of 20 feet and a diameter of slightly more

than 1 inch. The leaf crown is hemispherical or slightly more so and contains 10 to 12 leaves, each 3 feet long on 1-foot-long petioles. The narrow, dark green leaflets are to 16 inches long and are regularly spaced along the rachis from which they grow in a single flat plane, their tips pendent. The inflorescences are composed of 3-foot-long peduncles from whose ends the 1-foot-long flowering branches protrude. The dark purple fruits are ovoid and 0.75 inch long.

This species looks like a large *Chamaedorea* species and has the same landscaping uses as most of those species. It is probably still rare in cultivation, but undeservedly so; it is as beautiful as most *Chamaedorea* species.

Reinhardtia gracilis is a threatened undergrowth species in rain forest of southern Mexico, northern Guatemala, northern Honduras, eastern Nicaragua, and northeastern Costa Rica, from elevations near sea level to 4300 feet. The common name is window palm or windowpane palm. The epithet is Latin for "graceful." Four varieties of *R. gracilis* have been described, but they have few vegetative differences, certainly not enough for the gardener to be concerned with.

The species is found in nature mostly as a clustering species but also rarely as a solitary-trunked species. Mature stems sometimes grow to 10 feet high but usually are no more than 4 or 5 feet tall. Their diameters are never more than 1 inch. The upper parts of the stems are usually covered in a wrapping of the old leaf bases which are green, turning brown, with the lower parts of the stems green to gray and ringed. If clustered, the clumps are never more than 4 feet wide. The leaves are evenly pinnate and 6 to 12 inches long, with four to eight segments pointing forwards away from the trunk. Each segment is 3 to 6 inches long, wedge shaped, with its apex squared or more usually obliquely truncated, and with small indentations at the tip, the points corresponding to a fused pinna. The apical segments are usually much broader than the lower ones, and each segment has small elliptical "windows" at its base, near the leaf rachis. The petiole is 3 to 24 inches long, thin, and green. The inflorescences are composed of 2- to 3-foot-long peduncles from whose ends the short flowering branches are green but usually turn red when mature. They bear small whitish flowers of both sexes. The fruits are oblong and slightly less than 1 inch long; they turn black when mature.

This palm needs constant moisture and relishes high relative humidity. It also wants a rich, humus-laden, fast-draining soil. The species does not tolerate full sun or freezing temperatures. It is suitable only for an intimate site in which it can be seen up close; it is lost visually in any other situation. The plant is perfect for containers on a shaded patio or courtyard. It needs good light without direct sun, and languishes and dies in heavy shade. PLATE 760.

Reinhardtia koschnyana is a rare and critically endangered species in northeastern Honduras, eastern Nicaragua, the Caribbean slopes of Costa Rica and Panama, and extreme northwestern Colombia, where it grows in lowland rain forest. The epithet honors Teodor Koschny, an early 20th-century Polish botanist and the original collector of the species.

This is a tiny clustering species whose wiry stems grow to no more than 2 feet. The 8-inch-long leaves are unsegmented, apically and unequally bifid, and are borne on wiry, 4-inch-long petioles. The blade is linearly diamond shaped, with toothed margins, and its color is a uniform dark, glossy green on both surfaces. The spikelike inflorescences are 15 inches long and turn a coral color when in flower. The fruits are obovoid, blackish purple, and 0.5 inch long.

This tiny species must be carefully sited in the landscape lest it be lost among other vegetation. It makes a perfect container plant.

Reinhardtia latisecta occurs naturally in five disjunct populations in Central America: central Belize, northeastern Honduras, southern Nicaragua, and two locales along the Pacific slope of Costa Rica, always in lowland rain forest. The epithet is derived from two Latin words meaning "wide" and "section" or "segment." In the United States, this large, clustering species is called giant windowpane palm.

The stems attain heights of 25 feet with diameters of slightly more than 2 inches. The leaves are 3 to 5 feet long, obovate but divided into four to six segments of varying widths; the leaflets of the terminal pair are always much larger than the others. The margins of all segments are toothed and exhibit the little elliptically shaped "windows" at their bases adjacent to the leaf's rachis. The inflorescences consist of 3-foot-long peduncles from the ends of which emerge 8-inch-long flowering branches that are creamy white at first but turn reddish before the ovoid, 0.5-inch-long black fruits mature.

This is the most beautiful species in the genus. Its size assures that it will not be lost among other vegetation and its large, matte green, shapely leaves are a delight up close and from afar. Its only fault is its intolerance of cold. PLATES 761–763.

Reinhardtia paiewonskiana is endemic to low mountainous rain forest in the Dominican Republic.

This is a solitary-trunked species and the tallest in the genus, the stem attaining a maximum height of 40 feet with a diameter of 5 inches. The leaf crown is hemispherical or slightly more so and contains a dozen 6-foot-long leaves on 12- to 18-inch-long petioles. The emerald green leaflets are as long as 2 feet and are narrowly elliptical and long tipped. They are regularly and closely spaced along the rachis from which they grow in a single flat plane, becoming pendent with age. The inflorescence peduncles are 4 to 6 feet long with 18-inch-long terminal flowering branches that produce round, 0.75-inch-wide black fruits.

The species has a beautiful silhouette, reminiscent of the kentia palm, *Howea forsteriana*. It was described in 1987 and seems not to be in cultivation but should be a real winner in frostless Mediterranean regions. PLATES 764 & 765.

Reinhardtia simplex occurs naturally in northeastern Honduras, along the Caribbean slopes of Nicaragua, Costa Rica, and Panama to extreme northwestern Colombia, where it grows in low mountainous rain forest. The epithet is Latin for "simple."

The stems of this small clustering species attain a maximum height of 4 feet with a diameter less than 0.5 inch. The leaves are glossy deep green above, duller, lighter green beneath, and 8 inches long on 6-inch-long, wiry petioles. They are simple and undivided or else segmented into three leaflets, the terminal one much larger and linearly oval or diamond shaped, the other two at right angles to the rachis and linear wedge shaped, all with toothed margins. The inflorescences consist of 2-foot-long peduncles from the ends of which the short flowering branches produce obovoid, 0.5-inch-long blackish purple fruits.

RETISPATHA is a monotypic genus of rare spiny, pinnate-leaved, dioecious, nonclimbing or shortly climbing rattan palm endemic to Borneo, where it grows in low mountainous rain forest and is widespread but not common throughout the island, often forming thickets. The genus name is derived from Latin and Greek words meaning "network" and "spathe," an allusion to the netlike bracts subtending the flowering branches of the inflorescences. The epithet is Latin for "bushy" and alludes to the thicket-forming habit.

Retispatha dumetosa has no cirrus or flagellum to aid in climbing; what little climbing it does is limited to a clambering, scrambling, mostly leaning against other objects to which its very spiny upper stems and petioles help it adhere.

The stems are stout; their lower parts are free of sheaths and spines and are distinctly ringed, appearing like "sugar cane culms" (Dransfield 1982). The leaves are long, spreading, and slightly arching, with many regularly spaced, linear-lanceolate, pendent leaflets. The stout petioles are armed with groups of spines along their margins, and the leaflets are armed with bristles along their margins and midribs. The inflorescences are long and narrow, beginning erect and later becoming pendent. They consist of many overlapping netlike bracts subtending the short, congested flowering branches, those on staminate plants producing ovoid fruits with overlapping scales.

The species is not known in cultivation outside of a few tropical botanic gardens but would seem to be eminently worthy of being planted. Its stature would allow it to contrast beautifully with other vegetation. It needs a tropical or nearly tropical climate and copious and regular moisture in partial shade to full sun.

RHAPIDOPHYLLUM is a monotypic palmate-leaved, clustering, mostly dioecious, slow growing palm in southeastern United States. The genus name is from Greek words meaning "rod" or "needle" and "leaf." The epithet is from the Greek word for "porcupine" and alludes to the needlelike spines on the leaf sheaths. PLATE 766.

Rhapidophyllum hystrix is endemic to southwestern Mississippi, southern Alabama, southern Georgia, northern peninsular Florida, and extreme southern coastal South Carolina, where it occurs in the undergrowth on the coastal plain in deciduous forests or in swampy lowlands, often on limestone soils but always in moist sites. Common names include needle palm, blue palmetto, creeping palmetto, dwarf saw palmetto, spine palm, hedgehog palm, and vegetable porcupine. Except for a few sites in Florida, the needle palm is near extinction in habitat. This lamentable situation has arisen lately because of collection of specimens for the nursery trade as the seeds are slow to germinate and slow growing once they do sprout. In addition, the species poorly reproduces itself in the wild and that is mainly by vegetative means. It would seem to be a vanishing relict species, even in Florida.

The stems are short and mostly less than 3 feet high. They are 4 inches in diameter but usually appear much thicker because of the mass of petiole bases and fibers that cover them. The stems may also be densely clustered or sparsely suckering, the latter condition seemingly associated with shadier sites. In spite of the diminutive trunk stature, the total height of a palm can reach 12 feet. Old trunks often start to disintegrate near their bases and begin to fall over but have the ability to root from almost any point on the stem, thus slowly creating other adjacent individuals, clustering or not. The summits of the stubby trunks are covered in soft leaf base fibers and in dense clusters of upright black or dark brown needlelike spines, each of which is usually 6 to 8 inches long but may be 16 inches. The leaves are 4 feet wide and range from semicircular to slightly more so, with 15 to 24 nearly 1-inch-wide segments extending three-quarters of the way to the petiole, which may be 3 to 5 feet long, depending on how much sun the palm receives. The segments are deep green above and deep green with a silvery sheen beneath. The inflorescences are short and stubby like the trunk itself and are formed near the apex of the stem among the mass of dense fibers. They are most often monoecious but may also be all male, all female, or a mixture thereof. In any case the flowers are yellowish white or pale lavender and have a slight musky odor, especially at night. Individual populations never seem to bloom regularly, but rather they are prolific in some years and, in other years, may produce few inflorescences. The 0.5-inch-wide fruits are round and reddish purple to brown but are covered in white tomentum. They are densely packed in a tight cluster atop the trunk and sometimes germinate among the crowns' leaf fibers before they break apart and fall. They have a strong sickeningly sweet odor when ripe.

The species may be hardier to cold than any other palm. It is adaptable to zones 6 through 10 and reportedly has survived in 5 without protection. It luxuriates in partial shade; although it can adapt to full southern sun, it does not look as good, the leaves are smaller, the petioles shorter, and the clustering or suckering phenomenon much more dense. It is slow growing under all conditions, especially shady ones. The palm is adapted to several soils from heavy to sandy but prefers a rich, moist one; its most important cultural requirement is probably regular and adequate moisture.

The palm has extraordinarily beautiful leaves, especially in shady sites, and is a wonderful close-up specimen. It looks as good mixed in with contrasting vegetation against which its half-pinwheel leaves offer much needed visual relief. Some people disagree, but this palm looks its best if grown in shade with most of its suckers removed, which procedure allows one to see the beautiful form of the leaf crown. Its infamous needles are usually no problem as they are almost hidden in the center of the leaf crown. We've not heard of this species being grown indoors but can think of no good reason why it couldn't be.

The only human use for this species is an ornamental one that is now leading to its extinction. In the recent past the entire leaf crown was cut and shipped north for the florist trade.

RHAPIS is a genus of 12 mostly densely clustering, palmate-leaved, dioecious palms in southern China including Hainan Island, Southeast Asia, Thailand, and northern Sumatra. They are mostly small undergrowth species of dry or monsoonal evergreen forests at low to moderate elevations, usually on limestone soils. The leaves are borne in usually elongated crowns and are very deeply segmented (usually to the petiole) and often circular or nearly so; the segments are pleated and their apices bear small indentations. They are borne on slender but long petioles, and the upper parts of the stems are clothed in a tightly adhering, dense network of dark leaf sheath fibers. The inflorescences are short and congested, and the flowering branches bear either male or female blossoms. Female plants produce one-, two- or three-lobed, small, usually rounded fruits that are white to black when mature.

Two species are extremely common in cultivation, but the others are rare and seem little known even to botanists. Most species are surprisingly hardy to cold, considering their tropical or nearly tropical origins. They do not look good in the full sun of hot climates but, at the same time, are generally tolerant of neglect and drought. The most widely grown species, *R. excelsa*, makes one of the finest indoor subjects.

The genus is closely related to *Maxburretia* and *Guihaia*. Its genus name is Greek for "rod" or "needle," an allusion to the slender canes or stems. PLATES 767–771.

Rhapis excelsa has never been found in the wild but is believed to have originally occurred naturally in southern China and Taiwan on limestone hills and cliffs and in dry, evergreen forests at moderate elevations. All known plants originate from cultivated individuals in China. Common names are lady palm and bamboo palm, the latter sobriquet unfortunate as several other palm species share it; a better alternative vernacular is the one used by Lynn McKamey, a Texas grower who specializes in the genus: large lady palm. The epithet is Latin for "tall" and is ironic since the species is not, by far, the tallest in the genus.

The species forms dense and often large clumps (of 100 or more stems) with elongated leaf crowns. The new stems mostly grow along the perimeter of a clump, which phenomenon results in leaves from ground level up to the tops of the clumps. The stems grow to heights of 10 feet with maximum diameters of 1 inch. They are covered in all but their oldest parts with the characteristic tightly adhering network of dark gray to black fibers. The leaves are 18 inches wide, are borne on 18-inch-long, thin petioles, and are circular or nearly circular. The 12 to 20 segments of slightly varying widths extend to the petiole and are generally linear-elliptic and a deep, glossy green above and below. They are also leathery in texture, bluntly truncated at their apices with small indentations, mostly stiff, and almost never pendent in any part. The short inflorescences grow from the upper leaf axils and are cream colored, often with a pinkish tinge, and produce small round fruits that are greenish white when ripe.

A plethora of cultivars exist, most of which have originated in Japan and most of which are dwarf with variegated leaves. Many of these are extravagantly beautiful up

close; their use in the landscape, however, seems limited to intimate sites.

The species is amazingly hardy to cold considering its purported tropical and subtropical origins. It is unscathed by temperatures in the low 20s (F), even in regions where winter freezes are accompanied by moisture. It is also known to sprout from its rhizomes after the stems have been killed to the ground by cold. It seems to thrive on almost any soil type as long as it is well drained and not too acidic nor too alkaline, and it luxuriates in partial shade, which is a requirement in hot climates if the deep green leaf color is to be preserved. About the only fault of this species is that it is slow growing, especially if not given regular and adequate moisture.

That the leaves grow from the trunks for most of the trunk length and that the new canes or trunks grow mostly from the perimeter of a clump make this little palm species near perfection for informal tall hedge material in partially shaded sites. It is also almost unexcelled as a close-up specimen where its grace can be fully appreciated; like many other clumping palm species, it is more graceful and artistic if some of the crowded trunks are removed to better show off its wonderful silhouette. Few plants are as beautiful near water as *R. excelsa*. The dwarf forms, both variegated and of single hue, make exceptionally beautiful plantings along a walkway or among stones in partially shaded rock gardens. There is hardly a finer candidate for growing indoors. The lady palm endures neglect and abuse similar to the kentia palm, *Howea forsteriana*, and asks only for a site with bright light (but not sun) and regular watering. PLATE 767.

Rhapis humilis is, like *R. excelsa*, unknown in the wild, all known plants having come from cultivated individuals in China. It is assumed to have originated in southern China and possibly Taiwan in the same sort of habitats. The common name is slender lady palm. The epithet is Latin for "humble" or "small," an even greater irony than that of the above species since the stems of this clumper attain heights of 20 feet. The trunks have generally less fiber than do those of *R. excelsa*, are also thinner than the canes of *R. excelsa*, and are beautifully and closely ringed in the parts lacking fiber. The clumps are not as massive and the stems are significantly fewer in number. In addition, the leaf crowns are not nearly so elongated as are those of *R. excelsa*, and the leaves are wider but not usually as circular. The segments are generally more numerous and are longer, softer, pendent, and definitely pointed at their apices. The inflorescences are similar to those of *R. excelsa*, but only male plants are known.

The slender lady palm is more cold tolerant than the large lady palm and is adaptable to zones 8b through 11. It is not at home in hot climates, like those of southern Florida. It flourishes in Mediterranean climates, where the nights, even in summer, have lower temperatures. Like *R. excelsa,* it needs protection from the midday sun in hot climates. It appreciates the same soils as does *R. excelsa,* and its moisture requirements are the same and possibly less strict. The only method of propagation is by removing the suckers as no individual palm produces fruit. It is as slow growing as the large lady palm. There are a few cultivars with smaller stature or with variegated leaves, and these are more useful indoors than in the landscape.

This species is, if possible, more beautiful than is the large lady palm. It is taller and more elegant looking, and its softer, larger leaves are even more appealing than those of *R. excelsa.* As a giant hedge or barrier, it is unexcelled, and its silhouette is as lovely as that of any palm species. The only landscape situation it is not perfectly suited to is that of a specimen planting surrounded by space, and even there it is good if its silhouette is against a wall or contrasting vegetation. The species is almost as amenable to indoor culture as is *R. excelsa,* the mitigating factor being its size. PLATE 768.

Rhapis laosensis is a rare and endangered species occurring naturally in Laos and adjacent northeastern Thailand, where it grows in lowland rain forest. The epithet is Latin for "of Laos."

The stems of this small, sparse clumper are thin and reach 5 feet high. The leaves are composed of two to five, but usually three, diverging, pleated segments, each of which is 8 inches long, strap shaped or oblong shaped, with a small, abruptly pointed tip. They are soft, slightly recurved, and glossy medium green above and paler and duller green beneath.

This delicate, attractive species makes a beautiful tall groundcover. It is less tolerant of cold than are the above two species and seems adaptable only to zones 10 and 11 and possibly in warm microclimates of 9b. This palm needs more moisture than either *R. excelsa* or *R. humilis* and seems to flourish in humid regions. Because only female plants are known, propagation is mostly by removal of the suckers. PLATE 769.

Rhapis multifida is endemic to southern China adjacent to Vietnam, where it grows in monsoonal evergreen forests at low to moderate elevations, usually on limestone soils. The epithet is derived from two Latin words meaning "many" and "division."

The slender stems of this sparse clumper grow to heights of 8 feet. The mature leaves are 2 feet wide, semicircular to slightly more so, and contain 12 to 24 narrow segments that extend into the blade just short of the petiole. The segments of young leaves are stiff, but those of

older leaves are lax, slightly arching, and pendent. They are glossy medium green on both surfaces. The inflorescences are several branched and erect, with yellowish flowering branches covered in short, felty hairs. The round fruits are less than 0.5 inch in diameter.

This palm has the same cultural requirements as *R. excelsa* except it is not as hardy to cold, being adaptable to zones 9b through 11. It has the most beautiful leaves of the known species. They are extraordinarily attractive as silhouettes against contrasting vegetation or other objects. PLATE 770.

Rhapis subtilis occurs naturally in Cambodia, Laos, and Thailand, where it grows in monsoonal rain forest at low elevations. The epithet is Latin for "subtle" and, by extension, "thin," an allusion to the slender canes and petioles. It is usually called Thailand lady palm.

This small but dense clumper has stems to 6 or 7 feet tall. The leaf segments vary in form, from many narrow segments in a nearly circular blade, to single and unsegmented, wide strap-shaped or ovate leaves. All are glossy dark green above and below, and the segments are pleated and are borne on 1-foot-long, thin petioles. The forms with many, narrow segments look much like dwarfed versions of *R. humilis* and, when first introduced into cultivation by Watana Sumawong, were thought to be forms of it.

The species is not as cold hardy as most of the others, being adaptable only to zones 10 and 11, and it seems to greatly resent cold, drying winds and needs nearly constantly high humidity. The clumps are so dense and the rhizomes so brittle that it is nearly impossible to successfully remove suckers for propagation; but seed is readily produced from female plants. PLATE 771.

RHOPALOBLASTE is a genus of seven pinnate-leaved, monoecious palms in low mountainous rain forest of the Nicobar Islands, peninsular Malaysia, Singapore, the Moluccas, New Guinea, and the Solomon Islands.

All but one species is solitary trunked. All have slender, distinctly ringed trunks, handsome crownshafts, and large leaves, most with beautifully pendent leaflets. The much-branched inflorescences grow from beneath the crownshafts, often encircling them, and produce clusters of orange or red fruits.

These are among the world's most beautiful palms, but they are unaccountably rare in cultivation, even in tropical regions, possibly because they are slow growing. All are tender to cold and possible only in zones 10b and 11. They are true water lovers and much resent dry conditions, including desiccating winds.

The genus name was formerly *Ptychoraphis,* and the current name comes from two Greek words meaning "club" and "bud," a reference to the shape of the embryo. PLATES 772 & 773.

Rhopaloblaste augusta is a rare and endangered solitary-trunked species endemic to the Nicobar Islands, where it grows in low mountainous rain forest. The epithet is Latin for "noble" or "majestic."

This species is the tallest in the genus, the trunk attaining a height of 100 feet in habitat but seldom half that height under cultivation. It is never more than 1 foot in diameter above its swollen base and is light tan with widely spaced darker rings of leaf base scars. The crownshaft is 2 feet tall, not much thicker than the trunk, slightly bulging at its midpoint, and grayish light brown and velvety to the touch. The leaf crown is hemispherical or more so and is composed of 10 stiff, unarching (except at their tips), and spreading 12-foot-long leaves on short, almost nonexistent petioles that are only 3 or 4 inches long. The regularly and closely spaced narrow leaflets are 2 feet long and pendent, forming 2-foot-long curtains on each side of the rachis. The ellipsoid fruits are deep orange to red and less than 1 inch long.

The palm is enthrallingly beautiful with a silhouette that is beyond compare, and there is arguably no more beautiful sight in the plant world than three or more individuals of greatly varying heights. PLATES 772 & 773.

Rhopaloblaste brassii is endemic to New Guinea, where it grows in mountainous rain forest from sea level to an elevation of 3500 feet. The epithet honors Leonard J. Brass, a 20th-century botanist and collector in New Guinea.

The stem of this small, solitary-trunked species grows to 12 feet high with a diameter of 2 inches. The loose crownshaft is 2 feet tall, scarcely thicker than the trunk but bulging near its midpoint, cylindrical, a strange purplish green, and covered in a scurfy tomentum. The leaf crown is hemispherical or slightly less so and contains 10 straight, ascending, slightly arching 8- to 10-foot-long leaves on 8-inch-long, gray to tan rough-textured petioles. The dark green 2-foot-long leaflets are stiff and nonpendent and grow at a slight angle off the rachis that, in young leaves, creates a shallow V shape to the leaf but, in older leaves, are much more lax, spreading and half-pendent, to create a flat leaf. The inflorescences seem relatively gigantic on this species; they produce large clusters of ellipsoid, 0.5-inch-long, bright red fruits.

Although rare in cultivation, the species is deserving of much greater distribution as it is one of the most beautiful in the genus.

Rhopaloblaste ceramica occurs naturally on the islands of Batjan Pulau and Ceram in the Moluccas, where it grows in low mountainous rain forest. The epithet is Latin for "of Ceram."

It is a solitary-trunked species whose trunk attains a height of 60 feet in habitat with a diameter of less than 1 foot above the swollen base. It is light gray or tan and graced with widely spaced darker rings of leaf base scars. The crownshaft is 3 feet tall, light tan to almost silver, and distinctly bulged at its base. The leaf crown is hemispherical or slightly more so and contains 8 or 10 straight, slightly arching 10-foot-long leaves. The 3-foot-long narrow leaflets are regularly and closely spaced along the rachis and are pendent in older leaves, creating twin curtains of green along both sides of the rachis. The beautiful scarlet fruits are ovoid and more than 1 inch long.

This beautiful species is akin visually to *R. augusta* but shorter.

Rhopaloblaste elegans is endemic to the Solomon Islands, where it grows in lowland rain forest on limestone soils. The epithet is Latin for "elegant."

The stem of this solitary-trunked species attains a height of 40 or more feet and a diameter of 3 inches above its swollen base. The crownshaft is 3 feet tall, scarcely thicker than the trunk, cylindrical, and brownish green. The leaf crown is spherical or nearly so. The leaves are 10 feet or slightly more in length and are spreading and slightly arching. The numerous, narrow leaflets are 2 feet long, light green, regularly and closely spaced along the rachis, and lax and pendent but not forming the curtain effect of other species; rather, they gracefully arch downwards. The 1-inch-wide, round fruits are waxy and a beautiful cinnamon color when ripe.

The species is certainly among the most elegant of any genus, with its diaphanously thin, straight trunks and large, shimmering, light green arching leaves.

Rhopaloblaste singaporensis occurs naturally in the undergrowth of lowland rain forest of peninsular Malaysia and Singapore. The epithet is Latin for "of Singapore."

The stems of this clustering species grow to 10 or 12 feet high, with diameters of less than 1 inch. The crownshaft is loose, indistinct, and light brown. The 3- to 4-foot-long leaves are straight and spreading. The 18-inch-long, linear-lanceolate, long-tipped leaflets are regularly and closely spaced along the rachis from which they grow in a single flat plane. They are spreading, nonpendent, stiff, and glossy medium green above but paler green beneath. The 0.5-inch-long fruits are deep orange to red when ripe.

This graceful small palm makes a startlingly beautiful accent among other vegetation.

RHOPALOSTYLIS is a genus of two pinnate-leaved, solitary-trunked, monoecious palms in New Zealand, Chatham Island, Norfolk Island, and Raoul Island in the South Pacific. They are tall palms with distinctly smooth, ringed trunks and narrow, erect crowns shaped like a shaving brush; indeed, they define the term "shaving brush palm." The crownshafts are prominent, distinct, and often bulbous or greatly swollen. The inflorescences grow from beneath the crownshafts and consist of short flowering branches on a short peduncle. The fruits are rounded and red when ripe.

Both species strongly resemble each other, and future studies may unite the two (and the two varieties of *R. baueri*) into a single variable species. They are inhabitants of moist and cool, subtropical, coastal areas at low to moderate elevations where the temperature does not vary much from season to season or from night to day; as a result they are at home in cool and nearly frostless Mediterranean climates but are almost impossible to grow in hot or tropical climates. In their habitats, they are considered hardy to cold, which they are, but the cold conditions of Australia and New Zealand are different from those of United States, where great masses of chilly air can descend from the arctic in the winter, suddenly dropping the temperature from balmy to frigid conditions. The palms have been killed, even in southern coastal California, when these arctic outbreaks occur.

The genus name is from two Greek words meaning "club" and "pillar," an allusion to the form of the female flowers. PLATES 774–777.

Rhopalostylis baueri occurs naturally on Norfolk and Raoul Islands in the South Pacific, where it grows in subtropical rain forest at an elevation of 1000 feet. Australians call it Norfolk Island palm. The epithet honors the late 18th- and early 19th-century Austrian brothers, Ferdinand Lucas and Franz Andraes Bauer, who were botanical artists and accompanied Sir Joseph Banks to Australia and the South Pacific.

The trunk attains a maximum height in habitat of 50 feet with a diameter of 8 inches. It is light to dark green in all but its oldest parts and is distinctly ringed with light gray and closely set rings of leaf base scars. The plump, 3-foot-tall crownshaft is light to dark green and bulged at its base. The leaves are 12 feet long on short, almost nonexistent petioles. In trees exposed to the sun, they are stiff and erect, with regularly and closely spaced, narrowly elliptical, light green, 2- to 3-foot-long, stiff and long-tipped leaflets that grow from the rachis at a slight single to create a slightly V-shaped leaf. Palms grown in shadier conditions have slightly more spreading leaves with more lax and pendent leaflets. The ovoid fruits are reddish brown when ripe and 0.5 inch long.

A naturally occurring variety, **R. baueri var. cheesemanii**, is distinguished from the type by its endemism on Raoul Island, its larger and more rounded fruits, and the brown tomentum on its crownshaft. Because Raoul Island is isolated from Norfolk Island, the two varieties have, in the past, been treated as distinct species.

The species is hardy in zones 9b through 11 but only for the cooler Mediterranean climes; it refuses to grow in hot climates, although it is reportedly more tolerant to these conditions than is *R. sapida*. Regular and adequate moisture is almost as important as is climate, and specimens subjected to drought or too much sun become ratty looking and are not worth having. The palm flourishes in partial shade or full sun if not too exposed to drying winds, which make a mess of its beauty. The species is fast growing if given enough moisture and a rich soil. It prefers a slightly acidic, moist, and fast-draining soil but seems able to adapt to several types if they are not too alkaline or too acidic and if they have some humus. The palm reportedly makes a good container or indoor plant if given bright light and regular irrigation. PLATE 774.

Rhopalostylis sapida is endemic to New Zealand and the Chatham Islands to the east, where it grows in dense, wet forests at an elevation of 2000 feet. The epithet is Latin for "good to eat," an allusion to the growing point, which was used by the Maori as a cabbage. They supposedly also used the leaves for thatch.

The species is similar to *R. baueri* but shorter, the trunk attaining a maximum height of 30 feet. The crownshaft is more bulbous than that of *R. baueri*, and the leaves are 16 feet long. The fruits are a brighter, purer red.

The species is more tolerant of cold than is *R. baueri* and more intolerant of hot climates. In the Chatham Islands, it is the world's southernmost naturally occurring palm species. Individuals native to the Chathams reportedly have wider leaflets, more robust stems, and pinkish petioles. In Australia and New Zealand, the palms are called nikau palms, feather duster palms, shaving brush palms, and brush palms. PLATES 775–777.

ROSCHERIA is a monotypic genus of solitary-trunked, pinnate-leaved, monoecious palm endemic to the Seychelles Islands. The genus honors Albrecht Roscher, a 19th-century German explorer in East Africa. The epithet is from Latin and Greek and translates as "black" and "bristle," obvious allusions to the spines. PLATES 778 & 779.

Roscheria melanochaetes is a rare and endangered species endemic to Mahé and Silhouette islands, where it occurs in the undergrowth of low mountainous rain forest.

The trunk in habitat slowly grows to 25 feet with a diameter of 3 inches. It is usually straight and distinctly ringed in its younger parts. Young trees have rings of black spines at each node of the stem but, in older plants, these are sparse or even nonexistent; the crownshaft and lower portions of the petioles exhibit short black spines, even in mature plants. The crownshaft is 1 foot tall, scarcely thicker than the trunk, slightly bulging at its midpoint, and light green overlain with tiny brown scales, especially near its summit. The leaf crown is open, sparse, and rounded with six arching 4- to 6-foot-long leaves, usually with twisted rachises, on 6- to 8-inch-long petioles. The leaves are unusual in that the leaflets vary in shape and size; no two on a given tree seem to have the same dimensions. Some are elliptic with a single rib or midvein and with long-pointed apices, while others are much broader, with several ribs and obliquely truncated apices bearing indentations between each rib or midvein. All have several folds or pleats, especially prominent at the juncture of rachis and blade. The widths of the segments are mostly random as to their placement along the rachis but, in all cases, the leaflets of the terminal pair are wide, often the widest. The width of individual leaflets or segments is almost as broad where it grows off the rachis as it is at its midpoint. They are light olive to emerald green above, with a duller and brownish hue beneath, and are thin and membranous. Juvenile leaves are undivided except for their bifid apices. Newly emerging leaves are usually pink to red. The inflorescences are borne from the leaf axils, unlike most other crownshafted species in which they are borne beneath the crownshafts. They are 2 to 6 feet long and are much branched, the pendent flowering branches bearing both male and female flowers. The small, egg-shaped fruits are 0.25 inch long and are red when ripe.

The species is as unusual in appearance as it is beautiful. It is slow growing, intolerant of drought, and needs partial shade when young and at all ages in hot climates. It is tender to cold, as are all Seychelles species, being adaptable to zone 11 and marginal in 10b. It must have a moist soil with humus. These conditions are difficult to provide in many areas, even tropical ones.

ROYSTONEA is a genus of 10 large, solitary-trunked, pinnate-leaved, monoecious palms in tropical America, principally in and around the Caribbean Basin. The species are similar and often difficult to distinguish one from the other. Scientific differentiation is by inflorescence size, flower color and other floral details, as well as height and color of the stem.

The trunks are moderate in height to among the world's tallest, usually massive, often bulging at some point and, except for a few species, white or nearly so in all but their youngest parts, which are green and prominently ringed. The bases of the stems are usually much enlarged. All species form prominent, often large crownshafts. The leaf crowns are generally full, dense, and rounded, and the leaves large to very large, commensurate with the height of the trunk. No species has adult individuals with leaflets growing in a single flat plane off the rachis, but some species have much more plumose leaves than others; juvenile trees tend to have much flatter leaves than do adults of the same species. All the species reportedly have the ability to release their leaves easily in strong winds, a supposed adaptation to hurricanes that would otherwise fell the trunks. The inflorescences grow from beneath the crownshafts and are first enclosed in large, leathery, narrowly horn-shaped bracts. The flowering branches are many, spreading, and white when first released from the bracts. They bear unisexual blossoms of both sexes. The fruits are round or ellipsoid and are deep purple when ripe.

In this genus are some of the world's most famous palms. One (*R. regia*) is considered by many people to be the world's most beautiful; it is certainly among the most popular. All have grandeur that few other genera can compete with. All are unsuitable for arid regions unless well irrigated, and all are tender to cold, the hardiest being adaptable to zones 10 and 11. They seem to be survivors, however, sometimes refusing to die after being defoliated by cold, the only witness of their suffering being a constriction of the trunk marking the event; past conditions of drought effect the same visual phenomenon. They are almost without exception adapted to growing in calcareous soils, and yet grow faster and look better in a medium that incorporates humus—a thick mulch being second best. Under optimum conditions, all are fast growing once past the seedling stage, and some of the larger species are fast growing even when young. All are also adapted to full sun once past the seedling stage, and they grow more slowly if not given enough light.

The genus name honors Roy Stone, a U.S. Army engineer in Puerto Rico in the 19th century. PLATES 780–788.

Roystonea altissima is endemic to Jamaica, where it grows on hillsides and mountain slopes in the interior of the island from elevations of 200 to 2640 feet. The epithet is Latin for "highest," but the species is not the tallest in the genus.

The trunk attains a height of 60 feet in habitat with a diameter of 1 foot. It gently tapers from bottom to top, is usually light tan and, in its younger parts, is graced with widely spaced darker rings of leaf base scars. The crownshaft is 5 feet tall, deep olive green, not much thicker than the trunk, generally cylindrical, and slightly bulging at its base. The leaf crown is spherical and holds 15 slightly arching but spreading 12-foot-long leaves on short petioles. The 30-inch-long medium green leaflets are closely and regularly spaced along the rachis and grow from it at slightly different angles to create a slightly plumose leaf. The inflorescences bear violet male flowers, and the fruits are obovoid, 0.5 inch long, and a dark, purplish black when ripe. PLATE 780.

Roystonea borinquena is indigenous to Hispaniola, Puerto Rico, and the islands of Vieques and St. Croix in the U.S. Virgin Islands, where it grows in savannas, cleared areas, and at the bases of limestone hills from sea level to an elevation of 2640 feet. The epithet is Latin for "Borinque" (or "Borinquen"), a Spanish transliteration of the aboriginal name of Puerto Rico.

The trunk grows to 50 feet high with a diameter of 18 inches. It is sometimes bulging near its midpoint, is light gray to tan, and is distinctly ringed in its younger parts with darker leaf base scars. The crownshaft is 5 feet tall, not much thicker than the trunk, and deep emerald green. The leaf crown is spherical and holds 15 arching 15-foot-long leaves on 18-inch-long petioles. The 3- to 4-foot-long leaflets are deep green and grow off the rachis at angles which create a fully plumose leaf. The 4-foot-long inflorescences bear yellow male flowers and produce dark brown to black, rounded 0.5-inch-wide fruits.

Roystonea dunlapiana is indigenous to the Caribbean coasts of the Yucatán Peninsula (Quintana Roo) of Mexico, adjacent northern Belize, northern Honduras, and eastern Nicaragua, where it grows in coastal mangrove swamps and tidal estuaries. The epithet honors Robert V. Dunlap, an early 20th-century horticulturist in Honduras.

The trunk attains a height of 60 feet and a diameter of slightly more than 1 foot. It is pale gray to nearly white and usually slightly swollen above its midpoint, where it is also graced with darker rings of leaf base scars. The crownshaft is 6 feet tall, deep emerald green, slightly enlarged at its base, and cylindrical above that. The spherical leaf crown contains fifteen 12-foot-long leaves on 12- to 18-inch-long petioles. The 3-foot-long leaflets are medium green and grow from the rachis at several angles to create a fully plumose leaf. The inflorescence bract is 6 feet long and narrow. The male flowers are white, and the obovoid fruits are deep, blackish purple when ripe.

This is an outstandingly beautiful species, comparable in attractiveness and dimensions to the Cuban royal but is rare in cultivation. It makes a perfect seaside subject in tropical or nearly tropical climates with enough summer heat to keep it happy.

Roystonea lenis is a rare species endemic to extreme eastern Cuba, where it grows in open savannas on limestone soils at low elevations. The epithet is Latin for "mild."

The trunk grows to 60 feet high with a diameter of 18 inches. It is white or nearly so and is usually distinctly bulged at or near its midpoint; it is always much swollen at

its base. The deep green crownshaft is 6 feet tall, scarcely thicker than the stem, except near its base where it is slightly larger. It is otherwise cylindrical and tapers gently towards its summit. The leaf crown is spherical or nearly so and contains 15 plumose 16-foot-long leaves on 2-foot-long petioles. The male flowers are white, and the fruits are the typical blackish purple when ripe.

The species is similar in appearance to *R. regia* but usually has a more bulging trunk and rounder and harder fruits.

Roystonea maisiana is a rare species endemic to extreme southeastern Cuba, where it grows in open savannas at elevations from 1200 to 1500 feet. The epithet is Latin for "of Maisí," a region in Guantánamo, Cuba.

The light gray to white trunk attains a height of 60 feet in habitat with a diameter of only 1 foot and seldom bulges at any point above its enlarged base. The crownshaft is deep olive green, 4 feet tall, mostly cylindrical, and nearly the same thickness as the trunk. The leaf crown is hemispherical to nearly spherical and contains 20 arching 12- to 15-foot-long leaves on 2- to 3-foot-long petioles. The 3-foot-long dark green leaflets grow from the rachis at several angles to create a fully plumose leaf. The inflorescences bear white male flowers and produce typical blackish purple fruits.

The species is distinguished by its unusually long petioles and slender trunks. Although it seems not to be in cultivation, it is, because of its elegant proportions, more than worthy of being planted.

Roystonea oleracea occurs naturally in the Lesser Antilles, northern Venezuela, and extreme northeastern Colombia, where it grows along the edges of rain forest and seasonally flooded savannas from sea level to an elevation of 5280 feet. The epithet is Latin for "edible" and alludes to the palm's growing point.

It is the most widely distributed species in the genus, the only South American species, and the tallest in the genus. The trunk attains the remarkable height of 130 feet or even more in habitat, with a diameter of 2 feet. It is a light to medium gray and is slightly bulging, if at all, at any point above its swollen base. The crownshaft is 6 feet tall, deep green, slightly bulging at its base, and gently tapering to its summit. The leaf crown is hemispherical and has 20 gently arching 15-foot-long leaves on 2- to 3-foot-long petioles. The 2- to 3-foot-long, deep green leaflets grow at two slightly different angles from each side of the rachis to create a semiflat leaf. The male flowers are white, and the fruits are typically a blackish purple.

A naturally occurring variety, ***R. oleracea* var. *jenmanii***, is known only in cultivation and has erect leaves that create a shuttlecock form to the leaf crown.

There is no more majestic palm, but it is reportedly also the least hardy to cold. Photographs seldom give a true sense of its grandeur, and an avenue with this species planted along it is a grand sight. PLATES 781 & 782.

Roystonea princeps is endemic to southern Jamaica, where it grows in swampy areas near sea level. The epithet is Latin for "prince" or "chief."

The trunk grows to 60 feet high with a diameter of 1 foot. It is light gray to white and seldom bulging at any point above its swollen base. The crownshaft is 5 feet tall, silvery green, and cylindrical except at its base where it is slightly bulging. The leaf crown is spherical or nearly so with fifteen 12-foot-long leaves on 12- to 18-inch-long petioles. The emerald green, 30-inch-long leaflets grow from the rachis at several angles to create a plumose leaf. The male flowers are white, and the fruits are typically blackish purple.

The species is especially beautiful because of the long, supple, and mostly pendent leaflets. PLATE 783.

Roystonea regia is the second most widely distributed in the genus, from the shores of the Gulf of Campeche in Mexico (in the states of Campeche, Tabasco, Veracruz) and along the Caribbean coast of the Yucatán in Mexico (in the state of Quintana Roo), along the Caribbean coasts of Belize and northwestern Honduras, the Cayman Islands in the Gulf of Mexico, all of Cuba, the westernmost Bahamas, and the southern tip of Florida (in the counties of Collier, Monroe, and Dade). It grows naturally along the edges of rain forest, in wooded savannas, along rivers and streams, and in swamps from sea level to an elevation of 3000 feet. Were it not for its great beauty, it would be considered weedy as it readily naturalizes in tropical regions. Common names are royal palm, Cuban royal palm, and Florida royal palm. The epithet is Latin for "regal."

The trunk attains a height to 100 feet and a diameter of nearly 2 feet. It is light gray to white and distinctly ringed in its younger parts with darker leaf base scars. It exhibits at least one slightly swollen point along its columnar structure, and its base is enlarged. The crownshaft is 6 feet tall, emerald green, bulged at its base, and otherwise cylindrical. The leaf crown is spherical or nearly so and holds fifteen 12-foot-long leaves on 8-inch-long petioles. The 2- to 4-foot-long leaflets are deep green and grow off the rachis at different angles to create a fully plumose leaf. The male flowers are white, and the fruits are deep reddish brown to the typical blackish purple when ripe.

The palm wants regular and adequate moisture, a tropical or nearly tropical climate, and a humus-laden soil but grows in nearly pure limestone, especially if heavily mulched. Freezes and droughts are recorded in survivors by constrictions of the trunk. It often survives a freeze and has been known to return from the dead from temperatures in the mid 20s (F) after being defoliated. It should not be planted in the shade. In full sun and with good irrigation it can add 1 foot or more of new trunk per year.

This is the most widely planted species in the genus, and with good reason. It is magnificently beautiful and is a veritable symbol of the wet tropics and the tropical look. It is hard to misplace it in the landscape as it looks good even as a single specimen plant surrounded by space. Plantings of three or more individuals of varying heights are a vision of paradise itself, and its canopy-scape floating over lower vegetation is not only enthralling but also is how it looked in much of its habitat, like the Everglades of southern Florida. There is no more beautiful palm species. It is not known to be grown indoors, even in large atriums. PLATES 784–786.

Roystonea stellata is a 50- to 60-foot-tall royal endemic to Cuba. It is probably extinct now and is not known to be in cultivation. The epithet is Latin for "starred," an allusion to the apices of the fruits with their starlike stigmatic remains.

Roystonea violacea is endemic to the extreme southeastern tip of Cuba, where it grows in open savannas and on hills at elevations of 1200 to 1500 feet. The epithet is Latin for "violet" and alludes to the color of the male flowers and the young trunks.

The trunk grows to 50 feet in habitat and, especially when young, is an unusual dark tan to almost milk-chocolate color overlain with a slight purplish hue, with distinct light tan rings of leaf base scars; older trees usually have dark gray to dark tan stems. The 6-foot-tall crownshaft is light green, cylindrical, slightly thicker than the trunk, and slightly bulged near its base. The spherical leaf crown contains fifteen 10- to 12-foot-long leaves on 30-inch-long petioles. The 3-foot-long deep green leaflets grow from different angles off the rachis to create a plumose leaf. The male flowers are violet colored, and the fruits are round and the typical blackish purple when ripe.

This extraordinarily beautiful species is rare in cultivation. It is, by far, the most colorful species in the genus. PLATES 787 & 788.

SABAL is a genus of 15 or 16 variable solitary-trunked, palmate-leaved, monoecious palms in tropical and subtropical America. Most inhabit open, dry areas, but a few are denizens of swamps or forests. Some species are weedy, meaning that their seedlings spring up quickly after fire or other agents of destruction have cleared the land. In spite of the wide distribution of the genus, no species is known to grow naturally at an elevation above 5000 feet. Many species are extraordinarily similar in appearance to each other and are often difficult to distinguish by their leaves. Because the trunks of some species vary so much, even when palms are viewed in their entirety their identification can be confusing, especially in regions where more than one species occurs or is planted.

Some species are dwarf with subterranean trunks but most have aboveground stems from 10 to 80 feet tall. On some cultivated individuals the leaf bases persist for many years if not removed and often this look is considered ornamental, as with *S. palmetto* trunks and their crisscrossed hard, tough, and often whitish old "boots." In nature, this phenomenon rarely occurs, and the old trunks usually appear relatively smooth except up close. A couple of species like *S. pumos* and *S. rosei* have trunks with "knobs" indicating the locations of former leaf bases. Rings of leaf base scars are usually indistinct, but in a few tropical species they can often be discerned from a reasonable distance.

The leaves are borne on spineless petioles and are shallowly to very deeply costapalmate, sometimes appearing almost pinnate because of the costa which curves downwards and causes the bases of the segments to arch out from it at a steep angle, making the leaf distinctly V shaped. A hastula is always present at the top of the leaf juncture but may be long or short, tall or squat, and even almost indiscernible except up close. The apices of the leaf segments are sometimes deeply bifid, and there are often thin, curling lighter-colored filaments between the segments. The inflorescences grow from the leaf crown, are much branched, and bear slender panicles of whitish fragrant flowers. The round, ellipsoid, or pear-shaped, black or brown (when mature) fruits are usually much less than 1 inch long.

In this genus are some of the hardiest (to cold) palms. Indeed, *S. minor*, if not the hardiest is certainly near to being so. Almost without exception, these palms are adaptable to various soils, and a few can even thrive in waterlogged media. Most of them need a lot of heat in summer and are poorly adapted to regions with cool summers and colder winters. Most are slow growing, and a few of these are exceptionally slow. In seedling stage, all grow the saxophone type of underground stem and root system and, for many of these, form no aerial trunk for years.

Palm lovers disagree about the differentiation of species in this genus according to whether or not, for example, a given species forms an aboveground stem. At present, the most debated case involves *S. minor* and *S. louisiana*. Taxonomists consider them the same species, *S. minor*, with aerial or subterranean trunked forms according to the environment and habitat. The problem has been greatly exacerbated by scientific and horticultural literature. Even the late, much respected Robert A. Vines (following the

taxonomy of M. L. Bomhard) separated these two species. Liberty H. Bailey (1925) listed such epithets as *texana, blackburniana* (synonym *umbraculifera*), *exul, princeps* (no synonym), *glabra* (synonyms *adansonii, minus*), *megacarpa* (synonym *etonia*), *caerulescens, glaucescens, dealbata, mocinii, ghiesbreghtii, glauca, javanica, havanensis, longifolia,* and *longipedunculata* in addition to four valid epithets. Amazingly, some of these names are still bandied about and now there are such binomials as *S.* 'Riverside', a robust blue-green-leaved palmetto cloned from a single specimen found in Riverside, California. No one seems to know what it is, but it is most likely a form of *S. domingensis*. All this points out the great vegetative variability of these species.

Then there is the arborescent Brazoria palm, also called Brazoria hybrid palm, after a county in southeastern Texas. Robert A. Vines (1960) first pointed out the palm's existence and insisted it was *S. louisiana,* now a synonym for *S. minor.* It may be a hybrid between *S. mexicana* and *S. minor,* or a form of *S. minor,* or simply the most northerly population of *S. mexicana* (synonym *S. texana*). Texas naturalist Landon Lockett (1991) makes a strong case for its being a hybrid because the spectrum of morphological variability in the population fits in with the known parameters of hybrid variation of palms in general, and the "variation shown by the Brazoria palms is intermediate between the morphological characteristics of *S. minor* and *S. mexicana.*" Lockett proposes calling the hybrid *S.* ×*texensis,* the name palm lovers have used since. Besides recognizing the hybrid possibility in a genus in which hybridization does not readily occur, Lockett has tirelessly fought to protect this small population of 60 acres.

The etymology of the genus name was never explained by its author. Liberty H. Bailey among others conjectured that it may be a form of an aboriginal name from South America. If Bailey's guess is valid, the species in question would have to be *S. mauritiiformis* as it is the only one indigenous to that continent. Almost all species in the genus are called palmetto of one sort or another. PLATES 789–802.

Sabal bermudana is endemic to Bermuda, where it occurs in lowland marshes or on drier soil above the low spots. It is scarce in habitat and, if development increases, will be in danger of extinction. Common names are Bermuda palm and Bermuda palmetto. The epithet is Latin for "Bermudan."

This palm grows slowly to a height of 20 feet; in habitat, it increases less than 0.5 inch per year (Zona 1990). It has a tan or gray, indistinctly but closely ringed trunk, the diameter of which is 1 foot. The leaf crown is full, rounded, and dense with the deeply costapalmate leaves which are deep green, sometimes with a bluish cast. The inflorescences are shorter than the leaf crown and mostly hidden; they produce small, black pear-shaped fruits.

The palm looks much like *S. palmetto* but is usually more stout and robust appearing because of its short height, its large crown, and its thick trunk. It grows in partial shade but prefers full sun and thrives on calcareous as well as slightly acidic soils. In spite of its subtropical origin, its cold tolerance is probably on a par with *S. palmetto;* it is among the few *Sabal* species that tolerate areas with cool summer temperatures. It is extremely slow growing.

Sabal causiarum is indigenous to Hispaniola, Puerto Rico, and the small island of Anegada in the British Virgin Islands, where it grows in open places on sandy soil at low elevations, often in large groves. The common name is Panama hat palm. The epithet is Latin for "of hats" and has to do with Macedonian hats but succeeds in alluding to the main human use (other than the ornamental) for this palm species: the leaves have been used for many years to weave hats as well as baskets and other utensils.

When this palm is mature or nearly so, it is among the distinctive and more easily identified species in the genus. The trunks attain heights of 30 feet and are the stoutest in the genus, often with diameters of 2 feet or even more. They are mostly smooth and light gray and look like stout columns atop which the perfectly round, 10- by 15-foot dense crown of leaves resides. The large leaves on 5-foot-long petioles are deeply costapalmate and are deep green or bluish green with some whitish, thin curling threads between the segments. The inflorescences are as long as or slightly longer than the leaf crown, and the round, black fruits are 0.5 inch in diameter, causing the infructescence to hang beneath the crown.

The Panama hat palm is drought tolerant once established but responds with faster growth and better form and color if given adequate irrigation. It needs as much sun as possible, even in youth, and a free-draining soil. When young, the palm is tender to cold and usually does not survive temperatures below 20°F; however, older trees have been known to survive 10°F, although damaged, sometimes severely. The species is adaptable to zones 8 through 11, except in regions where temperature regularly reaches 10°F; under these conditions, even large specimens will surely die. Once past the seedling stage, the palm grows relatively fast.

This noble palmetto looks best in large groups or groves. To stand in such a grove is akin to being among the great columns of *Copernicia baileyana.* The other great landscaping use for this palm is to line a walk or promenade, even a thoroughfare, the resulting visual appeal being akin to doing the same with large royal palms; it's a shame the sabals do not approach the growth rates of the royals. It is also great as a canopy-scape. This is certainly one of the least likely candidates for indoor use. PLATE 789.

Sabal domingensis is native to western Cuba and interior areas of Hispaniola, where it grows on hills, in savannas, and in mountainous cut-over forests up to an elevation of 3000 feet. The epithet is Latin for "of Domingo," a reference to the largest city in the Dominican Republic near where the species thrives, or used to.

The palm attains the same stature as does *S. causiarum,* and its trunk is almost as massive; in fact, it is often difficult to distinguish the two species. The principal differences between them are the color and shape of the leaves and the fruits. The fruits of *S. causiarum* are slightly larger than those of *S. domingensis* and are pear shaped rather than round. The dark, sometimes bluish green leaves of *S. domingensis* have segments that grow in slightly different planes from the costa and give a fuller aspect to both single leaves and the palm's crown itself, and make more obvious the thin, whitish threads between the folds.

In some respects *S. domingensis* is more beautiful than *S. causiarum* as its leaves and crown seem significantly larger (but as rounded). The two species have the same cultural requirements and landscape uses except that *S. domingensis* does well without too much summer heat. The palm in habitat has the same human uses as does *S. causiarum,* namely, the weaving of hats from the leaves. In fact, one of the vernacular names in Haiti for the palm (*latanier-chapeau*) translates as "hat palm." PLATES 790–792.

Sabal etonia is endemic to Florida, where it is an important component of the scrub community and is abundant on sandy soils in the central and north central peninsula, along most of the eastern coast, and with one isolated population on the western coast in the Bradenton area. The common name is scrub palmetto. The epithet is a Latinized corruption of the Amerindian (Muslogee/Creek) name for a scrubland in central Florida where the species was first collected.

This is, for the most part, a dwarf species with a subterranean trunk; it occasionally forms an aerial stem to 6 feet high. The leaves are 2 feet wide and distinctly light green to yellow-green. They are costapalmate but not arching, and the segments, except in old, dying leaves, are stiff and extend almost to the petiole; there are white, curling threads among them. The inflorescence is shorter than the leaf crown but is thicker or bushier than those of most other *Sabal* species and produces 0.5-inch-wide, round, black (when mature) fruits, which usually bend the infructescence to the ground in trunkless individuals and beneath the leaf canopy in arborescent individuals.

The seedlings are difficult to distinguish from seedlings of *S. palmetto,* but are usually not as dark green, are less costapalmate, and have larger fruits. This little palm is drought tolerant and luxuriates in sandy soils that are calcareous to slightly acidic. It flourishes in partial shade or full, hot sun and is adaptable to zones 8 through 11 and marginal in 7. This one is quite refreshing as a border to taller and especially darker vegetation. PLATE 793.

Sabal gretheriae is from northeastern Yucatán Peninsula in the state of Quintana Roo, Mexico. The epithet honors Rosaura Grether, a botanist working with Mexican botanist, Hermilio J. Quero, who described the species in 1991. The palm is similar to *S. mexicana* but has broader leaf segments, an erect inflorescence with differing details of flowers and seeds, different flowering times, and a different internal anatomy. Only time and further study of the genus will determine if the binomial should be conserved or become a synonym of *S. mexicana*.

Sabal guatemalensis is, if it is a valid binomial, indigenous to the states of Oaxaca, Chiapas, and Yucatán in Mexico and to Guatemala, where it grows in dry areas near the coast and in low mountainous tropical thorn forests. The epithet is Latin for "of Guatemala." The species is related and similar in appearance to *S. mexicana* from which it differs only in details of the calyx of the flower, the fruits, and the seeds. It is probably not in cultivation outside of a few botanical gardens.

Sabal maritima occurs naturally in Cuba and Jamaica, where it grows near the coasts, in the low hills, savannas, and clearings, in forested areas from sea level to 2000 feet elevation. The epithet is Latin for "maritime," an allusion to the palm's habitat.

The species looks like a much more robust version of *S. palmetto*, the distinguishing features being its thick, smooth, and nearly white trunk and its larger leaves on longer petioles, which create a larger, more open crown. It is doubtless not as hardy to cold as *S. palmetto*; it reportedly has survived unscathed a temperature of 27°F. Otherwise the palm's cultural requirements are the same as those of *S. palmetto*. PLATE 794.

Sabal mauritiiformis is indigenous to southeastern Mexico, northern Guatemala, Belize, northeastern Costa Rica, the isthmus region of Panama, northwestern and northern Colombia, northern Venezuela, and Trinidad, where it grows in rain forest, savannas, and cleared forest areas, from coastal areas to 3000 feet elevation. The only common name, bay-leaf palm, seems inappropriate as a bay-leaf is not even a palm; this moniker is used only in Belize. The epithet is Latin for "formed like *Mauritia*," a similar-appearing genus of palmate-leaved palms in South America.

This species is readily distinguishable from all other *Sabal* species. The trunk attains a height of 80 feet in habitat and is straight as an arrow and less than 1 foot in diameter, making it an elegant sight when older. It is light tan or light gray in its older parts but a beautiful deep green in the younger parts. Adding to the great beauty of the stem are the closely set rings of darker leaf base scars. The leaf crown is also handsome as the shape, in unpruned trees, is a large obovate one, with the beautiful leaves silhouetted against the sky because of their unusually long petioles. Each 6- to 7-foot-long leaf is shallowly costapalmate, which would make it almost flat were it not for its long, pendent segments. Leaf color is olive to deep green above and silvery lighter green, sometimes with an almost bluish hue beneath. The segments in juvenile palms are unusually wide, deeply pleated, lanceolate, and deeply bifid or trifid; some are narrower and only shallowly cleft at the apex. They are all much more deeply divided, much narrower, and pendent at their apices in individuals past the juvenile stage. The inflorescences are 6 to 8 feet long, erect but arching, and extend beyond the crown. The fruits are round to pear shaped, black when mature, and 0.5 inch in diameter.

Reports of this species withstanding temperatures in the mid 20s (F) unscathed are rare and probably unreliable. The palms are defoliated by temperature in the low 20s (F), and most are killed by temperatures below 20°F. The palm grows well in partial shade when young but is slower and, when older, needs full sun. It seems to thrive on slightly calcareous soils but accepts any well-drained soil; a good one results in faster, more robust growth and better color. The more water, the better, although the tree is somewhat drought tolerant.

Few palms are more beautiful. The epithet tells a lot about its beauty, as *Mauritia flexuosa*, the plant after which it was named, is arguably the most beautiful palmate-leaved species in the Americas. The silhouette of this palm is galvanizing and makes an arresting canopy-scape. No palm is lovelier in groups of three or more individuals of varying heights. It thrives indoors with good light for a while and as a curiosity. PLATE 795.

Sabal mexicana occurs naturally from the extreme southeastern tip of Texas (Brownsville area), southwards through Mexico, Guatemala, Honduras, and El Salvador, where it grows in drier lowlands. At one time, it was common along the Rio Grande almost as far north as Laredo but has since been destroyed except for a small area near the mouth of the Rio Grande for agricultural purposes. It is called Texas palmetto in most English-speaking countries and, in Texas, Rio Grande palmetto or Texas sabal. The epithet is Latin for "of Mexico."

Very old individuals in habitat can grow trunks that are 50 feet tall and 1 foot in diameter. These are always straight and columnar and, in cultivation, are sometimes covered in the typical crisscrossing leaf bases; in nature they seldom retain these boots below a height of 25 feet, the remainder of the stem being gray to dark gray to dark tan with closely set and nearly indistinct rings. If not pruned, the leaf crown is rounded and massive; the deeply costapalmate leaves are uniform dark green, sometimes very dark green.

The species looks much like *S. palmetto* but is distinguished principally by its larger leaf crown, usually darker green leaves, always straight and columnar trunk, and its more robust appearance—because its height is not as great as that of *S. palmetto*, its trunk seems thicker. In addition *S. palmetto* has longer inflorescences and is rarely found in bloom when young, while *S. mexicana* often flowers with only 1 or 2 feet of trunk. The trunks are occasionally used for construction and the leaves for thatch. This species is as hardy as *S. palmetto* and is usually hardier in drier climates, in which it has withstood 10°F unscathed; in areas subject to wet freezes in winter it seldom is undamaged by that temperature. Otherwise, it has the same cultural requirements as *S. palmetto* except that it is more drought tolerant. Because it appears so robust, it readily lends itself to planting along avenues, and it makes wonderfully handsome specimens. PLATE 796.

Sabal miamiensis occurred naturally along the southeastern coast of Florida, in the Miami area of Dade County, on limestone outcroppings. This area is now developed and no sightings of the little palm in habitat have been made for years; thus, it is most likely extinct in the wild. The common name is Miami palmetto. The epithet is Latin for "of Miami." The short trunk is subterranean and never appears above ground. The species looks like *S. etonia* but has usually deeper green leaves, longer inflorescences, and larger black fruits.

Sabal minor is endemic to the United States in Texas, Oklahoma, Arkansas, Louisiana, Mississippi, Alabama, Georgia, South Carolina, North Carolina, and Florida, where it occurs in the undergrowth of evergreen and deciduous forest at low elevations in often swampy conditions. It is the most northerly ranging palm in the United States and in its genus. The distribution of the species in Texas is interesting because it relates to the question of what the large arborescent palms in Brazoria County might be, namely, *S. minor* is found as far south on the coastal bend as Corpus Christi and is found in the central part of the state not too far east of San Antonio and in the Dallas area. The species was reported as growing in Mexico in the state of Nuevo León at an elevation of 1000 feet in dry, subtropical pine-oak forest on rocky hillsides (Goldman 1991). Common names are dwarf palmetto,

bush palmetto, little blue stem, and swamp palmetto. The epithet is Latin for "smaller."

This species forms subterranean and aerial trunks according to habitat and environmental conditions. In the western parts of its range, it is often arborescent, sometimes with stems to 18 feet or more, while in the northern and southeastern parts of its habitat it usually has no aboveground trunk or only a short one. In what is called "The Big Thicket" of eastern Texas, it sometimes forms arborescent stems that are 10 feet long but basically prostrate and creeping along the ground under the bald cypresses (*Taxodium distichum*), American beeches (*Fagus grandifolia*), southern magnolias (*Magnolia grandiflora*), and other giant forest trees; little of this ecosystem still exists. In southern Louisiana the beautiful arborescent forms in Delta Country south of New Orleans, especially in the southern and natural segment of Jean Lafitte National Park, show erect stems that are to 8 or 10 feet tall and grow in swampland that is flooded for most of the year. The leaves are shallowly costapalmate and deep dark green, with deep, stiff, linear-lanceolate segments that are not cleft apically but are divided four-fifths of the way to the petiole; the segments are often in two groups separated by a gap in the middle of the blade that extends to the petiole, and there are usually no curling threads among them. The inflorescences are erect and slightly arching at their tips but are taller than the leaf crown. The round, black or dark brown fruits are 0.25 inch in diameter.

The palm is extremely hardy to cold, being adaptable to zones 6 through 11. Some forms (not the arborescent ones from Texas or Louisiana) are known to survive in zone 5, however, and this implies that the provenance of an individual palm has a lot to do with its cold hardiness. This species is a true water lover and one that relishes partial shade. Under such conditions, it reaches its full beauty, although it can survive (but not look good) being planted high and dry or in the full, blazing sun of southern latitudes. It prefers fertile, moist soil whether acidic or calcareous.

The species is as beautiful as any purely tropical palm when used as a giant groundcover under canopy. Otherwise, it seems totally out of place, especially as a specimen plant surrounded by space and in full sun. There is hardly a better or more beautiful palm for low, swampy areas under canopy, where it can give a tropical look to decidedly nontropical regions. It is not known to have been grown under glass or indoors, but there would seem to be no reason why it couldn't be, given bright light and much water. PLATE 797.

Sabal palmetto occurs as far north as Cape Fear in North Carolina and is found in coastal southern South

Carolina, all of Florida except the western panhandle region, the Bahamas, the Florida Keys, and southern Cuba. It grows mostly in low, swampy areas and along streams and rivers, but also in hammocks and open pine forests as well as along the coasts just inland of the dunes. Common names are palmetto, cabbage palm, or cabbage palmetto. The epithet is a corruption of the Spanish word for "little palm" and illustrates yet another instance of the variability of the species in this genus.

The mature trunks can attain heights of more than 80 feet in spite of what some of the literature claims. The tallest individuals in habitat seem to be in Florida. The trunks of these old patriarchs are never covered in leaf bases, and they are usually light gray to light tan. Younger individuals, especially in cultivation, are often covered with the distinctive and light colored, crisscrossing "boots." The leaf crowns of large specimens are relatively small compared to the total height of the palm and are always (unless pruned) a complete globe. The leaves are deeply costapalmate, the costa recurved, and are uniformly deep green. The arching inflorescences are usually slightly longer than the radius of the leaf crown and project beyond it. The fruits are round, black, and 0.5 inch in diameter. In the past, the leaves were cut for thatch and the growing point was harvested for food.

The palm is one of the world's hardiest to cold, thriving in zones 8 through 11, and marginal in 7b; but, as is the case with most *Sabal* species, it is not good in these zones where summer temperatures are cool, and it struggles to grow in areas such as the Pacific Northwest of the United States. The second most important factor for its successful culture is adequate and regular water. As for soil type, it tolerates but does thrive in saline conditions. It luxuriates for many years as an undergrowth subject and, in some ways, is more beautiful in partial shade than full sun, although it never reaches the great stature it is capable of without eventually having full sun. It is slow growing when young and moderately slow when older.

There is a landscaping phenomenon in which this native jewel is dug from its swamps and hammocks and planted in rows along Florida thoroughfares like telephone poles. In the dry season, they are drought stricken, and they show their suffering in the form of abnormally small crowns throughout the rest of the year, no matter how much rain falls in the rainy season. In spite of the fact that most of these palms have their handsome leaf bases on them, this usually beautiful phenomenon but enhances the severity and harshness of their plight. The final assault on their dignities is that their unnaturally small crowns are constantly pruned. They should, instead, be planted as a canopy-scape. Otherwise it is much better to leave them in their beautiful habitat. This palm is not known to be used indoors past its seedling stage.

Because the cabbage palmetto readily naturalizes, it is unthreatened in its natural range; however, there are but few mature specimens in Florida, where development, urbanization, and transplantation from the wild eat away relentlessly at their numbers. This decimation of the old beauties and their habitat is hard to grasp for those who are too young to have seen their abundance in habitat in the past, but, if they could only see the former magnificence, say from old photographs, they might help effect the return of this palm and its habitat in the future. Plate 798.

Sabal pumos is endemic to central western Mexico, where it grows in tropical deciduous forest of mountainous areas and in cleared pastures at elevations of 2000 to 4000 feet. The epithet is the aboriginal name for its edible fruits. The trunks are slender (usually 6 to 8 inches in diameter) but grow to 50 feet high in old individuals and, in nature, are clean with a knobby pattern of leaf base scars. This palm looks much like a slender *S. palmetto* and seems extremely rare in cultivation; in fact, it is a poorly known species in general. No data are available for its cold hardiness, but it is said to be drought tolerant and is probably as hardy as *S. guatemalensis* or *S. mexicana*. It would doubtless need full sun and a fast-draining soil.

Sabal rosei is endemic to Mexico along its northwestern coast from Culiacán southwards into the state of Jalisco, where it grows in mountainous tropical deciduous forests from sea level to 2500 feet. The epithet honors Joseph N. Rose, author of *The Cactaceae* and the palm's original collector. The species has similarities to *S. pumos* and is related to it but more attractive.

It has a slender trunk that is 8 or 9 inches in diameter but, with age, attains a height of 40 or more feet and, in habitat, is clean, straight, and covered with picturesque knobby leaf base scars, while in cultivation it often has a covering of whitish, crisscrossed leaf bases. The leaf crown is beautifully globular, much like that of *S. palmetto*; the leaves are deeply costapalmate and a uniform deep green with stiff, erect segments.

It is reported to have withstood a temperature of 22°F unscathed in Florida, where the climate is wetter than that of the palm's habitat; its cold tolerance is probably comparable to that of *S. palmetto*. It is a sun lover and is probably not particular about soil as long as it is freely draining.

Sabal uresana is endemic to northwestern Mexico in the states of Chihuahua and Sonora, where it grows in the foothills of the Sierra Madre Occidental in dry subtropical thorn forests from sea level to an elevation of 4500 feet. The epithet is Latin for "of Ures," a town in western Sonora and a part of the palm's habitat.

Old individuals in habitat reach heights of 60 feet with robust trunks to 18 inches in diameter. The leaves are a distinctive gray to blue-green on both surfaces. They are borne on petioles that are twice as long as the 3- to 4-foot-long, deeply costapalmate blades, the latter having many deeply divided thin segments whose ends are pendent; the leaf crown is usually dense and globular despite the length of the petioles.

This is one of the finest looking trees in the genus, although it is slow growing. It is also evidently hardy to cold, having survived unscathed temperatures in the low 20s (F) in a dry climate (Tucson, Arizona); it is probably not so resistant to cold in areas subject to wet freezes in winter where the low temperatures usually last longer and are accompanied by precipitation. PLATE 799.

Sabal yapa is indigenous to southwestern Cuba, the Isle of Youth, the Yucatán Peninsula of Mexico, and northern Belize, where it grows at low elevations in swampy forests, open savannas, and dry, exposed sites on limestone soil. The epithet is a corruption of one of the vernacular names for the palm in Cuba. Except for the leaf size and the color of the leaf underside, the palm is similar to *S. mauritiiformis*; the leaves of *S. yapa* are a uniform green on both sides and are slightly smaller. Like *S. mauritiiformis,* it is not hardy. It is more drought tolerant and is perfectly adapted to calcareous soils. Its silhouette and canopy-scape are as beautiful as *S. mauritiiformis*. PLATES 800–802.

SALACCA is a genus of 24 pinnate-leaved, spiny, clustering, dioecious palms in Myanmar, Thailand, Laos, Cambodia, Vietnam, peninsular Malaysia, Sumatra, Java, the Moluccas, Borneo, and the Philippines. They are undergrowth subjects in lowland tropical rain forest and are all quite spiny. These are mostly small species, many with subterranean trunks and most with stoloniferous clumping growth. Several of them have unsegmented and apically bifid leaves, and these are especially beautiful. The leaves can be large relative to the short or subterranean trunks, and they grow on long, stout, and spiny petioles. The blades themselves or the leaflets of the segmented leaves bear bristles and are a lighter color on their undersides. The inflorescences grow from among the leaf bases, are spikelike or more usually branching, and are accompanied by papery, quickly disintegrating bracts. Most of them are long enough to be pendent and lie partially on the ground where they are probably pollinated by beetles and where they often form roots to create new rosettes. The plants are either male or female. The fruits are usually round, red, and covered in overlapping scales, each with a sharp tip, showing the relationship of this genus to the rattans; several species produce fruit that is edible by human standards.

A number of species with unsegmented leaves have all male or female individuals in the wild, a fact which leads to the perplexing question of how they propagate themselves, especially since some of these species are widespread in disjunct populations.

Except for the species with unsegmented leaves, most species are rare in cultivation, especially in the Western Hemisphere. They are without exception intolerant of cold, being adaptable only to zones 10b and 11, but many species seem to tolerate well frostless Mediterranean climates if provided with enough water. Although several of them are known to resprout from their roots if frozen back, they are so slow growing that they usually die off if subjected to successive freezes. They are as intolerant of drought as they are of frost. They prefer a moist, fast-draining soil with organic matter, and they do not flourish on calcareous or poor soils. The larger species, especially those with segmented leaves, adapt to full sun, but the smaller species, especially those with unsegmented leaves, need partial shade at all stages.

The genus name is a Latinized form of the aboriginal name in Malaysia, a name which alludes principally to the highly esteemed (in habitat) fruits of the Malaysian species; Westerners usually find the taste of these fruits much too sour. PLATES 803–811.

Salacca affinis occurs naturally in northern Sumatra, peninsular Malaysia, and Borneo, where it grows in lowland and monsoonal rain forest and swamps. The epithet is Latin for "kin to," "similar to," or "neighboring," the allusion unclear.

This acaulescent species has subterranean clustering stems. The large ascending leaves are to 12 feet long, grow from the soil level in spreading rosettes, and are borne on 4- to 6-foot-long stout and spiny petioles. The 12- to 18-inch-long, glossy dark green leaflets grow from the rachis in closely spaced clusters and are of unequal widths, lengths, and forms. They are roughly broadly elliptic to obovate with truncated, jagged apices but may also be lanceolate and long tipped. The new growth is rosy colored, and there are short spines on the bottom of the rachis and bristles on the leaflet margins. The inflorescences are spikelike and the reddish edible fruits lack bristles on the scales.

The palm is attractive but also weedy looking. It looks good as an accent among other vegetation.

Salacca dransfieldiana is a rare species endemic to Kalimantan (Indonesian Borneo), where it grows in lowland rain forest. The epithet honors palm taxonomist John Dransfield of the Royal Botanic Gardens, Kew.

The unsegmented leaves of this acaulescent species grow in a rosette from the soil surface. They are ascending but also gracefully arching from the petiole. The blade is widely obovate, unsegmented, and deeply bifid apically, the terminal lobes with prominent indentations. It is 1 to 3 feet long and is borne on an 18-inch-long, spiny, tan petiole. It is also heavily grooved on both surfaces with the margins of the fused pinnae and is a glossy emerald green on top and a much lighter, silvery matte green below, often suffused with a bronzy hue. Only male plants are known.

Salacca flabellata is endemic to peninsular Malaysia, where it grows in lowland rain forest along the eastern coast. The epithet is Latin for "fanned," an allusion to the deeply notched leaf apices.

This is another species with unsegmented and deeply bifid leaves forming rosettes with rudimentary, short aerial trunks. The leaves are 3 to 4 feet long, ascending, erect, rigid, and unarching, deeply bifid apically, and borne on 2- to 3-foot-long petioles. The outer margins of the terminal lobes are deeply toothed, and the entire blade is deeply grooved with the margins of the fused pinnae. It is glossy medium green above and silvery green beneath, and the new growth is a beautiful grayish pink. The male inflorescences—there are only male plants—are pendent to the ground and often form adventitious roots where they touch the soil surface, creating in time a new rosette.

Salacca glabrescens occurs naturally in peninsular Thailand and peninsular Malaysia, where it grows in mountainous rain forest from 1000 to 2640 feet elevation. The epithet is Latin for "glabrous."

This nearly acaulescent species has creeping aerial stems to 3 feet long. The ascending. slightly arching leaves are 12 feet long on 6- to 10-foot-long, spiny petioles. The 2-foot-long leaflets grow from the rachis in widely spaced groups of three or four, each one stiff and straight, narrowly wedge shaped with either pointed or truncated, jagged apices; the leaflets of the terminal pair are much wider the others. All the leaflets grow at different angles within each group to give a loosely plumose or whorled aspect to the leaf and are deep green above but much paler beneath.

Salacca magnifica is endemic to Borneo, where it grows in mountainous rain forest from sea level to 3000 feet. The epithet is Latin for "magnificent." This acaulescent clumper is truly and wonderfully magnificent in appearance.

The great unsegmented leaves are linear-obovate, apically bifid, and 15 feet or more in length. They are ascending, stiff, and little arched on 2- to 6-foot-long, spiny, and stout petioles. The blade has the typical deeply grooved surfaces due to the margins of the fused pinnate segments and is deeply toothed along its margins, espe-

cially in its apical section. Leaf color is a glossy, bright medium green above but a beautiful silvery green to nearly white beneath. The blade is usually V shaped. The female inflorescences are erect and spikelike but mostly pendent in fruit. Male inflorescences are short and much branched. The fruits are pear shaped, 2 inches long, and deep rose or yellowish brown. PLATES 803–805.

Salacca minuta is endemic to peninsular Malaysia, where it grows in lowland rain forest. The epithet is Latin for "minute" or "small." The species is similar in most respects to *S. flabellata* but is much smaller and the leaf underside is covered with light brown tomentum.

Salacca multiflora is a rare and critically endangered species endemic to lowland rain forest in peninsular Malaysia. The epithet is derived from two Latin words meaning "many flowered." This species is similar to *S. magnifica* but half the size. PLATE 806.

Salacca sarawakensis is endemic to lowland rain forest in Sarawak on the island of Borneo. The epithet is Latin for "of Sarawak." The species is similar to *S. flabellata,* but the leaves are stiffer and unarching and their undersides are a pale yellowish green. Only female plants are known.

Salacca wallichiana occurs naturally from Myanmar southwards and eastwards through Indochina into peninsular Thailand and peninsular Malaysia, where it grows in swamps, clearings of monsoonal rain forest, along rivers and streams, and in the undergrowth of monsoonal evergreen forest. Its distribution has probably been greatly influenced by humans cultivating it. The epithet honors Nathaniel Wallich, a 19th-century superintendent of the botanical gardens in Calcutta, India.

The stems become aerial but are generally creeping and 6 feet long with whorls of vicious 3-inch-long, black spines. The ascending, erect leaves are unarching but become spreading, are 25 feet long, and are borne on 6- to 10-foot-long petioles. The 3-foot-long, limp and arching leaflets grow in groups of two to five and at differing angles from within each group to create a densely plumose leaf; the leaflets of the terminal pair are usually broader than the others. All the leaflets are linear-elliptic, with truncated, jagged apices, and are a deep, almost bluish green on both surfaces. The large, egg-shaped fruits are 3 inches long, reddish brown, and covered in overlapping scales with upturned bristly pointed tips. They are edible and considered a delicacy in habitat.

This species is different in aspect from *S. magnifica* but is also magnificent because of its immense size and heavily plumose leaves. PLATE 807.

Salacca zalacca occurs naturally in Sumatra and Java, where it grows in lowland rain forest and swamps, often forming impenetrable thickets. The epithet is a Latinized form of the aboriginal name for the species. This acaulescent, densely clustering species has large erect leaves springing from the ground in immense rosettes. The leaves are 15 feet long, ascending but arching, and borne on 6-foot-long, spiny petioles. The many leaflets grow from the rachis in a nearly flat plane but are arranged into closely set groups of three to five. Individual leaflets are 2 feet long, narrowly elliptic, dark green above and silvery green or pure silver beneath. The fruits are reddish brown to nearly red and are edible. In habitat they are relished and an item of commerce. The species is beautiful because of the silvery-backed leaflets and makes a wonderful accent when planted among other vegetation, either in partial shade or full sun. PLATES 808–811.

SATAKENTIA is a monotypic genus of pinnate-leaved, monoecious palm. The genus is allied to *Clinostigma,* to which it has many visual similarities. The genus name is a combination of two words, one a Japanese (in transliteration) surname honoring Toshohiko Satake, a 20th-century industrialist, amateur botanist, and lover of palm trees, and the second word, an out-of-date name for species in the genera *Gronophyllum, Gulubia,* and *Hydriastele.* The epithet is Latin for "of Liukiu" (Ryukyu). PLATES 812–814.

Satakentia liukiuensis is endemic to the islands of Ishigaki and Iriomote in the Ryukyu archipelago, where it grows on hills and near sea level in moist forests.

The trunk attains a height of 60 feet and a diameter of 1 foot in habitat, and usually has a mass of adventitious roots at its base. It is a light brown to grayish brown and exhibits closely set rings of leaf base scars. The smooth, dark olive green, reddish brown, or purplish brown crownshaft is 2.5 feet tall, slightly thicker than the trunk, sometimes bulging at its base, otherwise cylindrical. The leaf crown is spherical or nearly spherical and usually contains 12 to 14 spreading leaves, each of which is 8 to 10 feet long and borne on a short, 4-inch-long petiole in older palms, juveniles usually having longer leaf stalks. The leaves are gracefully arching, sometimes twisting, and bear regularly spaced lanceolate, 2-foot-long, dark green leaflets which grow from the rachis in a single, nearly flat plane and are limp and slightly pendent once unfurled. The inflorescences usually form a ring around the nodes below the crownshaft, each consisting of several stiff, horizontally spreading, whiskbroom-like branches on stout, ringed, short, and squat peduncles. The 0.5-inch-long, oblong fruits are black when mature.

The palm needs a nearly tropical climate and withstands only a touch of frost. It also wants regular and adequate moisture, a humus-laden soil, and full sun when past the juvenile stage. The crown and leaves look much like those of a coconut palm, giving this species the same landscaping uses. While still not common in cultivation, the species is rapidly gaining acceptance in southern Florida where it seems to do exceptionally well.

SATRANALA is a monotypic genus of palmate-leaved, dioecious palm. The genus name is a Latinized corruption of the aboriginal name. The epithet translates from Latin as "intersecting the forest," an allusion to its visual and genetic affinities with *Bismarckia* which is never found in forest.

Satranala decussilvae is a rare species endemic to northeastern Madagascar, where it grows in mountainous rain forest at elevations below 1000 feet.

In habitat, the trunk attains a height of 50 feet and a diameter of 7 inches. The leaf crown is open and less than hemispherical. The leaves are clear medium green on both surfaces, semicircular to nearly circular, and 8 feet wide on 5-foot-long petioles. The linear-lanceolate leaf segments extend halfway into the blade and are stiff and nonpendent. The leaf is weakly costapalmate and virtually flat.

The species is related to both *Bismarckia* and *Hyphaene,* which is evident by the form of the inflorescences. It is relatively new to cultivation, and all that is known regarding its culture is that the seeds are slow to germinate and the palm itself is slow growing. It cannot be hardy to cold and is certainly a water lover. Because it starts out as an undergrowth subject, it is probably adapted to partial shade at least when young.

SCHIPPIA is a monotypic genus of palmate-leaved, monoecious palm. The genus name honors William A. Schipp, a 20th-century Australian collector in Belize and author of a flora of that country. The epithet is Latin for "single colored," an allusion to the genus's distinctiveness from the genera *Coccothrinax, Cryosophila,* and *Thrinax,* which often have leaves with silvery undersides. PLATES 815–817.

Schippia concolor is a rare and endangered species endemic to Belize, possibly also in adjacent Guatemala, where it grows in lowland rain forest and mountainous pineland from sea level to 1600 feet elevation.

The solitary trunk slowly reaches to 30 feet high with a maximum diameter of 4 inches. The beautiful leaf crown is open and hemispherical or slightly more so with 12 semicircular to nearly circular 3-foot-wide leaves on 6-foot-long, slender unarmed petioles. The leaf segments are linear-lanceolate, extend two-thirds of the way into the blade, and are shortly bifid at their tips. They are glossy deep green above and paler green beneath. The 2-foot-long, much-branched inflorescences are white and bear white male and bisexual flowers. The round, 1-inch-wide, succulent fruits are white when ripe.

This is a silhouette palm, its airy leaf crown of exquisitely elegant proportions. It does not look good as an isolated specimen surrounded by space but is more than charming as a small canopy-scape or against a highly contrasting background so that its form can be easily seen. It is adaptable to zones 10 and 11 and possibly in the warmest microclimates of 9b. It needs regular and adequate moisture to look good and grow other than slowly but thrives on calcareous as well as slightly acidic soils. It flourishes in partial shade or full sun.

SCLEROSPERMA is a genus of three densely clustering, pinnate-leaved, monoecious palms in western tropical Africa. They are poorly known and are not in cultivation except possibly in a few tropical botanical gardens.

The trunks are subterranean or short. Leaves are large and ascending, and are borne on long, slender petioles. They are to 12 feet long and pinnately segmented into several wide leaflets or are unsegmented and apically bifid. The inflorescences are short and spikelike, the flowering branches extremely short and congested into a clublike formation at the end of the peduncle. The fruits are small, top shaped, and black when ripe.

The few drawings and photographs available show wonderfully beautiful small palms with relatively gigantic leaves, the unsegmented ones similar in general appearance to those of *Marojejya darianii* or many of the unsegmented *Salacca* species, and the pinnately divided leaves resembling large *Pinanga* species. The genus name is derived from two Greek words meaning "hard" and "seed."

SERENOA is a monotypic genus of palmate-leaved, clustering, monoecious palm in the southeastern United States. The genus name honors Sereno Watson, a 19th-century American botanist and curator of the Gray Herbarium at Harvard University. In the United States, common names are saw palmetto and silver saw palmetto. The epithet is Latin for "creeping." PLATES 818–821.

Serenoa repens is endemic to the United States in extreme southeastern Louisiana, southern Mississippi, southern Alabama, southern and coastal Georgia to the southeastern South Carolina coast, and peninsular Florida, where it grows mostly on the coastal plain regions in sandy, open (mostly pine) woodland and near the coast on sand dunes. The species is more than abundant in Florida, where many planned communities ban the palm from homeowners' properties. It may now be extinct in Louisiana.

The clustering trunks are subterranean until they are of some age at which time they usually emerge above ground and can grow to 20 feet long. The lower clumps are dense with leaves and it is only when fires in the pinelands remove most of the leaves that separate trunks can be seen. When above ground, they are covered in all but the oldest parts with a mass of fibers and leaf bases and are always creeping to some extent. The 3-foot-wide leaves are borne on 3- to 5-foot-long petioles with small backward-pointing spines and are a semicircle or somewhat more of segments that are deeply divided, stiff, and narrowly triangular or pyramidal, with a short notch apically. Leaf color varies from dull light grayish green to medium pure green to almost pure silver or bluish silver. The really silvery individuals are found only in the southern two-thirds of peninsular Florida on a narrow strip along the Atlantic; no one knows why this is the case but it may be that the eastern coast is less humid and windier than the western coast and therefore the sandy soil is probably more saline and there is usually more sunlight. These eastern forms usually have distinctly yellowish to almost orange petioles and leaf bases. The inflorescences appear year-round but especially in spring, summer, and fall. They are slender, branched, and shorter than the leaf crown, and bear small white bisexual blossoms, which produce 0.5- to 1-inch-long ellipsoid fruits that are shiny dark blue to black when mature. The flowers and fruits are mostly hidden by the densely packed leaves in younger plants, but the fruits are noticeable by their unpleasant odor when they are ripening.

The palm is hardy to cold and is adaptable to zones 8 through 11 and, with protection or a favorable microclimate, to zone 7. It is drought tolerant and fire tolerant, at least to the swiftly running fires that occur in habitat, leaving leafless but often live, scorched, and reclining trunks that were protected by the fibers and leaf bases, which then grow new leaves with the return of moisture. It grows in partial shade as well as the full blazing sun of southern Florida. It loves sandy soil and has great saline tolerance. In truth it is not particular about the type of soil, which in the palm's habitats is poor to terrible in quality and from acidic to very alkaline. As for moisture requirements, it grows in seasonally dry areas as well as swampland. Because of its great fibrous root system, the palm is almost impossible to transplant from the wild. In southern California the species is so slow growing that many growers eschew it as a landscape subject (Geoff Stein, pers. comm.).

The forms with silvery blue or blue-green leaves are usually considered more attractive than the plain green forms, but all forms make a dramatic, tropical-looking accent in the landscape. Great masses of the plants are tiresome to contemplate, however, even in nature. None of the colors seem attractive when isolated with surrounding space, and the great clumps look much better when integrated into a shrub border or mixed with tall but not overly umbrageous trees. This wild and unruly species is not known to be grown indoors and there are but few instances of its being grown in a container. Chemicals in the fruits of saw palmetto which might be advantageous in treating prostate problems were synthesized in the late 20th century.

SIPHOKENTIA is a genus of two solitary-trunked, pinnate-leaved, monoecious palms in the Moluccas and Indonesian New Guinea (Irian Jaya). The species are similar, with relatively large pinnate leaves and unequally sized leaflets; juvenile leaves are unsegmented and apically bifid. The small inflorescences grow from beneath the prominent crownshafts and are once branched, the flowering branches bearing unisexual blossoms of both sexes. The fruits are ovoid and mature to orange or red.

The genus is related to *Gronophyllum* and is distinguished by details of the female flowers. Both *Siphokentia* species are intolerant of frost and need partial shade and protection from the midday sun in hot climates. They are adapted to several soils but do best in those with humus; they need constant and copious moisture.

The genus name is a combination of the Latin word for "siphon" or "tube" (the sepals and petals of the female flowers are basally united into a tube, unlike those in the genus *Gronophyllum*) and *Kentia,* an out-of-date name for species of *Gronophyllum, Gulubia,* and *Hydriastele.* PLATES 822–824.

Siphokentia beguinii occurs naturally on the Moluccan island of Halmahera and adjacent islands, where it grows in lowland rain forest. The epithet honors Victor Beguin, a Dutch botanist and collector in the Moluccas and Indonesian New Guinea (Irian Jaya). The trunk attains a maximum height of 25 feet and is 2 or 3 inches in diameter. It is dark green in its younger parts and is heavily ringed with wide, tan leaf base scars. The crownshaft is 2 feet tall, not much thicker than the trunk, cylindrical, sometimes slightly swollen at its midpoint, and bluish or olive green. The leaf crown is hemispherical and often elongated, containing six to eight 4- to 6-foot-long spreading, arching leaves. The leaflets grow in a flat plane off the rachis, are limp and semipendent, and are irregularly shaped, except for those of the terminal pair, which are always the broadest. The leaflets range from linear-lanceolate to rhomboid, are glossy deep green above with duller matte color beneath, heavily ribbed with jagged tips, and are borne on short petioles. The inflorescences are short and resemble a whisk broom. The 0.75-inch-long fruits are oblong and deep red when mature.

With its variously shaped leaflets, this beautiful small palm adds great visual interest to plantings among other vegetation. PLATES 822 & 823.

Siphokentia dransfieldii is endemic to Biak Island of the northwestern coast of Indonesian New Guinea (Irian Jaya), where it grows in lowland rain forest. The epithet honors palm taxonomist John Dransfield of the Royal Botanic Gardens, Kew.

The species was described in 2000 and is already in cultivation because of its charming aspect. It is similar to *S. beguinii* except for details of the inflorescence and its much stiffer leaflets which are also of more uniform sizes and shapes: obliquely wedge shaped with truncated, jagged apices. It is also reported to be more robust under cultivation and has slightly larger but similarly shaped and colored fruits. PLATE 824.

SOCRATEA is a genus of three to five tall, mostly solitary-trunked, pinnate-leaved, monoecious palms in tropical America. Most are denizens of lowland tropical rain forest, but a few occur naturally in mountainous rain forest to a maximum elevation of 6000 feet. The most salient characteristics of these species are their large but open cones of spiny stilt roots at the bases of the trunks, and their wide, mostly plumose leaves with jagged apices. They form prominent crownshafts beneath which the relatively short once-branched inflorescences grow. The thick flowering branches bear white unisexual flowers of both sexes. The genus is obviously related to *Dictyocaryum, Iriartea, Iriartella,* and *Wettinia.*

In habitat the species have many human uses: the lower parts of the durable trunks are used for construction, the leaves are used for thatch, the spiny stilt roots are used for grating and grinding manioc or tapioca (*Manihot*) and plantains (*Musa*), and the fruits and seeds are eaten. Only one species is in general cultivation, and it is not common outside of tropical botanical gardens.

The species are completely tropical in their temperature requirements and are often killed by sustained temperatures below 55°F. They need constant and copious moisture as well as constantly high relative humidity. They are adapted to partial shade when young but, to reach their full potential, need sun when older. The genus name probably honors the ancient Greek philosopher Socrates. PLATES 825–828.

Socratea exorrhiza is the most widespread species in the genus, occurring naturally from southern Nicaragua, southwards through Costa Rica, Panama, and through most of Colombia, Ecuador, Peru, northwestern Brazil, the southern half of Venezuela, and all of the Guianas, where it grows in lowland and mountainous rain forest from sea level to 3500 feet. The epithet is from two Greek words meaning "outside of" and "root," an allusion to the stilt roots.

The solitary trunk grows to a height of 70 feet and is 6 or 7 inches in diameter at its thickest point. It is light tan in its younger parts and is graced with widely spaced rings of darker leaf base scars. In its older parts it becomes gray to nearly white and is supported by a 6- to 10-foot-tall, open cone of brown thick stilt roots that bear short and fat but sharply pointed, light yellow spines. The crownshaft is 6 feet tall, cylindrical except at its base where it is slightly swollen, and is deep bluish green to nearly blue. The leaf crown is hemispherical to nearly spherical and contains half a dozen 6- to 8-foot-long leaves on 1-foot-long petioles. They are stiff, straight, spreading, and slightly arching near their tips but are wide because of the 2-foot-long leaflets. The latter are linearly to broadly wedge shaped with a slanting, multitoothed or jagged apex; they are split to their bases into almost equally wide, narrow segments. Their color is medium to deep green to bluish green, and they grow from the rachis in bundles and at different angles to create a wide and plumose leaf. The flowering branches of the inflorescences are 1 foot long and produce ellipsoid, 1-inch-long deep yellow fruits.

This fascinating and beautiful species requires a wet tropical climate, is adaptable only to zone 11, and is marginal in 10b. It is impossible to maintain in frostless Mediterranean climates as a healthy individual. It has one of the most beautiful silhouettes of any palm and is enthralling as a canopy-scape or in groups of three or more individuals of varying heights. PLATES 825–828.

Socratea rostrata is indigenous to the slopes and foothills of the western Andes Mountains in Ecuador and Peru, where it grows in wet mountainous rain forest from sea level to an elevation of 6000 feet. The epithet is Latin for "beaked," a reference to the projection at the top of the yellowish, 1-inch-long, ellipsoid fruits. The solitary trunk attains a height of 80 feet and a diameter of 1 foot, making it the largest in the genus. It is otherwise similar to *S. exorrhiza*, if absolute magnificence can be a similarity.

Socratea salazarii occurs naturally in Peru along the eastern slopes and foothills of the Andes Mountains, in extreme western Brazil, and extreme northwestern Bolivia, where it grows in mountainous rain forest from 1000 to 2300 feet. The epithet honors Adolfo Salazar of the Peruvian forest service, who aided Harold E. Moore, Jr., in finding the species. It is similar in appearance and dimensions to *S. exorrhiza*, differing principally in its wide, unsplit leaflets and in its rarely clustering habit. The leaflets grow in only two slightly differing planes, creating a plumose leaf, and the leaflets of the terminal pair are broad.

SOMMIERIA is a genus of three small, solitary-trunked, pinnate-leaved, monoecious palms on the island of New Guinea. These are small undergrowth subjects in dense, wet, and humid rain forest.

The stems are short or nonexistent but sturdy and distinctly ringed when aerial. The leaf crowns are spherical because of the short-petioled but long, arching leaves that are unsegmented and deeply bifid apically or with four to six unequally sized leaflets. They are invariably linear-obovate, deeply pleated with the margins of the fused pinnae on both sides, have prominent, dark-colored midribs, and are glossy deep green above but chalky white or silver overlaid with a tan suffusion beneath. The inflorescences grow from among the leaf sheaths and consist of long, pendent peduncles at the ends of which single-flowering branches radiate in a starlike fashion. The tiny fruits are round, with bluntly pyramidal projections, pinkish or red, and much resemble diminutive litchi fruits.

These species are rare in cultivation even though the genus was discovered in 1877 and the first species technically described in 1955. They are elegant with leaves that look like gigantic seedling leaves of many other genera and have great visual affinities with mature individuals of the genus *Asterogyne*. They are finicky species, needing constant warmth, copious and regular moisture, a humus-laden soil, partial shade, and constantly high relative humidity. The genus name honors Stephen Sommier, a 19th-century European botanist. PLATES 829 & 830.

Sommieria affinis is the most widespread species in the genus, occurring naturally in Indonesian New Guinea (Irian Jaya) and into Papua New Guinea, where it grows in lowland mountainous rain forest. The epithet is Latin for "similar to," presumably an allusion to the first described species, *S. leucophylla*. Its trunk grows to 6 feet. The leaves are 3 to 5 feet long and unsegmented except for the deeply bifid apex. PLATE 829.

Sommieria elegans is endemic to Indonesian New Guinea (Irian Jaya). The epithet is Latin for "elegant." It is the tallest species in the genus, its solitary trunk growing to 12 feet. The leaves are 4 to 7 feet long and unsegmented except for the deeply bifid apex. They are a chalky silver or even white on their undersides, often with a bronzy hue.

Sommieria leucophylla is endemic to Indonesian New Guinea (Irian Jaya). The epithet is derived from two Greek words meaning "white" and "leaf," an allusion to the silver-backed leaves. The trunk attains almost the height of *S. elegans*, and its leaves often have four to six leaflets, the terminal pair larger than the others. PLATE 830.

SYAGRUS is a genus of 30 to 42 pinnate-leaved, monoecious palms, mostly in South America, with a single species in the Lesser Antilles. There are solitary-trunked as well as clustering species and a few that have subterranean stems. The species form no crownshafts, and the inflorescences grow from the leaf crown. They are once branched, the individual branches often ropelike, pendent, and white or straw-colored, bearing unisexual flowers of both sexes. They are accompanied by a sometimes large and tough woody bract that is usually spoon-shaped or boat-shaped.

The genus is closely related to *Cocos* (coconut), and many *Syagrus* species have edible seeds that are similar in taste to those of the coconut. In Brazil, several species grow in habitat together where there are at least four naturally occurring hybrids. In addition, there is the beautiful hybrid between *Syagrus romanzoffiana* and *Butia capitata* that comes about from growing these two species together in gardens. The genus name is derived from a Latin word that referred to some palm tree but definitely not one from this genus. PLATES 831–864.

Syagrus amara occurs naturally in the Lesser Antilles, except for Trinidad, where it grows in the hills and tropical forests along the coasts. It is one of the tallest species in the genus and is the only one not indigenous to the South American continent. It is called overtop palm in its habitat because mature individuals always grow significantly taller than the canopy of coastal vegetation among which they develop. The epithet is Latin for "bitter" and refers to the nearly liquid endosperm of the immature seeds, which is palatable and usually fermented to make a toddy.

This is a solitary-trunked species with stems to 60 feet or even more in habitat but 8 or 9 inches in diameter. The leaves are 10 feet long on 1-foot-long petioles. The many 3-foot-long dark green leaflets are arranged in closely set clusters and grow from the rachis in almost a single plane to slightly different angles from the rachis, creating a flat or a slightly plumose leaf; they are stiff in younger leaves but limp and pendent in older ones. The fruits are orange and 2 to 3 inches long.

The species is not hardy to cold and is adaptable only to zones 10b and 11, although nice specimens are to be found in the warmer microclimates of 10a. It grows in partial shade, especially when young, but, when past the juvenile stage, needs sun to grow faster and achieve its coconutlike appearance. While not fussy about soil type, it does better and grows much faster with a rich soil and with regular and adequate moisture. Mature palms look like slender coconut palms and even the fruits of the two palms are similar. While nothing can match the beauty of a coconut, this one goes a long way trying and should be treated in the landscape as if it were *Cocos*. It is tolerant of salty soils. PLATES 831 & 832.

Syagrus botryophora is endemic to Brazil, where it grows in the lowland rain forest of the central Atlantic coast. The epithet is from Greek words meaning "clusterbearing," an allusion to the grapelike clusters of yellow-green fruits. The species is solitary trunked with stems to heights of 50 or more feet in habitat and diameters of less than 1 foot. They are straight, columnar, and a beautiful green in their youngest parts, a light tan in their older parts, and a light gray in their oldest parts; they are also graced with distinct, widely spaced darker rings of leaf base scars in all but their oldest parts. The wonderful leaves are 10 to 12 feet long but strongly arching, sometimes almost forming a semicircle in bending back toward the trunk. The deep green, stiff, 2-foot-long leaflets grow from the rachis at an angle approaching 45 degrees, arching upwards to give the leaf a V shape.

This is one of the world's most beautiful palms. It is comparable in beauty to such pulchritudinous archetypes of the palm world as *Actinorhytis calapparia, Pigafetta,* and some of the larger *Gronophyllum* species. It is also among the world's fastest growing palms and with a rich soil, ample moisture, and a tropical or nearly tropical climate can add 6 feet of trunk per year until near its mature height. Under such optimum conditions, it grows so fast that its leaf crown tends to become elongated. It is one of the finest canopy-scapes, and specimen groups of three or more individuals of varying ages and heights are incomparable. Its only faults are that it requires a nearly tropical climate and it is still rare and hard to come by. Some of the literature indicates that it needs partial shade when young, but experience has shown that it flourishes in the sun from youth to old age.

The palm mentioned by James C. McCurrach (1960), *Arecastrum romanzoffianum* var. *botryophorum,* is now a synonym for this species, but McCurrach seems to have been referring only to a robust form of what we now know simply as *S. romanzoffiana.* Many *Syagrus* species, like species of many other genera, show this lack of or abundance of robustness according to their growing conditions, and the species under discussion can even be misidentified if not given the appropriate cultural conditions. PLATES 833 & 834.

Syagrus campylospatha is endemic to southern Paraguay, where it grows in open, dry scrubby savannas on sandy soils at low elevations, often almost hidden in the vegetation. The epithet is from Greek words meaning "curved" and "spathe."

This is a clustering species whose short trunks are mostly hidden underground, only occasionally emerging above the soil and then attaining heights of 3 to 4 feet. Its leaves are ascending and stiff, each little tuberlike trunk holding a 3-foot-tall shuttlecock of upright leaves with widely spaced, rigid silvery green to silvery bluish narrow, pointed, and sharp leaflets. The little leaf crown looks like a silver date palm bonsai.

The species is unusually hardy to cold and is adaptable to zones 9 through 11. Because of its underground stems, it returns as a perennial if frozen to the ground in zone 8. It needs sun and a well-drained soil. It is ideal for adding contrast to other vegetation and, because of its drought tolerance and stiff appearance, fits in perfectly with cactus and other succulents.

Syagrus cardenasii is endemic to central Bolivia, where it grows in the foothills of the eastern Andes Mountains in dry, open forest from 1200 to 5280 feet in elevation. In nature, it is found as a solitary-trunked and clustering species with trunks to 20 feet tall. The leaves are 8 feet long with widely spaced grayish green, stiff leaflets that grow at slightly different angles from the rachis. The short and erect yellowish inflorescences produce greenish brown edible fruits. The species looks like a dwarf, untidy cross between a date palm and a clustering queen palm. It is probably not in cultivation outside of a few botanical gardens.

Syagrus "cearensis" has been cultivated in Florida since 1959 under a wrong name and has been given the provisional binomial by Larry R. Noblick of the Montgomery Botanical Center in Miami until it is formally described and published. The proposed epithet is Latin for "of Ceará," a state in the palm's habitat. Whatever the future status of the binomial, this is a beautiful palm.

It is a mostly sparsely clustering species endemic to northeastern Brazil in the states of Ceará, Pernambuco, and Alagoas, where it grows in mountainous deciduous forest at elevations from 1200 to 2500 feet. The stems attain at least 30 feet with maximum diameters of 5 inches and are light tan to light gray with prominent darker rings of leaf base scars. The leaves are similar to those of *S. oleracea* but not as large.

The landscaping uses for this palm are as great as any in the genus and it is beautiful up close or as a canopy-scape. The species is adaptable to several soils and flourishes on calcareous ones. It grows well in partial shade, especially when young, but needs full sun when older for fastest growth and good form and color. It is not as fast growing as *S. romanzoffiana* or *S. botryophora* but is certainly not the slowest grower in the genus. It is drought tolerant but looks much better and grows faster with regular and adequate water. It is not cold hardy and is adaptable only to zones 10b and 11, but there are nice small specimens in warm microclimates of 10a. PLATES 835–837.

Syagrus cocoides is indigenous to southern Guyana and northern Brazil, where it grows mostly in lowland rain forest but also on the higher open hills and grasslands. The epithet is Latin for "similar to *Cocos*," although the two species are easily distinguished.

It is a solitary-trunked species attaining maximum heights in habitat of 35 feet, with slender, whitish, and indistinctly ringed trunks that are 4 inches in diameter. The 10- to 12-foot-long leaves have thin, dark green, narrow, pendent leaflets growing from the rachis at different angles to give the leaf a plumose appearance.

The palm is not hardy to cold, grows in partial shade but prefers sun, needs a rich but well-drained soil, and is a water lover. It is elegant with a rounded, compact leaf crown that lends itself wonderfully to use as a canopy-scape and is exquisite as a specimen group of individuals of varying heights. PLATE 838.

Syagrus comosa is indigenous to Brazil and the central eastern *cerrado* region, which is characterized by dry, monsoonal climate and low, shrubby dicot vegetation including many cactus species. The epithet is Latin for "tufted" or "hairy." It is important to note that, while the cerrado has seasons of drought, it also has a high water table and the rainy season can deliver copious water in a short time that results in flooding in many areas.

This is a solitary-trunked species whose stems grow slowly to maximum heights of 30 feet with diameters of 5 or 6 inches but sometimes remain hidden underground. They are covered in all but the oldest parts with triangular, closely spaced leaf bases. The leaves are 4 to 5 feet long, with closely set, wide, thick, and deep green to deep silvery green leaflets that grow from the rachis at more than one angle to give the leaf a semiplumose effect. The mature fruits are deep yellow-green.

The species has unusual cold hardiness for such tropical origins; it seems to be adaptable to zones 9b through 11 and is possibly safe in 9a, especially with protection or in a favorable microclimate. While it is drought tolerant, it grows faster (albeit still slowly) and looks better with regular and adequate moisture. It should not be grown in the shade. This unusual looking but beautiful species is rare in habitat and in cultivation. It has an architectural and sturdy, almost heavy look, and the many, closely spaced narrow leaf bases are beautiful to behold up close. PLATE 839.

Syagrus coronata is endemic to eastern Brazil, where it grows in the low savannas and cerrados, often near streams, but also in the *caatinga*, a dry region of short spiny dicot vegetation including cactus species. It is sometimes called licury palm. The epithet is Latin for "crowned" and refers to the large leaf crown.

The palm is solitary trunked, the stems attaining 40 feet high with diameters of 1 foot. They are covered except in their oldest parts with large persistent old leaf bases and petiole parts that are arranged around the trunk in loosely spiraling rows; when these finally fall off, undulating rows of horny, broad liplike projections remain that give the trunk a square, angled appearance. The leaf crown is large and dense, and the leaves are 10 feet long. The 1-foot-long leaflets grow from the rachis at different angles to give the leaf an almost fully plumose aspect; they are stiff, lanceolate, waxy underneath, deep green above, and silvery or whitish green beneath. The fruits are juicy, egg shaped, orange but covered in a brown felt.

The species is adaptable to zones 10 and 11, although it often matures nicely in warmer regions of 9b. It needs sun when past the seedling stage. The palm is drought tolerant but grows faster and looks better with regular and adequate moisture. It is not particular about soil type as long as it is well drained. It is not fast growing even in full sun but, after forming a trunk, is moderate in its growth rate.

The palm is beautiful even as an isolated specimen surrounded by space but looks better in groups of three or more individuals of varying heights; a grove is glorious. Because of the almost unique pattern of leaf bases and scars on its trunk, it is also architectural in aspect and provides unending pleasure in the up-close contemplation of its stem. It makes a wonderful large tub plant. It works for a while indoors but needs much light and eventually space.

Few palm species provide more uses for people. The trunks are used for construction and, in times of famine, the starchy pith is made into a flour substitute. The growing point is reportedly sweet and delicious. The leaves are fed to livestock and are used for thatch and making baskets and other utensils. The wax on the leaves is still used in the manufacture of soaps. PLATES 840–842.

Syagrus ×costae is a hybrid of *S. coronata* and *S. oleracea*. It grows in abundance in the state of Pernambuco in northeastern Brazil. It is similar to *S. coronata* except that it does not usually have its leaves and trunk arranged in a pattern of rows. It has the same cultural requirements as *S. coronata* and seems to be the only naturally occurring *Syagrus* hybrid in general cultivation around the world. It is extraordinarily beautiful. PLATE 843.

Syagrus duartei is a rare endemic to Brazil in the state of Minas Gerais, where it grows on dry, rocky outcrops at an elevation of 4000 feet. It is a solitary-trunked species that seldom raises its stem above ground, the erect leaves usually springing directly from the soil surface. When the stem does emerge from the rocky soil, it is dark brown, ropelike, tuberlike, and prostrate. The leaves are a glaucous medium to deep green and unarching, and have stiff, sharply pointed lanceolate leaflets that grow from the rachis at slightly different angles to create a slightly V-shaped leaf.

The palm is rare in cultivation and is mainly grown as a curiosity. It is adapted to sunny sites, is drought tolerant, and, because of its subterranean stems, would probably readily resprout from a killing freeze.

Syagrus flexuosa is endemic to eastern and central Brazil, where it grows in the cerrado and open woodlands to an elevation of 3800 feet. The epithet is Latin for "flexible," an allusion to the pliable leaves.

This is a clustering species whose trunks grow to a maximum height of 15 feet and are usually covered in old leaf bases; a few individuals in habitat do not seem to cluster. The leaves are 4 or 5 feet long, stiffly arching, and plumose, with many narrow, lanceolate dark green leaflets growing from the rachis at different angles. They are usually stiff but not rigid and are usually light or even whitish green beneath.

This nice little palm has the look of a soft, dwarf, spineless, and green *Phoenix* species. The solitary-trunked forms are especially beautiful. It is planted for ornament in habitat but, alas, is little known outside its range. It needs full sun from youth to old age and a fast-draining soil. It seems hardy to cold, having survived unscathed temperatures in the upper 20s (F); were it to be cut back from a freeze, it would probably return (albeit slowly) from the root. PLATES 844 & 845.

Syagrus glaucescens is endemic to central eastern Brazil, where it grows in dry and rocky cerrado from elevations of 2200 to 4000 feet. The epithet is Latin for "glaucous" and alludes to the color of the leaves.

This is a solitary-trunked species whose stems attain maximum heights of 12 feet and are usually less than 6 inches in diameter without the leaf bases. The leaf bases are similar to and almost as characteristic and striking as those of *S. coronata*: they are in vertical rows and lend an angled, squared appearance to the stem. The leaves are 3 or 4 feet long and have stiff, lanceolate, bluish or silvery green, slightly waxy leaflets that grow at slightly differing angles from the rachis to create a V-shaped leaf.

The species is more picturesque than beautiful. It is slow growing and demands full sun and a fast-draining soil. It is moderately hardy to cold, is adaptable to zones 10 and 11, and is marginal in 9b. PLATES 846 & 847.

Syagrus harleyi is endemic to northeastern Brazil in the state of Bahia, where it grows in low mountains at elevations of 1200 to 4500 feet, usually in rock crevices.

It is a clustering species whose stems rarely emerge above the ground. The erect, unarching bright green waxy leaves are 4 or 5 feet long with widely spaced, narrow leaflets that grow from the rachis at a slightly upward angle. The leaflets are rigid or flaccid according to their provenance: those from lower elevations of the habitat are soft and usually pendent but those from higher elevations are rigid.

The palm is surprisingly attractive for such a diminutive species and, if it can be planted where its delicate and lacy leaves can be displayed against a background of contrasting color, it makes a beautiful specimen. It is drought tolerant, needs full sun from youth to old age, and is unusually hardy to cold, thriving in zones 9 through 11, and is probably possible, if marginal, in 8b; its clustering and subterranean stems almost assure its return if the leaves are frozen back.

Syagrus inajai is indigenous to southern French Guiana, southeastern Surinam, and northern Brazil, where it grows in lowland rain forest as well as clearings and other open sites under 1500 feet elevation. The epithet is one of the Brazilian aboriginal names.

It is a solitary-trunked species, reaching a maximum height of 50 feet, with slender trunks no more than 6 inches in diameter. The leaves are 10 feet long with many narrow, dark green, limp, and pendent leaflets that grow from different angles along the rachis to give the leaf a plumose effect.

The visual aspect of this jewel of a palm is that of a slender-stemmed queen (*Syagrus romanzoffiana*). It is one of the most elegant looking in the genus but is not hardy to cold, being adaptable only to zones 10b and 11, although marginal in 10a. It requires a rich soil and constant moisture.

Syagrus macrocarpa is an uncommon species endemic to southeastern Brazil, where it grows in the cerrado on sandy soils. The epithet is Greek for "large" and "fruit," a reference to the 3-inch-long, egg-shaped, edible fruits that are orange when mature.

The solitary trunks grow to a maximum height of 25 feet and a diameter of 8 inches. They are smooth and tan or light gray with widely spaced but indistinct darker rings of leaf base scars. The leaf crown is full and round, partly because of the persistent and pendent, old dead leaves. The beautifully arching leaves are 6 to 7 feet long on 2-foot-long smooth petioles. The leaflets are 2 feet long, medium to deep green, and soft and pendent at their tips; they grow from the felt-covered rachis at different angles to create a plumose leaf.

The palm is similar to the queen palm (*Syagrus romanzoffiana*) but much shorter and thus has a more intimate and stockier, if not more robust appeal; its trunk also appears more solid and straighter and its crown larger. It is beautiful but is undeservedly rare in cultivation. It needs the same cultural practices as the queen palm but is not as hardy to cold, being safe only in zones 10 and 11. PLATE 848.

Syagrus oleracea is indigenous to a large area of interior sub-Amazonian eastern Brazil, southwestwards to eastern Paraguay, where it grows in moist monsoonal semidecid-uous forests. The epithet is Latin for "vegetable-bearing," an allusion to the edible fruits, seeds, and growing point.

This large solitary-trunked species grows to heights of 60 feet with diameters of only 1 foot. The trunks are usually straight, columnar, and almost white in their oldest parts. The leaf crown is full and round, and the individual arching leaves are from 8 to 10 feet long. The deep green leaflets are 1 foot long and grow either at angles along the rachis to create a V-shaped leaf, or at several different angles to create a plumose leaf.

The palm does not tolerate cold or drought and needs a rich, well-drained soil. It is adaptable only to zones 10b and 11, although it is marginal in 10a. This is certainly among the more beautiful species in the genus, with its tall, slender, and elegantly picturesque form. It is widely planted for ornament in its native haunts, especially lining the streets of larger cities, a landscaping use at which it excels. It is remarkably wonderful as a canopy-scape.

Syagrus orinocensis is indigenous to northern and western Venezuela and eastern Colombia, where it grows in lowland rain forest but also in mountainous rain forest to an elevation of slightly more than 1000 feet. The epithet is Latin for "of Orinoco," the great river between Colombia and Venezuela.

This solitary-trunked species occasionally occurs as a clustering specimen. The stems grow to 40 feet but are usually shorter. They are 4 or 6 inches in diameter, light gray, and mostly smooth and indistinctly ringed in their younger parts. The leaf crown is rounded but not dense, and the leaves are 8 to 10 feet long and beautifully arching. The medium to dark green leaflets are at least 1 foot long and are stiff but not rigid, growing at different angles from the rachis but mainly upwards to give the leaf a slight V shape.

The palm does not tolerate frost and is adaptable only to zones 10b and 11. It grows in partial shade and survives drought conditions, but it appreciates full sun, constant moisture, and a humus-laden, free-draining soil, under which conditions it is faster growing and more robust, although it is never really fast.

It is impossible to understand why this species is not more common in cultivation as it is one of the loveliest in the genus. It could serve as a paradigm for the pinnate-leaved forms of the family. Its canopy-scape is among the most pleasing in the family, and it is wonderful even when young as a close-up specimen. Planted in groups of three or more individuals of varying heights creates one of the world's most visually pleasing landscaping phenomena. PLATES 849 & 850.

Syagrus picrophylla is endemic to Brazil in the eastern central Atlantic tropical forest region, where it grows in mountainous rain forest at an elevation of 1000 feet. The epithet is Greek for "bitter" and "leaf," an allusion to the taste of the palm's growing point.

It is one of the smaller solitary-trunked species, growing only to a maximum overall height of 30 feet. The gray to tan trunks taper from base to tip and are 6 inches in diameter at their middle points. They are mostly smooth and show indistinct darker rings of leaf base scars. The leaves are 5 to 6 feet long and are mostly ascending with little arching evident. The leaflets are 1 foot long and widely spaced along the rachis but grow in clusters at different angles from it. Most are stiff but not rigid, but in some individuals, they are as limp as those of *S. romanzoffiana*. They are medium to deep green and grow at an angle which gives the leaf a slight V shape.

The species needs a good soil fortified with humus and regular moisture. It survives in shade but grows more slowly. It does not tolerate cold and succeeds only in zones 10b and 11. This attractive species has the look of a stiffer, dwarfed queen palm (*Syagrus romanzoffiana*). It is rare in cultivation outside its habitat but would make a stunning courtyard or patio subject as well as a miniature canopy-scape.

Syagrus pleioclada is endemic to Brazil in the state of Minas Gerais, where it grows in open, rocky savannas at elevations of 2800 to 4100 feet. The epithet is Greek for "many" and "branch," an allusion to the numerous short, gnarled inflorescence branches.

It is one of the most unusual species in the genus with its mostly subterranean and hidden stems that, when they emerge above ground, are squat, thick, and 1 foot or so tall. The leaves are exceptional: 3 or 4 feet long with widely spaced, long narrow, limp and pendent medium green, leathery leaflets.

It is not in cultivation perhaps because it is not terribly attractive but rather is a curiosity that looks more like an African cycad species than it does a tropical American palm. It is probably drought tolerant and, because of its mostly subterranean trunk, is likely to be cold hardy. Full sun would be necessary.

Syagrus pseudococos is endemic to southeastern Brazil, where it grows in low mountainous rain forest and clearings therein. The epithet is Greek for "false *Cocos*," an obvious allusion to its affinities with the coconut.

The trunks grow to 50 feet high and are usually less than 1 foot in diameter, white, and smooth, with beautifully distinct, widely spaced darker rings of leaf base scars and a heavy, bulging base. The leaves are 6 to 7 feet long on 1- to 2-foot-long heavy petioles. They are beautifully arching and bear 1-foot-long, deep emerald green, lanceolate, and stiff leaflets that grow from the rachis in clusters

and at slightly different but always upright angles to give the leaf a distinct V shape.

The species does not tolerate frost, needs full sun when past the seedling stage, and requires a deep, humus-laden soil as well as regular and adequate moisture, with which it is fast growing after its trunk is formed. Larry R. Noblick has shown by DNA analysis that this species is the New World's closest relative to the coconut; two of its vernacular names in habitat are *coco amargosa* ("bitter coconut") and *coco verde* ("green coconut"). It is almost as beautiful as that genus and it is nearly unfathomable why this species is not more widely cultivated. It is a veritable symphony of color with the intense green of its leaves against the tan or white trunks and, when in flower, its large, deep yellow inflorescences and great brown woody spathes. Its fully rounded crown is nearly perfect as a canopy-scape and, in groups of three or more individuals of varying heights, it is among the most dazzling specimen palms. PLATES 851 & 852.

Syagrus romanzoffiana is indigenous to southern and southeastern Brazil, eastern Paraguay, northeastern Argentina, and northern Uruguay, where it grows in monsoonal forests and swampy areas, always at low elevations. There is a high probability that it also occurs (or occurred) in extreme eastern Bolivia. It is almost universally called queen palm. At one time, the species was scientifically known as *Cocos plumosa,* and this now out-of-date binomial has almost reached the status of a common name; the palm is still known as *Arecastrum romanzoffianum* to most growers and nursery personnel. The epithet is a Latinized form of the Russian surname "Romanzoff" and honors an 18th-century count.

It is a variable species, the trunks growing to 50 feet in habitat but to 75 feet in cultivation under optimal conditions. Trunk diameters are even more variable in habitat, with individuals from the wetter, more tropical areas usually exhibiting the thinnest stems (6 inches in diameter), while those from the drier, less tropical areas manifest thick trunks (18 or 20 inches or even more). At one time taxonomists considered these regional forms to be separate varieties. The widely spaced rings of leaf base scars are always evident in the younger parts of a stem but are not overly distinct. The leaves are slightly less variable. They are 7 to 15 feet long but generally 12 feet and are plumose, the 1- to 2-foot-long, soft leaflets anywhere from light or yellowish green to verdant deep green, the variation in intensity of the hue often due to nutritional factors. There is a wonderful arch to each leaf near its apex, and the leaf crown is thus full and round. In general, old dead leaves do not last long on the tree. The inflorescences are usually long and pendent but may also be erect and short. Most are

5 feet long but some may be significantly longer; they all consist of many pendent yellowish branches bearing unisexual blossoms. The fruits are generally orange when mature, ovoid, and 1 inch long.

The species does not tolerate drought or calcareous soil. Unfortunately it is planted anyway in southern Florida so that the average person tends to think the species is normally chlorotic and therefore unsuitable for landscaping purposes. This is regrettable as the healthy palm is among the most beautiful that can be grown in nontropical regions, and even calcareous soils can be amended to the palm's liking with an organic mulch. It needs full sun once past the seedling stage and is adaptable in hot regions like southern Arizona if provided with regular moisture. Under optimum conditions, the species is one of the fastest growing palms and in its midlife can form at least 3 feet of trunk per year.

The queen palm is relatively hardy to cold and is usually unscathed by temperatures above 25°F. It is adaptable to zones 9b through 11 in areas subject to wet freezes in winter and to 9a through 11 in the drier climes. It is doubtless true that, if they can be found, individuals from the southerly habitats have more cold tolerance than those from the tropical areas of Brazil, which fact has led to several names in the nursery trade for differing forms with accompanying claims of unusual hardiness. The problem is that the names are simply created on the spot and probably do not correspond with any given provenance. One of the latest named forms has a slight silvery sheen to the undersides of the leaflets, robust trunks, and much smaller seeds. Its provenance probably is southerly but it cannot be documented. It is, however, significantly hardier to cold and survived the devastating freeze in central Florida of 1989 (David Witt, pers. comm.). These palms are the progeny of individuals grown by Dent Smith (founder of the International Palm Society), who obtained them from the Santa Catarina state of Brazil, whose southern boundaries extend to latitude 28° south.

The species is variable in nature, and it has been in cultivation for so long that differing forms are common. According to Noblick (1996) the species is known to hybridize in habitat with *S. coronata*, *S. oleracea,* and *S. schizophylla*, and some nursery forms are likely to be hybrids; unfortunately the other known potential parents in habitat are all more tender to cold than is pure *S. romanzoffiana*.

This is among the most beautiful, tropical-looking palms that can be grown outside of tropical areas. It looks enough like the royal palms (*Roystonea*) that it can be used to line streets and avenues. Its canopy-scape is thrilling, and a specimen group of individuals of varying heights is among the most picturesque landscaping tableau. The species is widely planted worldwide in tropical and subtropical regions; in fact, it is a weedy species that tends to naturalize. But, like the coconut, its ubiquitousness is sorely missed by those whose climate prevents growing it. The queen is widely grown in large atriums where its size and light requirements can be met. Otherwise, it is not a good candidate for indoors.

In cultivation, the species has hybridized with *Butia capitata* to form one of the most beautiful palm hybrids (see *Butia capitata* for more information on this hybrid).

The leaves and fruits are fed to livestock, and indigenous peoples in the palm's habitat eat the growing point. The seeds are crushed and fed to poultry, and the trunks are used as salt water piers because they are immune to attack by marine bore worms (Noblick 1996). The species is also widely planted for ornament in habitat. PLATE 853.

Syagrus ruschiana is endemic to central eastern Brazil in the states of Espírito Santo and Minas Gerais, where it grows in open areas in the low granite hills on steep slopes at elevations of 300 to 1200 feet.

It is a clustering species whose trunks can grow to 25 feet with diameters of 2 to 3 inches. The leaves are 10 feet long and 3 or more feet wide and beautifully arching, with closely and regularly spaced 2-foot-long narrow, limpish dark green leaflets growing in a single plane from the rachis. The long slender yellow inflorescences produce almost rounded, 1-inch-wide, bright orange fruits.

This extraordinarily beautiful species has leaves reminiscent of those of the kentia palm, *Howea forsteriana*, or even the coconut, *Cocos*. The clustering trunks add to the overall appeal, and yet the species is undeservedly rare in cultivation, possibly because of its isolated and small habitat, in which it nevertheless is abundant. PLATES 854 & 855.

Syagrus sancona is indigenous to two disjunct areas of northern South America: the first area is the Andean foothills of western Venezuela, central and western Colombia, and western Ecuador; the second region includes central and eastern Peru, west central Brazil, and northwestern Bolivia. It is found in lowland rain forest and clearings as well as in higher, drier areas to an elevation of 3800 feet. The epithet is a Latinized form of the aboriginal name for the species in Venezuela and Colombia.

This solitary-trunked species is the tallest in the genus, old trunks attaining heights of 100 feet and a maximum diameter of 1 foot except at their bulging bases. They are always straight as an arrow and would be columnar were they of greater thickness. They are light gray to almost white or light tan and bear widely spaced but indistinctly darker rings of leaf base scars. The leaf crown is fully rounded and dense and, in old individuals, seems small.

The leaves are 12 feet long and strongly arching, almost re-curved back to the trunks in some individuals. They are deep green with closely spaced wide leaflets to 3 feet long. The leaflets are limp with usually pendent apices, and they grow from different angles off the rachis to give the leaf a plumose effect. The yellow pendent inflorescences pro-duce 1-inch-long egg-shaped yellow to orange fruits.

This beauty is not hardy to cold and is adaptable only to zones 10 and 11. It requires constant moisture, especially in dry climates, to look good and for fastest growth but is not fussy about soil as long as it is fast draining and not overly acidic or overly alkaline. It needs sun from youth to old age and, under optimum conditions, grows fast when past the seedling stage and up to near maturity.

The appearance of this palm is often compared to that of the queen palm (*Syagrus romanzoffiana*). While this may be true, it is hard to imagine anyone mistaking the two palms if they have both formed trunks. It is unsurpassed as a canopy-scape and is almost overwhelmingly beautiful as a specimen planting of three or more individuals of vary-ing heights. It is not for small spaces. Only in large atriums or conservatories could this one be successful. PLATE 856.

Syagrus schizophylla is endemic to the northeastern Brazilian coastal forest known as the *restinga*. This is a veg-etation type with low, shrubby evergreen woody small trees and shrubs that grow on sandy soil—mostly prehis-toric sand dunes—near the coast as well as inland on the low hills. The only common name in English-speaking countries seems to be the arikury palm but this is not its English name. The epithet is Greek for "divided" and "leaf."

The palm is found mostly as a solitary-trunked speci-men but occasionally as clustering individuals. The trunks grow to 15 feet but are usually 10 feet high. They are slen-der but look thicker because of the persistent leaf bases and fibers; even with these adhesions the stems are never more than 6 inches in diameter. The trunks are distinctive be-cause these closely set, gray to tan narrow leaf bases give them the look of fine wickerwork. The species is the only one in the genus having spines, and these are limited to the long petioles and leaf bases. The leaves are 6 feet long on 2-foot-long spiny petioles. They are spreading and slightly arching; living ones never lie beneath the hori-zontal. The leaflets are stiff but not rigid and in older leaves are pendent. They are linear-lanceolate, regularly spaced, dull to olive or even deep green, and usually grow from the rachis in a single flat plane but may also grow at a slight angle to give a V-shaped leaf. The inflorescences bear beautiful 1-inch-long, egg-shaped reddish orange fruits. The palm's only human use seems to be its edible and sweet-tasting fruits. Unless one is ravenous for the taste, it would seem better to leave them on the little trees because of their beauty.

The species is slightly susceptible to lethal yellowing disease. The palm is intolerant of frost and drought: its habitat is reputedly wetter than the Amazon Basin to the northwest. It is not fussy about soil as long as it drains well, and it luxuriates in full sun as well as partial shade, although it is more slow growing, darker green, and usually has longer petioles in shadier sites; it is not fast growing in any situation.

This architectural-looking species looks its loveliest in up-close and intimate sites; it is the perfect patio palm. Its beauty is ruined if planted as a single specimen surrounded by space unless it is incorporated into lower vegetation above which its beautiful silhouette may be enjoyed. It does look much better as a specimen if planted in groups of three or more individuals of varying heights, but its small stature seems to mitigate against this situation also. If one is fortunate enough to have a clustering individual, almost any site is a good one. It does well indoors for a while if given lots of light and good air circulation. PLATES 857–859.

Syagrus smithii is a rare and endangered species indige-nous to southeastern Colombia, northeastern Peru, and northwestern Brazil, where it grows in rain forest to an el-evation of 2000 feet. The epithet was bestowed by Harold E. Moore, Jr., in 1963 to honor Earl E. Smith, an Ameri-can botanist.

It is a solitary-trunked species growing to a maximum overall height of 50 feet but usually 30 feet. The trunk is gray or tan, indistinctly ringed, and 3 inches in diameter. The leaf crown is full and rounded but not dense. The leaves are 8 to 10 feet long with dark green, 2-foot-long, narrow and long-tipped leaflets which, except for the ones near the base of the blade, grow in almost a single flat plane. Amazingly, the 8-foot-long leaves can reportedly also be undivided and entire, even in adult trees, in which case they are an elongated wedge shape with deeply bifid apices. The yellow, egg-shaped 3-inch-long fruits are un-usually large for the genus.

This species is almost as rare in cultivation as it is in hab-itat. It is doubtless frost intolerant but would probably lux-uriate in full sun or partial shade and would need regular and abundant moisture.

Syagrus stenopetala is endemic to northern coastal Venezuela, where it grows in semideciduous forest from sea level to 1600 feet elevation. The epithet is Latin for "narrow" and "petal," an allusion to the longer petals of this species as opposed to those of *S. orinocensis*. Some tax-onomists consider this palm a form of *S. orinocensis*, but Larry R. Noblick (1996) indicates that there are two differing taxa here and that *S. stenopetala* should be kept separate because of its clustering habit—if one accepts this binomial as valid, then *S. orinocensis* would only be a solitary-trunked species—with larger stature (trunks as tall as 80 feet), its thicker petioles, its slightly longer leaves, its stiffer and more erect leaflets, and its larger inflorescences. PLATES 860–862.

Syagrus stratincola is an endangered species indigenous to southwestern Surinam, southern French Guiana, and the northern area of the state of Amapá in Brazil, where it grows in lowland tropical rain forest and clearings therein. The epithet is Latin for "inhabitant of the strata," an allusion to the granitic rock (strata) of the palm's habitat.

This densely clustering species is occasionally found with a solitary trunk. The stems can grow to 45 feet high but are never more than 4 inches in diameter. They are light gray to pure white, smooth, and indistinctly ringed. The petioles are usually 18 inches long and the rest of the leaf to 8 feet long. The narrow, pointed, dark green leaflets are 18 inches long and are stiff and rigid; they are widely spaced and grow from the rachis at several different angles to give the leaf a loosely plumose effect and the look of that of a small *Phoenix* species.

The species is not in cultivation outside of a few botanical and collectors' gardens. It does not tolerate frost and needs sun and regular and copious moisture.

Syagrus vagans is endemic to north central Brazil in the states of Bahia and Minas Gerais, where it grows in open, dry caatinga at elevations of 800 to 2900 feet. The epithet is Latin for "wandering," an allusion to the underground stems.

The leaves of this clustering species grow directly from the rocky soil surface. They are 6 feet long, stiffly erect, with narrow and rigid, dusky to deep green leaflets. The leaflets grow from the rachis at an angle, making the leaf V shaped.

This species looks like an untidy mass of schizoid stiff leaflets; it is, nevertheless, sought after for cultivation. PLATE 863.

SYNECHANTHUS is a genus of two small, pinnate-leaved, monoecious palms in tropical America. One is solitary trunked, the other clustering. The species are related to and resemble those of *Chamaedorea*, the differences being in details of the flowers and the fruits and seeds. Neither *Synechanthus* species is hardy to cold, and both need partial shade at all stages of growth and a friable, humus-laden soil that is constantly moist but also fast draining. The genus name is derived from two Greek words meaning "united" and "flower" and refers to the arrangement of the flowers in the inflorescence. PLATES 865–867.

Synechanthus fibrosus occurs naturally from the Mexican state of Veracruz, southwestwards through central Guatemala, northern Honduras, and thence southwards through eastern Nicaragua and into northeastern Costa Rica, where it occurs in the undergrowth of rain forest from sea level to 4000 feet in elevation. The epithet is Latin for "fibrous" and refers to the leaf sheaths.

This is a solitary-trunked species whose mature, 1-inch-thick trunks can reach 15 feet tall; they are dark green with beautiful white rings of leaf base scars. The leaves are ascending and seldom lie beneath the horizontal; they are 4 feet long on 1-foot-long petioles. The glossy medium green leaflets are arranged into groups along each side of the rachis and are offset to give the leaf a slightly plumose effect; they are slightly S shaped and the two apical leaflets are wider than the rest. The long inflorescences grow from among the leaves, are branched only apically, and are usually erect until fruit formation. They bear tiny yellow flowers that produce 0.5-inch-wide, round, and fleshy fruits that change from green to yellow to orange and finally red when mature.

This delicate, ethereal-looking little palm needs to be sited where it can be appreciated up close. It's not always easy to accomplish, but a miniature landscape with this palm as a canopy-scape would be refreshing as an intimate site among larger areas of a garden or as a patio or courtyard feature. It has for many years been grown indoors in bright light or in greenhouses. In Belize the species is sometimes called the monkey tail palm because of the long, pendent inflorescence. PLATES 865 & 866.

Synechanthus warscewiczianus is a clustering species indigenous to southeastern Nicaragua, the east coast of Costa Rica, Panama, the west coast of Colombia, and northwestern Ecuador, where it grows in rain forest from sea level to 4000 feet in elevation. The epithet honors Josef Warscewicz, a 19th-century palm botanist in South America.

Its trunks can grow to 15 feet tall in sparse clumps that usually have one dominant stem and a few smaller, shorter trunks. The deep green, ascending leaves are 6 feet long and are sometimes entire and apically bifid or, more often, irregularly pinnately segmented, the segments of varying sizes and placement with the apical pair always much wider. The flowers and fruits are similar to those of *S. fibrosus*.

The clumping habit allows this palm to be used as a small specimen planting or as a component of a wall of other vegetation. PLATE 867.

TECTIPHIALA is a rare and endangered monotypic genus of solitary-trunked or clustering, spiny, pinnate-leaved, monoecious palm endemic to central Mauritius. The genus name is derived from Greek words meaning "covering" and a type of vessel, and refers to the small bracts that tend to obscure the flowers before they are fully open. The epithet is Latin for "fierce," an allusion to the spines.

Tectiphiala ferox grows in moist, marshy scrub vegetation in heavy, acidic soil at an elevation of 2000 feet. The species was described as sparsely clustering, but no such individuals now exist, possibly because of the slow growth habit.

The trunk grows to 20 feet high with a diameter of 6 to 7 inches. It is dark gray and exhibits closely set rings of leaf base scars, the rings bearing 6-inch-long black spines in the youngest parts of the stems. The crownshaft is 2 feet tall, greatly swollen at its base, and tapering to its summit. It is a deep rust or cinnamon in color because of the dense, velvety covering of tomentum. It is also covered in soft but long, black, flexible, and hairlike spines. The leaf crown is sparse and spherical because of the recurving, 6- to 8-foot-long leaves on short, stout, and furry petioles. The 18-inch-long, linear-lanceolate, and long tapering leaflets grow in closely set groups along the rachis and, in each group, at different angles to create a slightly plumose leaf. They are heavy and leathery but not stiff and are a medium to dark or even bluish green above but an astonishingly attractive silvery hue beneath. The inflorescences are initially covered in a spiny and hairy, elongated bract. They are once branched off a short, spiny peduncle, the flowering branches 18 inches long, few, and light yellow, bearing both male and female blossoms. The tiny ovoid fruits are blackish blue when ripe.

This unusually beautiful species is rare in habitat and in cultivation, being represented in only a few botanical gardens. It seems to need an acidic soil, constant moisture, and a tropical climate but is adaptable to full sun at an early age.

THRINAX is a genus of seven palmate-leaved, monoecious palms in the Caribbean Basin. A few grow to 50 feet but all have a delicate, almost ethereal quality with their slender trunks and nearly circular leaves. All except one are solitary trunked and, in the species that is the exception, its clustering is a rare phenomenon. The leaf crowns are relatively small, especially in older individuals, and are globular. Except for one outstanding instance, the trunks never have a shag of old dead leaves and are indistinctly ringed in their younger parts. The genus is closely related to *Coccothrinax* but is distinguished from it by the split leaf bases and white fruits in *Thrinax* versus the unsplit leaf bases and black fruits of *Coccothrinax*. The inflorescences

grow from the leaf crown and bear white bisexual flowers. The tiny round fruits are pure white or off white when mature.

Most species are slow to exceedingly slow growing, but all are adaptable to various soils as long as they are freely draining, even the calcareous and salty types. They need a site in full sun when past the seedling stage, and none are hardy to cold. Most are adaptable in zones 10 and 11 and are marginal in 9b. Except for the endangered Cuban species, the palms are called thatch palms because their leaves are widely used in house construction. The genus name is Greek and translates as "trident," an allusion to the leaf segments. PLATES 868–878.

Thrinax compacta is endemic to a small area of eastern Cuba, where it grows on mogotes (limestone hills). The epithet is Latin for "compact" and refers to the short inflorescences. This beautiful, graceful, and tall species reaches 50 feet high with a 1-foot-thick trunk. It has large leaves on long petioles that show them off in the large, globular leaf crown. The palm is rare, poorly known, and in cultivation only in a few botanical and collectors' gardens.

Thrinax ekmaniana is endemic to three small mogotes along the coastal area of northeastern Cuba, where it is an extremely rare and endangered species. The epithet is a Latinized form of the surname "Ekman" and honors a 20th-century plant collector. This is one of the world's most unusual palms and looks more like a large yucca than a palm.

This palm never attains a height greater than 15 feet, even in habitat, and its slender, 2-inch-thick trunk is hidden in the youngest parts (just beneath the living leaf crown) by a dense, rounded shag of dead leaves, which gives to older individuals the appearance of a big lollipop. The leaves are borne on 4-inch-long petioles and grow so close together in the crown that it is impossible to discern the outline of any individual leaf without extracting it from the palm's crown; in truth each one is three-quarters of a circle. The segments are rigid, taper to a stiff, sharp point, and are medium to deep green above but silvery green to almost silvery blue beneath. The inflorescences are long enough to exceed the foliage crown and are white with yellowish white bisexual flowers that produce 0.5-inch-wide white round fruits.

This species is not known to be cultivated anywhere. Measures have been taken to protect it in habitat, and seedlings are now growing there. PLATES 868–871.

Thrinax excelsa is endemic to Jamaica, where it grows in low mountains of the island's extreme eastern tip. It is called broad thatch palm in habitat and Jamaican thatch palm elsewhere. The epithet is Latin for "superior," an obvious allusion to the palm's beauty.

Individual trunks grow to 35 feet tall in habitat with a diameter of 8 inches. The leaf crown is large and beautifully rounded. The large leaves are almost circular and 5 to 6 feet in diameter with many linear-lanceolate segments that extend halfway to the petiole. They are a glossy medium to deep green above but a grayish and glaucous green beneath and are limp, with their apices usually pendent in the older leaves. The short inflorescences are difficult to see among the leaves, but the infructescences are pendent with the 0.5-inch-wide round fruits.

The palm is adaptable to most soils except for the quite acidic and waterlogged. It is not drought tolerant and should not be subjected to prolonged periods without moisture. It is tender to cold and adaptable in zones 10b and 11, although some nice individuals are found in warm microclimates of 10a. This species is faster growing than any other and makes a relatively quick and good show of tropical beauty. It is the most lush and most tropical-looking species in the genus because of its large leaves. It is beautiful and choice as a younger plant and is captivating up close and in an intimate site. When older it is beautiful as a specimen, especially in groups of three or more individuals of varying heights. In truth, it is hard to misplace. None of the thatch palms are suited to growing indoors, but this one probably has the most potential if given room and bright light. PLATES 872 & 873.

Thrinax morrisii is indigenous to the Bahamas, Florida Keys, western Cuba, Navassa Island (a tiny U.S. possession off the western tip of Haiti), Puerto Rico, and the Lesser Antilles islands of Anguilla and Barbuda, where it grows in open deciduous forests at low elevations and along the coasts. It is called Key thatch palm, silver thatch palm, brittle thatch palm, and peaberry palm in the United States and broom palm and buffalo-top in the Lesser Antilles. The epithet honors David Morris, a 19th-century British botanist.

The trunks grow to heights of 30 feet in habitat, with diameters of 8 inches, and usually have a small area of crisscrossing leaf bases and fibers beneath the leaf crown; otherwise, the stem is clean and relatively smooth. The leaves vary in shape and color according to the age and habitat of the palm: younger palms tend to have leaves that are not complete circles and that also are more bluish green than mature individuals, which are almost always circular. The undersides of the leaves are always a lighter green than the upper surfaces. Individual leaves are relatively small and usually 2 feet wide on long petioles that are 3 feet long. The leaf segments extend almost to the petiole, are linear-lanceolate and soft, and normally do not grow in a single plane. Both the inflorescences and the clusters of 0.5-inch-thick, round white fruits are almost hidden in the leaf crown.

The species is hardier to cold than the others and is adaptable to zones 9b through 11; isolated specimens thrive in warm microclimates (sometimes with protection) in 9a. The rounded, airy crown is beautiful as a canopy-scape, but the palm is equally satisfactory in an intimate site where its little starburst-shaped leaves dance in a breeze. The species can be grown indoors with a great amount of light. PLATES 874 & 875.

Thrinax parviflora is endemic to Jamaica, where it grows in open and rocky deciduous woods to an elevation of 2800 feet. The epithet is Latin for "small flower."

The palm attains a maximum overall height of 50 feet in habitat, with a trunk diameter of 6 inches. The leaf crown is globular and the 3- to 4-foot-wide circular leaves have heavily veined linear-lanceolate, often twisted and limp segments extending two-thirds of the way to the petiole with usually pendent apices. Leaf color is medium to deep green on both surfaces.

The palm is extremely graceful, especially when older, because of its diaphanously slender trunk and rounded but sparse leaf crown. It is uncommon in cultivation and deserves much wider acceptance. A few taxonomists recognize two subspecies based on details of the leaf segment tips and the length of the inflorescences. Although it is sometimes called mountain thatch palm, it is not hardy to cold.

Thrinax radiata is indigenous to the Florida Keys, Bahamas, western Cuba, Puerto Rico, Hispaniola, the northern and eastern coasts of the Yucatán Peninsula, and Belize, where it grows along the coasts. It is usually called Florida thatch palm in Florida. The epithet is Latin for "radiating" and alludes to the shape of the leaves.

This species rarely forms suckers but is usually a solitary-trunked palm with slender stems attaining maximum heights of 40 feet and diameters of only 5 inches. While the leaf petioles are 3 feet long, the leaf crown is rounded and dense in full sun, with 4-foot-wide leaves, which are circular and medium green above and a lighter, grayish green below. The leaf segments extend two-thirds of the way to the petiole and are pendent at their apices.

This is another relatively cold-hardy species and is adaptable to zones 10 and 11, with occasional handsome specimens seen in warm microclimates of 9b. It is slow growing in full sun and very slow growing in partial shade. The palm demands a fast-draining soil. It is tolerant of saline soil and air, and its limp leaves are marred only by hurricane winds. It is a perfect candidate for the beach as well as sunny inland areas. Its crown is open and airy when young or when planted in partial shade but is tightly globular and dense when older and in full sun—so much so that the leaves are usually obscured, making it a distinctive and picturesque canopy-scape. This is a poor candidate for growing indoors past the juvenile stage. PLATES 876 & 877.

Thrinax rivularis is endemic to a small area of northeastern Cuba, where it grows along the coast in salt marshes and along the streams of sparsely wooded low savannas in mostly serpentine soils. The epithet is Latin for "of the river."

This small species grows to a maximum height of 20 or 25 feet in habitat, with a trunk only 3 inches in diameter. There is often a small area of shag or pendent dead leaves beneath the small globular and dense leaf crown; otherwise, the trunks are smooth and almost white. The 3-foot-wide leaves are deep green above and a lighter, dusky green beneath. The leaf segments are stiff, nonpendent at their apices, and taper to a sharp point.

This palm looks as much like a small *Copernicia* species as a typical *Thrinax* species. It is extremely rare in cultivation and is reportedly not easy to grow because of its adaptation to the serpentine soil of its habitat. PLATE 878.

TRACHYCARPUS is a genus of eight solitary-trunked, palmate-leaved, mostly dioecious palms in northern India, Nepal, Myanmar, southern China, and northern Thailand. The species hail from mountainous forests of considerable elevations and include some of the world's cold hardiest palms. Three of the species were described in the 1990s.

One species is acaulescent; the rest form slender aerial stems that are covered in their younger parts with petiole and leaf base remains and the fibers associated with them. The leaf crowns and leaves are relatively small and compact, and the slender petioles are mostly unarmed; a few species having leaf stalks with only a few short, tiny teeth along their margins. The inflorescences grow from the leaf bases in the crown and are congested but much branched, the flowering branches mostly yellow, bearing either male or female blossoms on separate trees, occasionally with bisexual flowers. The fruits are small, variously shaped with hard and rough exteriors, and generally black when mature. In addition to floral details, the shape of their seeds differentiates the species. Were it not for two European nurserymen, amateur botanists, and avid trachycarpophiles, Martin Gibbons and Tobias W. Spanner, the world would know of only five of the species it now does and that knowledge would be half of what it is now. The genus name is derived from two Greek words meaning "rough" and "fruit." PLATES 879–890.

Trachycarpus fortunei is thought to be indigenous to central and eastern China, but its exact origin is unknown, so widely and for so long has it been in cultivation in that country. Common names are windmill palm, Chusan palm, and Chinese windmill palm. The epithet honors Robert Fortune, a 19th-century Scottish horticulturist, explorer, and collector, who established the tea plantation industries in India and Sri Lanka.

The trunk grows to 40 feet with time. The woody part is relatively slender, a maximum diameter of 8 to 10 inches, but it is usually covered in its younger parts with old, woody leaf bases, petiole bases, and the dark brown fibers associated with them so that the diameter of these parts is often twice that of the lower portions. These leaf bases and fibers can be removed mechanically to reveal an elegantly slender, distinctly and closely ringed stem. The leaf crown is dense and spherical or often obovate if the shag of dead leaves near its base is not removed. The leaves are deep green on both surfaces, 3 feet in diameter, and are borne on 18- to 24-inch-long petioles. The segments extend to varying depths into the blade, the deepest reaching nearly to the juncture of the petiole. The seeds are reniform.

This species is among the hardiest trunked palms. It is adaptable to zones 7b through 11 and is even found in warm microclimates of 7a. It is extremely rare or absent from tropical or nearly tropical areas but is at its best in cool Mediterranean climates such as are found in the Pacific Northwest of the United States, the southern and low elevations of Switzerland, and most of the Riviera region of Europe as well as southeastern Australia. In the right climate, with regular and adequate moisture and a decent soil, this species grows fast once past the juvenile stage and before it is mature. It is adapted to a range of soils, including slightly calcareous ones, and it flourishes in full sun except in hot climates. It should be protected from high winds, which spoil its elegance by tattering the leaves. The species is slightly susceptible to lethal yellowing disease.

The palm has a beautiful silhouette and makes a wonderful canopy-scape; it should not, however, be planted where its crown is regularly subjected to high winds. It looks nice even planted alone and surrounded by space but is even more satisfying in groups of three or more individuals of varying heights. While not as grand and majestic as the tropical royals (*Roystonea*), *Attalea, Jubaea, Livistona,* Canary Island date (*Phoenix canariensis*), or queen palms (*Syagrus romanzoffiana*), it is beautiful along streets or avenues. The species is not known to have been grown indoors but probably could be if given lots of light and moisture.

In China the durable leaf sheath fibers are used for making garments, brooms, and other utensils, and the same fibers are reportedly still used for containing the media in hanging baskets. PLATES 879 & 880.

Trachycarpus latisectus is a rare and endangered species endemic to India in West Bengal and Sikkim, where it grows in mountainous forest from 4000 to 8000 feet. The epithet is derived from two Latin words meaning "wide" and "section," an allusion to the width of the leaf segments. The species was described in 1997 by Gibbons and Spanner, who proposed the vernacular Windemere palm because this species is cultivated on the grounds of a hotel of that name in Darjeeling, India.

The trunk attains a height of 40 feet and a diameter of 6 inches. It is light gray and faintly ringed in its younger parts. The crown of living leaves is open and is hemispherical or slightly more so without the small skirt of dead leaves but is spherical or obovate with the skirt. The leaves are glossy light to deep olive green above and a lighter, glaucous hue beneath. They are circular or nearly so and 4.5 feet wide on 3- to 4-foot-long petioles. The thick, leathery segments extend less than halfway into the blade and are unusually broad at their midpoints and shortly bifid at their apices. The seeds are oval.

Gibbons (1993) has written that this species "is probably the only species in the genus which, owing to its wide altitude range from 3950 to 7900 feet, will adapt well to hotter regions." This is yet to be determined for there are still (2001) no individuals other than seedlings planted in such areas. The latter, however, seem to be doing well so far. The species is doubtless as cold hardy as *T. fortunei* and has similar cultural requirements. The leaf shape is the most beautiful in the genus. PLATE 881.

Trachycarpus martianus is indigenous to northeastern India, Nepal, and northern Myanmar, where it grows in mountainous rain forest from 3000 to 8000 feet. The epithet honors the 19th-century German plant explorer Carl F. P. von Martius.

The trunk grows to 20 feet tall and is 7 inches in diameter. It is light to dark gray and, in its younger parts, is distinctly ringed with closely set ridged and darker rings of leaf base scars. The leaf crown is open and hemispherical or slightly more so. The leaves of older trees are semicircular, but those of younger ones generally are circular. The rigid segments extend halfway into the blade, which is medium to dark green above and bluish gray green beneath. They are 3 to 4 feet wide on exceptional, 4-foot-long petioles, which are margined with a thick white tomentum when new, as are the young leaves themselves. The seeds are oval.

Individuals from the northerly parts of the palm's range (Nepal) have slightly smaller leaves with fewer segments and are hardier to cold and more drought tolerant than are individuals from the southerly parts (Gibbons 1993). Because of its open crown and stiff leaf segments, the palm is beautiful, especially in silhouette. It is reportedly more tender to cold than is *T. fortunei* and is probably adaptable only to zones 8 through 11. It seems to be more tolerant of warm to tropical climes and to need much more water than does *T. fortunei*. The species prefers somewhat acidic soil. PLATES 882 & 883.

Trachycarpus nanus is an endangered species endemic to southwestern China in Yunnan province, where it grows in moist evergreen forests or on drier steep hills, at elevations from 6000 to 7500 feet. The epithet is Latin for "dwarf."

The short, stout trunk remains subterranean or, when aerial, only grows 1 to 2 feet high and is heavily covered in old leaf base fibers. The leaf crown is small and compact with 2-foot-wide, semicircular leaves borne on 6- to 12-inch-long petioles with tiny teeth along their margins. The leaf segments are stiff and narrow and extend at least three-quarters of the way into the blade. They are deep green to silvery bluish green or even bluish silver, the latter hues being revealed only in full sun. Unlike all other species of *Trachycarpus,* this one has short erect inflorescences and erect fully loaded infructescences. The seeds are reniform.

The species is rare in cultivation. Seeds became available only after Gibbons and Spanner "rediscovered" the species in the wild in 1993. It is reported to be at least as hardy to cold as is *T. fortunei* and is probably more drought tolerant. Unlike *T. fortunei,* this species prefers slightly acidic soil. PLATE 884.

Trachycarpus oreophilus is endemic to the mountains of northwestern Thailand, growing in wet and cool monsoonal forests at elevations from 5280 to 7000 feet. The epithet is Latin for "mountain loving." The species was described by Gibbons and Spanner in 1997.

The trunk grows to 30 feet high with a diameter of 6 inches. The leaf crown is dense and hemispherical and contains twenty 3-foot-wide leaves on 20-inch-long petioles with tiny teeth along their margins. The leaves are semicircular to nearly circular, and the 60 or so stiff, rigid segments extend to half the depth of the blade. Leaf color is medium to deep green above and lighter grayish green beneath. The seeds are reniform.

The palm is rare in cultivation but is reportedly slow growing and needs a humus-laden, moist but fast-draining soil. It probably tolerates slightly calcareous soil conditions as it grows on limestone cliffs and slopes in habitat. It seems to be adaptable to zones 8 through 11, although no reports are available for colder regions. PLATE 885.

Trachycarpus princeps is endemic to southern central China, where it grows on limestone cliffs and ridge tops in monsoonal rain forest at elevations of 5000 to 6100 feet. The epithet is Latin for "prince" and alludes to "the stately bearing of this palm and the majestic way it looks down from its lofty position on the sheer cliff faces" (Gibbons 1993). The species was described in 1995 by Gibbons and Spanner.

The trunk grows to 30 feet high with a diameter of 8 inches. It is covered in all but its oldest parts by a thin mass of tight, dark brown fibers. The leaf crown is spherical or nearly so and contains two dozen 4-foot-wide leaves on 2- to 3-foot-long petioles that are covered in a bluish white waxy substance when new and are armed with tiny teeth along their margins. The leaves are semicircular with linear-lanceolate segments that extend halfway into the depth of the blade, which is bright medium green above and a beautiful glaucous, bluish white beneath. The seeds are reniform.

The species is not in cultivation because its habitat is remote and inaccessible. PLATES 886 & 887.

Trachycarpus takil is endemic to India in Uttar Pradesh province, where it grows in mountainous forest to an elevation of 8000 feet, and where it is nearly extinct. The epithet is a transliteration of the name of a mountain in the palm's habitat.

This palm resembles *T. fortunei* but is said to grow taller, have bigger leaves with stiffer and more numerous segments, a thicker and cleaner trunk, and a twisted hastula at the juncture of petiole and blade. The seeds are reniform.

Because of the elevation of its habitat, this species is probably the most cold hardy in the genus; it is reportedly adaptable to zones 6b through 11 and probably marginal in 6a, although it is no good in hot climates. It is fast growing once past the seedling stage (Gibbons 1993). PLATES 888 & 889.

Trachycarpus wagnerianus is unknown in the wild but may have originated in cultivation in Japan, where it was first discovered by the Western world. The epithet is a Latinized form of the surname "Wagner" and honors a German horticulturist of the late 19th and early 20th century who was the first European to import the plants from Japan.

The trunk grows to 30 feet or sometimes more and is 8 to 10 inches in diameter when free of the leaf base fibers that tend to remain for a good while. The leaf crown is hemispherical and often extended, especially in younger individuals. The leaves of younger individuals are nearly circular, but those of older plants tend to be hemispherical. At all ages they are relatively small, from 18 to 26 inches wide, and are borne on 2- to 3-foot-long petioles. The 40 or so segments are thick, leathery, stiff, and rigid, making the blade often "cupped." They extend three-quarters of the way into the blade and are glossy deep green above and a paler and glaucous green beneath. The seeds are reniform.

This is an easily identified species with small, stiff leaves. The new growth is margined with a short but dense white woolly tomentum. The palm is reportedly slow growing when young but fast as it forms a trunk. It is as hardy to cold as is *T. fortunei* and needs a humus-laden soil as well as regular and adequate moisture.

It is arguably the most beautiful species in the genus but, alas, is ill adapted to hot climates in which the nighttime temperatures are consistently high. PLATE 890.

TRITHRINAX is a genus of three palmate-leaved, monoecious palms in drier parts of southern South America. All are clustering palms with occasional individuals forming single trunks. All three species have persistent leaf sheaths that form downward-pointing spiny projections lasting sometimes for years on the trunks. The white or cream inflorescences are formed in the leaf crown and seldom exceed its length. They are much branched, the flowering branches relatively short, and are initially covered in several bracts. They bear bisexual flowers, which produce round white fruits that mature to yellow then to black or dark brown. All the species are drought tolerant and slow growing. Furthermore, all are cold resistant. The genus name translates as "three *Thrinax*" and probably alludes to the leaf segments. PLATES 891–898.

Trithrinax brasiliensis is endemic to far southeastern Brazil, where it grows in inland open, dry savannas. The only common name seems to be spiny fiber palm. The specific epithet is Latin for "of Brazil."

Most individuals are solitary stemmed but occasionally a clustering specimen is seen with two or three trunks. Old palms form trunks to 50 feet high but the norm, especially in cultivation, is half that height. They are covered in all but the oldest parts with a mat of dark gray fibers and rows of 2- to 4-inch-long blackish spines corresponding with the tops of the leaf bases. The leaves are 3 to 4 feet wide on 2-foot-long petioles and are slightly more than a half circle of deeply cut segments, each one being shallowly to deeply bifid apically. Leaf color is a deep green, light green, silver green, or even bluish green, and the segments are stiff but not overly rigid, especially in younger leaves; in older leaves the ends of the segments are often pendent.

The palm is hardy to cold in zones 9 through 11 where wet freezes occur in winter but 8 through 11 in drier climes; prolonged cold and precipitation are often lethal because the growing point becomes infected by fungus. The species is drought tolerant once established but grows faster and looks better with regular moisture, especially in drought conditions and periods of intense heat. It should not be planted in the shade where it grows extremely slowly and its growing point can become diseased in cold, wet weather. It requires a fast-draining soil.

The attraction of this species is its picturesque trunk, so pruning off the fiber mat and its accompanying spines leaves a characterless stem. One might as well plant a windmill palm (*Trachycarpus fortunei*), which grows faster and looks basically like this species minus its trunk covering. Removing the old, dead bottom parts of the petioles can be effective, however.

Because of its slow growth rate, this palm serves well for years as a close-up specimen. It is especially nice combined with rocks, cactus, or succulents. Old clustering individuals make beautiful specimens, even when surrounded by space. This palm is not known to have been grown indoors and is probably a bad candidate for doing so. PLATES 891–893.

Trithrinax campestris is indigenous to northern interior Argentina and west central Uruguay, where it grows mostly along and in ravines, dry river beds, and canyons at low elevations, but also in open intermontane savannas. The epithet is Latin for "of the fields." While still abundant in habitat, the species is quickly losing ground to expanding agricultural interests in Argentina.

This species often clumps, even when quite young. The trunks grow to 20 feet high and are usually clothed, except for the oldest parts, in a shag of dead leaves, reminiscent visually of the genus *Washingtonia*. Young plants or those from which the shag has been removed show a characteristic mat of closely knit curling leaf sheath fibers and downward-pointing spines. The distinctive leaves are less than hemispherical and diamond shaped or wedge shaped, and the entire blade is usually 2 feet wide. Leaf color is sometimes amazing, always beautiful: grayish green to almost silvery blue above and dull light or yellowish to grayish green beneath. The segments extend halfway into the blade and the 2-foot-long petiole, and are possibly the most rigid of any palmate-leaved palm, almost steel-like; they are shallowly bifid apically and the ends are pointed and tough enough to be dangerous.

This species is hardy to cold and is adaptable to zones 8 through 11 in areas subject to wet freezes in winter but 7 through 11 in drier ones. Its most important cultural requirements are sun and a soil with unimpeded drainage. There is hardly a more picturesque palm. Old clustering individuals are stunningly attractive even as specimens surrounded by space and, from a distance, look like small silvery washingtonias. This denizen of the semiarid plains fits into any setting as long as it is sunny. It is hard to overpraise this palm. The species is not known to have been grown indoors and is probably a bad candidate for doing so. PLATES 894–896.

Trithrinax schizophylla is indigenous to southeastern Bolivia, western Paraguay, southwestern Brazil, and northern Argentina, where it grows along rivers and streams in the dry, lowland subtropical thorn forests but always where it can find underground moisture. The epithet is from two Greek words which translate as "divided" and "leaf."

This one is found mostly as a clustering species but occasionally produces a single trunk. Individual stems grow to 20 feet high in habitat and are usually free of leaf bases, fibers, and spines except near their summits. The leaves are beautiful because of their color and the width of their segments; they are silvery yet glaucous light green, and thin and divided nearly to the petiole. They are borne on 2-foot-long petioles that show them off well because of the thin, airy looking segments.

The palm is adaptable to zones 9b through 11 and marginal in 9a. Its drought tolerance is on a par with the other two species, but it seems more adapted to partial shade than they are. The palm luxuriates if given regular and adequate moisture (David Witt, pers. comm.). PLATES 897 & 898.

VEILLONIA is a monotypic genus of pinnate-leaved, monoecious palm. The genus name honors Jean-Marie Veillon, a botanist in New Caledonia. The epithet is Latin for "white" and refers to the bloom on the crownshaft and inflorescences. PLATES 899–902.

Veillonia alba is endemic to New Caledonia, where it grows in rain forest from sea level to 2000 feet. It is solitary trunked, the stems growing to maximum heights in habitat of 50 feet. They are 6 inches in diameter and are light tan to light gray or almost white in the older parts of the stem but green in the youngest parts; there is a white waxy coating on the younger parts and widely spaced, deeply indented darker brown rings of leaf base scars on all but the oldest parts. The loosely formed crownshaft is bulging at its base, 4 feet tall, and waxy white but overlain, especially at its top, with a reddish brown feltlike tomentum. The leaf crown is sparse but full and rounded, and the leaves are large in comparison to the height and width of the trunk. They are 10 feet long, including the 2-foot-long petiole. The thick, heavy leaflets are 4 feet long and almost 3 inches wide at their midpoint and are linear-lanceolate, long tipped, and bright to deep green above and beneath. The much-branched, ropelike inflorescences are pinkish coral when new and covered with white waxy scales when in flower, giving a distinctly glaucous rosy hue. The ovoid fruits are reddish to greenish brown when mature and, as they grow, the inflorescence changes from a glaucous white to a grayish green infructescence.

There is hardly a more colorful and attractive palm species. It is like a gigantic candy cane. It is still rare in cultivation and is reportedly slow growing. It needs regular and copious water, a fast-draining soil that is not alkaline, partial shade in hot climates, and a tropical or nearly tropical climate. It reportedly does well in cool but frostless Mediterranean climes if given enough water.

VEITCHIA is a genus of eight pinnate-leaved, monoecious palms from rain forest of the South Pacific islands. These are without doubt among the tallest, most beautiful palms in the world and are an emblem of their homeland and all its exotic connotations.

The moderately tall to quite tall trunks are gray or tan in their older parts and beautifully ringed in all but the oldest parts. The exquisite deep green crownshafts are often silvery hued or almost gray-brown because of hairs or scales. These attractive columns reside beneath sparse but elegantly handsome leaf crowns of large pinnate leaves. The greenish white inflorescences grow from beneath the crownshaft, the much-branched, large panicles consisting of thick, waxy flowering branches that bear both male and female blossoms. The large clusters of fruits are orange to red.

All the species are intolerant of cold and adaptable only to zones 10b and 11. Some individuals survive in favorable microclimates of 10a, but they grow more slowly there and are overall less robust. The genus name honors James Veitch, a 19th-century British nurseryman. PLATES 903–911.

Veitchia arecina is indigenous to the Vanuatu islands, where it grows in mountainous rain forest from sea level to 1000 feet. Common names are Montgomery palm, in honor of Robert H. Montgomery, the driving force behind Fairchild Tropical Garden and donor of the land for the Montgomery Botanical Center, both in Miami, Florida; and sunshine palm. The epithet is Latin for "little areca" and suggests that Hermann Wendland saw a resemblance to the genus *Areca* when he bestowed the name in 1868. John L. Dowe reports that the species has become rare and endangered in habitat due to harvesting of the palm's growing point by European resort restaurateurs.

The trunk can attain a height of 80 feet in habitat but has, above its expanded base, a maximum diameter of only 1 foot or less and is almost white in its older parts. The beautiful, slightly bulging silvery light green crownshaft can be almost 5 feet tall but seems almost irrelevant in older palms because of the great beauty of the leaves. They are slightly ascending and slightly arching, borne on short petioles, and are 6 to 12 feet long with many deep green, 3-foot-long half-pendent leaflets growing from the rachis in one plane; they fall from the tree as they die and it is unusual to find an individual with live fronds that descend beneath the horizontal. The 3-foot-long inflorescences usually form a white ring beneath the crownshaft that, from a distance, looks like a little starburst of white blossoms. The fruits are bright red and hang in 4-foot-long clusters.

This incredibly beautiful species is slightly susceptible to lethal yellowing disease. It is adaptable to a range of soils, from acidic to calcareous. It must have constant, abundant moisture. It thrives in partial shade when young but needs the full tropical sun when older. Because its trunk is slender and its leaves become detached in strong winds, this palm usually remains standing in hurricanes and usually survives. It is fast growing after it starts to form a trunk. This is the only *Veitchia* species that can be grown in southern coastal California (Geoff Stein, pers. comm.).

Not many palm species look good planted anywhere, but this one does. It is difficult to find words to describe its beauty as a canopy-scape, especially in groups of three or more individuals of varying heights; its silhouette is simply astonishing. Although it can be grown indoors, this palm grows large quickly and needs an extraordinary amount of light. PLATE 903.

Veitchia filifera occurs naturally on two islands of Vanuatu, where it grows in mountainous rain forest at elevations of near sea level to 2200 feet. It is almost extinct. The epithet is Latin for "thread-bearing," a reference to the hairs on the crownshaft.

This palm is half the stature of *V. arecina*, and its crownshaft is an unusual brownish green or tan because of the covering of short brownish black hairs. Its trunk is also tan or light brown and is hardly more than 8 inches in diameter even in mature individuals. The leaves are borne on 8-inch-long petioles and are 6 to 7 feet long with many deep green linear-elliptic, 2-foot-long leaflets that are jagged on their apices and slightly pendent with age. This palm is not as fussy about moisture requirements as are the other species and is adaptable to various soils. It thrives in partial shade as well as full sun, even when older. This one is perfection itself and is suitable for almost any site in a smaller garden.

Veitchia joannis occurs naturally in the Fiji Islands, where it grows in mountainous rain forest from elevations near sea level to 2000 feet. The only common name seems to be the somewhat trivial joannis palm. The epithet honors John Gould Veitch, a plant explorer and son of nurseryman James H. Veitch.

This species is the tallest one in the genus. The nearly white trunks attain a height of 110 feet in habitat and are usually 12 inches but never more than 16 inches in diameter. The 10-foot-long leaves on 1-foot-long petioles carry 3-foot-long deep green, limp, and pendent leaflets. The beautiful red fruits are conical and 2 inches long.

This species has the same cultural requirements as the others in the genus, but is probably the fastest-growing species if given adequate moisture and a decent soil. It may be more cold tolerant than the rest, but it is certainly not tolerant of frost.

It is among the few rivals of the coconut palm for absolute beauty and grace. It is immediately recognizable from the other *Veitchia* species by its great height and full crown of leaves with pendent leaflets. There is no more beautiful silhouette or canopy-scape. It could not last too long indoors even if given optimum cultural conditions as it grows fast and tall. PLATES 904 & 905.

Veitchia metiti is a rare and endangered species from two islands of Vanuatu, where it grows in mountainous rain forest from sea level to 3000 feet elevation. The epithet is a corruption of the aboriginal name. The species was named and described by Odoardo Beccari in 1920 but lost to scientists for the next 76 years until rediscovered on the islands of Vanua Lava and Uréparapara by Sam Chanel, John L. Dowe, Jenny White, and Scott Zona.

This is one of the smaller species, growing to 40 feet overall in habitat. The white trunks are 6 inches in diameter, and the slender 3-foot crownshafts are light silvery green. The leaves are 8 to 10 feet long on 2-foot unusually long petioles. The limp, narrow, dark green leaflets grow from the rachis in groups of two or three and are 2 to 3 feet long. The ellipsoid fruits are red and 1.5 inches long.

Because of its relatively long petioles, thin leaflets, and elegantly slender trunks, this species is the personification of grace and is almost diaphanous. It is in cultivation only in tropical botanical gardens. Not much is known of its requirements other than its intolerance of frost; it probably is suited to various soils and full sun.

Veitchia simulans is endemic to the Fijian island of Taveuni, where it grows in mountainous rain forest from 1200 to 3000 feet elevation. It is under threat of extinction because of logging (Zona and Fuller 1999). The epithet is Latin for "similar to."

This medium palm attains an overall height of 40 feet. The tan or gray trunk is no more than 6 inches in diameter with closely set darker rings. The slender crownshaft is nonbulging, a deep, almost blackish green, and 18 inches tall. The 5- to 6-foot-long leaves are horizontally spreading and slightly but beautifully arching, with evenly spaced pairs of 2-foot-long, glossy deep green, and pendent leaflets. The fruits are ovoid, orange or red when mature, and 1 inch long.

This species is as beautiful in a smaller way as either *V. arecina* or *V. joannis*. It is intolerant of frost and drought and needs a humus-laden noncalcareous soil, but thrives in partial shade to sun at all ages.

Veitchia spiralis is endemic to the Vanuatu islands, where it grows in lowland rain forest and is now near ex-

tinction. The epithet is Latin for "spiraling," a reference to the arrangement of the fibers in the fruits.

The gray trunks grow to 50 feet high and are 8 inches in diameter. The crownshaft is 3 feet tall, tapering, and silvery green with darker hues at its apex. The leaves are 8 feet long on 6-inch-long petioles. The medium green leaflets are 2 feet long and 3 inches wide at their bases; they taper to a point or are squared off and jagged at their apices and are almost as pendent as those of *V. joannis*. The orange fruits are rounded and 1 inch in diameter.

This outstandingly beautiful palm is similar to the larger *V. joannis* and makes a beautiful canopy-scape. It requires a frost-free, warm, and moist climate but is adaptable to a range of soils that includes slightly acidic to calcareous. It needs full sun when past its juvenile stage. PLATES 906–909.

Veitchia vitiensis is endemic to the Fiji Islands, where it grows in mountainous rain forest from sea level to 3800 feet.

The gray to tan trunks of this medium species grow to 50 feet in habitat and are less than 1 foot in diameter except at their bases. The medium to dark green crownshaft is 18 inches tall and sits beneath 8- to 9-foot-long leaves that are usually beautifully and strongly arched (almost recurving) from their midpoint on. The leaflets are unusually widely spaced for the genus, medium to deep green, narrow and pointed at their bases but expanded to a width of 3 inches at their apices, which are squared off and shallowly and irregularly jagged; they are stiff and grow from the rachis at a slight angle which gives a shallow V shape to the leaf. The yellow to orange fruits are subglobose and small, 0.5 inch in diameter.

This palm has an elegant beauty when young and is as impressive as any when older. Its leaf crown is globular and is comparable to *Actinorhytis* and *Carpoxylon* species as a canopy-scape. It is among the most beautiful palms. PLATE 910.

Veitchia winin is indigenous to the Vanuatu islands, where it grows in mountainous rain forest from sea level to 1700 feet elevation. It is under pressure and becoming vulnerable because of expanding agriculture and logging (Dowe and Cabalion 1996). The epithet is one of the aboriginal names for the palm in Vanuatu.

The palm is similar to *V. arecina* but generally has a straighter and shorter trunk (to 50 feet) that is gray or tan and 1 foot or less in diameter and has a stiffer overall aspect. It thrives on acidic as well as calcareous soils and is more drought tolerant than most other species. It is, however, no more frost tolerant and needs a site in full sun. PLATE 911.

VERSCHAFFELTIA is a monotypic genus of solitary-trunked, pinnate-leaved, monoecious spiny palm in the Seychelles Islands. The genus name is a Latinized form of the Belgian surname "Verschaffelt" and honors a 19th-century nurseryman. The epithet is Latin for "splendid." PLATES 912–914.

Verschaffeltia splendida grows on the steep slopes of mountainous rain forest at elevations of 1000 to 2000 feet. The use of its stems has made it vulnerable. Some growers and nursery owners have coined monikers for this wonderful palm, such as splendid stilt palm, but the best one is probably Seychelles stilt palm.

The trunk can reach 80 feet high when old but is never more than 1 foot in diameter. It is covered in its younger parts with rings of downward-pointing 3-inch-long black spines, which are the remains of the leaf bases; shorter black spines on the petiole and rachis tend to slough off with age The bottom of the trunk is invariably a narrow cone of stilt roots that may be 6 feet tall; the species is exceptional in that these aerial or prop roots are not spiny. The leaf crown usually has 12 or more light to deep green leaves, which, because of their gentle arching, give a rounded aspect, although they do not usually fall beneath the horizontal. Each leaf is 6 to 8 feet long on a 2-foot-long petiole and in younger palms is obovate with jaggedly toothed margins but in older specimens is distinctly oblong. The blade is undivided when new except at its apex, and this is the main reason the species is splendid; in older palms mechanical factors invariably tear the leaves into segments of varying widths and numbers. The much-branched inflorescences grow from the midst of the leaf crown and are 6 feet long with unisexual blossoms, becoming pendent when the clusters of 1-inch-wide round, brown fruits mature.

The species is intolerant of drought and hot, dry winds and is adaptable to only zone 11; it is marginal in 10b, although gorgeous specimens exist in warm, protected microclimates of that zone. The palm is not fast growing and needs a fertile, humus-laden, fast-draining soil and constant moisture. It relishes partial shade when young but readily adapts to full sun when older except in the hottest climates; it is almost impossible to maintain in tropical desert regions because of the winds rather than the temperatures or great amount of sunlight.

This is among the world's most beautiful palm species. Its large leaves, even when segmented by wind, are indescribably lovely, and its overall form is perfect. It looks nice as a specimen plant, even with only one individual, but is simply stunning in groups of three individuals of varying heights and age. It seems to cry out for an intimate site where its beauty can be contemplated up close, but its ultimate size prevents such placement; when young, however, it is perfection seen up close. This enchanting species is easy to grow indoors when young. As it grows older, it wants such a large space and such good light that it usually becomes undesirable.

VOANIOALA is a rare and endangered monotypic genus of pinnate-leaved, monoecious palm. The genus name is the aboriginal name for the palm, which translates as "forest coconut." John Dransfield bestowed the epithet in 1992 to honor Jean Gerard, one of the discoverers of the palm in habitat.

Voanioala gerardii is endemic to a small mountainous rain forest on the Masoala Peninsula in northeastern Madagascar, where it grows at an elevation of 1200 feet. The trees are still cut down for the edible growing point. In 1995, fewer than ten individuals existed; six years later, only three wild specimens remain.

The trunk grows to a maximum height in habitat of 60 feet with a diameter of 1 foot and is light to dark tan with prominent indented rings of leaf base scars. The leaf crown is less than semicircular as the great 15-foot-long leaves are stiff and ascending. They are borne on massive 5-foot-long, heavy false petioles, which are actually the extended leaf bases. The dark green leathery leaflets are 5 feet long, stiff, and regularly spaced along the felt-covered rachis from which they grow in a single flat plane. The inflorescences are 5 feet long and grow erect from the leaf crown but are pendent with the 3-inch-long football-shaped reddish brown fruits whose fiber-covered seeds resemble miniature coconuts.

This palm looks like a stiff, massive coconut tree. The seeds are sold worldwide at premium prices and, while this practice probably assures that the species does not disappear from the face of the earth, it is very sad that conservation measures could not have been implemented in Madagascar in time to assure its continuation there. The palm is reportedly slow growing, so it won't be long before there will be no mature trees to see.

WALLICHIA is a genus of six or seven mostly small clustering as well as solitary-trunked, pinnate-leaved, and monoecious palms in India, Nepal, Myanmar, southern China, and Thailand. The genus is related to and similar to *Arenga* and *Caryota*. All three genera have monocarpic stems in which flowering commences from the leaf axils or nodes (rings) near the top of the stem, and moves downward on the trunk; the stem dies after all the inflorescences have produced fruit. The branched, spidery inflorescences of *Wallichia* are composed of all male or all female flowers, but both types of inflorescence are found on the same plant.

The small round, purplish or reddish fruits contain corrosive oxalic acid crystals that are characteristic of *Arenga* and *Caryota*. All three genera have unusually shaped leaflets.

Most *Wallichia* species occur in the undergrowth of wet forests in the mountains from sea level to 6500 feet in elevation. None of the species are hardy to cold, but many can withstand freezing or slightly lower temperatures, or recover nicely therefrom.

The widely used common name for the genus is the not very descriptive Wallich palm. The genus name honors Nathaniel Wallich, a 19th-century superintendent of the botanical gardens in Calcutta, India. PLATES 915 & 916.

Wallichia caryotoides is indigenous to India in the Himalaya mountains of the state of Assam and adjacent Myanmar, where it occurs in the undergrowth of valley hillsides in wet forest at elevations of 2000 to 4000 feet. The epithet is formed from the genus name *Caryota* and the Greek word "similar to" and is apt except that this *Wallichia* species runs the gamut of leaflet form for the entire fishtail genus.

It is a clustering species whose stems are mostly hidden underground, resulting in a 10-foot-square mass of 4-foot-long petioles springing from the ground and carrying 8-foot-long leaves. Widely spaced leaflets grow from the 7-foot-long beautifully arching rachis at slightly different angles. Each stiff leaflet is 1 foot long and wedge shaped with oblique apices, oblong or triangular overall. All the leaflets have lobes that are variously and usually jaggedly toothed, and leaflet color is deep green above and lighter green beneath. The inflorescences are 3 or 4 feet long and produce pendent clusters of 1-inch-long ovoid, purple fruits.

The palm wants a rich, well-drained soil, nearly constant moisture, and partial shade or at least protection from the midday sun in hot climates. It is hardy to cold, and temperatures of freezing or slightly below seem to not faze it. This attractive little thing is useful as a contrast in masses of other foliage, palms or otherwise, but does not look good as an isolated specimen surrounded by space.

Wallichia densiflora is an undergrowth palm in wet mountain valleys of the Himalayas in the Indian state of Assam, Nepal, and adjacent Myanmar at elevations between 2000 and 4000 feet. The epithet is from Latin words meaning "densely" and "flowered."

This palm is similar in overall appearance and dimensions to *W. caryotoides* but has more uniform leaflets. The leaves are 10 feet long with gracefully arching rachises. The equidistant 18- to 24-inch-long leaflets are 3 inches wide and are more numerous and more uniformly shaped than are those of the above species. Each leaflet is narrowly ovate to broadly lanceolate, irregularly toothed, slightly undulate on its margins, and long tipped; the leaflets of the terminal pair are usually united into an obovoid with a deep notch apically. Leaflet color is bright silky green above and satiny silver with hints of green beneath.

This palm is more attractive than is *W. caryotoides* but has the same culture requirements and the same landscaping uses. It has big satiny leaves, and the 12-foot tall clumps are reminiscent of robust *Alpinia* clumps.

Wallichia disticha occurs naturally in the Himalaya mountain range of northeastern India and Bhutan, Bangladesh, Myanmar, and into northwestern Thailand, where it grows in wet valley forests at elevations of 2000 to 4000 feet. The epithet is Latin for "distichous" and alludes to the arrangement of the leaves: on opposite sides of the trunk in a single plane. This arrangement gives the palm, from one profile, the look of a ladder, and makes the species the most unusual in the genus and among the most unusual palms in any genus. It is also the largest species in the genus.

This usually solitary-trunked palm occasionally occurs as a sparsely clustering individual. It grows to a maximum height of 30 feet overall, and the trunk of a mature palm is 1 foot in diameter and covered in all but its oldest parts in a tight, flat mat of dark brown or black fibers with a few lighter, looser striations arching between the persistent woody leaf bases. The leaf crown, if such it can be called, is extended, as in several *Caryota* species; in mature plants, leaves grow along half or more of the length of the trunk, while in younger plants leaves usually grow along the entire length. The leaf petiole is 2 or 3 feet long and holds an 8- to 10-foot-long blade whose rachis is stiffly ascending and arching only near its apex. The stiff, linear leaflets grow in clusters from the rachis at several angles to give the leaf a plumose effect. Each leaflet is 8 inches long, with slightly wavy margins that bear one or more shallow lobes, and with an obliquely cut, jagged apex; it is medium to dark green above and grayish green to silvery green beneath.

The species is not as hardy to cold as the previous two and is adaptable only to zones 10 and 11. It is not fussy about soil type, although it prefers one that is not too alkaline and it needs regular and adequate moisture. It grows in partial shade but prefers full sun, except in hot climates. It grows moderately fast, especially after its juvenile stage, but hardly lives more than 20 or 25 years.

This odd beauty is only good as a specimen plant, sited where its most unusual leaf arrangement can be appreciated. Like the solitary-trunked species of *Caryota* and *Arenga*, this palm takes four years to complete flowering, after which the plant dies. This attribute is the main reason the palm is not more widely planted. PLATES 915 & 916.

Wallichia siamensis is endemic to Thailand, where it grows in mountainous rain forest at elevations of 1500 to 3800 feet. It is similar in general form and dimensions to *W. caryotoides* and *W. densiflora*. Its leaves are, however, even more attractive because of their color. The leaflets are a deep, satiny green above and a grayish or silvery and satiny, almost shimmering color beneath with no hint of green. This trait creates an incredibly lovely effect when a breeze touches the leaves. The palm is not hardy to cold and needs protection from the hot sun. It is also less forgiving of poor soil than the others and needs constant moisture.

WASHINGTONIA is a genus of two large palmate-leaved, monoecious palms in southwestern United States and northwestern Mexico. The species are common in cultivation, especially in the United States, southern Europe, and the Middle East, and they have hybridized in growers' lots to the point that young palms for sale, especially in the United States, are as likely hybrid crosses as they are "pure" species. The good thing about this situation is that hybrids with a preponderance of graceful attributes from *W. robusta* may approach the cold hardiness of *W. filifera*. The genus name honors the first U.S. president, George Washington. FRONTISPIECE, PLATES 917–921.

Washingtonia filifera is indigenous to California, western Arizona, and northeastern Baja California, where it grows along streams and arroyos and near natural springs. Common names are California fan palm, desert fan palm, petticoat palm, and, in England, cotton palm. The epithet is Latin for "thread-bearing" and alludes to the whitish, thin, curling fibers on the leaves.

Mature trunks grow to 60 feet and are 3 to 4 feet in diameter with swollen bases. They are gray and often narrowly fissured in their older parts but brown or even reddish brown elsewhere. Unless trimmed, the trunks have a skirt of dead leaves beneath the crown of living leaves and, in nature, this skirt sometimes covers the entire trunk, which characteristic has led to the vernacular name of petticoat palm. The yellowish green to silvery or grayish green leaves are 6 to 8 feet wide, are greater than hemispherical, and are borne on 6-foot-long petioles which, in all but seedling plants, have sharp teeth along their margins. The segments usually extend more than halfway to the petiole, are pendulous at their apices in older plants, and are accompanied by curling, whitish threads between each segment. The inflorescences grow from the leaf crown and extend well beyond it. The whitish unisexual blossoms produce clusters of dark brown or black fruits that cause the infructescence to hang well below the canopy.

The species is hardy to cold and is, in dry climates, safe in zones 7 through 11. The trees are, like almost every other plant, much more tender to cold when young and, although they are usually unscathed by temperatures below 20°F when mature, may be severely damaged or even killed by the same temperatures when in the seedling stage, especially in wet climates. Henderson et al. 1995 cite an article by J. Cornett in *Madroño* (1987) that claims survival of a temperature of −11°F; if so, this temperature must have been short lived and one should note that Henderson states "survival" and does not mention damage. The species does much better in Mediterranean climates than humid tropical ones.

The palm is drought tolerant for short periods but looks better and grows faster with regular and adequate irrigation. It needs full sun from youth to old age and becomes etiolated without it. This species thrives especially in calcareous and alkaline soils as long as they are free draining.

The trunks of older palms are not attractive up close, and the trees look better as avenue borders or canopy-scapes where their wonderful crown silhouettes accent the horizon. Specimen groups of individuals of varying heights are stunningly attractive and tropical looking. This is not a good choice for indoor cultivation as it needs much light and grows so large so fast. PLATES 917 & 918.

Washingtonia robusta is indigenous to the southern half of the Baja California peninsula and to a small area in the Mexican state of Sonora. It, like the above species, grows near streams, in arroyos, and at natural springs in the desert. Common names are Mexican fan palm and thread palm. The epithet is Latin for "robust."

This species differs from *W. filifera* in having taller (to 90 feet in old individuals) and thinner trunks, fewer hairlike fibers on the leaves and leaf sheaths, and deeper green leaves in a tighter, more compact crown. While it is not an invariable diagnostic feature, a reddish brown area is often apparent on the bottom of the leaves of *W. robusta* near the juncture of blade and petiole (the colored area is more obvious in younger plants than in older ones); this patch is always lacking in *W. filifera*. The petioles of *W. robusta* are shorter and, in younger individuals, are reddish brown, especially near the base of the petiole, and always bear reddish brown spines, even when young. The older parts of the trunk are gray, and the newer parts are clothed in deep chestnut red or brown leaf bases, which in cultivation are often laboriously cut away to reveal the almost smooth and usually reddish younger trunk. The leaves are always bright or deep green. The inflorescences, flowers, and fruits of the two species are similar as well.

Washingtonia robusta is decidedly more tender to cold than is *W. filifera* and is safe only in zones 9b through 11. It is usually damaged by temperatures in the low 20s (F), although it has been known to survive the low teens (F) in dry climates where freezing temperatures are short lived and not accompanied by precipitation. The species is as tolerant of calcareous soils as is *W. filifera* and seems to need only a well-drained medium, although it grows faster and looks better with a decent soil. Like the California fan palm, it also needs full sun at all ages.

Mature palms are among the most elegant, graceful subtropical landscape subjects; their thin and extremely tall forms are ineluctably arresting in the landscape. This species is by far the most commonly planted palm in southern California, far southern Texas, and Phoenix and Tucson in Arizona. *Washingtonia robusta* has the same limitations for indoor growing as does *W. filifera*, although it is now often used in large atriums and other enclosures. PLATES 919–921.

WELFIA is a genus of one, possibly two, pinnate-leaved, monoecious palms in Central and South America. The inflorescences grow from beneath the leaf crown and are composed of massive 3-foot-long, single, thick, ropelike orange branches bearing both male and female flowers. The genus name is a Latinized form of the German surname "Welf" and honors a medieval family of economic importance in Europe. PLATE 922.

Welfia regia occurs naturally in northeastern Honduras, eastern Nicaragua, Costa Rica, Panama, northwestern and western Colombia, and into northern Ecuador, where it grows in mountainous rain forest from sea level to an elevation of 5280 feet. The epithet is Latin for "regal," an apt appellation.

The solitary gray trunk grows to 60 feet in habitat but is 6 inches in diameter, making for an elegantly slender silhouette. The 12- to 18-foot-long leaves on short, almost nonexistent petioles are erect but arching near their apices, seldom lying beneath the horizontal on the tree. The 2- to 3-foot-long evenly spaced, dark green, lanceolate leaflets grow in a single plane from the rachis, which is twisted from its midpoint to its apex. The new leaves are a beautiful cherry to deep red that lasts for a week.

This species is rare in cultivation. It is difficult to overwater in a well-draining soil, which should also be humus laden and slightly acidic. It thrives when young in partial shade but appreciates sun when older. It does not tolerate frost but should do well in cool but frostless Mediterranean climates if provided with enough moisture. This is among the most beautiful canopy-scapes and, when young, is handsome in any situation other than a single specimen surrounded by space.

WENDLANDIELLA is a monotypic genus of small pinnate-leaved, dioecious palm in South America. The genus name honors Hermann Wendland, a 19th-century Ger-

man botanist and gardener. The epithet is Latin for "graceful." PLATE 923.

Wendlandiella gracilis is indigenous to eastern Peru and extreme northwestern Brazil and Bolivia, where it occurs in the undergrowth of rain forest. It is mostly a clustering species, but some individuals form solitary trunks. The little green trunks are dainty and grow to 3 or 4 feet with a girth of less than 0.5 inch; they look like grass stems. The short, pinnate leaves have four to six leaflets, and most individuals look, from any distance, as though they are palmate, similar to a *Rhapis* species; some individuals have undivided leaves that are deeply bifid at the apex. This variation of leaf form corresponds to geographical distribution (Henderson et al. 1995) and has led to the erection of three varieties: *Wendlandiella gracilis* var. *gracilis* has separate but irregularly spaced leaflets; *Wendlandiella gracilis* var. *polyclada* has two leaflets; and *Wendlandiella gracilis* var. *simplicifrons* has the undivided and deeply bifid leaf. Leaf color is medium to dark green and the blade is indistinctly ribbed. The inflorescences grow from beneath the tiny leaf crown, and the female plants produce tiny ovoid red fruits.

The palm is not hardy to cold and is safe without protection only in zones 10b and 11, but it is small enough to be easily protected. It requires constant moisture in a well-draining, rich, and humus-laden soil and does not tolerate full sun. It is rare in cultivation and is certainly not a spectacular commodity: it looks like a dwarf bamboo. This small palm is endearing, however, and is perfect as a groundcover for shady and intimate sites. PLATE 923.

WETTINIA is a genus of 21 mostly solitary-trunked, stilt-rooted, pinnate-leaved, monoecious palms in South America. It is related to and has many similarities to *Socratea*. These species exhibit an interesting flowering process: inflorescences emerge from brown- or orange-hooded, leathery spathes resembling those of an aroid; the inflorescences are ropelike, grow in a circular pattern around one or more nodes (trunk rings) beneath the crownshaft, and bear either all male or all female blossoms that are thick, fleshy, and white. The middle and largest inflorescence is either male or female, but the up to 15 lateral inflorescences are usually male and are progressively smaller the farther they are from the center. The fruits are densely packed into large, sausagelike tomentose clusters that are usually twisted to some extent.

None of these species are frost tolerant, although many of them, because of their elevated natural habitats, relish cool climates. All are true water lovers but also need a fast-draining, humus-laden, slightly acidic soil. They grow equally well in partial shade and full sun but need protection from midday sun in the hottest climates. Not many of these species are in cultivation, which is a pity as they are sumptuously beautiful.

The trunks of all species are used in construction in South America because of the hard, durable wood. The genus is named "after King Frederick August of Saxony, of the house of Wettin" (Henderson et al. 1995). PLATES 924 & 925.

Wettinia augusta is indigenous to south central Colombia, Peru east of the Andes, and west central Bolivia, where it grows in mountainous rain forest to 2500 feet. The epithet is Latin for "noble" or "majestic."

The trunks of this sparsely clustering species usually grow to 15 feet but may reach 40 feet and are never more than 8 or 9 inches in diameter; they grow atop a small cone of stilt roots. The leaves are 5 feet long with evenly spaced 1-foot-long, deep green, linear, jagged-ended leaflets that are limp and pendent. The inflorescences bear white flowers and white tight clusters of fruits that are densely covered with white hairs.

This lovely species has ethereally thin trunks and, in most individuals, tiers of leaf crowns. It makes an excellent specimen and canopy-scape.

Wettinia fascicularis is indigenous to the Andes Mountains of northern Ecuador, where it grows in rain forest at elevations from 3500 to 6000 feet. It is threatened with extinction because of the clearing of the rain forest. The epithet is Latin for "fascicled" and refers to the deeply segmented leaflets, which seem to grow in bundles.

This beautiful species is solitary trunked, the stems reaching heights of 50 feet but diameters of barely more than 6 inches. The smooth, glaucous olive or bluish green crownshaft is 3 or more feet tall and slightly swollen at its base. The leaves are 6 to 8 feet long on petioles that are long for this genus. The olive green to deep green leaflets grow in all planes around the rachis and are split into as many as 12 segments, each segment a linear wedge with a jagged apex; the visual result is a leaf as plumose as that of the foxtail palm.

Wettinia kalbreyeri occurs naturally in montane rain forest on the slopes of the western Andes in Colombia and Ecuador, where it is found at elevations from 2000 to 6500 feet. The epithet is a Latinized form of the surname "Kalbreyer" and honors a 20th-century German palm collector in South America.

This solitary-trunked species attains a height of 50 or more feet with a trunk diameter of 6 to 8 inches. The crownshafts are 3 feet tall, deep green, and slightly bulging at their bases. The leaves are 6 feet long and plumose because the dark green leaflets grow from several angles around the rachis. The leaflets are split to the base into

two or more segments, each of which is linear, 18 inches long, and jagged on its apex.

Wettinia maynensis is indigenous to the foothills of the eastern Andes in Peru through central Ecuador and into southernmost Colombia, where it grows in rain forest from elevations of 800 to 5200 feet. The epithet is Latin for "of Maynas," a region in Peru.

The stems of this solitary-trunked species attain heights of 40 feet but are never more than 6 inches in diameter and are supported by a 3-foot-tall cone of spiny stilt roots. The light to medium green or even bluish crownshaft is only as wide as the trunk, 2 feet tall, and gently tapering to its apex. The leaf crown is sparse with usually six or seven leaves, but this characteristic emphasizes the beauty of the leaves. They are borne on short petioles, are 6 to 8 feet long and softly hairy, and have regularly and closely spaced, pendent leaflets, each of which is 18 inches long, ovoid-linear, and with an oblique, jagged apex. PLATE 924.

Wettinia praemorsa is indigenous to northeastern and central Colombia and northwestern Venezuela, where it grows in mountainous rain forest and cloud forests from 1300 to 8000 feet elevation. The epithet is Latin for "jagged" and alludes to the ends of the leaflets.

This palm is usually found as a clustering species. The stems grow to 50 feet but are often half that height and are never more than 6 inches in diameter; they sit atop 3-foot-tall cones of stilt roots and are crowned by 3-foot-tall silvery green cylindrical crownshafts that have a slight bulge at their bases. The leaf crown never has more than six large leaves, which are arranged to give an X shape to the crown. The leaves are 7 to 8 feet long with many widely spaced, 2-foot-long, irregularly lanceolate, deep green, soft and pendent leaflets with obliquely cut, slightly jagged tips. The leaflets usually grow in the same plane from the rachis, but many individuals have leaflets that are split lengthwise with each segment of the leaflet growing in a different plane, which then gives the leaf a plumose effect.

This is one of the handsomest species in the genus, its tiers of X-shaped leaf crowns and silhouettes creating an almost unbelievably beautiful effect. It is more than a pity that this palm does not like hot climates.

Wettinia quinaria occurs naturally in western Colombia and northwestern Ecuador, where it grows in rain forest from sea level to an elevation of 3000 feet.

This is a mostly clustering species. The trunks can grow as tall as 50 feet but are more often half that height, above a mass of stilt roots 3 to 4 feet tall, and beneath an almost completely cylindrical and barely bulging, grayish green, 5- to 6-foot-tall crownshaft. The leaf crown has four to six leaves, which, because of their disposition create an appearance, as Henderson et al. (1995) put it, "like an X when seen from a distance"; the arrangement also resembles a turning windmill. Each leaf is 8 feet long, steeply ascending, with an unarching rachis, and is borne on a short petiole. The deep green, regularly spaced leaflets are 2 feet long, limp, and pendulous, giving the leaf blade an almost curtainlike appearance.

This is arguably the most beautiful species because of the great leaves and the tiers of leaf crowns that create a veritably breathtaking tableau; there is nothing quite like this look. PLATE 925.

WODYETIA is a monotypic genus of solitary-trunked, pinnate-leaved, monoecious palm. The species was unknown to botanists until the early 1980s. It is now in great demand because of its extraordinary beauty, fast growth, and adaptability.

The genus name is a Latinized form of the surname "Wodyeti" and honors an aboriginal Australian who was the last man of his tribe to have knowledge of the flora and fauna of the region. The epithet is Latin for "twice divided" and refers to the arrangement of the fibers in the fruits. PLATE 926.

Wodyetia bifurcata is endemic to a remote area of the Cape York Peninsula in the Melville Range of Queensland, where it grows in monsoonal and rocky scrubland on sandy soils at elevations to 1200 feet. The common name of foxtail palm alludes to the plumose leaves. The species is endangered in its restricted native habitat because of the heretofore rampant collection of its seeds for ornamental horticulture. It is now protected in Cape Melville National Park, but rangers must still be on guard for illegal poaching of seeds and plants.

The trunks attain 50 feet of height in habitat. They are columnar, light gray to nearly white with widely spaced, prominent darker rings in their younger parts, and often slightly swollen near the middle of the stem. The smooth crownshaft is 3 feet tall in mature specimens, light to bluish green, the same diameter as the trunk at its base, and tapering from base to top. The leaves are borne on short petioles and are from 8 to 10 feet long with many medium to dark green leaflets growing from different angles around the rachis, the visual result being one of the most plumelike leaves in the family. Each leaflet is either apically cleft into two or more linear segments or lobed, the apical pair usually united. The much-branched inflorescences grow from beneath the crownshaft and hold small yellowish green flowers of both sexes. The 2-inch-long fruits are ovoid and deep orange to red when ripe.

The foxtail palm can endure drought but grows slowly and looks stunted and usually chlorotic. Its deep root system taps underground moisture. It is slow growing in shade but wonderfully fast in full sun. While it survives in calcareous soils, it needs a slightly acidic medium that is freely draining. The palm is not hardy to cold but usually survives short periods at 28°F unscathed.

The palm is similar to royal palm (*Roystonea regia*) but not as massive. It is among the best species for creating the "royal look" when planted in lines along an avenue or other promenades, and, as a canopy-scape, is nearly unrivaled. It resembles the Queensland black palm, *Normanbya,* but is heavier, more massive looking, easier to come by, and faster growing; it is the poor man's *Normanbya.* It is easily grown indoors if given enough light and space.

ZOMBIA is a monotypic genus of spiny, palmate-leaved, monoecious clustering palm from the West Indies. The genus name is from the Haitian Creole name for the palm, *latanier zombi,* which literally means "ghost palm." The only common name seems to be zombie palm. The epithet is Latin for "of the Antilles." PLATES 927–929.

Zombia antillarum is endemic to Hispaniola, where it grows on dry hills at low elevations. It is endangered because of habitat destruction.

The clumps are usually dense with spiny trunks to 10 feet high and, with time, 10 feet wide. The stems are covered except in their oldest parts with the beautifully intricate woven fibrous remains of the leaf sheaths and closely set rings of spiny, 2- to 4-inch-long light or dark brown downward-pointing needlelike projections. The leaves are borne on 2-foot-long petioles and the blade is a 3-foot-wide semicircle of narrow, lanceolate segments that are dull green above and silvery green beneath. The inflorescences grow from amidst the leaves and are 18 inches long; they bear small, white bisexual flowers that produce globular, white or greenish white 1-inch-wide fruits.

The zombie palm is drought tolerant but looks better and grows faster, although it could never be called fast growing, with average and regular moisture. It is not cold tolerant and is adapted only to zones 10 and 11. It prefers full sun but grows in partial shade but not as fast. It requires a free-draining soil and tolerates salt.

This palm is exceptionally beautiful in a site where its almost unique stems can be seen and, since its spininess is confined to the stems themselves, it can be used in intimate or close-up situations. Its natural tendency is to form dense clumps that obscure the trunks, resulting in a large mound of foliage in which not only the trunks but also the shape of the leaves are obscured. Thus, some judicious pruning out of the stems reveals not only the wondrous woven fibers and their spiny projections but also the ghostly white fruits in season. It is possible indoors but would need much light and good air circulation.

The Pronunciation of Scientific Names

The pronunciation transcriptions listed here are guides based on how English speakers in the United States pronounce the names. European, South African, and Australian readers may balk at some of the formulae. Uppercase letters indicate the primary stress syllable of a word. The ´ mark indicates the syllable that receives the secondary stress. In all cases, only one syllable is to be pronounced between each hyphen. Vowels and diphthongs are to be rendered thus:

a   is short as in the word *cat* or even shorter when at the end of a word
e   is short as in the word *elf*
i   is short as in the word *in*
o   is long as in the word *open*
u   is short as in the word *up*
g   is hard as in the word *get*
ow is to be pronounced as the "ou" in *ouch* and not as the "ow" in *show*
th is to be pronounced as the "th" in *thing* and not as the "th" in *the*

Alternative pronunciations illustrate the dictum that there is no one and only correct way to pronounce scientific names. This fact is commonly exhibited in specific epithets that end in "ata" or "ana." For example, *baileyana* is pronounced bay-lee-YAHN-a or bay-lee-AN-a; it is completely a matter of preference.

ACANTHOPHOENIX a-kanth´-o-FEE-nix
  A. rubra ROOB-ra
ACOELORRAPHE a-see´-lo-RAI-fee
  A. wrightii RYT-ee-eye
ACROCOMIA ak-ro-KO-mee-a
  A. aculeata a-kyoo´-lee-AHT-a
  A. hassleri HAS-l'r-eye

ACTINOKENTIA ak-tin´-o-KENT-ee-a
  A. divaricata di-var´-i-KAHT-a, di-var´-i-KAIT-a
ACTINORHYTIS ak-tin´-o-RYT-iss
  A. calapparia kal-a-PAHR-ee-a
  A. poamau po-ah-MAH-oo
ADONIDIA ad-o-NID-ee-a
  A. merrillii mer-RIL-lee-eye
AIPHANES EYE-fa-neez, ah-EE-fa-neez
  A. aculeata a-kyoo´-lee-AHT-a
  A. eggersii EG-g'r-zee-eye
  A. erinacea er-i-NAI-cee-a
  A. gelatinosa je-lat´-i-NO-sa
  A. grandis GRAN-dis
  A. hirsuta hir-SOO-ta
  A. lindeniana lin-den´-ee-AHN-a
  A. linearis lin-ee-AR-iss
  A. macroloba mak-ro-LO-ba
  A. minima MIN-i-ma
  A. ulei OOL-ee-eye
ALLAGOPTERA al´-la-GAHP-t'-ra
  A. arenaria ar-e-NAHR-ee-a
  A. brevicalyx brev-i-KAI-lix
  A. campestris kam-PES-tris
  A. leucocalyx lyoo-ko-KAI-lix
ALLOSCHMIDIA al´-lo-SHMID-ee-a
  A. glabrata gla-BRAH-ta
ALSMITHIA al-SMITH-ee-a
  A. longipes LAHN-ji-peez
AMMANDRA am-MAN-dra
  A. decasperma dek-ah-SPURM-a
APHANDRA a-FAN-dra
  A. natalia na-TAHL-aa-a
ARCHONTOPHOENIX ahr-kont´-o-FEE-nix
  A. alexandrae a-lek-ZAN-dree
  A. cunninghamiana kun´-ning-ham-ee-AHN-a
  A. maxima MAX-i-ma

[*ARCHONTOPHOENIX*]
- *A. myolensis* my-o-LEN-sis
- *A. purpurea* poor-POOR-ee-a
- *A. tuckeri* TUK-'-ry

ARECA a-REEK-a, AR-ee-ka
- *A. caliso* ka-LIS-o
- *A. catechu* KAT-e-kyoo, KAT-e-choo
- *A. concinna* kahn-SIN-na
- *A. guppyana* gup-pee-AHN-a
- *A. hutchinsoniana* huch'-in-so-nee-AHN-a
- *A. ipot* EE-paht
- *A. latiloba* lat-i-LO-ba
- *A. macrocalyx* mak-ro-KAI-lix
- *A. macrocarpa* mak-ro-KAHRP-a
- *A. mammillata* mam-mi-LAHT-a
- *A. minuta* mi-NOOT-a
- *A. multifida* mul-TIF-i-da
- *A. triandra* try-AN-dra
- *A. tunku* TOON-koo
- *A. vestiaria* ves-tee-AHR-ee-a
- *A. whitfordii* whit-FORD-ee-eye

ARENGA a-RENG-a
- *A. australasica* aw-stra-LAI-zi-ka
- *A. brevipes* BREV-i-peez
- *A. caudata* kaw-DAHT-a
- *A. engleri* ENG-l'r-eye
- *A. hastata* has-TAHT-a
- *A. hookeriana* hook-'-ree-AHN-a
- *A. listeri* LIS-t'-ry
- *A. micrantha* my-KRANTH-a
- *A. microcarpa* myk-ro-KAHRP-a
- *A. obtusifolia* ahb-toos'-i-FO-lee-a
- *A. pinnata* pin-NAHT-a, pin-NAIT-ta
- *A. porphyrocarpa* por-fy'-ro-KAHRP-a
- *A. retroflorescens* ret'-ro-flo-RES-senz
- *A. tremula* TREM-yoo-la
- *A. undulatifolia* un'-dyoo-lat-i-FO-lee-a
- *A. westerhoutii* wes-t'r-HOWT-ee-eye
- *A. wightii* WYT-ee-eye

ASTEROGYNE ass-te-RAH-ji-nee, ass'-te-ro-JY-nee
- *A. guianensis* gee-a-NEN-sis
- *A. martiana* mahr-tee-AHN-a
- *A. ramosa* ra-MO-sa
- *A. spicata* spi-KAHT-a, spy-KAIT-a
- *A. yaracuyense* yah-rahk'-oo-YEN-see

ASTROCARYUM ass-tro-KAHR-ee-um
- *A. acaule* a-KAW-lee
- *A. aculeatissimum* a-kyoo'-lee-a-TIS-si-mum
- *A. aculeatum* a-kyool'-ee-AHT-um
- *A. alatum* a-LAHT-um
- *A. chambira* chahm-BEE-rah

- *A. jauari* zhow-AHR-ee
- *A. mexicanum* mex-i-KAHN-um
- *A. murumuru* moo'-roo-MOO-roo
- *A. standleyanum* stand'-lee-AHN-um
- *A. vulgare* vul-GAHR-ee

ATTALEA at-TAL-ee-a, at-ta-LAI-a
- *A. allenii* al-LEN-ee-eye
- *A. amygdalina* a-mig'-da-LEEN-a, a-mig'-da-LYN-a
- *A. butyracea* byoo-te-RAI-see-a
- *A. cohune* ko-HOO-nee
- *A. colenda* ko-LEN-da
- *A. crassispatha* kras-si-SPAITH-a
- *A. cuatrecasana* kwah'-tre-ka-SAHN-a
- *A. funifera* fyoo-NIF-'-ra
- *A. humilis* HYOO-mi-lis
- *A. insignis* in-SIG-nis
- *A. maripa* mah-REE-pa
- *A. phalerata* fal-e-RAHT-a
- *A. speciosa* spee-see-O-sa

BACTRIS BAK-tris
- *B. brongniartii* bron-YAHRT-ee-eye
- *B. coloradonis* ko-lo-RAHD-o-nis
- *B. concinna* kahn-SIN-na
- *B. gasipaes* GAS-i-peez
- *B. glandulosa* glan-dyoo-LO-sa
- *B. grayumi* GRAI-y'-my
- *B. guineensis* gin-ee-EN-sis
- *B. hondurensis* hahn-doo-REN-sis
- *B. longiseta* lahn-ji-SEET-a
- *B. major* MAI-jor
- *B. mexicana* mex-i-KAHN-a
- *B. militaris* mil-i-TAR-iss
- *B. plumeriana* ploo-mer'-ee-AHN-a
- *B. riparia* ri-PAHR-ee-a
- *B. setosa* se-TOE-sa

BALAKA ba-LAHK-a
- *B. longirostris* lahn-jee-RAHS-tris
- *B. macrocarpa* mak-ro-KAHRP-a
- *B. microcarpa* myk-ro-KAHRP-a
- *B. seemannii* sai-MAHN-nee-eye

BARCELLA bahr-SEL-la
- *B. odora* o-DOR-a

BASSELINIA bas-se-LIN-ee-a
- *B. deplanchei* de-PLAN-shee-eye
- *B. favieri* fah-vee-AI-ree
- *B. gracilis* GRAS-i-lis
- *B. humboldtiana* hum-bolt'-tee-AHN-a
- *B. iterata* it-'-RAHT-a
- *B. pancheri* pahn-SHER-ee

B. porphyrea por-FEER-ee-a
B. sordida sor-DEE-da
B. tomentosa toe-men-TOE-sa
B. velutina ve-LOOT-i-na
B. vestita ves-TEET-a
BECCARIOPHOENIX be-kahr´-ee-o-FEE-nix
B. madagascariensis mad´-a-gas-kar´-ee-EN-sis
BENTINCKIA ben-TINK-ee-a
B. condapanna kahn-da-PAN-na
B. nicobarica nik-o-BAHR-i-ka
BISMARCKIA bis-MARK-ee-a
B. nobilis NO-bi-lis
BORASSODENDRON bo-ras´-so-DEN-drahn
B. borneense bor-nee-ENS-ee
B. machadonis mah-cha-DO-nis
BORASSUS bo-RAS-sus
B. aethiopium ee-thee-O-pee-um
B. flabellifer fla-BEL-li-f´r
B. sambiranensis sahm-beer´-a-NEN-sis
BRAHEA BRAH-ya, bra-HAI-a, BRAI-ya
B. aculeata a-kyoo-lee-AHT-a
B. armata ahr-MAHT-a
B. brandegeei bran-DEJ-ee-eye
B. decumbens dee-KUM-benz
B. dulcis DOOL-sis
B. edulis ED-yoo-lis
B. moorei MOR-ee-eye
B. nitida ni-TID-a
B. pimo PEE-mo
B. sarukhanii sah-rook-HAHN-ee-eye
BRASSIOPHOENIX bras´-see-o-FEE-nix
B. drymophoeoides dry-mahf´-lee-OI-deez
B. schumannii shoo-MAHN-ee-eye
BRONGNIARTIKENTIA bron-yahrt´-i-KENT-ee-a
B. lanuginosa la-noo´-ji-NO-sa
B. vaginata vaj-i-NAHT-a
BURRETIOKENTIA bur-ret´-ee-o-KENT-ee-a
B. dumasii doo-MAHS-ee-eye
B. grandiflora gran-di-FLO-ra
B. hapala HAP-a-la, ha-PAH-la
B. koghiensis kog-hee-EN-sis
B. vieillardii vee-ai-YAHR-dee-eye
BUTIA BYOO-tee-a, boo-TEE-a
B. archeri ARCH-´-ry
B. campicola kamp-i-KO-la
B. capitata kap-i-TAHT-a
B. eriospatha er´-ee-o-SPAITH-a
B. microspadix myk-ro-SPAI-dix
B. paraguayensis pah´-ra-gwah-YEN-sis
B. purpurascens pur-pyoo-RAS-senz
B. yatay yah-TAH-ee

CALAMUS KAL-a-mus
C. arborescens ahr-bo-RES-senz
C. aruensis ah-roo-EN-sis
C. australis aw-STRAL-iss
C. caesius SEE-see-us
C. caryotoides kar-ee-o-TOI-deez
C. castaneus kas-TAN-ee-us
C. diepenhorstii dee-pen-HORS-tee-eye
C. hollrungii hol-ROONG-ee-eye
C. javensis jah-VEN-sis
C. manan mah-NAHN
C. moti MO-tee
C. muelleri MYOO-l´-ry
C. ornatus or-NAHT-us
C. scipionum skip-ee-O-num
C. vanuatuensis vah´-noo-ah-too-EN-sis
C. vitiensis vit-ee-EN-sis
C. warburgii wahr-BURG-ee-eye
CALOSPATHA kal-o-SPAITH-a
C. confusa kahn-FYOO-sa
C. scortechinii skor-te-KEN-ee-eye
CALYPTROCALYX ka-lip´-tro-KAI-lix
C. albertisianus al-ber´-tis-YAHN-us
C. arfakiensis ahr-fahk´-ee-EN-sis
C. doxanthus dahx-ANTH-us
C. elegans EL-e-ganz
C. flabellatus fla-bel-LAHT-us
C. forbesii FORBZ-ee-eye
C. hollrungii hol-ROONG-ee-eye
C. micholitzii meek-o-LITZ-ee-eye
C. pachystachys pak-ee-STAI-kis
C. pauciflorus paw-see-FLO-rus
C. polyphyllus pah-lee-FYL-lus
C. spicatus spi-KAHT-us, spy-KAIT-us
CALYPTROGYNE ka-lip-TRAH-ji-nee,
ka-lip´-tro-JY-nee
C. ghiesbreghtiana gees-brekh´-tee-AHN-a
CALYPTRONOMA ka-lip´-tro-NO-ma
C. occidentalis or-ee-ENT-a-lis
C. plumeriana ploo-mer´-ee-AHN-a
C. rivalis RIV-a-lis
CAMPECARPUS kamp-ee-KAHR-pus
C. fulcitus ful-SIT-us
CARPENTARIA kahr-pen-TAHR-ee-a
C. acuminata a-kyoo´-mi-NAHT-a
CARPOXYLON kahr-PAHX-i-lahn
C. macrospermum mak-ro-SPER-mum
CARYOTA kar-ee-O-ta
C. cumingii koo-MIN-jee-eye
C. gigas GY-gas
C. maxima MAX-i-ma

[*CARYOTA*]
    C. mitis MIT-iss, MYT-iss
    C. no NO
    C. ochlandra ok-LAN-dra
    C. ophiopellis o´-fee-o-PEL-lis
    C. rumphiana rump-fee-AHN-a
    C. urens YOO-renz
    C. zebrina ze-BREE-na
CERATOLOBUS ser-a-TAHL-o-bus,
    se-rat´-o-LO-bus
CEROXYLON se-RAHX-i-lahn
    C. alpinum al-PYN-um
    C. amazonicum am-a-ZAHN-i-kum
    C. ceriferum se-RIF-e-rum
    C. echinulatum ee-kyn´-yoo-LAHT-um
    C. parvifrons PAHRV-i-frahnz
    C. parvum (PAHR-vum)
    C. quindiuense keen-dee´-oo-EN-see
    C. ventricosum ven-tri-KOS-um
    C. vogelianum vo-g'l-ee-AHN-um
CHAMAEDOREA kai-mee-DOR-ee-a
    C. adscendens ad-SEN-denz
    C. amabilis a-MAHB-i-lis
    C. angustisecta an-gus´-ti-SEK-ta
    C. arenbergiana ar´-en-burg-ee-AHN-a
    C. brachypoda brak-ee-PO-da
    C. cataractarum kat-a-RAK-ta-rum,
    kat´-a-rak-TAHR-um
    C. costaricana kos-ta-REEK-a-na,
    kost-a-ree-KAHN-a
    C. deckeriana dek´-e-ree-AHN-a
    C. elegans EL-e-ganz
    C. ernesti-augustii er-nest´-ee-aw-GUS-tee-eye
    C. fragrans FRAI-granz
    C. geonomiformis jee´-o-no-mi-FOR-mis
    C. glaucifolia glaw-si-FO-lee-a
    C. graminifolia gra-min´-i-FO-lee-a
    C. hooperiana hoop-'r-ee-AHN-a
    C. klotzschiana klaht-shee-AHN-a
    C. linearis lin-ee-AR-iss
    C. metallica me-TAL-lik-a
    C. microspadix myk-ro-SPAI-dix
    C. nubium NOO-bee-um
    C. oblongata ahb´-lahn-GAHT-a
    C. pinnatifrons pin-NAT-i-frahnz
    C. plumosa ploo-MO-sa
    C. pochutlensis po-choot-LEN-sis
    C. pumila PYOO-mi-la
    C. radicalis rad-i-KAL-iss
    C. seifrizii sy-FRITZ-ee-eye, see-FRITZ-ee-eye
    C. stolonifera sto-lo-NIF-e-ra

    C. stricta STRIK-ta
    C. sullivanorium sul´-li-van-ee-OR-ee-um
    C. tenella te-NEL-la
    C. tepejilote te-pai´-hee-LO-tee
    C. tuerckheimii toork-HY-mee-eye
    C. warscewiczii wahr-sai-WIK-zee-eye
    C. woodsoniana wood-son´-ee-AHN-a
CHAMAEROPS ka-MEE-rahps
    C. humilis HYOO-mi-lis
    C. humilis **var.** *cerifera* se-RIF-e-ra
    C. humilis **var.** *elatior* ee-LAI-tee-or
CHAMBEYRONIA shahm-bai-RO-nee-a
    C. lepidota lep-i-DOAT-a
    C. macrocarpa mak-ro-KAHRP-a
CHELYOCARPUS kee´-lee-o-KAHR-pus
    C. chuco CHOO-ko
    C. dianeurus dy-a-NYOO-rus
    C. repens REP-enz
    C. ulei OOL-ee-eye
CHUNIOPHOENIX choo´-nee-o-FEE-nix
    C. hainanensis hy-nah-NEN-sis
    C. nana NAN-a
CLINOSPERMA klyn-o-SPURM-a
    C. bracteale brak-tee-AH-lee
CLINOSTIGMA klyn-o-STIG-ma
    C. exorrhizum ex-o-RY-zum
    C. gronophyllum gro-no-FYL-lum
    C. harlandii hahr-LAN-dee-eye
    C. ponapensis po-na-PEN-sis
    C. samoense sah-mo-EN-see
    C. savoryanum sa-vor´-ee-AHN-um
COCCOTHRINAX kok´-ko-TRY-nax
    C. argentata ahr-jen-TAHT-a
    C. argentea ahr-JEN-tee-a
    C. "azul" ah-ZOOL
    C. barbadensis bahr-ba-DEN-sis
    C. crinita kri-NEET-a
    C. ekmanii ek-MAHN-ee-eye
    C. gracilis GRAS-i-lis
    C. gundlachii goont-LAHK-ee-eye
    C. hiorami hee-o-RAH-mee
    C. miraguama meer-a-GWAHM-a
    C. pauciramosa paw´-see-ra-MO-sa
    C. salvatoris sal-va-TOR-iss
    C. spissa SPIS-sa
COCOS KO-kos
    C. nucifera noo-SIF-e-ra
COLPOTHRINAX kol´-po-TRY-nax
    C. aphanopetala af´-a-no-PET-a-la
    C. cookii KOOK-ee-eye
    C. wrightii RYT-ee-eye

COPERNICIA ko-p'r-NIS-ee-a, ko-p'r-NEES-ee-a
- *C. alba* AL-ba, AHL-ba
- *C. baileyana* bay-lee-YAHN-a
- *C. berteroana* ber´-te-ro-AHN-a
- *C. brittonorum* brit´-toe-NO-rum
- *C. cowellii* kow-WEL-ee-eye
- *C. ekmanii* ek-MAHN-ee-eye
- *C. fallaensis* fah´-yah-EN-sis
- *C. gigas* GY-gas
- *C. glabrescens* gla-BRES-senz
- *C. hospita* HAHS-pi-ta
- *C. macroglossa* mak-ro-GLAHS-sa
- *C. prunifera* proo-NIF-e-ra
- *C. rigida* RIJ-i-da
- *C. tectorum* tek-TOR-um

CORYPHA ko-RYF-a, ko-REEF-a
- *C. umbraculifera* um-brak´-yoo-LIF-e-ra
- *C. utan* OO-tahn

CRYOSOPHILA KRY-o-sahf-i-la
- *C. cookii* KOOK-ee-eye
- *C. grayumii* GRAI-y'm-ee-eye
- *C. guagara* gwah-GAHR-a
- *C. kalbreyeri* kahl-BRY-´-ry
- *C. macrocarpa* mak-ro-KAHRP-a
- *C. nana* NAN-a
- *C. stauracantha* stow-ra-KANTH-a
- *C. warscewiczii* wahrs-se-WIK-zee-eye
- *C. williamsii* WIL-y'm-zee-eye

CYPHOKENTIA syf-o-KENT-ee-a
- *C. macrostachya* ma-kro-STAIK-ee-a

CYPHOPHOENIX syf-o-FEE-nix
- *C. elegans* EL-e-ganz
- *C. nucele* noo-SEL-ee

CYPHOSPERMA sy-fo-SPURM-a
- *C. balansae* ba-LAHN-see
- *C. tanga* TAHN-ga
- *C. trichospadix* try-ko-SPAI-dix
- *C. voutmelense* voot-me-LEN-see

CYRTOSTACHYS seer-toe-STAIK-iss
- *C. elegans* EL-e-ganz
- *C. glauca* GLOW-ka, GLAW-ka
- *C. kisu* KEE-soo
- *C. ledermanniana* laid´-d'r-mahn-ee-AHN-a
- *C. loriae* LOR-ee-eye
- *C. peekeliana* peek´-´-lee-AHN-a
- *C. renda* REN-da

DAEMONOROPS dee-MO-no-rahps
- *D. angustifolia* an-gus´-ti-FO-lee-a
- *D. calicarpa* kal-i-KAHRP-a
- *D. curranii* kur-RAN-ee-eye

- *D. jenkinsiana* jen-kin´-see-AHN-a
- *D. melanochaetes* mel´-a-no-KEE-teez
- *D. mollis* MAHL-lis

DECKENIA de-KEN-ee-a
- *D. nobilis* NO-bi-lis

DESMONCUS des-MAHNK-us
- *D. giganteus* jy-GANT-ee-us
- *D. orthacanthos* ort-a-KANTH-us
- *D. polyacanthos* pah-lee-a-KANTH-us

DICTYOCARYUM dik´-tee-o-KAHR-ee-um
- *D. fuscum* FOOS-kum
- *D. lamarckianum* la-mark´-ee-AHN-um
- *D. ptarianum* tahr-ee-AHN-um

DICTYOSPERMA dik´-tee-o-SPURM-a
- *D. album* AL-bum

DRYMOPHLOEUS dry-MAHF-lee-us, dry-mo-FLEE-us, dry-mo-FLO-yus
- *D. hentyi* HENT-ee-eye
- *D. litigiosus* li-tij´-ee-O-sus
- *D. oliviformis* o-liv´-i-FOR-mis
- *D. pachycladus* pak-ee-KLAD-us
- *D. subdistichus* sub-DIS-ti-kus

DYPSIS DIP-sis
- *D. ambositrae* ahm-bo-SIT-ree
- *D. baronii* ba-RO-nee-eye
- *D. bejofo* bai-JO-fo
- *D. cabadae* ka-BAH-dee, KAB-a-dee
- *D. catatiana* ka-taht´-ee-AHN-a
- *D. concinna* kahn-SIN-na
- *D. crinita* kri-NEET-a
- *D. decaryi* de-KAHR-ee-eye
- *D. decipiens* de-SIP-ee-enz
- *D. fibrosa* fy-BROS-a
- *D. hovomantsina* ho´-vo-mant-SEE-na
- *D. lanceolata* lan´-see-o-LAHT-a
- *D. lastelliana* las-tel´-ee-AHN-a
- *D. leptocheilos* lep-toe-KY-los
- *D. louvelii* loo-VEL-ee-eye
- *D. lutescens* loo-TES-senz
- *D. madagascariensis* mad´-a-gas-kar´-ee-EN-sis
- *D. madagascariensis* var. *lucubensis* loo-koo-BEN-sis
- *D. malcomberi* mal-KAHM-b'-ry
- *D. mananjarensis* ma-nahn´-ja-REN-sis
- *D. onilahensis* o-nil´-a-HEN-sis
- *D. pembana* pem-BAH-na
- *D. pilulifera* pil-yoo-LIF-e-ra
- *D. pinnatifrons* pin-NAT-i-frahnz
- *D. prestoniana* pres-to´-nee-AHN-a
- *D. procera* pro-SER-a
- *D. pusilla* poo-SIL-la

[*DYPSIS*]
  D. rivularis riv-yoo-LAR-iss
  D. saintelucei saint-LOO-see-eye
  D. sanctaemariae sahnk-tee-MAHR-ee-eye
  D. schatzii SHAHT-zee-eye
  D. tsaravoasira sahr´-a-vo-a-SEER-a
  D. utilis YOO-ti-lis

ELAEIS e-LEE-iss
  E. guineensis gin-ee-EN-sis, gin-ay-EN-sis
  E. oleifera o-lee-IF-´-ra
ELEIODOXA e-lee´-o-DAHX-a
  E. conferta kahn-FER-ta
EREMOSPATHA e-ree´-mo-SPAITH-a,
    er´-e-mo-SPAITH-a
  E. hookeri HOOK-´-ry
  E. macrocarpa mak-ro-KAHRP-a
  E. wendlandiana wend-lan´-dee-AHN-a
EUGEISSONA yoo-jee-SO-na
  E. brachystachys brai-kee-STAI-kis
  E. insignis in-SIG-nis
  E. minor MY-nor
  E. tristis TRIS-tis
  E. utilis YOO-ti-lis
EUTERPE yoo-TURP-ee
  E. edulis ED-yoo-lis
  E. oleracea o-l´-RAI see-a
  E. precatoria prek-a-TOR-ee-a
  E. precatoria **var.** *longivaginata* lahn´-jee-vaj-i-
    NAHT-a

GASTROCOCOS gas-tro-KO-kos
  G. crispa KRIS-pa
GAUSSIA GOWS-see-a
  G. attenuata at-ten´-yoo-AHT-a
  G. maya MAH-ya
  G. princeps PRIN-seps
  G. spirituana spi´-ri-too-AHN-a
GEONOMA jee-o-NO-ma
  G. congesta kahn-JES-ta
  G. cuneata kyoo-nee-AHT-a
  G. densa DEN-sa
  G. deversa dee-VER-sa
  G. epetiolata ee-pee´-tee-o-LAHT-a,
    ee-pee´-tee-o-LAIT-a
  G. interrupta in-te-RUP-ta
  G. laxiflora lax-i-FLOR-a
  G. longevaginata lahn´-jee-vaj-i-NAHT-a
  G. undata un-DHAT-a
GRONOPHYLLUM gro-no-FYL-lum
  G. apricum AP-ri-kum

G. brassii BRASS-ee-eye
G. cariosum kar-ee-O-sum
G. chaunostachys chaw-no-STAIK-iss
G. gibbsianum gib-see-AHN-um
G. ledermannianum lai-d´r-mahn´-ee-AHN-um
G. mayrii MY-ree-eye
G. microcarpum myk-ro-KAHRP-um
G. montanum mahn-TAN-um
G. pinangoides pin-ain-GOI-deez
G. pleurocarpum ploor-o-KAHRP-um
G. ramsayi RAM-zai-eye
GUIHAIA gwee-HY-ya
  G. argyrata ahr-jee-RAIT-a, ahr-jee-RAHT-a
  G. grossefibrosa gros´-s´-fy-BRO-sa
GULUBIA goo-LOO-bee-a
  G. costata kos-TAHT-a
  G. cylindrocarpa si-lin´-dro-KAHRP-a
  G. hombronii hom-BRO-nee-eye
  G. longispatha lahn-jee-SPAITH-a
  G. macrospadix mak-ro-SPAI-dix
  G. microcarpa myk-ro-KAHRP-a
  G. moluccana mo-LUK-ka-na
  G. palauensis pa-lah´-oo-EN-sis
  G. valida VAL-i-da

HEDYSCEPE hed-i-SEEP-ee
  H. canterburyana kant-´r-bur-ee-AHN-a
HETEROSPATHE het´-´-ro-SPAITH-ee
  H. cagayanensis ka-gah´-ya-NEN-sis
  H. delicatula del-i-ka-TOO-la
  H. elata ee-LAHT-a
  H. elmeri EL-m´-ry
  H. glauca GLAW-ka, GLOW-ka
  H. humilis HYOO-mi-lis
  H. macgregori mak-GRAI-go-ry
  H. minor MY-nor
  H. negrosensis neg-ro-SEN-sis
  H. philippinensis fi´-lip-i-NEN-sis
  H. phillipsii FIL-lip-see-eye, fil-LIP-see-eye
  H. salomonensis sal´-o-mah-NEN-sis
  H. sibuyanensis see-boo´-ya-NEN-sis
  H. uniformis yoo-ni-FOR-mis
  H. woodfordiana wood-ford´-ee-AHN-a
HOWEA HOW-ee-a
  H. belmoreana bel-mor´-ee-AHN-a
  H. forsteriana for-ster´-ee-AHN-a
HYDRIASTELE hy-dree-a-STEE-lee,
    hy-dree-ASS-te-lee
  H. beccariana be-kahr´-ee-AHN-a
  H. kasesa ka-SAI-sa
  H. microspadix myk-ro-SPAI-dix

H. rostrata ro-STRAHT-a
H. wendlandiana wend-lan´-dee-AHN-a
HYOPHORBE hy-o-FOR-bee
H. indica IN-di-ka
H. lagenicaulis lag´-e-ni-KAW-lis
H. vaughanii VAWN-ee-eye
H. verschaffeltii ver-sha-FELT-tee-eye
HYOSPATHE hy-o-SPAITH-ee
H. elegans EL-e-ganz
H. macrorachis mak-ro-RAI-kis
HYPHAENE hy-FEE-nee
H. compressa kahm-PRES-sa
H. coriacea kor-ee-AI-see-a
H. dichotoma dy-KAHT-o-ma
H. petersiana peet-'rz-ee-AHN-a
H. thebaica thee-BAI-i-ka

IGUANURA ig-wah-NOOR-a
I. bicornis by-KOR-nis
I. elegans EL-e-ganz
I. geonomiformis jee´-o-no-mi-FOR-mis
I. palmuncula pahl-MUNK-yoo-la
I. polymorpha pah-lee-MORF-a
I. speciosa spee-see-O-sa
I. wallichiana wah-lik´-ee-AHN-a
IRIARTEA ir-ee-AHRT-ee-a
I. deltoidea del-TOI-dee-a
IRIARTELLA ir´-ee-ahr-TEL-la
I. setigera se-TIJ-e-ra
I. stenocarpa sten-o-KAHRP-a
ITAYA ee-TAH-ya
I. amicorum ah-mee-KOR-um

JOHANNESTEIJSMANNIA yo-hahn´-nes-tysh-
    MAHN-nee-a
J. altifrons AL-ti-frahnz
J. lanceolata lan-see-o-LAHT-a
J. magnifica mag-NIF-i-ka
J. perakensis per-a-KEN-sis
JUANIA WHAHN-ee-a
J. australis aw-STRAL-iss
JUBAEA joo-BEE-a
J. chilensis chi-LEN-sis
JUBAEOPSIS joo-bee-AHP-sis
J. caffra KAF-ra

KENTIOPSIS kent-ee-AHP-sis
K. magnifica mag-NIF-i-ka
K. oliviformis o-liv´-i-FOR-mis
K. piersoniorum peer-sahn-ee-OR-um
K. pyriformis py-ri-FOR-mis

KERRIODOXA ker´-ree-o-DOX-a
K. elegans EL-e-ganz
KORTHALSIA kor-TAHL-see-a

LACCOSPADIX lak-ko-SPAI-dix
L. australasica aws-tra-LAI-zi-ka
LACCOSPERMA lak-ko-SPURM-a
LATANIA la-TAN-ee-a
L. loddigesii lo-di-GAI-zee-eye
L. lontaroides lon-ta-ROY-deez
L. verschaffeltii ver-sha-FELT-ee-eye
LAVOIXIA la-VWAH-ya, la-VWAH-zee-ya,
    la-VOIX-ya
L. macrocarpa mak-ro-KAHRP-a
LEMUROPHOENIX lee´-moo-ro-FEE-nix
L. halleuxii ah-YOO-zee-eye, ha-LOOX-ee-eye
LEOPOLDINIA lee´-o-pol-DIN-ee-a
L. major MAI-jor
L. piassaba pee-a-SAH-ba
L. pulchra PUL-kra
LEPIDOCARYUM lep´-i-doe-KAHR-ee-um
L. tenue TEN-yoo-ee
LEPIDORRHACHIS lep´-i-doe-RAI-kis
L. mooreana mor-ee-AHN-a
LICUALA li-KWAH-la
L. beccariana bek-kahr´-ee-AHN-a
L. bidentata by-den-TAHT-a
L. bintulensis bin-too-LEN-sis
L. cabalionii kah´-bahl-YO-nee-eye
L. cordata kor-DAHT-a
L. densiflora dens-i-FLOR-a
L. distans DIS-tanz
L. glabra GLAB-ra
L. grandis GRAN-dis
L. lauterbachii low-t'r-BAHK-hee-eye
L. longipes LAHN-ji-peez
L. mattanensis mat-ta-NEN-sis
L. naumanii now-MAHN-nee-eye
L. olivifera o-li-VIF-e-ra
L. orbicularis or-bik´-yoo-LAR-iss
L. paludosa pa-loo-DOE-sa
L. parviflora pahr-vi-FLO-ra
L. peltata pel-TAHT-a
L. peltata **var.** *sumawongii* soo-ma-WAHNG-ee-eye
L. petiolulata pee´-tee-o-loo-LAHT-a
L. platydactyla plat-ee-DAK-ti-la
L. radula RAD-yoo-la
L. ramsayi RAM-say-eye
L. reptans REP-tanz
L. rumphii ROOM-fee-eye
L. sallehana sahl´-le-HAHN-a

[*LICUALA*]
   L. sarawakensis sahr´-a-wah-KEN-sis
   L. spathellifera spath-e-LIF-´-ra
   L. spinosa spi-NO-sa
   L. triphylla try-FYL-la
   L. valida VAL-i-da
LINOSPADIX lyn-o-SPAI-dix
   L. microcarya myk-ro-KAHR-ee-a
   L. minor MY-nor
   L. monostachya mo-no-STAIK-ee-a
LIVISTONA liv-i-STON-a
   L. alfredii al-FRAI-dee-eye
   L. australis aw-STRAL-iss
   L. benthamii ben-THAM-ee-eye
   L. boninensis bon-i-NEN-sis
   L. carinensis kar-i-NEN-sis
   L. chinensis chi-NEN-sis
   L. decipiens dee-SIP-ee-enz
   L. drudei DROO-dee-eye
   L. eastonii ee-STO-nee-eye
   L. endauensis en-dow-EN-sis
   L. exigua ex-IG-yoo-a
   L. fulva FOOL-va
   L. halongensis hah´-lahn-GEN-sis
   L. humilis HYOO-mi-lis
   L. inermis i-NER-mis
   L. jenkinsiana jenk´-inz-ee-AHN-a
   L. lanuginosa la-noo´-ji-NO-sa
   L. lorophylla lor-o-FYL-la
   L. mariae MAHR-ee-eye
   L. merrillii mer-RIL-lee-eye
   L. muelleri MYOOL-l´-ry
   L. nitida ni-TID-a
   L. rigida RIJ-i-da
   L. robinsoniana rah-bin-so´-nee-AHN-a
   L. rotundifolia ro-tun´-di-FO-lee-a
   L. rotundifolia **var.** *luzonensis* loo-zeh-NEN-sis
   L. saribus SAR-i-bus, sah-REE-bus
   L. tahanensis tah-hah-NEN-sis
   L. victoriae vik-TOR-ee-eye
   L. woodfordii wood-FORD-ee-eye
LODOICEA lo-DOYS-ee-a, lo-doe-ISS-ee-a
   L. maldivica mal-DIV-i-ka
LOXOCOCCUS lahx-o-KAHK-kus
   L. rupicola roop´-i-KO-la
LYTOCARYUM lyt-o-KAHR-ee-um
   L. hoehnei HURN-ee-eye
   L. weddellianum wed-del´-ee-AHN-um

MANICARIA man-i-KAHR-ee-a
   M. saccifera sak-SIF-´-ra

MAROJEJYA mahr-o-JAI-jee-a
   M. darianii dar-ee-AHN-ee-eye
   M. insignis in-SIG-nis
MASOALA mah-so-AH-la
   M. kona KO-na
   M. madagascariensis mad´-a-gas-kar´-ee-EN-sis
MAURITIA maw-RIT-ee-a
   M. carana kahr-a-NAH
   M. flexuosa flex-yoo-O-sa
MAURITIELLA maw-rit´-ee-EL-la
   M. aculeata a-kyoo´-lee-AHT-a
   M. armata ahr-MAHT-a
   M. macroclada mak-ro-KLAD-a
MAXBURRETIA max-bur-RET-ee-a
   M. furtadoana foor-tahd´-o-AHN-a
   M. gracilis GRAS-i-lis
   M. rupicola roop-i-KO-la
MEDEMIA me-DEM-ee-a, me-DEEM-ee-a
   M. argun ahr-GOON
METROXYLON me-TRAHX-i-lahn
   M. amicarum am-i-KAHR-um
   M. sagu SAH-goo
   M. salomonense sal-o-mo-NEN-see
   M. vitiense vit-ee-EN-see
   M. warburgii wahr-BURG-ee-eye
MORATIA mo-RAT-ee-a
   M. cerifera se-RIF-´-ra
MYRIALEPIS mir´-ee-a-LEEP-iss
   M. paradoxa par-a-DAHX-a

NANNORRHOPS NAN-o-rahps
   N. ritchiana rich-ee-AHN-a
NENGA NEN-ga
   N. gajah GAH-ja
   N. macrocarpa mak-ro-KAHRP-a
   N. pumila PYOO-mi-la
   N. pumila **var.** *pachystachya* pak-ee-STAIK-ee-a
NEONICHOLSONIA nee´-o-nik-´-l-SO-nee-a
   N. watsonii waht-SO-nee-eye
NEOVEITCHIA nee-o-VEECH-ee-a
   N. brunnea BROON-nee-a
   N. storckii STORK-ee-eye
NEPHROSPERMA nef-ro-SPURM-a
   N. vanhoutteanum van-hoot´-tee-AHN-um
NORMANBYA nor-MAN-bee-a
   N. normanbyi nor-MAN-bee-eye
NYPA NY-pa, NEEP-a
   N. fruticans FROOT-i-kanz

OENOCARPUS ee-no-KAHRP-us
   O. bacaba bah-ka-BAH

O. bataua bah-TOW-a
O. distichus DIS-ti-kus
O. mapora ma-POR-a
ONCOCALAMUS ahnk´-o-KAL-a-mus
ONCOSPERMA ahnk-o-SPURM-a
O. fasciculatum fa-sik´-yoo-LAHT-um
O. gracilipes gra-SIL-i-peez
O. horridum HAHR-ri-dum
O. platyphyllum plat-ee-FYL-lum
O. tigillarium tij-i-LAHR-ee-um
ORANIA o-RAN-ee-a
O. archboldiana arch-bol´-dee-AHN-a
O. disticha DIS-ti-ka
O. glauca GLAW-ka, GLOW-ka
O. lauterbachiana lowt´-’r-bahk-hee-AHN-a
O. macropetala mak-ro-PET-a-la
O. palindan PAL-in-dahn
O. regalis REE-ga-lis
O. rubiginosa roo-bij´-i-NO-sa
O. sylvicola sil-vi-KO-la
O. trispatha try-SPAITH-a
ORANIOPSIS o-ran´-ee-AHP-sis
O. appendiculata ap-pen-dik´-yoo-LAHT-a

PARAJUBAEA par´-a-joo-BEE-a
P. coccoides kok-KOI-deez
P. sunkha SOON-ka
P. torallyi toe-RAL-lee-eye
PELAGODOXA pel´-a-go-DAHX-a
P. henryana hen-ree-AHN-a
PHOENICOPHORIUM feen´-i-ko-FOR-ee-um
P. borsigianum bor-sig´-ee-AHN-um
PHOENIX FEE-nix
P. acaulis a-KAW-lis
P. andamanensis ahn´-da-ma-NEN-sis
P. caespitosa sees-pi-TOE-sa
P. canariensis ka-nar´-ee-EN-sis
P. dactylifera dak-ti-LIF-e-ra
P. loureiri loo-RAI-ry
P. loureiri **var.** *humilis* HYOO-mi-lis
P. paludosa pa-loo-DOE-sa
P. pusilla poo-SIL-la
P. reclinata rek-li-NAHT-a
P. roebelenii ro-be-LEN-ee-eye
P. rupicola roop-i-KO-la
P. sylvestris sil-VES-tris
P. theophrasti thee-o-FRAS-tee
PHOLIDOCARPUS fo´-li-doe-KAHR-pus,
    fo-lid´-o-KAHRP-us
P. macrocarpus mak-ro-KAHRP-us
P. maiadum mah-YAH-dum

P. mucronatus myook-ro-NAHT-us
PHOLIDOSTACHYS fo´-li-doe-STAI-kis,
    fo-lid´-o-STAI-kis
P. dactyloides dak-ti-LOI-deez
P. pulchra POOL-kra
P. synanthera sin-AN-the-ra
PHYSOKENTIA fy-so-KENT-ee-a
P. dennisii DEN-nis-ee-eye
P. insolita in-so-LEET-a
P. rosea RO-zee-a, ro-ZAI-a
PHYTELEPHAS fy-TEL-e-fas
P. aequatorialis eek´-wa-tor-ee-AL-iss
P. macrocarpa mak-ro-KAHRP-a
P. seemannii sai-MAHN-nee-eye
P. tenuicaulis ten´-yoo-eye-KAW-lis
PIGAFETTA pig-a-FET-ta
P. elata ee-LAHT-a
P. filaris FIL-a-ris, fi-LAR-iss
PINANGA pi-NAING-a, pi-NAHNG-a
P. adangensis ah´-dahn-GEN-sis
P. aristata ar-i-STAHT-a
P. auriculata aw-rik´-yoo-LAHT-a
P. bataanensis ba-tah-NEN-sis
P. bicolana bee-ko-LAHN-a
P. caesia SEES-ee-a
P. capitata kap-i-TAHT-a
P. capitata **var.** *divaricata* di-var´-i-KAHT-a
P. chaiana chy-AHN-a
P. cochinchinensis ko-chin´-chi-NEN-sis
P. copelandii kop-LAN-dee-eye
P. coronata kor-o-NAHT-a
P. curranii KUR-r’n-ee-eye
P. densiflora dens-i-FLOR-a
P. dicksonii dik-SO-nee-eye
P. disticha DIS-ti-ka
P. elmeri EL-m’-ry
P. insignis in-SIG-nis
P. javana ja-VAHN-a
P. maculata mak-yoo-LAHT-a
P. malaiana ma-lai-AHN-a
P. negrosensis neg-ro-SEN-sis
P. patula PAT-yoo-la
P. perakensis per-a-KEN-sis
P. philippinensis fil´-i-pi-NEN-sis
P. pilosa pi-LO-sa
P. polymorpha pah-lee-MORF-a
P. punicea poo-NIS-ee-a
P. rivularis riv-yoo-LAR-iss
P. sclerophylla skler-o-FYL-la
P. scortechinii skor-te-KEEN-ee-eye
P. simplicifrons sim-PLIS-i-frahnz

[*PINANGA*]
  P. speciosa spee-see-O-sa
  P. veitchii VEECH-ee-eye
PLECTOCOMIA plek´-toe-KO-mee-a
  P. elongata ee-lahn-GAHT-a
  P. griffithii GRIF-fith-ee-eye
  P. himalayana him-a-lai-YAHN-a
PLECTOCOMIOPSIS plek´-toe-ko-mee-AHP-
  sis
PODOCOCCUS po-doe-KAHK-kus
  P. barteri BAHR-t'-ry
POGONOTIUM po-go-NO-tee-um
  P. ursinum oor-SY-num
POLYANDROCOCOS pah´-lee-an-dro-KO-kos
  P. caudescens kaw-DES-senz
PRESTOEA pres-TOE-a
  P. acuminata a-kyoo´-mi-NAHT-a
  P. acuminata **var.** *montana* mahn-TAN-a
  P. decurrens dee-KUR-renz
PRITCHARDIA prit-CHAHRD-ee-a
  P. affinis AF-fi-nis
  P. arecina ar-e-SEE-na
  P. beccariana bek-kahr´-ee-AHN-a
  P. hardyi HAHR-dee-eye
  P. hillebrandii hil-l'-BRAN-dee-eye
  P. kaalae kah-AH-lee
  P. lanaiensis la-nah´-ee-EN-sis
  P. lanigera la-NIJ-e-ra
  P. maideniana mai-den´-ee-AHN-a
  P. martii MAHRT-ee-eye
  P. minor MY-nor
  P. mitiaroana mee´-tee-ah-ro-AHN-a
  P. munroi mun-RO-ee
  P. pacifica pa-SIF-i-ka
  P. remota ree-MOT-a
  P. remota **var.** *aylmer-robinsonii* ail-m'r-rah-bin-
    SO-nee-eye
  P. remota **var.** *glabrata* gla-BRAH-ta
  P. remota **var.** *napaliensis* na-pah-lee-EN-sis
  P. schattaueri shat-TOW-'-ry
  P. thurstonii thur-STO-nee-eye,
    thur-STAHN-ee-eye
  P. viscosa vis-KOS-a
  P. waialealeana wy-ah´-lai-ah-lai-AHN-a
  P. woodfordiana wood-ford´-ee-AHN-a
PRITCHARDIOPSIS prit-chahrd´-ee-AHP-sis
  P. jeanneneyi zhahn-ne-NAI-yee
PSEUDOPHOENIX soo-doe-FEE-nix
  P. ekmanii ek-MAHN-ee-eye
  P. lediniana leh-din´-ee-AHN-a
  P. sargentii sahr-JEN-tee-eye

  P. vinifera vi-NIF-e-ra
PTYCHOCOCCUS tyk-o-KAHK-kus
  P. archboldianus arch-bol´-dee-AHN-us
  P. lepidotus lep-i-DOAT-us
  P. paradoxus ee-LAHT-us
PTYCHOSPERMA ty-ko-SPURM-a
  P. burretianum bur-ret´-ee-AHN-um
  P. caryotoides kar´-ee-o-TOI-deez
  P. cuneatum kyoo-nee-AHT-um
  P. elegans EL-e-ganz
  P. furcatum foor-KAHT-um
  P. hosinoi HO-si-noi
  P. lauterbachii low-t'r-BAHK-ee-eye
  P. ledermannianum lai-'d'r-mahn-ee-AHN-um
  P. lineare lin-ee-AHR-ee
  P. macarthurii mak-AHRTH-'-ree-eye
  P. microcarpum myk-ro-KAHRP-um
  P. mooreanum mor-ee-AHN-um
  P. propinquum pro-PINK-wum
  P. salomonense sal-o-mo-NEN-see
  P. sanderianum san-d'r-ee-AHN-um
  P. schefferi SHEF-f'-ry
  P. waitianum wait-ee-AHN-um

RAPHIA RAF-ee-a
  R. australis aw-STRAL-iss
  R. farinifera far-i-NIF-'-ra
  R. hookeri HOOK-'-ry
  R. humilis HYOO-mi-lis
  R. regalis REE-ga-lis
  R. taedigera tee-DIJ-e-ra
  R. vinifera vi-NIF-'-ra
RAVENEA rav-e-NAI-a, ra-VEN-ee-a
  R. glauca GLAW-ka, GLOW-ka
  R. hildebrandtii hil-d'-BRANT-tee-eye
  R. julietiae joo´-lee-ET-ee-eye
  R. lakatra la-KAH-tra
  R. madagascariensis mad´-a-gas-kar´-ee-EN-sis
  R. moorei MOR-ee-eye
  R. musicalis myoo-zi-KAL-iss
  R. rivularis riv-yoo-LAR-iss
  R. robustior ro-BUS-tee-or
  R. sambiranensis sahm-bir´-a-NEN-sis
  R. xerophila ze-RAHF-i-la
REINHARDTIA ryn-HART-tee-a
  R. elegans EL-e-ganz
  R. gracilis GRAS-i-lis
  R. koschnyana kosh-nee-AHN-a
  R. latisecta lat-i-SEK-ta
  R. paiewonskiana py´-a-vons-kee-AHN-a
  R. simplex SIM-plex

RETISPATHA ret-i-SPAITH-a
  R. dumetosa doo-me-TOE-sa
RHAPIDOPHYLLUM rap´-i-doe-FYL-lum
  R. hystrix HISS-trix
RHAPIS RAP-iss
  R. excelsa ek-SEL-sa
  R. humilis HYOO-mi-lis
  R. laosensis lah-o-SEN-sis
  R. multifida mul-TIF-i-da
  R. subtilis SUB-ti-lis
RHOPALOBLASTE rop´-a-lo-BLAS-tee
  R. augusta aw-GUS-ta
  R. brassii BRAS-see-eye
  R. ceramica se-RAHM-i-ka
  R. elegans EL-e-ganz
  R. singaporensis sing-a-por-EN-sis
RHOPALOSTYLIS rop´-a-lo-STY-liss,
  rop-a-LAHS-ti-lis
  R. baueri BOW-´-ry
  R. baueri **var.** *cheesemanii* cheez-MAHN-ee-eye
  R. sapida SAP-i-da
ROSCHERIA ro-SHER-ee-a
  R. melanochaetes mel´-a-no-KEET-eez
ROYSTONEA roy-STON-ee-a
  R. altissima al-TIS-si-ma
  R. borinquena bo-reenk´-AIN-a
  R. dunlapiana dun-lap´-ee-AHN-a
  R. lenis LEN-iss
  R. maisiana mah-ees´-ee-AHN-a
  R. oleracea o-le-RAI-see-a
  R. oleracea **var.** *jenmanii* jen-MAHN-ee-eye
  R. princeps PRIN-seps
  R. regia REE-jee-a
  R. stellata stel-LAHT-a
  R. violacea vee-o-LAI-see-a

SABAL SAI-bahl, SAH-bahl
  S. bermudana ber-MYOO-d'-na,
  ber-myoo-DAHN-a
  S. causiarum kow-see-AHR-um
  S. domingensis doe-meen-GEN-sis
  S. etonia ee-TOE-nee-a
  S. gretheriae GRAI-t'-ree-eye
  S. guatemalensis gwah´-te-mah-LEN-sis
  S. maritima ma-RIT-i-ma
  S. mauritiiformis maw-rit´-tee-eye-FOR-mis
  S. mexicana mex-i-KAHN-a
  S. miamiensis my-am´-ee-EN-sis
  S. minor MY-nor
  S. palmetto pahl-MET-toe
  S. pumos POO-mos

S. rosei RO-zee-eye
S. uresana oo-re-SAHN-a
S. yapa YAH-pa
SALACCA sa-LAHK-ka
  S. affinis AF-fi-nis
  S. dransfieldiana dranz-feel´-dee-AHN-a
  S. flabellata flab-el-LAHT-a
  S. glabrescens gla-BRES-senz
  S. magnifica mag-NIF-i-ka
  S. minuta mi-NOOT-a
  S. multiflora mul-ti-FLOR-a
  S. sarawakensis sahr´-a-wa-KEN-sis
  S. wallichiana wahl-lik´-ee-AHN-a
  S. zalacca za-LAHK-ka
SATAKENTIA saht-a-KENT-ee-a
  S. liukiuensis lee-ook´-ee-oo-EN-sis
SATRANALA saht-ra-NAH-la
  S. decussilvae dek-oo-SIL-vee
SCHIPPIA SHIP-pee-a
  S. concolor KAHN-kul-or
SCLEROSPERMA skler-o-SPURM-a
SERENOA ser-e-NO-a, se-RAI-no-a
  S. repens REP-enz
SIPHOKENTIA sif-o-KENT-ee-a
  S. beguinii be-GWIN-ee-eye
  S. dransfieldii dranz-FEELD-ee-eye
SOCRATEA so-KRAT-ee-a, so-KRAIT-ee-a
  S. exorrhiza ex´-or-RY-za
  S. rostrata ro-STRAHT-a
  S. salazarii sal-a-ZAHR-ee-eye
SOMMIERIA sahm´-mee-ER-ee-a
  S. affinis AF-fi-nis
  S. elegans EL-e-ganz
  S. leucophylla lyoo-ko-FYL-la
SYAGRUS sy-AG-rus
  S. amara a-MAHR-a
  S. botryophora bo-tree-o-FOR-a,
  bo-tree-AHF-o-ra
  S. campylospatha kamp-ee-lo-SPAITH-a
  S. cardenasii KAHR-dai-nahs-y'-ee-eye,
  kahr-dai-NAHS-ee-eye
  S. "cearensis" sai-ah-REN-sis
  S. cocoides ko-KOI-deez
  S. comosa ko-MO-sa
  S. coronata kor-o-NAHT-a
  S. ×costae KAHS-tee
  S. duartei DWAHRT-ee-eye
  S. flexuosa flex-yoo-O-sa
  S. glaucescens glaw-SES-senz
  S. harleyi HAHR-lee-eye
  S. inajai ee-na-ZHAH-ee, ee-na-YAH-ee

[*SYAGRUS*]
  S. macrocarpa mak-ro-KAHRP-a
  S. oleracea o-le-RAI-see-a
  S. orinocensis or´-i-no-SEN-sis
  S. picrophylla pik-ro-FYL-la
  S. pleioclada plai-yo-KLAD-a
  S. pseudococos soo-doe-KO-kos
  S. romanzoffiana ro´-man-zof-ee-AHN-a
  S. ruschiana rush-ee-AHN-a
  S. sancona san-KO-na
  S. schizophylla skits-o-FYL-la
  S. smithii SMITH-ee-eye
  S. stenopetala sten-o-PET-a-la
  S. stratincola strat-in-KO-la
  S. vagans VAI-ganz
SYNECHANTHUS sin-e-KANTH-us
  S. fibrosus fy-BRO-sus
  S. warscewiczianus wahr´-sai-wik-see-AHN-us

TECTIPHIALA tek-tif-YAH-la
  T. ferox FER-ahx
THRINAX TRY-nax
  T. compacta kahm-PAK-ta
  T. ekmaniana ek-MAHN-ee-ahn-a
  T. excelsa ek-SEL-sa
  T. morrisii mor-RIS-ee-eye
  T. parviflora pahr-vi-FLO-ra
  T. radiata rai-dee-AHT-a
  T. rivularis riv-yoo-LAR-iss
TRACHYCARPUS traik-ee-KAHRP-us
  T. fortunei for-TOON-ee-eye
  T. latisectus lat-i-SEK-tus
  T. martianus mahrt-ee-AHN-us
  T. nanus NAN-us
  T. oreophilus or-ee-AHF-i-lus
  T. princeps PRIN-seps
  T. takil TAH-keel
  T. wagnerianus vahg-ner´-ee-AHN-us
TRITHRINAX try-TRY-nax
  T. brasiliensis bra-zil´-ee-EN-sis
  T. campestris kam-PES-tris
  T. schizophylla skits-o-FYL-la

VEILLONIA vai-YO-nee-a
  V. alba AL-ba
VEITCHIA VEECH-ee-a
  V. arecina ar-e-SEE-na, ar-e-KY-na
  V. filifera fi-LIF-e-ra
  V. joannis jo-AN-nis
  V. metiti me-TEE-tee
  V. simulans SIM-yoo-lanz
  V. spiralis spi-RAL-iss, spy-RAL-iss
  V. vitiensis vit-ee-EN-sis
  V. winin WIN-in
VERSCHAFFELTIA ver-sha-FELT-ee-a
  V. splendida splen-DEED-a
VOANIOALA vo-ahn´-ee-o-AH-la
  V. gerardii zhe-RAHR-dee-eye

WALLICHIA wahl-LIK-ee-a, wahl-LICH-ee-a
  W. caryotoides kar´-ee-o-TOI-deez
  W. densiflora dens-i-FLOR-a
  W. disticha DIS-ti-ka
  W. siamensis sy-a-MEN-sis
WASHINGTONIA wahsh-ing-TO-nee-a
  W. filifera fi-LIF-e-ra
  W. robusta ro-BUS-ta
WELFIA WELF-ee-a, VELF-ee-a
  W. regia REE-jee-a, RAI-gee-a
WENDLANDIELLA wend-land´-ee-EL-la
  W. gracilis GRAS-i-lis
  W. gracilis **var.** *polyclada* pah-lee-KLAD-a
  W. gracilis **var.** *simplicifrons* sim-PLIS-i-frahnz
WETTINIA wet-TIN-ee-a
  W. augusta aw-GUS-ta
  W. fascicularis fa-sik´-yoo-LAR-iss
  W. kalbreyeri kahl-BRY´-ry
  W. maynensis my-NEN-sis
  W. praemorsa pree-MORS-a
  W. quinaria kee-NAHR-ee-a
WODYETIA wod-YET-ee-a
  W. bifurcata by-foor-KAHT-a

ZOMBIA ZAHM-bee-a
  Z. antillarum an-TIL-la-rum, an-til-LAHR-um

Landscape Lists

Drought-Tolerant Species

No palm is truly drought tolerant in the sense that most cactus species are, and even those palms growing in the Sahara do so at or near springs or other underground water sources. Furthermore, most palm species occur in tropical rain forest. Despite these disclaimers, a number of species thrive without copious moisture, can survive extended periods of deprivation, and can withstand drying winds.

Acrocomia (some)
Aiphanes eggersii (some)
Aiphanes lindeniana (some)
Aiphanes minima (slight)
Allagoptera species (great)
Arenga pinnata (some)
Arenga westerhoutii (slight)
Bismarckia (much)
Borassus (much)
Brahea aculeata (great)
Brahea armata (much)
Brahea brandegeei (some)
Brahea decumbens (much)
Brahea dulcis (some)
Butia archeri (much)
Butia campicola (much)
Butia capitata (some)
Butia eriospatha (some)
Butia paraguayensis (much)
Butia purpurascens (much)
Butia yatay (some)
Chamaerops humilis (much)
Coccothrinax (much)
Cocos (much once established)
Colpothrinax (some)
Copernicia alba (some)

Copernicia baileyana (some)
Copernicia berteroana (some)
Copernicia brittonorum (some)
Copernicia cowellii (some)
Copernicia ekmanii (much)
Copernicia fallaensis (some)
Copernicia gigas (some)
Copernicia glabrescens (some)
Copernicia hospita (some)
Copernicia macroglossa (some)
Copernicia prunifera (some)
Copernicia rigida (some)
Copernicia tectorum (some)
Corypha umbraculifera (some once established)
Dypsis decaryi (much)
Dypsis decipiens (much)
Dypsis madagascariensis (slight)
Gastrococos (some)
Gaussia (much)
Guihaia (some)
Hyphaene (much)
Jubaea (much once established)
Jubaeopsis (slight)
Latania (some)
Licuala peltata (slight)
Livistona alfredii (some)
Livistona carinensis (some)
Livistona chinensis (some)
Livistona decipiens (some)
Livistona drudei (some)
Livistona eastonii (much)
Livistona fulva (some)
Livistona humilis (much)
Livistona inermis (some)
Livistona lanuginosa (some)
Livistona lorophylla (slight)

Livistona mariae (some)
Livistona muelleri (some)
Livistona nitida (some)
Livistona rigida (some)
Livistona rotundifolia (slight)
Livistona victoriae (much once established)
Maxburretia (some)
Medemia (extreme)
Nannorrhops (very much)
Phoenix acaulis (some)
Phoenix caespitosa (much)
Phoenix canariensis (much once established)
Phoenix dactylifera (much once established)
Phoenix loureiri (slight)
Phoenix pusilla (much once established)
Phoenix reclinata (some)
Phoenix rupicola (slight)
Phoenix sylvestris (much once established)
Phoenix theophrasti (much once established)
Polyandrococos (some once established)
Pseudophoenix (much)
Ravenea hildebrandtii (some)
Ravenea xerophila (much once established)
Rhapis (some, except for *R. laosensis*)
Roystonea borinquena (slight)
Roystonea lenis (some)
Roystonea maisiana (some)
Roystonea violacea (some)
Sabal bermudana (some)
Sabal causiarum (some)
Sabal domingensis (some)
Sabal etonia (much)
Sabal guatemalensis (some)
Sabal maritima (some)
Sabal mauritiiformis (some once established)
Sabal mexicana (much once established)
Sabal miamiensis (much)
Sabal minor (slight)
Sabal palmetto (some)
Sabal pumos (much)
Sabal rosei (much)
Sabal uresana (much)
Sabal yapa (some)
Serenoa (much)
Syagrus campylospatha (much)
Syagrus cardenasii (much)
Syagrus comosa (much)
Syagrus coronata (much)
Syagrus ×costae (some)
Syagrus duartei (much)
Syagrus flexuosa (some)

Syagrus glaucescens (much)
Syagrus harleyi (much)
Syagrus macrocarpa (much)
Syagrus oleracea (slight)
Syagrus pleioclada (much)
Syagrus ruschiana (some)
Syagrus schizophylla (much)
Syagrus stenopetala (slight)
Syagrus vagans (much)
Thrinax compacta (much)
Thrinax ekmaniana (much)
Thrinax excelsa (some)
Thrinax morrisii (much)
Thrinax parviflora (much)
Thrinax radiata (much)
Trachycarpus nanus (some)
Trachycarpus princeps (some)
Trithrinax (much)
Washingtonia filifera (much once established)
Washingtonia robusta (some once established)
Zombia (some)

Water-Loving Species

Most palm species benefit from regular amounts of water, but several have extraordinary water requirements, even when established. Some are even considered aquatics.

Acoelorraphe
Archontophoenix tuckeri
Areca triandra
Areca whitfordii
Arenga microcarpa
Arenga obtusifolia
Astrocaryum murumuru
Bactris militaris
Bactris riparia
Calyptronoma
Chelyocarpus
Copernicia brittonorum
Copernicia gigas
Copernicia macroglossa
Copernicia rigida
Cyrtostachys renda
Dypsis crinita
Dypsis rivularis
Elaeis guineensis
Elaeis oleifera
Eleiodoxa
Eremospatha wendlandiana

Eugeissona tristis
Euterpe
Geonoma interrupta
Gronophyllum ramsayi
Gulubia costata
Heterospathe macgregori
Hydriastele wendlandiana
Laccosperma
Licuala bidentata
Licuala olivifera
Licuala paludosa
Licuala ramsayi
Livistona australis
Livistona benthamii
Livistona decipiens
Manicaria
Marojejya darianii
Mauritia
Mauritiella
Metroxylon sagu
Metroxylon salomonense
Metroxylon vitiense
Metroxylon warburgii
Nypa
Oncocalamus
Oncosperma tigillarium
Orania regalis
Orania trispatha
Phoenix paludosa
Phoenix roebelenii
Pholidocarpus
Phytelephas tenuicaulis
Pigafetta
Ptychosperma lauterbachii
Ptychosperma lineare
Ptychosperma macarthurii
Raphia
Ravenea musicalis
Ravenea rivularis
Rhapidophyllum
Roystonea dunlapiana (saline)
Roystonea princeps
Roystonea regia
Sabal minor
Salacca affinis
Salacca wallichiana
Salacca zalacca
Serenoa
Washingtonia robusta

Fast-Growing Species

Very few palm species are fast growing compared to dicot trees. Some are exceedingly slow. The following list includes those that are faster than the average, assuming they are given optimum growing conditions.

Acanthophoenix (moderately)
Acrocomia (moderately)
Actinorhytis (moderately)
Adonidia (moderately)
Aiphanes aculeata (moderately)
Archontophoenix alexandrae (moderately)
Archontophoenix cunninghamiana (moderately)
Areca catechu (quite)
Areca triandra (moderately)
Arenga listeri (moderately)
Arenga microcarpa (moderately)
Arenga obtusifolia (moderately)
Arenga pinnata (moderately)
Astrocaryum aculeatum (moderately)
Astrocaryum mexicanum (moderately)
Bactris gasipaes (moderately)
Burretiokentia vieillardii (somewhat)
Calamus (moderately)
Calyptronoma rivalis (somewhat)
Carpentaria (quite)
Caryota (quite)
Chambeyronia macrocarpa (somewhat)
Cocos (moderately)
Copernicia alba (somewhat)
Copernicia prunifera (somewhat)
Deckenia (moderately)
Dypsis lutescens (moderately)
Dypsis mananjarensis (somewhat)
Euterpe edulis (moderately)
Euterpe oleracea (moderately)
Gronophyllum ramsayi (somewhat)
Gulubia costata (somewhat)
Heterospathe elata (moderately)
Heterospathe phillipsii (moderately)
Hyophorbe indica (slightly)
Licuala paludosa (slightly)
Licuala peltata (slightly)
Licuala spinosa (slightly)
Livistona benthamii (moderately)
Livistona chinensis (moderately)
Livistona decipiens (moderately to quite)
Livistona drudei (somewhat)
Livistona jenkinsiana (somewhat)
Livistona mariae (somewhat)

Livistona merrillii (moderately)
Livistona nitida (moderately)
Livistona rigida (slightly)
Livistona rotundifolia (somewhat)
Livistona saribus (somewhat)
Livistona woodfordii (slightly)
Metroxylon (quite)
Nypa (moderately)
Oenocarpus (moderately)
Oncosperma (moderately)
Phoenix canariensis (slightly)
Phoenix dactylifera (slightly)
Phoenix reclinata (somewhat)
Phoenix roebelenii (somewhat)
Phoenix rupicola (somewhat)
Phoenix sylvestris (somewhat)
Pholidocarpus (somewhat)
Pigafetta (very)
Prestoea (slightly)
Ptychosperma elegans (somewhat)
Ptychosperma macarthurii (somewhat)
Ptychosperma salomonense (somewhat)
Ravenea rivularis (moderately)
Roystonea oleracea (moderately)
Roystonea princeps (moderately)
Roystonea regia (moderately)
Sabal mauritiiformis (somewhat)
Syagrus amara (moderately)
Syagrus botryophora (very)
Syagrus "cearensis" (slightly)
Syagrus cocoides (somewhat)
Syagrus inajai (somewhat)
Syagrus oleracea (somewhat)
Syagrus pseudococos (slightly)
Syagrus romanzoffiana (very)
Syagrus sancona (quite)
Trachycarpus fortunei (somewhat)
Veitchia (quite)
Washingtonia filifera (moderately)
Washingtonia robusta (quite)
Wodyetia (somewhat)

Unusually Slow-Growing Species

Compared to dicot trees, palms are slow growing. Some are extremely slow growing and these are listed below.

Acrocomia hassleri
Actinokentia
Alloschmidia

Areca multifida
Arenga retroflorescens
Attalea
Basselinia gracilis
Basselinia humboldtiana
Basselinia velutina
Brongniartikentia
Campecarpus
Ceroxylon
Clinosperma
Coccothrinax
Colpothrinax
Copernicia (other than *C. alba* & *C. prunifera*)
Gaussia spirituana
Guihaia
Hedyscepe
Heterospathe elmeri
Howea
Hyphaene
Itaya amicorum
Johannesteijsmannia
Jubaea
Jubaeopsis
Lavoixia
Lepidorrhachis
Licuala
Livistona alfredii
Livistona eastonii
Livistona humilis
Livistona inermis
Livistona muelleri
Lodoicea
Loxococcus
Lytocaryum weddellianum
Masoala
Maxburretia
Medemia
Moratia
Oraniopsis appendiculata
Parajubaea
Phoenix loureiri
Pinanga veitchii
Pritchardia hillebrandii
Pritchardia kaalae
Pritchardia martii
Pritchardiopsis
Pseudophoenix
Ravenea julietiae
Ravenea robustior
Ravenea xerophila
Rhapidophyllum hystrix

Roscheria
Sabal
Syagrus comosa
Syagrus glaucescens
Tectiphiala
Trachycarpus oreophilus
Trithrinax
Voanioala
Zombia

Groundcovering Palms

Short palms that creep by aboveground or underground stems can be used in the landscape as groundcovers. Others are amenable for mass plantings because of their size and form.

Areca minuta
Arenga caudata
Arenga hookeriana
Asterogyne
Brahea decumbens
Calyptrogyne
Chamaedorea adscendens
Chamaedorea brachypoda
Chamaedorea cataractarum
Chamaedorea elegans
Chamaedorea metallica
Chamaedorea nubium
Chamaedorea radicalis
Chamaedorea stolonifera
Daemonorops currani
Guihaia
Lepidocaryum
Licuala sarawakensis
Neonicholsonia
Pinanga disticha
Pinanga pilosa
Pinanga polymorpha
Reinhardtia gracilis
Reinhardtia simplex
Rhapis laosensis
Sabal etonia
Sabal minor
Wendlandiella

Hedge and Screen Palms

Whether practical or aesthetic in their basic function, or sometimes both, hedges and screens require palms that hold their leaves from top to bottom.

Acoelorraphe
Aiphanes eggersii
Aiphanes erinacea
Aiphanes hirsuta
Aiphanes macroloba
Allagoptera
Areca macrocarpa
Areca triandra
Arenga australasica
Arenga caudata
Arenga engleri
Arenga microcarpa
Arenga porphyrocarpa
Arenga tremula
Bactris brongniartii
Bactris coloradonis
Bactris concinna
Bactris gasipaes
Bactris guineensis
Bactris major
Bactris plumeriana
Bactris riparia
Bactris setosa
Brahea decumbens
Calamus arborescens
Calyptrocalyx forbesii
Calyptrocalyx hollrungii
Calyptrocalyx polyphyllus
Caryota mitis
Chamaedorea brachypoda
Chamaedorea cataractarum
Chamaedorea costaricana
Chamaedorea graminifolia
Chamaedorea hooperiana
Chamaedorea microspadix
Chamaedorea pochutlensis
Chamaedorea seifrizii
Chamaerops
Chuniophoenix
Cyrtostachys elegans
Cyrtostachys glauca
Cyrtostachys renda
Daemonorops calicarpa
Daemonorops curranii
Dypsis cabadae

Dypsis lutescens
Eleiodoxa
Eugeissona tristis
Euterpe oleracea
Geonoma interrupta
Hydriastele kasesa
Hydriastele microspadix
Hydriastele rostrata
Licuala rumphii
Licuala sallehana
Licuala spinosa
Mauritiella
Metroxylon sagu
Nannorrhops
Nypa
Oncosperma fasciculatum
Oncosperma horridum
Oncosperma tigillarium
Phoenix caespitosa
Phoenix paludosa
Phoenix reclinata
Phytelephas tenuicaulis
Pinanga adangensis
Pinanga cochinchinensis
Pinanga coronata
Pinanga densiflora
Pinanga dicksonii
Pinanga malaiana
Pinanga perakensis
Pinanga philippinensis
Pinanga polymorpha
Pinanga rivularis
Pinanga scortechinii
Prestoea decurrens
Ptychosperma lauterbachii
Ptychosperma macarthurii
Ptychosperma sanderianum
Raphia humilis
Raphia taedigera
Raphia vinifera
Reinhardtia latisecta
Reinhardtia simplex
Rhapidophyllum
Rhapis excelsa
Rhapis multifida
Rhapis subtilis
Rhapis humilis
Salacca
Serenoa
Syagrus campylospatha
Syagrus "cearensis"

Syagrus flexuosa
Syagrus harleyi
Syagrus ruschiana
Syagrus stratincola
Syagrus vagans
Trithrinax campestris
Wallichia caryotoides
Wallichia densiflora
Wendlandiella
Zombia

Climbing Palms

Vinelike palms exist in the tropics, and some of them have developed specialized organs for climbing. In almost all cases, these unique organs are formed only when the palm has attained some age and, more importantly, an above-ground stem.

Calamus
Calospatha
Ceratolobus
Daemonorops
Desmoncus
Eremospatha
Korthalsia
Laccosperma
Myrialepis
Oncocalamus
Plectocomia
Plectocomiopsis
Retispatha

Large Species

These are very tall palms that normally attain a total height of 60 feet or more, or are otherwise massive in their proportions.

Aiphanes grandis
Astrocaryum chambira
Attalea (most)
Beccariophoenix
Bismarckia
Borassus
Carpoxylon
Caryota gigas
Caryota maxima
Caryota no
Caryota rumphiana

Caroyta urens
Ceroxylon (most)
Cocos
Copernicia alba
Copernicia baileyana
Copernicia fallaensis
Copernicia gigas
Corypha
Deckenia
Elaeis guineensis
Eugeissona utilis
Gulubia costata
Gulubia cylindrocarpa
Gulubia longispatha
Gulubia microcarpa
Gulubia moluccana
Hyphaene
Iriartea
Jubaea
Kentiopsis magnifica
Kentiopsis oliviformis
Livistona australis
Livistona carinensis
Livistona drudei
Livistona jenkinsiana
Livistona mariae
Livistona nitida
Livistona rotundifolia
Livistona saribus
Lodoicea
Manicaria
Marojejya
Mauritia flexuosa
Metroxylon
Oenocarpus bataua
Oncosperma horridum
Oncosperma tigillarium
Orania glauca
Orania lauterbachiana
Orania macropetala
Orania regalis
Orania sylvicola
Orania trispatha
Phoenix canariensis
Phoenix dactylifera
Phoenix reclinata
Phoenix sylvestris
Pholidocarpus
Phytelephas aequatorialis
Pigafetta
Pritchardia hardyi

Pritchardia schattaueri
Raphia
Ravenea rivularis
Ravenea robustior
Ravenea sambiranensis
Rhopaloblaste augusta
Roystonea species (most)
Sabal causiarum
Sabal domingensis
Sabal maritima
Syagrus sancona
Veitchia arecina
Veitchia joannis
Washingtonia

Small Species

These palms are generally under 10 feet total height and are not of great widths because of clustering growth habits.

Acrocomia hassleri
Aiphanes hirsuta (some forms)
Aiphanes ulei
Allagoptera
Alsmithia
Areca guppyana
Areca ipot
Areca minuta
Arenga brevipes
Arenga caudata
Arenga hastata
Arenga hookeriana
Arenga porphyrocarpa
Arenga retroflorescens
Asterogyne
Bactris guineensis
Bactris hondurensis
Bactris mexicana
Balaka
Barcella
Basselinia gracilis (some forms)
Basselinia vestita
Brahea decumbens
Brahea moorei
Butia archeri
Butia campicola
Butia microspadix
Calyptrocalyx arfakiensis
Calyptrocalyx doxanthus
Calyptrocalyx elegans

Calyptrocalyx flabellatus
Calyptrocalyx hollrungii
Calyptrocalyx micholitzii
Calyptrocalyx pachystachys
Calyptrocalyx pauciflorus
Calyptrocalyx polyphyllus
Calyptrogyne
Chamaedorea (most)
Chelyocarpus repens
Chuniophoenix nana
Copernicia cowellii
Dypsis catatiana
Dypsis concinna
Dypsis louvelii
Dypsis pusilla
Dypsis sanctaemariae
Dypsis schatzii
Geonoma cuneata
Geonoma deversa
Geonoma epetiolata
Gronophyllum cariosum
Guihaia
Heterospathe delicatula
Heterospathe humilis
Heterospathe philippinensis
Hyospathe macrorachis
Iguanura
Iriartella
Lepidocaryum
Lepidorrhachis
Licuala (most)
Linospadix
Maxburretia furtadoana
Maxburretia rupicola
Nenga gajah
Neonicholsonia
Phoenix acaulis
Phoenix caespitosa
Phoenix loureiri
Phoenix roebelenii
Pholidostachys
Pinanga (most)
Pritchardiopsis
Ravenea hildebrandtii
Reinhardtia gracilis
Reinhardtia koschnyana
Reinhardtia simplex
Rhapidophyllum
Rhapis excelsa
Rhapis laosensis
Rhapis multifida

Rhapis subtilis
Sabal etonia
Sabal miamiensis
Sabal minor
Sommieria
Syagrus campylospatha
Syagrus duartei
Syagrus glaucescens
Syagrus harleyi
Syagrus pleioclada
Syagrus schizophylla
Syagrus vagans
Thrinax ekmaniana
Trachycarpus nanus
Wallichia caryotoides
Wallichia densiflora
Wallichia siamensis
Wendlandiella

Species Tolerant of Alkaline Soil

This category is a tricky one. Almost any palm can be made to survive in almost any soil type with heroic efforts of amendment, irrigation, and fertilization. For example, *Caryota* species generally need a fairly rich, humus-laden soil that is slightly acidic, and yet peninsular Florida, where the soil is slightly to quite alkaline, is full of most of these species. The species listed here thrive with moderate, not heroic, adjustments.

Acrocomia (slight)
Adonidia (some)
Allagoptera (extreme)
Aiphanes (slight)
Archontophoenix (slight)
Arenga (slight)
Astrocaryum (slight)
Bismarckia (some)
Borassodendron (slight)
Borassus (some)
Brahea (slight)
Burretiokentia vieillardii (slight)
Butia (some)
Carpentaria (slight)
Caryota (slight)
Chamaedorea (most)
Chamaerops (some)
Chuniophoenix hainanensis
Coccothrinax
Cocos (great)

Copernicia (great)
Corypha (some)
Cryosophila
Dictyosperma (some)
Dypsis cabadae (slight)
Dypsis decaryi (some)
Dypsis lanceolata (slight)
Dypsis leptocheilos (slight)
Dypsis lutescens (slight)
Dypsis madagascariensis (slight)
Elaeis (slight)
Gastrococos
Gaussia maya (some)
Guihaia
Heterospathe (slight)
Hyophorbe (some)
Hyphaene (some)
Jubaea (some)
Latania (some)
Licuala peltata (slight)
Licuala rumphii (slight)
Licuala spinosa (slight)
Livistona alfredii (some)
Livistona australis (slight)
Livistona benthamii (slight)
Livistona carinensis (some)
Livistona chinensis (slight)
Livistona decipiens (slight)
Livistona fulva (slight)
Livistona halongensis (slight)
Livistona jenkinsiana (slight)
Livistona mariae (some)
Livistona merrillii (slight)
Livistona muelleri
Livistona nitida (slight)
Livistona rigida (slight)
Livistona rotundifolia
Livistona saribus (slight)
Livistona woodfordii
Lodoicea (some)
Medemia (great)
Nannorrhops (some)
Nypa (some)
Oncosperma tigillarium (slight)
Orania (slight)
Pelagodoxora (some)
Phoenix caespitosa (some)
Phoenix dactylifera (great)
Phoenix loureiri (some)
Phoenix paludosa (some)
Phoenix pusilla (slight)

Phoenix reclinata (some)
Phoenix rupicola (slight)
Phoenix sylvestris (slight)
Phoenix theophrasti (great)
Polyandrococos
Pritchardia mitiaroana
Pritchardia pacifica (some)
Pritchardia thurstonii (some)
Pseudophoenix (some)
Ptychosperma (some)
Raphia
Ravenea hildebrandtii (some)
Rhapidophyllum (some)
Rhapis (some)
Roystonea regia (some)
Sabal (some to great)
Schippia (some)
Serenoa (great)
Syagrus "cearensis"
Syagrus schizophylla (some)
Thrinax (some to great)
Trachycarpus fortunei (some)
Trithrinax (some to great)
Trithrinax oreophilus (slight)
Veitchia (some)
Washingtonia (some)
Zombia (some)

Salt-Tolerant Species

Palms tolerate various degrees of salinity in the soil and air, ranging from slight to some, great, or extreme.

Acoelorraphe (some)
Acrocomia aculeata (slight)
Acrocomia hassleri (some)
Adonidia (airborne only)
Allagoptera (extreme)
Areca whitfordii (slight)
Brahea aculeata (slight)
Chamaerops (some)
Coccothrinax species (some to great)
Cocos (great)
Copernicia brittonorum (great)
Copernicia gigas (great)
Copernicia macroglossa (great)
Copernicia rigida (great)
Hyophorbe lagenicaulis (some)
Hyophorbe verschaffeltii (some)
Hyphaene (some to great)

Licuala paludosa (some)
Licuala spinosa (slight)
Livistona alfredii (some)
Livistona benthamii (some)
Livistona carinensis (some)
Livistona chinensis (some)
Livistona saribus (some)
Medemia (great)
Nannorrhops (some)
Nypa (some)
Oncosperma tigillarium (some)
Phoenix caespitosa (some)
Phoenix canariensis (airborne only)
Phoenix dactylifera (great)
Phoenix loureiri (some)
Phoenix paludosa (some)
Phoenix pusilla (slight)
Phoenix sylvestris (slight)
Phoenix theophrasti (great)
Pritchardia pacifica (airborne)
Pritchardia thurstonii (airborne)
Pseudophoenix ekmanii (some)
Pseudophoenix sargentii (great)
Sabal bermudana (some)
Sabal domingensis (some)
Sabal etonia (some)
Sabal gretheriae (some)
Sabal guatemalensis (some)
Sabal maritima (some)
Sabal mauritiiformis (slight)
Sabal mexicana (some)
Sabal miamiensis (great)
Sabal palmetto (some)
Sabal rosei (some)
Sabal uresana (some)
Sabal yapa (some)
Serenoa (great)
Syagrus amara (some)
Syagrus campylospatha (some)
Syagrus schizophylla (some)
Thrinax morrisii (some)
Thrinax radiata (great)
Thrinax rivularis (some)
Veitchia (airborne only)
Washingtonia (some)
Zombia (some)

Species with Colored New Growth

Actinokentia divaricata
Alsmithia
Archontophoenix tuckeri
Areca vestiaria form
Asterogyne martiana
Asterogyne spicata
Burretiokentia koghiensis
Calyptrocalyx
Calyptrogyne
Ceratolobus
Chambeyronia macrocarpa
Dypsis crinita
Dypsis fibrosa
Dypsis louvelii
Dypsis pinnatifrons
Geonoma densa
Geonoma deversa
Geonoma epetiolata
Gronophyllum montanum
Gronophyllum pinangoides
Gronophyllum pleurocarpum
Heterospathe elata
Heterospathe minor
Heterospathe woodfordiana
Iguanura bicornis
Iguanura elegans
Iguanura wallichiana
Kentiopsis magnifica
Laccospadix
Livistona fulva
Oenocarpus
Pholidostachys pulchra
Pinanga aristata
Pinanga caesia
Pinanga coronata
Pinanga densiflora
Ptychococcus paradoxus
Ptychosperma burretianum
Ptychosperma waitianum
Salacca affinis
Salacca flabellata
Salacca zalacca
Welfia

Species with Permanently Colored Leaves or Crownshafts

Allagoptera arenaria
Archontophoenix purpurea
Areca vestiaria
Arenga
Astrocaryum
Basselinia (most species)
Bismarckia
Brahea armata
Brahea decumbens
Butia capitata (many forms)
Ceroxylon
Coccothrinax
Colpothrinax wrightii
Copernicia alba
Copernicia "azul"
Copernicia cowellii
Copernicia fallaensis
Copernicia hospita

Copernicia prunifera
Cryosophila
Cyrtostachys renda
Dypsis lastelliana
Dypsis leptocheilos
Guihaia argyrata
Hyphaene (most species)
Itaya
Johannesteijsmannia magnifica
Kerriodoxa
Latania loddigesii
Mauritiella armata
Oraniopsis
Pinanga caesia
Pinanga coronata
Pinanga dicksonii
Pinanga speciosa
Polyandrococos
Sabal uresana
Serenoa repens (some forms)
Sommieria
Thrinax morrisii

Seed Germination Notes
for Selected Genera

The seed of all palm species benefits from bottom heat, which speeds up germination. During the day, the soil temperature should be kept at 80°F or higher, cooling off to the upper seventies at night. Most palm seeds are viable for a short time only and cannot be stored well. Unless otherwise stated below, seed should be planted soon after it is harvested.

Some genera are remote germinating, meaning the seed sends a radicle down into the soil. When the radicle reaches a certain depth, roots are sent down further and the first leaf is sent up. A deep container should be used when germinating seed of these species.

Acanthophoenix. See notes under *Areca*. Seed germinates within 60 days if it is not allowed to dry out completely before sowing.

Acoelorraphe. See notes under *Corypha*. Fresh seed germinates within 90 days.

Acrocomia. *Acrocomia* is a member of the tribe Cocoeae under the subfamily Arecoideae. All genera in this tribe have seeds similar to that of coconut with three "eyes" at one end and a thick hard shell. Older seed is viable but may take some time to germinate. It is not unheard of for the seed of *Acrocomia* to germinate up to five years after being planted. Germination tends to be sporadic, and in some cases seeds have more than one embryo, causing up to three seedlings to develop, one for each "eye." Carefully removing the hard shell before sowing has been shown to greatly speed up germination. Because the seed is more prone to disease and insect attacks without its shell, it should be planted in a sterilized potting medium such as perlite.

Actinokentia. See notes under *Areca*. Seed germinates within 60 to 120 days if it is not allowed to dry out completely before sowing. It should be harvested when fully ripe as slightly green seed does not germinate well.

Actinorhytis. See notes under *Areca*. Seed germinates within 30 days if it is not allowed to dry out completely before sowing.

Adonidia. See notes under *Areca*. Seed germinates within 30 days if it is not allowed to dry out completely before sowing.

Aiphanes. See notes under *Acrocomia*. Seed can take more than a year to germinate and does so sporadically.

Allagoptera. See notes under *Acrocomia*. Seed can take more than two years to germinate and does so sporadically.

Alloschmidia. See notes under *Areca*. The few available seeds have either been dried out or unripe, so germination was almost nil.

Alsmithia. See notes under *Areca*. Seed germinates within 60 days if it is not allowed to dry out completely before sowing.

Ammandra. See notes under *Phytelephas*. Seed can take up to three years to germinate and does so sporadically. It can be stored for several months as long as it is soaked in water for two to three days before sowing.

Aphandra. See notes under *Phytelephas*. Seed can take up to three years to germinate and does so sporadically. It can be stored for several months as long as it is soaked in water for two to three days before sowing.

Archontophoenix. See notes under *Areca*. Seed germinates within 30 days if it is not allowed to dry out completely before sowing.

Areca. *Areca* is a member of the tribe Areceae under the subfamily Arecoideae. Species of this tribe are among the easiest palms to grow from seed. Most seed in the tribe has a short viability only because it tends to germinate as soon as it ripens and falls from the tree. Seed that is allowed to dry out completely does not germinate well, and the smaller the seed, the more likely it will dry out before sowing. Germination tends to occur quickly, but in some species can take as long as a year.

Seed shipped in a bag for several days often begins germinating before reaching its destination. Fresh seed of *Areca* almost always germinates within 30 days and grows quickly.

Arenga. *Arenga* is a member of the tribe Caryoteae under the subfamily Coryphoideae. All the genera of this tribe are remote germinating. The radicles range from 1 to 3 inches, depending on the species, so a container at least 6 inches deep should be used. Fresh seed tends to germinate quickly, but several months can elapse before the first leaf appears above the soil. Seed should not be allowed to dry out for long. Fresh seed of *Arenga* germinates in 60 to 120 days with the first leaf appearing 30 to 120 days later depending on the temperature.

Asterogyne. *Asterogyne* is a member of the tribe Geonomeae under the subfamily Arecoideae. All genera in the tribe have small seed that, if allowed to dry out completely, does not germinate well. Fresh seed germinates within 30 to 120 days and rarely longer. Seed shipped in a bag for a couple of weeks often begins germinating before reaching its destination. Fresh seed of *Asterogyne* almost always germinates within 45 days.

Astrocaryum. See notes under *Acrocomia*. Seed can take up to three years to germinate and does so sporadically.

Attalea. See notes under *Acrocomia*. Seed can take up to five years to germinate and does so sporadically. Some species readily develop two or more seedlings from the same seed.

Bactris. See notes under *Acrocomia*. Seed can take up to two years to germinate and does so sporadically.

Balaka. See notes under *Areca*. Seed germinates within 30 days if it is not allowed to dry out completely before sowing.

Barcella. See notes under *Acrocomia*. Seed can take more than a year to germinate and does so sporadically.

Basselinia. See notes under *Areca*, Like many New Caledonia palms that seem to flower well but rarely produce much viable seed, this genus is no exception. Germination is difficult for *Basselinia* species and no definitive data are available, except that germination seems to be sporadic.

Beccariophoenix. Germination is fairly quick for this member of the tribe Cocoeae. Seed germinates at the same time and within 60 to 90 days or occasionally longer.

Bentinckia. See notes under *Areca*. Seed germinates within 60 days if it is not allowed to dry out completely before sowing.

Bismarckia. *Bismarckia* is a member of the tribe Borasseae under the subfamily Coryphoideae. All the species of this tribe are remote germinating. Seed begins to germinate within 30 to 120 days but can take up to a year or more. Depending on warmth and species, a month or more can elapse between the time the radicle first goes down to when the first leaf emerges from the ground. Seed of *Bismarckia* can take 30 days to 18 months to germinate. The radicle can go down as far as 12 inches, so the container in which seed is germinated should be at least 16 to 18 inches deep.

Borassodendron. See notes under *Bismarckia*. Seed generally germinates within 60 days but can take as long as 120 days. If it is allowed to dry out completely before sowing, seed does not germinate as well as if it is kept slightly moist. The radicle can go down 8 inches, so the container in which seed is germinated should be at least 12 inches deep.

Borassus. See notes under *Bismarckia*. Seed generally germinates within 60 days but can take as long as 120 days. If it is allowed to dry out completely before sowing, seed does not germinate as well as if it is kept slightly moist. The radicle can go down 18 inches, so the container in which seed is germinated should be at least 24 inches deep.

Brahea. See notes under *Corypha*. Seed germinates within 120 days and should not be allowed to dry out completely before sowing.

Brassiophoenix. See notes under *Areca*. Seed germinates within 30 days if it is not allowed to dry out completely before sowing.

Brongniartikentia. See notes under *Areca*. Seed can take 60 to 120 days to germinate if it is not allowed to dry out completely before sowing.

Burretiokentia. See notes under *Areca*. Seed germinates within 90 days if it is not allowed to dry out completely before sowing.

Butia. See notes under *Acrocomia*. Seed can take up to three years to germinate and does so sporadically. Often two or three seedlings develop from the same seed.

Calamus. *Calamus* is a member of the tribe Calameae under the subfamily Calamoideae. Species of this tribe are among the easiest palms to grow from seed. Most seed in the tribe has a short viability only because its tends to germinate as soon as it ripens and falls from the tree. Seed shipped in a plastic bag from a foreign country can begin germinating before reaching its destination. Seed that is allowed to dry out completely does not germinate well, and the smaller the seed, the more likely it will dry out before sowing. Seed of most *Calamus* species germinates within 30 days.

Calospatha. See notes under *Areca*. Seed germinates within 45 days if it is not allowed to dry out completely before sowing.

Calyptrocalyx. See notes under *Areca*. Seed germinates within 45 days if it is not allowed to dry out completely before sowing.

Calyptrogyne. See notes under *Asterogyne*. Seed germinates within 60 days if it is not allowed to dry out completely before sowing.

Calyptronoma. See notes under *Asterogyne*. Seed germinates within 60 days if it is not allowed to dry out completely before sowing.

Campecarpus. See notes under *Areca*. Seed germinates within 120 days if it is not allowed to dry out completely before sowing. The percentage of seed that germinates has never been good and may be the result of using seed that is not fully ripe. Seed is not generally available.

Carpentaria. See notes under *Areca*. Seed can take 30 days to one year to germinate if it is not allowed to dry out completely before sowing. In Florida, for some reason, seed germinates really well in late spring following the season in which it was sown.

Carpoxylon. See notes under *Areca*. Seed germinates within 90 days if it is not allowed to dry out completely before sowing.

Caryota. See notes under *Arenga*. Seed germinates within 30 to 90 days depending on how fresh it is.

Ceratolobus. See notes under *Calamus*. Seed is not generally available, so little information is known about its germination.

Ceroxylon. *Ceroxylon* is a member of the tribe Ceroxyleae under the subfamily Ceroxyloideae. Species of this tribe are among the easiest to grow from seed and seed germinates quickly. If it is allowed to dry out completely before sowing, seed does not germinate as well as if it is kept slightly moist, and the smaller the seed, the more likely it will dry out before sowing. Seed shipped in a bag for several days often begins germinating before reaching its destination. Fresh seed of *Ceroxylon* generally germinates within 60 days but can continue sporadically for several months.

Chamaedorea. See notes under *Hyophorbe*. Seed can take 90 days to a year or more to germinate and does so in a fairly short time. It can be stored for a few months but is best planted soon after harvest.

Chamaerops. See notes under *Corypha*. Fresh seed germinates within 90 days. Seed that is allowed to dry out completely and then rehydrated may take nine months or longer to germinate, and the percentage of seed that germinates is not as high as that of fresh seed.

Chambeyronia. See notes under *Areca*. Seed germinates within 90 days if it is not allowed to dry out completely before sowing.

Chelyocarpus. See notes under *Corypha*. Seed germinates within 45 days and should not be allowed to dry out completely before sowing.

Chuniophoenix. See notes under *Corypha*. Seed germinates within 60 days and should not be allowed to dry out completely before sowing.

Clinosperma. See notes under *Areca*. Seed is not generally available, so germination information is nonexistent. If it is allowed to dry out completely before sowing, seed probably doesn't germinate as well as if it is kept slightly moist.

Clinostigma. See notes under *Areca*. Seed generally germinates within 45 days of sowing. Long-term viability is not good.

Coccothrinax. See notes under *Corypha*. Fresh seed germinates within 90 days. Seed that is allowed to dry out completely and then rehydrated may take nine months or longer to germinate.

Cocos. See notes under *Acrocomia*. Seed can take more than a year to germinate and does so sporadically.

Colpothrinax. See notes under *Corypha*. Seed can take more than two years to germinate, even when fresh, and does so sporadically. Do not give up on any seed during that time.

Copernicia. See notes under *Corypha*. Seed germinates within 30 days and should not be allowed to dry out completely before sowing.

Corypha. *Corypha* is a member of the tribe Corypheae under the subfamily Coryphoideae. All the genera of this tribe are remote germinating. The radicle ranges from 1 to 3 inches, depending on the species, so a deep container at least 6 inches deep should be used. The seed of all genera in the tribe tends to germinate easily, but that of some species does so sporadically for up to three years in some instances, while that of other species germinates quickly after sowing. Seed of some genera can be stored in a cool, sealed environment for several months as long as it is soaked in water for two days before sowing. Seed of other species is best planted soon after harvest. Fresh seed of *Corypha* tends to germinate quickly within 120 days.

Cryosophila. See notes under *Corypha*. Seed germinates within 30 days and should not be allowed to dry out completely before sowing.

Cyphokentia. See notes under *Areca*. Very few seeds have been available, and they have been difficult to germinate, as have seeds of most New Caledonian species.

Cyphophoenix. See notes under *Areca*. Fresh seed germinates sporadically from 45 to 120 days. Time of harvest of the fruits is critical.

Cyphosperma. See notes under *Areca*. Very few seeds have

been available, and virtually no data are known. Seed viability is most likely quite short. Bottom heat as well as proper time of harvest seems crucial.

Cyrtostachys. See notes under *Areca*. Seed generally germinates within 90 days but can take 190 days or sometimes longer. If the tiny seed is allowed to dry out completely before sowing, it does not germinate. Seed should be harvested when fully ripe.

Daemonorops. See notes under *Calamus*. Seed germinates within 30 days if it is not allowed to dry out completely before sowing.

Deckenia. See notes under *Areca*. Seed germinates within 60 days if it is not allowed to dry out completely before sowing.

Desmoncus. See notes under *Acrocomia*. Seed can take more than a year to germinate and does so sporadically.

Dictyocaryum. See notes under *Iriartea*. Seed germinates within 120 days and should not be allowed to dry out completely before sowing.

Dictyosperma. See notes under *Areca*. Seed can take 60 to 90 days to germinate if it is not allowed to dry out completely before sowing.

Drymophloeus. See notes under *Areca*. Seed germinates within 30 days if it is not allowed to dry out completely before sowing.

Dypsis. See notes under *Areca*. Seed germinates within 90 days and does so in a short time. If it is allowed to dry out completely before sowing, seed does not germinate as well as if it is kept slightly moist.

Elaeis. See notes under *Acrocomia*. Seed can take two years or longer to germinate and does so sporadically.

Eleiodoxa. See notes under *Calamus*. Seed germinates within 45 days if it is not allowed to dry out completely before sowing.

Eremospatha. See notes under *Calamus*. Seed is not generally available, so germination information is nonexistent.

Eugeissona. See notes under *Calamus*. Seed germinates within 60 days and must be sown immediately as long-term viability is nil.

Euterpe. See notes under *Areca*. Seed germinates within 45 days if it is not allowed to dry out completely before sowing.

Gastrococos. See notes under *Acrocomia*. Seed can take more than a year to germinate and does so sporadically.

Gaussia. See notes under *Hyophorbe*. Seed can take 90 days to a year to germinate and does so in a fairly short time. It can be stored for a few months but is best planted soon after harvest.

Geonoma. See notes under *Asterogyne*. Seed germinates within 120 days if it is not allowed to dry out completely before sowing.

Gronophyllum. See notes under *Areca*. Seed germinates within 60 days if it is not allowed to dry out completely before sowing. Some batches of seed germinate far better than others for no apparent reason even though the same techniques are used. Seed should be harvested when fully ripe as slightly green seed does not germinate well.

Guihaia. See notes under *Corypha*. Seed germinates within 120 days and should not be allowed to dry out completely before sowing.

Gulubia. See notes under *Areca*. Seed germinates within 30 days if kept slightly moist.

Hedyscepe. See notes under *Areca*. Seed generally germinates within 90 days but can take longer. If it is allowed to dry out completely before sowing, seed does not germinate as well as if it is kept slightly moist.

Heterospathe. See notes under *Areca*. Seed germinates within 60 days if it is not allowed to dry out completely before sowing. It should be harvested when fully ripe and even then may not germinate well. Some batches of seed germinate far better than others for no apparent reason even though the same techniques are used.

Howea. See notes under *Areca*. This genus differs from other members of the Areceae as seed germinates sporadically from 30 days to as long as two years. Germination is best when seed is fresh and fully ripe before harvesting.

Hydriastele. See notes under *Areca*. Seed germinates within 60 days if it is not allowed to dry out completely before sowing. It should be harvested when fully ripe and even then may not germinate well. Some batches of seed germinate far better than others for no apparent reason even though the same techniques are used. Slightly green seed does not germinate at all.

Hyophorbe. *Hyophorbe* is a member of the tribe Hyophorbeae under the subfamily Ceroxyloideae. Seed of this tribe germinates either all at one time or sporadically for up to a year or more. Seed tends to be viable longer than that of many other palm species but is best planted soon after harvest. If it is allowed to dry out completely before sowing, seed does not germinate as well as if it is kept slightly moist, and the smaller the seed, the more likely it will dry out before sowing. Fresh seed of *Hyophorbe* germinates within 60 days to a year or more and does so sporadically.

Hyospathe. See notes under *Areca*. Seed germinates within 60 days if it is not allowed to dry out completely before sowing.

Hyphaene. See notes under *Bismarckia*. Seed generally germinates within 90 days but can take as long as 180 days or longer. The radicle can go down 12 inches, so the container in which seed is germinated should be at least 16 to 18 inches deep.

Iguanura. See notes under *Areca*. Seed germinates within 60 days if it is not allowed to dry out completely before sowing.

Iriartea. *Iriartea* is a member of the tribe Iriarteae under the subfamily Arecoideae. Species of this tribe are among the easiest palms to grow from seed. If it is allowed to dry out completely, seed does not germinate well, and the smaller the seed, the more likely it will dry out before sowing. Germination tends to occur within 30 days to 6 months depending on the species. Fresh seed of *Iriartea* almost always germinates within 60 days.

Iriartella. See notes under *Iriartea*. Seed germinates within 60 days and should not be allowed to dry out completely before sowing.

Itaya. See notes under *Corypha*. Seed germinates within 60 days and should not be allowed to dry out completely before sowing.

Johannesteijsmannia. See notes under *Corypha*. Seed germinates within 45 days and should not be allowed to dry out completely before sowing. The outer seed shell often cracks and breaks off, but this seems to cause little problem with germination and may even enhance it. If cracked, the shell should be removed so water does not become trapped between parts of it and the seed itself and cause disease.

Juania. See notes under *Ceroxylon*. Seed germinates within 90 days.

Jubaea. See notes under *Acrocomia*. Seed can take more than a year to germinate and does so sporadically

Jubaeopsis. See notes under *Acrocomia*. Seed can take more than a year to germinate and does so sporadically.

Kentiopsis. See notes under *Areca*. Seed germinates within 30 days for *K. piersoniorum*, 120 days for *K. oliviformis*, and sporadically over two years for *K. magnifica*. There is no standard rule for the species in this genus. If it is allowed to dry out completely before sowing, seed does not germinate as well as if it is kept slightly moist. Seed should be harvested when fully ripe as slightly green seed does not germinate well.

Kerriodoxa. See notes under *Corypha*. Seed germinates within 30 days and should not be allowed to dry out completely before sowing.

Korthalsia. See notes under *Calamus*. Seed germinates within 30 days if it is not allowed to dry out completely before sowing.

Laccospadix. See notes under *Areca*. Seed germinates within 60 days if it is not allowed to dry out completely before sowing.

Laccosperma. See notes under *Calamus*. Seed is not generally available, so germination information is nonexistent.

Latania. See notes under *Bismarckia*. Seed can take up to 18 months to germinate and does so sporadically. The radicle can go down 3 inches, so the container in which seed is germinated should be at least 6 inches deep.

Lavoixia. See notes under *Areca*. Seed is not generally available, so germination information is unknown.

Lemurophoenix. See notes under *Areca*. Seed has not been easy to germinate, but when it does, it takes six months or perhaps a bit longer. If it is allowed to dry out completely before sowing, seed does not germinate as well as if it is kept slightly moist.

Leopoldinia. See notes under *Areca*. Seed is not generally available, and the seed that has been tried was dried out and did not germinate. Seed should probably be kept moist prior to sowing.

Lepidocaryum. See notes under *Calamus*. Seed germinates within 45 days if it is not allowed to dry out completely before sowing.

Lepidorrhachis. See notes under *Areca*. Seed germinates within 60 days if it is not allowed to dry out completely before sowing.

Licuala. See notes under *Corypha*. Seed can take a couple of months to three years to germinate and does so sporadically. Ideally, it should not be allowed to dry out completely prior to sowing. Dried seed can be rehydrated, although it takes longer to germinate. Seed of this genus is viable longer than that of some genera is best planted soon after harvesting.

Linospadix. See notes under *Areca*. Seed germinates within 60 days if it is not allowed to dry out completely before sowing.

Livistona. See notes under *Corypha*. Seed generally germinates within 90 days unless it is allowed to dry out completely before sowing. Dried seed takes longer to germinate and does not germinate as well as if it is kept slightly moist.

Lodoicea. See notes under *Bismarckia*. Seed can take 90 to 360 days to germinate. The radicle can go down 6 feet, so best success is achieved by germinated seed directly in the landscape. Depending on how warm the ground is, a year or more can elapse between the time the radicle first goes down to when the first leaf emerges from the ground.

Loxococcus. See notes under *Areca*. Seed germinates within 30 days if it is not allowed to dry out completely before sowing.

Lytocaryum. See notes under *Acrocomia*. Seed germinates within 180 days but can take more than a year. Germination is sporadic.

Manicaria. See notes under *Areca*. Seed germinates sporadically over several months. If it is allowed to dry out completely before sowing, seed does not germinate well as if it is kept slightly moist.

Marojejya. See notes under *Areca*. Seed germinates within 45 days. If it is allowed to dry out completely before sowing, seed does not germinate as well as if it is kept slightly moist

Masoala. See notes under *Areca*. Seed germinates within 60 days. If it is allowed to dry out completely before sowing, seed does not germinate as well as if it is kept slightly moist.

Mauritia. See notes under *Calamus*. Seed germinates within 45 days. If it is allowed to dry out completely before sowing, seed does not germinates as well as if it is kept slightly moist.

Mauritiella. See notes under *Calamus*. Seed germinates within 45 days if it is not allowed to dry out completely before sowing.

Maxburretia. See notes under *Corypha*. Seed is not generally available, so little information is known about its germination. Since this genus belongs in the same subtribe as *Chamaerops*, *Rhapis*, and *Thrinax*, among others, it might germinate sporadically.

Medemia. See notes under *Bismarckia*. Seed can take up to 18 months to germinate and does so sporadically. Germination is virtually identical to **that of** *Bismarckia*.

Metroxylon. See notes under *Calamus*. Seed germinates within 60 days if it is not allowed to dry out completely before sowing.

Moratia. See notes under *Areca*. Seed is not commonly available. It appears to germinate sporadically over several months. If it is allowed to dry out completely before sowing, seed does not germinate as well as if it is kept slightly moist.

Myrialepis. See notes under *Calamus*. Seed is not commonly available, so germination information is nonexistent.

Nannorrhops. See notes under *Corypha*. Seed germinates within 30 days and should not be allowed to dry out completely before sowing.

Nenga. See notes under *Areca*. Seed germinates within 30 days if it is not allowed to dry out completely before sowing.

Neonicholsonia. See notes under *Areca*. Seed germinates within 30 days if it is not allowed to dry out completely before sowing.

Neoveitchia. See notes under *Areca*. Seed is slow to germinate, but some growers report that carefully cracking and removing the hard shell before sowing speeds up germination and increases the percentage of seed that germinates. Because the seed is more prone to disease and insect attacks without its shell, it should be planted in a sterilized potting medium such as perlite. If it is allowed to dry out completely before sowing, seed does not germinate as well as if it is kept slightly moist.

Nephrosperma. See notes under *Areca*. Seed germinates within 30 days if it is not allowed to dry out completely before sowing.

Normanbya. See notes under *Areca*. Seed generally germinates within 45 days if it is not allowed to dry out completely before sowing, but it can take up to 180 days. Germination is sporadic.

Nypa. *Nypa* is the only member of the subfamily Nypoideae. The large seed germinates easily and quickly, within days, after harvesting. Seed shipped in a bag for several days often begins germinating before reaching its destination. Seed should be kept wet but well drained with half the seed exposed to the air. Seed should not be allowed to completely dry out before sowing as this adversely affects germination rate.

Oenocarpus. See notes under *Areca*. Seed germinates within 90 days if it is not allowed to dry out completely before sowing.

Oncocalamus. See notes under *Calamus*. Seed is not generally available, so germination information is nonexistent.

Oncosperma. See notes under *Areca*. Seed germinates within 45 days if it is not allowed to dry out completely before sowing.

Orania. See notes under *Areca*. Seed generally germinates within 90 days but can take a bit longer. If it is allowed to dry out completely before sowing, seed does not germinate as well as if it is kept slightly moist. Unlike other members of the Areceae, *Orania* germinates remotely, and its radicle is up to 6 inches long.

Oraniopsis. See notes under *Ceroxylon*. Seed can take several months to a year or more to germinate and does so sporadically.

Parajubaea. See notes under *Acrocomia*. Seed can take more than two years to germinate and does so sporadically.

Pelagodoxa. See notes under *Areca*. Seed can take 30 to 180 days or longer to germinate and does so sporadically. If it is allowed to dry out completely before sowing, seed does germinate as well as if it is kept slightly moist.

Phoenicophorium. See notes under *Areca*. Seed germinates within 30 days if it is not allowed to dry out completely before sowing.

Phoenix. *Phoenix* is the only member of the tribe Phoeniceae in the subfamily Coryphoideae. All the species are remote germinating. The radicle ranges from 1 to 3 inches, so the container in which seed is germinated should be at least 6 inches deep. If is allowed to dry out completely before sowing, seed does not germinate as well as if it is kept slightly moist. Fresh seed germinates easily within 30 days and should be planted soon after harvesting.

Pholidocarpus. See notes under *Corypha*. Seed germinates within 30 days and should not be allowed to dry out completely before sowing.

Pholidostachys. See notes under *Asterogyne*. Seed germinates within 60 days if it is not allowed to dry out completely before sowing.

Physokentia. See notes under *Areca*. Seed germinates within 60 days if it is not allowed to dry out completely before sowing.

Phytelephas. *Phytelephas* is a member of the subfamily Phytelephantoideae. All the genera in this subfamily are considered vegetable ivory palms and germinate virtually identically. Seed can take 30 days to three years or occasionally longer to germinate and does so sporadically. It can be stored for some time but is best planted soon after harvest.

Pigafetta. See notes under *Calamus*. Seed germinates within 30 days if it is not allowed to dry out completely before sowing.

Pinanga. See notes under *Areca*. Seed germinates within 30 days if it is not allowed to dry out completely before sowing.

Plectocomia. See notes under *Calamus*. Seed is not generally available, so germination information is nonexistent.

Plectocomiopsis. See notes under *Calamus*. Seed is not generally available, so germination information is nonexistent.

Podococcus. See notes under *Iriartea*. Seed is not generally available, so germination information is nonexistent.

Pogonotium. See notes under *Calamus*. Seed is not generally available, so germination information is nonexistent.

Polyandrococos. See notes under *Acrocomia*. Seed generally germinates within 180 days but can take more than a year and does so sporadically.

Prestoea. See notes under *Areca*. Seed germinates within 60 days if it is not allowed to dry out completely before sowing.

Pritchardia. See notes under *Corypha*. Seed germinates within 30 days and should not be allowed to dry out completely before sowing.

Pritchardiopsis. See notes under *Corypha*. Seed is only available from a single tree, so germination information is lacking. The genus is in the same subtribe as *Copernicia*, *Livistona*, *Pritchardia*, and *Washingtonia*, so seed might germinate quickly.

Pseudophoenix. This genus is the only member of the tribe Cyclospaeae in the subfamily Ceroxyloideae. A hard shell covers the seed, making germination slow, sporadic, and seldom successful. A germination rate of 75 percent or better is possible when the seed is allowed to dry out for two to four weeks at which point it is easy to crack and remove the outer shell. The seed should then be soaked in room temperature water for two days. Because the seed is more prone to disease and insect attacks without its shell, it should be planted in a sterilized potting medium such as coarse perlite. The seed should be barely covered, then watered thoroughly, before placing the container in a semishady area. Bottom heat is important as is regular water. The seed must not be allowed to dry out completely. Within 60 to 120 days after sowing, a large number of the seed should sprout with some stragglers continuing to sprout for up to a year.

Ptychococcus. See notes under *Areca*. Seed generally germinates within 45 days and occasionally longer if it is not allowed to dry out completely before sowing.

Ptychosperma. See notes under *Areca*. Seed of most species germinates within 30 days, but seed of other species such as *P. waitianum* can take 6 months or longer. If it is allowed to dry out completely before sowing, seed does not germinate as well as it if is kept slightly moist.

Raphia. See notes under *Calamus*. Seed germinates within 60 days if it is not allowed to dry out completely before sowing.

Ravenea. See notes under *Ceroxylon*. Seed generally germinates within 30 to 60 days depending on the species.

Reinhardtia. See notes under *Areca*. Seed germinates within 45 days if it is not allowed to dry out completely before sowing.

Retispatha. See notes under *Calamus*. Seed is not generally available, so germination information is lacking.

Rhapidophyllum. See notes under *Corypha*. Fresh seed can take 90 days to a year or longer to germinate and does so sporadically.

Rhapis. See notes under *Corypha*. Seed germinates within 120 days and should not be allowed to dry out completely before sowing.

Rhopaloblaste. See notes under *Areca*. Seed germinates within 45 days if it is not allowed to dry out completely before sowing.

Rhopalostylis. See notes under *Areca*. Seed germinates within 60 days if it is not allowed to dry out completely before sowing.

Roscheria. See notes under *Areca*. Seed germinates within 30 days if it is not allowed to dry out completely before sowing.

Roystonea. See notes under *Areca*. Fresh seed germinates within 90 to 120 days, but dried seed can take six months to a year before starting to germinate and then does so sporadically for another year. Long-term viability is fairly good, but germination time is much longer for older seed.

Sabal. See notes under *Corypha*. Fresh seed germinates within 90 days. Seed that is allowed to dry out completely and then rehydrated may take nine months or longer to germinate.

Salacca. See notes under *Calamus*. Seed germinates within 60 days if it is not allowed to dry out completely before sowing.

Satakentia. See notes under *Areca*. Seed germinates within 6 months if it is going to at all. If it is allowed to dry out completely before sowing, seed does not germinate well. Furthermore, seed picked slightly green seems to germinate better than fully ripe seed.

Satranala. See notes under *Bismarckia*. Seed can take up to 18 months to germinate and does so sporadically. The radicle can go down 8 inches or more, so the container in which seed is germinated should be at least 14 inches deep.

Schippia. See notes under *Corypha*. Seed germinates within 90 days and should not be allowed to dry out completely before sowing.

Sclerosperma. See notes under *Areca*. The genus is in the same subtribe as *Marojejya* and might germinate similarly.

Serenoa. See notes under *Corypha*. Seed germinates within 120 days and should not be allowed to dry out completely before sowing.

Siphokentia. See notes under *Areca*. Seed germinates within 45 days if it is not allowed to dry out completely before sowing.

Socratea. See notes under *Iriartea*. Seed germinates within 60 days and should not be allowed to dry out completely before sowing.

Sommieria Seed germinates within 60 days if it is not allowed to dry out completely before sowing.

Syagrus. See notes under *Acrocomia*. Seed can take more than two years to germinate and does so sporadically.

Synechanthus. See notes under *Hyophorbe*. Seed generally germinates within 90 days and does so in a fairly short time.

Tectiphiala. Seed is not generally available, so germination information is lacking. The genus is in the same subtribe as a close relative from the same area, *Acanthophoenix*, and may germinate much the same way in which case it is important to have fresh seed that has not been allowed to dry out completely before sowing.

Thrinax. See notes under *Corypha*. Fresh seed germinates within 90 days. Seed that is allowed to dry out completely and then rehydrated may take nine months or longer to germinate.

Trachycarpus. See notes under *Corypha*. Fresh seed germinates within 90 days. Seed that is allowed to dry out completely and then rehydrated may take nine months or longer to germinate.

Trithrinax. See notes under *Corypha*. Fresh seed germinates within 90 days. Seed that is allowed to dry out completely and then rehydrated may take nine months or longer to germinate.

Veillonia. See notes under *Areca*. Seed generally germinates within 90 to 120 days but may take a bit longer. If it is allowed to dry out completely before sowing, seed does not germinate as well as if it is kept slightly moist.

Veitchia. See notes under *Areca*. Seed germinates within 30 days if it is not allowed to dry out completely before sowing.

Verschaffeltia. See notes under *Areca*. Seed germinates within 30 days if it is not allowed to dry out completely before sowing.

Voanioala. See notes under *Acrocomia*. Seed can take more than three years to germinate and does so sporadically. The shell is extremely thick and woody.

Wallichia. See notes under *Arenga*. Seed germinates within 30 to 90 days depending on how fresh it is.

Washingtonia. See notes under *Corypha*. Fresh seed germinates within 30 days. Seed that is allowed to dry out completely and then rehydrated may take three months or longer to germinate and does not germinate as well as fresh seed.

Welfia. See notes under *Asterogyne*. Seed germinates within 60 days if it is not allowed to dry out completely before sowing.

Wendlandiella. See notes under *Hyophorbe*. Seed is not generally available as plants of only one sex are in cultivation. Propagation is easy through division of the clumps.

Wettinia. See notes under *Iriartea*. Seed germinates within 90 days and should not be allowed to dry out completely before sowing.

Wodyetia. See notes under *Areca*. Seed germinates sporadically and generally within 90 to 180 days but can take as few as 30 days or as many as 270. In this way the genus differs from most other members of the Areceae. If it is allowed to dry out completely before sowing, seed does not germinate as well as if it is kept slightly moist.

Zombia. See notes under *Corypha*. Seed germinates within 90 days and should not be allowed to dry out completely before sowing.

Conversion Charts

Inches	/Millimeters
0.25	65
0.5	125
0.75	190

Inches	/Centimeters
1	2.5
2	5
3	7.5
4	10
5	12.5
6	15
7	17.5
8	20
9	22.5
10	25
11	27.5
12	30

Feet	/	Meters
1		0.3
2		0.6
3		1.0
4		1.2
5		1.5
6		1.8
7		2.1
8		2.4
9		2.7
10		3
100		30
1000		300

Glossary

Acanthophyll A leaf or leaflet modified into a spine, such as is found at the base of the pinnate leaf of *Phoenix* species.

Acaulescent Without an aboveground stem or trunk.

Acuminate Tapering gradually to a sharp point, with sides more or less concave.

Adjacent germination A type of germination in which the radicle and shoot are formed adjacent to the palm seed.

Anthesis The point in the life of a flower at which the pollen is shed or the stigma is receptive to the pollen.

Auricle An earlike lobe, usually a part of the leaf sheath or leaf petiole.

Bifid Divided into two usually equal parts, most often used to describe the apex of a leaf.

Binomial A scientific name consisting of two parts: a genus name (also called generic name) and the species name (also called specific epithet).

Bipinnate A pinnate leaf whose primary leaflets have been replaced by separate and smaller stalks that then bear their leaflets with or without individual stalks.

Boots The dead and usually split and lignified leaf bases (or sheaths) adhering to a palm's stem or trunk, such as are common in the genus *Sabal*.

Bract A modified leaf below a flower or an inflorescence. Palm inflorescences usually have several to many bracts.

Canopy-scape A term used in this volume to describe the use of a palm in the landscape wherein a palm's crown extends above adjacent or lower vegetation and, from any distance, is the primary if not the sole visual manifestation of the palm's whereabouts.

Caulescent Having an aboveground stem or trunk.

Cirrus, Cirri A modified and extended leaf rachis that allows a climbing palm to attach itself to a host.

Coriaceous Leathery in texture.

Costa A term used in this volume to describe the projection of the petiole into the leaf blade (or lamina) of a palmate-leaved palm species; sometimes called rib or midrib in the literature.

Costapalmate Said of palmate leaf with a discernible costa.

Cotyledon The first emerging leaf of a seedling; sometimes called the seed leaf.

Crownshaft A term used only with pinnate-leaved palm species to denote a tubular or cylindrical shaft above the woody part of the trunk; the tube is more or less columnar and consists of the expanded and tightly packed leaf bases (or sheaths) of the leaves presently on the palm.

Cultivar A variety or form of a species that originates in cultivation and is not found naturally.

Deltoid Triangular shaped, with the broader part near the point of attachment.

Dichotomous Having a succession of two-forked divisions.

Dicot, Dicotyledon Said of a seed that produces seedlings with two seed leaves (cotyledons) as opposed to those of monocots (monocotyledon), which produce seedlings with only one seed leaf. Dicots have woody tissues as opposed to monocots; almost all true tree species are dicots, the salient exception being the palm family. In addition, the flowers of dicot (dicotyledonous) plants have their parts in fours or fives as opposed to those of monocots whose flower parts are in threes or multiples of three.

Dioecious Having male (staminate) and female (pistillate) flowers on separate plants. The term is from two Greek words meaning "two houses."

Distichous Arranged into two ranks on opposite sides of an axis or stem.

Endemic Confined to a particular region.

Epithet The word in a binomial that follows the genus name and denotes the species.

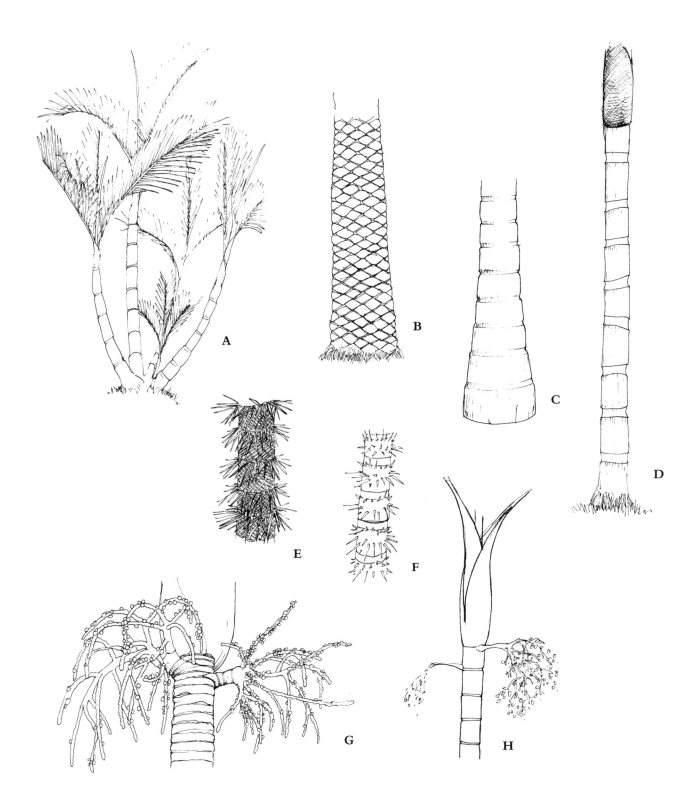

Palm trunks. **A:** Clumping trunks with pinnate leaves and no true crownshafts. **B:** Solitary trunk with diamond-shaped leaf scars. **C:** Solitary trunk with widely spaced, stepped rings of leaf scars and swollen base. **D:** Solitary trunk with widely and irregularly spaced rings of leaf scars, nonswollen base, and crownshaft that is nearly the same diameter as the stem. **E:** Trunk with rings of downward-pointing spines and adherent woven fibers from the old leaf sheaths. **F:** Trunk with rings of spines and no adherent fibers. **G:** Trunk with closely spaced rings of leaf sheath scars, infructescences borne beneath the swollen crownshaft. **H:** Trunk with widely spaced rings of leaf sheath scars, inflorescences borne beneath the loose crownshaft.

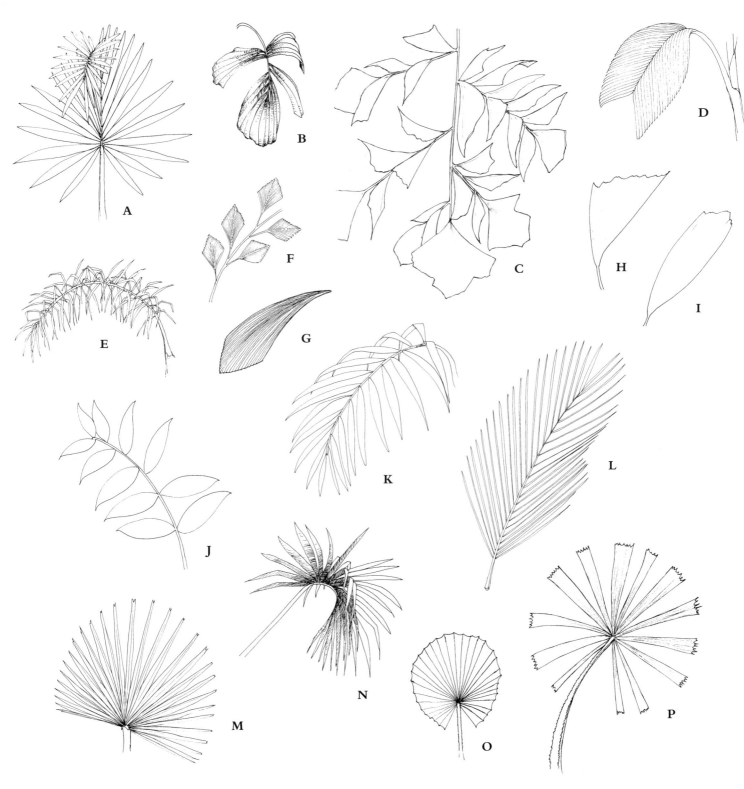

Palm leaves. **A:** Pinnate leaf with closely spaced leaflets near the base of the leaf and widely spaced leaflets at the apex. **B:** Pinnate leaf with groups of partially fused irregularly shaped leaflets. **C:** Bipinnate leaf of *Caryota* species. **D:** Unsegmented pinnate leaf with deeply bifid apex. **E:** Plumosely pinnate leaf. **F:** Diamond-shaped, alternating leaflets. **G:** Linear-obdeltoid leaflet with toothed apical margin. **H:** Irregularly diamond-shaped leaflet with toothed apical margin. **I:** Linear-oblong leaflet with toothed apical margin. **J:** Ovate-acuminate leaflets. **K:** Linear-acuminate leaflets. **L:** Narrowly linear leaflets. **M:** Palmate leaf with apically bifid segments and small hastula. **N:** Strongly costapalmate leaf. **O:** Nearly circular, unsegmented palmate leaf. **P:** Circular, segmented palmate leaf with apically toothed segments.

Falcate Sickle shaped.

Flagellum, Flagella A long, whiplike or tail-like modified and sterile inflorescence unique to the genus *Calamus* and used by the plant to climb a host.

Genus, Genera A collection of plants bearing similar characters. The taxonomic category that ranks below family and above species.

Glabrous Smooth, not hairy.

Glaucous Covered with a whitish or bluish bloom or a waxy or powdery substance that is easily rubbed away.

Hapaxanthic Of stems or trunks that flower and fruit once (usually terminally) and then die. Also called monocarpic.

Hastula A flap of tissue on some palmate leaves. This flap is variously shaped and protrudes from the point at which the petiole joins the leaf blade. The protruding organ may be tiny or large and may be found on either the upper or lower surface of the leaf, or on both surfaces.

Inflorescence A cluster of flowers originating from a single point on the stem or trunk and including all accompanying bracts and branches.

Infructescence The cluster of fruits formed on an inflorescence.

Intergeneric Between two genera.

Lamina The blade of a leaf. In palms, the lamina may include several leaflets (as in pinnate leaves) or a single expanse of tissue (as in palmate leaves).

Lanceolate Having a shape that is longer than wide, with the widest part near the point of attachment.

Leaf base The lowest or bottom-most part of a leaf; a widened (often greatly so) portion of the bottom of the leaf's petiole. Also called leaf sheath or sheath.

Leaflet The individual segment of a pinnate leaf.

Marcescent Withering but not falling. Used to describe palms whose dead leaves persist and usually hang (often in a skirt) beneath the crown of living leaves.

Mesic Of average rainfall, being neither wet nor arid.

Midrib The main vein(s) of a leaf. Also called midvein.

Midvein The main vein(s) of a leaf. Also called midrib.

Mogote A steep hill or small mountain of porous limestone in Cuba, full of solution holes and crevasses.

Monocarpic Of stems or trunks that flower and fruit once (usually terminally) and then die. Also called hapaxanthic.

Monocot, Monocotyledon Said of a seed that produces seedlings with only one seed leaf (cotyledon) as opposed to those of dicots, which produce seedlings with two seed leaves or cotyledons. Monocots do not usually produce woody tissues, as opposed to dicots, and, except for palms and a few other large monocots like the dragon tree (*Dracaena draco*), do not result in tree forms. In addition, the flowers of monocotyledonous plants have their parts in threes or multiples of three as opposed to dicots whose flower parts are in twos, fours, fives, or multiples thereof.

Monoecious Having male and female or male, female, and bisexual flowers on a single plant.

Monotypic Of one type, such as a genus with a single species.

Node The point on a stem from which a leaf, a group of leaves, or an inflorescence grows. In palm species these points are usually also indicated by differently colored or differently textured rings (complete or incomplete) along the older parts of the stem or trunk.

Obdeltoid Triangular shaped, with the thinner part near the point of attachment.

Obovate Egg shaped with the thinner part at the point of attachment.

Obtuse Blunt. Not sharp or pointed.

Palmate Shaped like a splayed hand. Said of a compound leaf with leaflets arranged from a common (fanlike) point.

Panicle A branched and elongated inflorescence of stalked flowers.

Peduncle The primary (basal) stem of an inflorescence.

Peltate Of a leaf attached to a petiole or stalk at its lower surface rather than to any part of its margin; the stalk is usually attached to the center of the leaf's underside and the leaf is usually rounded.

Perfect In a botanical sense, having male and female parts in the same flower.

Petiole The primary stalk of a simple or compound leaf. In palm species the stalk beneath the bottom-most leaves or leaflets, and above the leaf sheath or leaf base.

pH Potential of hydrogen. A measure of the alkalinity or acidity of a substance on a scale from 0 (most acid) to 14 (most alkaline), with 7 being neutral. Sulfuric acid has a pH of 0, while pure lye has a pH of 14. Most soils have a pH value of 5 to 9. Acidonger and do not raise or lower the pH value suddenly and unnaturally.

Pinna A leaflet of a pinnate leaf; pinnae (plural).

Pinnate Featherlike. Of a leaf with more than three leaflets growing from the central axis (rachis). The leaflets may grow on opposite sides of a rachis in a single flat plane or they may grow at angles off the rachis to create a plumose effect.

Pistil The female reproductive organ of a flower consisting of the ovary, the style, and the stigma. The ovary is the portion in which the seeds and fruit develop usually with expansion of the ovary. The style is usually a relatively elongated extension of the ovary atop which the stigma resides. The stigma receives pollen and stimulates the pollen grains to fertilize—by means of a pollen tube—the ovules in the ovary, which then develop into the seeds.

Pistillate Having a pistil. Said of a flower that is single sexed (female) or bisexual.

Plicate Folded at least to some extent. Also called pleated.

Plumose Featherlike with the segments arising from the midrib in more than one plane and resulting in a boa-like appearance.

Pneumatophore A specialized root that grows from normal subterranean roots but which rises above the water or soil surface and serves to aerate the subterranean or subaquatic root system. Few palms produce such roots, but when they do, the roots are usually contiguous with the stem or trunk or nearly so.

Prop roots Large, aerial roots at or near the base of a palm's trunk or stem, which usually provide support and stability to the tree and which are usually in the form of a cone. Also called stilt roots.

Rachis The primary and central stem of a compound leaf from which leaflets or subsidiary leafstalks arise, being above the petiole.

Radicle The first root formed by a sprouting seed.

Reins Narrow, usually threadlike pieces of leaf tissue accompanying the unfolding or newly unfolded (usually pinnate) leaf. In some palm species (for example, *Dypsis decaryi*), the reins last as long as the living leaf.

Remote germination. A type of germination in which the embryo first forms a petiole that may extend for some distance from the palm seed and, at the end of which, the radicle and first shoot are formed.

Reniform Kidney shaped.

Rheophyte A plant adapted to grow in a stream or other body of water; aquatic, but used only for terrestrial and nonmarine plants. Literally from the Greek "stream flow" and "plant."

Rhizomatous Having rhizomes.

Rhizome An underground or on-ground stem growing horizontally and giving rise to roots, stems, and leaves at its nodes or growing tips.

Root pruning A technique used for transplanting palms that consists of digging a trench around the root perimeter of the palm some months in advance of the transplanting, so that the cut roots will, to some extent, regenerate and heal with the benefit of the surrounding soil before the plant is moved to its new location.

Saxophone growth The seedling growth form of some palm species (for example, *Sabal*) in which the stem first grows downwards and then turns upwards to emerge aboveground. The resulting aerial stem often remains underground for many months or even years before emerging aboveground.

Serrate Sawlike. Having a toothed margin.

Sheath The lowest or bottom-most part of a leaf; a widened (often greatly so) portion of the bottom of the leaf's petiole. Also called leaf base or leaf sheath.

Spadix A large and usually woody bract which originally covers a palm inflorescence and from which the inflorescence later emerges. Also called spathe.

Spathe A large and usually woody bract which originally covers a palm inflorescence and from which the inflorescence later emerges. Also called spadix.

Spatulate Spatula shaped; a modified oblong shape with the apex much larger than the tapering base; an exaggerated obovate shape.

Spine A sharp protrusion on a leaf, branch, or stem. Used in this volume in its broad, nontechnical sense.

Stamen The male reproductive organ of a flower, whether single sexed (male) or bisexual, consisting of the filament and the anther.

Staminate Having a stamen. Said of a flower that is single sexed (male) or bisexual.

Stigma The apical (terminal) end of the pistil; the part of the pistil that receives pollen grains and initiates their germination.

Stilt roots Large, aerial roots at or near the base of a palm's trunk or stem, which usually provide support and stability to the tree and which are usually in the form of a cone. Also called prop roots.

Stolon A rootlike stem that creeps along the surface of the soil and roots at specific nodes, creating new plants that are genetically identical to the parent plant.

Subtend To grow directly beneath.

Taxon, Taxa A taxonomic category of any rank, such as genus or species.

Tomentose Having tomentum.

Tomentum A covering of short, densely matted hairs.

Trifid Divided into three usually equal parts.

Xeric Of, from, or adapted to dry habitats.

Bibliography

Bailey, Liberty Hyde. 1925. *The Standard Cyclopedia of Horticulture*. London: Macmillan.

Bailey, Liberty Hyde, and Ethel Zoe Bailey. 1976. *Hortus Third*. New York: Macmillan.

———. 1946. *Hortus Second*. New York: Macmillan.

Barrow, Sasha. 1998. *A Revision of Phoenix*. London. Reprinted from *Kew Bulletin* 53 (3).

———. 1994. "In Search of *Phoenix roebelenii:* the Xishuangbanna Palm." *Principes* 38 (4): 177–181.

Basu, S. K., and R. K. Chakraverty. 1994. *A Manual of Cultivated Palms in India*. Calcutta: Director Botanical Survey of India.

Bernal, Rodrigo. 1998. "The Growth Form of *Phytelephas seemannii*—A Potentially Immortal Solitary Palm." *Principes* 42 (1): 15–24.

Bernal, Rodrigo, Gloria Ramirez, and Rosman Ivan Morales. 2001. "Notes on the Genus *Ammandra*." *Palms* 45 (3): 123–126.

Blombery, Alec, and Tony Rodd. 1989. *Palms of the World: Their Cultivation, Care, and Landscape Use*. London: Angus and Robertson.

Borschsenius, Finn, and Rodrigo Bernal. 1996. *Aiphanes*. Monograph 70 of *Flora Neotropica*. New York Botanical Garden.

Borchsenius, Finn, Henrik Borgtoft Pedersen, and Henrik Balslev. 1998. *Manual to the Palms of Ecuador*. Quito, Ecuador: Department of Systematic Botany, Aarhaus University.

Boyer, Keith. 1992. *Palms and Cycads Beyond the Tropics*. Queensland, Australia: Palm and Cycad Societies of Australia.

Braun, August. n.d. *Las Palmas Cultivadas en Ciudades elevadas de la Parte Andina de América del Sur*. Caracas, Venezuela: August Braun.

———. 1995. *Las Palmas de las Sabanas de Venezuela*. Caracas, Venezuela: August Braun.

Broschat, Timothy K., and Alan W. Meerow. 2000. *Ornamental Palm Horticulture*. Gainesville, Florida: University Press of Florida.

Corner, E. J. H. 1966. *The Natural History of Palms*. London: Weidenfeld and Nicholson.

Dowe, John L. 1989a. *Palms of the South-West Pacific*. Queensland, Australia: Palm and Cycad Societies of Australia.

———, ed. 1989b. *Palms of the Solomon Islands*. Queensland, Australia: Palm and Cycad Societies of Australia.

Dowe, John L., and P. Cabalion. 1996. *A Taxonomic Account of Arecaceae in Vanuatu. Australian Systematic Botany* 9 (1). Victoria, Australia: CSIRO.

Dransfield, John. 1994. "What's In a Name?" *Principes* 38 (3): 145.

———. 1986. *Palmae (Flora of Tropical East Africa)*. Rotterdam/Boston: A. A. Balkema.

———. 1982. "A Day on the Klingklang Range." *Principes* 26 (1): 26.

Dransfield, John, and Henk Beentje. 1995. *The Palms of Madagascar*. London: Board of Trustees of the Royal Botanic Gardens, Kew.

Dransfield, John, and Scott Zona. 1997. "*Guihaia* in Cultivation: A Case of Mistaken Identities." *Principes* 41 (2): 70–73.

Ellison, Don, and Anthony Ellison. 2001. *Betrock's Cultivated Palms of the World*. Hollywood, Florida: Betrock Information Systems.

Essig, Frederick B. 1982. "A Synopsis of the Genus *Gulubia*." *Principes* 26 (4): 170.

———. 1978. *A Revision of the Genus Ptychosperma. Allertonia* 1 (7). Kauai, Hawaii: Pacific Tropical Botanic Garden.

Evans, Randall J. 2001. "A Monograph of *Colpothrinax*." *Palms* 45 (4): 189.

Fairchild, David. 1943. *Garden Islands of the Great East*. New York: Charles Scribners Sons.

Gibbons, Martin. 1993. *Palms*. Seacaucus, New Jersey: Chartwell Books.

Glassman, Sidney F. 1999. *A Taxonomic Treatment of the Palm Subtribe Attaleinae (Tribe Cocoeae)*. Chicago, Illinois: Board of Trustees of the University of Illinois.

Goldman, Douglas H. 1999. "Distribution Update: *Sabal minor* in Mexico." *Palms* 43 (1): 40–44.

Guzman, Enriquito D., and Edwino S. Fernando. 1986. *Philippine Palms*. Vol. 4, *Guide to Philippine Flora and Fauna*. Quezon City, Philippines: JMC Press.

Henderson, Andrew H. 1995. *The Palms of the Amazon*. Oxford and New York: Oxford University Press.

Henderson, Andrew, Gloria Galeano, and Rodrigo Bernal. 1995. *Palms of the Americas*. Princeton, New Jersey: Princeton University Press.

Hiep, Nguyen Tien, and Ruth Kiew. 2000. *New and Interesting Plants from La Hong Bay, Vietnam. Garden Bulletin of Singapore* 52.

Hodel, Donald R., ed. 1998. *The Palms and Cycads of Thailand*. Lawrence, Kansas: Allen Press.

————. 1992. *Chamaedorea Palms*. Lawrence, Kansas: International Palm Society.

Hodel, Donald R., and Jean-Christophe Pintaud. 1998. *The Palms of New Caledonia*. Lawrence, Kansas: Allen Press.

Johnson, Dennis V. 1998. *Tropical Palms*. Rome: Food and Agriculture Organization of the United Nations.

————, ed. 1996. *Palms: Their Conservation and Sustained Utilization*. Cambridge, U.K.: IUCN Publication Services Unit.

Jones, David L. 1995. *Palms Throughout the World*. Washington, D.C.: Smithsonian Institution Press.

Kahn, Francis. 1997. *The Palms of Eldorado*. Orstom.

Krempin, Jack. 1990. *Palms and Cycads Around the World*. Sydney, Australia: Horwitz Grahame Pry.

Langlois, Arthur C. 1976. *Supplement to Palms of the World*. Gainesville, Florida: University Press of Florida.

Lockett, Landon. 1991. "Native Texas Palms North of the Lower Rio Grande Valley: Recent Discoveries." *Principes* 35 (2): 64–71.

McCurrach, James C. 1960. *Palms of the World*. New York: Harper.

Meerow, Alan W. 1992. *Betrock's Guide to Landscape Palms*. Cooper City, Florida: Betrock Information Systems.

Moore, Harold E., Jr. 1972. "*Chelyocarpus* and Its Allies." *Principes* 16 (3): 77.

Muirhead, Desmond. n.d. *Palms*. Globe, Arizona: Dale Stuart King.

Noblick, Larry R. 1996. "*Syagrus*." *The Palm Journal* 126 (January). Bulletin of the Southern California Chapter of the International Palm Society.

Palm and Cycad Societies of Australia. 1987a. *Palms of Indonesia*. Queensland, Australia.

————. 1987b. "*Pinanga*." *Palms and Cycads* 16. Queensland, Australia.

Pintaud, Jean-Christophe. 2000. "An Introduction to the Palms of New Caledonia." *Principes* 44 (3): 132–140.

Principes (later *Palms*). 1956–2001. Journal of the International Palm Society, Lawrence, Kansas. Vols. 1–45.

Rodd, A. N. 1998. "Revision of *Livistona* in Australia." *Telopia* 8 (1). National Herbarium of New South Wales, Royal Botanic Gardens, Sydney.

Romney, David H. 1997. *Growing Coconuts in South Florida*. Homestead, Florida: David H. Romney.

Saw, G. L. 1997. "A Revision of *Licuala* (Palmae) in the Malay Peninsula." *Sandakania* 10 (April). Forest Research Center, Forestry Department, Sabah, Malaysia.

Stearn, William T. 1992. *Stearn's Dictionary of Plant Names for Gardeners*. London: Cassell.

Stevenson, George B. 1974. *Palms of South Florida*. Miami, Florida: George B. Stevenson.

Stewart, Lynette. 1994. *Palms and Cycads of the World*. Sydney, Australia: Angus and Robertson.

Tomlinson, P. B. 1990. *The Structural Biology of Palms*. New York: Oxford University Press.

Tucker, Robert. 1988. *The Palms of Subequatorial Queensland*. Queensland, Australia: Palm and Cycad Societies of Australia.

Uhl, Natalie W., and John Dransfield. 1987. *Genera Palmarum*. Lawrence, Kansas: L. H. Bailey Hortorium and International Palm Society.

Vines, Robert A. 1960. *Trees, Shrubs, and Woody Vines of the Southwest*. Austin, Texas: University of Texas Press.

White, Alan. 1988. *Palms of the Northern Territory and Their Distribution*. Brisbane, Australia: Palm and Cycad Societies of Australia.

Whitmore, T. C. 1998. *Palms of Malaya*. Bangkok, Thailand: White Lotus.

Zona, Scott. 1996. "*Roystonea*." *Flora Neotropica* 71. New York: New York Botanical Garden.

————. 1990. *A Monograph of Sabal*. Claremont, California. Reprinted from *Aliso* 12 (4).

Zona, Scott, and Frederick B. Essig. 1999. "How Many Species of *Brassiophoenix*?" *Palms* 43 (1): 45–47.

Zona, Scott, and Dylan Fuller. 1999. "A Revision of *Veitchia* (Arecaceae—Arecoideae)." *Harvard Papers in Botany* 4 (2): 543–560.

Photo Locations

Plate 2: Heathcote Botanic Garden, Ft. Pierce, Florida.

Plates 3–5: Montgomery Botanical Center, Miami, Florida.

Plate 6: Brownsville, Texas.

Plate 9: Singapore Botanic Garden.

Plate 12: Miami, Florida.

Plate 13: Fairchild Tropical Garden, Miami, Florida.

Plate 14: Tropical Research & Education Center, Homestead, Florida.

Plate 15: Jardín Botanico Nacional, Cuba.

Plate 16: Fairchild Tropical Garden, Miami, Florida.

Plates 17–18: Jardín Botanico Nacional, Cuba.

Plates 19–22: Fairchild Tropical Garden, Miami, Florida.

Plate 25: Fairchild Tropical Garden, Miami, Florida.

Plates 27–28: Flamingo Gardens, Ft. Lauderdale, Florida.

Plate 29: San Diego, California.

Plate 31: Montgomery Botanical Center, Miami, Florida.

Plate 32: Queensland, Australia.

Plate 33: Roth garden, Cairns, Australia.

Plate 34: Montgomery Botanical Center, Miami, Florida.

Plate 35: Terry Mead garden, Cairns, Australia.

Plate 37: Fairchild Tropical Garden, Miami, Florida.

Plate 38: Geoffrey Fowler garden, Queensland, Australia.

Plate 42: Flamingo Gardens, Ft. Lauderdale, Florida.

Plate 43: Fairchild Tropical Garden, Miami, Florida.

Plates 44–45: Ann Norton Sculpture Garden, West Palm Beach, Florida.

Plate 46: Arden Dearden nursery, Queensland, Australia.

Plate 48: Flamingo Gardens, Ft. Lauderdale, Florida.

Plates 52–54: Fairchild Tropical Garden, Miami, Florida.

Plate 55: San Diego, California.

Plate 57: Townsville Palmetum, Queensland, Australia.

Plate 58: Fairchild Tropical Garden, Miami, Florida.

Plate 62: Fairchild Tropical Garden, Miami, Florida.

Plates 64–66: Fairchild Tropical Garden, Miami, Florida.

Plate 68: Flamingo Gardens, Ft. Lauderdale, Florida.

Plates 69–70: Fairchild Tropical Garden, Miami, Florida.

Plates 72–73: Flamingo Gardens, Ft. Lauderdale, Florida.

Plates 74–75: Fairchild Tropical Garden, Miami, Florida.

Plate 76: Flecker Botanic Gardens, Cairns, Australia.

Plate 79: Earthworks nursery, Loxahatchee, Florida.

Plates 81–83: Fairchild Tropical Garden, Miami, Florida.

Plate 85: Townsville Palmetum, Queensland, Australia.

Plate 86: Wilson Botanic Garden, Costa Rica.

Plate 87: Fairchild Tropical Garden, Miami, Florida.

Plate 88: Teakettle Enterprises nursery, Belize.

Plates 89–91: Fairchild Tropical Garden, Miami, Florida.

Plate 92: Montgomery Botanical Center, Miami, Florida.

Plates 93–94: Fairchild Tropical Garden, Miami, Florida.

Plates 96–97: Montgomery Botanical Center, Miami, Florida.

Plates 98–101: Fairchild Tropical Garden, Miami, Florida.

Plates 102–103: Montgomery Botanical Center, Miami, Florida.

Plate 111: Lyon Arboretum, Oahu, Hawaii.

Plate 115: Fairchild Tropical Garden, Miami, Florida.

Plate 116: Paul Craft garden, West Palm Beach, Florida.

Plate 117: Fairchild Tropical Garden, Miami, Florida.

Plates 119–120: Fairchild Tropical Garden, Miami, Florida.

Plate 121: Flamingo Gardens, Ft. Lauderdale, Florida.

Plate 122: Fairchild Tropical Garden, Miami, Florida.

Plate 123: Mounts Botanical Garden, West Palm Beach, Florida.

Plate 124: Heathcote Botanic Garden, Ft. Pierce, Florida.

Plate 126: Fairchild Tropical Garden, Miami, Florida.

Plates 128–132: Fairchild Tropical Garden, Miami, Florida.

Plate 133: Heinz Nursery, Brownsville, Texas.

Plate 134: Townsville Palmetum, Queensland, Australia.

Plate 135: Quail Botanical Garden, San Diego, California.

Plate 136: Montgomery Botanical Center, Miami, Florida.

Plates 138–139: Balboa Park, San Diego, California.

Plates 140–141: Huntington Botanical Garden, Los Angeles, California.

Plates 144–145: Arden Dearden nursery, Queensland, Australia.

Plate 147: Tropical Research & Education Center, Homestead, Florida.

Plate 153: San Diego, California.

Plate 156: Moody Gardens, Galveston, Texas.

Plate 157: Horticultural Consultants, Houston, Texas.

Plate 158: Townsville Palmetum, Queensland, Australia.

Plate 163: Singapore Botanic Garden.

Plate 461: Fairchild Tropical Garden, Miami, Florida.
Plate 463: Heathcote Botanic Garden, Ft. Pierce, Florida.
Plate 464: Montgomery Botanical Center, Miami, Florida.
Plate 465: John DeMott Nursery, Homestead, Florida.
Plate 466: Jardín Botanico Nacional, Cuba.
Plate 467: Townsville Palmetum, Queensland, Australia.
Plates 468–469: Montgomery Botanical Center, Miami, Florida.
Plates 470–472: Fairchild Tropical Garden, Miami, Florida.
Plate 473: Atkins garden, Costa Rica.
Plate 474: Fairchild Tropical Garden, Miami, Florida.
Plate 475: Townsville Palmetum, Queensland, Australia.
Plate 476: Fairchild Tropical Garden, Miami, Florida.
Plates 477–478: Arden Dearden nursery, Queensland, Australia.
Plate 479: Terry Mead garden, Cairns, Australia.
Plates 481–482: Arden Dearden nursery, Queensland, Australia.
Plates 483–484: Wilson Botanic Garden, Costa Rica.
Plate 485: Townsville Palmetum, Queensland, Australia.
Plates 486–487: Marco Herrera nursery, Costa Rica.
Plate 488: Flecker Botanic Gardens, Cairns, Australia.
Plate 490: Singapore Botanic Garden.
Plate 491: Royal Botanic Gardens, Sydney, Australia.
Plate 492: San Diego, California.
Plate 493: Huntington Botanical Garden, Los Angeles, California.
Plate 494: San Diego, California.
Plates 496–497: Fairchild Tropical Garden, Miami, Florida.
Plate 498: Jan Pierson garden, Nouméa, New Caledonia.
Plate 499: Fairchild Tropical Garden, Miami, Florida.
Plate 500: Terry Mead garden, Cairns, Australia.
Plates 503–505: Fairchild Tropical Garden, Miami, Florida.
Plates 506–507: Flecker Botanic Gardens, Cairns, Australia.
Plates 511–512: Geoffrey Fowler garden, Queensland, Australia.
Plate 514: Flecker Botanic Gardens, Cairns, Australia.
Plate 515: Fairchild Tropical Garden, Miami, Florida.
Plate 516: Arden Dearden nursery, Queensland, Australia.
Plate 520: Fairchild Tropical Garden, Miami, Florida.
Plate 521: Geoffrey Fowler garden, Queensland, Australia.
Plate 522: Fairchild Tropical Garden, Miami, Florida.
Plate 523: Geoffrey Fowler garden, Queensland, Australia.
Plate 525: Geoffrey Fowler garden, Queensland, Australia.
Plates 527–528: Flecker Botanic Gardens, Cairns, Australia.
Plates 531–532: Summit Gardens, Panama.
Plates 537–538: Fairchild Tropical Garden, Miami, Florida.
Plate 539: Flamingo Gardens, Ft. Lauderdale, Florida.
Plate 540: Montgomery Botanical Center, Miami, Florida.
Plate 541: Robert Lee Riffle garden, Houston, Texas.
Plates 542–543: Flamingo Gardens, Ft. Lauderdale, Florida.
Plate 545: Flamingo Gardens, Ft. Lauderdale, Florida.
Plate 549: Townsville Palmetum, Queensland, Australia.
Plate 550: Flamingo Gardens, Ft. Lauderdale, Florida.
Plate 551: Fairchild Tropical Garden, Miami, Florida.
Plate 552: Atkins garden, Costa Rica.
Plates 553–554: Fairchild Tropical Garden, Miami, Florida.

Plate 555: Flamingo Gardens, Ft. Lauderdale, Florida.
Plates 556–558: Fairchild Tropical Garden, Miami, Florida.
Plate 559: Atkins garden, Costa Rica.
Plate 560: Fairchild Tropical Garden, Miami, Florida.
Plates 562–563: Fairchild Tropical Garden, Miami, Florida.
Plate 564: Montgomery Botanical Center, Miami, Florida.
Plate 565: Ann Norton Sculpture Garden, West Palm Beach, Florida.
Plate 570: Ann Norton Sculpture Garden, West Palm Beach, Florida.
Plates 574–575: Geoffrey Fowler garden, Queensland, Australia.
Plate 586: Montgomery Botanical Center, Miami, Florida.
Plates 587–593: Flecker Botanic Gardens, Cairns, Australia.
Plate 595: Fairchild Tropical Garden, Miami, Florida.
Plate 598: Montgomery Botanical Center, Miami, Florida.
Plates 599–601: Fairchild Tropical Garden, Miami, Florida.
Plates 607–608: Montgomery Botanical Center, Miami, Florida.
Plate 611: Summit Gardens, Panama.
Plate 612: Roth garden, Cairns, Australia.
Plates 613–615: Fairchild Tropical Garden, Miami, Florida.
Plate 617: Atkins garden, Costa Rica.
Plate 618: Fairchild Tropical Garden, Miami, Florida.
Plate 628: Fairchild Tropical Garden, Miami, Florida.
Plate 629: National Tropical Botanical Garden, Hawaii.
Plate 630: Townsville Palmetum, Queensland, Australia.
Plate 631: A: C: Langlois Retreat, Nassau, Bahamas.
Plate 632: Flecker Botanic Gardens, Cairns, Australia.
Plate 633: Montgomery Botanical Center, Miami, Florida.
Plate 634: Fairchild Tropical Garden, Miami, Florida.
Plate 635: Moody Gardens, Galveston, Texas.
Plates 636–637: Fairchild Tropical Garden, Miami, Florida.
Plate 639: Singapore Botanic Garden.
Plate 640: Fairchild Tropical Garden, Miami, Florida.
Plate 641: Ft. Pierce, Florida.
Plates 642–643: Fairchild Tropical Garden, Miami, Florida.
Plate 644: Montgomery Botanical Center, Miami, Florida.
Plate 645: San Diego, California.
Plate 646: Los Angeles County Arboretum, California.
Plate 647: Fairchild Tropical Garden, Miami, Florida.
Plate 652: Roth garden, Cairns, Australia.
Plates 656–657: Roth garden, Cairns, Australia.
Plate 658: Flecker Botanic Gardens, Cairns, Australia.
Plates 659–661: Wilson Botanic Garden, Costa Rica.
Plate 665: Townsville Palmetum, Queensland, Australia.
Plate 666: Montgomery Botanical Center, Miami, Florida.
Plate 667: Townsville Palmetum, Queensland, Australia.
Plate 668: Jardín Botanico Nacional, Cuba.
Plate 669: Marco Herrera nursery, Costa Rica.
Plate 670: Fairchild Tropical Garden, Miami, Florida.
Plate 671: Flecker Botanic Gardens, Cairns, Australia.
Plate 672: Bogor Botanic Garden, Java, Indonesia.
Plate 673: Fairchild Tropical Garden, Miami, Florida.
Plates 674–675: Jardín Botanico Nacional, Cuba.
Plate 676: Fairchild Tropical Garden, Miami, Florida.
Plate 678: Arden Dearden nursery, Queensland, Australia.

Plates 684–685: Fairchild Tropical Garden, Miami, Florida.

Plate 687: Roth garden, Cairns, Australia.

Plate 691: Arden Dearden nursery, Queensland, Australia.

Plate 693: Flamingo Gardens, Ft. Lauderdale, Florida.

Plate 694: Fairchild Tropical Garden, Miami, Florida.

Plates 697–698: National Tropical Botanical Garden, Hawaii.

Plate 700: Fairchild Tropical Garden, Miami, Florida.

Plate 701: National Tropical Botanical Garden, Hawaii.

Plate 703: Jan Pierson garden, Nouméa, New Caledonia.

Plate 704: Townsville Palmetum, Queensland, Australia.

Plate 705: National Tropical Botanical Garden, Hawaii.

Plate 708: Fairchild Tropical Garden, Miami, Florida.

Plates 711–714: Fairchild Tropical Garden, Miami, Florida.

Plate 716: Montgomery Botanical Center, Miami, Florida.

Plates 719–720: Flamingo Gardens, Ft. Lauderdale, Florida.

Plates 721–722: Fairchild Tropical Garden, Miami, Florida.

Plate 724: Riviera Courts Motel, Miami, Florida.

Plates 726–728: Fairchild Tropical Garden, Miami, Florida.

Plate 729: Teakettle Enterprises nursery, Belize.

Plates 730–732: Fairchild Tropical Garden, Miami, Florida.

Plates 735–736: Townsville Palmetum, Queensland, Australia.

Plates 737–738: Montgomery Botanical Center, Miami, Florida.

Plate 740: Terry Mead garden, Cairns, Australia.

Plates 743–744: Fairchild Tropical Garden, Miami, Florida.

Plate 745: Montgomery Botanical Center, Miami, Florida.

Plates 747–748: Fairchild Tropical Garden, Miami, Florida.

Plate 750: Mardy Darian garden, Vista, California.

Plate 753: Boots' nursery, Belle Glade, Florida.

Plate 755: Julie Rosenberg garden, Miami, Florida.

Plate 759: Montgomery Botanical Center, Miami, Florida.

Plate 760: Fairchild Tropical Garden, Miami, Florida.

Plate 768: Huntington Botanical Garden, Los Angeles, California.

Plate 769: Fairchild Tropical Garden, Miami, Florida.

Plate 770: John DeMott Nursery, Homestead, Florida.

Plate 773: Jardín Botanico Nacional, Cuba.

Plates 778–779: Searle Brothers Nursery, West Palm Beach, Florida.

Plate 780: Montgomery Botanical Center, Miami, Florida.

Plate 783: Fairchild Tropical Garden, Miami, Florida.

Plate 786: The Kampong, Coral Gables, Florida.

Plates 787–788: Jardín Botanico Nacional, Cuba.

Plate 789: Fairchild Tropical Garden, Miami, Florida.

Plate 791: Ft. Pierce, Florida.

Plates 792–793: Fairchild Tropical Garden, Miami, Florida.

Plate 795: Tropical Research & Education Center, Homestead, Florida.

Plate 797: Palmetto State Park, Texas.

Plate 798: Myakka River State Park, Florida.

Plate 799: Fairchild Tropical Garden, Miami, Florida.

Plates 801–802: Fairchild Tropical Garden, Miami, Florida.

Plate 803: Jan Pierson garden, Nouméa, New Caledonia.

Plates 804–805: Fairchild Tropical Garden, Miami, Florida.

Plate 807: Geoffrey Fowler garden, Queensland, Australia.

Plate 808: Flamingo Gardens, Ft. Lauderdale, Florida.

Plate 809: Geoffrey Fowler garden, Queensland, Australia.

Plate 810: Flamingo Gardens, Ft. Lauderdale, Florida.

Plate 811: Wilson Botanic Garden, Costa Rica.

Plates 812–813: Fairchild Tropical Garden, Miami, Florida.

Plate 814: Montgomery Botanical Center, Miami, Florida.

Plate 816: Fairchild Tropical Garden, Miami, Florida.

Plate 817: Ruth Sallenbach garden, Lake Worth, Florida.

Plate 820: Ft. Pierce, Florida.

Plate 822: Geoffrey Fowler garden, Queensland, Australia.

Plates 823–824: Fairchild Tropical Garden, Miami, Florida.

Plates 825–826: Wilson Botanic Garden, Costa Rica.

Plate 830: Bogor Botanic Garden, Java, Indonesia.

Plates 831–832: Fairchild Tropical Garden, Miami, Florida.

Plates 833–839: Montgomery Botanical Center, Miami, Florida.

Plates 840–841: Fairchild Tropical Garden, Miami, Florida.

Plate 843: Fairchild Tropical Garden, Miami, Florida.

Plate 844: Montgomery Botanical Center, Miami, Florida.

Plate 848: Montgomery Botanical Center, Miami, Florida.

Plates 849–850: Fairchild Tropical Garden, Miami, Florida.

Plates 851–852: Flamingo Gardens, Ft. Lauderdale, Florida.

Plate 853: Ft. Pierce, Florida.

Plate 855: Montgomery Botanical Center, Miami, Florida.

Plate 856: Fairchild Tropical Garden, Miami, Florida.

Plates 857–860: Montgomery Botanical Center, Miami, Florida.

Plate 862: Montgomery Botanical Center, Miami, Florida.

Plates 863–864: Fairchild Tropical Garden, Miami, Florida.

Plate 866: Wilson Botanic Garden, Costa Rica.

Plate 872: Fairchild Tropical Garden, Miami, Florida.

Plates 874–875: Fairchild Tropical Garden, Miami, Florida.

Plate 877: Fairchild Tropical Garden, Miami, Florida.

Plate 891: Huntington Botanical Garden, Los Angeles, California.

Plate 892: Fairchild Tropical Garden, Miami, Florida.

Plate 893: Huntington Botanical Garden, Los Angeles, California.

Plate 901: Mardy Darian garden, Vista, California.

Plates 903–904: Fairchild Tropical Garden, Miami, Florida.

Plate 905: Tropical Research & Education Center, Homestead, Florida.

Plate 906: Montgomery Botanical Center, Miami, Florida.

Plates 907–909: Fairchild Tropical Garden, Miami, Florida.

Plate 911: The Kampong, Coral Gables, Florida.

Plate 912: Flecker Botanic Gardens, Cairns, Australia.

Plates 913–914: Flamingo Gardens, Ft. Lauderdale, Florida.

Plate 915: David H. Romney garden, Homestead, Florida.

Plate 916: Flamingo Gardens, Ft. Lauderdale, Florida.

Plate 921: Ft. Pierce, Florida.

Plate 922: Fairchild Tropical Garden, Miami, Florida.

Plate 923: Searle Brothers Nursery, Ft. Lauderdale, Florida.

Plate 926: Townsville Palmetum, Queensland, Australia.

Plates 928–929: Fairchild Tropical Garden, Miami, Florida.

Index

Common names are cross-referenced to the scientific names by which the entries in the book are organized. Synonyms are also cross-referenced to the accepted scientific names.

Acanthococos. See *Acrocomia hassleri*
Acanthophoenix crinita. See *A. rubra*
Acanthophoenix nobilis. See *Deckenia nobilis*
Acanthorrhiza. See *Chelyocarpus, Cryosophila*
Acanthosabal. See *Acoelorraphe*
Acoelorraphe pimo. See *Brahea pimo*
Acrocomia armentalis. See *Gastrococos crispa*
Acrocomia crispa. See *Gastrococos crispa*
Actinokentia schlechteri. See *A. divaricata*
Actinophloeus. See *Ptychosperma*
Adelonenga. See *Hydriastele*
adonidia palm. See *Adonidia*
African oil palm. See *Elaeis guineensis*
African wild date palm. See *Phoenix reclinata*
Aiphanes acanthophylla. See *A. minima*
Aiphanes caryotifolia. See *A. aculeata*
Aiphanes chocoensis. See *A. macroloba*
Aiphanes corallina. See *A. minima*
Aiphanes elegans. See *A. aculeata*
Aiphanes erosa. See *A. minima*
Aiphanes fosteriorum. See *A. hirsuta*
Aiphanes kalbreyeri. See *A. hirsuta*
Aiphanes luciana. See *A. minima*
Aiphanes monostachys. See *A. hirsuta*
Aiphanes orinocensis. See *A. aculeata*
Aiphanes pachyclada. See *A. hirsuta*
Aiphanes schultzeana. See *A. ulei*
Aiphanes vincentiana. See *A. minima*
Alex palm. See *Archontophoenix alexandrae*
Alexander palm. See *Archontophoenix alexandrae,*
    Ptychosperma elegans

Alexandra king palm. See *Archontophoenix alexandrae*
Alexandra palm. See *Archontophoenix alexandrae*
Alfonsia. See *Elaeis oleifera*
American oil palm. See *Elaeis oleifera*
Ancistrophyllum. See *Laccosperma*
Andes wax palm. See *Ceroxylon*
Antongilia. See *Dypsis*
Archontophoenix elegans. See *Ptychosperma elegans*
Areca aliceae. See *A. triandra*
Areca calapparia. See *Actinorhytis calapparia*
Areca exorrhiza. See *Clinostigma exorrhizum*
Areca langloisiana. See *A. vestiaria*
Areca lutescens. See *Dypsis lutescens*
areca nut palm. See *Areca catechu*
areca palm. See *Dypsis lutescens*
Areca pumila. See *Nenga pumila*
Areca vidaliana. See *A. mammillata*
Arecastrum. See *Syagrus romanzoffiana*
Arenga ambong. See *A. undulatifolia*
Arenga borneensis. See *A. hastata*
Arenga saccharifera. See *A. pinnata*
Arikury. See *Syagrus schizophylla*
arikury palm. See *Syagrus schizophylla*
Arikuryroba. See *Syagrus schizophylla*
Aristeyera. See *Asterogyne ramosa, Asterogyne spicata*
assai palm. See *Euterpe oleracea*
Astrocaryum standleyanum var. *calimense.* See *A.*
    standleyanum
Australian cabbage palm. See *Livistona australis*
Australian fan palm. See *Livistona australis*

Bactris balanoidea. See *B. major*
Bactris cubensis. See *B. plumeriana*
Bactris gracilis. See *B. plumeriana*
Bactris horrida. See *B. guineensis*
Bactris jamaicana. See *B. plumeriana*